LAW
MISCELLANIES:

CONTAINING

AN INTRODUCTION TO THE STUDY OF THE LAW;

NOTES ON BLACKSTONE'S COMMENTARIES,

SHEWING

THE VARIATIONS OF

THE LAW OF PENNSYLVANIA FROM THE LAW OF ENGLAND,

AND WHAT ACTS OF ASSEMBLY

MIGHT REQUIRE

TO BE REPEALED OR MODIFIED;

OBSERVATIONS

ON SMITH'S EDITION OF THE LAWS OF PENNSYLVANIA;

STRICTURES

ON DECISIONS OF THE SUPREME COURT OF THE UNITED STATES,

AND

ON CERTAIN ACTS OF CONGRESS,

WITH

SOME LAW CASES,

AND

A VARIETY OF OTHER MATTERS,

CHIEFLY ORIGINAL.

———

BY HUGH HENRY BRACKENRIDGE,
A Judge of the Supreme Court of the State of Pennsylvania.

———

THE LAWBOOK EXCHANGE, LTD.
Clark, New Jersey

ISBN 978-1-58477-161-6

Lawbook Exchange edition 2001, 2021

The quality of this reprint is equivalent to the quality of the original work.

THE LAWBOOK EXCHANGE, LTD.

33 Terminal Avenue
Clark, New Jersey 07066-1321

*Please see our website for a selection of our other publications
and fine facsimile reprints of classic works of legal history:*
www.lawbookexchange.com

Library of Congress Cataloging-in-Publication Data

Brackenridge, H. H. (Hugh Henry), 1748-1816.
    Law miscellanies / by Hugh Henry Brackenridge.
      p. cm.
    Subtitle: Containing an introduction to the study of the law; notes
on Blackstone's Commentaries, shewing [sic] the variations of the law of
Pennsylvania from the law of England, and what acts of Assembly might
require to be repealed or modified; observations on Smith's edition of the
laws of Pennsylvania; strictures on decisions of the Supreme Court of the
United States, and on certain acts of Congress, with some law cases, and
a variety of other matters, chiefly original.
      Originally published: Philadelphia: P. Byrne, 1814.
    Includes index.
    ISBN 1-58477-161-5 (alk. paper)
      1. Law—Pensylvania. 2. Law—Great Britain. 3. Blackstone, William, Sir,
1723-1780. Commentaries on the laws of England. I. Title.

KFP80 .B7 2001
349.748—dc21

                                           00-059548

Printed in the United States of America on acid-free paper

LAW
MISCELLANIES:

CONTAINING

AN INTRODUCTION TO THE STUDY OF THE LAW;

NOTES ON BLACKSTONE'S COMMENTARIES,

SHEWING

THE VARIATIONS OF

THE LAW OF PENNSYLVANIA FROM THE LAW OF ENGLAND,

AND WHAT ACTS OF ASSEMBLY

MIGHT REQUIRE

TO BE REPEALED OR MODIFIED;

OBSERVATIONS

ON SMITH'S EDITION OF THE LAWS OF PENNSYLVANIA;

STRICTURES

ON DECISIONS OF THE SUPREME COURT OF THE UNITED STATES,

AND

ON CERTAIN ACTS OF CONGRESS,

WITH

SOME LAW CASES,

AND

A VARIETY OF OTHER MATTERS,

CHIEFLY ORIGINAL.

———

BY HUGH HENRY BRACKENRIDGE,
A Judge of the Supreme Court of the State of Pennsylvania.

———

PHILADELPHIA:
PUBLISHED BY P. BYRNE,
1814.

Alexander & Phillips,
Printers, Carlisle.

CONTENTS.

CONTENTS.

CONTENTS.

CONTENTS.

CONTENTS.

PREFATORY OBSERVATIONS.

IT struck me some time ago that it would be a work of utility for the *Student* of the Pennsylvania law; and *also* an exercise, or disquisition not without benefit to the *judge* himself, to examine in what particulars, the common and statute law of this state was different from that of the common, or statute law of England. This, it seemed to me might be best done by taking up the commentaries of Blackstone, and by notes to the text, marking these variations. Pursuing this thought, it occurred to me that an edition might be given under the title of the *Pennsylvania Blackstone*. Accordingly I had begun, and proceeded some length; writing out an introduction to such proposed edition; and some chapters tending to throw light on the connection between the law as it is in England, and with us; moreover going on with notes to particular passages in the pages of the commentaries as they came in order. But, on reflection it occurred to me that a printer would not be likely to find his account in publishing such an edition. For though like an almanac calculated for a particular latitude, it might without sensible variation in some parts, serve others, yet the bulk of the *notes, or observations*, having a respect to the law of Pennsylvania only, it must be confined in a great degree *to the students of this state;* and these, though daily growing in number, could not be supposed, for a great length of time to be sufficient to take off such an edition, even supposing it to supersede with them, any other. It was more than I could expect, even though a part of the notes of judge Tucker to his Virginia edition could be added, but which from the copy right under Congress, a publisher would not be at liberty to do.

It seemed to me also, that a principal advantage of the remarks which I found myself led to make, were *present* and *temporary;* so far at least as respected the successive amendments of the law by the legislature of this state, or the

A

particulars, in which, *speaking with deference*, they appeared
to have intermingled some things in their endeavours to improve the law, not altogether coinciding with my ideas of good
policy, or general convenience. If so, it might not be labour lost to suggest to the legislature for the time being;
or to the people from amongst whom they must, from time
to time be chosen, what might seem advisable to be a subject
of their consideration, as they might be led to consider the
law generally, or particular acts which had already passed,
or were meditated to be passed in future.

These were my reasons for dropping the idea which I
had at first entertained; and confining myself to a narrower compass; but more especially as I found that I would
not have leisure from my *official duties* to bestow much time
upon this *collateral object;* and in that case, it was not likely
that I could live to finish it.

" Vitæ summa brevis spem nos vetat inchoare longam."

Perhaps also I might add without an affectation of modesty, that upon experiment I was not quite sure, that it was
not an undertaking beyond my strength; or at least that it
would be thought so. Or even if not always thought, yet
abundantly *said;* I will not say, SUNG, amongst the profession. For what is extrajudicial cannot expect the same quarter from the learned of the law, as that which the judge is
bound to express, let it be right or wrong. He is considered as a volunteer, in what is said off the bench; and his
opinion, or notions as they will perhaps be termed, are canvassed with less *deference.* Hence perhaps the propriety of
a judge leaving to a posthumous publication, such lucubra-
tions as may have employed his time. But the secret
of my resignation on this occasion, is the not considering
myself as having attained such a height of reputation, that
if I did not add to it, I must descend from it. Not that
I will affect not to have deserved reputation; for I hate affectation in any shape; but not possessing any great cele-
brity on this head, it has not been fashionable to overrate
the small talents which I may possess. And to this I have
been most cordially reconciled; because, in troublous times,

it is safest to court the shade. And I have long since seen the vanity of human ambition. If so, it will be said, why do I write at all? Does it not argue some wish to please? For profit cannot be an object in such a performance. When I analyze my own feelings, I find it to be at bottom in a great degree the same principle which induced me, when a child to build houses of chips; or when a boy more grown to make a dam across a small stream, and to place a water wheel of thin boards to receive the fall. And this kind of pleasure in seeing the work of one's hands, "that it is good," would seem to be an emanation of the divine mind implanted in man, prompting him to improvements, in his small sphere, and according to the limited capacity of his invention. But it is this principle which distinguishes him from the brutal world, and is the foundation of his happiness; as well as an evidence of his superior nature. At the same time, I do not doubt, though I cannot so well recollect, that there was a secret consideration mixed with the amusement, that some one would see what I had done. So that man or boy, in literary or baby edifice, there is something of the

——————— *qua me quoque possim*

Tollere humo,————————————

At the bottom of every undertaking.

   Scire tuum nihil est nisi te scire hoc, sciat alter.

On a desert island without hope of society, one would read or write little. But it is not the motive that will be called in question, or ought to be, but the *execution;* though a good motive may form some excuse with the indulgent, and blunt the edge of censure; or at least it is with this view that it is urged, though, perhaps with not much effect. It is probably not much more than to say in conversation; you will excuse my detaining you, or I beg pardon for the trouble I have given. But even this is conciliatory, and is a compliment which decency exacts for the attention with which we have been heard.

PARTICULAR INTRODUCTION TO THESE
MISCELLANIES.

THE following notes and observations might seem to imply some presumption of thinking to instruct *the learned in the law*, were I not to disclaim this pretension, and profess myself to mean nothing more, than to instruct the *Student*, and less learned in the *legal science*. In fact, the *occasion* of most of these things was to assist one *studying* under my direction. It is unnecessary to say whether it was a son or another person. But being dictated to him or noted, and copied by him, it appeared to me that they might be also of some use to others. I will acknowledge that I had also another view in giving them publicity. It seemed to me that there were some of the observations which might be brought before the eye of the Legislature of this state, with a view to supply, abrogate, or amend acts of assembly. This was unquestionably a primary motive with me in the publishing; and I cannot but flatter myself, if they will deign to attend a little to the collection, they will be able to pick out something that may be useful.

At the same time there are many things which I cannot but think may be useful in other states of the Union; though chiefly calculated for that of Pennsylvania, looking to its laws and jurisprudence. I had once entertained as has been said, the idea, of preparing for the press, and publishing what might be called the *Pennsylvania Blackstone*. That was in fact, an edition of Blackstone's Commentaries, with notes in the manner of Tucker, referring to *the variations* in the law as it is in the state of Pennsylvania from that of England: the variations in the *introduction to the common law*, and in the statute law as it has been changed, or superseded, by our acts of assembly. But this appeared, upon more deliberation, and experience of the task, to be a work for which my official duties did not leave sufficient leisure. I have therefore thought proper to contract the design, and leave it to some one more learned in the law, or having more leisure that may come after. Some

outline of the law of Pennsylvania in the manner of Blackstone, would seem to me a desideratum for the student, and
would be of *use to the legislature.* There was also another
objection to such undertaking, without legislative aid. For,
being more peculiarly intended for the use of an individual
state, a sale could not be expected to be so general, as would
secure a *certainty*, or even a PROBABILITY of defraying the
expenses of a whole edition. These miscellanies are, in fact,
therefore, nothing more than some *materials* out of which
such a work might be composed, or *notes* of some of which,
such *an edition of the Commentaries might consist.*

It had been my plan, with the one studying under my
direction, at the *third reading* of the Commentaries to note, in
loco, the variation of *our* common law from that of England,
as not having been introduced, originally here; or as having
been altered by our own statutes; referring for this purpose,
to acts of Assembly, and to the reports of judicial decisions.
Before this, at the *second reading*, I had referred him to the
decisions of the English *courts*, chiefly such as are cited in
the margin of the Commentaries; so that, in reading these,
the bulk of the reporters in England were consulted; and
referring to the acts of Assembly, and the reports of decisions in this state, these were also read; which, whether more
or less pleasant, is, certainly, the only *profitable* way of reading. A particular point of law, or practice, is fixed upon
the memory, by thus dwelling on it and referring to several
books. The reason of the *principle* also, as a part of the
science, is better understood.

Be this as it may, it will account for my labour; which
might otherwise, appear somewhat *extra* to my judicial occupation; and will, at all events relieve me, in some degree,
from the imputation of considering myself as having such
pre-eminence in legal knowledge, that I could undertake to
write notes on a legal code; and, not rather leave it to those,
some of whom, at the bar, I could point out, as, if not having
more leisure, have unquestionably more ability. It is not
from affectation that I premise this; but, on the ground of
self-preservation. For there is nothing that produces person-

al dislike, and very deservedly, so much as the assuming consequence. We see it in society, and feel it every day. It behoves a man that would be safe from remark or injury, to conduct himself with humility; a lesson which is taught only *late in life*, and when one begins to find that the

———— *fallentis semita vitæ*

Is rather to be chosen than a glare of reputation. It is no doubt pleasing to the mind, to have some reputation above the common level. But it poisons all enjoyment of this, if it is not conceded with the good will of others. But enough of this; it will not suffice to make up a book of law with moral reflections.

INTRODUCTION

TO

WHAT MIGHT BE CALLED

THE

PENNSYLVANIA BLACKSTONE.

—————— ❋ ——————

IT must be the result of every man's experience, that happiness consists in the employment of the mind upon some object, the attainment of which, calls forth the energies of thought, or action. So that I consider the poet, as not going the whole length of the foundation of happiness, when he says,

"Reason's whole pleasure; all the joys of sense,
Lie in three words, health, peace, and competence."*

For though without these, little pleasure can be enjoyed; yet, even with these, little can be enjoyed, where there is wanting an occupancy of the mind. Hence it is, that Aristotle† places happiness in mental energy; an opinion says he, "ancient and universal among philosophers." The same thing is abundantly inculcated in that collection of wise sayings, which are ascribed to the Jewish King, Solomon, as meditated by himself; or, compiled under his direction. It will be seen from that *divine* composition, that the employment of the mind in *virtuous action*, is the means of happiness in this life; while, on the contrary, idleness is as comfortless in itself as it is disreputable, in the opinion of men.

* Pope.
† Gillies 254.

The historian Sallust, in his introduction to the Bellum Catilinarium, expresses the same idea: " *truly, he truly, at length, appears to live, and enjoy life, who intent on some business, seeks the reputation of some excellent achievement. or good art !" This is a sentence which may be called *golden*; and would deserve to have been inscribed on a column; or, over the gate of a temple by antiquity. For the employment of the mind, on some object of pursuit, is necessary to happiness. This is the nature of man, and the labourer who earns his daily subsistence, enjoys a greater portion of felicity, than the listless and vacant mind, which has no design to execute, and nothing to do. Give me an employment, or a profession, therefore, is the cry of nature to every one that has the conduct of youth.

The profession of the law under a Republican Government, not only leads to emolument, but qualifies for political eminence; if that were a thing desirable for one's own sake; which it is not; but, for the sake of the public, it is desirable. And it may not be in the way of private emolument, or happiness, for one of the profession of the law, to give his services to the public, on a special occasion: but for one's own sake, I have said that *political* distinction is not in general desirable. It is to the youthful of the profession, chiefly, that the glare of eminence in political life, is at all captivating: and, from the fire and passion of that age, they are the least fit for it. I count therefore him who confines himself to his profession, till he has arrived at the calm of years, as most likely to consult his own happiness, and at the same time, the interests of the public. For it cannot well be, that before this time, he has acquired an independence of estate; and much less, that he possesses that self-denial, and humility of spirit, which, experience in life, gives; so as to render him a useful member of a deliberative body.

But eloquence at the bar, gives great distinction. The name of the orator is not heard so much abroad; but, in pro-

---

* " Verum, enimvero, is mihi demum vivere, et frui vita videtur, qui aliquo negotio intentus, præclari facinoris, aut bonæ artis, famam quærit."

portion as his fame is concentrated, it burns the more steadily at home. It is, in the respect of those alone who are nearest us, and with whom we are conversant, that we find enjoyment. A *sphere more or less extensive* is of little moment.

But it is at the bar, that eloquence has the fairest scope; and, the most powerful effect. In the councils of the state, or of the nation, two formed parties will invariably prevail. The representative who does not range himself with one of these, can be of no account; he is heard by no one; because it is not what is reason, or good policy, that is considered; but what has been the previous determination of the party, or their leaders, out of doors. A speaker must know it therefore to be unnecessary to address those on the same side with himself; for they are already persuaded: and with regard to those on the opposite side, it must be the same thing as urging arguments to the walls. Hence it is, that, unless an individual can be at the head of a party, and lead it, he has little occasion for judgment; and none for eloquence. It is but a vain declamation on the side that he is, as a champion of their opinions; but without the least prospect of moving any one.

At the bar, on the contrary, a court or jury are to be persuaded. Were not even conscience to secure this for the speaker, in the breasts of Judges, and jurors; yet, respect for themselves, and their reputation amongst men, would, in general, secure it. For they are considered as deciding or giving a verdict, according to *the right* or *the wrong* of the case; and the credit of their understandings will depend upon it. Hence it is that having the human mind to deal with, free and unembarrassed as to the question, there is an encouragement to employ the resources of the orator, in canvassing the *law* or *fact* under consideration.

It may be worth while for me, now, to say a few words on the qualifications of a Lawyer. *Integrity* is unquestionably, the first qualification; *the love of truth and justice*. Without a consciousness of virtue, what man can even stand erect and present himself with a proper posture of body? but can he *open his countenance*, and shew that he is himself persuaded of what he says? Can he evince that indignation, against in-

justice, which the heart does not feel? It is impossible to
have a confiderce in one's self, unless conscious of integrity.
Hence it follows, that it is of the highest consequence, that
from the earliest years, the mind of one intended for an advocate, should be formed to virtue. Such is the connexion
between mind and body, that the feelings of virtue are
thought to contribute to health, and longevity; but, certainly,
to strength of intellect, and boldness of elocution. No man
can be great in any profession, much less in that of the law,
without *a soul of benevolence and truth*. It is a vulgar error,
that parts alone, meaning powers of understanding, can render great, *in a moral science*. The affections of the heart
have so much to do in sustaining right, and opposing wrong,
that if these are depraved, nothing great can exist. The in-
discriminate defence of right and wrong in the practice of
the law, is thought to deprave the mind. This impression
which prevails much, arises from a misconception of the duty, and the usual conduct of the profession. I have no idea
but that a lawyer, for his own sake, in giving counsel, will
advise to the best of his abilities; and in taking the cause
of a defendant, will point out to him the weakness of his defence, if there is a weakness; that the client may compromise,
and avoid costs. But it is his duty, if a defendant persists,
to undertake his cause; and to present it to the best advantage; and this in order to save him from the recovery of
more than ought to be recovered against him; and from *excess of damages*. For it being presumed, that a plaintiff having
had his choice of advocates, has chosen the ablest, a defendant
might be oppressed by the talents against him; and it is impossible for a Court and Jury to reach the whole truth, and
hit exact justice, unless the law, or facts of a case are well
discussed on both sides. The pleading and counter pleading of advocates, is a great help to the comprehending what
is equal in the meum and tuum of actions.

In the case of a plaintiff client, it is always, in the power
of a Lawyer, to decline the cause; if, on the plaintiff's own
shewing, it is not maintainable: and it is his duty to decline
it. Nor can I suppose, that he will not decline it, for his own

sake; since the failing in a suit, brings some disreputation upon a counsel; and is at least unpleasant. But it does not follow that because a plaintiff has failed in his suit, he had not reason to think, and so presented it to his counsel, as having a good cause of action. For evidence may have failed him which he expected to procure; or that may be brought against him of which he had not a knowledge. It is not safe for counsel; or, justifiable in them, to decline, in a matter of meum and tuum, and to undertake to say what is the justice of the claim; for he may err in his judgment of the law; and it is his business to serve his client, in bringing forward his case, before the proper judges; and presenting it to the best advantage, that it may receive a determination. I have no idea, that so doing, the counsel identifies himself with the cause; or makes the morality of it his own; nor does he feel that he does; though it is impossible, but that in a matter of dubious controversy, he may have a leaning in favour of that side which he espouses; and it is necessary that he should, in order to sustain the balance of a like leaning on the other side. But, if, in forming a verdict, juries will hang; or, in deciding, judges will differ, does it not prove that the right and wrong of the case, is not, always, so clear that counsel could pronounce upon it, undertaking it, that it was a clear matter. So far from it, that, such is the imperfection of human investigation, and even judgment, that the truth or justice of the case is not always reached. But, this I will say, that, if at all attainable, it will be owing in a great degree, to the advantage of an able discussion by counsel on both sides, presenting their respective cases, in the best point of view, for their several clients.

It is not to be understood that I would countenance sophistry, or quibbling, in attempting to persuade a court or jury; for no wise counsel will attempt this, as he must know that it cannot prosper. He may sail close upon the wind, in pressing a point; but not *in the wind's eye;* for if he does, to make use of a nautical phrase, his sails are instantly aback, and he will make no progress. Much less, in the conduct of a suit, do I take into view, what I reprobate, the catches of those whom I disclaim as lawyers, who avail themselves of the slips of counsel; and would take advantage of a mistake. These may be said to carry on the legal war, not according to the laws of civilized practice, but resembling savages, who make their attacks unseen, which is a species of assassination. This, at the same time, is, in general, as useless as it is vexatious; for, in most cases, it can give but the trouble of an application to the court to set right, on the payment of costs, and at the expense of the counsel who had not been duly vigilant. But these things are not known, but amongst the illiberal, who are at the foot of the profession. A nice and delicate sense of honour, and a contempt of undue advantage, that affects not the merits, is the characteristic of the noble minded of the profession; and these are always the *ablest* as they are the *fairest* in practice.

In order to qualify for the profession of the law, a *liberal education* is necessary. For, though there are instances of strong minds, that are but little indebted to a liberal education, making tolerable orators, and even lawyers; yet, it would have been of great advantage to them, to have possessed this. For something like a universal knowledge of literary subjects, would be desirable; because, in proportion as we have a knowledge of subjects, the mind is enlarged. For there is scarcely a subject of human knowledge, but that when the mind is brought to bear upon a point of at least *moral discussion*, it may not draw something from it to illustrate an argument or fortify a position. Not that I would have an orator to be able to support a thesis, in omni scibili et, de quolibet ente; but I would require some general information, on almost all subjects of science; especially that sphere of study which is fashionable, and I think useful, in our system of education. It is a question lately agitated whether the acquisition of what are called the learned languages, is useful. The perfect command of one's own vernacular tongue, in which the advocate is to speak or write, is certainly necessary; not the command of words merely, but the delicate selection of words, and choice of terms. In order to this, it is necessary to understand the precise meaning of words; and this is not to be collected from dictionaries; so well, at least, as from the roots of the words, which are found in those languages, from which our own is derived; and of which it is in a great measure made up, and composed. These are, of the ancient languages, the Latin and the Greek; of the modern, the French and the German. The farthest way about, is said to be, oftentimes, the nearest way home; and in order to be master of the English language, I would think it the shortest course to endeavour to obtain a knowledge of these; and more especially of the Latin and the Greek.

But by studying the structure of these languages we learn the structure of our own; in other words, the grammar of it; and nothing can contribute more to the richness and abundance of expression, in our own tongue, than a knowledge of these that are related to it. But the translation of an idea from one language to another, to which, in learning a language, we are accustomed, gives a facility in conveying an idea that is our own. And hence translation from another language, orally, or in writing, is an easy, and successful introduction to the speaking and writing our own.

But a great use in studying the analysis of language, is the habit of investigation; it being of all things the most difficult to fix the attention of the youthful and wandering mind. The tracing etymologies and examining the concords of speech, and the structure of sentences, is a good exercise for the judgment and suited to the understanding of early years.

But can any thing contribute more to form a taste for style than the study of these models of language, where there is every ornament and grace of expression: strength, at the same time, which will depend in a great degree upon *conciseness and brevity:* perspicuity also, without which there is neither strength nor grace. For were I to lay down a rule of style, it would be to endeavour to obtain *a precise and clear idea* of what is to be said; and, to express it *with the utmost brevity,* and in *the most perspicuous phrase possible.*

Where one is master of this, but which requires much pre-vious discipline of the mind, a diction may be indulged with the *embellishments of figure*, and the *flowers of imagina-tion*. But until this *rib and bone* of clear thought is obtaina-ble, all garniture but wearies. All this excellence of bre-vity, perspicuity, and grace, is distinguishable in the classi-cal writings. Hence it is that the diction of a good classi-cal scholar is distinguishable from that of one who has not had the advantage of this education, by a certain flavour, and, if I may so express it, *raciness* of diction that savours of the ancients. This, though not discernable in its cause in the hearer, is felt abundantly. There is a charm in such eloquence that is not equalled by him whose taste has not been so cultivated.

But it is not the etymon of radical words merely, that we acquire by the study of the learned languages; or even the helps to form our taste for style; or other advantage that has been hinted at; but in the course of acquiring these, we get impressed upon our minds many fine sentences, and ex-cellent maxims of good sense and morality with which the classic writers abound; and these, from the very difficulty of translating, become better fixed in the memory, than what is obtained with more ease and facility. But when we take into view the ancient mythology to which in our writings there is yet a great reference; and the knowledge of an-cient history, and ancient geography, with which these are connected; and which can, and ought to be studied at the same time; and also the lessons of rhetoric and criticism, which from these as a text the preceptor will explain, I do not know any more useful system, or course of study that can be taken. I would think it an up-hill work to undertake to make a lawyer without such a previous course of study, and such acquisitions. I say the more on this subject be-cause it is a prevailing idea, which *favours the indolent*, that the study of the dead languages is unnecessary. It is true, that from the slovenly and imperfect manner in which these languages are taught, with oftentimes bad pronunciation, and false quantity; and also from the neglect of them after the

academy is left, a slur is brought upon that part of the system of education. But it behoves that the acquaintance
which has been formed with the classics should be kept up ;

"Nocturna versate manu, versate diurna."

For, the reading the divine poets in these languages, and
in short of the poets in general, wonderfully feeds the imagination, and furnishes the orator with images and diction.
This brings me back a little to observe that the whole cir-
cle of the belles lettres, or what is called polite literature, is
necessary to eloquence. There is amongst all the fine arts,
in the language of Cicero, the commune vinculum ; and,
looking at them it may be said, in the language of Ovid ;

"Nec una facies omnibus, sed qualem decet esse sororum."

Hence these are called the *sister arts*. Runnington in
his life of Sir Mathew Hale, states of him, that when weari-
ed with studying law, he would recreate himself with Philosophy or Mathematics ; alleging "that no man could be
master of any profession without having some skill in all the
sciences." For, it will not be understood that I mean to
undervalue *mathematical learning ;* which is so universally
admitted to be necessary to assist the *reasoning faculty*, as
well as to enlarge the sphere of knowledge. But I say the
less upon this, because it is not questioned ; though I do
not think it a study proper to begin with ; or approve of
the system of Pestallozi, who makes it precede that of
Languages. It is the main study to fit the mind for mechanical pursuits ; and very properly constitutes the chief study in the military academies ; and though, doubtless, a public
speaker must be lame without a general knowledge of all
the parts that come under the idea of mathematical learning,
yet the *invention* and *imagination*, which constitute the orator, is not so much fed from this source ; and with regard
to moral truth, which is the soul of law, it has nothing to
do. The only practical branch of mathematics, of which
every lawyer ought to have a competent knowledge, is that
of the application of trigonometry to surveying ; and this
for the purpose of understanding the designation of proper-

ty, under the law of legal tenures, of real estate; and this cannot be without a knowledge of geometry, and the doctrine of angles.

Having incidentally made these observations I go on to observe, that the citadel of the law must be taken, if I may so express myself, by regular approaches; the difficulties of it must be encountered at long shot. Or, to lay aside a figure, the acquisition of this science must be rendered easy in the first advances to it, by a gradual introduction. History, ethics, and the constitution of government, or politics, is a natural and easy introduction to a science which is built upon these. And applying more immediately to what is called jurisprudence itself; and, especially our own municipal law, much will depend in gaining the attention, and facilitating the progress of the student, from the course of reading that is pointed out; under which I would recommend, the taking these commentaries* as a last task; and to read, and re-read with a reference to the authorities cited; and to others which may be noted; or to which he may be directed; essays and tracts, or particular adjudications. But the taking up abridgments and reports, and reading them flush through, is a waste of time; there is little left impressed upon the memory.

By such introduction and course of study as I have hinted at, rising like an inclined plane, the ascent to the summit is facilitated, which, when once gained, the hill top is pleasant, and it becomes delightful to look down upon the difficulties passed. It is under this image that the progress to a habit of *virtuous action*, is represented by the poet according to the translation of some one:

" Vices in throngs we may take in with ease,
Short is the journey and full nigh they dwell:
But in the road of virtue toil and sweat,
Th' immortal Gods have laid; long is the path
Thereto and uphill straight: and at the first
'Tis rugged all: but when the top you gain,
Thence smooth it lies."†

* Blackstone's.   † Hesiod.

But this I would not apply in such strong terms to the study of the science of the law, provided that the introduction to it has been, by taking advantage of the hill, as those who make roads; and, by ascending *obliquely*, attain eminence. In proportion as a proficiency is made in any science, or art, a taste is acquired for it; and it becomes not only easy, but pleasant; nor if skilfully managed, as has been hinted, are the first steps to the attainment of this science, so painful and laborious as they were wont to be, before this fine outline has been given in these commentaries of Blackstone; and when the student was under the necessity of encountering, in the first instance, the black letter of abridgments; or in the Norman French, the precedents of pleadings, and reports of the law. Even the black letter of Coke upon Littleton, at a more modern period, was discouraging to the tyro; and it was no wonder that many were drawn off from the task, and failed in attaining the profession.

I am aware that there is danger of too much indulgence in polite literature, so as to draw away from the necessary application to what is technical in the law; and yet without which the conduct of a suit, and an accurate knowledge of practice, as well as principles of common law, or statute, is not attainable. But the medium of an application to one and the other of these, must be aimed at. I have known a person who was so strongly attached to general learning and the belles lettres, that it become almost impossible to attach himself to the profound research of legal questions, and the deep study of science, so that he was under the necessity of retiring, for a time, from all opportunity of libraries, in order to become a lawyer; or to be in the way of becoming one.

When a competent legal knowledge shall have been obtained, so as to be admitted to the bar, it is a vulgar error to suppose that any acquirement, or even natural advantage, is substantially to be depended upon, but the being master of the science. Mere genius goes but a little way in making a lawyer; there must be a plodding; and hence it is that the plodding student will oftentimes reach the goal, when more

C

lively talents will not. It must be kept in mind, that general and liberal learning, is but an introduction, and a great embellishment and help; but without something like correct information, and knowledge of the science, the professional man may be said to be infelix summa operis; and a court would rather hear *him* who has some depth of judgment, but without volubility, or grace of diction, than all, that vociferation, with the best manner can do, where there is but the vox et præterea nihil; and to a jury even, closeness and clearness, in the illustration of matter of fact, or law is all prevailing. With the client himself, it is felt as hitting the nail upon the head; though, with a bystander, who is not bound by oath to give attention, or led by interest to consider the effect upon the understanding, declamation may be more pleasing; and flourishes, and gesticulations, and the sounding brass, and tinkling cymbal of the voice. Of good speaking, the great secret is good sense, and a knowledge of the subject. Of good writing, it is said by the poet,

Scribendi recte sapere est, et pricipium, et fons.

So also it may be said of speaking well; and no man will speak ill, unless through some want of habit, or impediment of tongue, provided that he understands his subject.

————————————Cui lecta potenter erit res,

Nec facundia de eret hunc nec lucidus ordo.

Thought is the body, and good expression the dress of thought. What is dress or ornament without a body? Hence the maxim, *think twice before you speak once.*

The not thinking, sufficiently, induces surplusage and repetition; for a consciousness that a thing has not been well said, leads to an attempt to say it better. Thinking before hand supersedes the necessity of this; and it is delightful to hear one speak who comes well prepared; whose words are, in the language of the scripture, " As goads, and as nails fastened by the masters of assemblies." Every word tells, so to speak; and to use another phrase of the same scripture, there is no " vain babbling." There is nothing that has contributed so much to depreciate the character of the advocate at the bar, as loose, tedious harangues, which proceed from a defect of classical education; or a want of due meditation on the matter to be argued.

It is a vulgar error, that forwardness and impudence is a qualification at the bar; on the contrary, modesty is characteristic of *the ingenuous mind, and bespeaks talents;* which is more likely to gain the attention of the court, as well as the public approbation, than *assurance without good sense, and legal knowledge to support it.* And, though noise and declamation, like a song, may please the uninformed suitors; yet when a man himself comes to be interested, and enquires for an able lawyer to defend his cause, he will look out for such as have a more solid eloquence.

Whether owing to the abuse of speaking at the bar, or to other causes, certain it is, that there would seem to be some prejudgment against the profession of the law in Pennsylvania. That there are other causes, I must admit. The denomination of people called Quakers, amongst themselves called *Friends,* do not admit a practitioner of the law to be in full communion. It is a regulation of discipline, not to go to law, but to decide all matters of meum and tuum by reference to members of the religious body : this is deduced somewhat from the example of the primitive christians, as appears from the censure of a contrary conduct in some instances, by the apostle : " Brother goeth to law with brother, and that before unbelievers."* With that body of people also who entertain the *puritan* doctrines, and who are the most numerous, presbyterians, &c. the name of lawyer is obnoxious ; and, somewhat, from a text of scripture familiar to them : " Woe unto you also, ye lawyers ; for ye load men with burthens grievous to be borne ; and ye yourselves touch not the burthen with one of your fingers."† But it is not considered that those of whom these words were spoken were *Jewish* lawyers ; and, of the Jews, it has been proverbial, at all times, that they are griping and usurious. And even of the Jewish doctors, before this time, and rabbies, the prophets had denounced the cupidity and the exaction : " The heads thereof (speaking of the *house of*

* 1 Cor. vi. 6.   † Luke xi. 46.

Jacob) judge for reward, and the *priests* thereof teach for hire, and the *prophets* thereof divine for money."* But I will not conceal that even the lawyers of our own times, in this *christian* state, are not altogether free from the reproach of taking higher fees than may comport with humanity, in many instances. The Stat. 32 Hen. viii. c. 9, respecting champerty and maintenance has not been introduced ; and the equality of condition, has doubtless been a reason of it ; and, oftentimes, parties not monied, preferring to stipulate for something out of what was recoverable, or, the giving of something unconditional, has introduced the practice, with the profession, of taking what are called *contingent* fees. This, nevertheless, cannot but be unavoidably accompanied with an over tenacity in pursuing a claim by litigation in court, after it shall have appeared in the view of indifferent persons, to be without foundation. Appeals, writs of error, and motions for new trials, are the fruits of this. In England it would not seem allowable in counsel to bargain for a proportion of the damages ;† "and even at common law there was a maintenance."‡ But, in the case of an attorney, I have not known the common law, in this particular, introduced here. For, perhaps, owing to the scarcity of a circulating medium, at an early period, it was tolerated, and has become common. But I take it, the bulk of the profession, at least the more eminent, would not be unwilling to have it understood to be unlawful ; for such bargains are often pressed upon them, and seldom where the client thinks his cause good. It seldom happens but that in case of a proposition of this nature, the suitor will keep back something very material in the statement that he gives, and on which the cause may turn.

Nevertheless, notwithstanding, owing to these or other causes, there may be some drawback on the popularity of the profession ; yet, in the nature of things, it *cannot but*

---

* Mic. lii. 11.

† The law severely contrabands,
  Our taking business off men's hands..........*Hud.*

‡ 15th Vin. 151.

be respectable. It is a proof of this, that it is perhaps too much coveted; persons applying themselves to the profession who cannot succeed in it: invita Minerva, and against nature. This results, in most instances, from parents designing their sons for a literary profession, whose particular genius they have not been able to ascertain. And it cannot be, in all cases, from a prospect of attaining great wealth, that the profession of the law is obtruded upon young persons. For though, with reasonable industry, a competent independence may be gained by the practice of the law, yet it seldom leads to great emolument. But the idea of knowledge gives power; and there is naturally associated with the idea of one skilled in the laws, that of power, *in a government of laws.* It cannot but occur to an individual, that he may have occasion for the assistance of an advocate, in defending his estate, or his reputation. For no man can be placed beyond the reach of being assailed, in both these respects. But, independent of any use to ourselves, the idea of superior information, and intellectual endowments, has a charm to the mind of man, from the love of excellence as we admire beauty in other matters. In proportion to the superiority of mind above body, the powers of intellect are valued. This is evident from the less estimation of a fine art in proportion as it is coupled with *manual labour.* Who would not rather be a Demosthenes than a Phidias? A degree of liberal knowledge is indispensable to the profession of the law, and the practitioner cannot but be supposed to possess more, in general, than the *husbandman,* the *mechanic,* or the *merchant;* though I must acknowledge that there are exceptions at the bar, as well as on the bench; mere clerks and note-takers, or whose minds are confined, in a great degree, to the narrow limits of technical learning, and, in their conversation, can talk of nothing but of John O'Nokes, or William Stiles, or John Doe, and Richard Roe.

I can have no difficulty in saying which is the greatest effort of the mind; the conducting an army or the management of a cause in court. Sallust,* who was himself a mili-

---

* Inprimis arduum videtur res gesta scribere.

tary man, has made it a question, which of these requires the greatest talent, the task of the general, or that of the historian. Although I will allow that this may be made a question; yet I consider the framing a narrative, with all the philosophy that may be interspersed, which is the task of the *historian*, as far behind that of the *orator*. And I can have no conception of any thing approaching nearer the *power* of an *angel*, than the management of an argument with the human mind; requiring an intuitive knowledge of the heart to distinguish what can persuade : those resources of argument, which can lead the understanding; that presence of mind which gives a command of diction, and which, from sober reasoning, can ascend to the regions of imagination, and turn and wind the fiery Pegasus of fancy, descending or re-mounting as the subject may require; the orator in his lofty flights, like the eagle,

" Sailing with supreme dominion
Through the azure deeps of air."*

Great generalship requires great judgment; but not more than a game of chess. An equal judgment, and presence of mind is required in the orator; the surprise of sudden emergencies calls for the talents of a commander; but not less are displayed, though apparently of less magnitude, where, in the course of a trial, *the evidence takes a sudden turn, and the front of your defence must be changed.* It is the image of a field of battle. But to presence of mind and judgment, the faculty of eloquence must be superadded ; that wonderful arrangement of ideas which must appear almost miraculous. An able lawyer could not but make a great general; but it does not follow that an able general would make a great lawyer; for the province is more extensive, and the task greater. A campaign or two will form a general; but the able lawyer is the work of years ; viginti annorum lucubrationes. It behoves to begin early and to discipline the mind much. The dictum may be applied in this case; " he who is industrious to reach the

* Gray.

wished for goal has done and endured much in his early years."*

It is difficult to make up for *the want of application in early years;* under which want of application, the American youth chiefly labour. Owing to the indulgence of parents, and family education, there is a want of tone in the mental system, which it is not easy to restore in the academies, or produce. And even here, there is oftentimes a want of a discipline sufficiently rigid: on the contrary not only too loose a rein, but a superficial course of study. And after leaving the academies, sufficient preparation is not enjoined, or allowed for the gaining a knowledge of a profession; and this from an impatience to get forward, and to fly unfledged from the nest. *Boys are men too soon,* and therefore, *always boys.* We see the skilful husbandman repressing the luxuriance of his grass, by cutting; *or lopping* his tree, to give it base, and make it spread. The American genius is vigorous abundantly; but there is an impatience to appear, in the capacity of men, and to undertake a profession; which cannot but be in the way of *attaining a great eminence.* A lofty structure requires a deep and broad foundation. " Nor would Italy, says the poet, be raised higher by valour and feats of arms, than by its language, did not the fatigue and tediousness of using the file disgust every one."†

The not having the means of support in going through a regular course of education, and waiting a reasonable time for an admittance to the bar, is a reason with many for this haste; but impatience is the cause with more. With those that want means, there is usually, industry and perseverance, to make up for this; but it requires industry and perseverance. A medium between easy and narrow cicumstances is desirable, but not the possession or prospect of an estate,

* Qui Studet optatam cursu contingere metam
Multa tulit, fecitque puer.
† Nec virtute foret clarisve potentius armis,
Quam lingua Latium; si non offenderet unum
Quemque poetarum limæ labor et mora.———

Horace.

independent of the practice. For when there is such a prospect, or possession, the necessary exertions cannot be excited that will make a lawyer. It may be said to be as easy,
in the language of the scripture, with a view to another object, for a camel, or cable as some suppose it ought to be translated, to go through the eye of a needle, as for the son of a
rich man to become a lawyer; or in fact almost any thing
else that requires labour. Such must remain amongst those,
the fruges consumere nati. The Novi homines, the res au-
gustæ domi men can alone surmount the drudgery of acquiring a knowledge of the law; or sustain the practice.
Were I to depict the making a man a lawyer, I would
change a little the image of that moral painting in the tabla-
ture of Cebes, where the virtuous man is represented as
climbing a rock, two female figures (sisters) *self-government*
and *perseverance*, standing above, and extending their hands
to encourage him. I would represent one clambering up a
precipice, and poverty, like an old and ugly witch, with a
flail, urging from below.

——" Duris in rebus urgens egestas."

It is one advantage of the law of primogeniture in England, though working seeming hardship to younger sons;
that they are put upon their own exertions; and with but
little means are under the necessity of tasking all their faculties for their subsistence; and for enabling them to rise in the
world. The church affords a living for some; and there is
a prospect of becoming dignitaries. But the army, the navy,
or the law, affords more generally a prospect of advancement.
These require great exertions in order to be competent to
the task; and necessity prompts, and calls forth all the powers of mind and body. Distinction is the consequence;
and hence it is, that the history of the peerage of Great Britain, contains an illustrious catalogue of those who have so
risen. Elder brothers, who enjoy the estates at home, are
little heard of but for their hospitality; their fox hunting;
or as giving, what may be called a dumb vote, in parliament.
Wealth is the bane of genius, while *poverty is the preceptress.*
Ingenii largitor venter. Wealth with its concomitant luxu-

ry, is the destroyer of virtue; whether with an individual or a nation.

The sentence that was pronounced upon Adam was not more a punishment than a preservative; a suffering than a medicine; " by the sweat of thy brow," &c. Labour and industry are the means necessary to restrain, and keep in subjection the passions. Adversity shews the necessity of the assistance of others, and must produce philanthropy in an ingenuous mind; and no greater secret can exist in getting forward in the practice of the law : civility and humility are popular qualities. It is the semblance of these that men affect when they court popularity for the sake of office, or advancement in the public councils. But the esse quam videri, is more easy, and at the same time, more natural.

An honest and faithful defence of a client in a good cause, is perfectly consistent with that indignation which may be expressed against the claim of an adversary, and may call for it, with respect at the same time for his general character. What hinders the distinguishing the claim from the man; save so far as it is an evidence of his injustice in the particular case. But I speak of general benevolence to society, and respect shewn to high and low. This is better than clinging to a particular denomination of the religious, from worldly motives; or affecting fanaticism; or espousing a party in politics. For this must detract from a consciousness of sincerity in one's self; and lessen the respect of the discerning, who may question the motive.

But what is the object of practice, but the acquisition of some estate; which, if wealth is an evil, ought to be avoided. The possession of wealth *is neither good nor evil in itself;* but immoderate wealth is *the cause of self-indulgence,* and *the occasion of evil.* This consideration ought to be a check on the cupidity of riches. I have seldom known a lawyer, or any man else who has left a great estate, that had a son, of much reputation, to succeed him. The pleasure of a gainful accumulation, is all that he has ever got for himself; and pride and sloth the sum of what he has acquired for his descendants. The want of motive to action is but ano-

D

ther name for the legacy that is left; and this want of motive entails listlessness, and lounging, and recourse to clubs
followed by intemperance. Such are to be pitied when under the necessity of amusing themselves by invitations to
convivial entertainments; and compliments for the company of those whom they respect or not as it happens. The
gout and the dropsy is in their viands, and their cups.
They must be indebted to the theatre in the winter, or to
watering places in the summer; where, if infirmities do not
lead them, the having nothing to do, will.

It may now be proper to suggest what it is that had put
me upon writing this introduction, with a view to an edition
of Blackstone's Commentaries. For though, considering my
station, it may not appear presumptuous, yet it might be deemed unnecessary. Tucker has given an edition, in which he
has taken a view of the outline of the constitution and government of the United States which has taken place of that
of England; and at the same time of the constitution of Virginia, and the laws under it. *Might not the same thing be necessary as to the constitution and laws of each state in the
union;* shewing what principles of the common law have been
introduced as applicable to our situation; what statutes, or
construction of statutes; or, in what particulars, the common
law has been changed by our acts of Assembly; or by the decisions of our courts? It must be of an advantage to the
student whose reference to these, under the respective heads
of the law, may be made, at the same time, *with the reading
these commentaries.* It will save a great deal of time to have
presented to his view these relations, oppositions, variations
and congruencies, under the particular head that is treated of
in this outline of the law of England. Not that I could expect
to have it in my power to go through with it, owing to the
little time I have to spare from official duties; and from the
date of life drawing to a close at no distant day. Nevertheless it may lead the way for some other person of more talents and leisure, and, beginning earlier in life, to complete
the object. For it is clear to me that something of this kind
ought to be done, as well for the use of the practising lawyer as for the service of the student.

LAW MISCELLANIES.

SOME VIEW OF THE ENDEAVOURS TO IMPROVE THE LAW BY THE LEGISLATURE.

IN the year 1787, going into the office of Wilson, (James) of Pennsylvania; great as a lawyer, but greater as an orator; I observed a folio bound up with blank leaves, intervening; and in which he had begun to add notes, under the respective heads of law; perhaps only as *Christian*, has since done; or perhaps with a reference at the same time to the principles of our common law, under the respective heads, as it stood upon our introduction of the common law; or, as it has been varied since, by acts of assembly or otherwise, in the manner of Tucker, as to the laws of Virginia; for as to the constitution of the United States it had not been then formed; for in fact it was a delegation to the convention that formed this constitution; and afterwards to the state convention which adopted it, and the subsequent judiciary appointment to the bench of the supreme court of the United States, that interfered with the going on with his design. It was a loss; because the mind of that man was great and comprehensive. He has left three volumes of his writings, chiefly lectures delivered as professor of law in the university of Pennsylvania, at the same time that he filled his judicial station. From the continuance of these lectures, his attention was drawn, says the editor of a posthumous publication of them (his son Bird Wilson) " by an object of more importance in which he was engaged." In March 1791, the house of representatives in the general assembly of Pennsylvania appointed him " to revise and digest the laws of the commonwealth; and to ascertain and determine *how far any British statutes extended to it*, and to prepare bills containing such alterations, additions and improvements, as the code, laws, and the principles and form of the constitution then lately adopted, might require." In a letter on the subject to the speaker of the house of representatives of the 24th Aug. 1791, he reports some outlines of his system, and the progress he had made. But, as stated by his editor, owing to the want of a provision by the legislature sufficiently ample for the pecuniary expenses necessary to the purchase of books, papers, &c. and the assistants, the design of framing a digest under the authority of the legislature was relinquished.

It was considered a great loss by intelligent men that the design should be abandoned; and, it continued to be thought of as what ought to be accomplished.

By an act of the 17th April, 1807, " the judges of the supreme court were required to examine and report to the next legislature, which of the English statutes are in force in this commonwealth, and which of those statutes in *their* opinion ought to be incorporated into the statute laws of this commonwealth." December 4th, 1808, that report was made. It cannot be understood that this report had the force of a decision by the court; much less that it could be considered, as to any statute so reported, to be conclusive; for it must remain the right of any person to contest it, in a judicial investigation, as to the being in force or otherwise; nor could even an act of the legislature make it conclusive a parte ante, as to property holden under the existence of any statute that had been introduced. For, in that case, it would have a *retrospective* operation, which, by the constitution, cannot be. The report of the judges, and any sanction the legislature could give it, must be still considered subject to the right which any one must have, to show, by themselves or counsel, in a judicial trial before a court and jury, that such statute had been introduced, though the legislature might from that time provide that it should not be in force. Nevertheless it was a wise and necessary policy to have such a step taken towards ascertaining what were in force. It was an advance to the obtaining some information on the subject. It had been indeed questioned whether an obligation could be imposed upon the judges to make such a report, it being extra-judicial wholly; but approving the object, the judges cheerfully undertook it; but considering such report as nothing more in law, than if made by any other four of the community, whatever weight it might have as being made by persons who were supposed competent. It was regretted by them only, that, consistent with their official duties, there was not sufficient leisure to make such enquiries and researches as were necessary to satisfy themselves. For as to what statutes had been introduced, it could be collected only from the memory of the practising lawyer, or notes of cases, in which any particular statute had been considered as extending. Notes were few, and printed reports none, from the settlement of the colony until after the revolution, and the state became independent. Those of Dallas were the first; and these from notes of but some cases furnished chiefly by the judges, or rather an individual judge, the Chief Justice. But these reports, even though imperfect as respects the whole state, have been of great utility; and much credit is due to the reporter for his undertaking as well as for the execution. It was chiefly from *the memory of the profession;* or the recollection of admissions or decisions in the course of their practice at the bar, or since they came upon the bench, that the judges could supply the defect of written evidence, as to what statutes had been introduced, and were considered as in force. There was not leisure or opportunity to consult the profession in these particulars, even those of them that were within a narrow compass, and had resided in the city; and, as to those in the country, it was out of the question. There was little or no opportunity of consulting these from their scattered residence. And yet the enquiry was, in part, a matter of tradition, and depended upon the usage. Unwritten common law evidence was, in many cases, all that could be got. No wonder then, that under this haste, the profession should be unwilling that this report of the judges should be considered as *final* or *conclusive.* It could not be

so considered even with every advantage of enquiry; for
that could only be where the point came in question in the
course of a trial, and on a judicial investigation; in which
case evidence could be called for, oral or written, to assist
the information which the judges might have of their own
knowledge. With these helps, and the argument of learned
counsel, able and better informed than themselves, as is
often or most usually the case, they might be enabled the
better to form a judgment.

The task was more extensive which was delegated to
Wilson (judge.) It was not only to say what statutes had
been introduced; and in fact to say what ought to be adopted, as applicable to the principles and forms of our constitution; but to prepare bills containing such alterations, additions and improvements as the code of laws and this constitution, and these forms might require. It was to do more;
to revise and digest the laws of the commonwealth. By an
act of March 10th, 1812, legislative encouragement was given for the printing the English statutes which are in force
in Pennsylvania as reported by the judges of the supreme
court, together with their report on that subject. This was
another step towards accomplishing what had been delegated to judge Wilson. But it was but a very small step. It
is nothing more than a printer could have done, and was
about doing; and well deserving this encouragement. But
it would be a great object, and require an able lawyer, or lawyers perhaps; for in a multitude of counsellors there is
safety; it would require lawyers, I say, to go further, and
to point out *what construction has been put upon these statutes by the English courts; and what construction has been
adopted here; what practice deduced under these in England,
or here.* This would be a most useful work. For even to
the bulk of practising lawyers, or judges, it is not familiar.
The language of these statutes also is in some degree obsolete, and by the people unintelligible. A translation, as it
might be called, into modern and popular expression, would
be necessary; for it can be but of little use to the legislature,
in examining these statutes, to have them presented to them

as they are, without explanation, or comment. It would be a task of ability to do this; and would require high talents to draw bills embracing the same thing in a modern style of enactment. But to frame such bills adapted to our constitution, and the forms of it, would be a matter of still greater difficulty. But the task delegated to judge Wilson embraced more; it was, *to revise and digest the laws of the commonwealth;* and this was perhaps a still more important object; and greatly conducing to the convenience of all the officers of the commonwealth; to the legislature; and must be greatly satisfactory to the people themselves. It would be desirable to have a single law on every particular subject, embracing the provisions of the several laws on that head, and contained in other acts and supplements. This would reduce the acts of assembly to a much lesser compass; and if done by a person or persons equal to the trust, might be drawn up with such simplicity and perspicuity of expression as would preclude much litigation. It is the result of much habit of composition to make use of words *unequivocal and unambiguous,* as well as to *arrange* properly. It requires clear thought, as well as a perspicuous diction, to frame a law. It is the *arrangement alone,* in our language, that secures perspicuity. In the ancient languages, or what are called the learned, there is *concord* or agreement; the relations of gender, number, case, person, &c. enabling to refer one word to another, and to couple, so as to assist the construction, or to ascertain the meaning. But in our language, unless with the most careful attention to the *arrangement* of words in a sentence, there can be but little more than a guess at the meaning of an act of assembly oftentimes, where words and sentences irreconcilable with each other, will occur. It is but a conjecture, in many cases, what the construction ought to be.

By an act of March 3d, 1812, the governor was " required to request the attorney general to draught and prepare a bill, consolidating the whole of the penal laws of this commonwealth, and suggesting what additions, alterations, and changes should take place in the system, for the purpose of laying before the next legislature." This is precisely what was delegated to judge Wilson, with regard to the laws in general, civil as well as penal; and though the injunction and request to the attorney general, is, under this act confined to the penal laws, yet, from what has been done, and the spirit evinced to improve the legal code, there can be no doubt but that the farther prosecution of the subject will be resumed, and delegated to some person or persons competent to accomplish what had been projected, and delegated to judge Wilson, and which the attorney general has been called upon to do in the case of *the penal laws.*

It will occur to any one to ask, and it has been often asked, why not compile a system of what is called the common or unwritten law; that the legislature having it under their view, may restrain or abolish as they think proper? It has been already done in the outline of these commentaries;* but embracing an outline of both common and statute law. But it is but an outline that in any reasonable compass could be given. But the common law, which is called our *birthright*, became ours in our colonial state, and was carried with us only so far as was applicable to our situation; and hence it would be a more practicable object to ascertain and select what parts or principles of the common law *we did not bring with us*, not being applicable to our situation. This, cut out of the mass, it would be more easy to show, than to say what *had been left behind.* In the notes to the outline given in these commentaries, it may be pointed out to the student, what of the common law has been left behind; referring to the contrary usages by which the common law has been changed; and to such parts and principles as are not applicable; at the same time referring to acts of the colonial legislature, or since the revolution, by which they have been abrogated. A more compendious outline of the common or statute law might be given, omitting all that is unknown to our code; but to the law-student, it would still be requisite to take a general view of the whole system of the English law; and this from the interlacing of the branches of the

* Blackstone's.

same stock. A knowledge of the ecclesiastical law, having no church establishment in this state, is, perhaps of all, the least necessary; yet, some general knowledge of it, cannot well be dispensed with. Nevertheless a compend or abridgment of the common law as retained by us, and of the statute law, British statutes introduced, or our own statutes, might be compiled for the use of such as are not of the profession. This, in the hands of the people, would be desirable; for, in that case there would be no great danger that every man would commence his own lawyer; but rather that knowing something of the law, he might use his knowledge to avoid litigation. Where the attainment of office is open to every man, some acquaintance with the common and statute law ought to be possessed if possible by every one. The science of law, says judge Wilson,* "should in some mea-
' sure be the study of every free citizen, and of every free
' man. Every free citizen, and every free man has duties
' to perform and rights to claim. Unless, in some measure,
' and in some degree, he knows those duties, and those
' rights, he can never act a just and independent part. In a
' free country, every citizen forms a part of the sovereign
' power: he possesses a vote, or takes a still more active
' part in the business of the commonwealth. The right and
' the duty of giving that vote, the right and the duty of tak-
' ing that share, are necessarily attended with the duty of
' making that business the object of his study and enquiry.
' In the U. States, every citizen is frequently called upon to
' act in this great public character. He elects the legislature,
' and he takes a personal share in the executive and judi-
' cial business of the nation. On the public mind one great
' truth can never be too deeply impressed, that the weight of
' the government of the United States, and of each state
' composing the union, rests on the shoulders of the peo-
' ple.'

Some years ago, in this state, a current set strongly against the common law of England; and it was within a point of being abolished by the legislature. This was owing

* Lectures on Law, part 1. chap. 1. 9.

E

to a total ignorance of what it was.   Editors of papers, who
had been prosecuted for libels, raised this hue and cry, as
it may be called, against the common law.   It may contribute therefore, as the prejudice has not altogether subsided,
nor the misunderstanding been removed, to give some idea
of that law; and this I shall do by a quotation from the
preface to Rolles' abridgment, said to have been written by
Sir Mathew Hale.   There is contained also in this preface
some idea of those parts of the law which, even in England,
have become antiquated; but much more so here.

    ' The common laws of England are not the products of
' the wisdom of some one man, or society of men in any one
' age; but of the wisdom, counsel, experience, and obser-
' vation of many ages of wise and observing men : where the
' subject of any law is single, the prudence of one age may
' go far at one essay to provide a fit law; and yet, even in the
' wisest provisions of that kind, experience shews us that
' new and unthought of emergencies often happen, that ne-
' cessarily require new supplements, abatements, or expla-
' nations; but the body of laws, that concern the common
' justice applicable to a great kingdom, or commonwealth,
' is vast and comprehensive; consists of infinite particulars;
' and must meet with various emergencies; and, therefore,
' requires much time, and much experience, as well as much
' wisdom, and prudence, successively, to discover defects
' and inconveniencies, and to apply apt supplements, and re-
' medies for them; and such are the common laws of Eng-
' land, namely the productions of much wisdom, time and
' experience.

    ' The common laws of England are settled and known;
' every entire new model of laws labours under two great
' difficulties, and inconveniencies, viz. 1. That though they
' seem specious in the theory, yet when they come to be put
' in practice, they are found to be extremely defective; ei-
' ther too straight or too loose, or too narrow, or too wide;
' and new occurrences, that neither were, or well could be,
' at first, in prospect, discover themselves, that either dis-
' joint, or disorder the fabric; and therefore such new mo-

' dels, continually, stand in need of many supplies, and a-
' batements, and alterations, to accommodate them to com-
' mon use and convenience, whereby, in a little time, the
' original is either wholly laid aside or in a great measure
' lost in its amendments, and become the least part of the
' law. Again, were such new entire models of laws never
' so good, yet it is a long time before they come to be well
' known, or understood, even to those whose business it
' must be to advise or judge according to them ; so that even
' a more imperfect body of laws well known, at least to those
' that are to advise or judge. is more of use and convenience
' to the good of society, than a more perfect and complete
' body of laws newly settled, and therefore to be newly learn-
' ed.

' The common laws of England are more particular than
' other laws ; and this though it render them the more nume-
' rous, less methodical and takes up longer time for their study,
' yet it recompences with greater advantages; namely, it
' prevents arbitrariness in the judge, and makes the law
' more certain, and better applicable to the business that
' comes to be judged by it. General laws are indeed very
' comprehensive, soon learned, and easily digested into me-
' thod ; but when they come to particular application, they
' are of little service, and leave a great latitude to partiality,
' interest. and variety of apprehensions to misapply them ;
' not unlike the common notions in the moralist, which when
' both the contesting Grecian captains most perfectly agreed,
' yet from them, each deduced conclusions in the particular
' case in controversy, suitable to their several desires and
' ends, though extremely contradictory to each other. It has
' therefore always been the wisdom and happiness of this law,
' not to rest in generals, but fitted almost to all particular
' occasions. But usage and disusage hath antiquated much
' of the law, and statute also hath taken off or abridged many
' titles ; and the various excesses, and alterations in point of
' commerce, and dealing, hath rendered some proceedings,
' that were anciently in use, to be no more useful ; and
' some that were anciently, useful to be now less useful :

' hence several great titles in the law are at this day in a great
' measure antiquated, and some abridged, and reduced into
' a very narrow compass and use."

The learned prefacer goes on to enumerate a number of
those titles, so antiquated in their application; or so abrogated by statute. Nevertheless it will be of use to the student to acquire some general knowledge of these titles, and
the law under them, in order the better to understand the
reason of those statutes which have come in their place; or
usages which have superseded. For which reason, some
learning on these heads, cannot well be dispensed with, as
throwing light on the law which now exists.

If titles are abrogated, or obsolete in England; and
usage is changed; how much more so in our colonization
from the mother country, and under our own statutes, and
adjudications. For, as has been seen, it is only so much of
the statute law as has been introduced; or so much of the
common law as applied to our situation, that is in force.
For this see note infra to page 39.

During that period in Pennsylvania, that the current set
so strong against the common law as what ought to be abolished, some sensible publications appeared in the newspapers, and excellent treatises by way of pamphlet from the press.
Of these, that by counsellor Hopkinson of Philadelphia, is
perhaps the best; but without his signature. It deserves to
be preserved; but having dwelt so long on this subject, I
cannot give even an extract.

A very useful step was taken by the legislature towards
giving the public some idea of our law: by an act of 28th
Feb. 1810, provision was made for publishing a new edition
of our acts of Assembly, "noting under each act the decisions of the courts of Pennsylvania, or of the United States,
which have been given upon the construction thereof; the
work to be examined and *approved* by the judges of the supreme court; and the governor authorised to appoint some
fit person to superintend the said publication." It has been
my understanding of the duty, in this case, that the examination and *approbation* must respect what of the work to be

examined and approved, was of such a nature, as to come within the province, more peculiarly, of the judges; and this must respect the *notes of judicial decisions.* Nor do I understand it that the approbation can be considered as going farther than to say, that, there had been reasonable industry used in collecting such notes. It could not be understood as undertaking to say that such decisions had taken place in the extent; much less to vouch for the correctness of the principles laid down. It could not be the intendment of the Legislature to give a father effect to the approbation of the judges; for that would be making these notes a part of the text, and the decisions equivalent to the acts themselves. My idea of the object of the legislature was to obtain information of decisions which had taken place under acts of Assembly with a view to supplement or alteration: some general knowledge of the construction which had been given by the judiciary branch, in order to such amendments by the legislature *as such construction would seem to require.* In subservience to the spirit with which this attempt hath been made to improve our jurisprudence, it may be suggested that a farther step might be taken. By the act of the 28th Jan. 1777, " The common law and such of the statute laws as had been in force, are declared binding." With regard to the common law, it is a well known principle that so much of it only, could have been carried by the emigrants to this state, as was applicable to their situation and therefore so much of it only in force. What of it was applicable must be determined by the courts; or, from time to time, by the legislature. In cases where the change of situation might not seem to warrant the courts to declare the common law not applicable, the legislature alone could interfere. As, for instance, in the case of a jus acrescendi, or survivorship in joint-tenancy, which by an act of the legislature has been lately taken away. There might be other principles pointed out, which would seem to have got a footing, and cannot be changed but by the legislature; such of them as would seem to have become *rules of property*, and above the power of the courts to alter. Thus, a principle of the common law has been altered in regard of the succession to real estate, in the case of an intestate ; not only, as to the proportion to be taken by the representative; but as to the offspring of the representatives taking the share of the parent in equal portions among themselves. See act of Assembly 13 Ap. 1791, and of 19th Apr. 1794. But in the case of a devise to one dying before distribution, and leaving children, it has been decided that an intention could not be inferred of giving to the children the devise to the parent, and therefore the children could not take at all, 1st Bin. 546. This would seem to require a provision that the children of a devisee shall take amongst them what the devisee himself would have taken, had he been alive at the time the estate came to be divided.

I suggest a farther step, that, under the act of April 1807, the judges of the supreme court were confined in their report, to English statutes before the revolution; but, as the common law remained the great mass of jurisprudence in both countries ; and even after the revolutionary period, the legislation of both frequently respected the same subject, the alteration of the common, or statute law, as it was before that time, might deserve to be looked into, and in some instances followed by statutes similar to those passed in that country since. To give an instance of what I mean ; in the case of *a writ of mandamus* as it was at common law, this writ has been rendered more effectual, and better guarded by the statute 9th Anne, c. 20. But which statute the judges could not report as introduced here ; because it did not appear that it had been introduced ; though they might well consider it as containing provisions, which, in whole or in part, were necessary to the like effect, in this commonwealth ; and which has been done in Virginia by an act of the legislature of 1798. A revision also of the law in the case of *writs of error* would seem to be called for, to some extent ; and the privilege of a freeholder in the case of process also ; and in some other cases which it would require time and attention to specify.

NOTE

INTRODUCTORY TO THE REPORT OF THE JUDGES ON THE
BRITISH STATUTES IN FORCE, &c.

By an act of Assembly of April 7, 1807: the judges of
the supreme court were required to examine and report
which of the English statutes were in force in this commonwealth, &c. The following is my note to the chief justice
(Tilghman) accompanying the whole of such acts as made
out, on my investigation, and according to my judgment.

" Which of the English statutes are in force in this commonwealth (Pennsylvania) is the first part of the point which
is to be examined. In order to ascertain this, it would be necessary to retrace our judicial history, and to see how it is
that any of these statutes can be in force. For this purpose
I take up our own statute book and examine whether there
is any law which goes to this, posterior to our present constitution. No law was necessary; for by the schedule to the
constitution which makes a part of it, it is provided " that
all laws of this commonwealth in force at the time of making
the said alterations and amendments in the said constitution,
and not inconsistent therewith; and all rights, &c. shall
continue as if the said alterations and amendments had not
been made." I am struck with nothing in this constitution
that is inconsistent with the *English statutes that were in
force before the adopting it.* The question then is open to
enquire which of the English statutes were in force before
the adopting this constitution.

In tracing this I find nothing until I go back to an act
of the legislature under the constitution altered and amended by the present constitution, which act is of the 28th Jan.
1777; and entitled " an act to revise and put in force such
and so much of the state laws of the province of Pennsylvania, as is judged necessary to be in force in this commonwealth." In this act it is provided that " the common law,
the principle which it contained might be adopted in usage.

and *such of the statute laws of England* as have been heretofore in force in the said province, (Pennsylvania) shall be in
force, except as in hereafter excepted." These exceptions it
will behove to note when we come to examine which of the
statute laws of England had been heretofore in force in the
said province; now state of Pennsylvania.

There is no law of the late province extending English
statutes generally; though there are acts adopting the provisions of certain particular statutes. But were not the English statutes in force in the late province independent of any
legislative act of the province; I speak of those acts that
had passed after the settlement of the province? "English
acts of parliament made in England, without naming the
foreign plantations will not bind them" 2 Peere Will 75.
"They are subject however to the controul of parliament,
though not bound by any acts of parliament, unless *particularly named.*" 1 Black. Com. 104. It would seem from
hence that the English jurists did not consider such statutes
in force here as did not particularly name the *plantations*,
and, by force of that term, comprehend the late province.
Several English statutes were enacted naming the *plantations;*
that is, extending the statute to the *plantations*. But the
force of a statute here, under that predicament never came
to be examined until the 6th of Geo. III. c. 12. which expressly declares "that all his majesties colonies and plantations in America, have been, are, and of right ought to be
subordinate to and dependent upon the imperial crown and
parliament of G. Britain, who have full power and authority
to make laws and statutes of sufficient validity to bind the colonies and people of America subjects of the crown of G.
Britain in all cases whatsoever." The attempt to carry this
power and authority into effect, gave rise to the revolution,
and solved the question that no English statute was in force,
in a colony, plantation, or province even by *particularly naming it*. It will not be alleged that the judicial power of the
province had authority to extend an English statute passed after
the settlement of the province and put in force here; or that
it could be in force in any way as an English statute, though

But in that case it could not be said that an English statute was in force, but a principle derived from it. This may be said to amount to the same thing with the statute being in force, and to be equally recognized by the act of January 28th, 1777, which provides " that such of the statute laws of England as have been heretofore in force, shall be in force except as herein excepted."

But I do not see that it can be admitted that an English statute could be said to be in force by its own enacting, even though the colonies are *particularly named in it;* notwithstanding as late as 1782, an expression is attributed to the court in the case of the lessee of Morris vs. Vanderen, which would seem to imply that the idea was then entertained that it would be in force. " It is the opinion of the court that the common law of England has always been in force in Pennsylvania; that all statutes made in Great Britain before the settlement of Pennsylvania, have no force here unless they are convenient and adapted to the circumstances of the country; and that all statutes made since the settlement of Pennsylvania, have no force here unless the colonies are *particularly named.*"

But if it be admitted that an English statute would be in force by particularly naming the colonies, so as to establish a rule of property, or a principle of municipal regulation, I do not see how we can justify the opposition to an English statute imposing a direct tax; much less to a statute which went indirectly to collect a revenue by duties on internal or external commerce.

Nor am I able to conceive that by an adjudication of the courts any principle could be legally derived from a statute passed subsequent to the settlement of the province, unless within that sphere where the judiciary have a power to adopt rules, independent of the legislature, and which must be confined to the rules *of pleading and the forms of justice.* Unless it be that the idea may at first have been entertained in the province, which prevailed in England, that a statute was in force in the plantations, where they were *particularly named;* and that from thence there was an acquiescence in

F

the application of them by judicial determinations; until the statute of 6 Geo. III. c. 12. and onward, presented this principle in so full a view, as to put an end to all acquiescence, in the most distant exertions of it. How far the principle, or provisions of a statute may have been adopted, and may have got a footing in our jurisprudence in this way, and how sanctioned by the 28th of January, 1777. becomes a matter of no easy ascertainment, if the duty assigned can be thought at all to embrace it.

Virginia has expressed herself, as to statutes before, and since the settlement of the colony, with precision on this point. " The same convention which established the constitution judged it expedient to pass an ordinance, declaring that all statutes or bills made in aid of the common law, prioi to the 4th year of James the 1st, and which are of a general nature not local to that kingdom, so far as the same may consist with the several ordinances, declarations, and resolutions of the general convention, shall be considered as in full force, until the same be altered by the legislative power of the colony." Tuck. Black. Appendix 444.

I take it that our legislature in the act of Jan. 28, 1777, could not have meant more; it is observable that the legislature of the province in many acts from time to time, have adopted the English statutes in the same words or to the same effect; which would seem to shew their sense to be, that without a legislative *sanction* no English statute, passed subsequent to the settlement of the province could be in force. This I think is the point of view in which it ought to be considered, and that we cannot undertake to say that any English statute is in force which passed subsequent to the settlement of the province. But if a statute should occur to our examination, which though since the settlement of the province has been passed by the English legislature, and *adopted by the adjudications of the courts*, it may come under the head of " such statutes as ought to be incorporated into the statute laws of this commonwealth;" and may be reported as such.

With respect to such of the English statute laws as were in force, at the settlement of the province, a great part have been suspended by acts of the legislature of the late province; or by our constitutions since the revolution; or, by acts of the legislature of the state. The question therefore will be narrowed, in the first instance, to what English statutes were in force at the *settlement of the province.*

By the charter of the province to William Penn, sec. 6, it is stipulated, "that the laws for regulating and governing of property within the said province, as well for the descent and enjoyment of lands, as likewise for the enjoyment and succession of goods and chattels, and likewise as to felonies, shall be and continue the same as they shall be for the time being, by the general course of the law in our kingdom of England, until the said laws shall be altered by the said William Penn, his heirs or assigns, and by the freemen of the said province, their delegates, or deputies, or the greater part of them." But this general extension of the laws of England cannot be taken without exception; and that exception must be taken from the general law, to which every stipulation must be subject, and which law is founded in the nature of colonization, which cannot carry with it all the regulations of the parent country, but such only as have *subjects to attach upon* and are not excluded by the change of situation. "If there be a new and uninhabited country found out by English subjects, as the law is the *birthright* of every subject, so wherever they go they carry their laws with them, and therefore such new found country is to be governed by the laws of England." Peere Will. 75. Salk. 411, 666. "But this must be understood with very many and very great restrictions. Such colonies carry with them only so much of the English law as is applicable to their own situation, and the condition of an infant colony." Black. Com. 107, and Tuck. ap. 443, "our forefathers migrating to this new country, brought with them all the laws of the parent state which were applicable to their own condition, and circumstances, and this extended not only to the common and unwritten law, but also to the written laws of the kingdom from whence they emigrated. But this principle extends only to the existing laws of the parent state, at the time of the colony being settled, and not to such as should be thereafter made."

In the case of the commonwealth vs. Mesca and others, 1 Dal. 74, 75, the chief justice makes a query, whether it was intended by the act, meaning that of 28th Jan. 1777 to include only such acts as were in force by an express extension of the legislature or to comprehend likewise such statutes as had been extended by the *judgment of the supreme court*, or received there in usage, which seemed to him to be in some degree uncertain. 1 Dal. 74. A statute expressly extended by the legislature, became an act of the colony, under the proprietary government, and had been comprehended under the preceding part of sec. 2. of the act of 28th Jan. 1777 ; " each and every one of the laws, or acts of general assembly that were in force and binding on the inhabitants of the *said province* shall be in force and binding on the inhabitants of this state." Whence it appears to me that the sentence of the section which follows, and provides for the statute laws of England can mean only such of the statute laws, as were in force by their own operation as applicable to the situation of the colony under the proprietary government.

Here opens the field which is now to be traversed ; which of the statute laws of England were applicable to the infant colony settled under the charter to William Penn ; and, were this left to the exercise of judgment as a question to be determined for the first time, by any one, the mind would be free to draw the conclusions as to what statutes were applicable, to the situation, and in force in the new colony. But it has been a subject of judicial consideration even since the first establishment of the courts, as a case arrived which would come under a statute of the present state, to say *whether that statute or any part of it, was applicable, and could be adopted here.* Hence it becomes a matter of evidence what statutes have been in force by the adjudications of the supreme court, and to be collected amongst other means of information, even from *oral testimony,* as would appear from the case aforementioned of the commonwealth vs Mesca and others, where the chief justice in addition to what was before stated, goes on to observe that "if this was a new case the judgment of the court would be different, on the ground however of the precedent we hold ourselves bound. 1 Dal. 75." This depended on the *oral testimony*, given in court, of a trial where the statute in question was held to be in force and the privilege of it extended to the accused. It may be easily conceived that when a statute come, in question in the first instance, it cannot always be a matter of easy determination whether it comes under the predicament of a statute which applies to the *situation and circumstances* of the new government. For being a matter of reason and judgment, requiring information, and sound discernment, the mind of a discreet man must deliberate carefully and decide cautiously. Hence the researches and argument of counsel learned in the laws, and policy of the respective governments, is useful to assist; and it is oftentimes a discussion of much length, to enable a conscientious, and prudent court, to make up an opinion, whether the point has been decided, in a particular case. To consider it as subject to a new discussion when the same statute comes again in question, would be an endless task, and involve *continual uncertainty*. Evidence therefore of a preceding determination, will be received, and bind, where the same principle again presents itself. This evidence must be the recollection of those present at the adjudication: or in a remote case, some memorandum, preserved in the notes of the judge; or the practitioners of the law; or introduced in practice, and communicated like the rules of a legislative body, or the laws of a game at school; the preceding decision being a guide to the next, until it grows into usage, and is known and considered as an established principle. "We know that many English statutes for near a century have been practised under in the late province, which were never adopted by the legislature, and that they might be admitted by usage and so become in force." 1. Dall. 75. This last must be the principal source of our knowledge on this head; for during the century which elapsed under the judicature of the province, scarcely a ves-

tige remains of the adjudications of the courts in any written
document; and yet it must have been during this time that
the provisions of the English statutes found their way into
our jurisprudence. At this day it is often a matter of solid
argument, and resting on the reason of the application or the
tradition of practice, whether a statute is in force, or not. And
the judges are now called upon to a task which in the opinion
of some might be better left to be investigated, as the point
arises, and comes to be disposed of on trial in th courts; and
this I take it remains the case in most of the states at this
day. But the state of Virginia has set the example to this
state, by endeavouring to ascertain and reduce to a certainty
what of the English statutes were in force at the revolution,
and which of them ought to be adopted. What has been done
on this head may be seen in Tucker's Black. Com. 443, '4, '5.
It was a matter of time in that state, and though taken up Oct.
1776, was not completed until 1792. It was done by committees of succesive legislatures with the assistance of professional men who were of the committees, or who contributed their
information, and advice as they were consulted. " At the
same session (1772) says Tucker, the assembly passed an
act repealing under certain restrictions, all statutes or acts of
the parliaments of Great Britain heretofore in force within
this commonwealth, with a proviso, that all rights arising
under any such statute or act shall remain in the same condition, in all respects as if this act had never been made."

From the above sketch it may be seen that it is not the
labour of an hour which has been enjoined upon the judges
of the supreme court of this state by the late act of the legislature; and though there are four judges, yet the labour to
every one must be the same, each finding it necessary to examine for himself.

But though it may be necessary to evolve many volumes,
and investigate much in this research; yet I cannot think
when statutes are referred to, the whole or a part of which
may be considered as in force, the section can be of great
bulk. For the greater part were of such a nature originally,
as could not apply to the situation of the colony, under the

charter to William Penn; or have been superceded by the
laws of the province; or of the since state. "Colonists carry with them only so much of the English law, as is applicable to their own situation; and the condition of the infant
colony; such for instance as the general rules of inheritance
and of protection from personal injuries. The artificial refinements and distinctions incident to the property of a great
and commercial people; the laws of police and revenue (such
as are especially enforced by penalties) the mode of main-
tainance for the established clergy, the jurisdiction of spiri-
tual courts, and a multitude of other provisions are neither
necessary, or convenient for them, and therefore are not in
force." 1 Black. Com. 102,103.

But when reduced by this criterion, the English statutes
must be still more abridged, by the original charter of incorporation, of the settlement; or in addition to this by the
conditions on the part of the proprietary with the first settlers; concessions, or charter of privileges granted them;
but still more by the acts of the legislature under the province. For though an English statute which might otherwise
extend, be not *expressly* repealed, yet it may by *implication*;
and is so considered, where it is on the same subject; notwithstanding it may adopt, but a part of the provisions of
the English statute in lieu of which it would seem to be introduced.

Nevertheless, though the statutes will be found to be few
in number, that can be said to be in force; yet in the application of them, they will embrace a wide extent; not only
from the immediate subject; but also from what has been
considered in England; and adopted by us, as within the
equity of them. As for instance, the statute of 1 Rich. II. c.
12. under which an action of debt is given against the *war-
den of the fleet*, for an escape; this statute is extended by
equity to all sailors and officers; and here as in other instances, whether depending on the express words of the statute,
or considered as within the equitable construction of it.
A duty is assigned of much delicacy, and requiring great deliberation. For though it may be presumed that the exi-

gency of the occasion, taught the necessity, or policy of applying any one at first; and experience being the best test of the expediency of any rule, it may be considered as the same thing to say what has been the adjudication, or the usage, as to say what ought to be; yet there will be found exceptions when the principle is taken up on original ground, and the mind is left at liberty to think for itself, with a view not to judicial decision, but legislative reform. As in the instance adduced of the state of 1 Rich. II. which gives the writ of debt on an escape, and subjects the officer to the whole demand, instead of the writ on the case at common law, under which might be taken into view the solvency of the debtor; and the probable damages sustained by the creditor.

It is true, that this last part of the duty assigned, the saying which of the statutes in force, ought to be incorporated, goes but to matter of opinion as to the policy or general convenience of any rule; yet it must be viewed as a trust of high confidence, and demanding the best attention that can be paid to it. And though the research and inquiry, under the first head, ascertaining what statutes are in force, embracing matter of fact in a great measure, may be of more labour, yet the last, the determining what ought to be incorporated, will require equal thought, and reflection. Hence it will be comprehended how much time the duty assigned must necessarily call for, and where that time can be taken but by intervals, to what length the completing the task must be protracted. And though numbers may at first sight, seem to promise a quicker dispatch, yet in fact it must be a cause of delay. For though it may answer the end in view, and doubtless will answer it, of greater wisdom, or judgment in the execution, yet where the same ground is to be gone over by every one, each being responsible, and under the necessity of examining the deductions of the others, so as to be able to concur, or if obliged to dissent, to fix the reasons, with precision in his mind; and to draw them out with satisfaction to himself; it will be understood why it is that a compliance more prompt has not been made with the fulfilment of what has been enjoined. I say fulfilment, because the moment the notification was made of the act of assembly under which the duty arises, the utmost attention was paid to it, and the minds of each turned to the object as much as the discharge of usual, and indispensable official duties, rendered possible."

So far my note to the chief justice. The report made to the legislature was directed by them to be printed; but no law has yet taken place incorporating, but these acts stand on the same foundations as formerly; nor can the courts be considered as absolutely bound by this report, but the question still open to further investigation when any particular statute comes in question. Some may be found to have been overlooked in the research which has been made, which, either from the nature of the provision, or from introduction, had been in force.

But though the above was the object to which the attention of the legislature was directed at this time; yet the effect or binding authority of British decisions, whether on the constructions of statutes, or on principles of the common law, was a question in the minds of the public. For by an act of assembly of the 19th March, 1810, " it shall not be lawful to read or quote any British precedent or adjudication, which may have been given or made subsequent to the 4th July, 1776; provided that nothing therein shall be construed to prohibit the reading of any precedent of maritime law, or of the law of nations." This would seem to have proceeded under the idea of these precedents or adjudications having been received by the courts as *authority* theretofore which was not the case. The following had been my ideas on the subject, a note of which I had made in order to hand it to some member of the legislature while the law which afterwards passed, was in agitation.

" A distinction is taken between a decision of the English courts prior to our entire separation from that government, by the declaration of independence on the 4th July, 1776, and a decision of those courts since that separation. I am not able to say that there is not a distinction. But it is in contemplation of law only; and, in fact, amounts to nothing. For all admit that though the decision posterior to

G

our independence will not govern as precedent, it will guide
as reason. Why is it that the anterior to our declaration of
independence shall govern as precedent? This depends on the
5th chapter of the charter to Wm. Penn, which, granting
power to establish courts of justice, reserves to the " King,
his heirs and successors, the receiving, hearing and determining of the appeal touching any judgment to be there made
or given." The acquiescence of a decision of the provincial courts is supposed to carry with it a tacit acknowledgment of correctness ; yet, in fact, we know that the distance
of the tribunal of appeal, and across a perilous ocean, and
the expense of prosecuting an appeal constituted in most cases
a *bar to the making it*. So that it cannot be inferred actually
that where there was no appeal, there was no dissatisfaction
with the principle of the decision.

But did not the provincial courts during the connection
with the English government possess a concurrent right with
the English courts to examine antecedent decisions ; and to
canvass the reason ; or correctness of them, as much as the
English courts themselves ? The English courts do enquire
into the reason and *correctness of decisions ;* and to this is
owing much improvement of the law. Did we dare to follow them in these decisions, reviewing and departing from
decisions ? We did follow them ; for there was not a judge
upon the bench who would not say, *such was the law, but the
late decisions are otherwise.* For, from the acquiescence there,
and the prosecuting no writ of error, to the court in the last
resort, the presumption was that it was the law ; and that
should a contrary decision be made here, and an appeal prosecuted under our charter provision, it would be reversed.
Hence so far as the common law or statute law of England
remained common to both countries, decisions on the same
law remained equally guides to both. But the decision of
the *mother country* only could be supposed to have weight to
guide. Why should they not be supposed to have weight
still? All the difference is that in the one case we could not
use our own reason without knowing that it might be pronounced erroneous in the court of the last resort there ;

and that now we may use it, without looking to such consequence. But shall we regard the reason and sense of them
less because they cannot say we *shall* regard it? Voluntary
submission is a legitimate authority. Decisions of the English courts since our separation have made great improvements on that portion of the law which is common to us
both. Where our reason tells us that it is an improvement
in giving light in the administration of justice, shall we not
follow it for its own sake, as much as if there was a principle which says we *shall* do it? All the difference, is, that before our separation we might be bound to follow *error*, and
now only *truth*. With respect to English decisions therefore, since our separation I am willing to take all advantage
of them as much as if they were forced upon me; so that
it is but in idea that I distinguish them as authorities. For
I do not think that the act of our legislature immediately on
our separation, and which is of the 28th Jan. 1777, by which it
is provided that the *common law* and *such of the statute laws
of England as had heretofore been in force* should be binding
here, can be construed as fixing upon us the decisions of the
English courts, either in matters of *common law* or *statute
construction;* so that the exercise of judicial investigation
should be restrained, and all question precluded. On the
contrary, I would entertain the idea that we have at least an
equal power with the English courts though we might exercise' it with less confidence, in the examination and application of decisions. And in the course of that examination
and application, what hinders to look at the recognition or
rejection of principle on the same subject; or at the comments of the expounders of the same text; and if we look
at them and find them reasonable, take them for our guides.
In fact we do take them just as much now as we would have
taken them before the revolution; and we might just as
well say we do, as that we do not. The great lights that
may be thrown on many parts of the law, and may be yet
thrown upon it, are not to be neglected. The science is improving there, and shall we refuse ourselves the advantage
of any help? I admit that respect for English authorities,

may become servility : but, that is as likely to be the case, or more likely, with regard to those before our separation, than those since. A judge of the court in the last resort here may claim the privilege of a judge of the court of last resort in England in reviewing English decisions ; which are only evidence of law ; and supposes a law of which they are the evidence ; and to which, if erroneous they ought to be brought back. But what shall be the test of that error? *I know nothing but the mind that is to judge.* The principle is to be got at ; and that is to guide. I have nothing to do in these observations, with that part of the law that is merely *arbitrary* and is not founded in reason, but where the *ita est*, is the only thing that can be said about it. There is such a thing as freedom of mind in a judge ; and *narrowness* of judges is spoken of in the commentaries of law ; and an *adstriction* to decisions is a fault. But it is in the application of principle to case that the error consists ; for I have no idea that a judge has a power to make a principle, any more than to enact a statute ; but in application of principle to case error springs ; for such case is said to prove such a principle, whereas it only proves that such a principle was applied in such a case. It is true that as a great part of the law is unwritten, it can only be from decisions, or chiefly, that we can ascertain the principle ; and in matters where reason has nothing to do these ought to be conclusive. But where reason can have a place, it is a maxim that *what is against reason cannot be law.* Here the advantage of the exercise of reason in deducing the principles of legal science, and the first lesson to a student of the law ought to be, to distrust authority. A mere automaton of decision, is little better than the machine that plays chess by springs.

But I have wandered from the point I had set out upon, the weight attributive to English decisions since our separation from that government. I shall only add a word or two upon the abuse of citing them. For I call it abuse to take up time in reading at great length from those decisions ; and to which I take to be owing, in a great degree, the popular prejudice against them ; and which has been near *excluding*

them altogether,* which I should consider to be a loss; for
there is much excellent sense to be found in them; and
which may be a great help in the administration of justice.
And it is with a view to contribute to prevent this total exclusion, that I have been willing to give these thoughts publicity. The public opinion is that the courts are governed
by decisions as if these made the law; and that, from the
force of education, and professional reading we are adscripti
glebis, and as much serfs in mind, as those were in body that
used to go with the clod. It ought not to be so; and with
some exceptions is not so; and it is a great matter that
it should be understood by the people, that unreasonable
prejudices may not be excited, or exist. My idea of decisions posterior to the revolution is this; that they are the
comments of men upon the same subject with that which we
have to consider. It is as if men who had set out from the
same place and having travelled together a certain distance,
had parted; but having occasion to refer to the point at
which they had set out, and the part of the ground travelled together, they should compare notes and correct their
journals, as well as to notice the improvements that might be
made, or to co-operate in making them. It it is true that this
drew upon us the purchasing and reading in courts, the
new books and late reports in England; but it saved, in a
great degree, as it does in England, the consulting old
books : for even there the year books, and Dyer, and many
others are little seen. Many of them are out of print, and
not to be got at with us at all. For these reasons I cannot
say that I would be unwilling to see our act of assembly
repealed, which goes to preclude the reading or citing in
court the later authorities.

* Since excluded.

ON THE STARE DECISIS.

IT occurs to me to express a few thoughts on the respect due to prior decisions. Certain it is that the stare decisis, is a salutary maxim, but it has appeared to me, that it has been carried sufficiently far in this country: in England there is such a thing as a departure from decided cases; and where there is not, we see nevertheless, in many instances, great dissatisfaction expressed with decisions. In the very first case, 2 East, 280, where lord Ellenborough takes his seat upon the bench, he uses these expressions: " If this question had come now to be decided for the first time, I should have been prepared to decide it upon the plain words of the statute which have been *broken in upon* by many cases, laying down rules of construction much less plain than the words of the statute itself." And again, 301, " As the case now before us, is in terms the same as that decided, I think it is better to abide by that determination than to introduce uncertainty into this branch of the law, it being often of more importance to have the rule settled, than to determine what it shall be. *I am not however convinced, by the reasoning of that case, and if the point were new I should think otherwise.*" And again, 3 East, 230, " If the case were res integra I should have done no more than apply my understanding." And 7 East, 60, " If this were a case in which we were called upon to decide for the first time upon a recent statute, there would be strong ground for the argument; but the uniform decision has been otherwise, and that opinion has always prevailed in practice, though perhaps the opinion obtained at first *without duly weighing the words.* But after so great a length of time, and such a *mass of property conveyed in this manner, it would be too much now to say, that all which has been done is erroneous.*"

We may see from these words of lord Ellenborough that a series of decisions is not always, with him, conclusive evidence of what is right, and the revising the decision resolves itself *into a question of expediency;* and that will depend upon two considerations, the " quod sit nota" of the rule; and that of property having been changed under it.

Lord Kenyon, the preceding chief justice, came upon the bench under the great weight of a name just before him, and having for associates men whom he found there, and who had participated in the decisions, which he would have had to encounter, had he undertaken to unsettle any of what had been considered as established during that period. Nevertheless he discovers a freedom of mind, occasionally, with regard to decisions before their time, as 3d T. R. 155, where he uses this expression, " The question must be admitted on all hands to be inter apices juris, if the objection could prevail, it would not be because it *is built on grounds of reason,* but because ita lex scripta est ; and then, however unreasonable we might think it, we would not be warranted in trampling on a series of decided cases to overturn it. But it does seem to militate against every *idea of reason and justice.* In a case of necessity I might be compelled to say, that what was supposed to be the old law was founded on mistake, and *that the law of the country has in modern times been better adopted to general convenience."* Here one may observe that this *adaptation* must have had a beginning, and this could only be in the breaking off from precedent.

In 4 T. R. 151, he gave a little vent to his impression, that too much respect might be paid to the opinion of a great judge ; he observes that " it is not now necessary to consider whether lord Holt were right ; in so *pertinaciously adhering to his opinion* before the statute of Ann, that no action could be maintained on promissary notes as instruments, but that they were only to be considered as evidence of the debt ; that question exercised the judgments of the ablest men of that time ; but the authority which his opinion had in Westminster Hall made others yield to him, and it was thought necessary to resort to the legislature to apply a remedy."

It gives me pleasure here to take notice that this question has been most ably examined in the appendix to 1 Cranch ; and the error of Holt, and his pertinacity abundantly exposed by an American writer, which to me appears valuable, in that it is doing something towards our emancipation from the too great authority of what a lord may have said.

In 4 T. R. 512, lord Kenyon states, " That it is incumbent on a party who wishes to establish a point contrary to all *justice and equity*, to produce some direct authority shewing that there is an inflexible rule of law established in opposition to justice." This by implication admits that rules of law may be established by decisions contrary to all justice and equity. On another occasion, he uses words which throw a light on the subject of decisions. " If this question," says he, " *were at rest*, either by reason of decided cases, or by the general opinion of Westminster Hall, I should not be inclined to disturb it now. But I perfectly well remember that when the Taunton case was argued, so far from the profession acquiescing in what was thrown out by the three judges immediately after the argument, great doubts were entertained about it."

And 5 T. R. 556, " The cases cited from Ventris, ought not to be treated lightly, or overturned without great consideration, because it has the sanction of lord Hale's name. But as at present advised, I confess it appears to me that the reasons given in support of that judgment are strong *to shew that the decisions ought to have been the other way."*

In 5 T. R. 682, he says, " I do not think that the courts ought to change the case, so as to adapt it to the fashion of the times; if an alteration in the law be necessary, *recourse must be had to the legislature for it.*" But in contrast with this dictum of lord Kenyon, I give the bold sentiments of the canonist Gomery, which I find quoted and approved by some chancery writers; " Non est inconveniens judicium esse uno tempore justum, et postea ejus contrarius justius. Opiniones secundum varietatem temporum senescant et intermoriantur, alioque diversæ renascuntur et deinde pubescant." This I take to be found in the nature of things; and though the principles of justice are always the same, yet the application of general rules, even in the like case, may from extrinsic circumstances become unequal and unjust.

And this is one great advantage of a jury trial, where the heart can feel the right which the head is at a loss to ascertain; and hence a consideration which ought to have a powerful effect in governing the discretion of a court in granting new trials, certain it is that even where a judge lays down the law, speaking of decisions, it ought to be sparingly said, *we are bound by it.* For though even a series of decisions may amount to a moral certainty of truth and reason, it is not conclusive; and in contemplation of law, any judge is supposed to examine a principle when he sanctions it, and if the decision is contrary to his own reason, he has a right to depart from it, and it can only be considerations of *expediency* that can hinder it. For in the language of lord Chancellor Finch, in the case of the Duke of Norfolk, " I must be saved by my own faith, and not another's; and must not decree against my own conscience and reason." Every man is supposed to use his own reason when he judges; and to be *assisted only by that of others,* who have gone before him.

The respect shewn to the sentiments of the jury by Lord Kenyon, appears from 1 T. R. 153, " I confess, says he, that the impression I received at the trial, was unfavourable to the defendant; *but the jury thought differently, and I see no reason upon mature deliberation to differ from the conclusion they have drawn.*"

Lord Mansfield, 1 Bur. 419, observes, " When solemn determinations acquiesced under had settled precise cases, and became a rule of property, they ought for the sake of property to be observed, as if they had originally made a part of the text of the statute." Yet in tracing his decisions it is impossible not to observe, that he is but little embarrassed with the old cases where they come in contact with his own reason. He has a felicity in getting over them and that is in most cases not by directly overruling, but by neglecting them though pressed in the arguments of counsel, and taking notice only of those that make for the opinion he has himself formed on principles of reason; or if he does take notice of them it is to give them the go-by with a " this is dis-

tinguishable." In some instances indeed he does not hesitate to speak with contempt of a case, as 3 Bur. 1281, " the
case in the exchequer cannot be rightly represented to us; for,
as it is represented, one of the two resolutions, viz. that upon
the statute of limitations, is wrong to the last degree, and
obviously so to every body."

In developing principles, the mind of this judge, often
pours a stream of light which puts out cases, or renders
them necessary as on the ejectment trial, 3 Bur. 1291, or in
1423, on a point of pleading; or respecting the will of a joint
tenant; 1498, or in that of Curret v. Vaugh, as to the bear-
er of a bill of exchange maintaining an action against the
drawer where he grants a new trial contrary to his own direction at nisi prius, misled as he alleges by cases; and though
strongly struck at the time, that upon general principles the
bearing of them was against law and justice. He did not
always take up water at the stream's mouth, but went to the
source; the " antiquos exquirere fontes," would be a good
motto for a sergeant's ring, though I have not seen it mentioned as used.

Another occurs to me from the poet Horace, which would
be a good motto, and expresses a principle which governs
too little,

—————————————— Sensus, moresque repugnant,
Atqui ipsa utilitas, juste, prope mater et æqui.
It would be too much to say of the judiciary,
—————————————— raro sensus communis in illis;
and yet mother wit seems to me to shew itself less than
might be expected in a science which contains the rules of
right and wrong in the transactions of men.

In 1 Bos. & P. N. S. 69, Sir James Mansfield says, " I
do not know how to distinguish this from the case before
decided in this court." It is of greater consequence that the
law should be as uniform as possible than that the equitable
claims of an individual should be attended to. The idea
that the equity of a particular case must be lost, for the
sake of a general rule, is not always satisfactory, or that a
general rule ought not to be changed though it is found to

work iniquity; notwithstanding there is the same power in the court to change it, that there was originally to make it. For it is said 1 Bos. and Pul. 207, N. S. by the same judge, that "certainly of late years the courts have been inclined to relax the strictness of the old rules respecting *proof*, which were thought to be attended with great expense and difficulty."

In the case of Wright v. Child, this chief justice discovers an independence of mind which might seem to militate with the doctrine of technical construction of devises in opposition to the popular meaning of the words; and though he concedes to the weight of authority against him, yet acknowledges it to be, at least in that case, against his own judgment. "This case says he, has been long depending, not so much on account of any doubts entertained by my brothers, as by myself; the rest of the court being of opinion, that the defendant is entitled to judgment. And therefore I now defer to the opinion of my brothers and of the judges of the court of king's bench, yet, I must declare that if it had fallen to my lot only, to decide the case, I should have decided it in favour of the lessor of the plaintiff. *I am bound to say that this is still my opinion.* In all the cases where questions of this sort have arisen, it has been next to impossible, *out of a court of justice to doubt of the testator's intention.*"

In 3 Bos. and Pull. 124, the case of Atkin v. Berwick is relied upon in the argument, and of which lord Alvanly observes; "It is singular that this case should have been often cited with disapprobation, and never overturned; but that different judges should have supposed it proceeded upon different grounds." Brook justice, speaks of it as "at different times confirmed," and Chambre says "perhaps if a case precisely similar to that were now to arise, it would not receive the same decision. It might be difficult now to support the case, as it was then decided, and it is remarkable that where this case has been mentioned upon various occasions, it has been constantly found fault with, and yet the judges have never particularly stated the parts with which

they quarreled, but have always confirmed the case upon
the whole, and held on the decision to have been right." It
may be seen from this, *the disposition of men's minds, to be en-
slaved to what is gone before:* In the gross, to feel a thing
wrong; but to think it a trespass upon the sacredness of
precedent, to undertake the examination, and to declare it
so.

3 Bos. and Pul. 245, Justice Heath observes that "with
respect to the case cited from Barnes, (Read, v. Garnet,) that
has been *overruled* by subsequent authorities and practice;
indeed many of the cases reported in that book are not law;"
and Brooke justice, "the reason upon which the decision
in Read v. Garnet is founded, proves it to be a case of no
authority," and in an excellent note by the reporter in the
case of Wennal v. Adney, the words are that the opinion
of justice Buller in the last case (Hawkes v. Saunders) was
to the same effect, and the same law was again laid down by
Lord Mansfield in Freeman v. Trenton. Of the two former cases, it may be observed that the particular point decided in them has been overruled by the subsequent case of
Deeks v. Strut, 5 T. R. 690. This shews that the judges
will test a decision *by the reason of it*, and *overrule* what has
been *ruled* before.

Referring to cases, 3 Bos. and Pul. Chambre, J. says;
"the language of those cases does not appear to me very
correct," and again, " before we get rid of these authorities,
we must be furnished with some principle of law, upon
which we may decide contrary to them." This implies the
exercise of his own reason in this judge, and the right to
develope principle, independent of what are called authorities. That a decision not founded in reason but contrary to
justice, will take place, we have an instance in the case of
goods coming into the hands of a bankrupt after his bankruptcy. The assigns shall take them and yet the creditor
shall not be allowed to prove the debt under the commission. The judges of the court of common pleas meeting
with this principle, 3 Bos. and Pul. in the decision express
themselves thus; the chief J. (Alvanly) " in looking into the

cases I find the question to be completely closed in West-
minister Hall ; and that we therefore are bound *to hold* that
though a bankrupt has altogether ceased to be a trader ; yet
that his warehouse continues open for the purpose of receiving goods ; and that the assigns have a right to take
possession of every thing that comes into their hands without paying a single farthing even though the consigns of the
goods are not entitled to come in under the commission."
And Heath, J. " It is much to be lamented that the goods
consigned to a bankrupt which arrive after the act of bankruptcy as in this case, should even be considered as part of
the bankrupt's effects. The hardships to which this rule of
law had given rise, was the occasion of introducing the doctrine of stoppage in transitu."

Brooks, J. " I exceedingly regret that such a rule of law
should have been adopted ; for it appears to me to be productive of very great hardships. But the cases are too de-
cisive upon the subject for the court now to adopt a contrary
doctrine." Chambre, J. " I am entirely of the same opinion." What would have hindered them in a conference
among themselves, say the twelve judges, to come to an understanding on the subject, and determine that as to all cases subsequently arising ; a contrary doctrine should prevail? This is not a case where it stands indifferent how the
rule shall be ; and the desideratum only can be, that it be
settled. A rent in the wall cannot more mar the beauty of
an edifice, than what is unreasonable, the consistency of
a moral science. For the law is not altogether a system
of arbitrary rules, like those of a game at cards, or of chess.
It depends upon the subject of the rules whether they may
be arbitrarily fixed ; or exist antecedently in the nature of
relations. All rules of practice, or which respect the modus
et forma of pursuing, or defending rights, are of an arbitrary nature, as, " if goods be bought to be paid for by a bill
at two months, and after the goods are delivered the bill is
refused to be given, shall the vender sue for the bills, or the
price of the goods ?" In Mussen v. Price, 4 East, 147, the
chief J. of the king's bench ; and in Dutton v. Solomonson,

3 Bos. and P. 584, the chief J. of the common pleas thought that he might sue for either; but the law being once settled no material inconvenience could result.

In Andrew v. Hutton, the chief J. of the common pleas, speaking of the case of Jeffreson v. Morton, says, " I cannot help thinking, with deference to the very learned judges by whom the case was decided, that if the matter had been *more fully discussed it would have been differently determined.* They would seem to have taken up the case in a wrong point of view, and I feel myself compelled to deny the authority of that case." 3 Bos. and Pul. 652. Nor is it only *a rule of practice*, but a *principle of law* that decisions will change. In a note to 3 Bos. and Pul. 654, we have a note of the words of lord Mansfield in a case before the court. " On the introduction of the statute of uses, there arose great dread of letting in perpetuities, by means of the extensive operation of that statute, and in the time of Eliz. and James, many cases were decided with a view to prevent that effect; with this view it was allowed to bar contingent remainders, before the person who was to take came into esse; others were held to be too remote in their creation. The cases proceeded in that view too far, and estates were too much loosened, and it became necessary to restrain them again; and in the time of the troubles, eminent lawyers, who were then chamber counsel, devised methods, which on their return to Westminster Hall, they put in practice; such as interposing trustees to preserve contingent remainders. It is not of long date that the *rules now in use have been establish-ed.* I remember the introduction of the rule which prescribes the time in which executory devises must take effect, to be life or lives in being, and 21 years afterwards."

A principle oftentimes comes to be varied from what it originally was, by application of it, and acquires an extent beyond its first dimensions. As said by lord Elden, 2 Bos. and Pul. 24, " With respect to the cases which have been cited, it is to be observed, that when a general principle for the construction of an instrument is once laid down, the court will not be restrained from making their own application of that principle, because *there are cases in which it may have been applied in a different manner.* The principle being once acknowledged, the only difficulty consists in making the most accurate application of it." Why is a decision cited but because the case decided is the same with that to be decided? But unless the case is precisely the same. the analogy is imperfect, and the application erroneous. Hence the exercise of judgment is as necessary as the recollection of precedent.

" The rule of stare decisis, is as justly applicable to private parties, as it is to general principles, *where the decision can be reasonably ascertained and supported,*" 2 Bos. and P. 191, and 298. The case is clear says justice Chambre, both on *reason and authorities.* This marks the distinction and implies a difference, and that *authority* is not always *reason.* And in 403, the same judge in another case, says, " I stand single in my opinion here, and opposed by a determination of the court of exchequer ; and that strengthened by a determination of lord Loughborough, at nisi prius, confirmed in this court. I am sensible of the weight of these authorities, but I feel myself under the necessity of enquiring into the foundation of those decisions. I feel the weight of authority against the opinion I am delivering, and I am fully aware of the propriety of adhering to former decisions, and the mischief of lightly departing from them ; but, as *certainty* is the chief reason for submitting to authority, such determinations as are not perfectly satisfactory in respect of the arguments on which they were founded, cannot contribute to certainty, which will be better attained by going back to reason than by following the determinations."

In 2 H. Blackstone, 450, Buller J. refers to it as a thing frequently said in courts, " the nonsense of one man cannot be a guide for another," which would seem to imply a right in all men that judge, to examine what is said, and determine whether nonsense or not, before they follow it. I take it to be the privilege, and what is more, the duty of every judge to examine for himself ; and to steer between the charybdis of unreasonable decision on the one hand, and the scylla of uncertainty on the other, as in his discretion shall seem practicable, in the administration of justice. These observations can have no relation to matters not founded on the construction of a statute; or on moral reason, but on abstract practice, and arbitrary rule, for which there is no reason but what is artificial, and the sic jubeo of decisions, where it is the regulation; or the adjudication of the courts that makes the rule, and is not the mere evidence of it, and supposes the prior existence of principle. Nor do I mean to insinuate that there are those who exclude wholly the canvassing the reason of a precedent; but that I would allow myself the questioning the reason of a precedent, as well as the application. Where one is shocked by a decision, there is some presumption against it, and if traced it may be found to be an error, and the time *when*, and the place ascertained where it bred.

With respect to our own courts in this country to which I bring my observations it would seem to me that we have been in the habit of paying more deference to English decisions than the most technical of the English judges themselves. They do sometimes by overhauling and distinguishing, make out to get clear of a case that seems to sanction what is unreasonable; but I do not know where that has been done in our courts. Be that as it may, I am not prepared to subscribe to our own decisions in all cases as conclusive authority. When we review the judicial history of this state, we shall find the constitution of the courts to have been such that for a length of time a decision could be considered as little more than the opinion of a single mind. Before the revolution, until the time of chief J. Chew, there was no great legal character on the bench of the supreme court; and after the revolution for a long time there was but one that had been bred a lawyer. When abler associates came upon the bench of this court, consisting still but of four judges, and two of them holding the nisi prius courts, the opinions given at nisi prius could be given but by two, and what use in bringing the matter before another two in bank, who being but of equal number could not be supposed to listen readily to reverse what had been sanctioned. Besides the judges sitting in bank at *an extremity of the state, rendered it impracticable in most cases, for suitors to sustain the expense of an appeal;* and for this and other reasons, we all know that the court of errors and appeals sitting at the same place, was to the midland and more especially to the western country *but a name.* I do not think, therefore, that so much weight ought to be attached to decisions in this state ; or that the not appealing should be considered as an acquiescence in the reason of them. On a principle of tenure of real property where an original, and not a *derivative* title comes in question, it must be with great repugnance I can submit to a decision. to which my judgment was opposed when at the bar, and which I cannot consider as having received the investigation of such a number of minds legally informed, so as to give satisfaction. I must acknowledge that I do not consider the principles of construction so far settled as to preclude examination. This I say as not undervaluing the judgment of others, but as accounting for that freedom of thinking which I may indulge in some cases, and which is not founded as may be supposed in the vain ambition of being singular, or of being thought pre-eminent ; but in the love of liberty, and repugnance to submission to what does not appear to me to be founded on reason, general convenience, or justice to individuals. I will admit that much has been done towards building a system of jurisprudence in the state, but I am unwilling to apply the maxim of *stare decisis* to all that has been done.

Under the head of Judicial opinion or determination, 15 Vin. 1. it is said the decisions of courts are the conservatives and evidences of laws. Or they are such as by way of deduction and dilation upon laws, are formed or deduced ; or they are such as seem to have no other guide but the common reason of the thing, unless the same point has been formerly decided, as in the exposition of the intention of clauses in deeds, wills, covenants, &c. where the very sense of the word, and their positions and relations give a ra-

I

tional account of the meaning of the parties, and in such
cases a judge does much better herein, than what a bare
grave grammarian and logician, or other prudent men could
do; for in many cases, there have been former resolutions
either in point, or agreeing in reason or analogy with the
case in question; or perhaps also, the clause to be expounded is mingled with some terms or clauses that require a
knowledge of the law to help out with the construction or
exposition; both which do often happen in the same case
and therefore it requires a knowledge of the law to render
and expound such clauses and sentences; and doubtless a
good common lawyer is the best expositor of such clauses.

I recur to observe a little on the act of assembly of the
19th March, 1810 : " It shall not be lawful to read or quote
any British precedent or adjudication, &c. This injunction
or prohibition has been complied with by the courts, though
I can have no doubt that it was under a misconception of
the legislature, as to the authority of British precedents,
or adjudications, that they judged it expedient to enact such
a law; and as to that obligation under which the courts
were supposed to consider themselves bound to respect such
precedents or decisions. Hence it is that the courts have
been forced to do that indirectly which they could not do
directly; and to suffer such adjudications to be read and
quoted through the medium of the reports of other states,
which, of necessity, must increase the lawyer's library; so
that in respect of time taken up in reading authorities, there
is nothing gained; and this, I take it, was one object in precluding such reading and quotation. But I have viewed
this matter in the light of a more extensive consequence.
It is interfering with judicial rights. Shall not a judge have
the privilege of informing himself from all sources of knowledge? It may be said there is nothing in this act to hinder
him from informing himself in his chamber and by private
reading. But it is in the way of the privilege of a party to urge
that information upon his mind, when, in the opinion of the
party or his counsel, an advantage may be thought to be derived from it. The legislature would start at the idea of

precluding the reading the holy scriptures, the principles and reasons of which, may, in many cases, be applicable as grounds of natural justice. For the law of God is a ground of the common law. They would equally revolt at the idea of precluding the sentiments of moral writers on any subject, even though these were British. The truth is they have no right to interfere with the mind of the judge, as to what he shall read, or suffer to be read to him. But more especially here, where the very substratum of his judgment in many cases, must be the comments that are made on the common law; and what can the distinction be, whether these comments are made by men who have lived, or by men now living, if they appear to carry reason and truth?

———————— "Knowledge at one entrance quite shut out."

Can this be considered in any other light, than that of trenching on the right of judgment; and narrowing the province of investigation? I feel the more for it, because it is an imputation upon the good sense of the state, and a reproach with the jurisconsults, and men of science of other nations. " Prove all things and hold fast that which is best," is an injunction of the scripture; and why not hear all things, which is the means of attaining just ideas on a subject discussed. The judiciary is a co-ordinate branch of the government; and which, if it is trusted with saying what the law is, may it not be left to its discretion to hear all reasoning on the ground of law, let it come from whatever quarter they may be willing to admit it?

A good deal has been said on the power of courts to judge on the constitutionality of a law. It would seem by the reasoning of some to be thought a self evident proposition; while others considered it extremely difficult even in theory to decide upon the question. But certain it is that if reduced to practice it must be a plain and broad case that will justify the interference, or render it safe to make the experiment. An omnipotent legislature will not readily yield to any thing but that which will carry the sense of the community with it; and this must be a transgression of the constitution extremely obvious indeed. A transgression may be plain and obvious from the *nature* and the *magnitude* of it. The British statute declaring the power to bind " the colonies in all cases whatsoever," was of a nature that justified resistance in the very first exertion of that power, from the principle which it contained. The very first attempt to exercise such a power, was resisted and gave rise to the war of the revolution. The power which the same government assumes in taking from American vessels, seamen naturalized in these states, and compelling them to serve as British subjects, because they have been once such, has been a cause of the present war; one cause at least; and seems to be the principal ground on which it is at this time continued. This claim is of such a nature that the *principiis obsta*, must apply, if it is at all to be resisted. For it is not the *number* of American seamen impressed, but the *right* of such impressment, or *taking*, that is to be determined.

To give an example on the other hand, of acts which, not from the *principle*, but from the excess and *magnitude*, become questionable, we may refer to the state laws increasing the jurisdiction of the justices of the peace; or abridging the province of jury trial by extending that of arbitrators; or taking away appeals from these, unless above a certain sum. No one will say, but that if all jurisdiction were given to the justices, or all to arbitrators, without appeal, and by this means the trial by jury *indirectly* abolished, it would be an invasion of the constitution; but, inasmuch as it cannot be considered an infringement of the constitution to give the justices some jurisdiction, for they had it under former constitutions, and it has not been taken away by the present, it will be impossible to say, at what point, the legislature ought to stop; and if undertaken to be said by the courts, it must be at some point of great excess that such a stand can be made.

Will not the act of our legislature taking from the courts the right of hearing any reading or quotation, involve the principle, that this may interfere to any extent; and is it not in the principle itself so obvious as to forbid a submis-

sion? I know of no case which has yet occurred, in the
jurisprudence of the country, that is equally alarming: and
I have no doubt that if the courts would refuse to submit,
the good sense of the country would be on their side, and
bring about a repeal of the law. I have no doubt but that
even the legislature which enacted the law would repeal it.
For it was owing to a misunderstanding of the fact that
British precedents or adjudications, since the 4th of July
'76 were read as authorities; or carry any more weight in
them than their intrinsic reason and good sense warranted.
There was a reflection upon the courts to suppose it possible that the reading or quotation of these could carry more.
But the truth is, what led to it in some degree, was an appearance of this, and an overweening attachment which some
judges seemed to discover to British decisions even of an ul-
terior date. But it was an evil that would wear off in due
time; but the remedy was worse than the mischief; the undertaking to restrain or abridge that information from all
sources; and without which they can be neither liberal nor
informed. The only means to prevent narrowness and to
give liberality, is to let all be heard.

I have said that another cause of the act of the legislature, or what led to it, was what had been seen and felt by
the country, in taking up the time of the court with so much
reading and quotation; and it was thought that if the province of reading was abridged, there would be less. But if
the later and more modern determinations are not read,
their place will be filled up from the old, which are without the corrections that time must be supposed to give in
the growing wisdom of one age above another; and the
adaptation to the increase of liberty and commerce; and
even if there were fewer books to be read and quoted, it will
not hinder to speak as much. For as long a sermon may
be made *upon a single verse as upon a whole chapter.*

I had been disposed to construe *quoting* in the act to
respect only the reading *a quota* of the case; or what applied to the point; or, to narrow this still more, by taking
it to mean a referring to the case merely; and this is what,

had I my will, I would allow counsel only to do, as to any adjudication, *unless called for by the court.* But I dislike a quibble; and therefore take it according to common parlance, and suppose it to mean a prohibition of making a reference to any British precedent or adjudication; and this I consider clearly as interfering with the right of judgment in a judge; because it abridges his means of information. But drawing out the consequence, it is interfering with the right of suitors, and with the province of juries and arbitrators, who have a right to hear reason, let it be of British or civil law, or other origin. Good sense and reason is of no country; it has its domicil in all regions, and deserves to be hospitably received, let it come from whence it will.

ON THE AMENDMENT OR ALTERATION OF LAWS.

I shall begin with an abstract of chief justice Hale's observations, "touching the amendment or alteration of laws."

"The business of amendment or alteration of laws is a choice and *tender* business, neither *wholly to be omitted,* when the necessity requires, and yet very *cautiously* and *warily* to be undertaken, though the *necessity* may, or at least, may *seem* to require it.

"Here we see there are two extremes, the over-hastily mutation of laws under pretence of *reformation;* and an over-strict adherence, in every particular to the continuance of the laws in the state we find them, though the reformation of them be never so necessary, safe, and easy.

"Every law that is *old* hath this advantage over any new law, in that it is better known already to the people who are concerned in it, than any new law possibly can be, without some length of time; by means whereof it must needs come to pass, that though a new law be possibly as good, and it may be, in some degree better than the old, yet many great inconveniences happen in that interval which will occur between the promulgation of the new law and the full and perfect knowledge thereof, in those who are concerned in that law. And if there were no other advantage of the continuance of old laws above the introducing of new, but this, yet it should make people very shy and careful in changes, and most perfectly to demonstrate, that the advantages of the change would be so great that it would preponderate this very single consideration, viz, the *notoriety* of the old, and the *novelty* of the new.

" It is most certain, that time and long experience is much more *ingenious*, *subtile* and *judicious*, than all the wisest and acutest wits in the world co-existing can be. It discovers such a variety of emergencies, and cases, that no man would otherwise have imagined ; such inconveniences also. And on the other side, in every thing that is new, or, at least in most things relating to laws, there are thousands of new occurrences, and entanglements, and coincidences, and complications that could not possibly be at first foreseen. And the reason is apparent, because laws concern such multitudes, and those of various dispositions, passions, wits, interests and concerns, that it is not possible for any human foresight to discover *at once*, or to provide expedients against, in *the first constitution of a law*. Now a law that hath abidden the test of time, hath met with most of these varieties and complications, and experience hath in all that process of time discovered these complications and emergencies, and so has applied suitable remedies, and cures. So that in truth, ancient laws especially, that have a common concern, are not the issues of the prudence of this, or that council or senate, but, they are the productions of the various experiences and applications of *the wisest thing* in *the inferior world*, viz. *time ;* which, as it discovers day after day new inconveniences, so it doth successively, apply new remedies ; and indeed it is a kind of aggregation of the discoveries, results and applications of *ages* and *events ;* so that it is a very great adventure to go about to alter it, without very great necessity, under the greatest demonstration of safety, and convenience imaginable.

"But *another extreme* is, an *opposition* to *all amendments*, as if what has been once settled for law must stand everlastingly without any alteration. By long use and custom, men, especially that are aged, and have been long educated in the profession, and practice of the law, *contract a kind of superstitious veneration* of it beyond what is just and reasonable. Laws were not made for their own sakes, but for the sake of those that were to be guided by them ; and if they be or are become unuseful for their end, they must be amended, if it *may* be, or new laws substituted, and the *old repealed.* How laws become, or are unuseful to their end upon two accounts : 1. When in their very constitution they are unjust, and impossible to be borne without remarkable and uncommon inconvenience—or 2. When a law, though never so good in its first institution, yet by reason of some accidental emergencies that do most usually happen in tract of time either becomes obsolete and out of use or weak, and unprofitable to its end or inconsistent with some superinduction that time and a variety of our occasions have introduced.

"So that it seems apparent, that as, on the one side something may seem fit to be done in relation to the amendment of the laws, yet, on the other side it is necessary, that exceeding caution be used, as well touching *the matter as the manner how*, and the *persons* by *whom*, and the seasons wherein such an amendment may be made. For the matter : 1. That nothing tend to the alteration of the government in any measure ; for that were to introduce ruin and confusion : 2. That nothing be altered that is a foundation, or principal integral of the law ; for these are very sound, and ought not to be touched lest the whole fabric be endangered. We must do herein as a wise builder doth with an house that hath some inconveniences, or is under some decays. Possibly, here or there, a door or window may be altered, or a partition made : but, as long as the foundations, or principals of the house, be sound, they must not be tampered with. The inconveniences in the law, are of such a nature, as may be easily remedied without unsettling the frame itself; and such amendments, although they seem small and inconsiderable, will render the whole fabrick much more safe and useful."

" Touching the manner and persons, these things are to be observed, 1. That it be done deliberately and leisurely. An attentive consideration will every day ripen the judgment of those that shall be employed in such a service farther than they can at first imagine. 2. Let every point be fully debated and impartially examined before it fix into a resolution. 3. *What can be done by the power and authority of the court and judges without troubling a legislature for such things.* And truly this would go a great way in the reformation of things amiss in the law. For it sometimes falls out that an unnecessary application to the legislature, in things that are otherwise curable, breeds unexpected inconveniences. What the poet says of miracles I may say in this case,

" Nec deus, intersit, nisi dignus vindice nodus,
" Inciderit ————————————————."

" 4. In these remedies that are given by the legislature. let it be particular and as little left arbitrio judicis as may be. Upon such a remission, forward men will do too *much*, but wise and cautious men will do too *little*. Wise and honest men desire to understand their rule; though some things are of such a nature, as must, in the particular application, be left to the judges and officers of courts, as the forming, and modeling of wills, process, pleadings, and other proceedings in conformity, and subserviency of what is to be settled by the legislature in this behalf. 5. Let no laws of this nature have a retrospect, but let the time that they shall be put in execution, have such a prospect, that men may not be surprized by the change of things, but may be fitted. for, and conusant of it."

The above is an abstract of chief justice Hale, to which I may add some observations of my own. It will be found extremely difficult, if not altogether impossible, to get a court to budge in a matter of *reform*, either in the *construction* of

K

the law, or in the *practice* at the bar. The causes are two. 1. Attachment to decisions; and 2. Timidity of mind in effecting a reform. Hence it is, that whatever improvement has been made, or will be made, *must come from the legislature.* I speak of that province or sphere within which the courts have *full power* to alter or reform *principle, or practice.* For beyond this, they can but suggest as other individuals, such amendments to the law, as it may have come in their way to see to be requisite. But within the sphere of *construction,* and rules of *practice,* they cannot but have power equi potens with the legislature. For *the practice of the court is the law of the court;* and no judge can be so constrained by a construction of statutes, as to be absolutely bound, to follow, what was originally *unreasonable* or *absurd;* or what may have become so, by a change of situation, and circumstances of a people. The stare decisis will be a consideration, but not a *talismanic charm* or spell, to bind the faculties of a judge and keep him from thinking a little for himself. So far as I have had experience, the error has been, the *too tenacious adherence to decisions,* both in matters of law and practice. But it may be said, it is the least dangerous extreme. Grant it, but still it is *an extreme.*

There are cases of construction where a change cannot be made without the interposition of the legislature; as where such construction has become *a rule of property, or contract;* and so in fact *a law* so far as respects what has passed under it; and it may require the publicity of a legal repeal of a construction which may be considered as having become a part of the statute; or of *the application of a rule of the common law.*

But in the nature of the case it cannot only be a court in the *last resort,* that can be competent to such a trust, or to undertake such a task. And, hence it is usual, and perhaps can only be from *some chief justice of a court,* or chancellor, that such improvement can arise. There have been great minds in such a situation who, have given philosophy, and liberality, to the science of the law;

" —— Enlarged the former narrow bounds,
With nature's mother wit."

A Mansfield, a Hardwicke, have had this praise. The bulk trudge on through the slough as Hodge did *even after the bridge was built;* so far are they from attempting *to build a bridge.* Such may have the praise of being what are *sound lawyers;* but must be contented with this, and cannot be called *great judges.* I will admit, that it is only one who has traversed all space of the legal science; or in the pithy language of the great Baron, have obtained the vantage ground of science, that can venture such a leap, or in fact ought to venture it. They will break their necks if without such *just confidence* in themselves founded upon the actual fact of reading and reflection and great original judgment, they attempt it. But where such a mind happens to be at the head of the highest court, little interposition of the legislature, or at least much less, will be required in matters that respect a reform of the law. Will any man say that the legislature of England, could, in many years, have given such a spring to the dictates of common sense and such reason as some judges have given in the course of a short sitting on the bench. The legislature can act only by detail, and in particulars, whereas the able judge can remove at once, or alter, what was originally faulty or has become disproportioned in the building. But no one but a *skilful architect,* and who can have the whole edifice in his mind, with its proportions ought to be suffered to attempt this. The legislature therefore, but in *special cases,* ought to be called upon for a reform in *the construction,* or practice of the law. But where a court who has power, will not reform a construction that is no longer applicable to the *circumstances* of a government, or the circumstances of a people; or a practice that has become absurd or unintelligible, what can the legislature do, but interfere? Where a struggle for a reform is founded in such pressure, it will have its vent even though it should blow up a valuable principle, or the *whole constitution together.*

NOTES ON

BLACKSTONE'S COMMENTARIES,

POINTING OUT VARIATIONS IN THE LAW OF PENNSYLVANIA
FROM THE COMMON AND STATUTE LAW OF ENGLAND,
WITH OTHER MATTERS OF A GENERAL NATURE.

———

" And it (law) is that rule of action, which is prescribed by
" some superior, and which the inferior is bound to obey." 1 Bl.
Com. 38.

Judge Wilson, attacks this definition in his lectures on
law;* and considers it of great moment to show that it is
incorrect, as being anti-republican. " A superior! let us
" make a solemn pause; can there be no law without a su-
" perior? Is it essential to law that inferiority should be in-
" volved in the obligation to obey it? Are these distinc-
" tions at the root of all obligation? There are laws that are
" human; does it follow that in these a character of supe-
" riority is inseparably attached to him who makes them?
" And that a character of inferiority, is in the same man-
" ner, inseparably attached to him for whom they are made?
" What is this superiority; who is this superior? by whom
" is he constituted; whence is his superiority deduced?
" Does it flow from a source that is human; or does it flow
" from a source that is divine? From a human source it
" cannot flow; for no stream issuing thence, can rise higher
" than the fountain.' Judge Wilson tells us that he hesi-
tates himself to give a definition of law, but takes a view of

* Lectures, part 1. chap. II. 61.

a number of those which have been given from Aristotle down; finds fault with most; but considers this of Blackstone as the most exceptionable, as leading to the most pernicious principles of arbitrary government. On the contrary, I am not able to find any fault with it, or to see any germ of despotism in it; and I answer his question, by saying that the community is the superior who prescribes the law, and the individual the inferior to whom it is prescribed. The whole is greater than a part. Judge Wilson lays it down as a position which he conceives overthrows the definition, that, " consent alone in a free government can make a law binding;" but is not this consent given by every individual at the framing of the constitution, that the laws made under it shall be obeyed? The whole body of the people is superior to a single one. " It is better that one man should die than the whole people perish." The salus reipublicæ, which was the Roman phrase; or the salus populi, which is that of our law, evinces the source and the obligation of our laws. We the people, the superior, frame the law; and you the individual, the inferior, must be governed by it. In the same manner as an individual member of the natural body is of less consideration; in other words of an *inferior* consideration to the whole; so is an individual member of the body politic, to the members collectively. It would seem to be but an affectation of republicanism, to carp at a definition so expressed, while the part is considered relatively to the whole as in subjection. Jus, justitia, juro, juramentum, injustitia, injuria, are all of the root Jubeo, which signifies to *command.* Lex est ratio summa insita in natura quæ ea quæ facienda sunt, jubet, prohibetque contraria. Cic. " In the same manner our English word *just* is the past participle of the verb jubere. *Right* is no other than rectum, the past participle of the latin verb regere. Thus when a man *demands* his right, he asks for that which he is ordered to have. A just man is such as he is *commanded* to be; qui leges juraque servat. Every thing that is ordered or commanded is right and iust."* The etymology of every word in the language

* Diver. of Purley.

that respects law, is from a root that implies the act of a *superior;* and it seems to me impossible to have any idea of a law but of that which is imposed. To reject these terms therefore, or a definition which retains them, would seem to me to savour of the French reform, when terms were rejected because the things were obnoxious.

The carrying a law into effect, in other words, the execution of the law shows a superior. A man does not ipso facto consent to be hanged. He may be said to consent constructively from having given, in contemplation of law, a previous consent to the law and the effect of it. But eo instante; in the act of inflicting the penalty, to suppose an assent would be absurd. It is enforced by a superior.

> None ever felt the halter draw
> With good opinion of the law.*

The correct idea is that quoad the law, or with relation to the making, the legislature is a superior power; but with relation to the constitution, which is the act of the convention which framed the society, it is not superior. It is diverso intuito, that superiority or inferiority is affirmed. But if any principle was to be deduced from these terms, such as the divine right of the magistrate, it would be of importance.

———

"—— Every law may be said to consist of several parts; one " declaratory, &c. another directory, &c." 1 Bl. Com. 53.

By an act of assembly for the gradual abolition of slavery, March 1, 1780, § 5. "The owner of any negro or mulatto slave, or servant for life, or years, now within this state, shall deliver in writing to the court of record of the county or city, in which he shall inhabit, the name and surname, and occupation of such owner, and the name of the county and township wherein he resideth; and also the name or names of any such slave, &c. with the age and sex, *in order*

* Hudibras.

to ascertain and distinguish, &c. which particulars *shall be entered in books,* &c. and that no negro or mulatto now within this state, shall. from and after, &c. *be deemed a slave or servant for life,* or for years, *unless his or her name shall be entered as aforesaid on such record.*" This law has been holden *directory* as to all particulars, except the *name;* and this by reason of the *negative* in the latter clause of the sentence; and even parol proof has been admitted to establish the *identity* where the slave or servant was recorded by a wrong name or colour; the object of the act being declared to be, to *ascertain and distinguish;* and this on the ground that this act was in derogation of the right of property in the master, taken from him, without an adequate compensation, and to be construed favourably for his claim of service. This also on the ground of general inconvenience, as from the ignorance of owners, or error of clerks, every requisite of the law had been, in few instances complied with.

It is a maxim of law, that an affirmative statute does not take away the common law. And if a statute, without any *negative words,* declare that deeds shall have in evidence a certain effect, *provided particular requisites are complied with,* this does not prevent their being used as evidence, though the requisites are not complied with, in the same manner as they might have been before the statute passed. Though, it is in the *general* true, that if an affirmative statute which is introductive of a new law direct a thing to be done in a certain manner, that thing shall not, even although there are no negative words, be done in any other manner. The power of construing a statute is in the judges; who have authority over all laws, and more especially over statutes to mould them according to reason and convenience, to the best and truest use. 6 Wil. Bac. 378.

By an act of 8th Ap. 1785, Sec. 9. it is provided "that every survey upon any warrant, shall be made by actual going upon and measuring off the land, and marking the lines to be returned upon such warrant, *after the warrant authorising such survey shall come to the hands of the deputy surveyor, to whom the same shall be directed;* and every survey made *theretofore* shall be accounted clandestine, and shall be void and of no effect whatever. The first part of this sentence has been held *directory* to the officer, and the survey *being void*, to refer only to the making it before the warrant comes to hand. This, because there could be no authority, to make the survey without the warrant; but the *going on the ground*, &c. refers to the mode and manner of making it.

This construction as to what was considered *directory*, was also applied, nobis dissentientibus, to surveys made under the act of April 3d, 1792. I dissented, because a main object of the survey being the *designation of boundary*, that settlers might know what was left out by the warrant holders in order to enter to settle, it was a substantial requisite under this act, to have the lines marked. It may be said that it is hard, that, from the neglect of the surveyor, *a party* should suffer; but it may be considered his own act, where he had the superintendance of seeing the survey executed.

It may be seen from these examples, that, in what is called the directory part of a statute, a distinction may be taken as to what is *merely directory;* and the not complying *strictly* with which, will not avoid the act done under it. The act pursuing the statute strictly as to such requisites, must be construed subject to the consideration of these not being matter of substance and contravening the whole policy of the act; but as having a reference to the mode or manner of doing a thing. For it is not in human vigilance, or the practical power of officers or party to observe all formalities.

By an act of 24th February, 1770, establishing the mode by which husband and wife shall convey the estate of the wife, a judge or justice is authorised to take the acknowledgment of such conveyance, in doing which *he shall examine the wife separate and apart from her husband, and shall read or otherwise make known the full contents of such deed and conveyance to the said wife; and if, upon such separate examination, she shall declare that she did voluntarily, and of her own free will and accord, seal, and as her act and deed deliver, the said deed or conveyance, without any coercion or compulsion of her said husband, every such deed or*

conveyance shall be good and valid in law. This, from an
early period, would seem to have been considered *directory*
to the officer; and however these requisites might have been
observed in taking the acknowledgment, yet in the certificate of the officer endorsed upon the deed, they were not always set forth as having been complied with. The question was whether in such certificate it must be set forth that
the requisites had been complied with. It is the presumption of law that an officer will do what he was directed to do.
Omnia recte et solemniter acta presumuntur. I had so ruled it in a case on the circuit; chief J. Tilghman had ruled
it otherwise, on his circuit, about the same time. The point
came before the court in bank; and it was ruled that so far
as respected the *substantial requisites,* the examining a part
&c. it must appear on the certificate, that these had been
complied with; a *substantial adherence* to the *manner* of acknowledgment prescribed by law, was indispensable; and
that it must appear upon the certificate. 2 Binn. 480.

A distinction was taken by the judges who ruled it,
(Yates and Smith) between a conveyance by the femme *of
land in her own right,* and of lands in which she might have
a right of dower; but this distinction was overruled by the
chief justice and myself, in Kirk v. Dean. 2 Binn. 341.

—— Ex post facto. 1 Bl. Com. 46.

No ex post facto law, nor any law impairing contracts,
shall be made. C. S. P. art. 9. sec. 7.

No ex post facto law shall be passed. C. U. S. art. 1.
sec. 10.

Ex post facto; ex jure post facto; or ex post facto law.
This embraces criminal as well as civil law. The impairing
contracts is but a species of the ex jure post facto. Retrospective acts are not always ex jure post facto; nor does the
term mean this, though it may be so applied.

L

EVERY individual of the community, is in contemplation of law, supposed to be present at the making of the law; and in fact it was the case in the ancient republics. When representation came to take place it ceased to be the case; and yet the idea is still retained in some measure. For though means are used to promulgate a law to those represented, who are supposed to be at a distance, yet the maxim still holds that they are supposed to know the existence of a law from the date. It is thus that in all affairs of men when a change takes place, all things are not immediately accommodated to that change. In England there is nothing to relieve an individual from the penalty of the law even where death is the penalty; and where there was even a moral or natural impossibility that he could be informed of it, but the interposition of the executive pardon. The same thing here. Why not have provided by the constitution that no law should take effect but in a certain time after the enactment. Or, as it is, why not always provide in the law itself, as is done in some cases, that not until after a certain time, and that sufficient to enable the citizens at the greatest distance to hear of it, should it take effect. The means provided of publication in the gazettes, forwarding to prothonotaries, sending copies to officers, &c. leaves still a space during which there is no moral, or perhaps, natural possibility of hearing of it.

By the act of 3 Cong. C. 115, the secretary of state is required to furnish the executives of the several states and of the territories north, west, and south of the river Ohio, with 4500 copies of the edition of the laws of the United States, by that act directed to be printed, and the like number of the acts passed at each succeeding session, to be divided among them according to the rule for apportioning representatives, and distributed as the executive shall deem most conducive to the general information of the people; and by the act of 5 Cong. C. 136, 5000 copies are directed to be printed and distributed in like manner. The act further directs, that every order, resolution, or law passed by congress, shall be published by the secretary of state in at least one, and not more than three, of the newspapers in each state. We may see from hence that it is still considered the principle that these laws take effect from the date.

———•◦•———

"But farther; municipal law is a rule of civil conduct prescri-
"bed *by the supreme power in a state.*" 1 Bl. Com. 46.

Judge Tucker takes exception to this definition; he prefers that of Justinian; jus civile est quod quisque sibi populus constituit; which he considers as comprehending the whole body of national institutions, from whatever source or authority derived; whether the immediate act of the people, or that of the ordinary legislature or founded on long and immemorial usage; whereas the former definition presupposes an act of the legislature in every case whatsoever; which he presumes was not the fact; or that all unwritten rules of law, are founded upon some positive statute, the memory of which has been lost. But cannot the law making power, act or enact without committing to writing? The word "*prescribe*" doubtless, signifies to write out. But it is used in common parlance to mean no more than to direct or order; and no more here. If we consult Tacitus on the manners of the Germans, which is the earliest monument of our Saxon ancestors; for these were Germans; we shall find that the manner of passing laws, or deliberating on any subject, was without writing; at least there is no mention made of it. He depicts minutely; but we hear of no clerk; nor does it appear that they had the use of letters. For Cæsar contrasts them with the Gauls, who had letters. Publicis privatisque rationibus litteris utuntur. Germani multum ab hac consuetudine differunt. Nam neque Druides habent.* It appears that their learning was from Britain; disciplini in Brittania reputa, atque inde in Galliam translata esse existimatur. There can be no doubt, therefore, but that the early Britons had the use of letters before the

---

* Cæs. Com. lib. 6.

Romans came amongst them; and the Romans had the use of letters from the earliest period; and might have introduced writing amongst the Britons had it not been known before. But it is not very probable that the Saxons coming in after the Romans, could be such apt scholars as in a short time to acquire the use of letters and to be in the habit of recording their public transactions. There remains no monument of a parliamentary record of the Saxon times; nor until a considerable time after the Norman conquest. "We possess acts of parliament," says Reeves, "from Magna Chart. 9, Hen. III. to the time of Ed. III. and from thence in a regular series to the present time. The statutes, except some very few enacted by the legislature before that period, are lost."*

When we talk of a custom we must remount to some convention; or gathering of the people to originate the rule. Even supposing but two persons in a community, there must be such assent, and so of more; so that I can see nothing in a distinction to be taken between the origin of an unwritten custom and a written law. They are both equally the act of a legislature.

The term Constitution is familiar to the English lawyer and civilian. This is chiefly common or unwritten law. It consists of the lex and consuetudines. It respects the system of government in all its parts, from the right of suffrage in the lowest frank-tenant, to the hereditary right of the monarch; embracing all the intermediate officers and offices, legislative, judicial, or executive. The sphere of each is known and the duties assigned; no encroachment to be made by one upon the other; the orbit of every power defined; moving in its proper groove. There is a multitude of instances where an interference is resisted; in the case of the king for instance in an attempt to give a proclamation the force of a law. It would be called unconstitutional for the lords or commons to vote themselves permanent, taking away the power of the king to prorogue or dissolve. We hear a great deal on the subject of preserving the consti-

---

* Reeves b. 1. c. 1.

tution; bringing it back to its original principles, &c. **The** saying, therefore, that in England there is no constitution, means only that there has not been a convention of the people within our memory, framing a constitution, uno ictu, and making a record in writing of the provisions therein contained; but it has grown up, and has been formed by time, until it has become, in some degree, fixed and understood. But in these states we have the frame of government reduced to writing with the provisions; and in all or most of them certain things stated which the legislative body shall not have the power of doing. In England the power of parliament is said to be omnipotent. It extends to every thing that does not contain an actual impossibility; and yet Coke (Sir Edward) has said somewhere, my recollection does not serve me, that a *law against reason is void.* If void the judges would be justifiable in declaring it a nullity. It is in my recollection that Cambden some where says that the judges have in contemplation of law, the power to declare an act of the legislature void; but they could not be expected to do it while those remained in power at whose instance the law had been obtained. Whether he respects an impeachment, or the power of the king to remove, may be a question. Under the constitution of the United States, there have been instances of the supreme court declaring a law void; but no instance that I know of in Pennsylvania under the present constitution though many arguments to the court on the subject of the constitutionality of laws, which would seem to imply the idea that the judiciary had the power to determine, which will probably come to a point at no distant day, and receive a decision. But it may be said of it at present, to be questio vexata, et adhuc sub judice lis est.

I have said, under the present constitution. For there are said to have been cases under that of '76 when there was but one branch in the legislature, and the Governor had no negative. But under the present constitution, there is less reason for the exercise of such a power, when there is a check of one upon another branch; and the veto of the Governor upon both. But it is stated, in the argument in Bonhams case, 8 Coke, 118, that, in many cases, the common law will

controul acts of parliament, and some times adjudge them to
be actually void. Many instances are there reduced in
which such a power may be exercised. And in Hardres
140, " the law and choice of nature is said to be superior to
all positive laws, and is called lex eterna or the moral law."
7 Rep. 12 b. Calv. case; " It is the law that was infused
into the heart of man at his first creation; and whatever positive laws are contrary to this law of nature and reason,
they are void of themselves." And, in Hobart 87, an act of
parliament made against natural equity as to make a man a
judge in his own cause, is void in itself; for jura naturæ sunt
immutabilia, and they are leges legum.

———

" The decisions therefore of courts are held in the highest re-
" gard, and are not only preserved as authentic records in the trea-
" suries of the several courts, but are handed out to public view in
" the numerous volumes of *reports* which furnish the lawyer's li-
" brary." 1 Bl. Com. 71.

Prior to the year books; there are said to be reports of
cases adjudged during the reign of Edward I. in manuscript
in certain public libraries. The year books are so called because they were published *annually* from the notes of certain
persons, who were paid a stipend by the crown for this employment. The establishment of reporters, is said to have
been first made by this king, (Edw. II) ; or more probably at
the latter end of the former reign. However, as we have
no fruits of such an appointment till the beginning of this
reign, we may suppose, it did not take place till then.

The year books were continued down to the 27th Hen.
VIII. and embrace some part of that year ; though during
that reign, there are Dyers reports, with some scattered
cases in Keilway, Jenkins, Moore, and Benloe ; and towards
the end of the reign, in Leonard, 4 Reeves, 414.

Pennsylvania has the credit of having given the *first* in
point of date, and not the last, in point of excellence, in the reports of A. J. Dallas ; the first volume of which, he pulish-

ed the 1st. May 1790; but, which embraces cases as far back
as 1754 : these collected with much research from that period downwards. But until the chief justiceship of M'Kean,
the cases are few ; and, except as to their antiquity, of minor importance. Chief justice M'Kean was a great man ;
his merit in the profession of the law, and as a judge has never yet been sufficiently appreciated. It is only since I have
been upon the bench, that I have been able to conceive a just
idea of the greatness of his merit. His legal learning was
profound, and accurate ; but, in the words of the poet,

        Materiem superabat opus————————

The lucidity of his explication; and the perspicuity of
his language ; which is the first excellence in the communication of ideas, was perfect ; but I never saw equalled his
dignity of manner in delivering a charge to the jury, or on
a law argument, to the bar. But, what is still more, his *comprehension* of mind in taking notes, so as to embrace the
substance, and yet omit nothing *material*, has appeared to me
inimitable. This, I say, thinking of him as a man out of the
world, as from the course of years, he must be supposed soon
to be.

The decisions also which these reports contain, and observations on points of law, of chief justice Shippen, render
them valuable ; not only on account of their intrinsic worth ;
but also as preserving some remains of the legal knowledge
of a great judge, and also of the most amiable of men ;
whose *integrity* and *manners*, attracted the respect and attachment of all persons.

        ————Qualem candidiorem————————————

These reports of Mr. Dallas are the only monuments of
the rudiments of our Pennsylvania law, and the early decisions ; and, being given in a concise, and perspicuous stile,
will last as long as the jurisprudence of the country ; being interwoven with it. Even the two first volumes which contain
fewer of the cases in the supreme court of the United States,
and district court, have not failed to attract the attention of

the practitioners of the law, in other states ; and have been cited in the courts, as containing many principles of common law, and practice, which render them instructive.

With regard to the reports of Mr. Binney which have succeeded to those of Mr. Dallas, I shall say nothing ; because, to these, I may apply to some small extent, the

——————— quorum pars ———————

This however I cannot help thinking; and I may take the liberty of expressing so much, that these reports have given me a chance to be remembered, longer than I would otherwise have been.

Mr. Peter A. Brown a young gentleman of talents, and industry has commenced a series of reports of cases in the *inferior courts*, with such others as he may be able to procure from the higher : This, that he might not interfere with Mr. Binney, who had published first, and occupied this sphere ; and, reports of cases in the courts of common pleas, orphans courts, and courts of quarter sessions, were wanted in addition to complete the history of Juridical proceedings. But though the sphere, in *contemplation of law*, may be the more humble, yet the ability may not be less ; and the labour more. Equal discernment and accuracy is required, and though the circulation, and emolument cannot be equal, yet the praise may be equal;

In tenui labor, at tenuis non gloria.

The report of a decision of any court; or of the opinion of any judge, must be, from the nature of it, examinable. The statement of the case, so far as may depend upon the record, may be given with exactness ; and the result of the decision ; for that can be taken from the record. But the sentiments delivered are supposed to be, and frequently are, the notes of the counsel, the judge, or of the reporter himself who catches in court, the argument or the opinion. This, with all the attention and quickness that is possible, cannot be done ; for the pen of the most ready writer, will not be able to keep pace, currente calamo with the oral expression ; and therefore the substance can only be obtained ; and even with regard to this, misconception, or omissions, are unavoidable. It follows therefore that the report of a case like a record cannot import absolute verity. But even after all, supposing the decisions of the court, with the reasons of them, to be given perfectly, these are but the *evidence* of law, and are examinable. The judges themselves who make a decision have a right to examine, and reverse their own judgment, in a subsequent case. This, subject to their legal discretion, under certain considerations must govern. For even though a decision may be contrary to legal principles, or the just construction of a statute, yet in cases where a principle is merely arbitrary, and from the artificial reasons of law, when it has become a rule of property, or practice, the advantage of certainty in the law will justify the sanction of it. This in all matters that are not contrary to *natural justice* or *public convenience.* The non ita refert quæ sit lex quam quod sit nota applies. It is not uncommon, therefore, for a court or judge to say, *were it a new case* we might think otherwise.

In case of an artincial rule of law, therefore, there can be no difficulty in the mind of a judge, in supporting former decisions, though contrary to his own judgment, as to what might appear to him, ought to have been decided. But subject to this consideration of expediency, he cannot be supposed not to have the right to reverse the former judgments of others, as well as of that which he himself hath given.

But supposing the case *new*, and that for the first time he delivers his opinion upon the point of law that is made in the argument, or arises from the case, how is it as to his right to continue his dissent from the majority of the court, as he now will discover it to be. His continuing to dissent when the question again arises, must be subject to the like consideration, as to the advantage of certainty in the law and judicial proceedings. It is a principle that in all collective bodies in a republican government the *majority shall govern;* and where a decision is not clearly contrary to natural reason and public policy, much more where it stands indifferent, it will be his duty to concede, even where

M

it depends upon the construction of a statute, the presumption to himself being that he has erred; and he will rest until the legislature shall, by a declaratory law, explain their own meaning. But I take it he has a right, in law and conscience, subject to the considerations aforesaid, to stick to his opinion, in all cases; because by a new judge coming on the bench, the judgment may be in favour of his decision. By maintaining his dissent also, the attention of the legislature may be attracted to settle the principle, whether of law or of construction. This the legislature have, in many cases, done, though it will be at all times a matter of the most delicate interference. But as this is the ultimate appeal, where judges in the court of the last resort, are divided, it may seem necessary. Hence it may be seen that it will behoove the legislature of a free people to read the judicial reports, and to make themselves acquainted with the construction put upon these acts by the judiciary, with a view either to declare the law as they intended it, or to repeal, or to supply. How is it that the members do not direct themselves to be furnished with the state reports that may be published, during the year, at every commencement of their session? and this at the expence of the public, whom, by this means, they may be the better able to serve. This would be an encouragement to reporters, by an increase of the emolument arising from the sale. The same officers that are directed to be furnished with the acts of assembly, might be directed to be furnished with these also. For judicial comments on the acts of assembly by the several courts, are necessary to be known, in order to discover what is defective in them, or needs amendment. Such encouragement to reporters would be unexceptionable. For it is a question whether an appointment by a fixed salary would be advisable. An experiment of this kind was made at an early period, in what were called the year books, or *books of terms and years*. These are said to be so called, because they were published *annually* from the notes of certain persons who were paid a certain *stipend* by the crown for the employment. This from the beginning of the reign of Ed. II ; and was continued until in the reign of Hen. VIII. When, says Reeves, 414, " The *opinion* of this establishment was altered, and it was thought more advisable to trust to the general inclination discovered in private persons to take notes, who, probably, from a competition, would do more towards rendering this department perfect, and useful, than any temptation from a *fixed salary*." But Blackstone on this subject, expresses himself in the following manner, 1 Com. 71. " It is much to be wished that this beneficial custom (reporters with fixed salaries) *had under proper regulations* been continued to this day. For though King James the 1st at the instance of lord Bacon, appointed two reporters, with a handsome stipend for the purpose ; yet, that *wise institution* was soon neglected ; and from the reign of Hen. VIII. to the present time, this task has been executed by many private and contemporary hands, who, sometimes, through haste and inaccuracy ; sometimes through mistake and want of skill, have published very crude (perhaps contradictory) accounts of one and the same determination."

The *decision* of a court is but *evidence* of what the law is ; and a *report*, is, but *evidence* of the *decision*, with the *reasons*, if any are given. The *weight* of the evidence will depend upon the supposed ability of the reporter. It is of great moment therefore, that this evidence, be the best in the nature of the case that can be got ; though, in the nature of things, it can be but imperfect, not only from the reporter misconceiving what is delivered ; but also from the not noting as quickly as the words are delivered by the judge, which is impossible, and therefore a great deal must be omitted in point of *identical* expression at least ; and by that means the sense may be lost, or impaired. It is not practicable to follow *closely* what is delivered, unless by professional stenographers, or short-hand writers.

By an act of 24th Feb. 1806, it is provided, that, " In all cases in which the judge or judges holding the supreme court ; courts of nisi prius circuit court, or court of common pleas, shall deliver the opinion of the court, if *either party*, by himself or counsel requires it, it shall be the duty of the said judges respectively to reduce the opinion so given, with their reasons therefor to writing, and file the same of record in the cause." It will follow from this that a judge must be *able to write*. By the common law this was not necessary. The *prothonotary* was the officer of the court who alone was expected to write; or *clerks* of the several courts. In the case of a *bill of exceptions* given by the statute 13 Ed. 1. c. 31. the judge could only be called upon, *to put to his seal*, not to write his name. But the arresting the trial until an opinion can be written out, is inconsistent with the *despatch of business*. And a *bare opinion* with the reasons of it, without a *statement of the facts* on which it is founded, and on which the law arises, can be of little moment. It is the business of a reporter to give these facts; for the calling on a judge to do this, would still more encrease his *clerk duties*, and engross his time. The duty enjoined by this act is inconsistent with the *faculty of thinking* to advantage, and the powers of judging. For it is impossible for one to be a *scrivener*, and at the same time, to have his mind *free* to *think* only. The manual occupation will interfere with the exercise of intellect. It is a great innovation upon the province of the judge; and I do not set it down under the head of an improvement in judicial trials. Were it not that it is a *right under the act*, which is but sparingly used by the party or counsel, it would be impossible to get through a trial in any reasonable space of time. In fact it is seldom used unless when a point is decided against the counsel, and they take revenge by giving the judge trouble.

If the act is not repealed, I would suggest a small amendment to it by way of supplement; "That it shall be the duty of the prothonotary to take down the opinion of the judge as delivered, with the reasons." This would delay business; but it would relieve the judge from the drudgery of the chirographer, and give the chance of a fairer handwriting to be filed. For a prothonotary has his name and his office from the idea of being a scribe. It might be enjoined also

on the party or the counsel in the cause to be the amanuensis
to prepare what was to be recorded, by way of assisting the
prothonotary, or clerk if he should require it; or the judge
should direct. This would be some check on the calling
for opinions, and the reasons of them. It may be said the
judge is not expected to take time for this clerkship in the
hurry of the trial, but in his chambers at the inn, or private
lodgings, when on the circuit. But it must be done on the
spur of the occasion; for the jury cannot go out till they
hear it; and, it is on a charge to them, that the opinions and
the reasons are most usually required. If it is on a demurrer, or in arrest of judgment, the objection *in part*, remains
as to time; but as to the *incongruity* of clerkship with the
office of a judge, it exists altogether. Even in term it is a
heavy labour to be bound to make out opinions and reasons
in all cases. The greatest dunce of a judge has the best
chance; for such generally like to write; for the faculty of
thinking is not familiar to them.

By an act of the 5th March, 1812, " where more than one
exception is taken or point made in any court of common
pleas, or other court of inferior jurisdiction, and the same
has been duly removed to the supreme court for their decision, the judges of the supreme court are enjoined, and required to give their opinion on every point, and exception taken and signed in the inferior court, which opinion so delivered, if required by either plaintiff or defendant, or *any
third person interested in the event of the cause,* shall be filed
in writing by the said judges, with the prothonotary of the
proper district." I approve of this act so far as it calls for
an opinion on *every point* and *exception* taken in the court below. But so far as enjoins the *filing in writing,* it is liable
to the objection, and would seem to require the amendment,
already stated; more especially as the right of calling for
the opinion to be filed is extended to *third persons*, not parties to the action, but who may conceive themselves some-
way *interested* in it.

· " Statutes also are either *declaratory* of the common law, or
"*remedial* of some defects therein." 1 Bl. Com. 86.

BY an act of assembly of the 21st March, 1806, it is provided " that in all cases where a *remedy is provided* or duty
enjoined ; or any thing directed to be done by any act or
acts of assembly of this commonwealth, *the direction* of such
acts shall be *strictly* pursued, and no penalty shall be inflicted, or any thing done agreeably to the provisions of the common law, in such cases, further than shall be necessary for
carrying such act or acts into effect." It could not be the
meaning of the legislature that *remedial* statutes should have a
strict construction contrary to the principle of law in construing statutes ; which is, that remedial statutes must be *liberally* construed, in advancement of the remedy; but the negative words, in this act of assembly, must be restrained to
an exclusion of what it negatives, a prosecution at common
law, and a penalty derived from thence ; and this, whether
the provision of the act shall be to provide a *remedy* or *en-
join a duty.*

It is a rule of construction that an *affirmative* statute does
not take away the common law ; and a party may make his
election to proceed upon the statute, or at the common law.
6. Wil. Bac. 377. It was with a view to meet this rule that
the act of assembly in this case has given a negative to such
construction. It had been done in particular cases, where
it was not the will of the legislature that the party should have
an election to proceed at common law or on the statute ; but
this was intended as a general sweeping *negative* in all cases,
in order to supercede the necessity of particular provisions.
I take it therefore that a great change of the law has been
made in this respect in Pennsylvania, but that it has no reference to the rule of construing remedial statutes *liberally* in
contradistinction from the rule of a *strict* construction of penal statutes.

1 Bl. Com. 141.

THERE is no compensation for the *soil* taken for the use of *roads* in Pennsylvania. 6 per. cent. or, 6 acres in the hundred acres, were allowed, in the proprietary grants ; so that, in a survey of 300 acres, 18 were allowed ; hence it is that the surveys are made, and returned into the surveyor general's office as containing 300 acres, and *allowance.* The demesne as of fee ; or the jus proprietatis, or absolute ownership of the whole 318 acres, is in the grantee, but subject to a right of the public in the whole quantity, to take at any time an occupancy for the use of roads ; or, rather, in consideration of this allowance, there is an *interest* in the public for the laying out, and the occupying the ground for what roads it may deem necessary to lay out through it.   In no case can it be supposed that more than 18 acres can be laid out and occupied for this use ; nor perhaps more than $\frac{1}{3}$d of that quantity. Two roads of 33 feet or 2 perches, the usual width, crossing the tract at right angles, or carried through it, in any direction, would not, by my calculation, take up more than 6 acres and little more than $\frac{1}{10}$th. And it must be rare if ever more than 2 roads of this width, or narrower roads in proportion to these, can be laid out through any tract of 318 acres. An under purchaser takes subject to this right of the public to lay out roads.   It may happen that a purchaser of a small quantity may have all that is taken for roads to pass through his lot, but he cannot complain.   The public are bound to make compensation only for the *improvements* on the ground, a building pulled down which is in the way of the road laid out ; orchard trees, or grass growing on meadow ground ; and this at a *valuation.* But trees that have not been planted, but in their natural state growing in a wood, are not to be valued ; but may be cut down, or taken for bridging and other uses in the making the road, in the same manner as stones or earth.

' And therefore he (the representative) is not bound, like a
' deputy of the United provinces, to consult with, or take the ad-
' vice, of his constituents upon any particular point, unless he
' himself thinks it proper or prudent so to do." 1 Bl. Com. 161

' The person chosen seems to be strictly the delegate of
' those by whom he is chosen, and bound by their instruc-
' tions whenever they think proper to exercise the right. If
' the maxim be true that all power is derived from the peo-
' ple; that magistrates are their trustees and servants, and
' at all times amenable to them for their conduct, it seems
' impossible to withhold our assent from the proposition,
' that in a popular government the representative is bound
' to speak the sense of his constituents upon every subject,
' where he is informed of it. *The difficulty of collecting the*
' *sense of the people upon any question, forms no argument*
' *against the right to express that sense when they shall think*
' *proper so to do.*' *Tucker. vol.* 1. *app.* 193.

In a democracy where the whole people convene for the
purpose of deliberating with regard to a general law, or public measure, no one is supposed to come forward with an
opinion already formed, and *not to be altered;* for that would
be inconsistent with the advantage to be derived from a united deliberation. The principle remains the same where the
whole do not actually convene; but the number is reduced
by representation. For it is equally inconsistent with the
advantage of united deliberation that any of the representatives come forward but with a mind open to the observations
of others. It is inconsistent with the rights of all for any
one not to be free to listen to the consideration of the interest of the whole. It is from a communication of sentiments
in a convention of the whole, that what shall be considered to
be the interest of the whole, can alone be collected. In this
case, have the constituents who are not convened a right to
foreclose the ear and understanding of the representative? In
that case the deliberation is supposed to be by the constituent; *and the expression* by the representative.

But taking it that the deliberation is at home, how is the
information of this to be communicated to the representa-

tive; what means are provided to collect the sense of the community; or to express it. There are laws securing free and equal proceedings in the election of the representative; but no provision for the taking the sense of the people, and sending it forward. The truth is the doctrine is a fallacy in theory: it takes for granted what does not exist, that the whole people have convened at home, and deliberated; for in that case, doubtless, the representatives of the whole would be bound by the whole.

For if this is not taken for granted, it will follow, that it must be contended, that the district sending a particular representative has a right to determine on a matter of general interest, independent of all conference with the other districts; and that this is expedient and compatible with the public safety. But it can only be in the representative body that the sense of one district can be supposed to be known to another. For as to what can be collected otherwise, there is no certain medium of communication. Of the right of the constituent to communicate, to instruct, to remonstrate there is no question. It is the right to *controul*, even supposing the sense of the district to be known, that is to be controverted. Under the constitutions of these states, where elections are for so short a period; it is not of so much moment what may be considered the *abstract principle;* as, *in practice,* the sense of the particular portion of the community from whence the representative is chosen, will govern him, so far as he is able to collect it; and it will require more fortitude; perhaps I might say more virtue, than falls to the share of most individuals, to resist the popular and temporary impulse. He will be a knave or a hero that can do it; that is, he will have bartered his duty for his profit; or, he will be a patriot, of self-denial, willing to sacrifice himself for the people. But I do not think that the danger of such possible bartering, is such as will warrant the denying a representative the right to think for those at home on a question which respects the general interest, freely and unembarrassedly as he would for himself, subject only to instructions as influencing his delibe-

N

rations, but not as *absolutely controlling his vote.* But independent of the expediency I rest the argument on the ground, that it is the republican principle of representative government, that every individual is presumed to advise with another before he makes up an opinion on what concerns the whole; for, " in a multitude of counsellors there is safety;" and as every individual constituent cannot be supposed to advise with another in a large community, it must be in that body where the number is reduced by representation, that this advisement can be presumed to take place. It is therefore contrary to all principle of right or expedience, that the constitutent out of doors should undertake to control the deliberations of those who constitute the representative body.

This principle, if correct, in the case of a representative to the legislature of a state, equally applies in the case of a representative to the general government; and a fortiori, where the election is not in the *primary* assemblies of the people, but by the representatives of the state; as, in the election of a senator of the United States. For these having elected the senator are functi officio; and he is not the representative of this *secondary* body, but of the *people;* and it is from that source that instructions must come if they are to *bind.* For it would be incongruous, that instructions should come from the primary assemblies to the representative in one house of congress, and from the secondary body to the representative in another, which might be discordant and draw a different way. But still I recur to the principle which is at the bottom of all this, that the deliberative body above has an interest in the free judgment of all the members, who ought not to be supposed to come there; not with their ears in their feet, it is true to use the language of Aristippus speaking of Dionysius, but with their ears in their pockets; or with the papers in their desks. It is better that even the interest of the whole should be mistaken in a particular case, than that the advantage of a free and united deliberation should be lost; the combined wisdom of the whole being controlled by the ideas of a part, having no opportunity of taking a near view of the question; and accompanied with such assistance as must be presumed to be derived from the reason and deduction of others. And such is the self-love of man, and the desire of present ease or convenience, that the danger does not arise from resisting, but from yielding to the wishes of the part by whom the representative is immediately elected: under the American constitutions particularly, where the individual can seldom find a temptation of honour or profit to swerve from the popular inclination of the moment; but in most cases must be actuated by what he considers as the salus populi or good of the whole. Where such sacrifice of popularity is made, the prima facie evidence always is, that of *virtue*, if not of *wisdom*.

Provisions against the possibility of a representative consulting self-interest contrary to his sense of the general good, in subservience to partial views, must be found, not in the restraint of instructions, but in the shortness of the period of his delegation, and the being incapable of receiving appointments under the government, for a period after the expiration of his term. These provisions if not in the constitution can be made by law.

" As to the qualifications of the electors." 1 Bl. Com. 172.

I am an advocate for the principle of universal suffrage; for I can see no consistency in any limitation, but what is *personal* and respects *age, and residence.* But this delightful principle of equality cannot be tolerated without endangering liberty, unless the stays or restraints upon public volition are proportionably powerful; for the mind of man like the water of the ocean is subject to sudden and great agitation. The breath of opinion like the atmosphere blows upon it, not with an equable and steady breeze; but, in flaws and strong winds. In proportion as the whole mass is acted on

and can be put in motion, the waves are the more tremendous.
The stays, or restraints are

1. The acting by representation; for, even in a small
state, where the whole can convene, this is found a great help
and contributes to the wisdom of deliberation. For though
" in a multitude of consellors there is safety," yet this is not
in the ratio of the number of heads, that consult, but of the
number out of which to select, and which gives the greater
chance of selecting men of understanding.

2. The division of power in the representation; the
law-making, the law-expounding, and the law-executing power. This we have under our Constitution, in the legislative
bodies, the judiciary, and the governor.

3. The subdivison of the law-making power, immediately emanating from the whole, and a representation emanating from the parts. This we have in the qualified negative
of the governor, and in the district delegates.

4. A subdivision of the representation from the parts,
in order to produce deliberation, and obstruct combination :
and, under this subdivision, a shorter period of revocation
in one body with a view to secure fidelity to the voice of
the constituent; in the other a longer period, in order to
lessen fear in the delegate of acting according to his own
judgment in opposition to temporary impulse, and popular
paroxism : this we have in the two branches, the annual
branch, and the quadrennial senate.

I am not about to write a comment on our constitution ;
but it will be seen that it possesses all these restraints and
stays ; and venture to assert that with the principle of *universal suffrage*, its date would be short without them. For
even where a qualification of property is introduced as a stay,
and citizens of a certain real estate only have the rights of
suffrage, yet a government founded on opinion, is subject to
internal commotion, and is with great difficulty preserved in
a state of freedom : It tends to anarchy or monarchy with al-
ternate heel until it goes down in despotism.

Our executive springs wholly from the stock; it rises on
the basis of the whole people. *Universal suffrage* raises it ;

and in this respect our government is as democratic as is possible short of the people exercising the executive power immediately by themselves which in a great community is impracticable. Nevertheless we have seen a struggle to break in upon this part of our constitution by the local delegates, by taking away the appointment of officers *from the people* through the state representative, and exercising it themselves.

The third and intermediate, the law expounding power, is but one remove from the immediate appointment of the whole people, and to a qualified extent, is in the power of the parts in the legislative body.

All this distribution is the result of much thought and long experience in the affairs of men. Our constitution has been framed with great deliberation.

The tenure of judicial office has been a subject of complaint. The stay here may support men who ought to be displaced, but there may be occasion for it when the attempt may be to bear down, and remove those who ought not to be displaced. The constitution is not made for a day. But the will of the people ought at all times to have effect. But the thing is to get at the will of the people; and even if they could assemble as one man to express their will, there is such a thing as rashness in a multitude. They would find it necessary to restrain themselves by taking time to deliberate. Perhaps to provide that in the case of those who administer their laws which subjects to much odium; and requires proportionable fortitude, it should be necessary that in the case of a change *two thirds among themselves should be agreed.*

It will be said this is a new idea, that the governor is the immediate and only immediate representative of the people. Is it not the fact? The local delegate is the actual representative of a district, and it is in contemplation of law only that he is the representative of the state. He is chosen annually, because it can conveniently be done. The governor is chosen with the solemnity of a triennial, and general election. He is a representative elected with more concern, and is of longer duration. Ephemeral productions in nature, are less

the objects of attention, than those which are of more importance in the scale of being, and of greater longevity. Not
that I mean to undervalue the local delegate, and virtual representative. He may be in fact the far superior personage ;
but it is in a political point of view, and representative capacity, that I consider the characters. But, in proportion as a
man is removed from local interests, his horizon is enlarged,
and his mind embraces the interests of the whole community.
The local delegate is charged with the accomplishment of
local objects, and for these he is under the necessity oftentimes of bartering his vote upon a general question. At all
events he is under the temptation of doing it. The general
representative is charged with the interests of the whole,
and has no local objects to accomplish. In this particular
alone, independent of all others, the constitution presents a
noble scheme of wisdom, and democratic equality.

It is contemplated in the nature of the case that an opposition of sentiments will arise between the local delegate
and the general representative. As is natural to the human mind it may produce warmth, and mutual accusations
of a mistake of the true interests of the people. Even a
contempt may be alleged and contumelious expressions
adduced as a proof of it. But it is to the conduct that a wise
people will look for the proof of this. Does the man slight
their interests by neglecting his duty? This will be the subject of enquiry with rational men, when it is to their passions, and not to their understandings. Nay, when the recurrence is to this it is a presumption that passion prompts
the movers more than reason, or that self-love in some shape
is at the bottom.

Certain it is that the whole body politic have not the
means of information upon a great scale. It is in contemplation of law only that they are supposed to be infallible,
and whatever the people do is right. Individuals in their
respective occupations have not the leisure nor the opportunity to investigate great questions. It is the part of a
faithful representative, *to respect the rights, but to distrust
the impulses of the people.*

But there are always ingenious men who will wish to try their hands at making a constitution, and the passion of constitution-making will not be satisfied with one essay. Hence it is that no constitution will be lasting; and there is such a thing as a *habit* of instability. A bone that is often out of joint is not easily retained in the socket.

It is an axiom that the people have a right to change their constitution; and a *majority* constitutes the people; and the *motion* towards a change must begin somewhere. Hence *the right* of any individual to propose a change. An oath to support the constitution is subject to the exercise of this right. But though the *vote of a majority* gives the right to change, yet it supposes *the vote of every one to be taken;* and therefore any attempt to change without having taken the *previous* question, convention or no convention, must be contrary to oath and right both. The existing legislature for the time being would seem to be the most expedient organ of communication with respect to this object, who, by way of *resolution*, not law, for they have no authority, could *fix upon* the ways and means of taking the sense of the people, and this ought to be by a universal vote of the citizens qualified to vote, and not, by proposing the choice of representatives in a convention without a vote by the whole people on the *previous question.* Where the sense of the necessity of a change pervades the whole community, it may not be attended at the time with an immediate convulsion? but where that is not the case, *it may produce a civil war.* For the man who from a surprise upon him, and exclusion in fact, by defect of ways and means of giving him an opportunity to make his will known, is not bound by what is done, and may resist, and it will depend upon the event whether it shall be stiled a *rebellion, or a revolution.* The taking the sense of the people therefore by the signatures, sent forward to the house, is not fair, or safe, and ought not to produce more than the devising ways and means to take the sense of the people. For can the executive authority do less than to issue his proclamation against a convention on any other ground, and in case of its taking place, calling on the

civil authority and militia *to suppress the insurrection.* It
would be his duty, and on his oath he could not dispense
with it; and if in this respect he is not vigilant, our established governments and liberty will be of short duration.

All the greatness of man is derived from his gregarious
nature, his love of association; yet of all things how difficult to retain him under any form of government but that
which of all others is the least favourable to his happiness,
and the great improvement of his nature. Tyranny in some
shape he will have. It is that which he constantly exclaims
against; and most of all hates, and fears, and yet as if under the dominion of witchcraft, he will run into his embraces. This mighty giant, this monster feeds on human
flesh; and yet in vain you warn against the approaches to
his den.

We will suppose that a revolution is brought about,
and a new constitution is formed, with all peace and quiet-
ness. This constitution must want the stays, the braces
of the present; because these very stays, or braces are the
impediments of which complaint is made, and which has
brought about the revolution. Will not that occur which
has always occurred, that the many first, the few next, but
in a short time the one will govern? Is the nature of man
changed? Is our air less elastic? Or is there a spirit in the
atmosphere less favourable to discord, that we should trust
ourselves more than experience has shewn it behoved, where
man has planted himself in all other climates and countries?

It is not the boy that applies the flambeau that causes
that mighty burning. The inflammable materials of the city
supply food. It is in the veins of the timber that the latent
sparks are found; that the flames are engendered, and burst
out. It requires no talents to set a town on fire. It is the
work of audacity alone.

Whence is it that some men have become great upon the
earth? Some by forming establishments, and doing good;
others by the greatness of the mischief they have accomplished. Rarely do even the actors find their account in
what is done. Ingratitude is in the way of the good man,

and is the reward of all his labours. Vain glory or the love of spoil prompts the bad, but it is in the nature of things that his own mind torments him at the present, and the revenge, and execration of mankind pursues him at the last.

It behooves men to weigh well before they begin a revolution. It may terminate short of a civil war, with great discretion, and wise conduct; but a great deal is put to risk. Legislators have been at all times aware of the unstable disposition of the multitude, and the use that is made of it by ambitious men. Solon exacted an oath from the Athenians, not to change his laws, for at least a period. Lycurgus, of the Lacedemonians that they would preserve his system, until his return, determining previously never to return. The legislator of the Jews an inspired lawgiver, saw, in the nature of his people, the propensity to change. He denounced curses on those who should subvert his institutions.—" Cursed let them be in their basket and cursed in their store."

Executive patronage under our constitution, is thought to put the Governor beyond the reach of the people; that when he has fenced himself with appointments under him, it is difficult, if not impossible to prevent his re-election. So far is this from being the fact, that it is his appointments which give him all his trouble, and lay the foundation of an opposition. We need not recur to a saying of Lewis 14th to prove this; that when he had conferred an office or an honour, " he made many dissatisfied, and one man *ungrateful.*" He is ungrateful, either because it is the nature of an obligation to produce ingratitude; or because the man thinks himself injured in getting less than his due. If I am to administer a government, and wish a continuance in office, or to escape enmities, let me have no appointments in my gift. It is invidious to select the qualified, or bestow emoluments. What a host does not a Governor raise up against himself, in the exercise of such a trust; there can be but one man in many appointed to office? and yet all, or most expect offices. So blind is self-love that few men suspect their incapacity, or call in question their desert.

I will not say; it would be unjust to say that there are

O

not cases where the disapprobation of an executive measure
may not spring from the purest motives of disinterested patriotism.   But I mean only to illustrate this point that the
power of conferring offices carries with it more to affect than
to protect ; and this depending on the nature of things when
so many are to expect and so few to receive.

It is evidently the general understanding of all who observe the springs of action in political characters, that their
antipathies have their origin in something personal.   This
may be true of those who obtain a leading in political affairs.
But doubtless there will always be a mass acted on by every
one of these to an extent proportioned to his influence, and
with whom there is no intrinsic motive or principle, of dis-
appointment, or hope.   Nevertheless it is still the pique of
disappointed ambition that in most cases gives the first impulse to a warm agitator who sets the public mind in motion.   Through whom is the voice of the people legitimately
known *immediately?* only through the governor.   For he
alone is chosen by the whole people.   And this is the great
glory of our constitution that the whole executive authority
emanates *immediately* from the whole body of the people,
and who, through this organ, at the same time, have an *immediate* though *qualified* volition in the legislative capacity.   It
is this and the principle of universal suffrage, that renders
our constitution as perfectly *democratic* as the nature of a government, by representation, will admit.

Through the Governor every taxable is actually represented ; but through the county delegate *virtually*, and in
contemplation of law only.   Is the fraction of a county represented at all but through the Governor?   It is but through
him that it can be represented equally.   It is not possible to
have it otherwise while the representation is by districts.   And
is it practicable to elect in all cases by a general state ticket?

But change the state representative, and let what would
seem to be the will of the *county delegates* prevail.   This is
all fair.   Bringing it to the test at once.   The only question
now will be, are *the people sure that the county delegates understand their true interest, and are right?*

I will be asked, what is a *democracy?*   I take my definition from a speech put into the mouth of Pericles, by Thucydides. It is to the Athenian people. "This our government is called a democracy, because, in the administration, it hath respect, not to a few, but to the multitude : a democracy; wherein, though there be an equality amongst all men, in point of law, for their private controversies; yet in conferring of dignities one man is preferred before another to a public charge; and that, according to the reputation, not of his power, but of his virtue; and is not put back through the poverty, or the obscurity of his person, as long as he can do service to the commonwealth. And we live not only free in the administration of the state; but also, one with another, void of jealousy towards each other in our daily course of life; not offended at any man for following his own humour, nor casting on any man censure or sour looks, which though they be no punishment, yet they *grieve:* so that conversing one with another, for the private, without offence, we stand chiefly in fear to transgress against the public; and are able always to be obedient to those that govern, and to the laws; and principally to such laws, as are written for punishment against injury; and such unwritten as bring undeniable shame to the transgressor." Hob's translation of Thucydides.

This definition or description, of a practical democracy, is drawn from real life. It is in the mouth of Pericles, a man of business; a sapient statesman; who had been bred and born in a democracy; versed in its affairs, and knew its errors, and its excellencies. One thing is remarkable, that a particular excellence which he notices, is the freedom of opinion. Where a government is founded on opinion, it is of the essence of its preservation, that opinion be free. It is not enough that no inquisition exists; that no lettre de cachet can issue; but that no man shall attempt *to frown* another out of his excercise of private judgment. Is it democracy to denounce a man in a paper, because he thinks differently on a measure of government with the editor? It is tyranny; and the man who can do this without reason, or moderation, is a tyrant, and would suppress the right of private judgment, if he had the power. I distinguish between stricture, and abuse. All depends upon the manner and the toleration. A man is not always a deserter from just politics, because he cannot agree with me in opinion, on a particular subject. Mutual toleration and forbearance, in our sentiments, with regard to the legality, or expedience of measures, is the soul of democracy. It is that which distinguishes it from despotism, as polite manners the fine gentleman in polished life; in civilized society. In a despotic country, it is the boot, or the thumb-screw or the cord, that brings a man to reason; at least the wheel and the pulley are used for this purpose. What better in a republic where a man is this day a patriot, and the next day a traitor, at the whim of him who bestows the appellation? In the livid dens of despotism, state prisons are the seminaries of submissive citizens. In a democracy, shall terror issue from lamp-black, and patriotism be put down under the name of opposition. When a man frowns upon me because I have dissented from him in opinion, on political matter, I discover clearly the grade of his political standing and improvement.

But it will be said, are not your democrats, all noisy, vociferous, intolerant and of a persecuting spirit? I say such are not democrats; they are spurious, and usurp the name. In a government founded on opinion, nothing ought to be a reproach, that is the exercise of private judgment. It is subversive of the essence of liberty. *A frown is the shadow of force, and he that uses the one, would have recourse to the other.*

These observations allude to what is practical in democracy, and cannot be established or prohibited by the laws; but constitute the manners which a democratic government inculcates, and is calculated to produce; and it will be observable, that there is a great deal of this among the body of the people, who have been accustomed to liberty. It is chiefly amongst the young in *the world*, or young in *the country*, that the contrary spirit shews itself. I am amongst those who carry my ideas in favour of the naturalization of foreigners, perhaps too far. I am for excercising the rights of hospitality to them, to all extent at once; making them citizens, and giving them the right of sffurage, and even office, the moment they set a foot upon the shore. For I cannot see on what ground, we can justify a refusal. But I do not mean to discuss this point at present. I introduce it to shew that I am liberal in my notions, with regard to the privileges of foreigners. But I admit, that it takes some time to give them correct ideas of the limits of liberty. It is, I believe, a saying of the Grand Pensionary, De Wit, of Holland, that " it takes a man half an age to enjoy liberty, before he can know how to use it." Nevertheless, I cannot see the inexpediency of admitting to a vote, the emigrant that comes amongst us, the first day he presents himself. He will be instructed by those that have been here before him. He must take his ticket from some one.—Is the ocean afraid of the rivers? Even when they come turbid with the swell of the mountains? The sea clarifies, or they are lost in it. Who complains, out at sea, of a spring flood muddying the waters? This ought to be a lesson, at the same time, to emigrants, that they " use their liberty, so as not abusing it." It is a strange thing to see a man come in the other day, undertake to set all right; and to denounce men of age and high standing, as guilty of defection. But what good is there in the world without an alloy of evil? What exercise of right without abuse? If I am wrong, it is the excess of liberality.

But I find another principle in the oration of Pericles, in the justness of which, I am more confident. That is, *the equal right of office to all the citizens.* As the greater contains the less, this involves the right of vote. The only *qualification* of which I can have any idea, as justifiable, is that of age; and I should have no objection to see this restricted to a greater age than that of 21,—say 45 years. At this time men cease to be fit for the militia, or other ministerial services. Let them then become legislators, and have the right of vote in *making laws, or chusing those that represent in making them.* This would take off a great deal of wildfire in our elections, and it would keep away vain young men from our public councils.

What absurdity does the idea of a qualification of proper-

ty involve! It unhinges the ideas of the ancient republicans;
that it was honourable to have enriched the republic, and to
remain poor themselves. To be wise, a man must be rich.
No, but to be honest, he must have an estate. But in getting this estate, he may have been a rogue. In general, he
must, in some measure, have neglected the improvement of
his mind. At least, it does not follow, that in proportion as
a man is poor, he is not to be trusted. They are frequently
the most generous souls who have amassed little wealth; on
the contrary the most ignoble, who have acquired great property. The man that has set his heart on riches, is lost to
benevolence, and public spirit. In the possession of office,
he is thinking of what can be made by it. " Nothing can be
great," says the stoic philosopher, Epictetes, " *the contempt
of which is great. It is great to despise riches. These cannot therefore be great.*"

But how can we measure the value of property, and fix
the criterion? Shall it be real property, a freehold? Is my acre
worth more than yours? Shall I have but an equal right? What
are the drawbacks upon my estate? My debts and credits?
It is the surplus that makes my property, even in the case of
the substantial fund of freehold. But property is not the
only stake. Person and character, are stakes. Every man
that has a head has a stake. There is no proportioning it.
In what is impracticable we can have no election. It is therefore an excellent principle, of our excellent constitution, that
all men have an equal *right of suffrage, und an equal right of
office.*

I should not like to live in a republic where a man must
be worth so much, to have equal rights; even could it be ascertained what I am worth; which, as I have said, is impracticable. How many men have I passed in life, less industrious than myself, and yet richer. They have had better luck, as we express it; or they have been more selfish,
and kept what they got. Can a man that is looking at the
stars, mind what is under his feet? We read of most
of the great statesmen of antiquity, and virtuous heroes, that
they were poor. It is no uncommon thing to find it added

that they themselves were buried, or their children educated at the public expence. The love of science ; and the love of the public is at variance with attention to private emolument. Shall it then be disreputable in a republic to be poor? Shall it operate as a crime and disqualify from the noblest function in society, the enacting laws?

But it is not so much, in the extension of the right of suffrage, as in a delicate and just use of it, that the democratic character consists. Will you see an upright citizen practise unfairness in an election; go upon the ground to canvass for himself, unless in the case of a ministerial office? and even in this, with great caution and forbearance. Will you see him substitute or change a ticket? much less introduce and obtain a vote for an unqualified individual? no upright man was ever capable of this. It is with the aristocracy or ambitious men that these arts are practised. They count it robbery to be stinted at an equal vote; and think it no injustice to make themselves whole by taking a plurality by whatever means in their power. This is all a usurpation of the sovereign authority; and in some republics has been punished with death. In countries where *the government is a fraud upon the people*, and the right of suffrage where it even partially exists, is but a name; it may be thought innocent to deceive, and to slur our votes. For it is a buying and selling throughout. The candidate buys the vote, and has in the mean time sold himself. He is oftentimes purchased, and paid in advance, and bribes with a part of the money that he gets. Not so in this heaven of liberty, where other stars glitter, where other suns and moons arise; this beautiful world of liberty, in these states. Perdition on the man that saps its foundation with intention; forgiveness, but reformation of error, to him who destroys it by mistake. And yet these last are more to be dreaded than the former. At least as much; because the error of opinion is equally fatal, though originating from a different principle of the mind, and oftentimes founded in virtue.

Who ever saw a good citizen keep an open house at an

election for a place in the legislative body? He is too poor, says one. He is poor because he is honest. At least being poor, he is honest. I have seen open houses kept in a republic; and private friendship, or personal safety has sometimes stood in the way of my endeavours to bring the persons to account. But disapprobation, and a portion of contempt has invariably attached itself to the transaction. What man can set the world right? The greatest self-denial is obliged to yield sometimes to personal considerations. Hence it is, that I have often been silent when I saw fraud, and unfairness before my eyes. Fraud in elections is at the root of all wickedness in the government of a republic. A man of just pride would scorn the meanness of succeeding by a trick; a man of proper sense would know, that in the nature of things, no good can come of elevation obtained by such means. Success by fraud, will never prosper. All men despise cheating at cards, or other games. He is turned out of company that is found guilty of it. And shall we restrain our indignation; or can we withhold our contempt when an individual is found cheating, not at a game of chance or skill amongst idle men; but in the serious business of real life, and the disposition of our lives, characters and fortunes? I pledge myself no good man is guilty of this; at least those guilty of it are not good men. They are not true brothers; real masons. They have been made at a false lodge; and will not be acknowledged. Thus it must be seen, I found republicanism in virtue; that is in truth, honour, justice, integrity, reason, moderation; civility, but firmness and fortitude in the support of right: quarter to error of opinion; and the aberrations of the heart; but death to ambition, and the vain desire of honour, without just pretension; and death to all knavery, and meditated hostility to the *rights of men.*

Digressing a little, or rather returning to what I have said on the first point, the right of naturalization, I admit that emigrants come when they will, are likely to be in opposition to the existing government, or rather, administration. This depends upon natural principles. The governments of Europe are most of them oppressive, and it is oppression that drives, in most instances, the inhabitant from amongst them. The poor or the most enterprising are those that emigrate. They have been in the habit of thinking of a reform, in the state of things in that country, from which they come; it is natural for them to think that a little touch of their hand may be still necessary here. Did you ever know a new physician called in that would not be disposed to alter the prescription, or to add to it? What occasion for him, if there was not something to be added, or retrenchment made? Or how can he shew himself, but in changing the medicines or the regimen. Extremes beget extremes in opinions, as well as in conduct. The extreme of government, where he has been, leads to licentiousness in his ideas of liberty, now where he is.

Besides it is in this revolution of administration, if he is an ambitious man, that he finds his best chance of ascending. He is therefore a demagogue before he becomes a patriot. I acquiesce, therefore, in the policy of our constitution, and our laws, which prescribe a kind of mental quarantine to the foreigner; though I incline to the generosity of those who think it unnecessary, and that such a great body of people have nothing to fear from the annual influx of a few characters, that may for some time, carry with them more sail than ballast. We had half Europe with us, in our revolution. We had all Ireland, the officers of government excepted, and even some of these. I therefore, do not like to see an Irishman obliged to perform a quarantine of the intellect. I think it contributes to sour his temper, and to fix a prejudice against the administration, under which the limitation has been introduced. However, this may be more splendid in theory than safe in experience, and I submit to the policy that has been adopted until the constituted authorities, shall think proper to regulate it otherwise. In the mean time, if this book should be read by any foreigner of high parts, and spirit, I would recommend it to him to suspend his judgment upon men and things, until he has examined well, the ground upon which he stands: to repress ambition and the desire of office, until unsought, it comes to him, during which time he may have become qualified to discharge it; and will have had an opportunity of finding out what he will finally discover, *that the best men are the most moderate.*

Intemperance of mind, or manner in a foreigner, gives colour to the imputation, that all are incendiaries. It becomes therefore, a matter of discretion, and just prudence, on his part, to be cautious in coming forward to take a lead in politics, until he has well examined the field of controversy. But because foreigners may abuse the privilege, I would not exclude them by a law, did the matter rest on first principles. I should think myself justifiable in excluding from my society, and the government I had formed, the inhabitants of another planet, could they come from thence ; because I do not know the kind of nature they are of; but men of this earth, of similar forms, and of like passions with ourselves, what have I to fear from them ? What right have we to exclude them ? We are not born for ourselves ; nor did we achieve the revolution for ourselves only. We fought the cause of all mankind ; and the good and great of all mankind wished well to us in the contest. With what anxiety did we look to Europe, for assistance. We derived assistance even from the good will of nations. It is an advantage to have a popular cause in a war. Have we a right to shut ourselves up in our shell, and call the society we have formed, our own exclusively? Suppose we had a right to the goverment exclusively, have we a right to the soil ? That is ours, subject to *the right of all mankind.* Pre-occupancy can give a right, but to a small portion of the soil to any individual. To as much only as is reasonably necessary for his subsistence. All the remainder is a surplus, and liable to be claimed by the emigrant. If he cannot get his right under the great charter of nature, without coming within the sphere of our government, and we hinder him to establish a society for himself within ours, why abridge him even for a moment; of the rights, immunities, and privileges of that which we have instituted ?

"Of the King's Prerogative." 1 Bl. Com. 246.

Is there any thing in the nature of a *prerogative* under our commonwealth? Unquestionably there is; and,

1st. In contemplation of law the *people* cannot be considered as having *done wrong*. Id quod sibi populus constituit, jus est. It is *lawful and right* whatever the people ordain. But *occasional representatives* may do wrong. For they may *transgress the constitution*. But the only remedy is the not delegating them again; and sending others who will repeal the act by which they had so transgressed; but,

2d. It is provided by the constitution, Art. 9. § 10. that "no man's property shall be taken, or applied to public use without the consent of his representative, and without just compensation being made." And this implies that the property of an individual may be taken away by law for a public purpose, the commonwealth making *just compensation*. This comes under the head of prerogative; for no individual can do this. The property cannot be taken away *directly*; so neither, I apprehend, can it be taken away *indirectly*; and the claim of a *priority* in a payment of debts, cannot exist under our constitution. For it is in fact taking away a man's property who has a right to be paid first; and to give this right of taking to the commonwealth where nothing will be left to discharge the debt due to the individual. In England a priority of payment, in the case of the king had some reason to support it, under feudal policy, according to the artificial structure of the system; but none under our commonwealth, where the people in whom the government is, may tax themselves ad libitum for its support. There is no necessity; and, there can be no *right* to alleviate the public burthens at the expence of a citizen, confiscating his debt, by giving a priority to the commonweath. There can be no necessity; for taxes can be laid and raised commensurate with the public exigencies; and bonds with sufficient security taken from official functionaries to secure duties to be performed or dues to be collected. There cannot be in the nature of the case a just compensation but the debt itself which will be its own measure, and this would amount to nothing more than the taking with one hand and paying with the other, which would be an absurdity. But;

3d. It is the nature of a *prerogative* of the commonwealth, that it cannot be *sued;* or at least this will not be permitted, but, sub modo, and by special law. The commonwealth cannot be sued; which though it may seem an unreasonable thing, yet the carrying a judgment against the state into effect, by compulsory process, constitutes the difficulty in the way of permitting a suit to be instituted in the first instance. For in the case of executory process there can be no writ to take a *corporate body*, and the inexpediency of permitting a levy on the public funds, money in the treasury, or lots on which the public buildings are erected, is such, as in the opinion of the legislature to prohibit it. Hence no general law enabling a creditor of the state to sue; and unless by law specially provided, and given in the particular instance, it has not been done; and this must be considered, rather with a view to inform the *conscience* of the legislature who will do right, and not as, ex adverso suing to a judgment. Laws have passed in some instances giving leave to individuals to bring suit; but this not under the idea that in case of debt or damages found, execution should issue; but that the state should satisfy; and in a case of real estate, direct *possession to be delivered.* For it must be understood that there shall be a saving of the principle, that in contemplation of law, the commonwealth should be supposed to *have done no wrong.* It is in order to ascertain what is right, that such legal process is instituted and enquiry made; But,

4th, The not being bound by *prescription of time* is a *prerogative* which our commonwealth posesses, unless when it is not taken away by particular statutes; and in no case, for an offence of malum in se, is it taken away. *At any length of time* the prosecution of the offender, for felony or misdemeanor, may be taken up. But,

5th, The *nonpayment of costs* is also a *prerogative* of the commonwealth, so that in the case of an acquittal on an *in-*

dictment or *information* no costs are allowed to the defendant, whatever may be the expences to which he may have been put ; but, he is left to recover of the prosecutor, where there is one ; but if not, the matter having been taken up at the instance of the attorney for the commonwealth ; or the court directing it ; or the court binding over to answer for a charge, he has no remedy ; for the *commonwealth does not pay costs.*

I return to say a few words on the head of prescription of time not running against the commonwealth, to shew that it is not unreasonable that it should be so in the case of *criminal proceedings.* For statutes of limitation are founded in the policy of quieting posessions in a case of real estate, and of preventing suits in the case of personal actions. But still more, in the *presumption,* that, in the case of debt, or account, payment has been made, when a creditor, within a reasonable time, hath not made a demand ; and in case of trespass called for satisfaction or brought suit. In the case of real estate the presumption is that a grant has been made ; or that the claimant has relinquished or abandoned. It is for the security of improvident individuals, that there should be a limitation of time, because the evidence of title may be lost or of money paid, or satisfaction made. But in the case of an offence against the public, the presumption is that the evidence has not existed, and the fact come to light as affecting the wrong-doer.

In the case of priority of payment, I will also add that, following the prerogative of the crown in England a preference was given at an early period, here, as appears by acts of assembly that are noted as expired, or repealed, or supplied. These are so early as 1705, 1710, and 1764, &c. entitled acts, " for giving priority of payment to the inhabitants of the government ; or directing the order of payment of debts of persons deceased, &c. That of 1764 which gave a preference to the commonwealth, after physical and funeral expences, has been supplied by that of 19th Ap. '94, by which debts due to the commonwealth *shall be last paid.* This is precisely as it ought to be, not because the commonwealth has a broad back ; but because the whole people have

a right to *postpone* themselves.   But the right to *prefer* themselves is more questionable; and as respects debts due before the act, it cannot be done consistent with the constitution.   Under a *general* law, and which bears upon debts to
arise, and a parte post, it is equal.   In this point of view, the
whole may have a right to prefer themselves, because every
constituent has in contemplation of law given his assent.
But as there never can be any necessity for such a general
act, I do not approve of it.

In the case of the U. S. there is no such *prerogative*, unless given by the constitution.   It is inferred from it under
the head of making all laws *necessary*.   The government of
the union is invested with the power, " *to* **pay** *the debts* and
provide for the common safety ; to raise and support armies ;
to provide and maintain a navy ; and to make all laws which
shall be *necessary and proper* for carrying into execution,
these and other powers."   The right to give a priority of payment as to debts due to the U. S. is claimed under this
clause.   It had been taken under sundry acts of the national
legislature, in certain cases, from an early period, after the
adoption of the constitution.   But by an act of the 3d March,
'97 this prerogative is carried to an *equal* extent, or *greater*
than, by the prerogative of England it has been done.   See
the reasoning of the counsel, and the decision of the court
2d. Cranch, 358.   And yet it is a provision of the federal
constitution, Art. 7 of amendments, that " private property
shall not be taken for a public use without a *just compensa-*
tion."   If our reasoning is correct with regard to the power
of the commonwealth of this state, a fortiori, it must hold in
the case of the U. S. under a *dubious construction* of the clause
of necessity.

The right of prosecution is ranked as a prerogative of
the crown ; and may also be considered as a prerogative of
the commonwealth ; so that *a felony cannot be compounded*;
and the right of *pardon* may also be considered in that
light : these and many other powers and privileges also,
which can only be vested in the body politic : and exercised
by the legislative or executive authority ; but I shall not no-

tice these as they would be numerous. In judicial trials it may be ranked as a *prerogative* of the commonwealth, that by a rule of the courts it shall have a preference in *the order of hearing;* but this extends only to *criminal cases ;* and not to those actions where the state is a party *in civil;* nor ought it to be.

NOTES ON

BLACKSTONE'S COMMENTARIES,

POINTING OUT VARIATIONS IN THE LAW OF PENNSYLVANIA
FROM THE COMMON AND STATUTE LAW OF ENGLAND,
WITH OTHER MATTERS OF A GENERAL NATURE.

———

"In the beginning of the world, we are informed by holy writ,
"the all-bountiful creator, gave to man "dominion over all the
"earth: and over the fish of the sea, and over the fowl of the air,
"and over every living thing that moveth upon the earth."* This
"is the only true and solid foundation of man's dominion over ex-
"ternal things, whatever airy metaphysical notions may have
"been started by fanciful writers upon this subject." II Bl.
Com. 2.

It is an objection to the theory of this commentator that
the authority of the legislator of the Jews is not *universally* acknowledged.

With such therefore who do not acknowledge this authority, the dominion of man over the *earth*, and all that it contains, must be established on other *evidence*. It may be asked
then, may it not be established by the *light of nature*, distinct from revelation; or in other words, placed on the
foundation of the *laws of nature themselves*.

However this very great commentator may sneer at the
"airy metaphysical notions of fanciful writers on the subject," it will be but a narrow foundation to all the world, to
place it on the authority of *Moses alone*.

* Gen. 1. 28.

What *law of nature* can give this dominion? What can be the *evidence of it?* His *superiority* over all other animals and the having the *power to subdue them*, is all the evidence that can be derived from *the light of nature.* And this evidence is sufficient; for *power* gives dominion, and is the *ultima ratio* of it. As between men and other animals, it may be put upon the ground of *mutual* benefit; but except in the case of the *dog*, the benefit would seem to be all on the side of man. The dog, of every species, seems by his *attachment to man*, and by the mutual interest of both, to be associated with man; but it is as subservient, to which condition, he seems willing to submit, that their mutual interest can exist. In fact, supposing a mutual benefit to exist on the side of any other animal from his association with man, it can only be under the idea, and on the actual ground of subserviency to this the lord of the creation. But can his *right* not only to the services of these animals, but to their lives be shewn by the *light*, or be derived from a *law of nature?* the *carnivorous teeth* of man, may be recurred to as the same evidence which nature exhibits in the brutal creation. Beast devours beast; and fish and fowl, even those that have not teeth, prey upon the inferior, or in other words the weaker as a *law of their nature.*

But as between men, and those whom he can subdue of his *own species* what is the law of nature. All respect their *peculiar species*, but it is *confined* to animals of the same species. For though *dog will not eat dog*, as the proverb is, yet he is hostile to the fox, which is not far removed from his kind; perhaps not farther than man is in many instances from man.

But though it may not be a law of nature that men should devour such as are in the shape of men, yet what hinders to compel their services if they have it in their power; more especially if at least one side is benefitted by it, which is disputed. For the holder of a slave is said by moralists to be equally injured by the holding, with the slave himself. But this leads to a disquisition into which I shall not enter. I shall confine myself to consider the sovereignty

Q

of man over the inanimate creation or *the earth itself.* Of
this *right of dominion* there is some evidence, above brute
animals. in favour of such as cultivate the earth; because
it is ameliorated or made more productive, by the skill and
labour of such.   But as to savages who do not cultivate the
soil, or sustain themselves to much extent, by that means,
they are in the same situation as to this evidence of right,
with the beasts.

   This leads to the question as to the right of men between themselves, with regard to portions of the earth. I have
discussed both this and the preceding question elsewhere;
and which discussion I shall save myself trouble by inserting here.   It is from a miscellany entitled Gazette Publications.   It comprehends also some thoughts with regard to
the discovery of a soil, as giving some priority of claim.

   " THE right of Great Britain to the soil of North-America, founded on the first discovery of the coast, however
just in its nature, yet was limited in its extent, by the right of
the natives, and the right of other nations.   The right of
the natives has been generally supposed not to limit but exclude all others.   For the law of nature vests the soil in the
first occupant, and these from the earliest times had possessed
the country.   But shall a few tribes thinly scattered over an
immense continent retain possession of it, while other parts
of the globe are overcharged with inhabitants?

   To set this matter in a clear point of view, we shall revert to the origin of that right which all men have, in common with each other, to the earth, the water and the air;
and this we shall find in the extensive grant to the first pair,
and in them equally to all their descendants.   This grant is
recorded in the first chapter and the first book of the sacred
law ; *And God blessed them, and God said unto them, be fruit-*
ful and multiply and replenish the earth, and subdue it : and
have dominion over the fish of the sea, and over the fowl of the
air, and over every living thing that moveth upon the earth.
The words of this grant convey no right of primogeniture,
or any other right by which one man may occupy a larger
portion of the soil than his neighbour; for rights of this kind

are the establishments of civil policy, and can have no place between individuals in a state of nature; or between different nations, who are in a state of nature; with relation to each other. The unequal distribution of the soil, would disappoint the manifest intention of the grant, which was to people and improve the earth; for it is unfavorable to population that societies or individuals should possess a greater quantity of soil than is necessary for their own subsistence.

To apply this to the aborigines or native Indians of America: Shall these tribes, inferior in number to perhaps one twentieth of the inhabitants of Europe, possess ten times the territory? It will be said that their manner of life makes a greater quantity of soil necessary. They live by hunting, and though their tribes are thinly scattered over the continent, yet the whole is no more than sufficient for a hunting ground; nay, with even this extent of country their subsistence is precarious, and they frequently experience the severest rage of famine, when the wild animals that make their food are rendered scarce, or have withdrawn to a different forest of the country. But do the laws of revelation or of nature leave every man at liberty to use what manner of life he pleases? This will deserve some consideration.

Before the fall, the earth spontaneously brought forth every *herb* and every *tree* for the use of man, and we may reasonably presume, that without cultivation it would then support a larger number of inhabitants than it can at present with the utmost labour we are able to bestow upon it. In this state of things it was not necessary to exercise the arts of industry; but when the curse attendant on the lapse of Adam, "glanced aslope upon the ground," and it became sterile, the cultivation of it was enjoined on man, not only as his punishment, but as now the only means by which he could support himself, and comply with the conditions of the grant, "replenish the earth and subdue it. The Lord God sent him (the first man) forth from the garden of Eden, to till the ground."

I acknowledge in the early times the cultivation of the earth was not so immediately enjoined as necessary; for the few inhabitants might live by pasturage, and for some space of time posterior to the general deluge, when the flesh of animals was given to the use of man, they might subsist by hunting; but on the closer settlements of families and nations, this manner of life became impossible to one, without engrossing more territory than could be spared to another, and as all could not subsist in this manner, no one had a right to claim it as an exclusive privilege.

The law of nature, where the law of revelation is not known, sufficiently enjoins on every man that he contract his claim of soil to equal bounds, and pursue that manner of life which is most consistent with the general population of the earth, and the increase of happiness to mankind : and it will easily appear that the mode of life by pasturage or hunting, requires a more extensive territory than by agriculture; and at the same time from the very circumstance of thin and scattered settlements in that state, the powers of genius are inactive, the arts and sciences remain unknown, and man continues to be an animal differing in nothing but in shape from the beasts of prey that roam upon the mountain. The life of these is therefore not human; for it is abhorrent from the way of life which God and nature points out as the life of man. " The Lord God sent him forth to till the ground ;" and common reason has discovered that from the goodness and benevolence apparent in the whole creation, and from that provision made abundantly for every creature, it must be most agreeable to the Creator that the earth be stored with inhabitants; and that in order to this end, a way of life be chosen in which individuals or particular nations may subsist with the least extent of territory.

The aborigines of this continent can therefore have but small pretence to a soil which they have never cultivated. The most they can with justice claim, is a right to those spots of ground where their wigwams have been planted, and to so much of the soil around them as may be necessary to produce grain to support them, their families, in towns upon the coast, or in the inland country, where they have inhabited. Perhaps they may have some priority of right to oc-

cupy a different country, should it be their choice to change
the situation where former circumstances may have placed
them.

The continent of North-America may therefore on the
first discovery of the coast, by any civilized European nation, be considered as, the greater part of it, a vacant country
and liable to become the property of those who should take
the trouble to possess it.   Nevertheless I do not mean
to justify the waging an unnecessary war against the natives, or the extirpation of them altogether; but yet I would
justify encroachment on the terrritory claimed by them, until they are reduced to smaller bounds, and under the necessity of changing their unpolished and ferocious state of life,
for fixed habitations and the arts of agriculture. At the
same time I think it still adviseable to purchase from them,
if it may be done conveniently; because it is a dictate of
humanity to decline insisting on the full extent of any claim
of property, if it may involve the shedding of the blood of
those, who though sunk beneath the dignity of human nature,
yet bear the name and are seen in the shape of men.

From the whole of this reasoning it will be evident, that
the right of Great-Britain to the soil of this continent, in
consequence of the first discovery of the coast, was limited
by the rights of the aborigines or native Indians found upon
it, but it was limited in a small degree, and the greater part
of this immense territory was then in strict view of revealed
and of natural law, without an owner or inhabitant.

The right of Great-Britain to the soil of North-America,
limited by the right of the natives, was also limited by
the right of other nations.   The terms of the grant
made to Adam, and renewed to Noah, equally embraced the
whole of their descendents. The earth lay in common, and
the occupancy of a portion of the soil, was that alone which
gave to individuals an exclusive right to hold it.   We must
restrict the right of occupancy to a moderate portion of the
soil, because it is inconsistent with the original condition and
express purpose of the grant, that an individual, or a nation
should possess a more extensive tract of country, than is ne-

cessary for their particular subsistence.   I have no doubt but that a nation greatly populous, whose numbers overcharge the soil, have a right to demand territory from a nation in possession of a soil equally fertile, and less abounding with inhabitants.

From the position which we have established, that it is the occupancy of a portion of the soil necessary for subsistence, that alone gives a right to hold it, it will follow that the circumstance of having first visited a country cannot give a right to any greater portion of the territory than is necessary for subsistence; and not indeed to any portion of it, unless the visitant remains to occupy and dwell upon it.   Perhaps it may confer a priority of right to occupy the soil while it shall be unoccupied by any other visitant.

We shall be sensible of this if adverting to the early emigrations, we consider that it would be absurd in Japheth the eldest son of Noah, wandering westwards from the mountains of Armenia, where the ark rested, to have advanced a claim to two or three countries, because in his way of life by pasturage or hunting, he had first passed the mountains, or first visited their boundaries.

The right of discovery was unknown in term or idea to the early ages, and it came first into view on the modern improvements in the art of navigation, when several of the sovereigns and states of Europe fitted out vessels to explore the seas, and to make discoveries.   The expence and labour of the enterprize, would seem to give a right to the soil of that continent or island which they had discovered.   But it may be said that an exclusive right of this kind would be unfavourable to the settlement of that country, and therefore could have no place even amongst the sovereigns and states of Europe, who by tacit and implied consent had submitted to it.   Much less could it have a place amongst the claims of other nations of the world, who in no way, by direct assent or implication, had come to such agreement.   In the mean time it will appear from history, that the claim of right, founded on the first discovery of the coast, was usurped by several of the sovereigns and states of Europe, rather than acknowledged by the others, who had not been equally adventurous or succcessful in expeditions of this nature. The Swedes and Dutch seem to have paid no regard to the claim of Britain, founded on the first discovery of Sebastian Cabot, who coasted North-America; for maugre his claim, the Dutch took possession of the country of New-York, and the Swedes of Pennsylvania. No state or individual ought to have regarded it; for no expence, enterprize, or labour of a nation, or of any individual, can give a right which in its operation would defeat the end in view by the Creator, which was, that the earth be fully stocked with inhabitants. To this great end, every claim and institution of a partial nature ought to be subordinate. The claim therefore of the first adventurers could with justice only be to so much of the soil, as they themselves immediately should occupy, and plant, and settle with inhabitants.—These things may be said plausibly; but it is to be considered that from the heart of Asia where man was first planted, it was an easy thing to emigrate and discover new countries. Hence it is that a pretence of right, from the first discovery of a country, would, in these early ages, have been vain, and we hear nothing of it. But when the whole eastern continent, and the islands of the coast had been visited and planted, it became an object of the industry of man, and required much sagacity, fortitude, and perseverance to explore the ocean, and effect discoveries. It was at the same time an affair of no small expence to fit out vessels for the voyage.

For these reasons natural justice would seem to give to the adventurers not only a priority of right to occupy a newly discovered country, but also a right to demand from others some consideration in services or money for admission to it.

The only reason to be urged against the claim from discovery is, that it is not favourable to the population of the earth that individuals, on any pretence whatsoever, should hold a greater portion of the soil, than is necessary for their particular subsistence. But it is to be considered, that it is favourable to population, because it is unfavourable to the

discovery of unknown regions of the earth, that the individual who by much labour and expence hath effected the
discovery, shall nevertheless enjoy no advantage resulting
from his ingenuity and enterprize, but a priority or right
to occupy an equal portion of the soil with him who, led
by the information of the first navigator, shall come to settle on it. The best argument in favour of the right of a
first discoverer, will therefore be, that by giving due encouragement to men who shall search the globe by sea and
land, and discover new soil, the whole earth will become peo-
pled, and it seems to be the will of the Creator, that the whole
earth be stocked with inhabitants.

" Tenant, in dower is where the husband of a woman is seized
" of an estate of inheritance and dies ; in this case the wife shall
" have the third part of all the lands and tenements whereof he
" was seized at any time during the coverture, to hold to herself
" for the term of her natural life."   2 Bl. Com. 129.

With respect to dower, the act of Pennsylvrnia, of 1794,
adopts the quantum allowed by the common law where there
is a widow and lawful issue, viz. one third of the real estate
for and during her natural life ; but in the case where there is
a widow and no lawful issue there is a different provision.
Sec. 4. " If the intestate shall leave a widow, and no lawful
issue, the said widow shall have one moiety or half part of
the real estate, including the mansion house, during her natural life, except in cases, where, in the judgment of the Orphan's court the estate cannot with propriety be divided ;
and in that case she shall have and receive the rents and profits of one moiety of the real estate during her natural life."
And concerning " the manner in which a woman is to be
endowed," by the same act, Sec. 22, it is provided, that upon
petition presented to the justices of the Orphan's court of the
county in which the lands lie, by the widow or by any of the

children of the intestate, or guardian, or next friends, if under age, the justices are empowered to appoint seven or more persons, indifferently chosen, on behalf and with consent of the parties, or where the parties cannot agree, to award an inquest to make partition; according to the purport and true meaning of the act.

These persons having made the inquisition are to make a return of it to the justices who are impowered then to give judgment, that the partition thereby made do remain firm and stable for ever.

But, where the estate, &c. cannot be divided without prejudice or spoiling the whole, the said seven or more persons, or the said inquest as the case may be, shall make a just appraisement thereof to the Orphans Court. After this, but not otherwise, the court may order the whole to the eldest son, or any of the other sons successively if they neglect or refuse; if no son, or all neglect or refuse, to the eldest daughter, &c. in the same manner, he, she or they, or some friend legally authorised, paying to the other children their equal and proportionable part of the true value of the estate, according to the appraisement.

But where the widow is living, and the whole premises are so adjudged, she shall not be entitled to the sum at which her share is valued, but the sum and the interest shall remain charged upon the premises, the child to whom the estate has been so adjudged to pay the interest annually to the mother during her natural life, in lieu and in full satisfaction for her dower at common law.

The law of Pennsylvania is different from that of England, as to the way in which a femme covert may be barred of her dower, by levying a fine, or suffering a recovery of the lands during her coverture; but which with us depends upon an act of assembly of 24 Feb. 1770, which is by appearing "before one of the judges of the supreme court, or before any justice of the county court of common pleas, of and for the county where the estate conveyed lies, and to acknowledge the convevance, the wife being examined separate and

R

apart from her husband," &c. Whether this respects the
lands of the femme in her own right before marriage; or
her right of dower acquired in the husband's estate by her
marriage had been distinguished; but it has been determined by the supreme court with a reference to both. For this
see 1 Bin. 470.

----◆----

"How dower may be *barred* or prevented." II Bl. Com 136.

THE question *of a devise given in lieu of dower and the
enjoyment* of the devise, and which might be construed *an
acceptance* barring dower was considered by the court in
the case of Webb and wife, v. Evans, reported 1 Bin. 565,
in which I am represented as *concurring*. I concurred in
holding it *under advisement*, but not in giving judgment; but
dissented in my mind from the opinion of Yeates and Smith
justices, and during the vacation had drawn up my reasons;
to be delivered at the subsequent term; but judgment in the
mean time being entered on the opinion of these judges;
or in some way it happened that I had not an opportunity.
It was not material, as my dissent would not have altered
the decision of the court. Nor did I dissent so much from
the law generally as laid down, but in the application of it
to the particular case.

But what I take to be a very material alteration of the
common law by our act of assembly of the 4th April, 1797,
was not noticed in the opinion as reported of the court:
and for that reason I subjoin my note. It is the *common
law* "that where a devise is *expressed* to be given in lieu
and satisfaction of dower; or where that is the clear and
manifest intention of the testator, the wife shall not have
both, but shall have her choice." Harg. Co. Litt. 366. By
our act it shall be taken to be in lieu of dower *unless expressed to the contrary*. My note on the case, as drawn up
was as follows.

" It is impossible for me to entertain any doubt in this case of the testator's intention, which was that the devises under the will should be in lieu of dower. The strongest circumstance against this, is the limiting the use of part of the messuage, and providing her with firewood, and keeping horse and cow, &c. to the time during which she shall remain a widow; which might lead to the conclusion that should she marry, she might determine this enjoyment under the will and recur to her dower. And I will admit, that I know of nothing on principle to hinder this; for though the right of dower accrues on the death of the husband, it is not necessary that the claim be made on the death; and certain enjoyments may be given, and used in lieu of a suspension of the claim; but it would not seem to me that this could be the meaning of the testator here. But that he limited these enjoyments during widowhood, in consideration that on marriage even should that happen immediately on his decease she would have at least four years and eight months before the eldest son came of age to enjoy the whole, and dispose of the issues; and seven years more to enjoy the one half, before the youngest son was of age, and after these sons both came of age, if married, she would have a husband to take her with him; or having had the issues for so long a time, she could provide for herself and him both. It is true she would have had to provide in the mean time for the maintenance and education of the children; but the eldest son, who would at the death of the testator have been turned of sixteen, could have been no charge, on either of these accounts, but must have been worth wages at work on the plantation. The second son turned of nine years, could not have been long, a burthen, but on the contrary soon worth more than his maintenance and education: such education as the testator's grade of education himself, must lead us to presume he contemplated.

The legacies to the three daughters were not payable, but respectively as they should arrive at the age of eighteen years. The eldest then of the age of thirteen, and some months ; so that there would have been the use of her legacy £150 for near three years before she came of age, and also of her own services, which considering the situation in life, of the testator, and the customs of the country, must have exceeded her support. The same could not be said with regard to the two youngest who had the like legacies ; but who were of the ages of not more than four and two years. But the inventory of the personal estate, exclusive, as I understand it, of what was specially devised to herself, for though she is directed to appraise the personal estate, and to take it at a moderate valuation, and out of it to pay legacies, yet he could not mean that it should be necessary to appraise what was specifically left to herself ; I say the inventory exclusive of this, and paying debts, amounted to the sum of £1000, and taking out of this the sum of £150, the legacy to the married daughter Hannah, there would remain £ 850 and the use of this until the three younger daughters came to their ages respectively to receive their legacies ; so that there would be considerable pickings out of this property, for a great length of time, especially when we take into view, the issues of the real estate in her possession, in a part of the country of good soil and generally highly cultivated, and not far from market, being in the neighbourhood of Lancaster. Adding to all this, the personal estate bequeathed to her, I can entertain no doubt of the intention of the testator that he considered himself as making a disposition which should be in lieu of dower ; and I think that in justice, she ought so to consider it. I know the language of the law, that to bar the claim of dower, the quantity of a bequest is not sufficient ; but it cannot but be a circumstance that will weigh, in considering the *intention.* But this is not the only circumstance here ; for though I will not say that the dispositions are absolutely inconsistent with the taking dower after the youngest of the two sons coming of age, which would be the time at farthest that she would be likely to claim it, when if married, she must claim it ; for in that case her use of the real estate would determine as to the whole, and the enjoyments provided during her widowhood, would cease ; yet nevertheless, on the score of the manifest intention of the testator, and her taking under the will and acting under it, I would hold her bound by it. Dower is favoured in law; and a good deal, from the early times, on this principle, that the personal estate was usually nothing, and it was on her dower only that the widow, could be supported. Hence the greater care in the provisions of the law for facilitating the recovery of dower, and the liberality in the decisions of courts in favour of it, the application of the strictness of which did not so well comport with a different nature of property; and hence an act of the legislature of this state, of the 4th April, 1797, Sec. 10, which provides "that if any testator after the passing of this act shall devise, or bequeath to his wife any portion of his estate, such devise, and bequest shall be deemed and taken to be in lieu and bar of her dower out of the estate of her deceased husband, in like manner as if the same were so expressed, unless the testator shall by his last will and testament declare otherwise, any law, usage, or custom of this commonwealth to the contrary in anywise notwithstanding." In this, as in many other cases, the legislature has been under the necessity of changing the law, from what it stood on decisions; aud perhaps it could not otherwise be done, the courts thinking themselves bound by what had been determined to be law by decisions; though, by the by, the decisions were never more than evidence of principles, which are supposed to exist in the law, before the decision is made according to them. But according to this evidence, that of decisions, the courts of this commonwealth would seem to have thought themselves bound to say, that notwithstanding the evidence of intention, if not express, or necessary, and incontrovertible from circumstances; or inconsistent with the taking under the will, dower should not be barred; yet so far as my knowledge of the understanding of the country went, this idea of the law was contrary to the general understanding; and it is evinced by this act of the legislature which I take to be precisely recognizing what was the general understanding. For surely no man who made a will, and made these arrangements, in the disposition of his property, did imagine that it could be broken in upon, or that

there could be superadded to it, a legal claim of dower. I
know that this case does not come under the act of assembly;
but I think myself at liberty to decide it in the spirit of it,
and that latitude which I take it, the courts are warranted to
take in the application of decisions to the nature of circumstances; and it is in this sense that the charter to William Penn,
grants the privilege of enacting laws, provided nevertheless
that the said laws be *consonant to reason*, and (as near as *may
be conveniently*) agreeable to the laws, statutes, &c. of England. And I take it that the courts of justice which by the
same charter the legislature of the province had a right to
establish, and the judges, in the application of the decisions
of the common law must be considered as having a like
latitude; and in fact it would seem to be so contemplated
by the charter; for the word "laws" in this section, would
seem to refer to the decisions of the courts as well as to the
acts of the legislature. It is only the *common law*, and
such of the statute laws of England, as have heretofore been
in force, that after the declaration of our independence, is
introduced by the act of assembly of the 28th of Jan. 1777
And I refer the "*heretofore in force*" to the words common
law, as well as to the statute laws, though in strict gramma-
tical construction, it can refer only to the statute laws; but
there is the same reason, for a reference to both; and I admit that decisions are evidence, and I will not contend but
that they may be evidence of the most weight in deciding
what of the common law was in force in the province, but
they are not the only evidence; for the reason of him who
has to decide on the application of a principle. is also evidence.

But without overthrowing English decisions; but applying without an adstriction to the mere letter, I cannot but
be of opinion that there is enough in the circumstances
of this case to warrant the inference that they amount to a
declaration plain of the testator's intention; and though the
testator could not by his will, deprive the widow of her
dower, yet as she has an interest under the will in the devise
of personal estate, and a great interest coupled with the trust,

and she accepted both, it would seem that she ought to be considered as accepting in lieu of dower.

But supposing the widow to have a right to dower, damages being given, and the dying seised having been found by the jury, and not having been *laid in the declaration* so that it can be considered as found, and the dying seised, or the having been seised, which is the same thing, being necessary to be found, to entitle to damages, I need not consider this, being of opinion on the principal point that the verdict ought to have been for the defendant.

II Black. Com. 140.

THE calender which is now generally adopted in the christian world, owes its origin to Romulus. Imagining the sun performed his course through all the seasons in 304 days, he divided the year into 10 months, making it to begin in the spring on the first of March. Numa giving the year 355 days, added two months, and transferred the beginning of the year to January. As this was still making the year too short, intercalary months were to be occasionally added. This producing confusion, Julius Cæsar with the assistance of the mathematician Sosigenus, undertook to rectify it. Taking up all the days which had been lost by the former method of reckoning, he formed one long year of 15 months or 445 days. After this had terminated, the *Julian* year commenced, January 1st. B. C. 46. As the annual revolution of the sun is completed in 365 days and about 6 hours he made the year to consist of 365 days, adding a day in every 4th year, to the 23d of Feb. or the 6th of the Kalends of March, which was to be twice reckoned. Hence bissextile, or *leap year*.

The Julian year however, was still imperfect; for as the sun performs his annual revolution or rather the earth performs its annual revolution round the sun, not exactly in 365 days 6 hours, but in 365 days 5 hours, 48 minutes and 45½ seconds, the solar year was shorter than the civil year by 11 min. 14½ sec. which in the space of about 130 years amounted to a whole day. This inconvenience becoming in the course of time too considerable to be unnoticed, Pope Gregory XIII. after unsuccessful attempts by former Popes and councils, abrogated the ancient Calendar and substituted a new one called the Gregorian Calendar or *new style*. It was published in the month of March, A. D. 1582. Ten days which had been gained by the old reckoning were taken from the month of October of that year, and the equinox brought back to the 21st of March as it had been settled by the council of Nice, A. D. 325. And in order to prevent a recurrence of a similar variation, every succeeding hundredth year was not to be counted a leap year, except every four hundredth year which should as usual be considered as a bissextile. Thus by making the years 1700, 1800, and 1900, common years instead of leap years, the error arising from the odd time would be corrected. The new style was adopted in Spain, Portugal, and part of Italy, on the same day as at Rome ; but it was not received in France until December, when the 10th was reckoned the 20th day, according to letters patent of Hen. III. In Great Britain such were the popular prejudices against it, that it was not easily admitted. However, as the inconvenience arising from the two modes of reckoning was much felt, an act of parliament in 1752 was obtained for this purpose. As 170 years had elapsed since the Gregorian alteration took place, the old style had consequently gained above a day more upon the course of the sun than it had when Gregory first promulged his alteration. It was therefore enacted that instead of cancelling 10 days, 11 should be left out of the month of September. On the 2d day of that month the old style ceased and the next instead of being the 3d was called the 14th. By the same act the beginning of the year was changed from the 25th of March to the first of January.

By an act of the assembly of Pennsylvania, 11th March, 1752, the act of parliament entitled " an act for regulating the commencement of the year, and for correcting the calendar now in use," was introduced, which provided, " that in and throughout all his majesty's dominions, &c. the supputation, according to which, the year, &c. beginneth on the 25th of March, should not be made use of from and after the last day of December, 1751, and that the first of January next following the said last day of December, should be reckoned, &c. to be the first day of the year 1752, and so on, from time to time, the first day of January in every year, which would happen in time to come should be reckoned the first day of the year; and that each new year should accordingly commence and begin to be reckoned from the first day of every such month of January next, preceding the 25th day of March on which the year would, according to the supputation aforesaid have begun or commenced; and that all acts, deeds, &c. &c. &c. which should be made, &c upon or after, &c. to bear date according to the new method of supputation, should be judged and taken as valid and effectual in law, as if according to the former supputation."

A provision is made in the same law relative to the calling the months *first and second*, &c. for the ease of the inhabitants of the then province, who scrupled to call the names of the months as they were commonly called March, &c.

It had excited no small alarm generally among the uninformed of the people, to talk of changing the date of the year, and many scrupled to reckon by what they call the new style. I have heard it said myself even in Pennsylvania, that they might change the style, but they could not change the seasons, for the winter would last just as long as it used to do, let them do what they would. It was even thought presumptuous to entertain such idea as the changing names of months, &c. It was considered to have its origin in some trick of the merchants on the continent, the Venitians in particular, for the sake of interest on accounts. I remember to have heard a learned Paisly weaver, as he thought himself, give this solution of the problem.

S

" The nature and degrees of kindred being thus, in some mea-
" sure explained, I shall next proceed to lay down a series of
" rules, or canons of inheritance, according to which estates are
" transmitted from the ancestor to the heir," &c. II Bl. Com.
207.

Land in Pennsylvania, comes to the heir, or representatives under the statute of distribution, *subject to the debts
of him from whom the estate has descended;* whereas at common law it was liable only to *debt by obligation;* and this
where the ancestor had bound himself and his heirs. An
obligation is by writing under seal; and differs from a *simple
contract debt,* in which case in England the land could not be
bound in the hand of the heir. " When a man binds himself and *his heirs*, by obligation to pay a certain sum at a day,
and dies, it is at the election of the obligee to sue the heir, or
the executors, or administrators of the obligor; and if so be
that the executors have assets in their hands, yet the obligee
may sue the heir if he will, because the obligor has bound as
well his heir, as himself."* Hence the form of an obligation, I bind myself and my heirs; or I bind myself, my
heirs, executors, and administrators, which is unmeaning in
Pennsylvania, where a man binding himself, makes his representatives liable, under every denomination, so far as he
has left lands or personal property. This is as it ought to
be, notwithstanding the *wife's right must be affected by the
principle.* Lands in her own right cannot be taken for debt
after the death of the husband, *nor in his lifetime* save so far
as affects profits; nor after her death save so far as affects
his right of tenant by the curtesy. But a man incurring
debts for the mutual benefit of both, as it must be supposed
to be, the law presuming a consideration received, it is reasonable that the wife's right of dower in lands not in her
own right, should be holden liable. Nevertheless it is an
inconsistency with this power in the husband to subject for
debts, that he cannot alien the whole without the consent of
the wife. It must be a voluntary act of her own, to convey

* For all the learning on this head, see 2 Plow. 439; and 3
Tuck. Bl. 418.

land in her own right or *otherwise*, so as to affect her own right of dower.

The liability of real estate for debts in Pennsylvania, depends upon laws agreed upon in England, and sundry acts of assembly of the colonial provience, directly establishing, or by *implication* recognizing this principle.

By the statutes of distribution in the case of intestates' estates, and particularly by that of the 19th April, 1794, great alterations have been made from the law of England. "Real estate shall be distributed to the *lawful children* of the intestate, such children always to inherit and enjoy as tenants in common in equal parts." This exclusive of the wife's right of dower in one third for and during her natural life. In case the person dying intestate shall leave several persons lawful issue in the direct line of lineal descent and all of equal degree to the person so dying intestate, the said estate exclusive of the right of dower in the widow, shall descend and be distributed to the several persons, as tenants in common in equal parts, *however remote from the intestate*, the common degree of consanguinity may be, in the same manner as if they were all daughters of the person so dying intestate: and in case the intestate shall leave lawful issue of different degrees of consanguinity to him, or her, the said estate shall descend to the lawful child, or children of the intestate, if either, or any of them shall be then living, and to the lawful issue of such of the children as shall be then dead, leaving lawful issue, as tenants in common, in equal parts, such share only as would have descended to his or their parent, if such parent had been then living; and each of the lawful children of the intestate always to inherit, and to receive such share as would have descended, and been distributed to him, or her, if all the children of the intestate who shall be then dead, leaving lawful issue, had been living, at the death of the intestate: and if there be no child of the intestate living at the death of the intestate, and only a grand child, or grandchildren who shall be then dead leaving lawful issue, then the real estate shall descend to such grand-child, or grandchildren of the intestate, and to the lawful issue of such of the

grand children of the intestate as shall be then dead, leaving
issue as tenants in common, such issue always to inherit if
one person, solely, and if several persons, as tenants in common, in equal parts, such share only as would have descended
to his, her, or their parent, if such parent had been then living.   And each of the grand-children of the person so dying intestate, who shall be living at the time of the death of
the intestate, always to inherit and receive such share as
would have descended, or been *distributed* to him, or her, if
all the grand-children of the intestate who shall be then
dead, leaving lawful issue, had been living at the time of
the death of the intestate and the same law of inheritance
and *distribution*, shall be observed in case of the death of
the grand-children, and other descendants to the remotest
degree."

The words distributed and distribution refers to the personal estate which takes the like course.   The provisions
are interwoven, and are the same, but having in mind only
the variations from the law of England in the case of *real*
estate, I have dropped in the act what refers to *personal.*

The 4th Sec. of the act respects the intestate leaving no
widow; or leaving a widow, and no lawful issue.   Sec. 5.
the case where neither widow, nor lawful issue is left, but
a father.   Here the rule of the common law " shall not ascend," is departed from, and material alterations made. Sec.
6. respects the disposition of the estate *after the death of
the father*, where it has so ascended.   Sec. 7. provides where
the *mother* shall inherit.   Sec. 8. where there is no widow,
nor *issue*, but a mother, and brother, and sister of their
representatives.   Sec. 9, treats of advancements to children.
Sec. 10, of posthumous children.   Sec. 11, where the half
blood shall inherit.   Sec. 12, where kindred in equal degree.

This act cannot be understood as having given a final blow
to the feudal system, but it has gone a great way towards it.
The law of *entails* must go before our law of the tenure of
real estate can be, in all particulars, accommodated to a republican government.

This act, I speak of that of 1794, has been drawn by one who has had a comprehensive view of the system of the English law respecting the descent, and inheritance of real estate, and in making the alterations has committed no error, which it is of all things the most difficult to avoid where a structure is to be altered, and a part taken away, or supplied. For hence it is that we see amendment and supplement without end.

But this will serve to give an idea of what I mean. A workman, master of his art, has the whole in his mind before he begins, and the *proportions* are all hit at once.

This act has been drawn by one who has understood the *arrangement of words*, which is one standing cause of the obscurity of our acts of Assembly, and the extreme perplexity of being able judicially to say what *is unequivocally meant*. This act is invaluable as a model of perspicuous *arrangement* and *unambiguous expressions*. I might say of the acts of the legislature generally, had they said all things so,

" O, si sic omnia dixissent."

Might it not be advisable, by a supplement to *the law of devises*, to have a similar provision, viz. " That *where real or personal estate is devised, and the devisee dies after the death of the testator, but before the contingency, on which he is to take, happens, his lawful issue shall take per capita, or by the head, what is devised to him.*" I have in my mind, the decisions in the case of the lessee of Smith against Folwell, 1 Binney, 546. It is true, it may be said, that the testator may provide for *such* or *any other contingency;* but it is not within the *foresight* of common persons to look to such contingencies, and provide for them ; and they are not aware of the difficulty on the rule of the common law, of taking *per stirpes*, or by the *stock*, and not *per capita*, or by the head, which is in the way of representatives succeeding to the devise, as may be seen in the case referred to in the report which I have cited. This provision perhaps, with another relative to the *construction of devises*, might be the subject of legislative interposition. I speak of that much agitated question in England, as well as here, *what shall be the effect of technical terms in a last will and testament.* See 2 Binney, 13 ; 3 Binney, 374, and other cases in our reports and decisions under this head.

I did not take notice in the early part of this note, that by the *common law* the king's prerogative extended to the lands of the debtor; though by the statute of magna charta this prerogative was restrained to the taking the lands of the king's debtor, only where *goods and chattels were deficient.* But by the statute 33 H. 8. c. 39. this prerogative was restored; and perhaps *enlarged* from what it was at common law; but not carried so far as would seem to be by the laws of the United States and the decisions of their courts in case of a preference in the payment of debts. Judgments in the case of a *private* person take place of the king's debts by obligation, short of a judgment.

Lands descend therefore in England subject to the debts of the ancestor *by obligation*, where the heir is named, and in the case of the king's debt by obligation, *whether named or not ;* and this by force of the statute in that case provided.

It may serve to give a clearer view of the subject, to contrast the rules of inheritance, as laid down by Blackstone, with the changes by our act of assembly.

The first rule, says the commentator, is, that " inheritances shall lineally descend to the issue of the person who died last seised, in infinitum ; but shall never lineally ascend. '

By our act, sec. 6. if the intestate die, leaving neither widow nor lawful issue, but leaving a father, the whole of the real estate shall be enjoyed by the *father* of the intestate, for, and during his natural life.

In like manner, Sec. 7. if the intestate die leaving neither widow nor lawful issue nor father, but leaving a mother, the whole of the real estate shall be enjoyed by the *mother*, for, and during her natural life.

At the end of the same Sec. it is provided that if " the intestate shall leave no brothers or sisters, nor their representatives, then the estate shall go to the father in fee simple, unless where the estate has descended from the part of the mother."

In a supplement to the above act, passed 1797, it is provided in Sec. 5, that if any intestate shall die seised of real estate in fee simple, and shall leave no widow, nor lawful issue, father, brother, sister, or their representatives, then the said estate shall go and be vested in fee simple in the mother, unless where such estate has descended from the part of the father, in which case it, or such part thereof as shall have come from the part of his or her father, shall pass and be enjoyed, as if such person, so dying seised, had survived his or her mother.———

2d. " The male issue shall be admitted before the female."

In Pennsylvania no preference is given to the male issue, but all the children, lawful issue, or their representatives, are entitled to succeed to equal parts of the real estate, and hold as tenants in common.

3d. " Where there are two or more males in equal degree; the eldest only shall inherit; but the females altogether."

The provisions of our act have changed this rule. With us there is no such thing as the right of primogeniture; and the males as well as females inherit equal parts.

4th. " The lineal descendants, *in infinitum*, of any person deceased shall represent their ancestor; that is, shall stand in the same place as the person himself would have done, had he been living."

Our act adopts this canon, but in the application of the rule, there is no preference of the eldest son or his representatives, as in England. In Pennsylvania *all* the children, grand-children, or great-grand-children, as they succeed to the inheritance, take equal shares, regarding in the distribution the method of inheriting *per stirpes* by the roots.

5th. " On failure of lineal descendants, or issue, of the person last seised, the inheritance shall descend to his collateral relations; subject to the three preceding rules."

By our act, when the lineal descendants are exhausted, the father or mother succeed, and where there are brothers and sisters the real estate shall descend to and be enjoyed by

the brothers and sisters of the intestate, or their representatives, *after* the decease of the father or mother, as tenants
in common, in equal parts.

" Being of the blood of the first purchaser."

The Jews, Greeks, and Romans looked no farther than
the person who died seised of the estate. The looking back
to the first purchaser, is derived from the feudal system, and
I presume is not a rule in Pennsylvania, except in the case
where the brothers and sisters or representatives of the half-
blood, being otherwise entitled to inherit, cannot take where
the inheritance came to the intestate by descent, devise, or
gift, of some one of his or her ancestors, in which case all
those, who are not of the blood of such ancestor, shall be excluded from the inheritance.

6th. " The collateral heir of the person last seised must
be his next collateral kinsman of the whole blood."

By our act the half blood are not totally excluded. By
Sec. 2. on failure of lawful issue, father or mother, brothers
or sisters, or their lawful issue, of the whole blood, then brothers and sisters of the half blood, and their lawful issue, shall
inherit the same as aforesaid, in preference to the more remote kindred of the whole blood, unless where such inheritance came to the person so seised by descent, devise, or gift
of some one of his or her ancestors, in which case all those,
who are not of the blood of such ancestor, shall be excluded
from such inheritance.

And by a supplement to this act, 1797, Sec. 7. " if there
are no lawful issue, widow, father or mother, brothers or sisters, or their representatives, of the whole blood, then brothers and sisters of the half blood shall inherit the said real
estate in fee simple, &c. as tenants in common, in equal parts,
except such parts of the real estate as came to such intestate
by descent, devise or gift of some one of his or her ancestors,
in which case, all those who are not of the blood of such ancestor, shall be excluded from such inheritance, and such
part of the real estate."

7th. " In collateral inheritances the male stocks shall be
preferred to the female; (that is, kindred derived from the

blood of the male ancestors, however remote, shall be admitted before those from the blood of the female, however near) unless where the lands have, in fact, descended from a female."

By our act is given no preference to the males in lineal succession, nor in the succession of collaterals.

This last, will seem in some degree to be but a repetition of what precedes ; but giving a different view by means of the contrast, it will be of use to the student. For of all things it is the most difficult to get an impression made upon the understanding or the memory, where the rules are merely abstract, and little depending upon natural reason. There must be " line upon line, precept upon precept, here a little and there a little ;" and this is the great secret of indoctrinating the early mind in any science.

" The fourth species of assurance, by matter of record, is a " common recovery." II Bl. Com. 357.

THE statutes of entail, were *impliedly* recognized as extending to Pennsylvania by the act of 27 Jan. '49, '50, entitled an act baring estates tail, 1 Smith's laws, 203. The preamble is, that, " forasmuch as the entailing of estates without a proviso by law for baring them, would introduce perpetuities, prevent the improvement of such estates, disable tenants in tail to make provision for the younger branches of their families, prove of general detriment, and be attended with manifold inconveniences, for preventing thereof," &c.

By this act, the recoveries *before suffered*, were *validated* and *confirmed* as well as those *thereafter* to be made.

But by an act 16 Jan. 1799, entitled " an act to *facilitate* the baring entails," it is provided " that whereas common recoveries are now considered as a mode of *conveyance*, by which tenants in tail, are enabled to convey and dispose of their lands and tenements ; but, the said mode of convey-

T

ance is attended with a *heavy expence*, and, in many cases, with great inconvenience. Be it enacted," &c.

In consideration of these acts of the legislature, not only recognizing the *statutes of entail* as *introduced* in Pennsylvania, but having rendered the baring them so easy, by a mere deed of conveyance, &c. I did not withhold my signature from *the report of the judges, on the subject of the English statutes;* but I have had, since, reason to wish that I had noted an exception with regard to the statutes of *entail.* My reasons of which I was not then aware, and which in great part did not exist, at least so strongly in my view, will be seen from my *dissent* in several cases, Binney's reports, where the questions were under *devises,* whether an estate in fee, or in tail was taken. It will be seen in these cases, that the judges, from whose opinion I *dissented,* not only adopted the strictest rules of the English courts in the construction of devises; but as I would seem to have thought, *even in the application of the rules to the particular case.* This however would be only matter of opinion with me, and must be judged of by others, on the strength of the reasons given. But certain it is, that the court adopted, in its utmost strictness, the English rule, that where a *technical term* is used, the devisor shall be presumed to mean it in the *technical sense,* unless it *can be collected from other parts of the will, that he did not mean it in a technical sense.* I would just reverse this rule; viz. that a devisor shall *not be presumed* to use a word in a technical sense, unless it can be collected from the whole of the will, that he did mean so to use it.

We all know who are the usual *scriveners,* or drawers up of last wills and testaments in Pennsylvania; the school-master of the neighbourhood; a commissioned justice of the peace, or some one that has been about the courts and has some reputation for clerkship. The school-master has his Clerks' Assistant, or vade mecum, or some book of *bad precedents,* from which he picks terms without distinguishing the use: the justice in like manner, or other person, little learned in the law, and yet affecting much. The terms, *heir, issue, begotten,* &c. get in, or the arrangement of the words, by *implication* is such as to be construed to mean what in fact never was intended. I am therefore of opinion to *abolish the entailing estates altogether.*

The person taking the estate, not dreaming that he was an heir *in tail* never thinks of baring it; but conveys it to an innocent purchaser, who makes improvements, and at a distant period, a defendant looking at the will, or some one for him, finds it out that he may claim the estate as *entailed* under the devise, and takes it with all the labour of the purchaser, the judges declaring it an estate tail, by reason of a technical term, or arrangement of words, that by implication, would seem to make it such. These things ought not to be so.

"Entails" says judge Tucker in his note, 2 Bl. Com. 119. "were formerly greatly favoured in Virginia; the statute *de donis conditionalibus*, extending to the colony, no act of assembly authorising entails of lands, occurs in our code. In 1710, as we have seen, they were protected from being defeated by a fine and recovery. In 1727, slaves were subjected to limitations in tail, by being annexed to lands entailed, and were to descend and pass in possession, reversion, and remainder, with the lands themselves, c. 4. Sec. 12. Edi. 1769. By the act of 1734, c. 6, Sessions acts, an abstract of which is preserved in Mercer's abridgment, title, entails, " any person seised in fee-"tail of any lands, tenements, or hereditaments, not exceed-"ing the value of £200 sterling, and not being parcel of, "or contiguous to other entailed lands of the same party, "might sue out a writ from the secretary's office in the na-"ture of an *ad quod damnum* to the sheriff of the county, "commanding him to inquire, by the oaths of good and "lawful men of his county, of the value of such lands, and "whether, &c. and if such lands shall be found not to exceed "the value as aforesaid, and to be a separate parcel, and an "inquisition to that effect be made and returned to the office, "then a deed of bargain and sale reciting the title, and such "inquisition, wherein a valuable consideration shall be ex-"pressed, and *bona fide* paid, acknowledged, or proved "by three witnesses, before the general court, within eight

" months after the date thereof, should be sufficient in law
" to pass the fee simple estate to the purchaser, and the
" right of the issue of the vender, and all other persons in
" remainder or reversion, should be barred, &c." This act
was amended by the act of 1748, c. 1. §. 16, which requires
the surveyor of the county to attend and survey the lands
in the presence of the jury, and to give them an account of
the number of acres. And where the tenant in tail had no
issue capable of inheriting the lands, if there were a remainder over, the remainder man, or, if an infant, his guardian
or next friend should have notice to attend the survey, and
see that the valuation was fairly made; and the deed of bargain and sale was to be recorded in the general court within
eight months. Edi. 1769. Estates, above the value of £200
sterling, were barred by private acts of assembly passed for
that special purpose."

" But when the revolution took place, a different mode of
thinking succeeded; it was found that entails would be the
means of accumulating and preserving great estates in certain families, which would, not only introduce all the evils
complained of in England, but be utterly incompatible with
the genius and spirit of our constitution and government.
At the first session, therefore, after the declaration of independence, an act passed, declaring tenants of lands, or slaves
in tail, to hold the same in fee simple. This act avoids all
estates tail in possession, reversion, or remainder theretofore
created by deed, will, act of assembly, or any other ways or
means, or thereafter to be created, any words, limitations, or
conditions in the deed, will, or act of assembly, or other instrument to the contrary notwithstanding; and further declares, that every estate, so created, shall be held in full and
absolute fee simple. This act is further confirmed by the
acts of 1785 and 1792, which declare, that every estate in
lands which hath been limited since the seventh day of October, 1776, or hereafter, shall be limited, so that as the law
aforetime was, such estate would have been an estate tail,
shall be deemed to have been, and continue an estate in fee
simple. The act of May, 1783, declares, that all estates in

lands or slaves which have become, or shall become escheat-
able to the commonwealth, by virtue of the " act declaring
tenants of lands or slaves in tail, to hold the same in fee simple," for defect of blood, shall descend, and be deemed to
have descended agreeable to the limitations of the deed or
will creating the same. But that act does not extend to
lands or slaves which had been escheated and sold. L. V.
Oct. 1776, c. 26 May 1783, c. 27. Edi. 1785. Sessions
acts of 1785, c. 62. Edi. 1794, c. 90. Sect. 9, 10, 11."

" In the construction of these acts, it has been decided, that
by the act of October 1776, for docking entails, all remainders, as well *contingent* as vested, are utterly barred, whether the entail be created before or after passing the act.
And though executory devises of lands, after a devise thereof in fee simple, may still be created as before that statute,
yet the court will not, in order to avoid the effect of the statute, construe that to be an executory devise, which, before,
would have been held to be a contingent remainder. Carter,
vs. Tyler, and also 1 Call's Rep. 165."

" And in this case, Pendleton, president, said, a parent may
guard against an improvident child's wasting his estate, by
limiting his interest in, or power over it. He may give an
estate for life, and limit remainders over, upon it; but how
far he may go in limiting estates for life, one after another,
so as to effect a perpetuity, we leave to be decided when the
experiment shall be made. At present, we can safely say,
that whenever the conveyance gives an estate-tail in lands,
the act vests in that tenant, an estate in fee simple. Ibi-
dem, 185."

" See also Hunters v. Haynes. 1 Wash. Rep. 71. Where
a devise to A. for life, with remainder to B. and the heirs
of his body lawfully begotten forever; but in case B. should *die
without such issue*, then to C. and his heirs for ever. In this case
the court decided, that although B. died without issue in the
life-time of A. yet his next heir should have the land in preference to C. the next remainder man. For, by the operation of the act of 1776, B's vested remainder in tail, was turned into an absolute fee simple, and descended to his heirs after the death of the tenant for life."

" We have now considered the several species of common as-
" surances, whereby a title to lands and tenements may be trans-
" ferred and conveyed from one man to another. But before we
" conclude this head, it may not be improper to take notice of a
" few general rules and maxims, which have been laid down by
" courts of justice, for the construction and exposition of them all."
II Bl. Com. 379.

THERE has been no point of law upon which I have been
more dissatisfied with the decisions of the English judges
than with regard to the *construction* of last wills and testaments. The rule which they have laid down, and their reasoning upon it, or application of it, is so inconsistent and contradictory, that I have been at a loss to know what to make
of it.   According to one, the *technical* term is to govern; according to another, the *intention* is to govern; or the construction is to be a *compound* of both. The only judge, or
elementary writer, that I find to speak common sense on the
subject, is Hargrave, in his observations, concerning the rule
in Shelly's case, in which I am happy to find my own way of
thinking on the subject perfectly established. Harg. Tracts,
574.

His language is, " Surely the rules of interpreting words
must be the same throughout. If a single word or a whole
sentence, has, by habit, obtained an appropriate sense, the
law ought to presume in favour of that sense in preference
to any other; unless from other passages in the same instrument, or from some *peculiar circumstances* attending the case,
there is evidence sufficient to satisfy the mind of the judge,
that the author of the instrument under consideration really
intended to convey a different meaning.   For the sake of
preventing the assumption of a boundless and arbitrary discretion, it is fit that great respect should be shown to former
decisions as to the weight of evidence requisite to repel the
legal or technical sense of words, but *some discretion must necessarily be left;* because to insist *that men shall only use
words in one certain sense would be a monstrous tyranny;
and there is such an infinite variety in the language and circumstances which may occur to distinguish one case from ano-*

ther, that, to lay down one general rule of interpretation so absolute as to be indispensible, would be making legal interpretation to torture like the bed of the fabulous attic robber Procustes, and so, every instrument would be cruelly stretched or curtailed into the same meaning. All this is plain sense as to the interpretation of words, and, more or less ever has been, the language of our judges in deciding upon conveyances and written instruments of every kind, with, however, a peculiar extension of indulgence to last wills and testaments."

But when they come to construe, or apply the rule, even judge Blackstone, in the case of Perrin and Blake talks of *rules more or less flexible, accommodating* or *obedient* which I cannot comprehend ; and I am happy to find that Hargrave in his observations is of the same opinion. *Intention or technical term must govern; there cannot be a compound of both.* It has been on this principle that I have been under the necessity of dissenting in some cases of a devise of real estate, from the decision of the court of which I am a member, looking at a will as I would at any other writing by persons not supposed to know any thing about law terms ; and also looking at all that can be collected from the will relative to the family of the devisor, and the nature of the property devised. Dehors the will I would not go ; or bring evidence *aliunde* as to the *construction;* and this is the only limit I would put to my interpretation. I would certainly consider, whether, from the language of the will, it appears to have been drawn by a person *technically* learned or otherwise ; and I would assist myself by what I could collect, or had collected of the popular use of terms ; as also of the common usage in employing persons to draw wills, such as schoolmasters, or half learned persons in the society where the will was drawn.

There are a variety of things I would consider ; in short from whatever sources I might draw my knowledge or information, I would take up a will as I would a letter or any other paper coming from the person, and inquire what was meant. *Intention* with me should be absolute ; and I would fetter it with nothing deducible from art or science of which

I could not suppose the person writing to have a correct knowledge.

Under this head let me refer to judge Tucker's note, 2
Bl. Com. 381 ; particularly the remarks which he cites from
Pendleton, president, to wit, " that the intention of the testator is declared by all the judges both ancient and modern,
to give the rule of construction : but after laying down the
true rule built upon *intention*, they admit that if there were
no words of limitation, the common law rule must prevail ;
by which they tied a gordian knot, which they have since
struggled to untie. It would have been better to have cut it
at once."

He cites 1 Wash. Rep. 102, 103, 271, 302, 338. 1 Call's
Rep. 13, 14, 16, illustrating this that the intention must be
collected from the will itself; " which is true," says he, " if
we admit those words to be explained by the *relative situation* of the parties ; and *the circumstances of the testator* ;
which a multiplicity of cases prove *ought* to be considered.
But it is said, the *intention* is not to prevail against *settled* and
fixed rules of construction. If we could discover those settled rules, continues the president, we would pursue them ;
but, after all our researches, we are much inclined to affirm what was said by judge Wilmot, 3 Bur. 1533, that cases
on wills served rather to obscure, than illumine questions of
this sort. So it is said by the court, 3 Wil. 141. that cases
on wills may guide as to general rules of construction,
but, unless a case cited, be, in every respect, *directly in point,
and agree in every circumstance*, it will have little or no weight
with the court, who always look upon the *intention* of the
testator as the polar star to direct them *in the construction of
wills*."

" Upon the two principles of inconvenience and hazard, compar-
" ed together, different nations have at different times, established
" different rates of interest." II Black. Com. 462.

BY the statute of the 12th Anne, c. 16. (1713) entitled
" *an act to reduce the rate of interest,*" which remains the English law, no lender upon *any contract*, shall take directly or
indirectly for loan of any monies, wares, merchandise, or
other commodities whatsoever, above the value of 5 pounds
for the forbearance of 100 pounds for a year and so after that
rate for a greater or a lesser sum, or for a longer or shorter
time; and that all bonds, contracts, and assurances whatsoever for payment of any principal, or money to be lent or covenant to be performed upon or for any usury, whereupon
or whereby there shall be reserved or taken above the rate
of 5 pounds in the hundred shall be *utterly void;* and that
all and every person or persons whatsover which shall, upon
any contract to be made, take, accept and receive, by way or
means of any corrupt bargain, loan, exchange, chevizance,
shift or interest of any wares, merchandise, or other thing or
things whatsoever, or by any deceitful way or means, or by
any covin, engine, or deceitful conveyance, for the forbearing or giving day of payment for one whole year of and for
their money or other thing, above the sum of 5 pounds for
the forbearing of 100 pounds for a year, and so after that rate
for a greater or lesser sum, or for a longer or shorter term,
shall forfeit and lose for every such offence *the treble* value of
the monies, wares, merchandises and other things so lent,
bargained, exchanged or shifted."

The student when he reads the decisions of the English
courts upon this statute, will be naturally led to enquire whether this statute has been introduced, or made the law here.
It has not been introduced, or acted upon; for we have an
act of assembly of our own of the 11th March, 1723, which is
different, and varies in some particulars from the English statute. With a view therefore to be enabled to compare our
act with the British statute, I will extract what is material
of it, as has been done above, totidem verbis in the Stat. of
Anne; that, " no person shall, *directly nor indirectly*, for

U

any bonds or contracts, take for the loan or use of money or any other commodities, above the value of 6 pounds for the forbearance of 100 pounds, or the value thereof, for one year, and so proportionably for a greater or lesser sum; and that if any person, &c. shall receive or take more, &c. on any such bond or contract upon *conviction* thereof the person or persons so offending shall forfeit the money and other things lent, the one half to the governor, the other half to the person who shall sue for the same."

A difference in one particular will be observed here that the bond or contract is not declared *void* as by the English statute; so that though an interest of more than 6 per cent. could not be recovered, yet the sum *originally lent* might be recovered on the bond.

But by Sect. 2. the taking more than 6 per cent. is rendered highly penal. But it is not an indictable offence, though the word *conviction* is used; for the kind of conviction is stated in the act upon which the forfeiture shall be recoverable, and that is by action of debt, &c. It is called a qui tam action from the words of the writ, qui tam pro republica quam pro se ipso sequitur. These words of the writ as in other cases, are recited in the declaration.

The Jews were prohibited from taking interest from each other; " Thou shalt not lend upon usury to thy brother; usury of money, usury of victuals, usury of any thing that is lent upon usury. Unto a stranger thou mayest lend upon usury; but unto thy brother thou shalt not lend upon usury." Deut. xxiii. 19, 20.

I can find but little concerning usury among the Greeks. It does not appear that any legal standard was established. Money lenders were enjoined to be moderate in their profits; which were in general previously stipulated by the parties.

Among the Romans, the interest of money was called Foenus, Usura, fructus, merces, and impendium. It would seem to have been discouraged by the Decemvirs: " Primo 12 tabulis sancitum est nequis unciario foenore amplius exerceret." Tac. An. Lib. VI—16.

The rate of interest, which was an inveterate grievance of the city (veterem duram and gravissimam molem) increased and fell as the influence of the wealthy, or clamours of the populace were most predominant. At one time (A. U. 408) 6 per cent. (foenus semiunciarum) was usual. Towards the end of the Republic, and under the first Emperors, 12 per cent (usura centesima) was tolerated. After the death of Anthony and Cleopatra, it fell to 4 per cent. Dio. Lib. 21. Finally Justinian took up the subject and regulated it. Persons of illustrious rank were confined in all cases to the moderate profit of 4 per cent. Manufacturers, and persons in other employments were allowed 8 per cent. In contracts of insurance (trajectitiis contractibus) twelve was permitted : and six (dimidiam centesimæ) was made the ordinary and legal profit to all other descriptions of persons, and in all other contracts. Code 4. 32, 26.

It is on this principle, the prohibition of our statute, that the licence of the state, by a charter of incorporation becomes necessary, in order to take the case out of the statute, in case of discounts upon money lent by banks. What is called a bonus is usually given by the company for such a privilege. There is an inconsistency between this law, and the taking more than 6 per cent. upon bank stock. It would seem that this statute ought to be *repealed* or *enforced* against the money lenders of a self-constituted company.

The opinions of abstract writers on the subject of usury are different. Those who are enemies to interest in general, hold any encrease of money to be indefensibly usurious. Principally resting on the prohibition of it to the Jews by Moses, the school divines have exclaimed against the practice; and the canon law has absolutely forbidden it as a heinous sin. But the precept of Moses is clearly a political and not a moral injunction. His permission of it to strangers, proves that he did not think it *malum in se*.

Grotius seems to condemn it in a moral point of view, although he grants (De Jur. Bell. and pac. l. 11. c. 22) that a compensation allowed by law not exceeding the proportion of the hazard run, nor the want felt, by the loan, is repugnant neither to the revealed nor natural law.

The common arguments against interest are considered by Rutherforth, in his Institutes ; book II. c. 27.

The distinction of the security being void by the English statute, and not by our act, See 1 Smith's laws, 157. referring to 2 Dall. 92.

NOTES ON

BLACKSTONE'S COMMENTARIES.

POINTING OUT VARIATIONS IN THE LAW OF PENNSYLVANIA,
FROM THE COMMON AND STATUTE LAW OF ENGLAND,
WITH OTHER MATTERS OF A GENERAL NATURE.

III Black. Com. 5.

On the law of nuisances as respects cities, towns, or villages.
Premising that I have no particular case in view, I will
venture to lay down some principles of law on this head, and
to refer to some authorities in support of them. For, when
a people come to be informed of their rights and duties, by
knowing what the law is in the relations of society, and the
use of property, it will go a great way with reasonable men,
to induce them to *reform abuses and to correct what is wrong.*
For the purpose therefore of giving a clearer view of the subject, I shall state what I have to say under the following
heads.

1. *A matter may be a nuisance in a city, town, or village,*
that would not be a nuisance elsewhere.

When a town is laid out, it is in small portions of ground,
with a view to a contiguity of building. Whatever goes to
prevent this, or to hinder, goes to delay or defeat *the becom-*
ing a town. Hence, it follows that no man has a right to
use the parcel of ground that he purchases, so as to deprive
his neighbour of the enjoyment of that which he has also
purchased; and, on which he may meditate to improve; or
mean to reside. It is inconsistent with the original purpose

of the grant. Whatever therefore shall discourage the improvement of the town by building; or render residence in it *uncomfortable*, must be a *nuisance*. A legal definition of a nuisance therefore is, " *that which renders the enjoyment of life and property, uncomfortable.*" 3 Bur. 337.

It follows that what gives a *reasonable cause of apprehension from fire*, must be a nuisance. Who would think himself safe with a magazine of gunpowder on an adjoining lot; or even a small quantity uncovered and exposed to accidental sparks from the chimney tops of houses, or to other causes of inflammation. Are combustibles of *hay*, *straw*, or materials *easily inflammable*, not also dangerous? It never was in the contemplation of purchasers in a town that the harvests of the grounds adjoining should be brought in, and stowed away upon the in-lots; *and exposed without cover as in a country situation.* It is on this principle that

2. *What would not be a nuisance at one degree of improvement in a town, will be a nuisance at another.*

Rome not being built in a day, as the proverb is, so the lots of a town will not come all at once to be built upon. And while the buildings are sparse, and distant from each other, they partake, in proportion, *of the country.* But as the building progresses, the reason ceases, and the indulgence with it. A man on his own farm may erect his own hogsty. But in a town he cannot keep hogs, or erect even a dove cote, or pigeon house, so near my dwelling as to *offend by the smell. Either of these is a nuisance.* Rol. 141. 9 Coke, 57. 16 Vin. 25. It is on this principle of contiguity of building that

3. *What may be a nuisance in one part of the town, will not in another.*

"A soap boiler in Wood street, a Callender man in Bread street; a brew house on Ludgate hill, is a nuisance; for such trades ought not to be in *the principal parts of the city*, but in the *outskirts.*" 2 Show. 327.

A lime kiln so near my house that the smoke offends, is a nuisance. 9 Coke, 59.

A butcher must confine his shambles to a convenient place,
Com. Dig.

"It would be endless to enumerate all the instances of
nuisance. The principles on which the law proceeds, is to
use your property so as not to injure that of another." 3
Selwyn, 974.

But I go on to state another principle of which all are not
aware, viz.

4. *That what may be indulged in the hand, or under the
management of one person, will be a nuisance in the hand of
another.* It is on this principle that a crazy man will not be
suffered to run abroad, or retain possession of weapons, even
though he has stabbed no one; because, the presumption
from his insanity is that he will stab, and a reasonable fear
or ground of apprehension, will justify the arresting and
confining him as a *public nuisance.* So of a careless man, or
a man with *careless servants* in the use of such things from
which danger may arise.

This leads me to speak of remedies in the case of nuisance. And,

1. *A man may be called upon to find pledges of the peace,
or give security for his good behaviour, whose management
even in the use of his own property, becomes dangerous to his
neighbours.* Preventive justice is the best principle of the
law. Præstat cautela quam medela.

2. *The person who is injured by having his situation rendered uncomfortable by reason of a nuisance, may enter upon
the soil of another, and abate the nuisance; that is, may remove it.*

"A person injured by a nuisance, may enter and abate
the nuisance, though on the part not his own ground. 2 Inst.
405.

"A nuisance may be abated, or removed, by those persons who are prejudiced by it. But every man may abate a
common nuisance." 16 Vin. 40.

"Any one may break it down." 16 Vin. 46. But,

3. "Justices of the peace have a power of nuisance, by
virtue of the statute, 1 Ed. 3. c. 16. by which they are creat-

ed to enquire of all public nuisances." Per. Holt, Chief Justice, Mod. 255.

The great remedy is therefore by abatement.

A redress is by action in the case of a *private* nuisance. But I speak of those which concern the whole, which is a public nuisance, and for which an action does not ly ; because the whole are concerned. " Of a common nuisance, none shall have action but shall *present* it." 16 Vin. 46.

For individual hurt done by a public nuisance, an individual may have action, as from an obstruction in a high-way, or street, against him who has placed the obstruction in the way, or negligently left it there, whereby a particular injury is sustained.

By the common law, " if a servant keep his master's fire negligently, so that his neighbour's house is burned down, an action lies, 1 Black. 431. And if an action lies on the consummation of the injury, why may not I have security of the peace on giving proof of the negligence which may lead to it ?

I am led to this remark, from careless persons going into *stables with candles in their hands*, at late or early hours ; or with *segars* smoking. This is a just cause of apprehension of danger.

But remedies by action or indictment, out of the question, one great object of the incorporation of a city, town, or village, is a more *summary inquiry* into nuisances and removal of them. It can by this means, be ascertained with more discretion what might be tolerated for a *time* or in *any place.* Relative situations can be taken into view. A *stack yard ;* buildings not closely joining ; rubbish from a building carrying up, not wholly obstructing the street ; where and how a butcher's shambles may not render uncomfortable, &c. &c. &c.

" The next and principal object of our enquiries is the redress of injuries by *suit in courts*," &c. III Bl. Com. 22.

By the constitution of Pennsylvania, art. v. " the judicial power shall be vested in a supreme court, in courts of oyer and terminer, and general gaol delivery, in a court of common pleas, orphans court, registers court, and a court of quarter sessions of the peace, for each county, in justices of the peace, and in such other courts as the legislature may from time to time, establish."

A justice of the peace, as the term imports, is a *conservator of the peace.* He has jurisdiction over all offences against the public peace in the first instance, and, on complaint made on oath, or on his own view, he may issue his warrant to a constable who is his proper officer, and commit to gaol, or bind over to the court of quarter sessions of the county; to which it will behove him to certify the recognizance taken of the offender if bailed, and of the prosecutor, if there is one, and the witnesses that may substantiate the charge in order that the court may proceed therein; which they will do, if they consider it an indictable offence, by directing the prothonotary to hand over to the attorney for the commonwealth that he may frame bills to go to the grand jury. The prosecutor, or witnesses bound over to attend are then sworn in court, and sent up with the bill.

The powers and duties of a justice of the peace are to be collected from precedents at common law, treatises, and statutes on the subject.

But to the jurisdiction of a justice of the peace there has been superadded, from the earliest settlement of this state, certain powers and duties in civil cases or controversies, between individuals of the community. This jurisdiction having been found convenient has been extended from time to time, both as to the *quantum* of the demand, and as to the *nature* of the demand of redress. In the first instance it was confined to a debt or demand under 40s; extended subsequently to a debt not exceeding £5, with an appeal to the court of common pleas of the county; but not to extend, " to actions of debt for rent, debt upon bonds for performance of cove-

X

nants, actions of covenant, replevin, or upon any real contract, to action of trespass on the case, for trover and conversion, or slander, or to actions of trespass for assault and battery, or imprisonment, or to such actions where the title to land, shall, in any way, come in question." This jurisdiction afterwards was extended to debts and demands not exceeding £10 with the like appeal.

Thus stood the law until the adoption of the present constitution, when, by an act passed 19 April, 1794, the jurisdiction was extended to debts and other demands not exceeding £20 under every regulation, restriction and exception of the act of the 1st March 1745—4th April 1798, a farther advance was made in the *nature* of the demands cognizable before the justice, extending to all cases of *rents* not exceeding £20; and by act of assembly 1st March 1799, farther extended to actions for recovery of damages for any trepass wrong or injury against the real or personal estate of the defendant in cases not exceeding 20 dollars; and to cases of rent not exceeding 53⅓ dollars, with the right of removal and repeal although the cause in dispute may not amount to £10. But on the defendant making oath that the *title to lands* will come in question, the suit shall be dismissed. This jurisdiction not to extend to actions of ejectment brought to obtain possession of lands and tenements, actions of replevin in cases of *actual distress*, actions of slander, actions on *real contracts* for the sale and conveyance of lands, and tenements, civil actions for damages in personal assault and battery, wounding, or maiming, or to actions for false imprisonment. 17th March, 1806, justices authorised on complaint for assault and battery, or assault only, to dismiss on the *agreement of the parties*, provided the said justices, or justice, shall be fully satisfied that the settlement of such complaint will not injure the safety of the citizen, or the peace of society. 10th April, 1809, extended to actions of trover and conversion to the amount of 30 dollars, provided it shall not prevent a party from his remedy by action of replevin, or detinue as regulated by law. 20th March, 1810, this jurisdiction is enlarged to all causes of action arising from *contract* either *expressed* or *implied*, in all cases where the sum demanded is not above 100 dolls : except in cases of real contracts, where *the title to lands or tenements* may come in question, or actions upon promise of marriage; this with regulations as to *referees*, and restrictions as to appeal, or removal, and stay of execution.

Thus much may suffice as to some outline of the civil jurisdiction annexed to the powers and duties of the justice of the peace, whose judicial authority is without the assistance of a jury, but with that of *referees* under certain regulations.

It was not without opposition in the legislature that the jurisdiction of the justices was thus increased. A branch of it, the governor refused his signature; so the act of 2d Jan. 1804, *reviving and making perpetual* the act of 1st March 1799, was passed by two thirds of each of the other branches, and became a law. Nor out of doors was there a perfect acquiescence, as a case appears to have been brought before the supreme court, in which was questioned the constitutionality of such increase. 1 Bin. 416.

The next grade of courts, in the ascending scale, is that of the court of quarter sessions in each county, which, as at present constituted, consists of a president, and two associates; these last though not necessarily *legal characters*, yet are of great use, consilium et auxilium, contributing the advice of good sense and moral reason and giving weight to authority; but more especially they are serviceable in taking recognizances, and judging of the quantum of bail; in the assessment of fines; appointment of county auditors; and of viewers and reviewers in the laying out and locating of roads; and granting tavern licences, &c. &c. &c.

The president though not a sine qua non in holding this court, is the president of a district, consisting not of fewer than *three*, and not of more than *six* counties. This president and the associates, any two of whom shall be a quorum, shall constitute the respective courts of common pleas in each county; which last court has jurisdiction of *civil* matters only; but, it is provided by the constitution that the judges of the common pleas, any two of whom shall be a quorum, shall constitute *the court of quarter sessions of the peace*, the orphans court. The register of wills, together with the said judges, shall compose the *register's court* of each county.

The judges of the court of common pleas in each county, shall, by virtue of their offices, be justices of oyer and terminer, and general gaol delivery for the trial of *capital* and other offenders therein: any two of the said judges, the president being one, shall be a quorum; but they shall not hold a court of oyer and terminer and general gaol delivery in any county when the judges of the supreme court, or any of them, shall be sitting in the same county. This I presume must mean when *sitting as a court of oyer and terminer and gaol delivery in the same county.*

The court in the *dernier resort* is the *supreme court*, as the term imports. From this court writs of error and certiorari are directed to the several courts of inferior jurisdiction, and appeals sustained where the law gives an appeal, for the review of matters of law there arising.

In the city of Philadelphia there is a mayor's court subordinate to that of the court of quarter sessions. There is also a *district court* of common pleas of a *co-ordinate* but not *superior* jurisdiction to that of the common pleas which remains attached to the court of quarter sessions, or connected with it, in so far as the component members are judges of both courts. This district court may be considered *superior*, as to the *sum* in demand; for it takes cognizance of higher demands; the jurisdiction of the common pleas attached to the sessions being limited to the amount of the justice's jurisdiction; so that appeals from them, or certioraries directed to them, make the subject of the jurisdiction; whereas that of the district court begins here and is without limit. This last court is but of a *temporary* duration of six years, by the act constituting it; but such is its evident *utility,* or, rather *necessity,* that, doubtless, it *will be made permanent.*

The supreme court still continues to have *original* jurisdiction in the city of Philadelphia, in matters exceeding 500 dollars ; and for this purpose, courts of *nisi prius* are holden ; but it is expected, that at no distant day, these will be taken away ; and, this court, as it ought, will then exist a court of errors and appeals *merely*. This is all that is wanted to render the system perfect ; so far as respects arrangement, and the distribution of powers and duties. The supreme court has an immense jurisdiction independent of the trial of issues in fact. It has " to examine and correct all and all manner of errors of the justices and magistrates of this province (now state) in their judgments, process and proceedings in the said courts, as well in all pleas of the crown, as in all pleas real, personal, and mixed ; thereupon to reverse or affirm the said judgments as the law doth or shall direct : and also to examine, correct and punish contempts, omissions and neglects, favours, corruptions and defaults, of all or any of the justices of the peace, sheriffs, coroners, clerks and other officers ; and also shall award process for levying fines, forfeitures and amerciaments, that shall be estreated into the said court ; and generally shall administer justice to all persons, and exercise the jurisdiction and powers hereby granted concerning all and singular the premises according to law, as fully and amply, to all intents and purpose whatsoever, *as the justices of the court of king's bench, common pleas* and *exchequer*, at Westminster, or any of them may or can do.

This system I consider good in the outline, but it wants some filling up, to do the system justice. For as to the quantum of duty ; or I might rather say, *drudgery* that devolves upon such of the district presidents, as have more than three counties to attend, it is oppressive ; and, the salary, in proportion to such labour, totally inadequate. It is the more so, as most of the districts comprehend a mountainous country, in the interior of the state. This ought to receive a remedy. For the system has not a fair chance of experiment under such disadvantage.

As to the supreme court, two judges added, in due time, will be advisable, as the finances of the state increase, and the public mind becomes more enlarged as to the importance of having the law settled, with the advantage of more judgment; or at least more to judge.

I object to *four* judges; even *three* are better than an equal number;

————————Impari numero gaudet deus.

In the city of Philadelphia, it has been suggested that a maritime and commercial court, so called, might be constituted, taking cognizance of all transactions of that nature, which in this growing and trading metropolis, might be necessary with writs of error to the supreme court.

Courts of arbitration, as they may be called, are *ancillary* to all the courts; and with some lopping and improvement, this part of the system might receive approbation.

We have no chancery court in Pennsylvania: nor do we feel any great want of it; for *equity is a part of our law;* and all our courts exercise *equitable jurisdiction*, with the exception of an appeal to the *conscience* of the party, and the decree of a specific performance, which under the constitution, might be given, in the proper cases to the courts of law.

The act establishing a court of chancery in Pennsylvania, was passed the 28th of May, 1715, and repealed by the lords justices in council the 21st July, 1719. It is understood to have been adjudged that the proceedings which took place under the said act before its repeal, were binding.

By an act 22d May, 1722, Sec. 25, *special* courts are grantable to *defendants* in the *common pleas*, by reason of *sudden departure* out of the then province, now state.

By an act of 10th April, 1782, the privilege of having a special court was extended to *plaintiffs* as well as defendants; and to cases in the *supreme* court as well as common pleas; but was again taken from the plaintiffs by an act of the 27th March, 1789.

By an act of 13th April, 1791, a court of *errors and appeals* had been constituted, consisting chiefly of the *presidents* of districts. To these *severally* writs of error were directed, in the first instance, from the *supreme court;* and in the *last resort* from these *conjunctively* to the supreme court. So that each could have his revenge for a reversal of his *several* judgments, by a voice in the consistory of the *whole* in the reversal of the supreme judgment. In this constitution of the judiciary, there was something like a resemblance of Cottom Mathew's snake in his report to the philosophical society, that ran with its *head* foremost one while, and with its *tail* foremost afterwards.

By an act 24th Feb. 1806, this court was *suspended* as "to sustaining any new cause," and after holding two terms for unfinished business to be then *abolished* and the powers and duties to be vested in the supreme court.

By an act of the 20th March, 1801, what were called *circuit* courts, were substituted in lieu of courts of *nisi prius*, so far as respected the counties exclusive of the city and county of Philadelphia. This court was found unwieldy and inconvenient, and has been since abolished; and without a revival of the nisi prius courts; for which, under the constitution of the courts by presidents of districts there would seem now to be no necessity.

" The high court of chancery is the only remaining, and, in " matters of civil property, by much the most important of any, " of the king's superior and original courts of justice." III Bl. Com. 47.

IT will naturally occur to the student, to enquire, what have we to do with *chancery law* in Pennsylvania, since we have no court of chancery? We have to do with it; and the student after a course of reading *general law*, will come to read *treatises*, tracts, or reports of *equity* law. As for instance, *Fonblanque*, or the treatise on equity, referring to Atkyn's, Peere William's reports, &c. For *equity* is nothing more than *exceptions* from *general rules*. Thus we say, such is the general rule; but this case does not come within it. There are circumstances which *distinguish*, so that the general rule cannot apply. The court of chancery in England, takes a peculiar cognizance, or exercises a peculiar *ju-risdiction* over these *exceptions*, and therefore the law with respect to these, is to be collected from the *chancery reports.* And it becomes as necessary to read these in this *state* where we have no chancery court, as in England, or in other states of the Union, where they have.

It is asked by lawyers from other states, or reflecting in-dividuals, how are we able to accomplish the ends of justice in our administration of the law, having no court of chancery in Pennsylvania? Why not? Cannot the same courts which take notice of the general rule of the law, take notice also of the exception which forms an *equity*, or takes a case out of the general rule? We have an advantage over administra-tion of the law by courts of chancery in England, or in other states, in this particular, that we have the assistance of *a jury* to whom the *facts* may be referred upon which constitutes the exception, and upon which the *equity* arises. This is a great aid to the courts, and more satisfactory to the people. It cannot but be some abridgment of the *trial by jury*, that the *conclusion of fact* from the evidence should be drawn in any case, by *the court*, and not by *the jury*.

By the constitution of Pennsylvania, art. 5, sec. 6, " the supreme court and the several courts of common pleas, *be-side the powers heretofore usually exercised by them*, have the power of a court of *chancery* so far as relates to the perpetu-ating testimony, the obtaining of evidence from places not within the state, and the care of the persons, and estates of those who are not compotes mentis: and the legislature shall vest in the said courts, such *other powers* to grant re-lief in *equity* as shall be found necessary; and may from time to time, enlarge, or diminish those powers, or vest them in such other courts as they shall judge proper, for the due administration of justice." Our courts of law before this constitution, had exercised the powers of a court of chance-ry, as to the equity province of it, and we look into the grounds of decisions there, as much as the lawyers in England themselves do; and as to the farther powers giv-en by this constitution, for perpetuating testimony, &c. we look into the *precedents*, and *practice* of chancery as guides, where we choose to make use of the wisdom of those who have gone before us. There is no book therefore of chancery law, which may not be useful to the student; and *necessary* indeed, in most cases to be consulted, and read.

III Bl. Com. 98.

THERE being no *ecclesiastical* court, or *equity* court in Pennsylvania, which have a concurrent jurisdiction in the case of *legacies; acts of assembly* became necessary on this subject. That of the 21st March, 1772, entitled an " act for the more easy recovery of *legacies*, is that under which we proceed against executors, or administrators. And this may be by action on the case, debt, detinue, or account rendered, as the case may be, for such legacy after it becomes due ; and in that case shall recover with costs. It may be debt where it is a sum certain, and *assets* after debts paid, exist, sufficient to discharge ; or it may be case for the *part* of the sum after debts paid ; or case, and not debt, for the whole, as for money had and received to the use, giving special notice of the cause of action. But in the case of a specific chattel, it must be *detinue ;* or on the case for the detention of, and praying damages, not for the detention but for the value.

The term *devise* is appropriate to real estate ; legacy to personal. This distinction also, in the use of the terms, *devisee*, and *legatee ; devise*, and *bequest*, &c. of which let the student take notice who would wish to be correct, as all ought to be, in the use of terms. As for instance, *evidence* is a general term which applies to *written*, and viva voce of witnesses ; but *testimony* is applicable to that by *witnesses ;* and it is not correct to say *an evidence*, but a *witness*. I always think it an *evidence* of want of *precision*, and a distinguishing mind, where a lawyer at the bar, does not attend to this ; for it may be said, in this, as in other matters of lesser moment,

Y

———————————— Inest sua gratia parvis.

It will be seen, that by our act, Sec. 7. where no time is limited, for the payment of a legacy, the executor, or administrator shall have the space " of one year to discharge the same."

An executor is considered as a trustee in England for creditors, legatees, &c. and under this idea it is that the court of equity takes jurisdiction. How far he is a trustee for the next of kin as to the *residuum*, after all debts and legacies have been discharged, see the chancery decisions on this head. The claim of the executor in this case has been much reduced, and would seem to be in a fair way to come to nothing. But it is astonishing that in Pennsylvania, where by act of assembly a compensation had been allowed for his trouble, at the discretion of the orphans court, yet it was not until May, 1811, in the case of Wilson v. Wilson, 3 Binney, 557, that it was finally settled that he was not entitled to claim for himself, but as to the *surplus* was to be considered a trustee for the next of kin.

———

" Some agreements indeed, though never so expressly made, " are deemed of so important a nature, that they ought not to rest " in verbal promise only, which cannot be proved but by the me- " mory (which sometimes will induce the perjury) of witnesses." III Bl. Com. 159.

BY the act of 29 Car. 2. (1676,) entitled an act for prevention of frauds and perjuries, " all leases, interests of freehold, or terms of years, or any uncertain interest of, in, to or out of any messuages, manors, lands, tenements or hereditaments, made or created by livery and seizen only, or by parol, and *not put in writing*, and signed by the parties so making or creating the same, or their agents thereunto lawfully authorised by writing, shall have the force and effect of leases or estates at will only, and shall not either in law or equity be deemed or taken to have any other or greater force or effect," &c.

Sec. 2. "Except nevertheless all leases not exceeding the term of three years from the making thereof, whereupon the rent reserved to the landlord, during such term, shall amount unto two third parts at the least of the full improved value of the thing demised."

The act goes on, sec. 4. that no action shall be brought whereby to charge any executor or administrator, &c.

Our act with the same title and precisely in the same words of the first and second sections which relates to real estate proceeds no farther. It would seem to be copied so far as it goes from the British statute, made near a hundred years before. Real estate would seem to have been left in the meantime, in matters of transfer, to the testimony of witnesses ; and having had no court of chancery, except for a short space during this period, persons contracting as purchasers of real estate, must have been left to recover in an ejectment for the possession, or by action on the case to recover damages for the non performance of the agreement. Even without writing, an action of damages would lie in England now, or in Pennsylvania before our act passed ; and in England a court of chancery would decree a specific execution of the contract where there was evidence of part execution, such as posession given, or money paid. It is a query whether the receipt for the money must not be in writing. But at all events the terms of the contract must be precisely proved. It is the same law with us on an ejectment brought, which, in default of a chancery court, is our only remedy for obtaining the possession. We had a law before this relative to a seven years' possession entered upon under an equitable title, which is still in force, and is a statute of limitation to the claim of him in whom the legal title remains after an agreement made to convey, and delivery of possession.

" *Entered on upon an equitable right*," are the words of the *Pennsylvania* act of assembly of 1705, entitled " the law about seven years' quiet possession." It will be a question with the student, what is to be understood by *an equitable right*. It is a right short of what is called a *legal* right, or a right under *the general rule* which gives a right to lands. This must be *by a writing under seal*. A writing not under seal; or an agreement without writing will constitute an equitable right; but not an *agreement merely, proved by witnesses*, will suffice. Some performance of the agreement must be proved. Will proof of the payment of the consideration, or a *principal part* of it, be sufficient? This is a question in England, to which *a query* is added. But the inclination of the law seems to be, that it will; because, in such case, the parol evidence is applied to the act of *receiving*, which is a consequence of and collateral to the act of contracting, and consequently affords a further evidence of the bargain, than the parol proof of such bargain only; namely, an act done in pursuance of it, which furnishes a distinct fact, that appears to be the proper subject of discussion before a jury, who, in such case, would be competent judges of the credit of the parties, and might, by their verdict, decide, whether the payment of money was in part performance or not. 1 Pow. Con. 306. 7—8, and 4 Dall. 152.

The giving possession in pursuance of an agreement, is clear evidence of a part performance, and may be proved by witnesses. The being suffered to remain in possession, and the making improvements with the knowledge of the person agreeing to convey, is still stronger evidence of the contract, and will give an equitable right. I do not well know therefore what is the use of this act of assembly. It would seem that at the time there had been a doubt whether evidence of the giving possession, not having a court of chancery in this state, could be admitted; or if evidence of the giving possession could not be had, the suffering to remain in possession for a length of time should be proof of an agreement to convey. This length of time was made seven years as a statute of limitation within which time an ejectment must be brought.

In a court of chancery the party agreeing to convey may be called upon to say on óath whether he did not so agree. In that case if he acknowledges the agreement, there is an end of the matter.

Where possession is not given the party claiming such a contract to convey in this state where we have no court of chancery to decree the performance, and the giving a conveyance, can have only *the remedy of an action to recover damages;* but in such case, the jury will, and ought to give such damages as will compel the party to convey, by making it his interest rather than to retain the land. Note; that it is to be understood that in all these cases of an agreement to convey land, the terms of the contract must be proved; the consideration; the quantity, &c. In all these cases there must be a reasonable certainty; perhaps a precise certainty established; for, the party claiming the benefit of such contract, without writing, ought to be held to *strict proof of these particulars.*

By the common law a parol contract was as good for lands as for chattels. It is the statute of 29th Charles II. which was made to prevent persons from swearing verbal agreements upon others, that has introduced a distinction, and the exceptions to this statute are, what is said to constitute an *equity;* that is to admit evidence by parol.

III Bl. Com. 199.

WHAT was it that introduced the necessity of the fiction in ejectment? It is here distinctly stated to be, the defect of a remedy on behalf of *a tenant for years,* enabling him to recover the possession against the lessor, or a stranger, who had put him out; in which case he was obliged to desert the courts of law, and go into chancery to obtain redress; for at law he could only recover damages, but not the *possession.*

The courts of law, in order to give redress without rendering it necessary to go into a court of chancery, *contrived* the feigning the lessee for years to be a lessor himself, and to pursue for a wrong to his tenant. And in order to avoid the statute of maintenance, it is a part of the fiction that he had *entered* and *was in possession*. It was a principle of law also that the grantee of the reversion " might at any time by a common recovery, have destroyed the term of the lessee for years."

But what was there to hinder the parliament to have made provision as to all these particulars? There was nothing that I know of but, that the feudal lords might object to this. It was probably an apprehension that such a bill could not be carried in the house of lords, that it was not brought forward in the legislature. It was doubtless of necessity that the courts devised this fiction; for a fiction was never introduced, but where the application of the general principle, will work an inconvenience. Hence the maxim, in fictione juris semper subsistit equitas. This last reason had ceased under our colonization. What could hinder then our own legislature to provide for all that was gained by this fiction of proceeding? This fiction carried with it the advantage, that there might be a trial toties quoties by *feigning a new lessor* and *a new lessee;* so that a recovery in one case could not be pleaded in bar to another. For it was a principle " that when a man's possession is once established in a possessory action, it can never be disturbed by the same antagonist." But it was *found* to work an inconvenience to suffer the possession to be disturbed *toties quoties;* and therefore application became necessary to a court of chancery, to set some limit to the fiction; and after two verdicts in favour of the same title, an injunction was decreed.

But the management of this fiction, even as moulded and fashioned by the courts for the purposes of justice, and however well understood by the profession, carried with it some inconvenience in the practice. Where the term laid in the declaration had *expired*, from the continuance of the cause in court, the courts would give leave to enlarge the term. But where the *time of the demise*, or leasing alleged, had been laid too far back, so that evidence of title anterior to the demise laid, could not come in, they would not give leave to *contract* it to a later date. The courts had begun to give this leave in England, to avoid a fine, &c. But it had been refused here, and a nonsuit the consequence; even to avoid the statute of limitations, it had been refused. A confession of lease entry and ouster, where it had been omitted to be called for, and not entered, the courts thought themselves not justifiable in directing the filling up this part of the fiction, and a nonsuit must take place.

But the fiction of lease entry and ouster was unintelligible to the country; and the form of the declaration, alleging the entry to be with " swords, staves, and knives," where none were used, appeared an absurdity. It is of moment in a republican government, where the people will not be satisfied with what they do not comprehend, that not only the substance of the law shall be understood; but also that the forms of legal proceedings, should be brought as much as possible on a level with common apprehension. But it is a difficult matter for men who are not acquainted with the principles of a science, and cannot discern *the cause of what is wrong* to apply themselves to substitute, or amend. Any one will grant, that a mechanic, or an architect only, is competent to diminish, or enlarge, or vary the structure of a machine, or the plan of a building. If an application had been made to the attorney general, as has been done in a late case on the penal law; or to some other person of legal abilities, to frame a bill to supply the place of this *fictitious* proceeding in ejectment, embracing all the advantages of it, and avoiding the inconveniences, it would have been advisable. But let us see what has been done by the legislature themselves.

By an act of the 24th March, 1806, the form of a writ of ejectment is devised, and proceedings enjoined. It was evident to men of legal science, on the publication of the act, or promulgation, that the law was entirely defective, and *most unskilfully* drawn; yet it was not considered an injury to our jurisprudence, that some step had been taken towards the getting quit of the necessity of the use of a fiction; and it was not doubted, but that some improvement might grow out of what had been done.   Accordingly by a supplement a year afterward, some of the most *material defects* in the law were supplied.   What yet remains to have it accommodated to all purposes of justice, with regard to a claim of possession ; or of property; or of an *interest* in *real estate*, will in due time be discovered, and the remedy may be applied.

———————

" For every man's land is in the eye of the law inclosed and set " apart from his neighbour's, &c." III Bl. Com. 209.

THIS principle of the common law would seem to be restrained by the act of 1700 of this commonwealth, and other acts pari materia.   The principal act is chap. 56, entitled an act for regulating and maintaining of fences ; 1st. Smith's laws 18.   It was decided in Addison's district; and may have been elsewhere, that this act, or these acts giving a special and summary remedy, did not take away the common law ; but, though decided in my favour, in a case at that bar, I did not approve of the doctrine laid down by the court, in all particulars.   It did appear to me, that it was a change of the common law to some extent, in consideration of the settlement and state of the country ; where it was contrary to the convenience of the inhabitant, to have it supposed that the owner of cattle could keep them from trespassing upon the uninclosed ground or wood-land of another.   It could not be but by running at large that the stock of the settler could be supported before there were inclosed pastures ; and the obligation of having keepers to hinder them from trespassing would be inconsistent with the situation of the improver in a new country.   These acts therefore qualifying the right which the owner of the soil had in his uninclosed grounds, appeared to me necessary ; and that an action of trespass would not lie unless the owner of adjoining grounds had done something towards excluding an entry on his possessions, such as is prescribed by the act in question.

Be this as it may, the proceeding at common law notwithstanding this act, would seem to be restrained by the act 21 March, 1806. 4th Sm. Laws, 332, Sec. 13, "that in all cases where a remedy is provided or duty enjoined, or any thing directed to be done by any act or acts of assembly of this commonwealth, the directions of the said acts shall be strictly pursued, and no penalty shall be inflicted agreeably to the provisions of the common law in such cases further than shall be necessary for carrying such act or acts into effect."

In the case referred to, the president laid it down, that, " In England, the law is a fence round every man's ground ; and trespass may be maintained for passing over the uninclosed ground of another against his will. Every man must take care to keep his cattle from going on the land of another. In this country our circumstances have led us to *suppose* that every man must take care of his land that the cattle of others go not on it.

" The act regulating fences gives a new and summary remedy for trespasses on lands, enclosed with fences of the description therein mentioned; but takes not away any remedy which existed before, and at the time of the passing that act. The person injured whose fences are of that description, may proceed under that act, *or at common law.* And if the fences are not of that description, the person injured, though he can have no remedy under that act, may have remedy at common law."

The decision of the president was correct in the main point of this case; for the *defendant had thrown down the fence,* and *turned his cattle in.* This took the case out of the act. In other words the act did not apply to it; *it was a trespass at common law.* Add. Rep. 259.

Z

III Bl. Com. 264.

THE writ of *mandamus* in Pennsylvania, stands as it did at common law. The British statute 9 Anne, c. 20, being *since the charter to William Penn*, and not being introduced here, could not be reported by the judges as in force in this commonwealth. But the provisions of this statute are salutary, and deserve to be introduced by an act of the legislature ; and perhaps could not be done in better terms *substantially* than in the words of the British statute. For it is true, as is said, in the marginal note to this statute, Ruffhead's edition, that it is *clearly and correctly drawn*. It was drawn by Mr. *Justice Powell*, 1 Black. 95.

So far as respects the *mandamus*, it is entitled an act for rendering the proceedings more *speedy and effectual*.

The *first* provision is as follows ; " that where any writ of *mandamus* shall issue, such person, or persons who, by the laws, are required to make a return to such writ, shall make his, or their return to *the first writ of mandamus*.

Sec. II. And that as often as any writ of mandamus shall issue, and a return be made thereunto, it shall and may be lawful to and for the person, or persons suing or prosecuting such writ of mandamus, to plead to, or traverse all or any the *material facts* contained within the said return ; to which the person or persons making such return, shall reply, take issue, or demur : and such further proceedings, and in such manner shall be had therein for the determination thereof as might have been had if the person, or persons suing such writ had brought his, or their action on the case for a false return, and if any issue shall be joined on such proceedings, the person, or persons suing such writ, shall and may try the cause in such place as an issue joined, in such action on the case, should or might have been tried ; and, in case a verdict shall be found for the person, or persons, suing such writ, or, judgment given for him, or them upon a demurrer, or by nil dicit, or for want of a replication, or other pleading, he or they, shall recover his or their damages, and costs, in such manner,

as he or they might have done, in such action on the case as
aforesaid; such damages and costs to be levied as in other
cases; and a peremptory writ of mandamus shall be granted
without delay, for him or them, for whom judgment shall be
given as might have been if such return had been judged insufficient; and in case judgment shall be given for the person, or persons making such return to such writ, he, or they,
shall recover his, or their costs of suit to be levied in manner aforesaid.

Sec. III. Provided always that if any damages shall be
recovered by virtue of this act against any such person, or
persons, making such return to such writ, as aforesaid, he, or
they shall not be liable to be sued, in any other action or suit,
for the making such return, any law, usage or custom to the
contrary, thereof in any wise notwithstanding.

Sec. IV. That it shall and may be lawful for the courts
respectively, to allow to such person, or persons respectively
to whom any writ of mandamus shall be directed, or to the
person, or persons who shall sue or prosecute the same, such
convenient time respectively to make a return, plead, reply,
rejoin or demur as to the said courts respectively shall seem
just and reasonable.

Sec. V. That this act shall be extended to cases of the
like nature with those contemplated by the statute of the 9
Anne, c. 20. which British statute would not seem to have
been introduced here, but which as referring the trial of facts
to a jury, is consonant with the spirit of our constitution, and
ought to be adopted.

The above is the substance, and in the words of a bill
which I would suggest to the legislature.

By the same statute 9 Anne, c. 20. It is provided in
the case of a proceeding by *information* in the nature of a
writ de quo warranto.

" That in case any person or persons shall usurp or in-
trude into, or unlawfully hold and execute any office or fran-
chise to which that statute has a reference, it shall and may
be lawful to and for the proper officer in each of the respective courts, with the leave of the said courts respectively, to

exhibit one or more information or informations in the nature
of a quo warranto, at the relation of any person or persons
desiring to sue, or prosecute the same, and who shall be
mentioned in such information, or informations, to the relator, or relators, against such person, or persons, so usurping, intruding into, or unlawfully holding, and executing any
of the said offices, or franchises, and to proceed therein in
such manner, as is usual in cases of information in the
nature of a quo warranto, and if it shall appear to the said
respective courts, that the several rights of divers persons,
to the said offices, or franchises, may properly be determined, on one information, it shall, and may be lawful for
the said respective courts, to give leave to exhibit one such
information against several persons, in order to try their respective rights to such offices, or franchises, and such person or
persons, against whom such information, or informations, in
the nature of a quo warranto, shall be sued, or prosecuted,
shall appear and plead as of the same term or sessions, in
which the said information, or informations, shall be filed,
unless the court, where such information shall be filed, shall
give further time to such person, or persons, against whom
such information shall be exhibited, to plead; and such person, or persons, who shall sue, or prosecute, such information, or informations, in the nature of a quo warranto, shall
proceed thereupon with the most convenient speed that may
be, any law or usage to the contrary, in any wise notwithstanding.

" And in case any person, or persons, against whom any
information, or informations in the nature of a quo warranto,
shall, in any of the said cases, be exhibited in any of the
said courts, shall be found, or adjudged guilty of an usurpation, or intrusion into, or unlawfully holding and executing any of the said offices, or franchises, it shall and may be
lawful to and for the said courts respectively, as well to
give judgment of ouster against such person, or persons, of
and from any of the said offices, or franchises, as to fine such
person, or persons respectively, for his or their usurping, intruding into, or unlawfully holding and exercising any of

the said offices or franchises. And also, it shall and may be lawful to and for the said courts respectively to give judgment, though the relator, or relators in such information named, shall recover his or their costs of such prosecution; and if judgment shall be given for the defendant, or defendants in such information, he or they for whom such judgment shall be given, shall recover his or their costs, therein expended against such relator or relators, such costs to be levied in manner aforesaid.

" And it shall and may be lawful to and for the said courts respectively to allow to such person, or persons respectively, against whom any information in the nature of a writ of quo warranto, in any case shall be sued or prosecuted, or to the person, or persons who shall sue, or prosecute the same, such convenient time respectively to make a return, plead, reply, rejoin, or demur, as to the said courts respectively shall seem just and reasonable."

It may be seen that by such a bill passed into a law, a trial by jury is given in the case of a contested fact; and here it has happened that this statute of Anne has either not been extended by usage, and adoption of the courts; or that this being the case, it has not been enacted with the same or similar provisions by the colonial legislature, or by the legislature of the state since the adoption of the constitution under the revolutionary establishment, would seem to me to have been owing to an oversight; or that a case did not occur which brought the advantage or necessity of such an enlargement of the remedy into view, and an application of the jury trial where matters of fact came to be the subject of enquiry.

But the *supreme court*, who alone can issue writs of *mandamus*, and receives *informations* in the nature of a *writ de quo warranto;* except in the city and county of Philadelphia, where courts of nisi prius are yet holden, have not the power to summon a jury, and try an issue of fact in the other counties, or any of them; and therefore it will be necessary to add a clause enabling the courts at their term to direct issues to be tried in their respective counties where the cause of complaint arises; and in case a county is interested, to any other county of the district in which that county lies, and which is nearest, or most convenient to that vicinage.

That the supreme court, under the present arrangements, has not the power to summon a jury, and to try an issue was determined in the western district of the supreme court 9th September, 1811. See 4th Binney, 117.

In consequence of this decision, a bill was brought forward in the legislature in the winter of 1812, in the case of the mandamus, and of the information in the nature of the writ de quo warranto; and the object was to supply the provisions of the statute of 9 Anne, c. 20. and adapt them to our situation. But the bill was exceptionable in this, that instead of merely supplying what was deficient in our law on this head, it undertook to comprise and specify all and singular the powers of the court in the case of the mandamus, and the writ de quo warranto, which it had already by the common law; which was unnecessary, and dangerous, because what was not specified, must by *implication be lost ;* and the specifying so far as it went brought into view, what could not be well comprehended by the legislature, as to all the *qualifications of the powers ;* for these must be collected from precedents and decisions. The bill therefore, as was to be expected, fell through and did not pass. There remains therefore a defect of justice on this head as to some objects, and the want of the benefit of a trial by jury in the case of contested facts, so far as respects the counties of the state out of the city and county of Philadelphia. It will be probably moved again in the next legislature, and these observations may assist in the deliberations on this subject.

III Bl. Com. 304.—Set off.

IN the digest to which the commentator refers in the margin, the term is *compensatio.* The etymology of which is *compenso,* a compound of con and penso, which signifies a *weighing together.* *Pendo* is the root which signifies to weigh. *Pensum* the supine of the verb as the grammarians say ; and *pensum* a thing weighed. Hence pensum a *task* or *thing weighed out for manufacture.* All this refers to the weighing out one commodity against another, in an original barter, or in part retribution of a commodity originally weighed out and received. Hence we see from the *derivation* of the term the history of the thing itself.

When *barter* ceased, and gold and silver became a medium of commerce, it passed by *weight,* and not by the *nominal* and *arbitrary* value of a piece of coin ; and which could only be by the consent of a nation amongst the *people* of that nation, or by the courtesy of other nations, to receive it at that value. Weighing therefore, in the nature of the case, must take place and exist *still,* where gold and silver, or other scarce metal passes by weight. If a man owes twenty pounds, and can weigh out only ten, he can *compensate,* or *set off* only ten.

It may be worth while to extract here for the sake of the classical student, the various dicta of the codes which are here *digested,* or collected in the *pandects.*

Definitio. *Compensatio* est debiti et crediti, inter se, contributio.

Effectus. Unusquisque creditorem suum, eundemque debitorem, petentem, summovet, si paratus est compensare.

Utilitas. Ideo compensatio necessaria est, quia interest, nostra potius non solvere, quam solutum repetere.

Quod natura debetur venit in compensationem.

This will suffice out of that chapter which contains a summary of the whole law upon this subject.

Stoppage or *set off,* is the term in the common law of England. For, at the common law, the demand of a debt might be *stopped* by something set off, and going to the whole of the demand, or to a *part.* The question was, what could be set off to stop the demand in law if a suit were brought. Any thing going *directly* in discharge of the demand, and made and accepted with a view to that discharge, there could be no doubt, might be set off. Or any thing done in pursuance of a fulfilment of a contract, or payment of a debt, on the principle of *natural justice*, could not but be set off. But what was not so immediately connected with the contract, as necessarily to be in discharge of it, might be considered as *collateral* to it, and the necessity of a set off did not immediately follow. The common law was narrow upon this point. See Montagu on the law of set off, and the authorities there cited, page 1. An extent was given to the law of set off in chancery, or the equity courts in England; but still not to the extent of giving a remedy, to the extent which *natural justice*, or *public convenience* would require. Hence the statutes of set off. 2 Geo. II. c. 22. Sec. 13: and 8 Geo. II. c. 24, Sec. 4 and 5.

That of 2 Geo. II. is in these words; that where there are mutual debts between the plaintiff and defendant, or if either party sue, or be sued, as executor or administrator, where there are mutual debts between the testator or intestate, and either party, *one debt may be set against the other.*

That of 8 Geo. II. c. 24. extends this provision which had been limited by the former statute to continue for the term of five years, and it is in these words; " And whereas the provision for setting mutual debts one against the other is highly just and reasonable at all times, the said clause in the said first recited act for setting mutual debts one against the other, shall be and remain in full force forever."

And by sec. 5. it is enacted, that " by virtue of the said clause in the said recited act contained, hereby made perpetual, mutual debts may be set against each other, either by being pleaded in bar or given in evidence under the general issue, in the manner therein mentioned, notwithstanding that such debts are deemed in law *to be of a different nature,* unless in cases where either of the said debts shall *accrue by reason of a penalty contained in any bond or specialty;* and in all cases where either the debt, for which the action has been or shall be brought; or the debt intended to be set against the same, hath accrued or shall accrue by reason of any such penalty, the debt intended to be set off, shall *be pleaded in bar,* in which shall be shewn *how much is truly and justly due on either side;* and in case the plaintiff shall recover in any such action or suit, the judgment shall be entered for no more than shall appear *to be truly and justly due to the plaintiff* after one debt being set against the other."

This act of 8 Geo. II. not only gave *perpetuity* to the former; but also a greater extent than, in the construction of some judges, had been put upon it. This construction had been that the provision of a *mutual set off* did not apply to debts of a *different nature*. By debts of a *different nature* is meant, of a different *class of actions* referring to the technical boundaries which had been fixed between actions of debt, actions of *trespass on the case*, &c. But even under these words, *debts of a different nature, the construction was restrained* to what, in its nature, was a *debt* or demand *certain* arising on *contract*. In the case of a *specialty* or writing *under seal*, a set off might be made, but it must *be pleaded*, it could not be given in evidence with notice. And in the case of a penalty pleaded as a set off, it could not be allowed; and the debt *really due* was narrowed to what could be shewn by payments; for under the plea *unliquidated damages* could not be set off; that is, the jury at the bar, would not be suffered to hear all circumstances, and liquidate the damages a defendant had sustained by reason of non-compliance with a contract with the plaintiff.

It is also observable, under these statutes, that no provision is made, that if the defendant under his plea, or *notice of set off*, could shew that he had overpaid, or that his set off was such as *brought the balance in his favour*, he could not have judgment for it, but must bring his action for the balance; in which case if even an overhauling of the whole controversy could be avoided, yet, a counter suit must follow, and *new costs* be incurred.

Before these statutes of 2 Geo. II. and 8 Geo. II. which passed in the year 1729, we had an act of assembly of Pennsylvania of 1705. And it has been with a view to refer the student to this act as going farther than the English statutes, that I have made this note. For, though, our act was before theirs, yet they did not chuse to follow it to the whole extent, if they had at all heard of it, which is possible; but not probable that they had not heard of it, as every act of the colonial legislature was liable to a repeal by the king and council, and could not but be reported'to them, and in that case could not well but come to the knowledge of at least one branch of the legislature, *the house of Lords.* But whether owing to the embarrassment of a court of chancery upon whose wonted jurisdiction they did not wish to trench; or to the advantage of having it, as not rendering it necessary, in their opinion, to go so far in some particulars, the whole extent was not given by the words of those acts, which by the provisions of our act of assembly, is established. In order the better to compare the two English statutes with our act of assembly, we shall extract it here.

It is entitled, " An act for defalcation." The etymon of this term is from Falx a latin word for a *pruning knife.* Hence falco to amputate, or *prune.* Defalco, the compound, to *prune from :* So that vi termini, it expresses the pruning a demand by shewing that it is less than it purports to be, by reason that it ought to be made less by something shewn against it. Let us now see the act.

" If two or more, dealing together be indebted to each other on bonds, bills, bargains, accounts or the like, and commence an action in any quarter of this province, if the defendant cannot gainsay the deed, bargain or assumption, upon which he issued, it shall be lawful for such defendant to plead payment of all or part of the debt, or sum demanded, and give any bond, bill, receipt, account, or bargain, in evidence, and if it shall appear that the defendant hath fully satisfied the debt or sum demanded, the jury shall find for the defendant, and judgment shall be entered, that the plaintiff shall take nothing by his writ, and to pay the costs. And if it should appear that any part of the sum demanded be paid, then so much as is found to be paid, shall be defalked, and the plaintiff shall have judgment for the residue only, with costs of suit. But if it appear to the jury, that the plaintiff is overpaid, then they shall give in their verdict for the defendant and withal certify to the court how much they find the plaintiff to be indebted, or in arrear to the defendant more than will answer the debt or sum demanded ; and the sum, or sums so certified, shall be recorded with the verdict, and shall be deemed as a debt of record, and if the plaintiff refuses to pay the same, the defendant for recovery thereof, shall have a *scire facias* against the plaintiff in the said action ; and have execution for the same with the costs of that action." There is nothing said about *executor* or *admi-nistrator* in our act as being unnecessary ; because a provision which is made for the original parties, must extend to the *representatives.*

" *Mutual debts*" are the words in the English acts. This answers to the word, debitum, or what is due, in the Roman law, and can have no reference to the *technical* distinction of a debt *by specialty ;* or of a certain sum by contract, or *in account settled.* It must have a more extensive meaning, and be clear of what is merely technical in the denomination of demands. But our act introduces a specification of *bonds*, bills, *bargains*, promises, accounts, or the like. The word *bargain* has a sweeping effect, and cannot but let in *unliquidated* damages. So that a defendant in answer to a *demand on one bargain* may be let in to give evidence of a claim on his part, *on another.* But still it must be a *bargain* in the course of *dealing together.* It is no objection and ought to be none, that the damages on such bargain, are not *liquidated*, because *on notice* given, they can be liquidated by the *same jury* that hears the plaintiff's demand. And in case of *a penalty* we make no distinction, because we can enquire in the case of a bond what was the *real debt ;* and we can set off what is really due. Even in England the *liberal* mind of Lord Mansfield, saw that this could be done. " He said he expected that it would have been put upon the foot of setting off the sum that the defendant imagined to be *really due for the damages he sustained.* But he now perceived that it was insisted the *whole penalty might be set off.* He said it is clearly most unjust and contrary to the intention of the acts of parliament, that the whole penalty should be admitted to be pleaded by way of set off when, perhaps, a very small sum was really due for such damages as the defendant had actually sustained." The judges were fettered by the principle that the penalty could not but be considered as the real debt, in a *court of law*.

For the *construction* of our act of assembly as to what demands may be set off, see Smith's laws, 51.

As to the pleading, or giving in evidence *with notice*, there is a provision subsequent to this act by that of the 14 Feb. 1729, 30; of which see in the same note to Smith's edition of the laws of Pennsylvania.

The *scire facias* given by our act of assembly, which is in the nature of a summons to shew cause why *execution* shall not go for the sum *certified* to be found for the *defendant*. This provision is a *novelty*, and not adopted by the English acts, though for what reason, I am not able to comprehend. For unquestionably it must be considered an improvement.

Where in case of a set off a balance is found for the defendant, but for this provision he must bring his *action* and *declare*. The scire facias, here, is a declaration at once, and will set forth the ground on which the demand is made without *circuity*. It is in the nature of a new action as every scire facias is, but *springing out of the former suit*, the connection and relation is immediately seen without pleading, or averment; and delay is avoided, and expence to the parties.

Though a set off is a matter of right to a defendant, yet he is not bound to make it. He may prefer as it may be advisable, to do in many cases, *the keeping demands separate, as things taken singly may be better understood*.

I have been the more particular in an analysis of this act of assembly, that the student may distinguish the reason of the construction of the law of set off by the English judges, and by the decisions of our courts, and also that *the respect due to the good sense of our early legislators may appear*.

" Also, all actions of trespass, (quare clausum fregit, or other-
" wise) detinue, trover, replevin, account, and case, (except upon
" accounts between merchants) debt on simple contract, or for ar-
" rears of rent, are limited by the statute last mentioned (21 Jac.
" 1 c. 16.) to *six* years after the cause of action commenced;
" &c." III Bl. Com. 307.

THIS statute is a provision of wisdom and humanity, but
it must be restrained to the reason of it. It is founded on
the policy of protecting honest but improvident individuals
who are not careful in taking vouchers of their payments,
and there is a presumption arising in human transactions that
a debt not demanded for a length of time, is paid, because
creditors do not usually, except in particular cases, a continuance, &c. suffer debts to lie over, without being demanded,
a great length of time. The length of time which the statute has fixed upon, as a general rule, when the presumption shall be considered as having arisen is six years; but whatever will meet that presumption, and remove it, shall take
the case out of the statute. It is not therefore a promise to
pay the debt, but an acknowledgment of it, that meets the
presumption, and takes a case out of the reason of the law.
As, in contracting the debt, there is seldom, or never, an *express* promise to pay, or totidem verbis, as I will pay, *the
law is said to raise it,* or to *imply* a promise, so it is said that
by *an acknowledgment of the debt,* the former promise is revived or *continued,* which is sometimes the phraseology
or, in other words that a new promise is implied, or raised,
nor need the acknowledgment be *express*, it may be inferred
from *circumstance,* or *expressions* that imply the not having paid the debt.

What will take a case out of the statute, must be what
will constitute an exception to it. In that case it is as if it had
not been; with regard to any effect upon the case.

It was early felt by the judges that a case not within the
reason of the statute ought not to be considered as within it.
It would be " establishing iniquity by law," so to consider it.
But on a simple contract *debt,* to which the statute alone applied, in order to avoid *wager* of *law,* or a defendant swear-

ing himself clear, an action *on the case* must be brought, and
the declaration laid with an assumpsit. In order to meet
this form the defendant pleads non assumpsit, *infra sex annos*
which prima facie brings him within the provision of the
statute. The plaintiff instead of replying *specially* the fact
of an acknowledgment, or confession of the debt within
that time, joins issue on the plea of non assumpsit; probably,
at an early period the narrow minds of the common law judges, not being bold enough to encounter the statute, on the
reason of it, and it not being known that the special replication of an acknowledgment would be admitted, or from
mere oversight such replication not having been made. In
a hard case therefore the common law courts would be disposed to adopt the *astutia* of considering an assumpsit, to
arise from an acknowledgment of the debt, and to be a new
promise. But it is but a *fiction* and is embarrassing to the
mind of the *student;* for it is not consistent with the truth of
the case, and is in fact, not a new promise, nor even evidence
of a new promise, but of the old not having been complied
with, or fulfilled. It is for this reason, that I wish we could
get quit of this language *reviving*, or *continuing* a promise,
and take common sense in our forms of pleading. The truth
is, the plaintiff says, the defendant did contract to pay. The
defendant says, I have paid. For if I had not paid, is it
probable you would not have called upon me before this? I
have paid, but I have lost the proof of that payment; ergo
the statute of 6 years. But says the plaintiff you have acknowledged within the 6 years that you have not paid; for
which reason you cannot claim the benefit of the provision.
The matter conducted in pleading in such shape as this,
would be intelligible. Assumpsit, non assumpsit; replication, acknowledgment; and hereupon issue joined. It would
avoid the whole mummery of *new promise*, or reviving; or
continuing the debt.

In the case of an express promise taking the case out of the
statute, an issue on non-assumpsit infra sex annos may be
joined, without logical blemish, or the necessity of astutia
to support a fiction.

III Bl. Com. 352.

THERE never was a power under the judiciary system of Pennsylvania, as at first adopted, or since, to change the *venue;* and this, owing to the organization of the courts, and the laws providing for the return of jurors. The supreme court, as at first constituted had no *original* jurisdiction, nor has had since at any time unless within the city and county of Philadelphia. No *original* writ therefore could issue from the supreme court to any county, as was the case with the superior courts in England. Every cause must come into the supreme court by removal. Issue having been joined in the court below, or joined in the supreme court after removal thither, the venire issued to the sheriff of the county from whence the cause had been removed, commanding him to summon jurors; or rather to distrain them: for, following the English theory, they were supposed, in contemplation of law, to have made default before on a summons served. The sheriff was commanded to have these at the sitting of the supreme court in term, *nisi prius,* that is, unless the judges of the supreme court came into the county before that term holden. But this was matter of form merely, and without reason, following the theory of the judiciary system of England, and adopting the precedent of the writ. It was not the understanding that any trial was to be had at *bar,* or the jurors to attend at the sitting of the term. For it is provided by the act constituting the court, 22d May 1722, "that upon issue joined in the supreme court, such issue shall be tried in the county, from whence the cause was removed, before the judges of the supreme court or any two of them, who are hereby empowered and *required* to go the circuit, into the respective counties; and to do generally all those things that shall be necessary for the trial of any issue as fully as the justices of *nisi prius* in England may or can do. This reserves to the court in term, the giving judgment; or hearing motions for a new trial; or in arrest of judgment. It may be seen therefore that under this act there can be no *trial at bar;* by calling a jury from the county;

nor can there be a *change of the venue* by calling a jury from one county to another.

By an act of 25 Sept. 1806, original jurisdiction under certain restrictions, was given to the supreme court within the county and city of Philadelphia; and in that case there might be, and frequently were trials at bar, all the judges sitting; but it has been since restored, but limited by act of 24th Feb. 1806, and a removal in civil actions restrained; but *no issues in fact are to be tried in bank;* and nisi prius courts to be holden by a single judge; so that trial at bar cannot, at this time, exist in any place. I consider all these particulars a great improvement of the system; and I would consider it a farther improvement to have the trials of *issues in fact* taken away from the supreme court, even at nisi prius sittings in the city and county of Philadelphia, as is the case in the other counties in the state.

As to trial by jury, too much cannot be said for it in a *criminal* case, where the necessity of *unanimity* is more reconcileable to reason. For there is a *presumption* of law in favour of the accused, that he is innocent; and it is the maxim, that if there is a doubt, acquit. Where one or more of the jury doubt so much as to stand out, after being kept together a reasonable time, and no appearance of agreeing, it may be evidence that there is ground of doubt; and it being necessary to keep the jury together in the case of felony, without meat or drink until they are agreed. It is a reason that such a principle may be admitted in foro conscientiæ to justify a concession in favour of the accused.

In a civil action there is no *legal presumption* on one side or on the other; and the court have a power to allow the jury to eat and drink; and may permit the finding a privy verdict, and separating; or upon cause may discharge. Trials per pais 250. By our act of assembly 21 March, 1806, this power is impliedly sanctioned in the oath prescribed to be taken by the jurors; " a true verdict give according to the evidence unless *dismissed* by the court, or the cause withdrawn by the parties."

It might seem expedient to give the district courts the power to change the venue in the case where a county was interested, which is quasi a corporation; and the presumption might be that an impartial trial could not be expected.

III Bl. Com. 377.

IT is the understanding of some judges that a *writ of error will not lie upon a case stated.* I cannot say that I have ever known it so decided. But the adding to the state- ment for the opinion of a court that it " shall be consi- dered *in the nature of a special verdict,* would seem to imply that there is some necessity for such addition. I do not see, that, unless at nisi prius, there can be any necessity for it. There, indeed, there may be a good reason. Because facts stated by the parties, are in the nature of, or, rather, in the place of a *special verdict :* and this, because, as the commentator says, the facts must be as if the jury had found them; and be made a part of the proceedings. But where the statement is made immediately to the court in term, and made ipso facto, a part of the proceedings, they do appear upon the record; and there would not seem to be a necessi- ty, or, even a *propriety*, in tacking to the tail of a statement, that it was to be considered in *the nature of a special verdict.* The truth is, I take it, that the appendage has been trans- ferred from an exigence where it was proper, to an occasion where it was not wanted; and this without examination of the reason of the use. Because, that, in a case stated, at nisi prius, it was added, that it should be in the nature of a spe- cial verdict, for which there was reason; when a case came to be stated for the opinion of the court, in term, pursuing the *form* of a case at nisi prius, it was added that it should be in the nature of a special verdict without distinguishing the difference.

I could assign a reason, and it is the only possible reason that I could assign, for this sublevamen, or wing to the statement; or *tail*, as I have already called it, viz. that it is to be understood in submitting to the opinion of the court, that *a writ of error is not to be brought;* but, it would be more intelligible that this should be expressed, and to have it said, that a writ of error was not to be brought.

But in term, and in a *case stated* to a court in *the last resort*, our supreme court, it is still added, that it is to be in *the nature of a special verdict.* It cannot therefore be to save the bringing a writ of error that this is added. The truth is, it is unmeaning, and without any visible use. It ought therefore to be rejected. It can answer no possible end but to puzzle the student to know what to make of it. He must think it either mystery, or magic, or nonsense, where it is supported by no visible, *artificial*, or *moral* reason.

" Thus much for judgments; to which costs are a necessary " appendage, &c." III Bl. Com. 399.

It will be useful for the student to have some idea of the difference of the law of Pennsylvania from that of England in regard to costs. It is observable that in original writs in England; or writs instituting process, there is a *condition* directory to the officer serving these writs; that, if he (the plaintiff) *shall make you secure of prosecuting his claim, &c.* This security was at the beginning a matter of substance; and real persons were required; not, as since, merely nominal, John Doe and Richard Roe. But when the law ceased to be, that the plaintiff, for his false clamour, or groundless complaint, should be amerced, these sureties became nominal; and, had it not been for the *form* of the writ being still preserved with this condition, even John Doe and Richard Roe, might have been left out. But in Pennsylvania we have no such condition in our writs; and therefore John Doe and Richard Roe need not be attached to the writ, or declaration pursuing the writ. Pledges of prosecution are idle words, and need not be introduced.

What was the necessity, of security to prosecute the suit, at an early period? It was because that parties, plaintiff or defendant, were liable to an amercement; the plaintiff for complaining falsely; the defendant for groundlessly resisting a just claim. But when costs were given by statute; or came to be given in certain cases, which the common law eo nomine did not allow, all idea of amercement ceased, and the costs are the amercement; or answer the same, and a better purpose; some allowance to the party for what has been expended in prosecuting or sustaining a suit. But it is under the idea of an amercement that the form still remains of calling the plaintiff in the case of a nonsuit.

It is on the same principle that the paying a fine to the king in case of a judgment against a party has ceased in England, costs being deemed a sufficient restraint against a vexatious suit, or groundless defence. But it is still under the idea of vexation in the *bringing* the action, that *executors* and *administrators* in England do not pay costs; for the reason given is that they cannot be supposed to be cognizant of the ground of action, in those whom they represent, in such a manner, as that the law can infer a vexation. But fine and amercement ceasing, and costs being in place of these in England, the *exemption* of executors and administrators from costs, ought to have ceased also. Here it has never been introduced; and no distinction taken as to these from other parties to a suit.

The *absurdity* did not exist at the common law, so far as respected the plaintiff, that he could have no allowance for his costs of writ, service by the sheriff, and return, docketing by the clerk, filing of papers, and continuance of suit, together with subpoena for witnesses, &c. An allowance was made for these in the damages assessed by the jury, in *all cases where damages were recoverable.* But as the jury could make but an estimate or guess as to these, the costs actually laid out, were a most certain criterion; and, therefore given by the statutes; and these added by way of increase of damages, by the court. For even before the statute of Gloucester " the justices in Eyre were wont at their iters to assess the costs of the plaintiff, when he prevailed, at a reasonable sum exclusive of and unblended with the damages which he recovered; and that custom prevailed till the introduction of the modern justices of assize and nisi prius; at which time it became necessary that the costs should be taxed by the court above, and not by the judges on their circuits." Gilb. hist. c. p. 266. When the jury therefore gives a verdict even in the case of debt or ejectment, they say we find for the plaintiff six cents damages, and six cents costs, in order that the court may consistently add the increase of costs to the damages. In cases where the verdict is for damages, and not an ejectment, or a debt on bond with a penalty, or in covenant with a penalty, &c. they say only we find so much damages, and six cents costs.

But is there any thing to hinder the jury still to include costs in the damages and under that idea to say we find so much damages *without costs.* I should think there is not; it is the usage and practice. Under the statutes which provide that damages being found under a certain sum, there shall be no costs, or no more costs than damages, the jury who are the arbiter of damages, and with whom it must be to bring the damages under the sum, may say we find *with* or *without* costs. This is no more than to say, we have lessened the damages with a view to that. For costs are *in a legal sense included in the word damages,* 2 East. 296; and if said to be added by the court, it is the same thing as if added by the jury themselves. Damages are *exemplary* as well as *compensatory;* and it is not therefore the exact compensation that is alone to be the measure. See the error in the reasoning, 2 Cain, 213. The case in Salk. 207. was the result of good sense, and according to the reason on which the statutes passed. The jury giving costs, even where the damages found would not otherwise justify the court to encrease, took the case out of the statutes and formed an exception.

The impracticability of making but an estimate of the costs in the action, is a reason against including; or being supposed to include; but it is an embarassing circumstance to be obliged to find damages to a certain extent, in order to carry costs, in a case where a jury may think that the plaintiff had good cause of action, but that the excuse or extenuation of damages, which, from evidence which the plaintiff could not anticipate, might reduce in such a way that small damages, *on the defendant paying costs*, might suffice. Reason and convenience appear to me in favour of this principle, as extending to all cases in which damages are to be recovered and costs given. Such finding by the jury ought to be considered as taking the case out of the general rule.

It is a different matter, and more difficult, to say what the jury may do, where an action is commenced in an *inferior* court, and removed by the plaintiff; and where it is provided that no more costs shall be recovered than damages. I should think in such a case a jury could not find a less sum, and say, *with costs*, because it is the *policy* of the law to avoid the delay which the removal of a cause gives, and also to save the time of the *superior* court for the determination of the more important actions. But under our acts of assembly in the case of *referees*, the trial by jury being taken away, in the first instance, there is less reason on an appeal, to limit the power of the jury in this particular, so as to say, with or without costs. See 1 Bin. 61. 4 Bin. 5. In the case of penal actions, or actions on penal statutes, where a certain sum, in the nature of a mulct, is to be recovered, the jury cannot give less; costs must follow. Under the statute 22d, 23d, Cha. II. reported by the judges of the supreme court to have been introduced here, where the judge must certify in order to entitle to costs, it is inferable from the policy of the statute, that the jury cannot say, with or without costs, so as to exclude the necessity of the certificate.

III Black. Com. 406.—WRIT OF ERROR.

By an act of Assembly of 6 March, 1812. Sec. 11. it is provided that " when more than one exception is taken, or point made in any court of common pleas; or other court of inferior jurisdiction, and the same has been duly removed to the supreme court for their decision, the judges of the supreme court, are enjoined and required to give their opinion on every point, and exception taken, and signed in the inferior court." It is no small reproach upon *the courts of error*, that it should be found necessary to make such a provision. It had its origin in the indolence, or *weakness*, or *timidity* of judges, and unwillingness to take more upon them in deciding points of law than became unavoidable in the undertaking to affirm, or reverse a judgment. But the *defendant* in a writ of error was still left at a loss to know whether the other errors which had been assigned were erroneous; so that it might behoove him to pray amendments; or, if a plaintiff, to discontinue, and bring a new action. In this country, it was following the English judges, and their *errors*, that led to this. It was their mode of proceeding; I mean of the English judges, that if one error assigned, was fatal to the action or proceedings, to look no farther into the record. By this means they consulted their own ease, and perhaps the interest of attornies, and special pleading, but, by no means of the parties in the suit. I am pleased therefore, with this amendment of the legislature. But there remains yet another step to be taken, and which, I think, was originally in the bill, and if so, would seem to have been struck out; for it is not in *the law*. It is what by way of supplement, may be yet added. I will endeavour so to explain myself that I may be understood by the legislative body with a view to such a supplement.

"A writ of error lies where a party is aggrieved by any error, in the *foundation, proceeding, judgment,* or *execution of a suit.* It is in the nature of a commission to the judges of the same or a superior court, by which they are authorised to examine the record upon which a judgment was given; and on such examination, to affirm or reverse the same according to law.

"Errors in law, are *common* or *special.* The common errors are, that the declaration is insufficient in law, to maintain the action. Special errors are, the want of an original writ, bill, or warrant of attorney or other matter appearing on the face of the record, which shews their judgment to have been erroneous.

"Errors in *fact*, consist of matters not appearing on the face of the record, which if true prove the judgment to have been erroneous; as that the defendant in the original action being under age appeared by attorney. That a femme plaintiff or defendant was under coverture, at the time of commencing the action, or that a sole plaintiff or defendant died before a verdict or interlocutory judgment." 2 Tidd's practice, c. 43.

In *the foundation of the action*, the first error that is assignable, is *the want of jurisdiction;* and it is a maxim of law that *consent cannot give jurisdiction*. Now in the case of a justice of the peace in this state, it is a great hardship, that if on a writ of error, it shall appear *on the face of the proceeding* that he has exceeded his jurisdiction by *a cent*, even though the defendant has appealed, and not made a plea to his jurisdiction, or made the sum demanded a ground of exception before the justice, but waved all this, and taken the chance of a trial, he shall nevertheless be permitted to take advantage of this on a certiorari, which is in the nature of a writ of error. For though it is true that consent cannot give jurisdiction, where it respects the *nature of the action*, yet it is not necessary that this be applied where it respects only the *quantum of the demand*.

In like manner where errors alleged is in the *process* from a court; or where different causes of action are joined in one writ; or where proper persons are not made parties; or the declaration varies from the writ; or has counts that cannot be joined; or does not go to maintain, or give ground of action; or the evidence does not agree with the declaration; or the verdict with the evidence; or the judgment with the verdict; or the execution with the judgment; in all these cases, *if exception is not taken to each of these, and the point made in the court below,* why should a party be at liberty to assign that for error because appearing on the record, which had never been moved or thought of, or brought forward in the court below, and it can be by *implication* only, that it can be supposed to have passed upon it, the matter having passed sub silentio, and no notice taken of it by the party in the first instance. The clause therefore which I would propose

is this, that where a *certiorari* is taken to a justice of the
peace, or writ of error to a *court of record*, no exception
on the certiorari to the proceedings of the justice, shall be
taken; and on the writ of error to the court of record, no
error shall be assigned which had not been made a ground
of exception to the court below, and on which the court had
not expressly decided; and at the proper degree of the proceedings when such exception ought to have been taken, or
point made.

———

" The next species of execution is against the goods and chat-
" tels of the defendant; and is called a writ of fieri facias," &c.
III Bl. Com. 417.

THE law gives preference to priority; prius in tempore,
potior in jure is the maxim. The fieri facias put first into
the hands of the officer, has the right to a levy to be first
made under it; and the levy first made, attaches in favour
of that creditor. But this may be lost by *delay*, either where
the delay may be evidence of covering that property collu-
sively with the debtor; or where the delay itself will amount
to a *fraud in law*. It may be a fraud on those who give credit on the evidence of goods in a man's possession. This
would be a fraud in fact; or it may delay a posterior execution; and this would amount to a *fraud in law*. A man
must use the preference the law gives him, so as not to *delay or defeat* the right of another. This both at common
law, and under the statute of Elizabeth.

But will a fraud in *fact* be inferred; or a fraud in *law*
arise from the suffering the property levied on to remain in
the possession of the debtor; or rather the officer not taking it immediately into his actual, as it already is in his legal
possession? That is by such removal and change of situation
as will be exclusive of all evidence of a possession by the
debtor. Must the officer remain with the property, and hold

this visible and actual possession of it? It is at the risk of the officer not to do it; but the law will not raise the impu-tation of fraud, nor will a jury be bound *necessarily* to infer fraud from *the bare leaving goods in the possession of the debt-or, under-circumstance, for a time;* so far as respects a credi-tor; or a plaintiff in another execution, under what circum-stances will the lapse of time not be conclusive? These must be left to the court when the question is to them; or to the court and jury where the fact is in issue. What *time* will conclude? That must be left to the same consideration. A day, a month, *a longer time* may be seen in the English books not to conclude. A very short time in other instances has been holden to warrant a conclusion of fraud in fact, or of fraud in law. " If a creditor by fieri facias seises the goods of the debtor and suffers them to remain *long* in the debtor's hands; and another creditor obtain a subsequent judgment and execution, it is evidence of fraud in the first creditor, and the goods in the hands of the debtor remain liable," 1 Vez. 245, 6. Take notice, it is the word *long* that is used. What time shall be construed *long* cannot be laid down by a ge-neral rule. 1 Wilson 44, which is sometimes referred to on this head, gives a case where the jury found *fraud;* not from the *time* but from the *circumstance,* and *manner of the levy.* The time was but four days; and the sheriff did not remain, nor his bailiffs in possession of the goods; but the manner of the taking in execution was, by riding round the farm and saying, " I seise all this corn and cattle." 7 Mod. referred to in Wilson, says nothing of the time; and the plaintiff had " got the sheriff to seise the goods and would not let him proceed further." That was held a fraud, nothing appearing to *explain and rebut the imputation;* or rather circumstances appearing to support it; as the paying taxes for the *farm,* and the goods in the mean time, 10 Vin. 561. The case 1 Ray. 251. The time was not a day; but the plaintiff *refused to proceed;* and the creditor who had another execution in the sheriff's hands took the goods. For it seems, said lord Holt, " that the plaintiff in the first execution had a design

C c

only to keep the execution in his pocket, to *protect the defendant's goods by fraud.*"

The permitting an *exercise of ownership* for a day, or less time may be such a badge of fraud as will justify a court or jury to infer it. As, " in the case of a bill of sale of liquors, and the permitting the debtor to continue to retail them." Every case of this kind must stand upon its own bottom; for no general rule can apply, unless we say, that from *the moment* the goods are seised, the officer must be in the actual possession, and proceed with all possible dispatch, to offer them for sale and to make sale of them. The law of England has never been carried to this extent. But *unreasonable and unexplained* delay, alone, or such circumstances as will evince a design to defeat for a time, or altogether, will warrant *the inference of fraud.*

I know of no difference in the case of this state (Pennsylvania) from that of England where *actual fraud* can be made out; that is an intention to cover property from creditors, or to delay their executions. On what the law shall raise an implication of fraud, there may be a difference; for in the application of a rule *of construction*, we are bound to look at the difference in the spirit and genius of the system of a different community; and the *usage* or what is *customary* goes to explain or rebut the implication. The law of Pennsylvania has been, from the earliest period, favourable to the obtaining credit, and is indulgent to debtors.

The law has had a gradation, a more or less tenderness to the debtor, from a consideration of the circumstances of the people. By the law of 1800, now obsolete in practice, for the appraisement of goods, a postponement of sale for seven days is provided; and in case the goods appraised will not sell for so much as the same are appraised, and valued to be worth by the said appraisers, or any two of them, the creditor shall receive them for his pay.

Another law of 1700, also obsolete in practice, provides " not only that in a levy upon real estate, the chief plantation, or messuage, shall be taken in execution last, but it shall not be exposed before the expiration of one whole year after judgment is obtained." These provisions in the case of real estate have become obsolete in practice, being considered as superadded, or supplied by the act of 1705, taking away the sale under a fieri facias where real estate is levied on, and providing that a venditioni exponas shall issue only on the return of the fieri facias, where on an inquest taken, the land levied will not extend so as to pay the debt in 7 years. This privilege has been construed by the courts to extend to what are called improvement rights. In case of personal property why not pursue the spirit of the law in the case of real estate?

The early cultivator of the soil in Pennsylvania could not *oftentimes* take out a grub without credit for an implement of husbandry; nor plough the ground without cattle; nor build a cabin, or live in it without some sort of furniture, and vessels of a culinary nature, or a bed, or a blanket; and execution levied upon these, and rigorously carried into effect might leave him, in a little time, as if he had had no credit. It is on this principle that the insolvent law provides for the unfortunate, the retaining family articles, and implements of the respective occupation not exceeding the value of £5; I mean a respect to the circumstances of the husbandman as well as the early state, of trades, and other occupations. The improvement of the country has a good deal depended on it.

In the case of a levy on personal property, it is the usage that has superseded the appraisement of goods and delivery to the creditor, or of giving some delay in a proceeding to sale. Certain it is, that, *it is* the usage to let the goods remain and not to change the actual possession instantly in all cases. This with the consent of the plaintiff; or at the discretion of the officer himself taking security. A subsequent fieri facias put into the hands, of the officer and *notice to him, or the plaintiff in the first*, that if the sale was not made, a levy should be made under the subsequent, might alter the rights of the parties, and lead to a postponement of the prior, to the subsequent. But I do not think that of itself, it ought to be considered as implying fraud.

In the state of New York, 8 Johns. 20, " the agent of the plaintiff delivered an execution to the sheriff, and directed him to levy it on the property of the defendant, but said to the sheriff that he supposed he did not wish to distress the defendant, and that if the property remained in the possession of defendant after the levy, the plaintiff would not hold the sheriff responsible if it was squandered, and that he need not take a receipt for it. The sheriff after levying on the goods of the defendant did nothing further until after the execution had expired, and a second execution was delivered to him when he sold the property on both executions. It was held that as there were no instructions from the plaintiff to delay the execution after the seizure ; nor any agreement between the plaintiff and defendant to let the first execution sleep in the sheriff's hands ; nor any evidence of such a delay as would afford a legal presumption of fraud, the first execution did not lose its preference." This is the marginal note but it is the language of the court in the opinion given, " that if a *long time* had intervened between the one execution and the other, it might have been ground for the jury to have inferred the consent of the plaintiff to the delay, and might have established the *legal presumption of fraud.* The courts of the United States sitting in Pennsylvania have expressed a disposition to *differ*, and in one case, 4 Dal. 359, a regret at differing from the decisions of the state courts, in this *particular of jurisprudence.* But had they any right to *differ* in laying down *a principle*, however in the application of one to a particular case ? by Sec. 4. of the act to establish the judicial courts of the United States, it is provided that " the laws of the several states except where the constitution, treaties or statutes of the United States shall otherwise require or provide, shall be regarded as rules of decision in trials at common law in cases where they apply." Will not this embrace the *common law of the state;* and where are they to find this, where it departs from the common law of England, but in the decisions of the state courts ?

Our decisions are evidence to these courts of our unwritten law, and ought to bind, otherwise *the abridgment of their jurisdiction by a constitutional amendment will be called for more loudly than it is.*

But it will be said that the giving way to *a reasonable time under all circumstance* will be a continual source of difficulty, and give rise to litigation in every particular case. It is attended with that difficulty : but this is not the only case known to the law where what is *reasonable as to time*, is taken into view. This from the necessity of the case, and the impracticability of fixing a rule as to time consistent with a *humane administration of the laws.*

In the case of Berry v. Smith, in the circuit court of the United States before Judge Washington, according to a manuscript report furnished me, there was a fieri facias, Jan. 1, 1811 : on the same day delivered to the sheriff 12 o'clock, with directions not to levy it till further instructions. Same day plaintiff's council called at the house of the defendant to inform him of the issuing the execution, and to request his taking immediate measures to discharge it. The defendant was not at home. Next day plaintiff's counsel called again between one and two, and found defendant at dinner. He then called him to the door, and informed him of the issuing of the fieri facias : said there was no desire to break him up, or to distress him, if it could be avoided consistently with the plaintiff's safety; that the execution delivered to the sheriff would secure the property ; and that the defendant must immediately see the plaintiff's agent, and make some arrangement with him to prevent further proceedings under the execution. 3d. Jan. plaintiff's counsel not hearing from the defendant or his agent directed the sheriff to proceed to make his levy; and accordingly the sheriff went to the house of the defendant and levied. But did not then remove the goods; but left them with the defendant according to the orders of the plaintiff, endorsed on the writ "till further orders." This levy made the 3d. But on the 4th, 1 o'clock, fieri facias in favour of another creditor, levy and the same goods seised. The defendant then being in his house, and no sheriff or officers being there, and removed the said goods. The defendant informing the marshal on the

levying, that the sheriff had been there. Neither the plaintiff nor his agent knew of the issuing of the fieri facias, or
of the levy, or of the removal until after it was done."

This was decided to raise the inference of a fraud in law.
With much respect for the abilities of that judge I must
bear testimony against that decision, though his reasons are
sensible and manly. And I think that even in the English
courts it would be deemed rigorous, and winding up too
strictly the law. The rule which I would lay down is "that
*if the goods are forthcoming at the next court to which the
writ is returnable,* and money made to answer the exigence
of the writ, the law shall not *raise a fraud. Until that time
the goods to be subject to the levy.* And this I know to be
the custom of the country, and the understanding of the practice in Pennsylvania. Not until the last day of the term is the
sheriff called upon *to bring the money into court.* The return of the writ may be called for, the first day of the term,
but the money not expected to be made until the last day.
If the writ shall have issued but a short time before, though
a levy has been made, it would not amount to a fraud in
law to postpone a sale for ten days after the terms, or to
the adjourned court, which is usually six weeks after the
terms. This is the practice of the country.

But fraud in fact either in the entering the judgment, the
taking out the writ to cover, the putting into the hand of the
officer with instructions to postpone, or in the levy, and sale
colourable or otherwise, a single particle of fraud would avoid,
according to the stage of the transaction and let in, a *concurrent, or subsequent execution.*

This indulgence of the courts to the debtor where ground
can be laid for a special application to the contrary, is founded in humanity, and the necessity of paying some regard to
the difficulty of poor but honest defendants discharging debts
to avoid the ruin of the country. And the salus populi
suprema lex est. It is establishing justice in mercy. For
the tearing away property by an execution amongst the groans
of the distressed, and the tears of families, is hard enough
even with all the softening that can be given it. And the

Shylock that would say to the officer, "I stand upon my bond" remove and sell instantly, would be considered in most cases, an unfeeling creditor; and on the contrary the law would not hastily raise an imputation of fraud to the party from a customary indulgence, or a reasonable stay of sale.

I cannot but confidently be of opinion that if this *usage of lenity and tenderness is superseded by a rigid common law, or beyond* common construction of what shall be a fraud, the appraisement law must be revised by the courts, or the interposition of the legislature be called for to moderate in some way, which might be less convenient to creditors than the indulgence which the *usage* allows.

The *rigour* of an *instant removal* of goods levied on under an execution was softened at an early period, in our sister colony of Virginia. This by an act of assembly of 1748, c. 8, by which it is provided "that if the owner of goods taken in execution shall give sufficient security to the sheriff to have the same *forthcoming* at the time of sale, it shall be lawful for the sheriff to accept such security, and suffer the goods to remain in possession, and at the risk of the debtor until the time of sale."

This continues to be the law. See Tucker's Black. note page 421. For the law, under this head as holden in the state of New York, See 9 Johnson, 135, 197, 243 and 337.

———

"The fourth species of execution is by writ of Elegit," &c. III Bl. Com. 418.

By the common law real estate was subject to the payment of debts, only, in the case of debt due to the king by obligation or recognizance : or where lands had descended, the ancestor having bound himself and his heir by obligation. But by statute they were made liable to be taken in execution sub modo and to a certain extent. But in neither of these cases could a sale be made, but the land only taken un-

til from the issues and profits the debt was paid. See 2
Plow. 439.

An inheritance in a foreign country (plantation) was liable to be taken for payment of debts, and to be esteemed as
a chattel interest till the debts are satisfied. 2 Vent. 358.

The laws of the plantations themselves *where they have
made provision* must govern as to the taking lands in execution, or sale by executors.

Under the charter of Penn, certain laws were agreed upon
in England with the adventurers, amongst which was this,
that "all lands and goods shall be liable to pay debts, except
where there is legal issue; and then all the goods, and one
third of the land only." 5 Smith's laws, 416. In appendix
No. 3. By an act of the *colony* 1687, this was made a law.
By an act of 1684 all lands whatsoever, and houses are
made liable to execution; and to be sold subject to certain
regulations. And by an act 1693, are made liable to be sold
by the executor, or administrator, *for the payment of the decedent's debts.* By an act of 1700, widows and administrators, under the order of the orphans court, were empowered
to sell lands for the payment of debts. See appendix. 1 Dall.
state laws, for all these acts of assembly superseded, or repealed.

Doubts would seem to have been entertained with regard
to the proceeding under these laws, for what reason is not
recited in the act of 1705, which is entitled an act "*for the
better confirmation,* &c." But by subsequent laws and decisions, no doubt now remains, in Pennsylvania, but that lands
are liable to be taken in execution for the debts of decedents;
not, *until extinguished by the issues and profits,* but to be sold
absolutely. 1 Dall. 481.

In the case of *living* debtors they must be sold subject to
an inquisition, whether the issues and profits subject to all
reprises, by which is meant judgments and mortgages, will
satisfy the debt in seven years. But in the case of *deceased*
debtors, query whether they may not be sold absolutely,
without an inquisition. For if real estate is to be considered
as *goods and chattels* for the payment of debts in the case of

a *deceased* person, it would be an *inconsistency* to say that such real estate could not be sold as goods and chattels are without an inquisition. I am not at present informed what has been the construction in this particular from any practice sanctioned by the courts. But it would seem unreasonable that the debtor should be deprived of the benefit in law provided in his favour, giving him seven years to discharge by the issues and profits; and, that the *contingency* of the *decease* of the debtor should put his *representatives* in a worse situation than he had himself been; and taking these acts of assembly that are pari materia, it would seem that the representatives are entitled to the privilege of extinguishing the debt by the issues and profits in seven years. This being the case, though the lands are subject to be sold as goods and chattels for the payment of debts, yet they must be still subject to an inquisition.

But it would seem from the necessity of an inquisition being holden, that executors, without an authority under the will cannot sell, but must *suffer an execution to issue* on judgments against the testator, or against themselves. *Administrators* cannot sell but under the direction of the orphans court. This authority is given for the payment of debts, or the maintenance of orphans. It would seem that in this case the right of the debtor must be still saved to extend the lands; and therefore the analogy is not strict; or can be carried to the whole extent of considering the real estate of the deceased as goods and chattels. It was to cure some irregularities of sales by executors or administrators, not having authority by the will, that the act of 1705 would seem to have passed. I speak of administrators cum testamento annexo, where no authority was given to sell for the payment of debts.

D D

"Freehold lands which he had at the time of the judgment
"given." III Bl. Com. 418.

THIS might seem to imply, and has been cited for that
purpose, that lands purchased *after the judgment*, could not
be taken in execution. But the authority to which the commentator refers, 2 Institutes, 395. does not restrict to this.
The words are, "Such land as the defendant had, at the time
of the judgment given, unless it be conveyed away, by *fraud
and covin to deceive his creditors.*" This *exception* shews
what effect of the judgment it is that he is speaking of, (Lord
Coke) and that it relates to lands actually owned at the time
of the judgment, not having been bona fide conveyed away
before the judgment. Nor, has it any reference to the effect
of a judgment upon *after purchased lands*. That an execution may be levied upon after purchased lands, not aliened
before execution, there can be no doubt. But whether the
judgment attaches on such lands eo instante that they are
purchased ; or, whether they are taken by virtue of the execution, as, in the case of goods and chattels, is a question.
In England it would seem that the judgment is considered
as attaching, and drawing under it the lands purchased after
the judgment, so that, though aliened before the execution, it
would seem to be the law. In Pennsylvania, it has been otherwise. And indeed in England, when traced to the origin
of the doctrine, would seem to have a very doubtful foundation. And so far from extending such a principle here, I
cannot say I would have any objection to confine the execution to the *lien* of the judgment, as in the nature of a *general
mortgage*, so that those lands only should be considered as
pledged, or liable to be taken, which the debtor had at the
time of the judgment. But that these lands being first exhausted, towards payment of the judgment, a scire facias
might then issue to the terre-tenants of other lands, and it
might be shewn that they were not the lands of the debtor at
the time of the judgment ; and *have since been purchased by
them, the terre-tenants.* This would be in the spirit of what
the legislature have already done, in restricting as to limitation of time, *the lien of a judgment.*

III Black. Com. 452.

A wager is not considered as a nudum pactum, or contract *without consideration* in the law of England. The *mutual promise* is a consideration. In case of a certain event taking place, I will pay you £10 on condition that if it does not take place you will pay me £10. It is a *species of gambling* though it does not come under the usual denomination of it. There may be said to be a quid pro quo, risk against risk. But *gain* to one at the expence of *loss* to another, is not in the nature of a *moral* contract, where some certain benefit is contemplated on both sides. Alterius incommodo suum augere commodum, magis est contra naturam quam mors, quam paupertas, quam dolor.

It is strange therefore that it should still remain a contract known to the law, and that an action is maintainable in a court of justice, upon *a wager*. It is still more so, that it should receive so much the countenance of the law, as to be the mode of declaring on *a feigned issue*, where the *court of chancery* directs a matter of fact or law to the common law courts, with a view to an equity case depending, and a decree to be made. This mode of declaring has been introduced in Pennsylvania; and is the form of stating the case where a matter of fact or law is sent to the *common* pleas by the orphans court, in like manner as from the chancery in England, where the opinion of the common law judges is to be taken on a question of law, or where a matter of fact is to be ascertained by jury. In either case this might be easily avoided, by simply stating the law point to be decided, or the matter of fact to be tried. The reason given in England, for admitting this form of declaring is to avoid the prolixity and expence of special pleading. That does not hold here, where there is neither prolixity nor expence arising from the pleadings; all being put in brief. This needs no act of assembly, but simply that the court in the *last resort*, giving it to be understood that such form of declaring may be dispensed with, and a statement according to the truth of the case admitted. For a court in the last resort, such as we

have in Pennsylvania, the supreme court, has a greater latitude, and is less embarassed in altering a matter of practice;
or a rule of law as to form of action, than either the court of
common pleas, king's bench, or exchequer in England. For a
writ of error lies from the king's bench to the common pleas,
and from the law side of the exchequer, a writ of error lies
into the *court* of exchequer chamber before the lord chancellor, lord treasurer, and the judges of the court of king's bench,
and common pleas, and from thence it lies to the house
of peers. This et sequentia, see 3 Black. 410. It must be
a matter of less difficulty therefore here to alter, or change
rules, than in that country from the constitution of their courts,
and the expence attending appeals. For this reason it ought
to appear absurd in our supreme court, to hear the judges declaring as in the common pleas, 1 Taunton, 542. " The cases
have decided," says Mansfield, " *(for what reason, I cannot
perceive)* that a count for goods sold and delivered, is not an
action upon a contract." And Chambre, justice, " I am very
sorry we *are bound to conform to such a rule,* but the cases are
all so."

It is on this principle that so far as my voice could go,
I have declared more than once against declaring on a feigned issue in such a way, not only because I think that it may
be better done or at least more conformably to common understanding, to state the point of law on which an opinion is
required, or a matter, the issue in fact of which is to be determined by a jury; but for this reason also that it will avoid
the giving countenance to the principle of a wager, by adopting the form in a judicial proceeding.

A wager, however, is restrained by the common law to what
is *lawful.* It must be unlawful for a person to wager that he
will *transgress a penal statute.* This comes under the head
of malum prohibitum; but still more it must be unlawful to
wager that he will commit a battery, for this is malum in se,
and a breach of the peace, contra bonos mores, or what is
against good morals must be unlawful, as the ground of a
wager that the wagerer will strip himself, and shew himself
naked from a balcony, or other place.

But the common law will still farther restrict the subject of a wager. What must affect the *reputation* or *the feelings* of a *third person*, is unlawful. What will lead to an indecent investigation, will not be sustained by a court, as with regard to *the sex of an individual.* On a wager against public policy, also, no action can be maintained.

There is a species of wagering which, I take it, the common law would hold unlawful, so that an action could not be maintained; such as upon a man's own speed or strength, or that of others; or such uncommon exertions, as must be unprofitable or pernicious. Even in the case of animals, races against time, or carrying or drawing against each other, or against weight, is a species of cruelty, and cannot but be considered wantonness, and an abuse of useful powers; so that in these cases also, wagering ought to be held unlawful, and no action to recover ought to lie.

Wagering has been excluded from the law of insurance by statute in England. "The practice of insuring *ideal risks* under the names of interest or no interest, nor without farther proof of interest than the policy, or without benefit of salvage to the underwriters, was increasing to an alarming degree, and by such rapid strides as to threaten the speedy annihilation of that lucrative and most beneficial branch of trade. All these various kinds of insurance just enumerated, (and many others, which the ingenuity of bad men found no difficulty in devising) having no reference whatever to actual trade or commerce, were very justly considered as mere gaining and wager-policies: and therefore the legislature thought it necessary to give them an effectual check, and, by positive rules, to fix and ascertain what property or interest a merchant should be permitted to insure." Park. 348.

All wagering on the event of an election ought to be considered as unlawful in a republican government; where it is essential to the exercise of the privilege and the choice of representatives, that the voter be confined to considerations of policy in the selection, and be swayed by no motive of pecuniary profit or advantage. It leads to undue exertions also, where a stake is depending further than the public good, and is introductive of unusual heat, and sometimes breaches of the peace. No action ought to lie in these cases. Where there is a deposit in the hand of a stake-holder, it ought not to be recovered of him by the party succeeding. But query, whether it would not be for the public good, that by an act of the legislature all such wagering should be swept away by making it a misdemeanor, and an indictable offence to bet, and deposit, or take the mutual promise of parties to such contract. The freedom of unbiassed suffrage is of great moment, and great sums at risk by monied men on the event of an election, cannot but do mischief. The wealthy bet because they can afford to lose, and the bulk are led to place confidence in the stake, as a pledge that in their judgment such a candidate will be successful. It is an art of canvassing that prevails much, and misleads the weaker judgment.

———————

Extract of a letter from Joseph Reed, recorder of the city of Philadelphia.

PHILADELPHIA, Oct. 5, 1813.

" I HAVE been much pleased with the perusal of a few sheets of your intended publication, by Byrne. As a didactic work, I think it well calculated for the use of the student, and will, I hope, in time, promote a complete revision of the code of Pennsylvania law. On a perusal of the sheets, I am inclined to think there are some few errors in point of fact, which I beg leave candidly and respectfully to suggest to you —In page 19 of the introduction, you have observed, that the quakers do not admit a practitioner of the law to be in full communion.—This, I am informed, is not the case, there are several instances in this city of gentlemen of the profession being in full communion with the friends. Mr. John Hallowell, I know is, and values his privilege as a member of the meeting, very highly.—Before the western insurrection, I might have named several others, viz. Messrs. Rawle,

Morgan, &c.—Mr. John Tod, the former husband of Mrs. Madison, remained in full communion with the friends, until his death in 1793.—In page 38 of the Law Miscellanies, you have stated that a legislative provision is necessary " to en- " able the children of a devisee to take among themselves " what the devisee himself would have taken."—This was done by the act of the 19th March, 1810, which has probably escaped your notice, or perhaps your observation was made before the passing of the law.

" I have thus, sir, taken the liberty of stating what has occurred to me on a perusal of a part of your work; if I am right, I know you will thank me for the information, and if I am wrong, you will I am sure appreciate my motive, and excuse the liberty I have taken."

The title of this publication, a miscellany, will naturally admit, or rather call for a greater liberty of insertion than otherwise could be tolerated ; but, independent of this, there would be a perfect propriety in admitting any thing that would serve to correct what had been said or hinted at. I there- fore did not think I could do better than give the extract from the preceding. I shall be disposed to do the same in any case where I may be honoured with the notice of what has been written.

As to the act, 19th March, 1810, I believe what I had written was before it passed ; and I overlooked it in correct- ing the original note. But this act of 19th March, 1810, does not come up to all that I had in view ; and was in my mind in the observation made upon a reference to 1 Bin. 546. That was the case of the representatives of a brother and sis- ter devisees, which is not provided for even yet under that act, as it would not seem to extend to the case of *collateral rela- tions*, but is confined to *lineal descendants*, and respects the dying before the testator ; and does not provide for the case of an executory devise at a future period, and after the death of the testator. The feudal principle of taking *per capita*, was in the way in the case of the lessee of Smith v. Folwell, 1 Bin. 546.

It would seem to me that the legislature are but little in the way of reading our decisions; otherwise their attention could not have been but drawn to this subject long before this time.

NOTES ON

BLACKSTONE'S COMMENTARIES.

POINTING OUT VARIATIONS IN THE LAW OF PENNSYLVANIA,
FROM THE COMMON AND STATUTE LAW OF ENGLAND,
WITH OTHER MATTERS OF A GENERAL NATURE.

———•+•———

" But by Stat. 22 Car. II. c. 7. no person is allowed to work on the Lord's day," &c. IV Bl. Com. 63.

" *To work*" is not an expression in the statute; though it is in the 8th commandment given to Moses; "*shalt not do any work.*" Exod. c. 20, sec. 10. The words of the statute Chas. II. c. 7. are that, " no tradesman, artificer, workman, or labourer, or other person whatsoever, shall do or exercise any *worldly* labour, business or *work* of their *ordinary calling* on the Lord's day." It has been holden that it is not unlawful, under this statute, to bargain for the sale of a horse, the vendor not being a *horse-jockey;* and so, not in the way of his *ordinary calling.* 1 Taunt. 130. The punishing the offendor in Connecticut for letting his *beer work*, was carrying the matter to the other extreme.

Our act of assembly of 1705, copied in part from that of Cha. 2d. c. 7. judiciously omits the words *ordinary calling*, and steers clear of this difficulty, or rather absurdity, in distinguishing work done in the way of a man's *ordinary calling*, from that of work done in any other way; and in the act of assembly 22d Ap. 1794, which is the last act, and supplies all antecedent, as to this particular, the words are, if any per-

E E

son do, &c. such persons *so offending* shall, &c. By these acts
all *wordly labour* is prohibited, whether in the way of a *man's
ordinary calling* or otherwise; and which, doubtless, also
was the intent of the statute, Cha. II. c. 7; but, *as penal laws*
are to be construed *strictly*, the judges have thought themselves warranted in taking the distinction, or bound to take
it.   For it is under the statute alone that it could be cognizable not being *a misdemeanor* at common law; though as to
this, there has been some contrariety of opinion. It depends
upon the question whether the commandment given to Moses is in force under the *christian dispensation*.   It cannot be
denied but that the *reason* of the institution goes some length
in extending it to all times, and under all dispensations; " In
six days the Lord made heaven and earth, &c. and rested the
seventh; wherefore the Lord blessed the Sabbath day and
hallowed it."*   But the author of our religion, would seem
to have claimed the authority of *dispensing* with the keeping
it; at least, with the *Jewish strictness.*

" The son of man is lord also of the sabbath." Mark 2.
sec. 28. Certain it is that the Jewish Sabbath does not appear
to have been kept, or at all attended to under his immediate
disciples; but whatever respect was paid in the observance of
any day, it was to *the first day of the week*, the hebdom of
the resurrection, and so called the *Lord's day*. On this day the
brethren met to "break bread," as appears from Acts 20. sec.
7; " upon the first day of the week when the disciples came to
break bread," &c. and this day appears to have been regarded, and no other day, from that time forward, whether for
the purpose of *meeting*, and confirming each other in the
faith, making charitable collections for the poor brethren;
or settling matters of order and discipline in the church; or
for the purpose of joining in religious devotion.

In the case in Taunton, 130, the counsel on one side argue that, " no canon, no opinion is to be found in any writer
upon Ecclesiastical law, treating bargains made on a Sunday as
illegal. The Jewish law prohibited them, but several of the
councils have expressly declared that *christians shall not*

* Exod. 20. sec. 11.

judaise." On the other side it was contended "that a sale
on Sunday was illegal *at common law;* that in christianity
as well as judaism, the 4th commandment is retained; and
that which is an offence against it, when committed by a *Jew,*
is equally such when committed by a *Christian;* that no case
had been cited where a contract made on a Sunday has been
enforced by law."

The court take notice that it is said by Lord Coke, that
the *Christian Religion* is part of the common law ; 2 Inst. 220.
Where he cites a law of King Athelstan, dic autem domini-
co nemo mercaturam facito; id si quis egerit, et ipsa merce
et trigenta præterea solidis mulctatur; and note that *no merchandise* should be on the Lord's day. But it does not appear, say the court, that the common law ever considered
those *contracts void* which were made on a Sunday.

That the contract should not be void, and yet the act a
misdemeanor as contra bonos mores would seem to be an
inconsistency. But the legislature in England, as well as here
having legislated on the subject, it can only be according to
the prohibitions that it is a *misdemeanor* or the act *void.*

The Stat. Cha. 2. c. 7. goes farther than merely prohibiting
secular work and employment, and enjoins what is to be
done on that day ; "Every person or persons, shall on the
Lord's day, apply themselves to the observance of the same,
by exercising themselves thereon in the duties of piety
and true religion publicly and privately." But by our act
22 April, '94, it is left to the conscience of the party, or the
censure of the religious society to which they belong, if they
belong to any, as to the duties in which they may employ themselves. It restrains only the doing worldly labour on that
day. The compact of our political association embracing
jews, or seventh day baptists, or others who do not use that
day for the purposes of devotion, must be comprehended,
so far as respects the exercise of public employment of a
worldly nature.

It may be observed that whether of *divine* or *civil* institution merely, the observance of one day in seven, is a great
political good; and it cannot interfere with the rights of

conscience in jew or others, who are left at liberty to observe
other days of their own chusing.   If it is even at the expence
of being thrown out of a portion of time for their occupations, in addition to that out of which they throw themselves,
private convenience must give way to general good.

———•+•———

IV Bl. Com. 136.

THE Commonwealth v. Dennis and others. At the trial
of this indictment, the testimony for the commonwealth
being closed, it was moved on behalf of one of the defendants, that the jury pass upon him (that defendant) in the
first instance, *nothing having been proved against him.* But
the court would not say that there was no evidence ; on the
contrary, there was evidence upon which it was not impossible but that the jury might convict. But why not let the
jury pass upon him that in case even of conviction ; the offence charged, not being of such a nature as to exclude his
testimony even on conviction, he might be sworn a witness
for the other two defendants. *They had an interest in his
testimony,* and it had deprived them of it in joining them in
the same indictment. The inclination of my mind, at first,
on general principles of justice, was to let the jury pass
upon this defendant, against whom the least was proved,
and in whose case some doubt of his acting might be thought
to exist. But more advised, I thought proper to refuse the
motion, and directed the verdict to be taken against the
whole.

I saw a difficulty in the particular case. For the indictment being for a riot, if the first was convicted it would be
of a *riot;* and yet by his testimony, I mean the convicted,
the remaining two might be acquitted of the riot, by his testimony, *an assault and battery only* proved, which would involve an inconsistency upon the record.

The same in the case of conspiracy, where two being
necessary to constitute the offence, the conviction of one and

acquittal of the other, on the testimony of the convicted, would involve the same inconsistency : and the private mischief of the loss of testimony to one must give way to the general inconvenience of admitting it in such cases.

But in the case of other misdemeanors ; an assault and battery, for instance, this inconvenience would not exist; and even though some evidence is given against one of *several defendants*, yet why not take a verdict in the case of one to let in his testimony for the others ? But it does not seem to be the policy of the law to carry the matter far. And it is only in a case where *no evidence* is given, that the defendant is considered as having a claim of right to have a verdict taken *separately in his case.*

The plaintiff cannot hinder letting judgment go by default against one, and then he becomes a witness for the co-defendants, even in a case where there *is evidence.* But this is his act. But he cannot move to have his name struck out of the declaration, there being no evidence against one, for this would be putting it to the court, to say whether there is evidence. But he can move to let the jury pass upon his case separately.

The present Lord Ellenborough in a late case which I do not cite, but which I have looked at to inform myself as to the reason of others ; for I do not understand the late act of Assembly as precluding the looking at English decisions either by counsel or by court, but the *citing them only.* And in a late case on an indictment against several defendants for a misdemeanor in obstructing a proceeding under a penal law ; two pleaded guilty, and the other not guilty, and offered those before him, as witnesses, there being an end of the matter as to them, agreeable to the case in 1 Strange 633. But the reason given in a modern case, for rejecting the evidence appears to be *fallacious.* " There is," says he, " a community of guilt. They are all engaged in an unlawful proceeding. The offence is the offence of all ; not the act of the individual only." Is not this assuming the fact that the others in whose case this co-defendant was about to give evidence, *were guilty.* It might be that his evidence, as it was the object of offering it, would go to shew that these men, notwithstanding what had appeared, were innocent.

The counsel admit in the argument in this case, that where no evidence is againt the co-defendant, yet the jury must pass upon him and acquit before he can be heard.

The court adopts this language that in that case he might be sworn.

The being liable for costs is spoken of; and these out of the way, by being acquitted, or by being fined, the competency is admitted.

A defendant in an information against whom no evidence given, is admissible for the others. 2 Bar. 582. But, I take it, a verdict must be taken before he can be heard.

In misdemeanors, parties indicted separately from the parties on trial, or not indicted, though concerned in the transaction, are competent witnesses; and the same rule holds good in many species of civil actions, when the witness is not made a defendant.

As if A. and B. be indicted for assaulting the same persons, and tried separately, they are good witnesses for each other. 1 M'Nally, 204.

And so where A. B. and C. are tried in three several actions on the statute, for a supposed perjury, in their evidence concerning the same thing, they may be good witnesses in such action. 2 Hawk. pl. cr. c. 46.

It may seem unreasonable that a plaintiff or prosecutor, should have it in his power, by joining in an action or indictment to deprive a defendant of testimony that he would otherwise have had. But there being no evidence, in the opinion of the court, will restrain this arbitrary joining, and making a defendant, by giving leave to strike the name out of the declaration, or by directing a verdict to be taken for him. But if in all cases defendants in misdemeanors joined, could be witnesses for each other, it would tend to defeat every action, and indictment.

It would seem to be giving an undue advantage and the policy of the law would not seem to have come so far.

Since making the above note with a view to report to the court, notice having been given by the counsel of an intention to move in bank, I have met with something to the point, and supporting some of the ideas I have thrown out. This in 13 East, beginning 411, in the notes to the case in that page, referring to several cases of the ante-revolutionary period. The King *v.* Nichols, 17 G. II. 1742. The defendant was indicted for a *conspiracy* at Hick's Hall. The jury found him guilty of a conspiracy with one Bygrave. They likewise found that Bygrave died before this indictment found ; and therefore pray the advice of the court whether the defendants were guilty as laid in the indictment? By Lee c. justice. " It is certain that in all conspiracies, there must be *two*, at least, or no indictment will lie, and therefore if one be acquitted, the other cannot be guilty." But that case differs ; because one being acquitted, the conviction of his companion on the same record must be directly repugnant and contradictory to the other. But here no such contradiction, where the one is dead, any more than where one of the defendants refuses to come in plead, yet judgment may be given against the other.

Rex *v.* Kinnersly cited by Eyre, c. j. in Kinnersly's case, indictment for that A. and B. cum multis aliis, illicito, riotorè, routosè assemblaverunt, &c. A. acquitted ; yet B. convicted on the score of the cum multis aliis being, which saved the appearance of contradiction on the record.

In the case of the Commonwealth *v.* M'Clean and another, the jury having first passed upon M'Clean, and he being acquitted on the plea of *insanity* set up for him, it occurred as a question, whether the other defendant, it being a *conspiracy* that was charged, must not be discharged from the indictment, it requiring *two*, and it being alleged that A. could not be guilty of a conspiracy with B. who had no mind. It seemed to me at the time that he might have conspired in the act, though it could not be said in the will of the other; but of this I had doubts, and had a conviction taken place would have expected a motion in arrest of judgment; but the other was acquitted.

This all bears upon the difficulty I have suggested, and which governed me in the case of the Commonwealth *v.* Deuris and others, the impossibility of admitting the defendants to be witnesses for each other without involving the inconsistency of one being found guilty of a riot, and the other acquitted, there being no cum multis aliis laid in the indictment.

——◦——

IT is provided by the constitution of Pennsylvania, that " in prosecutions for the publications of papers, investigating the official conduct of officers, or men in a public capacity, or, where the matter published is proper for public information, the truth thereof may be given in evidence." There is in this sentence, after the diversative conjunction or, what the grammarians call an ellipsis, a greek word which signifies deficiency, or the want of that which must be supplied in the mind, to make the sentence complete. In completing this sentence in our minds, we must go back, and take up what part of the sentence preceding the conjunction, is necessary to connect what follows the conjunction. In doing which we shall read the whole thus, " In prosecutions for the publications of papers investigating the official conduct of officers, or men in a public capacity; or in prosecutions for the publication of papers where the matter published is proper for public information, the truth may be given in evidence."

This may seem to carry the provision farther than the *investigation of official conduct;* for it may be said, that a matter may be proper for *public information*, though not relating to *official conduct.* But on that construction, there would have been no necessity for the specification of *official conduct;* for it would take in *all conduct*, where the matter published was proper for public information; and, therefore in applying the second branch of the sentence, we are warranted in applying it to other than the conduct of officers, or men

in a public capacity; and to consider the words, "the publication of papers, where the matter published may be proper for public information," as introducing a provision in
the case of those who are *not officers*, or *men in a public capacity*. But the restriction to *official conduct* in the first
branch of the sentence, must, from analogy, restrain the provision, in the second branch, to the *official qualifications* of
of such as are candidates for offices. To extend it farther,
would carry it beyond all rule that could be laid down, as
to what should be a matter proper for public information.
But as to what is matter proper for public information, the
officer who prosecutes, must judge, in the first instance;
and it would seem reasonable, and in the spirit of the privilege of *giving the truth in evidence*, that the accused should
have notice from the indictment itself, that it is such a case,
as the prosecutor for the state, considers to be within the
privilege to *give the truth in evidence*. This reason will a
fortiore apply, if matter proper for public information is carried beyond the official conduct of officers, or the official
qualifications of *candidates for office*. But ever restraining
this as we do, there would be great advantage to the accused,
in having the information from the indictment itself, that the
truth might be given in evidence, and this information would
be given from the allegation that the matter of the publication in question, was prosecuted because *false*.

But can an indictment, in contemplation of law, be prof-
fered, which does not charge *an offence?* The investigation
of official conduct, or where the matter published is proper
for public information, may be a duty: it is certainly a privilege. There must be an offence charged; or how can a
grand jury be justified in finding a bill? An indictment for a
trespass, without alleging a *breach of the peace*, cannot be
supported. And so in the case of every misdemeanor, and
of every crime; the act alleged to have been committed,
must of itself, constitute an offence against the public. *Falsehood* on the subject matter of the indictment is here made
the essence of it, by admitting the truth to justify. The
law of libel is changed in this particular; and the prosecu-

F f

tion must be modelled according to the change. The necessity of alleging the falsehood of the libel in an action for a libel must be the same on an indictment, where the same proof is made to constitute a defence. There is no distinguishing or getting over it on principle of individual safety or public policy; or the analogy of precedent. Nor ought we to use astutia or strain a construction to get over it; but rather in the spirit of the constitution, amplify and give a liberal construction to a remedial provision; and which, the nature of our republican institutions seems to demand, for nothing can be so conservative of a free government as perpetual vigilance, and free discussion of the integrity, or wisdom of the administration of affairs, or of the qualifications for official duty in such as are called upon, or offer themselves for office or delegation. The *manner* in which this is done may be *exceptionable;* but the thing is *necessary,* and without which the spirit of liberty could not be preserved. I incline therefore, even in a doubtful construction, to lean to that most favorable to the *freedom of the press;* and the privilege of citizens to be heard on the official conduct of officers, or men in a public capacity, or where the matter published is proper for public information.

That this is a *remedial provision* of the constitution, will be known from a consideration of what had been understood to be the rule before the constitution, viz. " that on an indictment for a libel the *truth could not be given in evidence,* it being immaterial with respect to the essence of a libel, whether the matter of it were true or false, since the *provocation* and not the *falsity* was the thing to be punished criminally; though the falsehood of it might aggravate its guilt, and enhance its punishment." 4 Black. 150. For which, so far as respected private persons and matters not proper for public information, there might be reason; but for which, in the cases specified, the public interest, in the opinion of the framers of the constitution, required a *different rule.* Now if the truth is to be given in evidence in the cases specified, why shall not the *falsehood be alleged?* Will not the truth amount to a justification? It could not be the meaning that the truth might be given in evidence in extenuation of the offence; for that would go to the court, and not to the jury; for though it might affect the punishment, it would not change the nature of the verdict, there being no such thing as a verdict of *less* or *more* guilty, but simply guilty or not guilty. The truth therefore must justify; and is admissible in evidence with a view to that effect. Shall not the falsehood then be charged in the indictment? in the case of an information, it is charged; and no information unless where, in the nature of it, an exception lies, will be allowed to be filed but on affidavit of the falsehood of the libel. Doug. 372. The grand jury can have the oath of the prosecutor who claims the interference of the commonwealth, and in the specified cases, may be sent up by the officer for the commonwealth; and there is the same reason as in the case of an information, why he should first lay a ground by an averment of his innocence, in regard to the allegations of the libel, before the indictment is sustained, so far as to be found; and with a view to this, falsehood must be charged. " The charge must contain such a description of the crime, that the defendant may know what crime he is called upon to answer, that the jury may be warranted in their conclusion of guilty or not guilty upon the premises delivered to them; and that the court may see such a *definite crime*, that they may apply the punishment the law prescribes." Cowp. 682. An affirmative verdict couples the probate with the allegata; and we cannot legally apply the verdict to more than the allegata, or charge of the indictment, which of itself containing no offence, no culpability can exist; and the technical finding culpabiliš or guilty, can refer only to the act alleged, which is not criminal. It will not be seen from an inspection of the record that the court had before them a conviction whereon to ground a judgment. For it stands indifferent whether the publication is an offence or justifiable. But maliciously publishing, as laid in an indictment, will not that constitute a crime? Taking it in the popular acceptation of the word it will not. For meaning personal enmity, it can affect only the political, or moral nature of the act. For even malice expressly proved, in doing what is justifiable, will not make it blameable, though it may take away from the merit of the act so far as respects the doer; and where what is done is wrong, *the best intention* cannot justify the act; for evidence of the quo animo can absolve from guilt only, where it goes to shew *that the actor did not mean to do the act*, or a criminal act of which it was the consequence. It cannot alter the nature of the act, though it may reduce the *degree* of the malignity; and be considered by the judge in affixing the punishment, where the law gives him a discretion. Evidence of express malice in the case of a malicious prosecution will not support an action, provided there was *probable cause* for the prosecution. This proves that *malice* in the popular acceptation of the term, can go but in aggravation of a wrong committed, and is not of the essence of the wrong. The *malice which the law knows*, is quite a different thing; it is the bad mind which is inferred from the bad act, and the act must be established before badness of mind can be inferred. Ex malitia, publishing, is the characteristic of the act of *falsely* publishing; and I do not find that in the case of any other offence, the allegation of an ex malitia will supply all the allegation of a crime in the act done. It will not in felony; nor will it supply the defect of force and arms in a trespass, so as to render it indictable. It may not be necessary to constitute a seditious writing that it be false; for it is not the truth of the words that is in question, but the tendency and object of words to unsettle the government, or obstruct the laws.

The truth of speculative opinions cannot be traversable; or the policy of a law; and therefore in seditious attempts, by publications, to unsettle the government, and excite opposition to the laws, the falsity of opinions need not be averred; but in an indictment, though the court on which a verdict has been for the commonwealth, charges the " combining and intending by the publication seditiously to disturb the peace, tranquillity, and happiness, of the people of the state," yet it is as a consequence of the libel on the person of the officer; and it would seem that it could not be considered an indictment for sedition, and out of the provi-

sion of the constitution for a personal libel; for an indictment might be so framed in every case as to give it the appearance of an indictment for the sedition, and so defeat the
provision.

But if falsity must be alleged in every bill sent up to a
grand jury, in the case of a publication personally libellous,
how shall the jury ascertain the falsity where in the nature of
the case the prosecutor cannot be sworn to the falsity; as
where the defamation consists of general abuse, as depravity
of heart, disaffection to institutions, intentions hostile to liberty, &c. I answer that if an indictment can ly at all, in our
republican government, for such freedom of opinion with regard to public officers, the grand jury who must presume
in favour of the officer will be justifiable in making the accusation of falsity, and the finding is but an accusation. But
if maliciously will supply the term falsity, how will the grand
jury be justifiable in finding the maliciously, which is but
an implication from the falsity, and yet it will not be said
that without the term maliciously, the publication barely set
out in the indictment could support an indictment. The
truth might have been given in evidence and the words proved false; but not appearing on the record, it must stand as
if judgment had gone on the barely publishing the words.

When the truth may reasonably be expected to be given
in evidence, in all cases where it exists, the leading the way
for it, by charging falsity, may seem to be unnecessary; but
I must feel myself absolved from the rules of strict construction, which the law applies to criminal proceedings, before
I could think otherwise.

Bad precedents are set in good cases, is a principle which
will apply in all cases, and which though it may regard *form*,
yet will protect *substance*, and fortify the provision of the
constitution, by shewing from the form of charging the offence, what defence may be set up; and more especially, as
a distinction might creep in between admitting the truth in
extenuation, and in justification; and it might be, grow into
a construction, that though admitted to the jury, it was in
order to reach the court, and direct their discretion in modi-

fying the sentence. On this last consideration which perhaps outweighs all, I think the alleging the publication to
be false, ought to be held essential.

IV Black. Com. 150.

By an act of Assembly, 1809, it was provided " that no
person shall be subject to prosecution by *indictment* for the
publication of papers examining the proceedings of the legislature, or any branch of government, or for investigating
the official conduct of officers, or men in public capacity."
And sec. 11. " That, in all actions or criminal prosecutions
of a libel, the defendant may plead *the truth thereof* in *justification, or give the same in evidence.*" This act was subject
to a limitation of three years, " *and from thence to the end of
the next session of the legislature.*" I have not seen in the
title of acts of the last session, a continuance of this act : It
would seem therefore *to have expired.*

It was a great safety *to the judiciary* to be relieved from
the necessity of imposing fines in case of prosecutions under
the law as it before stood. For the imposing fines in the
case of men in public capacity prosecuting, never failed to
draw with it much obloquy from the libellers, and the people not discriminating the *liberty* of the press, from the
abuses of it, most usually ranged themselves in their sympa-
thies on the side of those prosecuted. Hence it was that
fines were remitted ; or where imprisonment made a part of
the sentence, in the case of editors of Gazettes especially,
their subscriptions were increased ; and where the authorities of the publications were given up, or where they avowed
their writing, it was a passport to public favour, and oftentimes to the suffrages of the community for a public trust.
This proved that such prosecutions by indictment in the case
of libel were far from being popular.

The judiciary found a safety in being relieved from the
necessity of imposing fines, or sentencing to imprisonment ;

for, though their own flanks were left uncovered, from this protection of the law being withdrawn, so that an indictment could not be sustained on their behalf for matters relating *to official conduct;* yet they could not but find it safer to be exposed to general calumny, than to be under the necessity of drawing upon themselves the attacks of the malevolent, or their friends, who were personally irritated; and, came forward to take a revenge *through the medium of the public, papers.*

But, the libellers themselves would not seem to have found their account in this law. For prosecutions by *action being* now the only mode of obtaining satisfaction by the persons aggrieved, and the juries assessing damages which they began to do pretty liberally, they could not raise the cry of persecution, not *for conscience sake,* but for what was equally *sacred,* the liberty of the press; which was alleged; however unreasonaably, in their case, to be concerned.

Owing to these or *other causes,* I do not find that during *this interregnum* of the law, as it might be stiled, libelling had increased; and yet, the natural consequence would seem to be, that it would have increased. For it would seem to have been a great matter for the libellers, to have it provided for them under sec. 11. that *the truth shall in all cases of indictment be given in evidence.* So that where a *public* or *private person was the subject of the libel,* he must be under the necessity of proving the calumny *false;* which, even *though false and groundless,* might not be convenient, or pleasing thing to do. For all libel, usually consists in *caricature* or *exaggeration* of the picture, and it might not be easy to discriminate and shew to the conviction of the world, what was *excess,* and what was *real.*

But what is more, there are many things which may be, and often are in the hands of the malicious made the subject of slander, which though in a great degree groundless, yet may have some foundation in *collateral circumstances;* so that the *refutation* must affect those concerned, or others, not *to the extent,* but in *some degree.* They might judge it better, therefore to bear the whole, than to have the matter stirred. What might affect *domestic peace, or the reputation of a neighbour*, might also be a reason for not wishing to have the matter brought into public view.

How the act might have been for the administration of justice generally salutary, and otherwise, is another question. The power which the courts had *by the common law* to impose fines, or imprison in the case of defamers, was not a trust for themselves, but for the people. If the people chose to take it away, it was their affair : they were principally interested. The officer for the time being, judicial or otherwise, had not more an interest in the suppression of personal abuse than the rest of the community.

It might have been one reason why *libelling* did not seem to prevail more during the period we speak of, that, before this time it had proceeded to the utmost excess, and the public mind had begun to revolt at the *licentiousness* of the press ; not only the conduct of individuals, in discharge of public functions, legislative, judicial, or ministerial, was misrepresented ; but matters which did, in no way concern the discharge of their duty were made the subject of animadversion, and reproach. Nor was this all ; but such as had pretensions to office were attacked in order to defeat ; and the effect of the defamation in this particular was felt by the community. A certain editor was known to boast *that he could write down any man in six weeks.* Cobbet and Callender, I do not mention *resident* or *living* persons, had done good service indirectly, though they did not mean it, in bringing into disrepute the language of what the English call Billingsgate ; and that abuse which knows no restraint of decency, delicacy, or refinement. They had set such an example that all men saw the consequence of *approving*, and the more viperous ceased to be encouraged in their burlesque, and malicious, and often *false colouring and representation.*

It was thus that in Massachusettss, in the time of those fanatics the Mathers, when credulity in witch-craft prevailed, and whole families were put to death on this suspicion, it was in vain that reason and philosophy interposed. Not until the accusation became so general as to alarm the bulk, would they for a moment be brought to doubt of *the credit of the testimony ;* or to see the absurdity of the belief.

The constitution of this commonwealth, by *implication* would seem to give *the prosecution* by indictment. For though the term may apply to the prosecution by a civil suit, yet the provision of giving *the truth in evidence*, which had been always allowable in civil actions, shews the term to have a reference to a proceeding as for a misdemeanor. It cannot therefore be said, not to be an abridgment of *constitutional right*, for men in a public capacity not to have *the privilege of prosecuting by indictment;* and where the matter published, is *not proper for public information*, to have *the truth given in evidence.*

In the case of a *private person*, the prosecuting by indictment is not taken away by this act, but the specification in the constitution of men *in a public capacity*, and a matter *proper for public information*, where *the truth may be given in evidence*, carries with it an *implication*, that in a prosecution by indictment, in the case of a *private person*, the truth cannot be given in evidence. So far therefore this act was *a departure from the spirit of the constitution.*

But is it not reasonable that the truth *in all cases* should be given in evidence? The reason of the common law, which has grown up from experience, would seem to have not. And if we apply our own reason, it would not be difficult, a priore, to carry the giving the truth in evidence farther than the constitution would seem to have done. This is in the case of men in public capacity, and where the matter published, is *proper for public information.*

It might be said, that all men in public office are fair game, and may be hunted down by bringing into view even their foibles, extra-judicial aberrations, and exaggerating, or caricaturing them. Or more plausibly it might be said, that extra-judicial immorality, or even a deviation from the *dignity* of official station; and the

—decens et decorum—

might deserve to be stigmatized. But allow this to a satyrist, and where will it end? Give an inch and he will take an ell. He will not be content with a candid examination of the defect or error, but carry it far beyond the truth, like some of those minerals that eat away the fungus, and then corrode the solid flesh. Will it not be sufficient that *all matters of this nature may be brought before the legislature,* who have the constitutional power of removing from office ; and in which case and that of infirmity and incapacity it is alone perhaps the *constitutional proceeding.* For in the case of a *misdemeanor in office, the redress by impeachment is provided.*

But, in the case of *private* persons who endeavour to pursue, in humble life,

      ——The noiseless tenor of their way,
Or who court the shade, and have chosen the
      ——fallentis semita vitæ,

Why drag their frailties from their dread abode ; why introduce, though *true,* what does not concern the community ? It is unprofitable to the public and increases *the miseries of human life* to individuals, which are enough, God knows, in all conditions, situations, and relations. That even *the truth ought not to be told at all times,* is a proverb as old as the experience of man. Breaches of the peace would be unavoidable in such licence were permitted for a length of time. For I lay out of the question that breaches of the peace, have not perhaps multiplied within these three years, during which time this act has existed. For I look to the *permanent effect,* and this must be deduced from the *nature of things,* and *the experience of ages,* rather than the experiment of a period.

In *the nature of things* it is impossible, but that where matters are brought into view of no *public concern;* whether in the case of *public men,* or private *persons,* and where the matter is rather vexatious than infamous, wounding to the feelings, more than injurious to the estate, a breach of the peace should not ensue, and it is upon this experience that the common law is founded, in not suffering such matters to be at all broached or any thing heard about the *truth of them.* For being nothing to the community whether *true* or *false,* but of great consequence that *the peace be preserved,* it is the principle that truth or no truth is no justification of libelers in such cases. On the contrary it is the law, that the greater *the appearance of* truth given to the libel, it is the more provoking, which maxim misunderstood, has led to that dic-

tum, that " *the greater the truth, the greater the libel.*" Or
perhaps it may be explained by saying, that the greater the
weakness, or aberrations which humanity would keep out of
view, it is the more provoking to have it brought before the
public, and the more irresistibly impels to outrage ; and for
which reason, the law will more guard against such provocation and consider it the greater libel.   Be that as it may, the
policy of the law is the preservation of the peace.   And, is it
reasonable that the law should extend the prosecution by indictment to *assaults* and *batteries*, and permit no excuse of
words or writing to be set up as justification, or even given
in evidence on the plea of not guilty, as matter of excuse ;
but to the court only after verdict ; and yet that *the truth of*
an indictment for words, or writing the truth should be admitted to justify the speaking, or writing, when the proving
the words false, or even malicious, would not *justify*, or on the
trial even *excuse* the battery ? Shall the *flagellum*, or whip of
calumny have greater privilege than the *club of strength?*

Intending these strictures more for the legislature, than
the profession ; for I would not take it amiss if the greater
part of lawyers *should think themselves above my instruction*,
I do not enter into a consideration *of the law of libels*.   But
so far only as to take notice of the observations of Barrington on the statutes quoted by Judge Tucker in his edition of
the commentaries ; for I have not Barrington by me at the
present, to refer to ; viz. "That the general rules laid down
by the court of Star-chamber in Pickering's case, 5 Coke 125,
from whence the doctrines contained in *the text* are borrowed, are either extra-judicial, or not maintained, one of which
Lord Coke himself contradicted on another occasion ; and
that the reason of the questionable doctrines contained in that
case, arises from every one of those rules being borrowed
from the civil law, that, when we consider *the source* from
whence these doctrines have been brought to us, the reasonableness of them ought to be examined before we yield our
full assent to *all of them*."

It is my way of thinking that the *reasonableness of all
doctrine ought to be examined*, and this on the ground of pub-

lic policy, and general convenience; but I will acknowledge that I am not able to discover any thing unreasonable in the doctrines as laid down in the *text* of Blackstone.

Some of the doctrines laid down, 5 Coke, 125, may be derived from the civil law; but so far as the *text of Blackstone goes there would seem to be nothing that has not its source in the common law, or sanctioned by it.*

It may be observed that Blackstone does not adopt every principle *laid down in the star-chamber case*, particularly that " where a man finds a libel, if it concerns a magistrate or other public person, the *finder ought presently to deliver it to a magistrate* to the intent that by examination and industry, the author may be found out and punished." This principle I do not approve. For I think the finder is not under an obligation to take any notice of it in the case of a public person, unless it concern *the community*, but is at liberty to burn it, as it is admitted he may do, in the case of a libel on a private person. But taking it that it is a writing which affects the safety of the government, and in which case it is, I presume, that it is meant to be enjoined as a duty, I do not say that I find even this exceptionable. But the court of star-chamber got an ill name, and deservedly, from many usurpations, and the proceedings in the case of libel as in other matters, being by information, and *without a jury*, it was justly odious, and even its doctrines, where salutary, were suspected and unpopular; and hence, to brand a doctrine with the name of star-chamber, carries with it a degree of reprobation.

IV Bl. Com. 194.

BY an act of March 3d, 1812, the governor was required " to request the Attorney General, to draft and prepare a bill consolidating the whole of the penal laws of this commonwealth; and, suggesting what additions, alterations, and changes should take place in the system, for the purpose of laying before the next legislature." I know not whether the attorney general may think proper to suggest any alterations, or change, with respect to the punishment of death in any case. But, be that as it may, the expression of the will of the legislature to hear what may be suggested, generally, on the penal code, has emboldened me, though not within the legislative request, to suggest what has occurred to me, in my reflections on the subject of *capital punishment in the case of murder in the first degree;* which now remains the only case, in which, the punishment is *capital.*

In limine, or, at the threshhold of an examination of what relates to this, we are arrested by the language of Revelation; " whoso sheddeth man's blood, by man shall his blood be shed." Gen. 9th, 6.

The context, as the divines would say, is in these words; " and surely your blood of your lives will I require; at the hand of every *beast,* will I require it; and at the hand of man; at the hand of every man's brother, will I require the life of man."

Were it not for the preceding words, I should have been disposed, to have considered those of the text, as containing a *denunciation merely,* of what, in the course of things, would most usually, and most naturally happen; viz : that, in revenge of the person slain, some one would be prompted to slay the slayer; so that, in a course of retributive justice; and, in this sense, it might be said, " whoso sheddeth man's blood, by man shall his blood be shed :" but the words of the context do not leave room, in fair and candid construction, for such a meaning, to be put upon them : it must be taken, as enjoining *the avenging of the blood of man.*

But is this injunction to be considered, as respecting men in a state of nature; or, in a state of society? Doubtless, not to men *in a state of nature only;* but also in a state of society; because being promulgated to Noah, who was in a state of society; though his family consisted but of eight persons; it cannot but be considered as extending to that association; and, to all others that might spring from them. This must silence the allegation of those who undertake to say, that *no power can exist in the social state*, to put a man to death; *I speak of moral or lawful power*.

But, taking it up, independent of Revelation; and, on the principle of reason, why is it that the lawfulness of putting to death in a state of society, shall be questioned? It is said to be because the individual entering into the social state, can surrender to the community, no power, but that which he himself, in a state of nature had possessed; and having no power over his own life, he could not surrender that which he had not. But this *is a fallacy;* for, it is not a power over his own life which he surrenders; but *the right to preserve it*, at the expense of the life of him who would take it away.

It is this right of self-preservation which is surrendered; and unless in a case, where self-preservation is inconsistent with delay, the taking the life of an assailant is not warranted by any municipal law. But this right of self-preservation so surrendered to a community, warrants the interference of the body politic to protect from the assailant, who attempts homicide; and, if that cannot be done, to provide against what may be presumed to be likely to be atttempted by the same offender against the life of others. What can this provision be? The most certain, unquestionably, will be *putting an end to the power of action in the offender.* This must render it physically certain that this individual who has shown himself to be hostis humani generis; or, in the light of an enemy of mankind, will not again have it in his power to take away the life of another. But would it not be enough, if it could be rendered *morally certain*, that he should not have it in his power again, to take away the life of any one? Does not the highest degree of probability approach so nearly to absolute, as to be scarcely distinguishable from it: to be, in fact, to all practicable purposes, the same thing? A man so confined as to be to all human probability, out of the way, and not likely to have it in his power to take the life of another, would seem to be much the same thing as a dead man to the social state; and no longer endangering the safety of an individual of the community.

But still he is not dead; physically dead, says the objector; and the " whoso sheddeth man's blood," &c. is in the way. I grant it is; but this injunction, cannot be considered more than *a general rule*, and subject to exceptions. What was the occasion of this precept to Noah? It was the destruction of the whole race of man, by a flood, eight persons excepted. What was the object? The preservation of man in order to replenish the earth. Will it not be inconsistent with this object to take away the life of a man, provided the preservation of human life can be equally guarded and attained? This is the exception; and as the jurists say, makes it a part of the rule; it must be considered as co-existent with it, and involved in the nature of it. Where the letter of the law is inconsistent to any extent, with the spirit of it, the spirit must prevail. This is a rule of interpretation in all laws human and divine.

But the legislator of the Jews who has recorded this precept; for we assume it that he was the author of the five books, or Pentateuch, as the Septuagint calls it, has given us a practical application of the precept; and has laid it down in his law, that, "the murderer shall be put to death."— Numb. xxv. 6. This goes, in express terms, to sanction the right of a society to inflict death. But what was the state of the Jewish society to whom this law was given? Were they in a situation to be able to preserve themselves from homicide, without such extermination of an individual who had committed murder? In a wandering state of society, in a wilderness, had they the means of self-preservation by confinement, and keeping to hard labour. This being the case, could the injunction be understood otherwise than as having relation to the condition of the people? Can it be of binding obligation at all times, and in all cases to put to death; and not rather subject to the reason of the law given to Noah, *the preservation of the life of man?* Shall the slayer be slain, who not only can be put in a way to be restrained from a possibility of committing homicide; but may be also rendered useful, in his confinement to hard labour? It would seem to be subverting the end of all punishment, *precavention and reformation.*

The precept "whoso sheddeth man's blood by man shall his blood be shed," still recurs. What has been the *application* of this precept from the earliest existence of *christian communities?* Christianity *is a ground of the common law, which is our birthright;* and, yet, this law admits the power of the society *to pardon.* What is this but *to dispense* with the injunction given to Noah, that "whoso sheddeth man's blood by man shall his blood be shed?"

By our constitution, the executive magistrate is vested with *the power to pardon.* A felony of murder is not exempted from this power. If the magistrate, who in this particular represents the power of the society, can pardon, *he can reprieve.* Can there be any thing in his way to hold the criminal in confinement for life *under the idea of a reprieve?* Could this be said to be otherwise than a dispensing with the law of God; and yet our law, immemorially and our late and present constitution warrants this.

If our magistrate has the power of reprieving in this way, it may be said, why not exercise it? There is one thing wanting, which, may be a reason for not exercising it; and this is the not having a power under a reprieve, *to employ at hard labour;* and thereby, to relieve, in some degree the community from the burthen of the convict's support. He has the power to continue a reprieve without limit; but it must be at an expence, which, did the law go to embrace this case, might, in a great measure, be avoided; or rather the service of a criminal turned to an indemnification to some extent, for the injury to the society.

It is remarkable that it makes a part of the text and context of the scripture in this place, that, in the case of *a beast* causing the death of a man, it shall be put to death; "your lives will I require at the hand of every beast:" and agreeable to this is the injunction of the Jewish Legislator. "If an ox gore a man or a woman, that they die, then, the ox shall be surely stoned." Yet in *christian countries*, this has never been carried into effect; the putting the beast to death in any way; and yet this makes a part of the injunction to Noah; and if this is dispensed with under all christian institutions; for I know of no exception, why not admit of the like softening in the rigor of the precept, under the christian dispensation, in the case of a homicide by man? Under our common law, in the case of a beast, causing or even occasioning the life of man, it is forfeited to the king. 1 B. Com. 300. Why not the like commutation for death in the case of man; *the forfeiture of the labor for life of the culprit to the community.* My deduction is that the injunction to Noah is not of universal application under all circumstances; and under the christian dispensation is taken away altogether. So that, though I *hold it lawful to put to death for murder,* yet I resolve it into a question of *expediency,* and, subject to *the reason of the law,* the security of the peace, and the preservation of the life of man. If, consistent with this, the criminal can be spared, it is inexpedient to put to death. If, on experience, the state of society should be found to be such as to permit this, without endangering the community, I should think capital punishment unnecessary; and it is only in a case where unavoidable, and necessary, that I should think it justifiable.

"*Ense recidendum immedicabile vulnus.*"

In the state of society in which Noah, and his immediate descendants, must, for a length of time, be, and, under the circumstances, in which the Jews were: more especially, before their fixed habitations in Judea, and, improved establishments, it might be impossible, and it was certainly *morally* impossible, that the people could be safe, and a murderer be permitted to live; but *a very different degree of proof was required, from that under the common law of England,* which, yet, continues to be our law. For, by the Jewish laws, "whoso killeth any person, the murderer shall be put to death by *the mouth of witnesses;* but *one witness* shall not testify against any person to cause him to die." Numb. xxxv. 30. And again, "at the mouth of two witnesses or three witnesses, shall he that is worthy of death be put to death, but at the mouth of one witness, he shall not be put to death." Deut. xvii. 6. Query, ought not the testimony of these witnesses to be direct; and, to the actual fact of killing; and not to *circumstances only*. I would take it, that the testimony must have been positive, and to *the actual fact of killing*; and not to be deduced from *the presumption of circumstance*. Under our law, one witness is sufficient to convict; and, even, *where the testimony goes but to circumstance*. In this respect, our law is more *sanguinary* than that of the Jews: and, even, though the injunction of Moses might be said to be given in this case, as in another, " because of the hardness of their hearts." Might it not then be a reason for a commutation of a capital punishment for imprisonment for life, that, especially, where a conviction had taken place, on the credit of *one witness*, or *from circumstance on the evidence of more than one*. Unless the code is so ameliorated, in this particular, it is more sanguinary than even the Jewish law; for the lesser degree of evidence being sufficient to convict, makes the law more sanguinary. Nevertheless this is under the *christian dispensation*, which has been considered as softening the rigour of the Mosaic precepts in many instances.

It is not my meaning to suggest an alteration of the law in regard to circumstantial evidence being sufficient to convict; for *circumstance often speaks stronger than words ;* and *there could be no security from assassination*, unless the law were so ; but it will be a consideration for the doctrine of *continual reprieve* which I advocate ; as on a conviction from circumstantial evidence, if providence should at any time, bring to light the innocence of one condemned, as has sometimes happened, it might not have been altogether out of the power of the society to *relieve his person from confinement; and his name from infamy.*

But the restraining the malefactor from doing hurt, as *to future time*, in his own person, is not the only object of punishment. *The example* to others will be a preservative against what they may do. This will bring it to the question; which is most likely to affect, the carting to the gallows, or to the place of hard labour and confinement for life. I do

not take it there would be much difference as to the effect.
For I count but little on the effect of a *present terror*, however *shocking the spectacle*. The best means of preventing
the catastrophe, will be found in restraining the passions by
a useful occupation, and impressing moral and religious instruction on the mind. Præstat cautela quam medela. In
the countries of Europe, Britain in particular, where the effect of capital punishment has been tried abundantly, it has
not been effectual; not more so than transportation and exile;
which in most cases has been substituted for it. We have
no Botany-bay to which we can transport; but we can accomplish the same thing by confinement and hard labour.
What then would be the amendment, in this particular,
which I would propose to the penal code? It would be, that,
on conviction for murder in the first degree, the convict shall
undergo *for life* the same punishment, which on a conviction
for murder in the second degree, he shall be sentenced to
undergo for years; the time specified in the act for the amelioration of the penal code of the 22d April, 1794. This
will be *imprisonment at hard labour for life; and death in case
of an escape.*

————

IV Black. Com. 286.

The following observations are an extract from a publication, at the time certain judges of the supreme court were
impeached for the alleged misdemeanor of enforcing a process of contempt for a *constructive trespass*, in the case of a
certain Passmore. The judges were acquitted; but by an
act of assembly, 3d Ap. 1809; and extended 4th Feb. 1812, the
power of the judges to issue attachments, and punish in the
case of *constructive* contempts before alluded to, is taken away.
This is precisely one object which I had in view in these observations published subsequently to the acquittal. But it is
what it behoved the legislature to have done before the impeachment instituted, unless it had been supposed an abuse of the

power in the particular case. And I will not say that it was not an abuse. For the great question in Passmore's case, was, whether, at the time, *there was a suit depending*, having been out of court and before referees. But it was true, it might come back, and be *before a jury.* However this was *the only hook* in the case, and if all had been waived but this, something solid might have been advanced in the prosecution. For the doctrine of a constructive contempt for a publication respecting a suit in court, had been expressly recognized as the law of Pennsylvania, in Oswald's case, 1 Dal. 319. I will not enter into the question whether the doctrine of constructive contempts was properly applied *under a republican government.* But this I will say, that, after the recognition the courts had given it in this state, even after the adoption of the constitution of 1776, it was competent only to the legislature to *restrict* it, as by the act *alluded to,* has been done.

I do not enter into the question I have said, whether the suit in Passmore's case, being before referees, could be said to be depending, as it might come back to court, but I take it that for this reason it could not be said to be *terminated;* but this was the only point in the case. Yet I think it was not judicious nor necessary to have taken it up as a contempt, but to have left it to an indictment, as meriting *peculiar and exemplary* punishment; a libel, a challenge, and a posting, required a heavier proceeding of the law.

The public mind could not understand why it should be called a contempt of the court, what was a *contempt of law only*, and nothing in face of the court had taken place. It was with a view to this that I published the following observations, explaining the reasons on which the common law was founded in this particular.

To explain the meaning and effect of a *consequential contempt.* For it is a thing buried in obscurity by the very phrase that is used to express it. A contempt of the court! One would suppose that it can mean only, treating the court with contempt. That is the meaning of what is called the *direct* contempt; which is "in open insult and resistance to the powers of the court, or the persons of the judges who preside there." 4 Black. 283. But there is what is called the *consequential contempt*, and which is but constructively a contempt, and does not mean a disrespect of the court, but *of the law*. The court which administers the law, is put by a figure for the *law itself*.

It is the technical term, the word contempt that misleads. It is not the court that is despised. Nor do they feel it as such. It is the law; it is the administration of justice that is *slighted*. Common sense can understand this. The scripture has the idea, and the language of the constructive contempt. "He that despiseth you, despiseth me; and he that despiseth me, despiseth him that sent me." It is not the court that is despised; but the law which they are bound to administer. We say "against the peace and dignity of the commonwealth," in an indictment; and yet the commonwealth, that is the body of the people, know nothing of the matter, and feel neither peace nor dignity affected. A tall man, which in the old language means a strong man, impels another with his foot upon what are called the posteriors. The commonwealth, in fact, that is the body of the people, never hear of it, or take any heed of the consequences; nevertheless the law pursues, and punishes in the name of the commonwealth.

But a principal of these contempts, is *an interference with a case depending in the courts of justice*. It is the policy of the law to provide against this, by giving the suitor a right to call upon the court, for a summary interference to restrain it.

But why not turn the matter over to a jury; and let them in the first instance find a bill? I grant that where the libel is upon the court itself, it might be prudent, and would answer the end as well, to let the fact come forward established in that way. But where the cause in court is affected; where any blemish is thrown upon that while it is depending; the right of a third person intervenes; the right of the suitor who calls upon the court to interfere by a *summary proceeding*. Can the court refuse in this case? "I call upon you, Messieurs Judges, for protection; for redress; you have the power; it is *the law of the land*. You are sworn to dispense the law; it is your duty. I demand my right. My case shall be considered pure until it is determined otherwise by a final hearing and decision. Will you tempt me to break the peace; to murder this man that has attacked my interest and my honour, by his publication, relative to the controversy that is in law between us. If you withhold the summary redress, which the law gives, you tempt me to break the peace; and his blood be upon your heads. Shall I lie by, and let the imputation rest upon my cause, or affect the decision, and take my chance of a circuitous prosecution, when the law gives me an immediate protection, in the shape of supporting your dignity? I have a right in the power which you possess; and I call for the exercise of that power."

This is called the power of the court; but it is founded upon *the right of the citizen.* It is the duty of the court to proceed in this way, when called upon; because the suitor has the *election* of the proceeding, by calling on the court; or by *indictment for the libel.*

But under an attachment, you call upon a party to say whether he is not the author of the writing. That is against a principle of the common law; no one is bound to accuse himself; and by a clause of the constitution, no one is compellable " to give evidence against himself." But the parts of the law must be taken together: exceptions subject to the general rules. The proceeding by attachment, and compelling to answer on interrogatories put, existed under the common law, whose maxim it was, " no one is bound to accuse himself." It is a *special case* out of the general principle: and there is good reason for the exception. But whether reason, or not, the exception is as old as the principle. For this proceeding, and such interrogation is of immemorial usage; it is as old as the constitution of the courts themselves. If our constitution had meant to do away this exception, it would have voted it in express terms; more especially as it had been exercised by the courts before the formation of the constitution; and by implication recognized by the legislature itself, in the case of Oswald, taken up by the house. But the constitution gives the courts, " *the powers usually exercised.*" This power was usually exercised, and therefore it is given.

But there is reason for it, independent of law, and constitution. The administration of justice requires it. How can I fix a libel on the author? The presumption is, that my adversary in the cause depending, is the author of the *writing* that affects the merits of it. On this presumption the law gives me a right to call upon him. Who else can be supposed to interfere but my adversary; or some one with his privity? The necessity of the case justifies this exception to the general rule. He may go on behind the scene and prejudice the public mind against me and my cause, and leave me to my redress afterwards. The law will not allow this. If it is not a principle of the law, it ought to be a principle. But it is a principle as old as our Saxon ancestry, from whom the trial by jury is derived. It is coeval with the trial by jury, and necessary to its preservation. It is a safeguard of the trial in which the bulk of the people are especially interested. Before they give it up let them think. Leave it to the suitors in court, and at least one side will always object to it; probably both. All that wish a fair and unprejudiced decision will object to it. They will not be satisfied with being turned round to an indictment, and the slow process of a jury trial to establish the fact of the libel. But they will wish more, that the party interested, shall be purged on his oath, as to his agency in the publication. In this case, they have the conscience of the party to establish the guilt. And the looking forward to him, will lessen his hope of *escaping detection. It is a great privilege to an honest man. It is the rogue only that needs fear it.*

But though the bare circumstance of being a party to the suit depending, may found such *presumption* of being the author of the writing, as will justify the calling on the party to answer, by a rule to shew cause why an attachment should not issue, yet it is never done, and perhaps ought not to be done, without an affidavit of *some fact to lay a ground for the motion.* This in the case of a third person, is absolutely necessary; for no presumption of the nature already stated, can exist.

But the negative of the party to the suit depending, or of a third person, on oath, dissolves the rule, and there is an end of the summary interposition. This is a *privilege peculiar to this special proceeding :* and not possessed in the case of an indictment by a *grand jury.* It softens the extraordinary remedy, by suffering a man *to be a witness for himself: and what is more ; taking what he says, to be the truth, and so far as respect the attachment, incontrovertible.*

But if this power, though founded on law, and the constitution, should be deemed contrary to the *spirit of liberty, or good policy,* a clause of a few lines, can put an end to it: viz. " That in the case of *consequential contempts, by interference in a cause depending,* the proceeding shall be by indictment, in the first instance; and in no other way." It will relieve the court from a burden, which they conceive a duty ; and experience will determine whether the alteration of the common law in this particular be *an evil or a good.*

But of what use can a rogue's oath be ? He is not supposed to have a conscience. But he can look to an indictment for perjury. But suppose he did not know, or at least think there was a cause depending; and that he did not mean a contempt. It is not what he thought, or what he meant; but was there *a case depending*, and what did he do ?

But at this rate you abridge *the liberty of speech, and of writing ;* you make it dangerous to canvass a general principle of law; for some suit may be depending on which it may turn. The law goes no such length. I am at liberty to canvass a general principle. It is a consideration *of the particular case* from which I am excluded; or the application of *the facts to the law.* The legality of general warrants was abundantly canvassed, at the time Wilkes was the subject of one of them; and no exception taken to the freedom of the press in this particular. The constitutionality of the *sedition law* of the United States, was brought into view pending indictments under it; and no exception. I am canvassing a general principle at present; and there are impeachments depending where it may be brought into view. That is nothing; for it is *the facts of the case* that will be ultimately considered.

The courts may have this power, and yet may exercise it with *partiality, oppression, and tyranny.* This *will render the exercise of any power impeachable.* For this the accused must put themselves upon the country; or if clearly and palpably, *a court have no such power at all,* and yet exercise it, it is a *misdemeanor.* For error in judgment where there is a right to judge, is not impeachable; but the exercise of a power unknown to the law, even though unaccompanied with express malice, is impeachable, and will subject to a *reprimand, &c. according to the circumstances.* The rights of the citizen are thus secured; and far be it from me to abridge them, even in idea, by any reasoning I may offer.

NOTES

LAWS OF PENNSYLVANIA.

BY an act of Assembly of 28 Feb. 1810, provision is made for a publication of the laws, to be *examined and approved by the judges of the supreme court*, and the Governor is authorised to appoint some fit person inter alia "*to insert the notes of judicial decisions.*" *To what must the examination, and approbation* of the supreme court be considered as extending? It could not respect type, press-work, or fidelity of the publication, compared with the *enrolled acts;* or even the *arrangement* of the laws; but what was immediately within *the province of their judgment, the insertion of the notes of judicial decisions.* Nor could this *examination and approbation* be considered as vouching for the correctness of the decisions; but, only at most, for the correct statement of these decisions. Nor even that indeed, for *no record is kept of decisions,* but only of causes in which such decisions are made. And this, without recurring to the prothonotary's dockets, was not in their power. It would require a labour of years to ascertain all these. But as to the *reasons* of the decisions in a particular case, this could only be collected from the notes of judges; or others who had taken notes. And these notes could not always be considered as *correctly* taken, unless *noted by the judge himself* at the time he delivered his opinion. Nor had any one judge the notes of other judges in his power; much less, of those taken by the counsel at the bar; or, by others. And what is more, in the case of judges who had set on the bench before him, and were deceased, unless from papers left behind them, which might, or might not be furnished, there was no opportunity of information. The notes of judges, or of others, is private property; and even an act of assembly could not enforce the procuring them.

But an impracticable consequence must follow if their examination, and approbation was to involve a consideration of the *law* of the decisions. For that would require of them with the reasons given, much time, and be inconsistent with the prescribed official attendance, and necessary hearing and adjudication of causes in court.

A great mischief would also follow, that these decisions should be sanctioned, or disapproved *without argument in the particular point of law*, when it comes again to be considered. For though the stare decisis is a salutary maxim; and the non ita refert, may be taken into view; yet every party, in his particular case, *has a right to contest his decision; for decision is but the evidence of law;* and the judge himself has a right to depart from the decision of others; and, even from his own, in a new case. It cannot therefore be supposed that the legislature in imposing the duty could mean to *forestal* the opinions of the identical judges at a future day, by such a revision. They could mean, only; and certainly did mean no more, than to call for some judgment *in bulk* upon the work, as to the reasonable industry, *and pains bestowed in collecting decisions.* Whether these were right, or wrong, they could not be considered as expressing an opinion. Nay, on the contrary, if decisions *in the individual opinion of* any of them; or of the whole erroneous, were left out, it would be a reason for *refusing their approbation.* The public had it in view; and had a right to know, as far as possible *what decisions had taken place.* This doubtless, with a view to provide by law where they might think it necessary to interpose. This, by acts *declaratory* of what they conceived the law to have been, *or explanatory* of acts of the legislature, where the construction put upon them by the courts, appeared, as they might think, to be erroneous: or, to supply or amend where there appeared to *be a defect in the acts themselves.*

Nevertheless, though on my part it was considered, and as it appears would seem to have been considered by the other judges, as extending to nothing more than as I have stated; yet I did not consider my self as precluded from giving an opinion, if I chose to do it, on any decision that had been made. And I cannot say that there are not *some* of which I do not approve. From some of them indeed, I have *dissented* in a judicial capacity; and in *most* if not in *all* of these *I stick to my opinion.* But not in any case, where I think it wrong. Because I am *more covetous of the praise of candour in retracting error, than even of correct judgment, in the first instance.*

A few of the notes which I made in reviewing this publication, which deserves not a little credit, for its labour of industry, and collection of decisions, I take the liberty of subjoining here : they will be but few of which I shall take notice. These chiefly which respect the law of *legal tenure* in Pennsylvania.

————◆————

SINCE writing the above it occurs to me to subjoin a few observations more particularly upon the task enjoined upon the judges of the supreme court, in examining and approving the edition of the laws, with *notes of decisions* as prescribed by the act 28 Feb. 1810. It would be a reflection upon the understanding of the legislature, and an indecency to suppose for a moment, that they could mean that the judges were to approve of the *decisions reported*, but only of *the report* of the decisions. For it could not but be considered as much within the view of the legislature to have *erroneous decisions* reported as those which the judges might think *correct*. For the object of the legislature must have been, to see what the decisions were ; whether *erroneous* or *correct ;* with a view to interpose, where it might appear to them, their own acts required explanation, or amendment. Declaratory laws settle the intention of the legislature. These decisions so reported will be read in court, but no *greater*

*weight will be attached to them, than their own intrinsic rea-
son* will seem to justify. Chief justice Shippen, expressed
the idea to me that decisions merely *nisi prius*, and these
constitute a great part, had *better be burnt;* because they
might mislead. But as the legislature *have called for them*
they could not consistent with duty be omitted, and the judges
could not with delicacy but approve the *reporting*, because
the keeping any of them back, would be contrary to duty in
the reporter, and the giving countenance to this by the judges,
would be a participation in the fraud. So far from *approving* these decisions in any other view of the matter, I do entirely disapprove of *many of them;* in other words dissent
from them ; and especially such as have a *relation to the
lands within the purchase of* 1768 *; and those lying west of
the Allegheny river under the act of* 3 *April*, 1792.

In contemplation of law a *nisi prius* decision not appealed from by a motion for a new trial, acquires in some degree
the force of a decision of the court above ; but it can only
be in a degree ; for the court sitting above is at a distance ;
and it becomes a matter of expence to appeal. In Pennsylvania, where until of a late period, the court in bank sat
in the city of Philadelphia at the distance of many hundred
miles from the county in which the nisi prius trial was, it was
a matter of increased expence to prosecute an appeal; because
fresh counsel must be employed in that case, the counsel at
nisi prius not attending, as they could not with any possible
convenience at such a distance. And even the fresh counsel
that might be employed at the then seat of government could
not always be well acquainted with the local laws of the interior, so as to do the case equal justice with those even of inferior talents that had more knowledge of the acts of assembly
applying to rights in a particular quarter ; and this, from a
more careful study of them. I have known the *poverty of a
defendant*, in many cases, to operate as a bar against an appeal ; so that whatever might be the effect of not appealing
from a nisi prius decision in contemplation of law, it in fact
amounted to nothing, so far as respected the decisions in the
counties remote from the sitting in Bank.

But, it was discouraging in any case to appeal where two of the judges sitting at nisi prius, left but two others in the supreme court to whom the appeal could be made ; and the two sitting at nisi prius, had in their turns the revision of the decisions of the two behind, who in the mean time were on the circuit elsewhere, and thence could not be supposed in fact, whatever it might be in contemplation of law, to have a leaning to support what the other two had done ; not to judge severely " lest they themselves should be judged." In a court so constituted, an appeal was a *mockery.*

It was an appeal, I will not say from Philip drunk to Philip sober, for I mean no such reflection ; but it was almost the same thing as an appeal *from Philip* to *Philip.*

I admit that during a period there was what was called a court of appeals, not independent of the supreme court, but with a simul cum of other characters. But this court was holden at the seat of government, and it was a matter of still greater expence after a decision on the appeal, in the supreme court, to pursue it farther to a hearing in the last resort. The terms holden as they now are in *districts,* and by judges who have not sat at *nisi prius,* or have to review the decisions of each other, with regard to causes in the counties, is a great improvement on the system.

Thus much I have thought is necessary to say, with regard to the extent of that approbation which the judges of the supreme court may be considered as having given to the notes of decisions, as reported in pursuance of the act of the legislature.

UNDER the act of the 1st Ap. 1784, in the edition of the laws which the judges were to examine and approve, we have a note of much utility tracing the history of land titles in Pennsylvania. In this note a concise and clear view is given of the controversy of Penn with Lord Baltimore, respecting the boundaries of their respective grants.

But I have overlooked, or there is not comprehended in it, an account of the controversy of Penn with Virginia, to which dispute the commonwealth succeeded in the place; for it had not been *compromised* under the proprietary government. The ground of controversy with Baltimore whose grant was called Maryland, respected a degree of latitude; of which under the agreement with Penn half a degree was given up; but the Maryland boundary running west, terminated before the extent of five degrees of longitude to which Penn was entitled to go. He had a right therefore to run south at the extremity of the Maryland boundary, a degree. Then a line due west to the extremity of the fifth degree of longitude from the river Delaware. There was therefore in dispute with Virginia, a degree of latitude, for the distance of 23 miles due west, after passing the charter boundary of Maryland.

But independent of this, Pennsylvania claimed a line north parallel with the Delaware, but not according to the curves of that river. Virginia claimed according to the curves, the sinuosities of which river would throw considerable bays in many parts into Virginia. Office rights had been issued both from Virginia and Pennsylvania, and had been laid upon this ground, that according to the claims of each respectively, *settlements* also had been made under the laws, or usages of both.

By an act of first April, 1784, an agreement previously made, containing a compromise of the respective claims, is ratified and confirmed by the state of Pennsylvania, viz. "that the line commonly called Mason and Dixon's, be extended due west five degrees longitude, to be computed from the river Delaware, for the southern boundary of Pennsylvania, and that a meridian drawn from the western extremity thereof to the northern limits of the said states respectively, be the western boundary of Pennsylvania, for ever, on condition that the private property and rights of all persons acquired under, founded on, or recognized by, the laws of either country previous to the date hereof, be saved and confirmed to them, although they should be found to fall

within the other, and that in the decision of disputes thereon, preference shall be given to the elder or prior right, which-
ever of the said states the same shall have been acquired under, such persons paying within whose boundary their lands
shall be included, the same purchase, or consideration money which would have been due from the state under which
they claimed the rights." Such are the material conditions
of the agreement, and ratification. It will be seen from the
annexed diagram what was the nature of the dispute, and
the term of the compromise as it respects boundary.

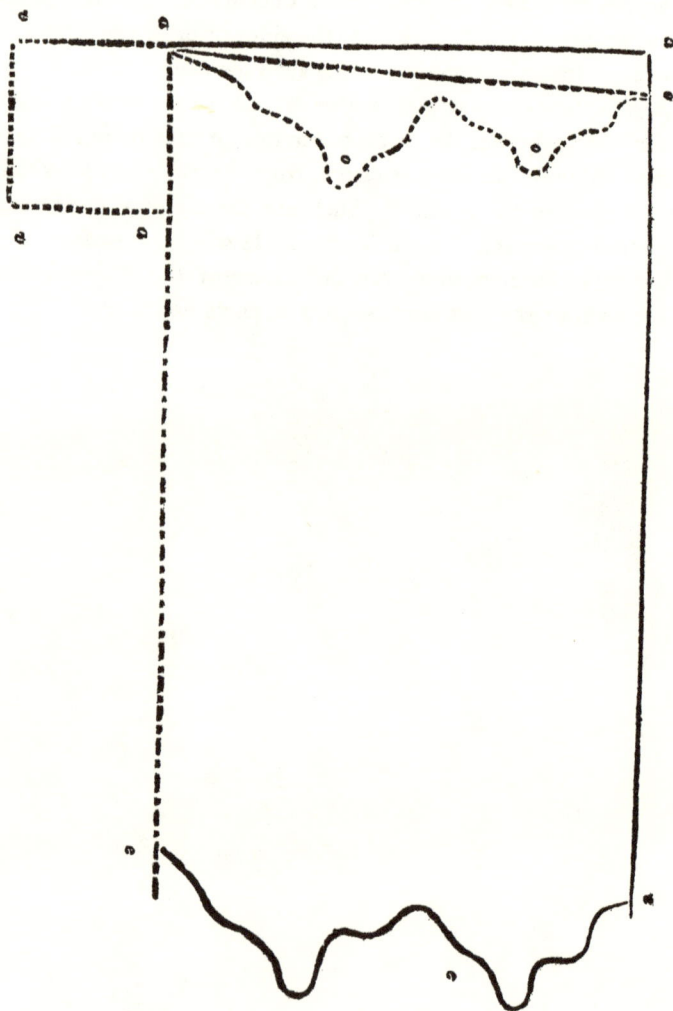

a — a. Line due north—of compromise.
a .... o. Boundary claimed by Pennsylvania.
o o o. Curves originally claimed by Virginia.
a a e. Mason's and Dixon's line.
a a v v. Ceded to Virginia under agreement.
e e e. River Delaware.

The zig zag of a western boundary, parallel with the meanders of the Delaware on the east, would have been difficult, or impossible to ascertain, with mathematical exactness. The curve consisting of irregular arches reducible to no segment of the sphere, could with no *convenience*, at least, be traced upon the ground in ascertaining the western boundary. What would justify the taking the *chord* of an irregular arch, would warrant that for which Pennsylvania contended, the taking the chord of the whole curved line of the Delaware, connecting the two extreme points of the north and south longitude. That is, from the Delaware at the place of beginning on the south running five degrees in longitude, and from the place of beginning on the north running the same distance from the Delaware, and connecting their terminations with a right line. This would seem by far the most likely to have been intended in the grant of the charter to Penn. It is totally improbable that any thing else could have been in contemplation in designating the extent, because the carrying it into effect by measurement, would have been impracticable. The court of justice would have put a construction on a writing which would have led to such inconvenience, because it would have been unreasonable, if not absurd. The claim of Virginia would therefore appear to me not to have been well founded. This independent of the principle of law, that every thing is to be taken most strongly against the grantor. And the *whole of the soil*, both of Virginia and Pennsylvania, was in the king of England when he granted the charter to Penn. So that this principle applied, and bound Virginia as to the right of soil at least, *if it did not as to jurisdiction.*

By the compromise Pennsylvania obtained the jurisdiction, or rather the claim of Virginia was withdrawn so far as respected this. She quieted her possession, and title also so far as respected the state of Virginia, but subject to *rights of individuals* who claimed under Virginia. These if prior to Pennsylvania titles, must come in. It was then in fact ceding *the rights of individuals* under Pennsylvania; or rather taking them away; for the courts of justice bound by the

K K

law ratifying the agreement, sustained ejectments under Vir
ginia claims where they were prior. General Washington
after the peace of 1783, instituted ejectments, and succeeded
in recovering under a prior Virginia claim, a large tract of
country containing a number of settled plantations which
had been defended and cultivated during the Indian depredations upon that quarter, at the expence of life in many instances. It was sufficiently distressing to be obliged to leave
their cultivated fields, meadows, orchards, and buildings.
The general did not offer to make compensation for these.
Nor in strict law, was he bound to do so. He could not be
considered as under more than an imperfect obligation. It is
possible he might have thought of this, had he not taken it
for granted, as he had a right to do, that the state of Pennsylvania who had taken away the property from the settlers,
by ceding to Virginia, would have provided a compensation.
This by strict law the state was bound to do. For though
the ceding the jurisdiction is at all times a right of the society; yet the exercise of the *dominium eminens*, could not,
under the constitution of 1776, or under the present, be justifiable without providing a compensation. This was the
case some years afterwards in the adjustment of the Wyo-
ming controversy, with Connecticut. But nothing of this
was heard of with regard to lands taken away by the Virginia
claims in this disputed territory. And at this late period,
it is not probable that we shall hear more of it. It remains
now, not a matter of legal discussion, but of history.

" Whether a sale of defendant's lands, under a younger judg-
" ment, affects the lien of an *older* one, *remains undecided*." I
Smith. 68, referring to a dictum of Judge Yates, 2 Bin. 218.

I am not able to name the case, nor can I say with certainty that it became necessary to decide the case *expressly*
on this point, and that the opinion expressed was not a dictum of the court, and what might be called in *strictness*, ex-

tra-judicial. But this I well recollect that C. J. Shippen, Yeates, Smith and myself on the bench, it was expressed, Yeates, as I understood it, of a contrary way of thinking, that the sale of a defendant's lands under a younger judgment, *could not affect the lien of an older one.* It might have been perhaps the case of a mortgage that brought the principle into view. But if it had never been decided, can there be any doubt about it?

A gives a pledge to B; say a *piece of plate.* Can A selling that pledge, give the purchaser a right to take it, or do more than put him in his place and enable him to take it paying B? What has B to do with A selling the pledge, or C purchasing it? It cannot change his interest in the thing pledged. The money advanced still remains due upon it. Will it avail the purchaser C to say the pledge was sold to me for *so much,* and I will pay you that? Might not B say, I will have the whole of the money advanced upon it, *or my interest in the plĕdge must remain.*

If a judgment is a lien, must not the land *liened,* or *tied,* remain bound until the debt for which it is bound be discharged? Can it make any difference whether it is *land* that is pledged, or a *chattel?* I cannot comprehend how the idea could have arisen, that it makes any difference. If land is pledged under a mortgage, that mortgage must be satisfied, before any other can come in. What is it to the *first mortgagee,* whether the land is sold under a second mortgage or, *what it may be sold for* under a second mortgage? He is safe, and his mortgage must be paid off, before the purchaser under a second mortgage can take it freed from the encumbrance. What is the difference between a mortgage, which is a *specific lien* upon *one or more tracts,* and a *judgment,* which is a general lien, and binds what lands the debtor has at the time of the judgment. I do not enter into the question why it may not *bind lands after purchased by the debtor.* But it is not questioned but that it will bind all the lands he has at the time. It binds as perfectly as in the case of a mortgage of a single tract. The only difference is in the manner of *foreclosure, and the proceeding to a sale.* I think it pro-

bable the case decided in the supreme court was that of a
mortgage; but it decides the *principle;* and if land sold
under a *second* mortgage, for less than the mortgage money
on the first, could not affect the right of the first to have it
sold again, how should the sale under a younger or second
judgment affect? It may have been the case of a mortgage
that was decided in the supreme court, but the principle
went the whole length; and the case of a sale under a *younger*
judgment, could not but be spoken of, and *considered the same.*
Who ever heard of a sale under a younger mortgage, cutting out the lien of a prior? There must have been something
special in the circumstances of the case, that could have raised the question, or brought it before the court.

The purchaser at sheriff's sale takes it cum onere of every
encumbrance by the debtor prior to the date of the judgment
on which the sale is made. It is his business to look into
every encumbrance, and the sheriff who is the mere agent of
the law in selling has nothing to do with the encumbrances.
It is the business of the purchaser to examine into this, *and
to bid no more than he thinks proper to give, taking the encumbrance into view.* He obeys the exigence of his writ and
sells, and out of what money comes to his hands he pays off
the judgment under which the land is sold if so much is
obtained, and the *surplus to the debtor* as directed by the
act of assembly in the case of *chattels.* As to the notion of
the sheriff being liable to see how the purchase is applied, he
has nothing to do with it.

Am I bound who am a judgment creditor, to do more
than to watch my own lien, and the sale under it, if I choose
to have a sale made? I am not bound to attend the sale under a *younger* judgment, or to see what it will bring, as I
cannot be affected by it. It is the younger creditor to attend to this, knowing that his judgment cannot come in until the other is satisfied. If the money bid will not amount
to what will discharge the prior judgment, or will amount
to no more, he gets nothing. Unless the land is of sufficient
value to answer prior encumbrances, the purchaser loses by
so much. This is a doctrine which younger judgment cre-

ditors, or purchasers at sheriff's sale, may not relish, but the injustice and *inconvenience* of having the law otherwise understood must be manifest. A judgment creditor *at a distance may have his lien taken from him, if a sale under a younger judgment, could dissolve it.*

It will be said, what is a younger judgment creditor to do if the older is not pressed to a sale? must he lie by until the older presses? not at all. If he thinks that the land will bring more than the older judgment, he can proceed upon the younger, and purchase himself; or some one else purchasing, pay off the older judgment, which he will then have a right to do. For he succeeds to the place of *the debtor* against whom the judgment was. The same in the case of a mortgage. He has then the equity of redemption in him, and has a right to pay off the first mortgage, and hold the land discharged of the mortgage. The whole error lies in the not considering as it ought to be that *a sale by the law is* a sale by the *debtor* himself: and he can make title only of what interest remains in him; and this is what interest remains after paying off all encumbrances *prior.*

The case of a mortgage is precisely the same with that of a judgment creditor except as to the necessity *of holding an inquisition to condemn the lands;* and the kind of writ, the levari facias which by the act of assembly is directed to issue. The point therefore having been decided in the supreme court, in the case of a mortgage, did decide the principle that *a sale under a younger judgment, could not affect the lien of an older one.*

2 Smith's Laws, 127.

Plumstead's lessee v. Rudibach, Westmoreland.

The defendant offered to prove that his father, Christopher Rudibach, settled on these lands before the Indian purchase, in consequence of a military permit from Colonel Boquet which he alleged was lost by the casualty of office; but that his uninterrupted possession since his death would be presumptive evidence thereof, and that he had made considerable improvements thereon. Defendant had obtained a warrant for the land, December, 1784.

The evidence was excepted to and overruled.

I disaprove both of the decision and the reasons of the court.

Lessee of Sherer v. Mc'Farland, Westmoreland.

I disapprove of this decision and the reasons.

Drinker's lessee v. Hunter: Northumberland; I disapprove.

Buchannan's lessee v. Mc'Clure: Northumberland, 1808. My dissent appears, 1 Bin. 385. And totis viribus, I continue of the same mind.

Benoni Dawson v. William Laughlin; 2 Smith, 207.

A recovery cannot be had on a mere settlement without a survey. I say it can: shall not one regain by law, the possession of his house or improved ground, without a survey?

Lessee of Samuel Ewalt v. Martha Highlands; Alleghany. 2 Smith's Laws, 208.

I was of counsel in this case for Ewalt, and I am constrained to say the report of the facts is not correct. And here I take the liberty of observing that no report of any judge can import absolute verity. It is not a *record*, though I have heard a judge affect to call it so. What a judge notes upon his paper, is not read to the counsel in the cause. They have no opportunity of taking, nor have any right, to take exception to the statement at the time. It is a matter with the judge himself and is his own memorandum, with which a party in the cause has nothing to do. The report in the case of the lessee was *defective*, and it is erroneous in this, that the nonsuit would appear to have been suffered on the merits, where, in consequence of a conveyance being over-ruled, as not competent to be given in evidence, and this on a technical objection, the date of it being after the *demise laid in the declaration.* Yet it was under the idea that a nonsuit was suffered on the merits, that it went before the board of property, and this from the report of the judge. It was a rule with the board that on a verdict, or nonsuit, the granting a patent should depend. And on this principle the heirs of Highland obtained the patent which though not conclusive, has always such weight, on a *settlement right,* that it becomes up hill to contend against it in a court of law.

Lessee of Robert Morris v. William Neighman, 1779.

This involved some principles under the act of 3 April, 1792. 1; whether, a warrantee forfeits his right under the warrant by not making a settlement on the lands within two years.

2; Whether, if a forfeiture be incurred, the defendant might not enter, and the condition being broken, take advantage thereof.

As to the necessity of making a settlement within two years, there was an exception in the act; "the being by force of arms of the enemies of the United States prevented from making such actual settlement, &c."

An Indian war did prevent until a certain period. What was that period? The court say the war continued *in fact* until the treaty was concluded by General Wayne; and until that treaty was ratified by the president and senate of the United States. I would query, did not the treaty put an end to hostilities in fact; and as *to ratification* it must be considered as relating to that peace established.

But on the 2 1 point; the court lay it down, that no individual can take advantage of the breach of the condition "unless through the instrumentality of the state by granting new warrants in a specified form."

It was contended and might be made a question on the other side, whether the act of the legislature itself did not provide, that advantage should be taken of the forfeiture, in a different manner, viz. *by the entry of an individual*, without a warrant. "It shall be lawful to and for this commonwealth to issue new warrants to other *actual settlers* for the said lands." Must not applicants have *actually settled* before the warrant could issue? If so, *an entry for the condition broken* is allowable.

Hazard v. Lowry. A note is added by the editor, page 214. "This judgment" says he "fully confirms the doctrine of Morris v. Neighman, and the point is settled." On the contrary it did not touch the all-sweeping doctrine in Morris v. Neighman, viz. " *that an entry could not be made without a vacating warrant.*" The person entering could see the tract *vacant*, and that it had remained *vacant for more than two years since the pacification by the treaty of General Wayne;* but how could he tell, or the commonwealth ascertain the warrant it had been surveyed under.

It was impossible to ascertain it, where the description in applications, refer to some *leading warrant*, as it is called, and it could only be by measuring over again, the whole country that it could be known what warrant would take a particular tract. The idea of a *vacating warrant* never ought to have come into the mind, in such a case. Nor the idea of not having a right of entry without a warrant. It is contrary to the policy, 'and express words of the act. The point is *not settled*, and I take it never will be in that way.

Attorney General v. grantees under the act of 3d April, 1792.

---

2 Smith's Laws, 105.

" His religious principles" says the editor, speaking of William Penn, the grantee of the charter under Charles, II. " did not permit him to wrest the soil of Pennsylvania, by *force* from the people *to whom God and nature gave it.*" What is the evidence of God, or nature having given it, save the

mere circumstance of possession; or *the being found upon it.*
God and nature have given the whole earth to man as a common inheritance. But the right to a particular part can be
no more than his proportion of the soil to the individual.
This, taking into view *quantity and quality.* Power may
engross more, but it is incorrect in that case to resolve it
into right. It is the common *cant*, that the natives had an
exclusive title, under the *law of nature* to this continent;
but it cannot bear the test of an investigation. They had
a right only to so much of it as was their proportion of
the whole earth. This is taking up the matter on the strict
principle of *natural right.* Upon this principle, can it be
said, that a few scattered tribes could claim the whole of
this continent. So soon as discovered, the nations of Europe had a right to enter upon it, the share being too much
which they occupied in proportion to their population.
But I do not question the *expediency* of obtaining by fair
means, and even by purchase, the possession of a part.
This was advisable; as an individual may buy his own to
avoid a law suit; or give something in consideration of quieting a claim. It may be said that considering their mode
of life, hunting, a larger tract was necessary to an individual savage, than to a civilized man living by the cultivation of
the soil. What have we to do with mode of life where
right is in question? My ideas on this head were expressed
some years ago, in a treatise *on the Indian right of soil.*

On what is it founded? Having had a foot first on the continent?
Then one Indian might claim the whole : spend his winter in the torrid zone—his summer in one or other of the frigid, and spring and
fall in the temperate. That would be unreasonable. Will two Indians have this right? There must be more than that. Two tribes?
It would be too much to take up the whole continent with two
tribes. How many must there be to give the right? Just as many
as there are. If there was one less, would they have the right?
Yes. Two less? Yes. How many might there be less, and the
right exist? I cannot tell—nor no one else. There must be some
fixed principles on which all right depends. Under the great
law of nature, it is a right to as much as is necessary for our sub-

sistence. By pasturage or hunting? No; by agriculture. Because in this way of life most can subsist at the same time.

But men by the municipal laws of society hold more than an equal quantity. What has this to do with the great out-wheel of natural law, which gives the earth to man in common. The municipal law binds as citizens; the law of nations as societies; but the law of nature as men. Say, as the number of inhabitants upon the earth is to its extent, so the right of each individual to his share. God gives a man no more when he dies than space to lie down upon, and how, more in life than to enjoy reasonably? Let the appeal be made to him. Great spirit; says the Indian, here is a white man that wants some of my land. How much have you? Ten miles square. The tenth of that may serve. To hunt upon? No; but to plant corn, raise hogs, and live like a man. But did not you give me all this? I have given none of you more than another. There is the earth, and the dividing of a sea or a river makes no partition. It is true, I do not permit the inhabitants of Jupiter or other planets to come down to your earth, but have placed a law of nature to hinder it: but on the same planet, I know nothing of what is called the right of the natives, beyond at most a right of preference to chuse their ground, or to hold that which they already cultivate.

Nevertheless, as has been said, it was not inexpedient to purchase, more especially as the wild man, or savage must be considered as having some right within the extent ceded, that is to his proportion as an individual of the human race in common with the civilized, and those living more humano, and not in the manner of beasts. But in these purchases, the utmost *fair dealing* ought to have been observed; which was not always the case. As for instance in the case of what is called the *walking purchase;* of which the Indians complained, as having had an advantage taken of them. The *quick* step is distinguished in military tactics from the *slow;* and on a wager taken on to walk from York to London, in a given time, the bet is not considered fairly won where the pedestrian *runs* instead of walks; and it would not seem to have been according to the understanding of the contract, to take the *chord* of the arch on the Delaware,

instead of the curves. This could not but have produced greater heart-burning in the simple mind, than even a claim of
right plainly made and asserted. I refer to what was called the *walking purchase* spoken of, 2 Smith, page 116.

The case of the Attorney General v. the grantees, under
the act of April 1792, has been reported, 4 Dal. 237, and
this has been read in court; or referred to as containing
the construction of the court on the act in question. As
this report carries with it the appearance of a concurrence
of the other judges on the bench, in the sentiments delivered by the presiding judge, (Yates) it becomes proper for me
to have it known that I did not concur in that construction
as to some particulars, and I did make it known to the presiding judge himself at the time, and did take it, that he
made it known in delivering his charge to the jury, that in
some things, he delivered his own opinion only; or at least
did not deliver mine. For admitting that I did concur with
him in the sentiments necessarily arising on the point in issue,
yet not as to some, or at least to one sentiment, incidentally
introduced. For, by a reference to the case of Morris v.
Neighman, the effect of the warrant, as voidable by an entry
without warrant, would seem to be introduced: and the doctrine in one point of the decision in Morris v. Neighman,
by implication sanctioned; viz. that *a right of entry is not
given to the settler on the non-compliance with the condition
of settlement by the warrantee.* To this doctrine I could not
subscribe; for an entry appeared to me to be given by the
strongest implication; and that the warrant was voidable,
equally by the *entry* of the settler, as by the new *warrant* of
the commonwealth. For in the language of the presiding
judge himself " the lands becoming forfeited by the omission
of certain acts enjoined on the warrant holders, they *became
vested in the whole body of the citizens, as the property of the
commonwealth, subject to the disposition of the lands.*" Now
if they become vested in the citizens must they not be in as
of their former estate, and to the disposition of what law
could this estate be subject, but of that law already provided :

and if an entry under that law was given without warrant, on the lands as before in the commonwealth, why not now?

I will admit that the condition of the grant by warrant under the act of April 2, 1792, is not a *condition precedent;* but that the grantee in the warrant has estate in fee simple by virtue of the grant. But I take it that by necessary implication, it is a *conditional limitation ;* the effect of which must be, that on the non-fulfilment of the condition, an *entry* is given to him for whom the grantor has provided; and from the express words of the act, would it not seem that the state (the grantor) has provided for the entry of *an actual settler* on the non-compliance with the condition of settlement on the part of the warrantee. " In default of such actual settlement and residence, it shall be lawful to, and for this commonwealth to issue new warrants to other *actual settlers* for the said lands." And " if words of condition be used on the creation of an estate, and on breach of the condition, the estate be limited over to a third person, and does not immediately revert to the grantor, or his representatives, as if an estate be granted by A to B, on condition that within two years, B intermarry with C, and on failure thereof then to D, and his heirs; this the law construes to be a limitation and not a condition." 2 Black. 155. Now it would seem to me that granting new warrants to other *actual settlers* is a provision in favour of such citizens of the commonwealth as might be disposed to appropriate by settlement. For it is as much as to say, the condition not being complied with, a right of entry is given to others who upon settlement and residence shall be entitled to warrants. It might be some question whether warrants could issue to other than persons actually settled. For as the object of the state had been defeated by the first grantees, in a principal part of the object of the law, the settling the country, it would be reasonable that it should provide against a like non-compliance, a second time by granting only to such as had actually settled. But be this as it may, it would appear to be against the policy of the law to suspend the right of entry until it could be ascertained by an inquisition of issue of office, that the condition had not been complied with: more especially when from the difficulty of ascertaining the precise spot on which the survey was made under a *particular warrant*, it must be a work of time to point it out, and ground an application for a new warrant. But sanction the entry, and in the mean time the settlement goes on, and when the warrantee comes forward with his warrant, if he ever does, his own shewing will point it out. But let it be considered and which perhaps it ought to be, *an estate defeasible on a condition subsequent;* and applying the law, that in such case, a stranger could not take advantage of the condition broken, the estate being voidable, and not void. 2 Coke Lyt. 214. Yet the question will remain, whether a citizen desirous to settle can be considered to be a stranger. Had not every member of the state, an interest in the occupancy of these lands could the body politic be considered otherwise than as a trustee for the whole; where every individual of the community was in the light of a cestui que use as to a right of entry and settlement of this vacant country? This is a construction of the act most consistent with the policy of securing the improvement of it. It is certainly the least favourable to the engrossing large tracts of uncultivated country, and most favourable to the poorer sort, for whose benefit the means of acquiring land for the support of a family by labour without money, in the first instance would seem to have been intended. Nay, for whose benefit, the provisions of the law, or any other construction, must be in a great degree, an illusion; for the country being overspread with warrants almost generally immediately on the opening of the office, or rather before it is opened, what chance had they to any great extent, but from the *voidable nature* of the grants on the non-compliance of the warrantee with the condition specified?

The negative of this doctrine was laid down in the case of the lessee of Morris v. Neighman, 4 Dal. 209, "that even if it were a case of forfeiture, no individual could take advantage of it by entering on the land; the advantage could only be taken by the commonwealth, whose officers might issue new warrants in the form prescribed by the act of assembly." But this was at a circuit court before not more than two judges of the supreme court, and this in the course of a jury trial; and if there was not an appeal from the direction of the court in this particular, it was because (and being of counsel for the defendant I have a right to know) the charge of the court, and the facts of the case were against him on another point, viz. that his entry though two years after the date of the warrant, yet was before the general pacification of the country, during which time, the limitation ran, and the forfeiture was saved, there being a prevention of settlement, by the Indian hostilities. It is true what was suggested in Morris v. Neighman, so far as related to this point, was but impliedly sanctioned by a reference to that case, on another point; nevertheless, involving great consequences, in the construction of the statute, I did not choose that it should pass as receiving my concurrence in this particular. Nor as to what was laid down in that case with regard to the time during which the prevention ought to be considered as lasting, whether until Wayne's treaty or after, I was not prepared to give an opinion, and therefore was not willing to be considered as recognizing the one given; for which reason I objected to the introduction of a reference to Morris v. Neighman's case, or an implied sanction of the extent of the doctrine laid down in it. More especially as it was evident from the very act under which this extra court then sitting was constituted, that so far as a legislative exposition could have weight, it was in the face of this doctrine; and this by unavoidable implication from the following clause of the preamble. "As much confusion might arise, if the state were to continue to grant lands which in consequence of *former acts* may have become the property of others." How could they have become the property of others, otherwise than by grant, if not by the entry of the settler?

In all other matters laid down by the presiding judge, in the direction to the jury, in the case of the Attorney General v. grantees, I acquiesced then, and am well satisfied now of the correctness of the principles.

———◆———

THE litigation which has arisen in regard of *original title* to real property, in Pennsylvania, has been owing, in a great degree, to the deception of purchasers, and the fraud and negligence of officers intrusted with the carrying grants into effect. The grant, under whatever name, or in whatever quantity, it may have been, was a matter between the proprietaries whilst they continued the owners of the soil, and those to whom they chose to grant. It was in the evidence of appropriation that the community became interested. Had the whole country been a woodless plain like Egypt, a place of beginning marked by a stone or other monument, would have been all that could have been obtained. Courses by the compass, and distance by the chain, must have done the rest. But the variation of the compass and the unavoidable inexactness of measurement, would have rendered the identity of the specific ground appropriated, in length of time uncertain. It was a dictate of good sense therefore, and was of general convenience, the country being a timbered forest, to adopt the expedient of the natural *boundary* of trees, marked, as a corrective where they could be found; and when these so marked can be ascertained, they are always to govern. The instructions from the surveyor general to his deputy, from the earliest period, were to go upon the ground and run the courses and distances, *and mark the trees.* But as in this case the trouble of going on the ground and the expence of paying chain carriers, and a marker of the trees, and of provisions furnished for these, must be incurred by him for whom the survey was made, there was a temptation to dispense with the going on the ground; or the actual running, and marking the boundary trees. But more frequently the surveyor himself intrusted to make the survey as officer and as agent, took it upon him to dispense with going on the ground, and made the survey on paper merely. This he could do, by stating a beginning on some other survey actually made, and taking the courses and distances of that survey, or part of them, for the courses and distances pretended to have been now run. His temptation to do this, was the saving himself trouble, his fees being charged the same as if he had gone upon the ground. A neighbour wishing to appropriate, or informing one who wished to appropriate, knowing there had been no surveyor on the ground, or boundary tree marked, would speak of this land still vacant; nor would the return to the office of a survey, on this ground, give him information of which he could reasonably take notice; because there having been, in fact, no survey made on the ground in question, he must conclude it to be some other ground, on which the survey was made. And here sprung the first error of our courts of justice in sanctioning a survey where a conflicting claim came in question, which had not been made by going on the ground, and actually running the lines. These were the directions of the proprietary office for the granting lands, and where this was not done, it must be the fault of the grantor, or the fraud of the officer, and the ground ought not to have been considered as yet legally measured off; but as belonging to the unappropriated mass, and liable to be disposed of to others. For though the officer must be considered as the agent of the proprietary the grantor of the soil, yet he must be viewed also, in the light of the agent of the grantee and as against whom as agent, the grantee has redress by complaint to the principal, or by action at law against himself. His acts to a certain extent must be considered as the acts of the grantee; and third persons, innocent, bona fide purchasers, ought not to be affected by the irregularity of carrying a grant into effect according to the implied or known terms of the contract. Where it becomes a wrong to others; that is the occasion of their taking the same land as unappropriated, this wrong ought not to be taken advantage of by the authors of it. It is contrary to the maxim.

But the irregularity was not only in not going on the ground to run the courses and distances, according to the instructions of the office or the authority of the warrant, and taking for boundaries, the surveys of others made at other times, but in taking up the courses and distances made under a different warrant returned afterwards on a survey not on the ground for which it called; or courses and distances run with a view to a warrant that might be taken out, and which when taken out was returned as made at a date subsequent to the date of the warrant, and with which date the marks on the trees would not correspond; and which the testimony of the vicinage would refute having knowledge of the time when the survey was actually made. Notoriety of appropriation is a great object; and it was the act in pais the carrying the grant into effect by actual admeasurement, and laying off by marks that even the unlettered could read, that was in the view of the owners of the soil, and ought to have been regarded by every purchaser. The neglect of this, or omission, was *a legal fraud* upon the public who had an interest in the notoriety of appropriation. For the proprietary William Penn, took his charter subject to an implied condition of settlement. For this is not only the object of all colonization; but it is held out in the charter as the object of the grant, " the enlarging the English empire, and promoting useful commodities." This from the preamble of the charter; and again in Sec. 5. " that this new colony may more happily increase by the multitude of people resorting thither, we for us, our heirs and successors do give and grant by these presents, power, licence and liberty unto all liege people and subjects both present and future of us, our heirs and successors, excepting those who shall be specially forbidden to transport themselves, and families to the said country," and doubtless the proprietaries under this charter, had this object honestly in view, because, if from no other reasons, their interest was connected with it. Every purchaser had an interest in the population of the country; for the improvement of the settlement was the improvement of his individual farm. Every stroke of an axe struck by his

M m

neighbour, in clearing the country was half a stroke for
him. Could any thing more effectually defeat the object
of the crown in granting, or of the proprietary in taking the charter; or of the purchasers interested in the improvement of the country, than irregularity in the appropriation, defeating the notoriety of it, and misleading settlers.
It was a monstrous evil, and the judiciary at an early hour
ought to have set their faces against it. The proprietary
board of property did; and I take it that, in the examination of their proceedings, it will appear that in general they
discovered a willingness to save an applicant from the wrong
likely to be suffered, either in his settlement, or warrant from
a want of notice of what purported to be a prior appropriation, but which had not been regularly carried into effect. Be
that as it may, the commonwealth succeeding to the ownership of the soil, would seem to have had their attention drawn
to these irregularities which had prevailed, and to the mischiefs of them. For by an act of 1785, entitled an act to
provide further regulations whereby to secure fair and equal
proceedings with the land office, and in the surveying of
lands, Sec. 9. 3 Dall. 316, it is provided that "every survey
hereafter to be returned into the land office of this state,
upon any warrant which shall be issued after the passing of
this act, shall be made by *actual going upon and measuring
of the land, and marking the lines to be returned upon such
warrant, after the warrant authorising such warrant, shall
come to the hands of the deputy surveyor to whom such warrant shall be directed, and every survey made theretofore, shall
be. accounted clandestine, and shall be void, and of no effect
whatever,*" and every deputy surveyor, upon request to him
made, shall give a receipt in writing, signed by him, to the
person delivering any warrant of survey; in which receipt
shall be set forth the day and year when, and the order in
which the same warrant shall have come to the hands of such
deputy surveyor, and also the grantee's name and surname,
and the number of acres to be surveyed thereon, and also
the number of the same warrant."

The mischiefs that did exist before the passing of this act, were the *not going on the ground and marking the lines* by which act in pais there could be notice, to the whole community; but returning a survey as marked which in fact was not marked; but what was an equal mischief, the taking a survey that had been made under another warrant, or under no warrant, and returning it as marked of the date purporting to be surveyed; which would be contradicted by the marks upon the ground, and the testimony of the vicinage; and to give this act a construction according to the rules of construing statutes, the most in advancement of the remedy of these mischiefs, it would seem reasonable to extend it as avoiding all surveys not made by going on the ground, and marking the trees, but at least it must be construed as avoiding all surveys made *before the warrant came to hand*, even though the survey had been upon the ground. If a special return were made on such a warrant stating a return on a survey made for another purpose, could it be received in the face of this act? Is not a general return therefore concealing the fact; or rather stating what was not a fact, a deception upon the office, and an evasion of the law? I would take it to be in contemplation of law *a fraud* however unintended by the officer or the warrantee for whom the survey was made.

There are circumstances under which the warrantee would have an interest over and above the saving expences of a survey, in having it returned upon the old lines actually run for other purposes, unless indeed the warrant was so special in the description as to amount to a designation equal with a survey, and by that description to attach from the grant. For in the case of a warrant, not specific, it might be an object to give it a bed as soon as it existed, and before there could be time to survey it actually; and this, to exclude the laying other warrants perhaps prior; or settlements which might be made before the officer, with chain carriers and provisions could get upon the ground, and we know races against time have not been uncommon to get the return of a survey made. I do not mean to say that we shall presume fraud;

but that where circumstances exist that tempt to fraud, the suspicion is not resisted by a consideration of the total absence of all motive. That it is in contemplation of law a fraud, I infer, because it is against the express words of the act, and against the reason and policy; and in its nature must work an injury. What notice can any one get from the description of most warrants, though entered in a book of the surveyor of the district? What notice from the return of a survey? It is the marks on the ground that a settler will look for. These he has a right to have, and of these he is bound to take notice. The age of the survey can be distinguished; and will a settler be bound to read a survey in appearance years old, as one which had been recently made? It will prove to him that no survey has been made which can correspond with the existence of the warrant. His conclusion must be that there is no survey. The considering the entry of a warrant in the surveyor's books as a notice of the ground which it calls for, is assuming that the warrant contains *a particular description of the ground*. This is required by the act of assembly under which the warrant issued, and where, agreeably to the act, the warrant contains a particular description, it may come near to all the notice of a survey. But even there it cannot separate the tract from the common stock precisely, and it is only a survey that can do it. This the purchasers are interested in having, and have a right to call for. The act has prescribed a particular description in the application; it has prescribed an entry with the surveyor *of the district*, an actual survey on the ground. The land office has admitted, in many instances, applications without a particular description, and the entry of the warrant in the surveyor's books gives no notice. This furnishes an additional reason why the provisions of the act shall be respected in regard of going on the ground.

By an act of assembly of the 12th of March, 1783, a district of country was surveyed and returns made into the surveyor general's office with a view to a sale, but which as to a portion of the tract surveyed did not take place, so that a number of the lots so surveyed, remained on hand. At the opening of the office, April 3d, 1792, for the sale of the lands, west of the Ohio, and comprehending this district, it fell into the common mass and was for sale, not under the act of March, 1783, but under the new act of 1792. These lots not to be sold at vendue, and as they had been surveyed in lots of 200 or 300 acres, but made subject to the new law, and the conditions warranting and the returns of surveys made under the law of March, 1783, were in the office as of that date. The marks on the trees were of that date. Could any settler entering under the act of April, 1792, ever dream that marks on the ground, made nine years before, could be considered as a survey lately made. As between the warrantee and the commonwealth, such return of survey might not be *void;* but it is impossible for me not to hold it *voidable* where a third person is affected. Even if notice were brought home to a settler of the circumstances of the case, I should not think he was bound to take notice of the acceptance of such returns; for the surveyor general had no power to take such surveys off the file and attach them to a warrant. But the contrary of this would seem to have been determined by a majority of the court; and in contemplation of law the majority must be right. But the minority owe it to justice to dissent; and in the construction of a statute especially. In the language of Justice Chambre, 2 Bos. and Pul. 403, " where I find no ambiguity in the act, and think that the act has not been expounded, but contradicted, I feel it my duty to adhere to the authority of the statute." I can have no doubt but that under the act of assembly a survey returned without going on the ground is *voidable;* and a survey made even by going on the ground before the warrant comes to hand, is void. The inclination of my mind is to hold them void in both cases. For that I take to be the true construction, if not according to the *strictness* of the term in both cases, it is according to the intention of the act. I admit that the first clause may be considered *directory,* the not going on the ground; and the return only voidable; for the arrangement of the words, may bear a distinction.

A source of litigation with regard to lands lying west of the Allegheny river, was the conduct of the secretary of the land office in admitting applications.

The law of the third of April, 1792, provides that " upon the application of any person who may have settled and improved, or is desirous to settle and improve a plantation, to the secretary of the land office, which application shall contain a particular description of the land applied for; there shall be granted to him a warrant for *any quantity of land not exceeding* 400 *acres.*" This restriction respected the quantity of land that was to be put into any one warrant, but not the number of warrants that any one might take out. The object was to secure reasonable fees to the commonwealth, and towards the support of the land office, making many, and therefore small grants. But it was construed that no man should have more than *one warrant* in his own name. Hence the expedient of the names of friends, or fictitious names, and the necessity of conveyances from these increasing the expences of the grant, by conveyancing, and recording which the law did not contemplate, or render necessary; it was the oversight, or misconstruction of the land office.

But this was a small matter compared with the monstrous error which accompanied it, the construction of the preceding clause of the section; the application " containing a particular description of the land applied for." Did not this imply such a description as to distinguish it from all other lands, and which no one could make who had not traversed it, and taken some natural boundary, or designated it by an artificial? Yet after what is called a *leading location*, others were admitted as describing by reference; thus, an application for a tract of land at the mouth of a certain river, and for another adjoining, and a third adjoining that, and so on to the end of the chapter. Such applications could be made, and in fact were made, and admitted, from a map, or even without a map; many just from the name of a stream which from the relation of a traveller was said to run through the country. Hence the number of applications filed the first day of the opening of the office. The whole country was applied for in an instant; nay a greater extent of country would not have satisfied the applications that were filed. No man meaning to settle bona fide, could obtain a warrant for a tract that was not anticipated by a pretence of application under this admission of the land office. It was a fraud in the first instance upon the public, and the intentions of the law. This through the ignorance of the secretary of the land office, who admitted the applications. The Governor was in fault that did not on this great and momentous occasion attend to it; or perhaps he misconceived the thing himself, and gave countenance to the error. But hence the intention of the law has been in a great part defeated. This intention was, in a great part, the accommodation of the settlers, and the settlement of the country. But what is perhaps a more lasting evil, hence has arisen the endless litigation and insecurity of title in the country. Such is the value of mind, whether in discernment or application. A touch of a finger at the end of a lever moves a great weight. A small matter of care and judgment at the beginning of a purpose, changes the event of great undertakings.

Speaking of the unwarrantable and mischievous indulgence of the land office, in admitting applications in the case of the law of April 1792, I am not calling in question the titles derived under them; but regretting the admission as contrary to the contemplation of the law, and *an injury to the purchaser.* It has been of incalculable evil consequence. *Innocent foreign* purchasers especially have reason to complain.

The juror's oath altered by act of 21st March, 1806. *(Pennsylvania Legislature.)*

BY an act of assembly of the 21st March, 1806, it is enacted that the oath or affirmation to be administered to jurors, viz. " I, A. B. do swear (or affirm as the case may be) that I will well and truly try the issue joined between C. D. plaintiff, and E. F. defendant, and a true verdict give according to the evidence, *unless dismissed by the court, or the cause withdrawn by the parties.*" It has been the subject of merriment with *scientific men* out of the state, that the legislature should have thought such a qualification of the oath of a juror necessary. But it is because the legislature thought it necessary otherwise than in accommodation to the scruples of weaker and more uninformed jurors. For it is known that in administering the oath according to the form heretofore used, the courts had oftentimes a great deal of trouble in explaining to conscientiously scrupulous persons, or those who affected to be so, which was the most common case, the notice of the exception implied in all undertaking to do an act, that if a stop was put to the doing the act, and it ceased to be required of them, they were not bound to do it, but were discharged from the obligation. Thus if A promises to marry B, but B refuses, A is discharged. If A contracts to build a house for B, and B says he will not have it built, A is discharged. An oath to *give* a verdict, implies a willingness to take it on the part of those to whom it is to be given. A verdict cannot be given but to a court that is willing to take it. Nor will a court take it but for the use of parties in a suit. It is therefore implied in the nature of an undertaking to give a verdict, that a court for the use of one or other of the parties, or both, is willing to take it. There is nothing undertaken to be done in human life, but the undertaking is accompanied with this tacit condition, that it remains physically, or morally possible to do it, or that those for whom it is to be done, are willing to have it done. When a candidate shall have been elected, or appointed, and is sworn into office, his oath is to execute the trust; is it necessary for him in order to satisfy his conscience, to have this *saving* that he will enact it, unless *the office is taken from him,* to which he has been so elected, or appointed? The truth is, it is a laughable matter to well informed men; but as a scruple of this kind had got a footing in common understanding, though where, and whence it originated, it is difficult to conceive,

it introduced no inconvenience, but the making the oath of
the juror a little longer, to introduce the *implication* by *express* words. The first time that I ever heard of such a
scruple was from a juror in the western country, at the first
organization of Washington county, who seemed to have
some difficulty upon this head, from his habits of casuistry,
and the scrupling articles of church government and discipline.
I forget whether the court were able to satisfy him by explaining the *tacit condition* of the oath ; or whether they excused him from *taking the oath*, and of course from *serving*
as a juror. But be it as it might, he got the credit of being
a man of *tender conscience ;* and it began to be no uncommon
thing to allege such a difficulty in the taking the oath; whether from *conscience* or from *policy* it could not be said. The
last time that some difficulty of this kind occurred in my recollection, with a juror, was in a court at Chambersburgh.
Judge Smith, with whom I sat, said it was *the law.* I attempted to explain the *reason of the law*, but the judge interrupted me, and ordered the juror to be sworn. I take it,
that it was this very circumstance which gave rise to this addition to the oath of a juror. It will be seen therefore, that
it did not originate with the legislature, but with the scruples
of the people, which *whether honest in all cases, or affected*,
gave the court trouble. For as the legislator of the *Jews*, is
said to have given some laws to the people in the wilderness,
" *because of the hardness of their hearts ;*" so our representatives have thought it advisable to accommodate, in some instances, to the *weakness* of the people whom they represent,
and with whose concerns they have been entrusted. Legal
characters of other states, or individuals of good sense, to
whom I have made this explanation of the amendment in
question, were satisfied, and deduced no inference of a want
of understanding in our legislature, to conceive such an a-
mendment necessary ; an amendment changing the form of
an oath from that of the common law, and which had been *in
use*, and *the implication of it generally understood* for an immemorial period of years.

N s

I will observe here, as an apology for what has been introduced, that a judge, especially, cannot but feel a peculiar interest in all that concerns the credit of the legislature of his state; in all that relates to their provisions, as well as to the language of their acts, whether ambiguous, or the arrangement defective. I had it once objected to me by a *Virginia* lawyer; an expression of the old act of assembly, I think Galloway's edition, that the state house yard should be " surrounded by a brick wall, and remain an *open inclosure* forever;" but I put him down by that act of the legislature of Virginia, which is entitled, a " *supplement to an act, entitled an act, to amend an act, making it penal to alter* the *mark* of an *unmarked* hog." The solecism was at least as great in one case as in the other; our act of the 17th Feb. 1762, has altered that phraseology, by saying that the " same shall be, and remain a *public green and walk forever.*"

An enquiry into the causes of that obloquy, under which the supreme court of this state laboured from the year 1800, down, during a period of several years.

This was owing to several causes; I shall begin with the *weakest*, and conclude with the *strongest*.

1stly, The supreme court itself, consisting of *four*, three of these were so connected by *affinities*, that they seemed to be but one person. For it is necessary, not only, that judges be independent of the people to a certain extent, but also, for the public confidence, that they be independent of *each other*. *Affinity*, and habits of close connexion, cannot but beget a suspicion of such resignation of individual opinion, as to be unfriendly to the freedom, and voluntary exercise of individual judgment. There is such a thing as even *a weaker brother*, or assistant judge in all *ministerial* matters at least, managing the arrangement, and not without influence by address, and representation in conciliating a determination to his way of thinking even in matters of a *judicial nature.*

For these reasons I did think, and now think with the public, without intending the least reflection upon the character of the judges, that the circumstance of a seeming attachment from family considerations with some of them, however accidental it may have been, and not the result of intrigue with the governor, that so many of a connexion having got upon the bench, was a drawback, if I may use a mercantile phrase, on the confidence of the public with regard to the judges who composed the bench at that time. But,

2dly; What was perhaps a more obvious circumstance, the *same three* of the four were from *wealth and connexion,* and supposed *political way of thinking,* all of the *aristocracy* of the commonwealth. For the two natural divisions of society are into the *few* and the *many;* or the aristocracy, and democracy under whatever name it may be disguised, or whatever character it may assume. I will not say that the *judiciary power* is not safely lodged in any case with that which may be deemed of the aristocracy of the state; but in general, I do not approve of it without such a due admixture, as will approximate to the common people. It is impossible that a man of wealth and powerful connexions, should not consider these of *better mould,* or meliore luto than the bulk; and have a leaning, perhaps imperceptible even to a good man, in favour of people that keep carriages, and who entertain, and are entertained by him. It will be observable if not in an individual case, yet at least in a tone of mind disposed to wind up the construction of statutes, favourably to the *inequality* of estates and conditions. But,

3dly; The arrangement of *their own services.* It was a radical error that the whole four judges, suffered themselves to be occupied a considerable part of their time, sitting upon a jury trial. It was a monstrous mis-application of their services, or arrangement of their duties. I saw the error, and knew the dissatisfaction that it occasioned both with bar and country; but though remonstrating to the court themselves, and to individuals of them I could not prevail in effecting an alteration. Each admitted the evil, but no change could be brought about. How or why the obstinacy of the habit which had been established, I may suspect, but I can not develope. The bar have always to me disclaimed any approbation of it, or that they were the cause of its *continuance*. But be it as it may, this was a substantial cause of dissatisfaction with the court, producing a delay in trials. For, as four men cannot walk four miles, sooner than one man, it is of no use to have four as to the effect of expediting the journey. The truth is, *it was a source of great delay, to have four on a jury trial.* A paper offered in evidence must be read by the presiding judge, and a note taken of it. It then comes to the second who must read, and note also; and to a third, and a fourth who has the same right to read and note; and, if he does not, at least read, he is under a disadvantage in understanding the cause. By the time it came to a fourth, *which* was my place, I found by both bar, and country, such an impatience at the vexatious delay, that I was led to dispense with looking at it at all; and to content myself with catching the substance from the argument of the counsel, or the hearing it cursorily read by them, without *seeing* it, which at all times fixes the impression of the contents more forcibly upon the mind.

> *Segnius irritant animum demissa per aures*
> *Quam quæ sunt occulis subjecta fidelibus.*

It happened that the two assistants immediately preceding me, took notes at great length, so that in copying a paper, there seemed to be no end. The delay of trials, therefore, by this, and other means, was a great cause of dissatisfaction with the administration of justice. I say *other means;* because, the trial was protracted *by the taking notes at great length of the testimony of witnesses;* and there was a constant cry of, " *wait* until I take that down," expressed by bar, or court.

The bringing many books, and reading cases at great length, was another means of the delay of trials; *together with the long comments made by counsel on the application of the authorities.* But I come now to a

4th, Or greater cause, than all these; the *constitution of circuit courts.* These had succeeded to the *nisi prius* courts, and were of the same nature, save that judgment *could be rendered*, at these courts, but *subject to revision in term.* It was the arrangement that *two judges* sat on trials at these courts ; though not made necessary by the act under which these courts were constituted. This was unnecessary, and injudicious, being subject in some degree to the same inconvenience with four sitting at nisi prius, in the city and county of Philadelphia. The time and services of the judges could have been distributed *singulatim* on jury trials. The augmentation of judges to this extent, prevented the dispatch of business ; for one could dispatch a trial, at least in the same time with two ; and hence there was less business done by half than might otherwise have been done. But taking the number of judges into view, it was impracticable, with any arrangement that could be made, to give satisfaction to the country, under the constitution of the circuit or *country nisi prius courts.* Of the greater number of causes depending, but few could be tried in the course of the time allotted for a county, and much time could not be allotted for twenty six or thirty counties. But as *all* the suitors must have a chance of having their actions brought forward, all must be put down for trial; and *witnesses* summoned, and attending in the respective cases. This made it a matter of great expence to the parties, and it was a source of great pain to the judges to be under the necessity, though but little prospect of reaching a case, to detain suitors, and witnesses for the trial. For an action could not be continued over until another sitting, without the consent of both parties. And the court, consistent with their duties elsewhere, could not sit more than once in the year. In fact it was an absurdity in the constitution of the court to be bringing judges from a distance *to each county of the state* to try matters of fact, which could not be supposed to be in contemplation by the new constitution, under which, *districts*, were established ; and a president, a legal character, was appointed to preside. Nisi prius courts had been continued for some time after the framing and adopting the constitution ; but this was an *inconsistency* with the provision which had been introduced ; and which had rendered it unnecessary, when carried into effect. At a circuit court,

it was found impossible to send away suitors satisfied, by
having their causes tried, when, from the *multiplicity* of actions on the docket at a circuit court once a year, but a few
could be tried; and the people not discerning always what
prevented it, laid *the blame upon the judges.* It would require twelve judges, one of these holding a circuit or nisi
prius court, every three months, to keep down, or discharge
the business without delay through the state. The system is
much preferable, of district judges, with writs of error to a
court of the last resort. Presidents alternating with each
other in adjoining districts, under some regulation, *might be
an improvement.* But in that case it would be unreasonable
not to allow *journey expences* according to the extra riding.
Something of this nature has been done in a particular case,
but provision ought to be made by a general law, *to a certain
extent, in all cases.* But, a

5th, And leading cause of that obloquy under which all
courts of justice, and the supreme court especially, laboured
from 1800 down, was to be found in *the temper of the times.*

The pressure of the preceding causes, had been felt by
the people, joined to others more latent, and of a personal
nature, so far as respected manners; and there was an unea-
siness, and struggle to throw off the whole judiciary. With
a certain description there was a struggle to throw off the *law*
altogether. This was the case pretty generally with those
editors of journals, who had been in the habit of arraigning
characters at their bar, and did not much relish there being
an appeal to the courts of law, in cases of libel. The common
law itself, therefore, became a subject of *defamation;* and
batteries were erected in every county; and gazettes
playing upon it in every direction. What was *common
law,* seemed to be uncertain, and could not be understood.
No one likes the restraint of law. The idea is always popular and pleasing, to be able to do without it. The language
of John Cade, in Shakespeare, is much the same with the popular and prevailing sentiments, at a certain period in Pennsylvania.

Even learning itself began to be considered as a disqua-
lification for office; at least for the legislature.

So far as respected law it seemed to be pretty generally

the opinion that it could be dispensed with in the decisions of questions of property; indeed, in every matter of demand, or even trespass, unless with some reservation of appeal in certain cases, the idea was, that *good sense*, without a knowledge of legal rules, might suffice. Hence the increase *of the jurisdiction of the justices of the peace; and the system of arbitrations.*

The then governor, who had been chief justice of the state, undertook to stem these innovations as *unconstitutional.* This naturally led to the *meditating a change of the constitution itself.* It requires great judgment and knowledge of the popular current in favour of what is called *reform*, to know how far to stem it, or how far to fall with it, until its force is spent. Where a reform is really judicious to a certain extent; if it is resisted, short of that extent, it swells to a torrent, and goes to a greater excess than it would otherwise have done. The people would have the jurisdiction of the justices encreased; and arbitrations introduced, that they might make the experiment. I was for having it done; and was sorry that any impediment or obstruction was thrown in the way. I well knew that the rage would satiate itself, and on experiment what was found salutary, would be retained; and what was otherwise would be amended or abrogated. I could pretty well see where it would ultimately rest; and that would not be far from where it began, as to arbitrations. The single amendment that I saw necessary in the law as to arbitration, was this, that at the instance of the defendant on the return of the writ into court, *a reference might be ordered by the court to be conducted under their direction.* And, at the discretion of the court themselves, in any case, *where a cause appeared proper for a reference, it should be ordered.* This would take place chiefly in matters of account; or in controversies of lesser moment.

I am favourable to the increase of the jurisdiction of the justices; and perhaps from the depreciation of the circulating medium, it might be still farther augmented. Be that as it may, I consider it much more favourably than I do *an indefinite reference to arbitration.*

A *discontent* with the judiciary branch, would seem, in

some measure, to have subsided. *The chief justice, at least, is above all exception.* The delay in the administration of justice, which as we have pointed out, was a great cause of it, has been in part removed. By an act of 24th February, 1806, it was provided that "no circuit court of the supreme court, shall be held otherwise than by a *single judge.* By this act also, the *high court of errors and appeals*, which was also a cause of delay, was *suspended*, so as to sustain no new cause ; but, with a power to hold *two terms* at which all the causes then before them should be determined and whereupon the said court should be abolished."

By an act of the 11th March, 1811, *circuit courts* were abolished, which had been a distressing grievance to the judges of the supreme court, and a great ground of delay of trials, and consequent dissatisfaction of the country. By this act it was provided that, *no issues in fact should be tried in bank;* a thing which the judges of the supreme court themselves, as I have already pointed out, ought long before, to have corrected, and which they had the power to do.

By the act of 24th February, 1806, the state had been divided into two districts of the supreme court, called the *Eastern* and *Western:* And by act 10th April, 1807, a *middle* district was established. And now by the act of 11th March, 1811, two new *district terms* were added; so that so far as respected the hearing causes in Bank, justice, if not brought home to *every man's door*, must be said, at least, to be brought *nearer to it.* All these were great improvements ; for writs of error, to a court in Bank at Philadelphia, were to a great part of the state, but a *mere illusion, and a name.* And yet before these *terms* were established, writs of error could ly only to that in Philadelphia, for it was the *term* for the whole state. *For this reason, a case at nisi prius, in the remote counties especially, not appealed from, founds but little presumption of an acquiescence in the law decided. And hence nisi prius decisions in Pennsylvania are of the less weight. The great bulk of these referred to in Smith's edition of the laws, ought to pass for nothing, except so far as to give information as to a knowledge of the history of the law, and the way of thinking of individual judges.*

By an act of the 30th March, 1811, "the district court for the city and county of Philadelphia," was established; to take jurisdiction, "where the sum in controversy shall exceed one hundred dollars," and to which court, "all suits, and causes depending in the court of common pleas of the city and county of Philadelphia, where the sum in controversy exceeds one hundred dollars shall be transfered, and the original jurisdiction of the said court of common pleas of the city and county of Philadelphia where the sum in controversy exceeds one hundred dollars, shall thenceforth cease and determine." This gave great relief to the court of common pleas, and, by such *tail race*, so to speak, the wheel of this court continued no longer *to wade*, as the phrase of the millers is. It is farther provided by this act, "that no suit shall be removed from the district court by certiorari, or habeas corpus; but, that in all cases, the final judgment of the said district court may be examined and affirmed, or reversed *on a writ of error from the supreme court.*" By this provision, a great relief is given to the *supreme court*, lessening the number of trials at nisi prius, so as to present a prospect of the wheel of that court, no longer continuing to wade also. For though there is a sufficiency of business for the *nisi prius* of the supreme court, even sitting 33 weeks in the year which is prescribed by law, yet it is in the power of the court by this means to keep the business pretty well done, and we hear now of little or no complaint of the delay, which has been justly termed a denial of justice; for it is a denial to a certain extent. All things considered, the system of the judiciary establishment in Pennsylvania, is the best in the union, but is even yet susceptible of some amendments. As I have already hinted, one of these is, the reducing the number of counties in some of the presidential districts to the constitutional limit of three. It is preposterous that there be four, five or six counties in a *mountainous* district; and not more than three, in some cases, in the *level* country, and where the seats of justice are more adjoining. It *is an unequal distribution for the same salary. The earliest attention* of the legislature, ought to be drawn to this; more especially

O o

as in the mountainous country of the *western* districts, a greater croud of business, from ejectments depending, has been thrown upon the dockets, from the abolition of the circuit courts. It is what reflects much credit upon the late and *present administration* of the state government, that the attention of the legislature has been so much drawn to amendments, both of the *judicial* codes, and *judiciary* system; and though sometimes *touched unskilfully*, in the opinion of scientific men; yet, *no question can be raised, but that a disposition has been shewn to do what was for the best.*

On the Naturalization Laws of Congress, and the principle involved in *the right of expatriation.*

CAN the subject of a foreign power, be *detained* contrary to his subjection? It would be *immoral* to detain a bale of cloth; and why the property of *a man?* But is he *detained* by our naturalization laws? It might not be *immoral* were we only to refuse the aid of our *municipal law*, for the apprehending and delivering him to his sovereign. But do not our naturalization laws oblige us to go farther; and to protect him against the claim of his sovereign demanding him? That cannot but be *implied;* for *allegiance* and *protection* are reciprocal.

But it cannot be construed, it will be said, as going further than to protect while under our municipal law. But the going that length must imply that he is his own property, and may be protected, at least, to that extent, *against the claim of his sovereign.* As to the protecting him while in our service, and out of the municipal jurisdiction, can involve a question of *power* only, not of *right*. If we have a *right* to protect him while under our municipal law, we have a *right* to protect him while out of it, and on the *high seas* if we can do it. The allegation therefore is idle, that *there is a distinction in the case, between the right to protect within our municipal jurisdiction, and out of it.*

But our right to protect to any extent must depend upon the right of the naturalized to withdraw himself from his allegiance; or, in other words, *expatriate himself.* Do not we sanction therefore, this right or claim of a right to expatriate himself, when we receive the *abjuration* of his allegiance, and admit him to become a citizen? We expressly exact from him that he shall "absolutely and entirely renounce and abjure all allegiance and fidelity to every foreign prince, potentate, state or sovereignty whatever, and *particularly by name,* the prince, potentate, state or sovereignty whereof he was before *a citizen or subject.*" See the naturalization acts, and particularly that of the 14th Ap. 1802.

If it was an immoral act in the naturalized to do this; if it was contrary to his duty *political or moral;* are we altogether just, and free from blame, who receive the abjuration? Are we not rather to be considered in the light of a particeps criminis and partakers of his guilt? His precedent obligation to his *sovereign* or *country,* if we can suppose an *inextricable* obligation to exist, must render the taking such an oath, immoral; and as it could not be taken to us unless we accepted it, we are at least instrumental, as the phrase is, to this breach of obligation. I do not just say in the language of Hudibras

———— A breach of oath is duple,
And either way admits a scruple
And may be ex parte of the maker
More criminal than the injured taker;
For he that strains too far a vow
Will break it like an o er-bent bow,
And he that made and forc'd it broke it,
Not he that for convenience took it.

But the protecting him against the *precedent obligation,* whether *at home* or *abroad,* must bring us clearly, and on every principle of law *natural, moral, or political,* under the denomination of his offence as *accessaries* or *as principals.* Or if we *distinguish,* it is at least the holding out an inducement, and taking benefit from the *iniquity,* if we do not procure it.

In law there is a distinction between the *stealing* and
the *receiving* stolen goods; but in morality, the distinction can only be in the degree of guilt. The nature of the
crime is the same. The one may bespeak more hardihood,
or address, but the minds of both are equally depraved *and
regardless of social duty.* The subject naturalized robs his
country of *himself*, or steals *himself* from it; and we participate in the *robbery or stealth*.

In order then to justify our naturalization laws and make
them honourable, it becomes *necessary* to assert *the right of
expatriation*. It becomes necessary to do more; to assert it
even in the face of a nation, or of those nations, a principle
of whose laws, it is, that a citizen, or subject *cannot expatriate himself.* This is the case particularly with England, in
whose case *no exception is made;* and it is notorious that we
receive the naturalization of *subjects* of that power.

But if we assert the right of *exuere ligeantiam* in the
case of British subjects, can it be made any question whether such a right exists with ourselves in these states, I
mean the right to put off or *strip ourselves of our allegiance*.
If a British subject has a right notwithstanding the principle
of his law, can it be a question *in our case* with regard to
whom it may be a question, whether such a principle of the
common law, was carried with us in our emigration from
that country. It is a principle *at least* of the European
country, from whence our emigration chiefly has come;
and it is in the face of this principle that we undertake *to naturalize.* Can we justify this, upon any ground but by saying that the principle is contrary to natural right, and that
we will not regard it. If locally unreasonable, and unjust
with these countries, can it be reasonable or just here? Can
it be expedient in those countries, when we must attack even
that foundation in saying that it is unjustifiable? To what
would I bring my argument? It is to those who question
the right of expatriation from these states; who allege that it
is a principle of the common law which we have carried with
us to these early colonies; and recognized by our laws and
institutions; particularly the laws of those states, and in par-

ticular Pennsylvania, who have expressly recognized the introduction of the common law without an exception of this principle; and the exclusion of which can be maintained only on the ground, that colonists carry with them only so much of the common law *as is applicable to their situation.* I bring my argument also to that decision of the judges of the supreme court of the United States; *or of any of them,* who have questioned the right of the citizens to expatriate, and throw off their allegiance, under any circumstances, *and in any case or at any time.* The naturalization laws *must be repealed or the right must be asserted.*

It may be said that, in the act of naturalizing, it is understood, or ought to be understood, that the naturalized person is to be considered as intitled to the protection of the laws only while here; to the rights of a citizen but still liable nevertheless to the *demand* of his sovereign; and to be surrendered when *demanded.* Be it so, that it is so to be understood by the U. S. naturalizing, and the person naturalized, which is *not the fact,* but suppose it so, would it not be a departure from the duties of one good neighbour to another, and, as in common life, a cause of dissatisfaction, if not of *litigation,* so between nations a cause of war, and a just cause of war, to *harbour runaways* from the service of each other, not of *hired* persons only, but of *servants for life.* And still more to *entice,* and seduce from service, by confering on them every *privilege of one born in the family?* The truth is, the right must be asserted in its *germ* and *progress,* or the naturalization laws, must be *modified,* or repealed *altogether.* They certainly must have proceeded on the ground that every individual in every political society, has a *natural,* and political right to leave it except *during war.* And this exception is expressly made by the naturalization act " That no alien who shall be a *native citizen,* denizen or subject of any country, state, or sovereign with whom the U. S. shall be at war at the time *of his application,* shall be then admitted to be a citizen of the U. S."

I do not enter into the question how far the principle of the nemini licet exuere ligeantiam, is founded in reason.

political conveniency, or original compact, or general consent. But looking at it in relation to the naturalization law
it is evident that both cannot stand together ; one or the
other must go by the board.

———•—•——

SINCE writing the above, it came into my mind to see
whether I could not throw out a few *hints* on the subject of
the right of expatriation, and consequent naturalization,
which is founded upon it.

I call these *hints*, because I cannot undertake a formal
dissertation, not having either *leisure*, or *abilities* to do the
subject justice. Does not nature seem to point out the right
from what we see *even in the inanimate world ?* The tide
ebbs and flows ; and " *the wind bloweth whence it listeth.*"

It is essential to the salubrity of the waters, and of the
atmosphere, that there be a *current*.

In the *vegetable* world, *seeds* and *plants* are said to flourish by a change of *soil*.

In the *animal* kingdom we hear of *crossing the strain* in
order to improve the breed. The *human species* is said to
degenerate both in *physcial* and *moral* qualities, by the in-
ter-marriage of near relations. *Dwarfs* and *idiots*, after a
length of time, have been observed to be the *offspring :* If
so, in a degree, the effect will be the same where the society
is *small*, the cause being the same.

But be these things as they may, there can be no question but that the *civilization* of man, and his *intellectual improvement* must be assisted by a free *ingress*, and *egress*
from one people to another. The collision *polishes ;* the
communication of ideas *improves* the understanding. Arts
and sciences are not the invention of one man ; but of many ;
nor are they brought to perfection by one nation ; but by many ; and that through successive generations of men upon the
earth. If a *denial*, therefore, of the right of expatriation con-
travenes the physical, and moral improvement of the species, and the amelioration of the condition of man, it must
be the voice of nature that such *right* exists.

What is there against it, but the *obligation* due to *a parent* and to *country?* But, it must depend upon the question, what will contribute to the greater sum of happiness to the species. For the general result must determine, the particular right. The lesser must give way to the greater. Much may be said in favour of the obligation due to the parent; and it will be just as easy to shew that the *subserviency* of *the whole life* is due, as that it terminates at the years of maturity, or 21 : or, that a parent has the right to inflict death, as he gave life : and the *Roman law* gave this power to a father. But this would be taking matters in an extreme to which no one could consent; or rather at which every mind would revolt. But what is there to limit the right if we take it on the footing of obligation? I know of nothing but the consideration stated, the happiness of the individual, and of the whole.

The same thing in the case of that *claim*, or *right*, if you chuse to have it so, which the society has *over all that are born under it.* It must be determined not on the principle of obligation; but of the greater general good to the species.

I had conceived an early prejudice against this claim in the case of Patkul, put to death by Charles 12th of Sweden, on the ground of the *ne exuere ligeantiam*, notwithstanding he had been 30 years in the service of the Emperor of Russia.

M'Donald's case also, Foster's Reports, 59, served to impress me unfavourably towards this as a principle of the common law. He was a native of Great Britain, but "had received his education from his early infancy in France; had spent his riper years in a profitable employance in that kingdom where all his hopes centered." Speaking of the doctrine of natural allegiance, the counsel in his case, represented it as a slavish principle not likely to prevail in these times, especially as it seemed to derogate from the principles of the revolution. This feeling was strengthened by a course of thinking on the one side, from our situation, and that of *emigrants*, in the revolutionary war and since. I had felt a predisposition, before I undertook to throw out these hints, to be able to satisfy myself, that this principle of the ne exuere, might be found to rest on no good foundation.

The fact is that I had become reconciled to a *resistance* to it; and there is no question with me as to the *right*, but the *power*, only. And I believe it is now brought to such a point that the *ultima ratio* must determine it.

It will not be understood, that I mean to say that the cause of the present war, or the continuance of it, is the naturalizing British subjects, though it may have led to it on the part of the enemy, and is *the pretence for continuing it.* For whether these states had naturalized or not, they might *employ* British seamen, or it might be alleged that they did employ, and the *redress* as they would call it by *the act of the party*, in the law phrase, would be resorted to; which would produce the consequence of *taking* or *mistaking* the American for the British in the caption. So that, unless it *is left to be a matter between the governments, and of national investigation, and not of individual interference, it will be impossible, that controversy can be avoided.*

Of certain acts of congress, and the construction put upon those acts by the courts of the United States.

By an act of 4 Aug. 1790, sect. 45. it is provided, " that where any bond for the payment of duties shall not be satisfied on the day it became due, the collector shall forthwith cause a prosecution to be commenced for the recovery of the money thereon, by action or suit at law, in the proper court having cognizance thereof; and, *in all cases of insolvency*, or where any estate in the hands of executors, and administrators shall be insufficient to pay all *the debts due from the deceased*, the debt due to the United States on any such bond, *shall be first paid.*"

And by an act of 2d May, 1792, sec. 18, it is provided that " the cases of insolvency in the preceding act mentioned, shall be deemed to extend, as well to cases in which a debtor not having sufficient property to pay all his or her debts, shall have a voluntary assignment thereof for the benefit of his or her creditors, or in which the estate and effects of an *absconding*, concealed, or absent, debtor shall have been attached, by process of law, as to cases in which an act of legal bankruptcy shall have been committed."

By an act of 3d March, 1797, sec. 5, it is provided "that where any *revenue officer, or other persons*, hereafter becoming indebted to the United States, by bond, or otherwise, shall become insolvent; or where the estate of any deceased debtor, in the hands of executors or administrators, shall be insufficient to pay all the debts due from the deceased, *the debt due from the United States shall be first satisfied;* and the priority hereby established, shall be deemed to extend, as well to cases in which a debtor, not having sufficient property to pay all his debts, shall make a voluntary assignment thereof; or in which the estate and effects of an absconding, concealed, or absent debtor, shall be attached by process of law, as to cases in which an act of legal bankruptcy shall be committed."

This *prerogative* assumed by the United States is alleged to be founded on sec. 8 of the constitution of the United States, "The congress shall have power," &c.——

" 18 : To make all laws which shall be necessary," &c. Now I am not one of those who have been for stinting these *powers* so much as has been contended in the case of a *national bank*. For I think such a means of economy is absolutely necessary, and the money concerns of the union cannot well be transacted without; at least, not to so much advantage for the general good. But I hold it *not necessary to take away the property of an individual to serve the community*. Is it not *taking away my property*, when a debt due to me is taken away, and the *demands* of the United States against my debtor must be satisfied, before I can come in. In the case of a *revenue officer*, it might be justifiable in a case where I have trusted him after he had been appointed a revenue officer, because I had notice that he had been so appointed, and it was at my own risk, and *with a knowledge of this privilege of the United States* that I gave him credit. But having given him credit, *before he was an officer*, shall that *fund* on which I gave him credit be swallowed up by

P p

the United States who after my debt, and cause of action had accrued, had thought proper to appoint him such.

But the act goes further than even the case of a *revenue officer;* it extends to the case of any *other person* who shall become indebted to the United States. Thus, if I sell a tract of land to an individual, transfer property of any description, or contract with him for services, and render it whereby a debt becomes due; and for which I may even take his obligation under seal, or what is more, have brought a suit and obtained *judgment;* yet a demand of the United States subsequently founded, or established, will take a *priority; or sweep the whole from my grasp.* I have been informed by the very gentleman who draughted the bill, that the words *other person,* were not in the bill as originally draughted; but were put into it as it passed through the houses, a representative observing to him that *it would all have enough to do.* His idea was that such a provision would be necessary. Necessitas nullam habet legem, is a maxim as ancient as the Latin language; and, that necessity has no law, is as old as good English; and even in old Saxon or the broad Scotch, it is said, needs must when the devil drives. But what is there to drive to this? Has not the congress power to lay taxes *ad libitum?* Why then filch away from an individual his debt due to him, for the sake of the public? *It is the prerogative of the king of Great Britain;* but how came it to be that of the United States, unless it is given under this term *necessary?* It is not given, but *by a species of political cowardice in the representatives,* taxes are avoided because the laying of these might affect their immediate popularity. The *individual wronged* has but one mouth to exclaim against the injustice; but the multitude that feel taxation to which they are bound to submit have many mouths. The representatives, for the time being, are unwilling to lay taxes though equal on the whole community; and they *consult themselves* at the expence of Tom, Dick, and Harry, who are in the towns, or in the woods; and whose voice individually cannot be so much heard. They are in the habit of starting at the word tax, like Asmodeus, at the smell of burnt fish; but are not shocked at the broad view of *individual injustice*. This section of the act ought to be repealed; and the provision restrained to the case of a *revenue officer* trusted, and the debt to an individual which became due *before* the appointment. This is the farthest that the act of the legislature of the Union, on the score of natural, and moral, or legal, and political justice, had a right to go. Knowledge to all the citizens that the United States have *a priority of lien* upon all the property of a revenue officer, would save from the giving him credit, or if given, would take away from the creditor in such case, the right to complain. The United States have it in their power to exact *security* to any amount from a revenue officer, or *other person* with whom they may contract; and this is their *remedy a priore* against delinquencies, and not a posteriore, the relieving in a case of *default* at the expence of a citizen who is in common with the whole body politic bound to contribute his proportion to the exigencies of a peace or war establishment. It cannot therefore be *necessary* to take the property of a citizen in this way; and if not necessary, is unjust. Under what idea but that of being *necessary* can it be taken? The Congress have no power, but that which is given them. They have no *common law prerogative* as in the case of the *king of Great Britain*, or which the commonwealth of a state may exercise where it is given by law, because that law has the assent of every citizen; or, in contemplation of law, is supposed to have it. Though even in this case, it may be questionable; and ought to be questioned. In the state of Pennsylvania, debts due to the commonwealth, instead of being preferred, are postponed; and much to the credit of the people who have rejected this badge of royalty, as *uncongenial with a republican government*. This amendment was made upon the former law of an ante-revolutionary period which followed the common law in the case of the kingly prerogative. It is not only reasonable that if a loss in the case of an insolvent debtor is to be borne, it should fall upon the *many* instead of falling upon *one*, but I deny that the commonwealth has a right to make it otherwise; for the property of one individual cannot be taken away, without a *compensation*. And a preference of payment in the case of an insolvent, or where *the property of a. deceased person*, cannot discharge the whole, is the same thing as taking away what belongs to an individual without giving him a compensation; yet on behalf of the United States this is claimed as a right, and enacted by law. Is this law constitutional? There can be no doubt of the right to enquire into the constitutionality of a law of the United States. For the judiciary of the union admit that right, and exercised it themselves. They go a little farther, and claim the right of enquiring into the *constitutionality* of a law of a *state :* witness the case of Vanhorne and Dorance where a law of the state of Pennsylvania was held to be against the constitution of that state, not because it took away property without giving compensation, but for not giving it in *money ;* though by the common law of England, and by the law of just retribution, it ought not to be in *money* but in *kind*. It was given in kind, a fee for a fee, or *land* for *land*. But if, as to the *medium* of the compensation, the courts of the union, were so squeamish, how is it that they have overlooked this *law*, which takes away a right, or *interest* in a debtor's property, and makes *no compensation ?*

But the fact is, that instead of questioning the law, they have, by their construction, extended the operation, or effect of it. So far from questioning the law, they have sanctioned *the application* of the maxim to the case, " *that the interest of all should prevail over that of an individual.*" 3 Cranch, 82. This maxim is true, where *both* cannot *stand together ;* but not true as applied *in this* case ; but rather the idea that *the public* has a broad back, and ought to sustain a loss, rather than an individual, where one or the other must sustain a loss : divided among the whole, the loss of a *particular* debt is small, but may be ruinous to a single citizen. But by construction, they have extended the operation of the laws of the United States, on this head, as it would appear to me, beyond what either *the letter*, or the *spirit* would require. For this, see the argument by the counsel, for the defendant in error, in the case of the United States v. Fisher et al. 2 Cranch,

358. The observations of counsellor Ingersoll on the head of *prerogative*, with us, termed privilege, supersedes all that I could have to say, in stating how far this privilege is carried, even beyond that of the kingly prerogative in England. It may suffice to extract a few of his observations. " It may be useful (says he,) to consider the prerogative of the Kings of England in this particular, at the least liberal period of its juridical history, where unreasonable preferences of the sovereign over the subject, fill and deform its every page. By the statute of 33 Hen. 8. chap. 39. sec. 74. " his debt, shall in suing out execution, be preferred to that of every other creditor who hath not obtained judgment before the king commenced his suit, 3 Bl. Com. 420. This only makes the commencement of the king's suit equivalent to a judgment in favour of a subject."

" The king's judgment also affects all lands which the king's debtor hath at, or after the time of contracting his debt. 3 Bl. Com. 420. This relates to lands only. The personal estate escapes the royal grasp. Even there the distinction for which we contend has always been observed. The preference in favour of the king is principally confined to cases where public monies have been received by an accountable officer to public use. It does not extend to transactions of a common nature."

By the statute of 13 Elizabeth, chap. 4. " The lands and tenements, goods and chattels of tellers, receivers, collectors, &c. and other officers of the revenue, are made liable to the payment of their debts."

" These are the models which the act of congress was intended to imitate. The lands of such revenue officers are liable to process, under the king's judgment, even in the hands of a bona fide purchaser; though the debt due to the king was contracted by the vendor many years after the alienation. 3 Bl. Com. 420. Here the distinction is still kept up between the revenue officers and others."

" If goods are taken on a fieri facias against the king's debtor, and before they are sold, an extent come at the king's suit, tested after the delivery of the fieri facias to the sheriff, these goods cannot be taken upon the extent, but the execution upon the fieri facias shall be completed. 4 T. R. 402. Rorke v. Dayrell.

" Even Queen Elizabeth, with all the supremacy of absolute sway, did not carry her prerogative claims to the extent now urged for a *federative republic*, and representative democracy."

" With the several exceptions already stated, and which are confined principally to revenue officers, the king of England has no *priority* in the recovery of his debts over the meanest peasant of his dominions."

Mr. Ingersoll goes on to shew why the *construction* of the act in question ought to be *restricted* to the case of *receivers of public monies.*

" How strange and improbable it is," says he, " that congress should give a preference so much exceeding the royal prerogative of England? Unless such a construction be absolutely necessary, the inconvenience attending it will undoubtedly prevent its adoption. Besides the destruction of private credit, and the ruin of individuals, it would repeal all the state laws of distribution of intestate estates ; it would prostrate all state priority, which in those cases has been long established. It would produce a collision between the prerogative of the states, and the United States. Suppose the treasurer of a state should become indebted to the United States, the latter would take his whole property, in opposition to any law of the state which had passed to secure herself against the default of her officers."

" If that act is to have the extended *construction* contended for on the part of the United States, the act is *unconstitutional and void.* If *liens general or specific ;* if judgments and mortgages are to be set aside by the prerogative of the United States, it will be to impair the obligation of contracts by an *ex post facto law.*"

" *Under what clause of the constitution is such power given to congress ?* Is it under the general power to make all laws necessary and proper for carrying into execution the particular powers specified ? If so, where is the *necessity*, or where the propriety of such a provision, and to the exercise of what other power is it necessary ?"

" *It is in direct violation of the constitution*, inasmuch as it deprives the debtor of his trial by jury without his consent."

Johnston, J. Do you admit the law respecting the final adjustment of accounts at the treasury to be constitutional as to revenue officers ?

Ingersoll. We neither admit, nor deny it as to them. But we deny the power of the congress to give the United States, a preference in all cases of persons who may become indebted to them in every possible manner.

It was not necessary for counsellor Ingersoll to go that length in the case before the court. But it has been seen that I deny the right to give a preference in any case.

Patterson, J. Do you contend that by the 5th sec. the priority of the United States, will avoid even a mortgage to an individual?

Ingersoll. I say that the opposite construction leads to that.

I will take upon me to say the same thing. If the act, and the construction put upon it by the court, is carried out to its consequence, it cannot be otherwise. What is a specific lien more than a general lien as to the effect of it? It had been considered as applying to the general lien of a *judgment*, and why not to the specific lien of a mortgage? A judgment binds the lands so that the debtor has but an interest in these, subject to the payment of the debt. In the case of a mortgagee it is the same. If a distinction is made, it is not founded on law or reason, but an *arbitrary construction of the court.*

But it is not the construction of the court, that I encounter, or think it worth while to trouble myself with; it is the acts themselves that I call in question, as to *the powers of congress to enact.* I wish to go to the foundation of *the illegality of such legislation.* The *substratum* or scaffolding being struck away, the construction will fall of course.

It was a case in which the commonwealth of Pennsylvania was concerned, that led the supreme court of this state to consider this question. I think it was the case of a *judgment* in favour of the state against Nichols. Execution had been levied, and the money brought into court. A motion was made on the part of the United States to take it out, in favour of a debt due to them by the same defendant. It was refused by the court. I have not heard what became of the *appeal*, being a case of *concurrent jurisdiction ;* but I could not but see that if pressed, and decided in favour of the United States, it might terminate in the same disagreeable controversy, with that of Olmstead and the Commonwealth.

The truth is the whole system of *legislation* and *construction* in hac parte, is unconstitutional and void. There might be the like reason for introducing the prerogative of the sovereign of England if there was the like *necessity*. Every fiscal prerogative of that country, was in lieu of taxation to support the government. It had its foundation at a time, and under a state of things when no taxes were laid, but feudal services exacted by the sovereign ; or at least when the only establishment for the King's household, or support allowed him, was from this source. What have we to do with any thing of this kind under our government, where a provision is made by law for this purpose ; and where the *great source* of revenue, is, or ought to be the free contribution of the people, by way of *equal tax through the medium of their representatives.* Of this nature is, what they pay *voluntarily* by duties of imports ; or which may be laid upon internal manufactures, or negociations ; or *directly* upon the real or personal estate of individuals in proportion to their property. It may be said, it will occasion *insurrections* to exact a revenue by *direct* contributions ; that money cannot be extorted; it must be taken circuitously, and clandestinely from a free people. If that should be found the case, it will prove them unworthy of a free government. But let us have an open and direct application to the virtue of the people, until it shall be proved that they have not virtue sufficient to justify the experiment, or the continuance of the application, to their understanding,—and not to their blind sides, as it may be expressed, by surreptitious, and indirect means : more especially if these means are in their nature unjust, and a robbery of individuals. Of this nature I take all priority, or preference in the payment of debts due to the United States, over the private claims of a citizen. *Prior lien, or attachment*, as between citizen and citizen, ought to be the law of the land, as between the citizens of the union, and the union itself.

On the extent of the judicial power of the courts of the United States.

I DO not enter into the question, whether the congress may not " from time to time, *abolish* such inferior courts, as they may from time to time ordain and establish." On this head see Tucker's Blackstone's Commentaries, Appendix, 361. But the *inferior* courts abolished by the act 29th April, 1802, did appear to me, according to the title of the act under which they were established, to be " a more convenient organization of the courts" of the United States. The administration of the laws, under the judicial power of the United States, was, by those courts, brought *nearer to the doors* of suitors, jurors, and witnesses. These called upon, and attending from an *extreme of a state* to some one place within it, was *inconvenient*, not only from the *expence*, but the *loss of time*, and in some cases, personal *inability* to attend, at so great a distance. It would seem to me that some *arrangement* of this nature, must be re-established, if the judicial power of the union, *continues to be extended as it now is*. The resolution of J. Breckenridge, then senator, since attorney general, offered in the senate of the United States, appeared to me to be a natural, if not *necessary* consequence of the *abolition* of these *inferior courts*. This was to abridge the extent of the judiciary power of the union, confining it to " cases arising under the constitution, the laws of the United States, and treaties made, or which shall be made, under their authority; to all cases affecting embassadors, other public ministers and consuls; to all cases of ad-

miralty and maritime jurisdiction; to controversies to
which the United States shall be a party; to controversies
between two or more states, and between a state and citizen
of another state." Here the power might have a close; and
by an *amendment* to the constitution, what remains might be
struck away. This is " to controversies between citizens of
different states, between citizens of the same state, claiming
lands under grants of different states, and between a state,
or the citizens thereof, and foreign states, citizens or subjects."

It is not only to the *inconvenience* under the *present* system that the objection lies; but there is a radical objection
at bottom to such extent of judicial cognizance, of the United
States' courts under any arrangement, or *organization:* that
is, the *moral* improbability to say the least of it, that the
judges of these courts, can have a competent knowledge of
the laws of the particular states, to enable them to decide on
local questions according to the *acts* of the legislature, and
the established construction thereon; or according to local
usages, and practice. But it may be answered, that there
can be no necessity of having a knowledge of the *construction* of the acts of the legislature; or of the practice of the
courts, since not bound exclusively by these. Hoc gravamen
est; this is the rule; it is the *evil* that they are not bound.
It would at least be expedient that they should have a knowledge of these. That is *impracticable.* It is not the lucubrationes viginti annorum; but an hundred years that could suffice for this. The life of man would not suffice, with the
greatest application, to acquire such minute information of
the laws, usages and practice of each particular state in the
union, as could satisfy a conscientious judge himself, that he
did not err in deciding controversies, according to the laws,
usages, and customs of each. And, it is not to be wondered
at if under such disadvantage they would seem to have erred
in many cases, or, at least, have not secured that confidence
in their decisions, which their talents, and integrity, not under such disadvantages, would doubtless have secured with
the bar, and with the country.

It would seem to me that if attorney general Brecken-ridge, had brought forward his resolution for an amendment of the constitution, in the first instance, and before the *aboli-tion* of the *inferior* courts established, of which I have spoken, it might have been carried in the senate, and adopted by the states; at least it would have been more advisable to have taken the sense of the people in this way. For if it had been thought advisable to have *retrenched* the judiciary pow-er of the union in this way, there would have then, been no necessity for these *inferior courts* which had been so esta-blished, and the province of duty being lessened by the ju-risdiction struck away, these courts could with more propri-ety have been abolished; and more especially as little or no business out of the sea-ports, and commercial towns, would have remained. Such amendment to the constitution must take place; or these courts in some shape, on the score of *conveniency*, at least, must be restored.

Of Errors, as it would seem to me, in decisions of the Supreme Court of the United States.

CUI bono, it may be said; of what use to *review* deci-sions; since it is the maxim, non ita refert quod sit lex, quam quod sit *nota*. The *nota* must mean *settled;* because what is *unsettled*, cannot be known. And it must be the ef-fect of fluctuating determinations, that the law must remain *uncertain*, and therefore unknown. But it is with no idea of contributing a mite towards the changing a determination, or the principle of it, that this examination is undertaken. It would be absurd to suppose it. Even a judge of that court; or even the *whole court*, could not change *the determination*, though they might have it in their power to change the prin-ciple; or, in other words, their opinion of what was the law in a like case. But of what use can it be that an individual undertakes to think differently from what a court has decid-ed? I cannot say that I can give any other reason than my own ambition, to let people see that I also have an opini-

on; and am capable of remarking, where there may appear
to be error. But what other reason can be given in many
cases of *criticism?* For instance, it is of no use to remark an
historical error, in the divine poem of Milton, as in that
verse;

    " When Charlemain with all his peerage fell
    " By Fontarabbia———."

Yet, the fact is, that *Roland* fought the battle; and Charle-
main was not present, and neither *fell* there, or any where
else; but *died in his bed.* The verse might be altered to
meet the *truth* of history; and, at the same time, without
spoiling the *measure.* But I have no idea that the printers
will make the alteration in the next edition. However, will
it not be pardonable, not only to have made the observation;
but also to shew how the alteration could be made? Would
it not read as well, and perhaps not be less poetical, to say,

    When all the peerage fell of Charlemain
    By Fontarabbia———

But it may be stiled *presumption* in me to attempt a remark upon a decision of the supreme court of the United
States. I would admit this, did it not furnish an objection
against all criticism, where the subject is of transcendant
eminence and dignity: Thus, in the case of Milton as already mentioned; whose genius is superior to what mine can
pretend to be; as far as

    " Thrice from the centre to the ethereal pole;"
or the orbit of the sun himself,

    " Nine times the space that measures day and night."

Yet it is allowable even in such cases, to speak of a *speck*
which the microscopic eye of a *mosquetto,* can perhaps alone
discern. It savoured of *profanity* in him who said, though
he meant it but as wit, that 'had he been consulted in the
formation of himself, he would have put the calfs of his legs
before, that *he might not break his shins.*' But, of all things
human, and beneath divine, it is lawful to hazard a correc-
tion.

Having premised this, and taking up the reports of

Cranch, I find the case of *William Marbury v. James Madison, Secretary of State of the United States.* 1 Cranch, 137.

The first question that ought to have been made in this case, was, *have inferior courts, a power given to them by the constitution, or the laws, to issue a mandamus?* In the *constitution* there is nothing said about such a power in the *one* court or the *other*. Independent of the act establishing the *judicial courts of the United States*, neither *supreme* or *inferior* court had the power; unless we should suppose that the supreme court succeeded to the power of the court of *King's Bench;* being the highest court of the union, and it being necessary for the administration of justice, that such writ, which has been called a high prerogative writ, should issue. But the legislature of the union would seem to have thought that it was at least questionable, or that it had been questioned, whether such a writ could issue even from this *the highest court.* For by the act to establish the judicial courts of the United States, it is provided that the supreme court shall have power amongst other things, " *to issue writs of mandamus in cases warranted by the principles and usages of law, to any courts appointed, or persons holding offices under the authority of the United States.*" Was a law necessary to give such a power to the *supreme court*, and could an *inferior* court exercise it, without a provision *specially* giving it. It cannot be said to be *impliedly* given; for these courts themselves are made the *subject of a mandamus* to whom it is to issue; and it would be an inconsistency to say, if these courts refuse to do a thing, or to give *redress*, they might issue a mandamus to themselves in the first instance. Or, in the case of *other persons holding offices*, which are the words of the act, is there any power given to them under the act to issue *a mandamus?* The supreme court shall have *appellate jurisdiction from the circuit courts.* But there must be *original* jurisdiction first given, before there can be *appellate.* Can any one suppose, for a moment, that any such high prerogative power would be given by the congress to an inferior circuit court? There is no such power given even to any of the higher courts in England. It is a prerogative of the sovereignty, and so called; and can issue only from that bench which controls all inferior jurisdiction; and where alone of all the courts, *in plena majestate*, the king himself, is supposed to be present.   Can any one suppose then that a writ of such high and supereminent authority could be intended to be given, unless we were concluded by express words, from doubting of the trust; what is more to courts of inferior jurisdiction *established by the act*, under our republican government?   Here we may naturally suppose the citizen *more jealous*, of such writs of high prerogative.   No; it never came into the head of any person before this decision, that an *inferior court of the United States had the power to issue such a writ.*

The king's bench has the power to issue this writ of mandamus, to the court of common pleas, who, it might happen, might refuse to proceed to judgment, that a writ of error might be brought; or for other cause might be the subject of the writ of *mandamus;* to the exchequer also.   What did the congress mean more than to give a similar power over inferior jurisdictions to the supreme court of the union. The inferior courts of the union had a right to raise their heads, indeed, if it could be supposed that such a power was given to them.   Even in their own case where they refused to do a thing, they must first, it seems, *issue a mandamus to themselves*, and decide upon it, before it could be brought before the supreme court, of the United States.   This would be sitting *as judges in their own case*, if the mandamus had been directed to them commanding them to do an act.

If there is no *original* jurisdiction in an inferior court, there can be no *apellate;* for an *appeal* implies a decision from whence an appeal is made.

But by art. 3, sec. 2, n. 2, " in all cases affecting embassadors, other public ministers, and consuls and those in which a state shall be party, the supreme court shall have *original* jurisdiction.   In all the other cases *before mentioned*, the supreme court shall have apellate jurisdiction."   That must be in all other cases, where the inferior courts have original jurisdiction given them; for original and apellate are relative terms, and where the one does not exist, the other can have no place.   The truth is that with regard to a *mandamus*, the relation of the terms does not exist, because it is the supreme court alone to whom any jurisdiction is given in this case.

What then, to use the language of the court, could constitute " *the peculiar delicacy of the case, the novelty of some of the circumstances, and the real difficulty attending the points which occur in it ?*" I can see no difficulty in any of the points, nor is there any *novelty* of *principle* in the determination. But I will acknowledge there was, a *peculiar delicacy*, as the court express it, *in the case.* It was whether the *judiciary* should enter into a contest with the *executive.* They could not but see that if the mandamus issued, it must be directed to the *marshal*, who was the officer of the executive, and who might be instructed *not to obey;* and if an attachment issued against the marshal, for not obeying, who was to put him in jail but *himself?* The court would be placed in an *undignified* situation in such a case, who had issued a writ which they could not *enforce.*

On the marshal's return to the writ that he was instructed by the executive not to pay regard to it, what remained but to represent this to the legislature that the executive might be *impeached*, if they should be of the same opinion with the court, as to the power of issuing the mandamus. But the legislature might be of opinion that the writ was not grantable in *such a case*, and instead of impeaching the president, *impeach* the judges who had issued it. Or, by repealing the *law* under which the supreme court was constituted, these judges might be got rid of altogether. For though the constitution provides that there shall be a *supreme court*, yet the *identity of judges* has nothing to do with this. There could be a supreme court with one set as well as another. The legislature had shown what they could do, *in a case just before*, that of the *circuit courts;* and they might be disposed to do the like in the case of the supreme court.

Not that I would insinuate that if the matter was *perfectly clear* to the judges, they would hesitate for the sake of their own standing, to grant the writ. But weighing the *embarrassment* of what might be the consequence, they may naturally be supposed to have had a leaning, or predisposi-

tion to avoid it. Or, to use the *legal term*, may have thought
some *astutia* justifiable in finding reason to avoid it.   But it
might not be for *their own sakes* merely, or any regard to
the commissions which they held, but for the sake of the
constitution which might be injured in their case, and for the
sake of that *precedent* which might be set at a time when one
party had succeeded to the administration on the overthrow
of another.   So far am I from finding fault with the judiciary in this instance, that I will admit the prudence of what
they did ; or, in other words, the *expediency*.   And if there
could be a case where the issuing the writ was *discretionary*,
this was such a case.   But I am speaking of the *legal correctness* of the decision as to the power of granting the mandamus, which was put upon the ground of a want of *original
jurisdiction in such a case*. The court saw the *delicacy* of the
case as involving not their own standing merely, but the *sta-
bility* of the judiciary branch of the government, which might
be endangered, by an *unreasonable*, and as they would seem
to have thought, a *questionable stand* to support it.

A principle of self-preservation, not of themselves merely but of the *post* which they occupied to use a *military* phrase,
may have dictated the withdrawing from a contest which
might be attended with unfavourable consequences, and at
all events disagreeable.   It is said of the Nile receding from
the blaze of conflagration, when Phæton misguided the cha-
riot of the sun,

Occuluitque caput.——
And of the *Earth* itself on that occasion,

Suum que

Retulit os in se.——

It was not certain what the *return* of secretary Madison
would be ; but it might be a refusal *to make a return :* in that
case *an attachment* must issue, which the marshal might refuse to *serve*. These circumstances could not but be foreseen, and are what we may presume, were in the view of the
court, when they speak of it as a case of *peculiar delicacy*,
and attended with circumstances *novel* in their nature.

The following official opinion of the attorney general of the United States has been transmitted to the different collectors, for their government.

SIR,

I have read and considered the papers and documents referred to me relative to the case of the *mandamus*, issued by the circuit court of the United Sates for the district of South Carolina, to compel the collector of the port of Charleston to grant clearances to certain vessels.

The first question that naturally presents itself, is, whether the court possessed the power of issuing a *mandamus* in such a case ?

A mandamus in England is styled a prerogative writ, and in that country is awarded solely and exclusively by the court of king's bench.

The constitution and laws of the United States establish our judicial system. To these we must refer in order to ascertain the jurisdiction of the respective courts, the extent of their powers, and the limits of their authority.

The " *Act* to establish the judicial courts, of the United States," passed on the 24th September, 1789, declares and defines the jurisdiction of the several courts thereby created, and among these the jurisdiction of the circuit courts. Upon a careful and attentive perusal, it will be found to delegate to the circuit courts no power to issue writs of *mandamus*. In the thirteenth section of that act this authority is expressly given to the supreme court of the United States. In like manner it is specially provided by the act of the 3d of February, 1801, that the supreme court shall have power to issue writs of *mandamus*. This last act having been repealed, and the former revived, the question must rest on the true construction to be given to the original act.

The eleventh section defines and limits the jurisdiction of the circuit courts. It is specially appropriated to this single object. There are no expressions in this section which can fairly be interpreted to confer the authority of issuing writs of mandamus. Nor can the power be either implied or inferred from any language it contains. It is true, the proceeding by mandamus in England is on the crown side, as it is termed, of the court of king's bench. But it is a prosecution relative to a civil right to enforce it, and to obtain prompt redress ; and not to punish criminalty as in the case of an offence. The provision therefore that the circuit courts, " shall have exclusive cognizance of all crimes and offences cog-

R R

nizable under the authority of the United States, except when the act otherwise provides, &c." cannot warrant such a proceeding. Besides the same act does provide that the supreme court shall issue writs of mandamus.—An authority given perhaps because its jurisdiction extended all over the United States.

In the first place, the law gave the collector complete discretion over the subject. According to the opinion he might form, he possessed competent authority to grant, or refuse a clearance And I apprehend where the law has left this discretion in an officer, the court, agreeably to the British practice and precedents, ought not to interpose, by way of mandamus.

Secondly. In this case, there was a controuling power in the chief magistrate of the United States. There was, in fact, an express appeal given to the president by the very words of the act of congress, which authorizes the collectors to detain vessels, " until the decision of the president of the United States be had thereupon." By the mandamus, the reference to the president is taken away, and the collector is commanded to clear the vessel without delay. Agreeably to the English authorities under such circumstances, it is not the course, I believe, to issue a mandamus.

Thirdly. The parties, it seems, had their legal remedy against the collector, and it is not usual, if not unprecedented, to grant a mandamus in such a case.

Fourthly. A mandamus is not issued to a mere ministerial officer to compel him to do his duty. The court will leave the parties to their remedy, by action or even by indictment. In England, in a very late case, they declared that they would not grant a mandamus to a ministerial officer, such as the treasurer of a county, for the proper remedy was by indictment.

I am aware of a precedent in which it seems to be admitted, that a mandamus may issue to the commissioners of excise, to compel them in a proper case, to grant a permit. The case is more analagous to the one now before us, than any other, I have been able to discover, after a diligent research. But in this instance, the point was not made, nor the question argued. Besides, the commissioners of excise in England form a board for superintending the collection of that branch of the revenue. They constitute, in many respects, a court of inferior jurisdiction, which, in particular cases takes cognizance in a summary way, of offences against the excise laws. A mandamus might be granted to such a tribunal, when it would not be issued to a mere ministerial officer acting under them in collection of the revenue

The fourteenth section, immediately succeeding that which gives this authority in plain and positive terms to the supreme court, solely, if not exclusively (and the affirmative frequently, and in this case justly, I think implies a negative) contains the following provision : " All the before-mentioned courts of the Unit-ed States (including the supreme, as well as the circuit and dis-trict courts) shall have power to issue writs of *scire facias*, *habeas corpus*, and all other writs not specially provided for by statute, which may be necessary for the exercise of their respective juris-dictions." This clause cannot affect the case, I conceive. The mandamus is a writ, which we have seen is specially provided for by law. This section was evidently not designed to give any ad-ditional jurisdiction to either of the courts, but merely the means of executing that jurisdiction already granted to them respectively. The issuing of a *mandamus* in the case under consideration was an act of original jurisdiction. Precisely as much so as it would have been in the supreme court, to have exercised the power in the case of Marbury vs. Madison. In that case, the supreme court declared, that to issue a mandamus to the secretary of state, would be, to exercise an original jurisdiction, not given by the constitu-tion, and which could not be granted by congress, The constitu-tion having enumerated or declared the particular cases in which the supreme court should exercise original jurisdiction, though there were no negative expressions, the affirmative they consider-ed implied them. It was on this principle alone they refused to exert their authority.

The practice I believe, has uniformly been, so far as I can trace it from the books of reports, that have been published, or from re-collection and experience on the subject, to apply to the supreme court for a *mandamus*. This court it is true has determined not to issue the writ, when it would be an act of original jurisdiction. But this I apprehend, can afford no ground for the circuit court's assuming an authority, which the supreme court have declined, un-less by a legislative act the power be delegated to them.—This power is not inherent, nor necessarily incidental to a court of jus-tice even of general jurisdiction. For in England but a single one, of several courts having general jurisdiction, possesses the autho-rity. Neither the chancery, the common pleas, nor the exchequer, though classed among the king's superior courts, and having ge-neral jurisdiction over the realm, can exercise this power. It is the peculiar privilege of the king's bench alone. Our circuit courts have a mere local and subordinate jurisdiction. Their analogies therefore with the four courts of England having general and superior jurisdiction, must be very weak, and still weaker their claim to the pre eminent distinction of the king's bench, which possesses solely the exclusive authority of issuing the mandamus.

For these reasons I am induced to believe from the best consideration I have been enabled to give the subject, that the circuit court of South-Carolina had not authority to issue a mandamus to the collector of the port of Charleston.

It is scarcely necessary to remark, that when a court has no jurisdiction, even consent will not give it, and much less will the mere tacit acquiescence of a party in not denying their authority.

Independent of this serious and conclusive objection to the proceedings adopted by the court, there are others entitled to consideration. For supposing the court did not err in the exercise of jurisdiction, and admitting the British doctrines on the subject, without restriction or limitation could be extended to this country, there are legal exceptions to the course they have pursued, supported by the English authority.

It results from this view of the subject, that the mandamus issued by the circuit court for the district of S. Carolina, was not warranted by any power vested in the circuit court by statute : nor by any power necessarily incident to courts, nor countenanced by any analogy between the circuit court and the court of king's bench, the only court in that country possessing the power of issuing such writs. And it further appears that even the court of king's bench for the reasons assigned, would not, agreeably to their practice and principles, have interfered in the present case by manda-mus.

It might perhaps with propriety be added, that there does not appear in the constitution of the United States, any thing which favours an indefinite extension of the jurisdiction of courts, over the ministerial officers within the executive department. On the contrary, the careful discrimination which is marked between the several departments, should dictate great circumspection to each in the exercise of powers having any relation to the other.

The courts are indubitably the source of legal redress for wrongs committed by ministerial officers, none of whom are above the law. This redress is to be administered by due and legal process in the ordinary way. For there appears to be a material and obvious distinction, between a course of proceeding, which redresses a wrong committed by an executive officer, and an interposition by a mandatory writ taking the executive authority out of the hands of the president, and prescribing the course which he and the agents of any department must pursue. In one case the executive is left free to act in his proper sphere, but is held to strict responsibility; in the other all responsibility is taken away, and he acts agreeably to judicial mandate. Writs of this kind if made applicable to officers indiscriminately, and acts purely ministerial and executive in their nature, would necessarily have the effect of transferring the powers vested in one department to another department. If in a case like the present, where the law vests a duty and a discretion in an executive officer, a court cannot only administer redress against the misuse of the authority, but can previously direct the use to be made of it, it would seem that under the name of a judicial power, an executive function is necessarily assumed, and that part of the constitution perhaps defeated, which makes it the duty of the president to take care, that the laws be faithfully executed. I do not see any clear limitation to this doctrine, which would prevent the courts from compelling by mandamus all the executive officers, all subordinate to the president at least, whenever charged with legal duties in the treasury or other department, to execute the same according to the opinion of the judiciary and contrary to that of the executive. And it is evident that the confusion arising, will be greatly increased by the exercise of such a power by a number of separate courts of local jurisdiction, whose proceedings would have complete and final effect, without an opportunity of control by the supreme court. So many branches of the judiciary, acting within their respective districts, their courses might be different, and different modes of action might be prescribed for the citizens of the different states, instead of that unity of administration which the constitution meant to secure, by placing the executive power for them all in the same head.

What too becomes of the responsibility of the executive to the court of impeachment, and to the nation? Is he to remain responsible for acts done by command of another department? Or is the nation to lose the security of that responsibility altogether? From these and other considerations, were this branch of the subject to be pursued, it might be inferred that the constitution of the United States, by the distribution of powers of our government to different departments ascribing the executive duties to one, and the judiciary to another, controls any principles of the English law, which would authorize either to enter into the department of the

other to annul the powers of that other, and to assume the direction of its operations'to itself.

These remarks are respectfully submitted to your consideration. They are to be made with due deference to the opinion of
the court, with one of the judges constituting which, I am personally acquainted, and for whose character I feel the sincerest regard.

Yours, very respectfully.
(Signed)   C. A. RODNEY.
                                            July 15, 1808.

M'Ilvaine v. Coxe's lessee. 2 Cranch. 280.

It still *sticks* in my mind that it may be thought *presump-*
tion and *impertinence*, to undertake to examine any decision
of the supreme court of the United States. But it ought to be
considered that the decision of the highest court; and even of
the highest, in continuance, and by the repeated decisions of
different judges, are but *evidence* of what is *law*. And this
evidence, is strengthened by the *unanimity* of judges on the
same bench; and by a *series of decisions* taking place to the
same effect. It still further strengthens this *evidence*, that
there has been an *acquiescence*, by the bar, and by *the public*.
The sense of the profession goes always a great way; and *de-*
servedly, in fixing what is law, or otherwise, upon a particular
point; for *frequently*, if not usually, there are *greater men at*
the bar, than on the bench; and the judges themselves will
always pay regard to the sentiments of the servientes ad legem, or the barristers of learning and ability. But what is
more, great respect is due also to *general sense* and *public*
opinion. In proportion to the general sense of the community, is the evidence of a decision, weakened, or strengthened.

The sense of a community is evinced, more especially by
the disquisitions of the learned on the subject. What was
originally wrong, unless great inconvenience was to be the
consequence, ought not to prevail. The general sense of the

mass of the people ought to have weight in shaking a decision. I will not apply to this the maxim, quod initio non val*e*t, tractu temporis, non convalescit; but this I will say, *convalescere non debuisset.*

Has there ever been a single voice heard, in these states, but that of *reprobation,* of the decision of Chief Justice Ellsworth, in the case of *Isaac Williams,* February 27th, 1797? that the nemo exuere ligeantiam, existed *a principle of our common law;* and was carried by the emigrants to these colonies from England? If we examine the substratum of the principle, it will be seen to fail, as, *applicable to our situation.* But I will not undertake to examine that, in the present case; at least at the present stage of my observations. It is sufficient to illustrate my position; viz. that an *acquiescence* in a decision adds weight to it; and I speak of the acquiescence of the public mind, as well as of the *individual* opinions of *elementary* writers, or *essayists* of every description.*

The present case of M'Ilvaine and Coxe lay in a *narrower* compass; or at least was determined on a principle short of the *general one,* of the nemo exuere ligeantiam. For this principle did not apply to a revolutionary case, where it cannot but be admitted, that each of the community has *a right to chuse his side.* The question was, *whether by remaining some time in the state of Jersey after the declaration of independence, Coxe had not chosen his side and elected to become a subject of the new government.* I will admit, for the present, that by remaining *one moment* after the declaration of independence, longer, than was *absolutely necessary to get out of it;* he became a citizen of the *new commonwealth,* and owed allegiance; this I admit for the present, and in order to exclude all difficulty on the ground of *qualified* allegiance.

In affirmance of this inference of law, that by remaining in Jersey after the declaration of indepedennce, he became a citizen; the act of 4th October, 1776, declares, " that all persons there abiding, not only owe allegiance, but are mem-

* For this reason it may be excusable, if not justifiable, and a *duty*, where any of a community dissents from a decision, to come forward and express it.

bers of the then government." Doubtless Coxe leaving
the state afterthis, and joining the British, might, in *strictness*,
and according to abstract rigid law, be considered as having
been guilty of *high treason;* and if found within that commonwealth, proceeded criminally against for such offence. If
holden a subject, his *descendant* could inherit what had not
been confiscated; or taken away by the commonwealth. Qui
sentit commodum, sentire debet et onus; and to reverse the
maxim, qui sentit onus, sentire debet et commodum. Why
should he be amenable as a citizen, to suffer loss of property,
or life, and not be considered as entitled to the benefit of
inheritance, to his posterity? Agreed therefore, "that it
would have been competent for that state to allege allienage
in Coxe. That a treaty of peace intervened which is a supreme law, it is insisted, says judge Cushing, 4 Cranch, 114,
" that the treaty of peace operating upon his condition at that
time, or afterwards, he became an alien to the state of New-
Jersey, in *consequence* of his election then made to become a
subject of the king, and his subsequent conduct confirming
that election." " In vain," continues that judge delivering the
opinion of the court, " have we searched that instrument *for
some clause or expression, which by any implication could
work this effect.*"

I take it to result, by necessary implication, and legal inference from this clause of the treaty, art. vi. " There shall
be no future confiscations made, *nor any prosecutions* commenced against any person, or persons, for, or by reason of
the part which he or they may have taken in the present war."
This cannot but be considered as a repeal of the Jersey law;
and in that case no impediment was in the way of a British
adherent during the war, to return to his state, if he should
chuse to elect to be considered a citizen. I consider him placed in the situation precisely, with that of having chosen his
side, and quitted the state before the commencement of the
war. In that case a new government being formed he was
excluded, and could not become a citizen, without some act
on his part revesting himself of that privilege. I will agree
that he might be allowed *a reasonable* time, say his *whole life,*
to come in. But never having come in, citizenship did not

result in him. For not until he had resumed his character, and put himself in the condition of a citizen, could he be intitled to *hold land*, on the facts found in the special verdict, and from which the court had a right to draw, and could not but draw the conclusion of expatriation. I could not consider him as having died *seized;* and in that case, real estate could not descend to the heir. For suppose him, until his latest breath, to have a right, under the treaty, to revest himself with the right of a citizen, in contemplation of law, a moment must exist on his expiring, before the transit could be made of the estate, to his *grantee.*

But I would be willing to favour every possible *legal astutia* to save the descent of an estate, and inheritance under the circumstance of a revolutionary period; but I am opposed to every thing that would give countenance to the idea of not being able to expatriate. The principle of the *nemo exuere* I detest. All notion of this being a principle of the common law carried with us from a feudal country in our emigration, I would scout from our code. It had its origin in a *military establishment;* and agreeable to military ideas, he might be considered a *deserter*, who would leave the ranks, except upon furlough, so to speak, and might be punished as such. It is on account of giving the most distant countenance to the supposed introduction of this principle that I dislike the decision in this case.

———◆———

Simms and Wise v. Slacum. 3 Cranch, 300. Error to the circuit court of the district of Columbia, and the judgment reversed, *judge Paterson dissenting.*

I take the opportunity of expressing the great respect which I entertain for the memory of judge Paterson, though there have been cases decided by him, or where he has joined in the decision, which I have thought wrong. His natural talents were respectable; and his legal knowledge, the result of all, that application could do. But the integrity of his

S s

mind was pure, and his manners amiable. I had known
him from an early period in life; but not with intimacy,
being my superior in years, and in standing. But all that
I ever observed of him was dignified, and noble. I cannot
say, but that in this case, where, in looking at the report, I
saw that he *dissented*, I had a *predisposition* to find him right,
against the majority of the court; and this I had the satisfaction, abundantly, to find; and this I undertake to say, without fear of contradiction from the *majority* of the learned in
the law, maugre, the weight of a decision of the supreme
court. I shall just take the liberty of submitting, for the
proof of this, the decision of the court, with judge Paterson's reason of dissent *contrasted.*

MARSHALL, Ch. J. delivered the opinion of the majority of
the court.

This case depends on the construction of an act of the legislature of Virginia, which allows the prison-rules to a debtor whose
body is in execution, on his giving bond, with sufficient security, not to go out of the rules or bounds of the prison; that
is, while a prisoner. The condition usually inserted is, not to depart therefrom till he shall be discharged by due course of law,
or shall pay the debt. The act further provides, that the prisoner,
on delivering a schedule of his property on oath, to a tribunal constituted for the purpose, and pursuing certain steps prescribed in
the law, shall be discharged, and all his property shall be vested
in the sheriff, for the benefit of the creditors at whose suit he is
in execution.

In the case at bar, the forms of the law were observed, and a
certificate of discharge obtained, after which the debtor departed
from the rules. Conceiving this discharge to have been obtained
by fraud, the creditor brought a suit upon the bond, and the court
instructed the jury, that if a fraud had been practised by the debt-
or, although neither the justices who granted the certificate, nor
the security, partook thereof, yet it avoided the discharge, and left
the security liable in this action. To this opinion the defendants'
counsel excepted, and upon that exception the cause is before this
court.

The certificate of discharge may be granted either by the court
sitting in its ordinary character for the transaction of judicial business, or by two magistrates who are constituted by law an extraor-

dinary court for this particular purpose. Whether granted in the one mode or the other, it is of equal validity. In either case, the judgment of discharge is the judgment of a court, and, as such, is of complete obligation.

The judgments of a court of competent jurisdiction, although obtained by fraud, have never been considered as absolutely void; and therefore, all acts performed under them are valid, so far as respects third persons. A sheriff who levies an execution under a judgment fraudulently obtained, is not a trespasser, nor can the person who purchases at a sale under such an execution, be compelled to relinquish the property he has purchased. All acts performed under such a judgment are valid acts; all the legal consequences which follow a judgment are, with respect to third persons, precisely the same in one obtained by fraud, as if it had been obtained fairly.

When the person who has committed the fraud attempts to avail himself of the act, so as to discharge himself from a previously existing obligation, or to acquire a benefit, the judgment thus obtained is declared void as to that purpose; but it may well be doubted, whether a penalty would be incurred, even by the person committing the fraud, for an act which the judgment would sanction. Thus, if a debtor taken on mesne process escapes, he may be retaken by the authority of the sheriff, and if not retaken, the sheriff may be liable for an escape; but if he fraudulently obtains a judgment in his favour, in consequence of which he goes at large, it has never been imagined that the sheriff could retake him on suspicion that the judgment was fraudulent, or be liable for an escape on the proof of such fraud.

Thus too, where, as in Virginia, an injunction has been adjudged to discharge the body from confinement, if a debtor in execution, by false allegations, obtains an injunction whereby his body is discharged from prison, or from the rules, it has never been conjectured that the injunction thus awarded was void, and the acts performed under it were to be considered as if the injunction had not existed. In that case, it would not be alleged that there was an escape, and that the security to the bond for keeping the rules was liable for the debt, because the discharge was fraudulently obtained; but the discharge would have all its legal effects, in like manner as if no imposition had been practised on the judge by whom it was granted.

The judgment rendered in his favour may not shield the fraudulent debtor from an original claim, but it is believed that no case can be adduced, where an act, which is the legal consequence of a judgment, has in itself created a new responsibility, even with respect to the party himself, much less with respect to third persons, who do not participate in the fraud.

It would seem, then, upon general principles, that a debtor who has departed from the prison-rules under the authority of a judgment of discharge, granted in due form by a competent tribunal, has not committed an escape even to charge himself, much less a third person. Such a discharge might not be permitted to protect him from the original debt, even if the case had not been particularly provided for by statute; but the act of departing from the rules, after being thus discharged, could not charge him with a new responsibility to which he was not before liable, much less will it impose on his security a liability for the debt. Departing from the rules, after being discharged in due course of law, is not a breach of the condition of his bond.

This opinion receives great additional strength from those arguments, drawn from the objects and provisions of the act, which have been forcibly urged from the bar.

The objects of the act unquestionably are, not to increase the security of the creditor, but to relieve the debtor from close imprisonment in the confined jails of the country, and to consult his health, by giving him the benefit of fresh air. But as this indulgence would furnish the means of escaping from the custody of the officer, and thereby deprive the creditor of his person, it was thought necessary to guard against the danger which the indulgence itself created, not to guard against dangers totally unconnected with this indulgence. Security, therefore, ought, in reason, to be required against a departure from the rules without a lawful authority so to do, because the means of such departure were furnished by being allowed the use of the rules; but security against a fraud in obtaining such authority need not be required, because the means of practising that fraud are not facilitated by granting the rules. They may be used by a debtor in close jail, as successfully as by a debtor admitted to the rules.

It is also a material circumstance in the construction of the act, that ample provision is made for the very case. A new capias may be awarded to take the person of the debtor. This remedy is not allowed in the case of an escape; and it is strong evidence that the legislature did not contemplate a departure from the rules under a certificate issued by proper authority, as an escape; that the remedy given the creditor is competent to a redress of the injury, replaces him in the situation in which he was before it was committed, and is not founded on the idea that there has been an escape.

The argument founded on the provisions respecting the property of the debtor, also bear strongly on the case. They confirm the opinion, that a departure from the rules, under a certificate of dischrage granted by a proper tribunal, ought not to be considered as an escape. So, too, does that provision of the act which requires notice to the creditor and not to the security.

Without reviewing the various additional arguments which have been suggested at the bar, the court is of opinion, that upon general principles, strengthened by a particular consideration of the act itself, a departure from the rules under such an authority as is stated in 'the proceedings, is not an escape which can charge the security in the bond for keeping the prison-rules, although that authority was obtained by a fraudulent representation on the part of the debtor, neither the magistrates nor the security having participated in that fraud.

There is error, therefore, in the instruction given to the jury, as stated in the third bill of exceptions, for which the judgment is to be reversed, and the cause remanded for further trial.

Judgment reversed.

PATERSON, J. As to the third exception, which embraces the main point in the cause, my opinion differs from the opinion of the majority of the court, and accords with the direction given by the court below. The condition of the bond is, " that Simms do well and truly keep himself within the prison-rules, and thence not to depart until he shall be discharged by due course of law, or pay the sum of 1,285 dollars and 45 cents, to George Slacum, assignee," &c. The act that will not exonerate the principal, will not exonerate the surety, from the obligation which they have entered into; for the surety stands on the same floor as the principal, and assumes the like character of responsibility, in regard to the terms specified in the condition of the bond. The benefit of the act of insolvency, if obtained by fraud or perjury on the part of Simms, will be unavailing, and his going beyond the limits of the prison, in consequence or under colour of a discharge, thus procured, will be an invalid and unwarrantable departure. Fraud infects the decision; and the legal principle is, that the fraudulent person shall not be suffered to protect himself by his own fraudulent act. If he should, then a judgment, which is laid in fraud, will, as in the present case, operate to the extinction of a legal, pre-existing obligation or contract. But a discharge, fraudulently obtained, is of no virtue—of no operation; and is, in truth and in law, no discharge; it has neither legal effect, nor even legal existence as to the party himself, and the surety, who stands in his shoes. If the judgment be of no avail as to the principal, it will be of no avail as to the surety; it cannot be ineffectual as to the one, and operative as to the other. The discharge must be legal to be valid, and to exonerate the surety from the special condition of the bond. The judgment itself is a fraud on the law; and I can discern no difference between the debtor's going beyond the prison bounds voluntarily, or under colour of a judgment so obtained; except, that the latter is a case of deeper die, and less excusable in a legal and moral view than the former.

Although Simms is liable to be imprisoned by virtue of a new process, yet he may have gone out of the jurisdiction of the court; or if not, Slacum will be deprived of the benefit of the bond which Simms and Wise executed.

The sheriff stands on different ground; for he is exonerated from all liability, by an express provision in the statute. Besides, if the justices have jurisdiction of the subject, and should not exceed their jurisdiction, it is not incumbent on the sheriff to examine into the regularity, fairness, and validity of their proceedings and judgment; he looks at the instrument of discharge, which, emanating from a competent authority, it is his duty to obey. But though the discharge may excuse the sheriff, as an officer of the court, it will not excuse the party, nor his surety. As to them it is inoperative, and of no legal efficacy.

———◦•◦———

The United States v. Fisher et al. assignees of *Blight*.

IT cannot be a question, but that it is more pleasing to the mind to find itself with the *majority* of a court in giving an opinion; and, where constrained to *dissent*, it cannot be unpleasing to find that this dissent is approved by the bar; or even by intelligent persons, out of doors; more especially if these persons are of a standing and just pretension to legal knowledge. Even an expression of the sense of the multitude, is not, in all cases, wholly to be disregarded: It cannot be ungrateful to have one's judgment approved, even by a *simple mind*, because, it goes some length, however small, in reconciling to ones-self what it has done; and giving the satisfaction of believing that we had not conceived amiss of the law, and justice of the case; but to have it approved by the intelligent, is still a greater satisfaction to the mind. It also contributes to inspire confidence in our own strength, and to secure independence of opinion on other occasions. This holds still more, or at least equally, where the judgment of a court below, is to undergo the revision of a court of error. So that though a judge, or a court below would from *conscience;* or if this was the weaker power, on principle of delicacy, and a sense of honour; or what is more, a principle of self-preservation, be willing not only to avoid the act, but also to escape the imputation of attempting, in the most distant degree, to influence the revision of his opinion, yet it would give him more pleasure to have his judgment affirmed rather than reversed; unless, indeed, from reasons that had occurred to his own mind, or delivered by the court above, he should come to alter his opinion. In that case, he would be unworthy of the name of judge, that would not acquiesce, and be internally satisfied. And it is only in the case of a weak understanding that *cannot well afford to be thought wrong*, that, under these circumstances, pain would be felt, or unfavourable impressions of inferiority would occur.

It is no uncommon thing for a reader of *reports*, or rather, it is too common to look at nothing more than the decisions of the court, and to take it for granted, that the *minority* are in the wrong. The *presumption* is doubtless against them: and the maxim is, stabitur presumptioni donec in contrarium probetur. But what proof can be offered, but the examination of the *reasons*. And without examining, the conclusion of error is unfair. There cannot be a more useful exercise of mind to the *student* than an examination of cases, where the court have been divided. Or where the court above has *reversed* the decision of an inferior; as in the present case, which was an appeal from the decision of judge Washington, on a writ of *error from the circuit court of the district of Pennsylvania.* It may have been seen from some things already stated on the subject of the *acts of congress,* that I think the decision of *Judge Washington,* and for the reasons given in this case of Blight perfectly *correct.* It was not necessary for him to call in question the constitutionality of the acts of congress, on this head ; or of the act immediately before him ; the *construction* that ought to be put upon it being the only question. The court above reversed his *construction ;* but his reasons stand, and will prevail. It is not likely that a construction so palpably *erroneous* as that of the *superior* court, can receive the sanction of an adjudication, by succeeding judges. At all events, it cannot be, but that the attention of congress will be drawn to it, and the act will be so amended, as to be *restrained in the extent of such construction ; or repealed altogether ;* and which in my judgment it ought to be ; as being *unnecessary* to carry the *powers* given into effect; and, therefore, unconstitutional, and void. The congress is charged with the *common defence,* and the *payment* of the national debt ; but the very power first given, sec. 8, n. 1, " to lay and collect taxes," &c. supersedes all necessity of a recurrence to *preference,* and thus taking away the property of an individual, without compensation. And what compensation could be given but the thing itself. For it is the debt due that is taken from the creditor by the preference given to the union.

The question is, says judge Washington, " have the United States a right in all cases whatsoever to claim a preference of other creditors in the payment of debts."

WASHINGTON, J Although I take no part in the decision of this cause, I feel myself justified by the importance of the question in declaring the reasons which induced the circuit court of Pennsylvania to pronounce the opinion which is to be re-examined here.

In any instance where I am so unfortunate as to differ with this court, I cannot fail to doubt the correctness of my own opinion. But if I cannot feel convinced of the error, I owe it in some measure to myself and to those who may be injured by the expense and delay to which they have been exposed to shew at least that the opinion was not hastily or inconsiderately given.

The question is, have the United States a right in all cases whatever to claim a preference of other creditors in the payment of debts. At the circuit court the counsel for the United States disclaimed all idea of founding this right upon prerogative principles, and yet, if I am not greatly mistaken, the doctrine contended for places this right upon ground at lest as broad as would have been asserted in an English court.

The whole question must turn upon the construction of acts of congress, and particularly that of the 3d of March 1797. The title of the law is " an act to provide more effectually for the settlement of accounts between the United States *and receivers of public money.*"

The first section describes more specially the persons who are the objects of the law ; points out the particular officer whose duty it shall be to institute suits against those public delinquents thus marked out; declares the rate of interest to be recovered upon balances due to the United States, and imposes a forfeiture of commissions on the delinquent.

The 2d section defines the kind of evidence to be admitted on the part of the United States, in the trial of suits in all cases of delinquency.

The 3d section gives to the United States in such actions, a *preference* of all other suitors in court, by directing the trial of such causes to take place at the return term upon motion, unless the defendant will make oath that he is entitled to credits which have been submitted to the consideration of the accounting officers of the treasury, and rejected.

The 4th section takes up the case of the defendant, and declares under what circumstances he shall be entitled to the benefit of off sets.

The 5th section brings us to an important part of the trial, and furnishes a rule to govern the court in the judgment, it is to render, in cases where the claim of the United States might, by reason of the insolvency of the debtor, go unsatisfied, unless preferred to that of a private citizen.

The 6th section is general in its terms, and relates to executions where the defendant or his property is to be found in any district other than that in which the judgment was rendered.

T T

This is a concise view of the different parts of this act, and I shall now examine more particularly the expressions of the 5th section taken in connection with those which precede it.

The words are " that where any revenue officer or *other person* hereafter becoming indebted to the United States by bond or otherwise, shall become insolvent, the debt due to the United States shall be first satisfied," &c.

It is conceded that the words " or other person" are broad enough to comprehend every possible case of debts due to the United States, and therefore a literal interpretation is contended for by those who advocate the interest of the United States. On the other side, a limitation of those expressions is said to be more consonant with the obvious meaning of the legislature, which contemplates those debtors only who are accountable for public money.

Where a law is plain and unambiguous, whether it be expressed in general or limited terms, the legislature should be intended to mean what they have plainly expressed, and consequently no room is left for construction. But if, from a view of the whole law, or from other laws in *pari materia*, the evident intention is different from the literal import of the terms employd to express it in a particular part of the law, that intention should prevail, for that in fact is the will of the legislature.

If a section be introduced which is a *stranger to* and unconnected with the purview of the act, it must nevertheless take effect according to its obvious meaning, independent of all influence from other parts of the law. Nay, if it be a part of the same subject, and either enlarges or restrains the expressions used in other parts of the same act, it must be interpreted according to the import of the words used, if nothing can be gathered from such other parts of the law to change the meaning. But if in this latter case, general words are used which import more than seems to have been within the purview of the law, or of the other parts of the law, and those expressions can be restrained by others used in the same law, or in any other upon the same subject, they ought in my opinion to be restrained.

So if the literal expressions of the law would lead to absurd, unjust or inconvenient consequences, such a construction should be given as to avoid such consequences, if, from the whole purview of the law, and giving effect to the words used, it may fairly be done.

These rules are not merely artificial; they are as clearly founded in plain sense, as they are certainly warranted by the principles of common law.

The subject intended to be legislated upon is sometimes stated in a preamble, sometimes in the title to the law, and is sometimes, I admit, mistated, or not fully stated. The preamble of an act of parliament is said to be a key to the knowledge of it, and to open the intent of the law-makers: and so I say as to the title of a law of congress, which being the deliberate act of those who make the law, is not less to be respected as an expression of their intention, than if it preceded the enacting clause in the form of a preamble. But neither the title or preamble can be resorted to for the purpose of controuling the enacting clauses, except in cases of ambiguity, or where general expressions are used inconsistent or unconnected with the scope and purview of the whole law.

They are to be deemed true, unless contradicted by the enacting clauses, and it is fair in the cases I have stated to argue from them.

The object of this law then, as declared by the title, is to provide for the effectual settlement of debts due to the United States, from *receivers of public money*. To effect this, suits are directed, the species of evidence to support the claim on the part of the plaintiff is pointed out, and a speedy trial provided; on the part of the defendant, a limited right to oppose the claim by offsets is provided, and the claim of the United States is to have a preference of other creditors, where the debtor is unable to satisfy the whole. Here then is one entire connected subject—the different provisions of the law constituting the links of the same chain, the members of the same body. It will not, I presume, be denied, that the three first sections of the law apply to those only who are declared by the title to be the objects of its provisions. The 4th section is the first which uses general expressions, without a reference to those who had before been spoken of; and yet I think it will hardly be contended that this section is not closely and intimately connected with the same subject.—When we come to the 5th section the reference to the three first sections is again resumed, with the addition of the words " or any other person." So that instead of the words " revenue officers or other persons *accountable for public money*," used in the first section, this section uses the words " revenue officers *or other persons indebted to the United States*."

Now it is obvious that these expressions may have precisely the same meaning, so as to comprehend the same persons, although the latter may be construed to include persons not within the meaning of the first section. For *persons accountable for public money*, are also *other persons than revenue officers indebted to the United States;* and the latter may, by a construction conformable to the other parts of the law, mean *persons accountable for public money;* and by an intended construction, they may comprehend others, who in no sense of the expressions used, can be said to be accountable for public money.

It is then to be inquired, is the court bound by any known rules of law to give to the words thus used in the 5th section a meaning extensive enough to comprehend persons never contemplated by the title of the law, and most sedulously excluded by the three first sections? Does justice to the public, or convenience to individuals demand it? Is such a construction necessary in order to give effect to any one expression used by the legislature?

Shall we violate the manifest *intention* of the legislature, if we stop short of the point to which we are invited to go in the construction of this section?

To all these questions I think myself warranted in answering in the negative.

As to the first. Do the principles of equity, or of strict justice discriminate between individuals standing *in equali jure* and claiming debts of equal dignity?

The *nature of the debt,* may well warrant a discrimination; but not so, if the privilege be merely of a personal nature. The sovereign may in the exercise of his powers secure to himself this exclusive privilege of being preferred to the citizens, but this is no evidence that the claim is sanctioned by the principles of immutable justice. If this right is asserted, individuals must submit; but I do not find it in my conscience to go further in advancement of the claim, than the words of the law fairly interpreted, in relation to the whole law, compel me. But I do not think that congress meant to exercise their power to the extent contended for. First, because in every other section of the law they have declared a different intent; and secondly, because it would not only be productive of the most cruel injustice to individuals, but would tend to destroy more than any other act I can imagine all confidence between man and man. The preference claimed is not only unequal in respect to private citizens, but is of a nature against which the most prudent man cannot guard himself. As to public officers and receivers of public money of all descriptions, they are, or may be known as such ; and any person dealing with them, does it at the peril of being postponed to any debts his debtor may owe to the United States, should he become unfortunate. He acts with his eyes open, and has it in his power to calculate the risk he is willing to run.

But if this preference exists in every possible case of contracts between the United States and an individual, there is no means by which any man can be apprized of his danger, in dealing with the same person.

2. Is this broad construction necessary in order to give effect to the expressions of the law ? I have endeavoured to shew that all *accountable agents* are other *persons* than revenue officers indebted to the United States. The words then " other persons" are satisfied by comprehending all those persons, to whom the first section extends.

3. Is this construction rendered necessary to fulfil the manifest intention of the legislature ? So far from it, that to my mind, it is in direct opposition to an intention plainly expressed by all the other parts of the law. To prove this I again refer to the title of the law ; to the three first sections, which are in strict conformity with it, and that too by express words ; and to the fourth section, which is so plainly a part of the same subject, that it cannot be construed to go farther than those which precede it. Is the fifth section a stranger to the others ; unnaturally placed there without having a connection with the other section ?

If this be the case, I have already admitted rules of construction, strong enough to condemn the opinion I hold. But let us examine this point.

The object of the four first sections is to enforce by *suit*, where necessary, the payment of debts due to the United States from a particular class of debtors. It points out the officer who is to order the suit, declares at what term the cause shall be tried, lays down rules of evidence to be regarded in support of the action, extends to the defendant the benefit of making offsetts under certain qualifications, and then most naturally, as I conceive, comes the fifth section, relating to the judgment which the court is to render in case a contest should ensue between the United States and individual creditors on account of inability in the debtor to satisfy the whole. What if an individual creditor should attach the property of the debtor before the United States had taken steps to recover their debt? Or if the debtor should assign away his property, or it should be claimed by assignees under a commission of bankruptcy; or the defendant being an executor, should plead fully administered except so much as would be sufficient to satisfy judgments, bond debts, or other debts superior in dignity to that of the United States? This section establishes a plain rule by which the court must proceed in rendering its judgment whenever those cases occur. What would have signified all the other provisions of the law, unless a rule of decision had been prescribed in cases where otherwise the United States might never obtain the fruit of those steps which their officers were pursuing?

Can a section in a law which professes to afford a remedy in a particular process of law, be said not to belong to the law, when it leads to the point of a judgment, which is the consummation of the proceedings in the case? I think not; and therefore I cannot acquiesce in the opinion that the 5th section is unconnected with the other parts of the law.

I have before observed that the 4th section is the first which uses general expressions, without reference to those which had before been particularly mentioned; but that when we come to the 5th section the reference is again taken up, with the addition of those words which produce the difficulty of the case.

Now I ask in the first place, what necessity was there for departing from the mode of expression used in the 4th section, which for the first time is general, without particular reference to any of the persons before described. Would it not have been as well in the 5th as in the 4th section, to say " that where *any in-* " *dividual* becoming indebted to the United States, shall become " insolvent," &c. What reason can be assigned for the specification of *revenue officers*, one class of persons mentioned expressly in the 1st section, intended in the 2d and 3d by plain words of reference, and clearly meant in the 4th, when it must be admitted that the words used in the 4th section, or the words " other persons," in the 5th would have comprehended revenue officers if they were broad enough to include every description of persons indebted to the United States. Unless they are construed to limit and restrain the generality of the words " other persons," they are absolutely without any use or meaning whatever. If the preceding sections had applied only to *revenue officers*, then from necessity we must have construed the words " other persons," as broad as their natural import would warrant, because otherwise, they would have been nugatory, and we would have found no rule in the law itself, by which to limit the generality of the expression.

But when the law professes in its title to relate to all accountable agents besides revenue officers, and the first section specifies amongst these agents, " revenue officers," we have a rule by which to restrain the sweeping expressions in the 5th section, viz. " or other person accountable, or indebted as aforesaid." This construction renders the law uniform throughout, and consistent with what it professes in every other section.

2d. In confirmation of this construction, the 62d section of the bankrupt law does, in my opinion, deserve attention. If the United States were, at the time that law passed, entitled to a preference in every possible case, by virtue of the general expressions in the law have just been considering, what necessity was there for limiting the saving of the right of preference to debts due to the United States, " as secured or provided by any law heretofore passed." This mode of expression leads me to conclude that the legislature supposed there were some cases where this preference had not been provided for by law. If not, it would certainly have been sufficient to declare, that the bankrupt law should not extend to, or affect the right of preference to prior satisfaction of debts due the United States."

It will be seen from the above, that the whole object of judge Washington's opinion, and it was all that was necessary for the point in issue, or matter in controversy, was the construction of the terms " or other person." In this, no doubt, he was correct, for the whole of the language of the acts taken together cannot but show, that these words had been foisted in, or stand so isolated as to be incongruous with the rest. They must be rejected or explained: taken by themselves they involve the most manifest inconsistency with other parts of the act.

But it is my choice to go farther than Judge Washington and attack the root, the *constitutionality* of these laws, or of this law. The *doctrine is monstrous, that the congress should be thought to have the power to give the union a preference in any case whatsoever.* To the act providing *that the commencement of a suit should constitute a lien, I have no* exception. But to cut out other *heirs*, or *prior debts due* and, take the whole, is that to which I except.

Rhinelander v. Insurance Company of Pennsylvania. 4 Cranch, 29.

" This was a case certified from the circuit court for the district of Pennsylvania, in which the opinions of the judges of that court were opposed to each other." And in the decision of the supreme court, one judge is spoken of as *doubting*.

I do not know any question to chich the " *non it arefert*" would apply with less propriety, than in this case.

As a new question, it could be determined only on the principle of mercantile convenience, which is the great principle upon which every question of this nature ought to be decided. It was stated by the court to be a new question. In the case of Hamilton v. Mendez, says chief justice Marshal, lord Mansfield leaves it completely undetermined whether *the state of the loss, at the time the abandonment is made must fix the right of the parties to recover on an action afterwards brought.*" The supreme court of Pennsylvania, chief justice Tilghman, &c. sitting, it was holden that at least the *libelling*, as in that case, would justify an abandonment. I did not understand it to be laid down in that case of Dutilgh v. Gatliff, that nothing short of having *libelled*, would justify. But that at least a capture, and carrying in for adjudication, and libelling, would. This was a matter *short of condemnation*.

Taking up the matter upon original ground, I would enquire what is it that would constitute a *deviation*, such as to excuse the underwriter; or what is it that would constitute such *delay*, as would affect the right of abandonment as for a total loss ? If a point insured against, occasions a detention to such extent, or produces a deviation, will not the measure of the one be the measure of the other ? I would take it that the moment the peril attaches, and has *an effect* to the amount of the *whole*, an action for a *total loss* accrues. I know no medium that can be taken between this, and a *final condemnation*, without great embarrassment. I would have held it, were it a new case that the right of abandonment arises on the attachment of the peril: but not that the injured was bound to abandon, on that happening, but might take time in using means with *due diligence* to escape from it. Independent of *marine regulations*, or *the contract* of the parties, I would have taken this to be the law; because, independent of regulation, or the contract of the parties, I could conceive of no other general rule that would work throughout, and secure an indemnity. Upon the abstract principle, I had taken it, that though Lord Mansfield had not decided it, yet that whatever would have justified the abandonment, supposing the *insurer, and insured to be upon the spot at the time the peril happened*, and the assured to have offered to abandon, his right was the same when the intelligence of *that fact* came to hand, without regard to what in the mean time had taken place. This rule is *simple*, and intelligible, and any other rule leads to embarrassment.

Some certain time is usually stipulated in the policy after which, on abandonment, payment is demandable of the writer. Suppose that period to elapse, and *payment* to be made, there must be a *repayment*, on it turning out that a *detention* was over, or that a *restoration* had taken place. There may be an *opening* and *shutting* of abandonment, if it is to depend upon a new state of the fact. In all cases the *insurer*, who usually wishes to escape the having an abandonment thrown upon him, will say, wait till I see whether the *state of the fact* may not be changed, and which may relieve me from the necessity of *accepting* the abandonment. In that case a clause of 30 days, or other time is useless; or, rather inconsistent with the idea of the state of the *fact* case. The very inserting such a clause proves, that, in the understanding of the contracting parties, the payment on abandonment could have no relation to the state of the fact changing from what it was, when the intelligence set out if I may so speak, that afterwards came to the insured, and on which the abandonment was made.

Suppose on suit brought, in answer to an allegation of the declaration, that a vessel had been taken, it was pleaded, that she had been restored, on demurrer would not that be holden a departure; because the question was not what had happened, after she was lost to me, but whether she had ceased to be in *my power* at any time, whether from physical, or moral force ; so that for a time I was disabled from the prosecution of my voyage. It is matter of election with me whether to waive an abandonment instantly on the attachment of the peril, or to endeavour to release myself. If I chuse not to abandon on the peril attaching, the doctrine of abandonment in *reasonable time*, or otherwise, will then come into view.

Chief Justice Marshall says that "*commercial contracts are seldom rightly expounded by a course of artificial reasoning.*" I am at a loss to know by what otherwise they are to be expounded but the application of reason where *the rule is said not* be *fixed*, and the *ab inconveniente* must guide. It is of more consequence with me than a dictum of my lord *somebody* to this or that effect ; or even a *decision* of several my *lords*. For *decisions* are but evidence of the *reason of* others, but the reason itself deduced from the *inconveniente*, is paramount, in settling what the decision ought to be.

But the *non ita refert* will induce an acquiescence where the rule may be helped by *the contract of the parties* when known and established. As in this case, where for the sake of uniformity *in the law of insurance*, the courts of the states have conceded to *this rule of the supreme court of the union*. It has been done in Pennsylvania, and I presume elsewhere. But that has nothing to do with the principles on which it ought to have been placed, and an examination of the opinions of different members of a court who have dissented, or *doubted in the introduction of the rule.*

———

Ex parte Bollman, and ex parte Swartwout. 4 Cranch, 75.

In this case Johnston justice dissented ; and my object is *to examine his opinion.* And at this moment of entering on it, I do not know whether I shall support his dissent, or declare against it. For I write as I read. And it is chiefly because I saw there was a *dissent* in a case of great importance, I mean involving a principle of great importance, that I have been led to examine it.

"I am far, says the Judge, very far from denying the general authority of adjudications. Uniformity in decisions is often as important as their abstract justice. But I deny that *a court is precluded* from the right, or exempted from the necessity of examining into the correctness, or consistency of its own decisions, or those of any other tribunal." This is excellent, and I am so pleased with it, it is so congenial with my own way of thinking, that I shall be sorry if I shall be under the necessity of finding this Judge wrong in the case before me.

He adds further, "strange indeed, would be the doctrine, that an inadvertency once committed by a court, shall ever after impose on it the necessity of persisting in its error. A case that cannot be *tested by principle* is not *law;* and, in a thousand instances have such cases been declared so by courts of justice." This is manly; and spoken like a man of sense, and of *independent* mind, that has a consciousness of its own strength. He proceeds. "The claim of the prisoners as founded on precedent, stands thus. The case of Hamilton is strikingly similar to the present. The prisoner had been committed by the order of the district judge on a charge of high treason. A writ of habeas corpus was issued by the supreme court, and the prisoner bailed by their order. The case of Burford was also strictly parallel to the present. But the writ in the latter case having been issued expressly on the authority of the former, it is presumed that it gives no additional force to the claim, but must rest upon the strength of the case upon which the court acted.

"It appears to my mind, continues the judge, that the case of Hamilton bears upon the face of it, evidence of its being entitled to like consideration; and that the authority of it *was annihilated* by the very able decision in Marbury v. Madison."

What evidence could it bear upon *the face of it*, but the reasons upon which it went: or the mere circumstance of the court taking jurisdiction? But the decision in Marbury v. Madison, annihilated the *authority* of this case. In this case, says the judge, it was decided that congress could not vest in the supreme court, any *original* powers, beyond those to which this court is restricted by the constitution. That an act of congress vesting in this court the power to issue a writ of *mandamus* in a case not within their *original* jurisdiction, was *unconstitutional and void.* In the case of Hamilton the court does not assign the reasons on which it founds its decisions, but it is fair to presume that they adopted the idea which appears to have been admitted by the district attorney, in his argument, viz. that this court possessed a concurrent power with the district court, in admitting to bail. Now a concurrent power in such a case must be an *original* power; and the principle case, Marbury v. Madison, applies as much, to the issuing of a *habeas corpus*, in a case of treason, as to the issuing of a *mandamus* in a case not more *remote* from the original jurisdiction of the court."

All this is *correct.* The court are involved in *an inconsistency;* but what will he say to me, who deny the case of Marbury v. Madison, *to be law*, and set up the cases of *Hamilton* and *Burford?*

Disembarrassing the question from the effect of *precedent,* he says he will proceed to consider the *construction* of the sections of the act of congress, on which the issuing a *habeas corpus* must depend. That is right; let us neither *hold the court* to Marbury v. Madison, nor support them by Hamilton and Burford.

It is necessary to presume, says the judge, that the case of treason is one in which this court possesses neither *original,* nor *appellate* jurisdiction. The 14th section of the judiciary act, so far as it has relation to this case, is in these words : All the before mentioned courts (of which this is one) of the United States shall have power to issue writs of *scire facias,* and *habeas corpus,* and all other writs not specially provided for by statute, which may be necessary for the exercise of their respective jurisdictions, and agreeable to the principles and usages of law." "If the power to issue the writs of *scire facias* and *habeas corpus,* be not restricted to the cases within the *criminal* or appellate jurisdiction of this court, the case of *Marbury* and *Madison*, rejects the clause as unavailing; and if it relate only to cases within their jurisdiction, it does not extend to the case which is now moved for."

Doubtless the judge has the court here in a dilemma; but was it fair to talk of Marbury and Madison, when he had professed a disembarrassment of the question *from the effect of precedent.*

But again, he says, " on considering this act it cannot be denied, that if it vests any power at all, it is an *original* power. It is the essential criterion of appellate jurisdiction, that it reserves and corrects the proceedings in a cause already instituted. I quote, says he the very words of the court in the case of Marbury v. Madison."

I perceive that through the whole of the opinion he embarrasses himself with the case of Marbury and Madison; and the argument is, in some degree, ad hominem, that is to the court who had so decided in that case. But I wish to treat them fairly, and to take no advantage of what they had decided in that case, but to see what they ought to decide in this. I turn to the constitution, and the judiciary act itself.

Having done so, I look at the opinion of the court as delivered by chief justice Marshall; and I find it correct, throwing Marbury v. Madison out of the way, which he *distinguishes from the case before him,* with some astutia affecting to consider it as the case of *an appeal.* It is not on that ground, I would put it, but consider the court as having power under the act of congress, to issue a habeas corpus in the first instance. The clause is, " that either of the justices of the *supreme court,* as well as judges of the district courts, shall have power to grant writs of habeas corpus for the purpose of an enquiry into the cause of commitment." The power is concurrent, with judges of the district courts; and not being given to these exclusively in the first instance, the judges of the supreme court either of them, or a fortiore, the whole of them sitting in bank, have *original* jurisdiction in this case. For if they have concurrently jurisdiction, they have original. For the *constitution* giving the supreme court *original*, in some, and appellate in all, does not exclude the power of congress to give original, where it must be appellate.

But the fact is, that the issuing the writ of *habeas corpus*, being but *incidental* to the jurisdiction as to *trial*, it does not come in view as to *jurisdiction*, either in the meaning of the constitution or of the act of congress. It is *collateral*, and sideway to the jurisdiction, whether original or appellate. A justice of the peace, or a judge of the court of common pleas or in his capacity of a justice of the pleas, may commit or bail for offences not triable before the justice, or before the common pleas. Justice of the peace, or other magistrate of any of the United States, for any crime, or offence, against the United States may arrest, imprison, or bail. And even where " a person is committed by a justice of the supreme, or a judge of a district court, for an offence not punishable with death, if there be no judge of the United States in the district to take the same, it may be taken by any judge of the supreme, or superior court of law of such state." Judiciary act, sec. 33. Yet these judges, or courts could not take jurisdiction of the offence, to try it. It follows necessarily from the provision, that each of these authorities must issue the habeas corpus, ad inquirendum, or to see whether the facts alleged amount to *capital*, before they can say, whether their power is precluded from a liberation.

I am therefore obliged to be with the majority of the court, and to say, that the habeas corpus ought to have issued.

Craudson and others, v. Leonard. 4 Cranch, 434.

THIS case involved the doctrine of the conclusiveness of " *the sentence of a foreign court of admiralty*." It had not before become *necessary* in any case to decide it ; though it had been argued in the case of Fitzimmons v the Newport Insurance company. It was decided in favour of the *conclusiveness* of the sentence, by four judges, Marshal, Cushing, Washington and Johnston, justices, Chase and Livingston *dissenting*; Todd not being present at the argument gave no opinion. The weight of a decision is proportionably shaken by a want of unanimity. The doctrine had begun to be shaken in the English courts in the case of Lothian v. Henderson, 3 Bos. and Pull. 499, Graham, B. dissenting from the majority of the court in a very able argument *against the conclusiveness of the sentence.*

The bar would never seem to have acquiesced perfectly. 2 East, 476. it is said, the counsel were proceeding to contend that the *sentence of condemnation*, admitting it to be pronounced by a competent tribunal, was not conclusive as to the question of neutrality, which was collateral to the question of prize or no prize. But the court said " that after the repeated determinations to the contrary, it would be nugatory to open that discussion again." The question is, said Lawrence, whether this sentence of condemnation be conclusive evidence that the property insured was British, and consequently that the warranty of its being neutral was not complied with. The argument was attempted to be carried into a wider field than we think it fit now to enter into, since the case of Hughes v. Cornelius, and a long string of authorities which have followed that decision. We must now therefore take it for granted, that, if this sentence were given by a court of competent jurisdiction, it is conclusive upon the point then in judgment." Thus it may be seen that the *stare decisis*, not *principle*, was that which governed.

And 5 East, 160. it is said by lord Ellenborough, that, " since the judgment of the house of lords in Lothian v. Henderson, it may now be assumed as the settled doctrine of a court of *English law*, that all sentences of foreign courts of competent jurisdiction to decide questions of *prize*, are to be received here, as conclusive evidence in actions upon policies of insurance, upon every subject immediately and properly within the jurisdiction of such foreign courts, and upon which they have professed to decide judicially."

I do not wonder at *English courts* holding this doctrine ; because having the command of the sea, and capturing, whether justly, or unjustly, I do not say, more than other nations, they have more captures to bring to market, and therefore, it suits them that such doctrine, should prevail, inasmuch as it would lessen the value of their prizes, at an admiralty sale, if there could be a doubt of being able to give a title.   Yet their judges say very little, or rather nothing on the reason of the principle, but shelter themselves under the authority of lords, &c.

1 Camp. 418. in the case of Fisher v. Ogle, lord Ellenborough observed, with the concurrence of the other judges, " It is by an overstrained comity that these sentences are received as exclusive evidence of the facts which they positively aver, and upon which they specifically profess to be founded."   And again, 1 Camp. 429.   " I am by no means disposed to extend the comity which has been shown to these sentences of foreign admiralty courts.   I shall die like lord Thurlow in the belief, *that they ought never to have been admitted.*   The doctrine in their favour, rests upon an authority in Shower (Hughes v. Cornelius, 2 Show. 232) which does not fully support it, and the practice of receiving them, often leads in its consequences, to the greatest injustice."

This doctrine of *conclusiveness*, had been adopted implicitly from the English courts, in all, or most of the states, before and since the revolution, without the least examination of the principle.

O imitatores ; servum pecus—

There was some reason for it before the revolution, because, it hold a doctrine that suited the then *colonies*, being part of the British empire, and sharing with her in this *buccaneer principle*, so as finding our account in it.   But how it could exist, during the revolutionary war, and since, could have been only from a defect of examination.   After the war and during our situation as *a neutral nation*, the consequences had been felt, and persons insured, had begun to cast themselves about, to provide against the rule, by special clauses in the contract ; such as *warranted American ;* but the proof to be made here. *There cannot be a stronger evidence of the badness of the rule, than the necessity of excepting it, by a special provision in the contract, to the contrary.*

This doctrine was shaken by a decision in the New-York state, 1805, by the court of errors and appeals, 2 Caines, 217. And the courts of Pennsylvania, although they sometimes appeared, indirectly, to recognize the theory of the courts of England, had honestly endeavored to escape from the practical operation, which often leads (says lord Ellenborough) to the greatest injustice, until they were involved in the necessity of giving judgment in Dempsey's case.*

---

* In this case, in the supreme court, I was confined to my chamber, by indisposition, and did not deliver the opinion which I had drawn up; but gave it to the public, not as an opinion drawn up to be delivered, but as an abstract essay, in Poulson's Advertiser of January 6th, 1808, and not with my name; but it is as follows:

On the conclusiveness of a sentence of a foreign Court of Admiralty.

THE effect of a sentence of a foreign Court of Admiralty, as between the assured and assurer, where there has been a warranty by the assured, that the property assured was neutral; but where it has been condemned in a foreign court on the ground of being *enemies property*, is the question proposed to be examined.

When two nations are at war between themselves, a sense of justice will induce each to avoid injuring an individual who is not of the belligerent nation; or, if a sense of justice does not govern, *self-preservation will.* For it cannot be the interest of either to injure an individual, lest it provoke the nation to which that individual belongs; and involve it in a war with that power, adding to itself another enemy; and drawing on itself the enmity of the whole community of nations, who will see its own danger in the example. For this reason it becomes the policy of each, to take every precaution against an injury to an individual; and while each is committing depredations on its adversary, to have some power subordinate of the particular government of each country, to take cognizance of prize, and confine this to the property of the enemy; and to which authority an individual who thinks himself injured may apply; and hence the institution of *Courts of Commissioners*, or the giving power to *Admiralty or other Courts*, for the

I had an opportunity afterwards at March term, 1808 in the case of Calhoon v. Insurance Company of Pennsylvania, to express my sentiments upon this point coming incidentally in question; and this the more, because I fore-

purpose of examining in cases of injury. It must be incident to such authority, to order restitution of the specific property, with damages; or condemn as enemies property, and decree a sale on behalf of the government, and for the use of those concerned. The sale is made as of property which has become the prize of the nation, by the hands of her subjects, and the nation is interested in protecting the purchasers. Because, otherwise, there would be no purchasers, or the prize would not bring its value. The specific property sold in the market of the foreign Court, must be protected, and immunity at the same time must be secured to the purchasers from any suit or prosecution in any forum, for the asportation of the property. What has the nation of the captor to do with the matter any farther? Where the property of a neutral nation is taken, why shall the neutral nation regard the change of possession, by the adjudication, and sale of the belligerent nation, and be restrained from recaption, by an act of the government, or the right of reprisal exercised by the act of the injured individual? Because it may be the immediate cause of war with the nation to whom the purchaser belongs, or with the nation who made the sale, and is interested in making good the transfer. It is therefore more her interest to admit the conclusiveness of the sentence, and the validity of the transfer, and to put the matter into a train of investigation with the capturing government. Or she may *also be a capturing nation in her turn*, and have property at market under the same predicament. It is the public policy of the neutral nation therefore, that the sentence of the foreign Court be considered as conclusive on *the subject of the capture, so far as respects the validity of the transfer, and that the proceeding in rem shall be supported ;* and that no collateral suit shall be sustained between the foreign owner and the late purchaser which shall bring the jurisdiction of the forum, or the regularity and justice of the judgment in question. But as respects contracts, which, though they may involve the question of neutral property, yet do not tend to nullify or defeat the judgment, by affecting those who hold under it, it is wide of the national concern, and a matter of profit or loss between those who pay a premium, and those who take a risk upon it.

saw from the arrangement of the courts, that I could not be present in the courts of errors and appeals, to which the case of Dempsey had been removed; and wished my sentiments to be known, that I might not be supposed to have concur-

Let us examine, whether from the nature of the contract, the foreign judgment can at all affect it. It is on the *same point*, but is it between the *same parties*, or those claiming under them? This is necessary to enable a judgment of any Court to be given in evidence in any case. The Chief Justice of the King's Bench (Mansfield) assumes this as a principle clear and admitted. "All the world are parties to a sentence of a Court of Admiralty." But the Lord Chancellor, (Eldon) expressing himself to have the concurrence of the present Chief Justice of the King's Bench, (Ellenborough) entertained a different idea on this particular. His words are, " that notion I apprehend, and am informed, is a mistaken notion, and that the assured on a policy of assurance could not be admitted parties to the proceedings in a Court of Admiralty."—3 Bosan. and Pull. 545.

But suppose all persons who may conceive themselves to be affected have a right, and have notice *actual* or constructive, to come in and make themselves parties to the proceedings in a Court of Admiralty; let us examine from the nature of the contract of insurance, what must be the understanding of the parties, with respect to defending the claim of neutrality before an Admiralty Court, or with respect to the effect of the sentence. For what is the premium paid, but for the risk of capture, and the effect of that capture? You, the assurer, undertaking that the property is neutral; I, the underwriter, undertake that it shall not be captured. But it has been captured and condemned, therefore it was not neutral. The underwriter plays a saving game in this case. On capture, the right of abandonment arises, and the right of action accrues, to the assured; the underwriter pays the value, but on acquittal, takes the property; on condemnation, he pockets the premium, and pays nothing. Put this matter to mercantile men, and they will acknowledge that it is absurd, and what they had no idea of in the *contract of insurance;* nor can they comprehend the mystery of the conclusiveness of a foreign sentence, on a stipulation which pre-supposed in the very nature of it, the possibility of an *unjust condemnation.* The consequences of the doctrine must shew the inconsistency with the nature of the contract, and what is contemplated under it. It can only be in the case of capture and acquittal, that the assured

red in sentiment, though not upon the bench, with the supreme court, in that case.

July 29th, 1808, in the court of errors and appeals, judge Cooper, delivered his opinion since published, which exhi-

has any right of action ; and this right may be divested by the condemnation ; and if an action has been instituted, it must be discontinued at the costs of the plaintiff; or if the money has been recovered, it must be paid back, with the costs of recovery. All these inconsistencies appeared to the Judges, in the case of Lothian and others, vs. Henderson and others, and they could get over them only with the unsatisfactory reconcilement, that the principle had been established.—3 Bosan. and Pull. 499.

The leading case is, that of Hughes vs. Cornelius; Sk. 59 ; 2 Show. 232 ; and Tho. Ray. 473. We have the special verdict in Shower, which shews it to be an action by the owner of a ship against the vendor, under a sentence of the Court of Admiralty in France ; which sentence, though falsified by the facts found by the special verdict, was held to be conclusive ; and the property thereby altered, though the sentence be unjust. This carries the doctrine no farther than we are willing to allow, and the reason given would be conclusive with us ; which was, that though it be in another King's dominions, we ought to give credit to it, lest they may not give credit to our Courts of Admiralty. This case was decided in the 34 Ch. 2, the year subsequent to our charter, but on that circumstance I lay no stress ; for a decision before the charter can be no more than evidence of what the law was before, and a decision since, cannot be less. But a great ground of the common law is reason, and every principle is examinable by reason.—Now, the reason given, does not bear it out farther than the protecting the sale by the order of the Court of Admiralty. But it is no uncommon thing, to have the doctrine carried beyond the principle. Hence the perversions of the common law, by the decisions of Judges. The superstructure overjuts the base, by the misconceptions of narrow, or through the oversight of great minds.

A case is referred to in the books, 2 Ray. 893. That was on a bond with condition that if the defendant should answer the value touching such a ship and goods, and in case the law should adjudge the said ship and goods to be prize ; plea that the law did not adjudge the ship and goods to be prize ; replication that the French Admiralty court did adjudge ; demurrer ; judgment. And justly, because the circumstance of non-condemnation was the *condition of* bits *the utmost comprehension of mind*, which is *the character-istic of a great judge;* and is the finest specimen of legal rea-soning, that ever fell from a bench. Nevertheless, it was rul-ed contrary, the supreme court of the United States, having

the bond. The condemnation was conclusive by the nature of the contract. This gives no countenance to the doctrine of *conclusive-ness on the abstract principle.*

From all that can be found in the books, at least from my read-ing, nothing appears to sanction the idea of carrying the doctrine of conclusiveness farther than the proceeding *in rem*, until we come to the great case of Bernardi and Matteaux in the year '81, and to the decision in which, though even since the declaration of our independence, I pay just as much respect as if it had been before the charter of Char. 2; and that is nothing, farther than reason will support.—The decision of a Court is but the reason of a Court, and no prescriptive length of time will bar the reason of another; opinion, however old, is but matter of weight, not con-troul, and respect and servility are distinct things.

It is but by implication that the doctrine would seem to have been carried farther in this case. For though the case involved the principle, yet it was put on the ground of being out of it; that the sentence had not proceeded on the ground expressly of the pro-perty not being neutral; that it did not appear from the sentence that the ship and cargo were condemned as enemies property. The warranty on the part of the assured was that of neutral ship and neutral property; and it would have been competent to him to have produced the sentence as conclusive evidence of the loss, had there been a necessity for him to have gone beyond the cap-ture, to prove the loss total. But for the assurer to produce it, to excuse himself from payment of the loss, could not be compe-tent, because it would be irrelevant, and could prove nothing for him, to support his defence. It was an effect of the capture a-gainst which he had insured, and could not serve his defence; or even if it were relevant, it could not be competent, because it was *res inter alias acta*, and the assured was no party to the sen-tence. Is it thought of giving notice to the assured to make good his warranty, on the trial before the Admiralty Court; or does he in fact consider himself as bound to take notice of it. He abandons to the underwriter the possession and management of the property. His understanding is, that it will be sufficient for him, to make good

before this time, Feb. 1808, in the case before us, decided in
favour of the conclusiveness of foreign sentences. It may
be presumed that it was for the sake of uniformity, between
the state court, and that court in their decisions, that it was

his warranty before a Court and Jury of his country, if defence
should be set up on this ground, when he comes to pursue his policy.

The competency of the Admiralty sentence was conceded in
the argument, from an oversight I take it, and no point made on
this ground. It seems to have been conceded even that it was
conclusive for him, provided the sentence had gone expressly on
the point of not being neutral property.—The attention of the
court was not called to consider on which side the sentence was
produced. Or as Lord Eldon says, in the case of Lothian and
Henderson, " The practice of receiving those sentences as conclusive evidence for collateral purposes, and not merely in suits
between the identical parties in the foreign courts, may possibly
have first obtained in those cases where the Plaintiff himself produced the sentence in order to prove the loss !

The Admiralty sentence, as to whatever it meant to decide,
says the Chief Justice, (Mansfield) we must take it as conclusive,
and bottoms this on the reason which he had before given " that
all the world are parties to a sentence of a Court of Admiralty."
—But the reason failing, the law fails. But the principal point
not being made in the argument, the decision must have less
weight. In this case we first observe the struggle of a sense of
justice with the doctrine, and a disposition to lay hold of what
will take the case out of the general principle. This is accomplished finally by putting it on the ground of the ambiguity of the
sentence. Lord Mansfield said " he thought the justice of the case
might be got at, on the ground of the ambiguity of the sentence."
This is the commencement of the doctrine which has been since
adopted, that ambiguity, obscurity, injustice or contradiction on
the face of the sentence, &c. would exclude the conclusiveness,
and the Courts have discovered an astutia on all occasions, to take
the case before them out of the general principle.—This was foreseen by Lee in his argument, " urging the danger of opening the
sentences of foreign Courts of Admiralty, which are usually infor-
mal, and expressing his apprehensions, that the consequence of
this determination would be, that, in all cases of this sort, there

so ruled by the court of errors and appeals. I take the liberty of saying that if lord Ellenborough's dicta and judge Cooper's opinion had appeared, before the decision of the supreme court of the United States, it might have changed

would be controversies about the ground of the foreign sentence." On this Lord Mansfield said, "that this supposed inconvenience, would be entirely obviated, if the foreign Courts would say, in their sentences, *condemned as enemies property.*"

But not having it in his power to command this correctness in the sentences of the foreign courts, it was an inconvenience which it was not in his power to obviate; it is rather curious that he should expect the Courts of Admiralty of the powers at war with Great Britain, so to amend their sentences, as to excuse English underwriters from paying losses—they would be careful not to take the hint.

Mayne vs. Walter, 22 Geo. 3, it was ruled by the same Chief Justice (Mansfield) if the ground of the decision appeared to be a foreign ordinance manifestly unjust, and contrary to the laws of nations and the insured has only infringed such a partial law, that, shall not be deemed a breach of his warranty so as to discharge the insurer. In that of Salucci vs. Johnston, 25 Geo. 3, it was ruled that though the vessel be condemned as prize, yet if the grounds of the sentence appear manifestly to contradict such a conclusion, the court here will not discharge the underwriters by declaring that the insured has forfeited his neutrality.—Calvert vs. Bovat, 38 Geo. 3, in the opinion of the Chief Justice (Kenyon) " the justice and honesty of the case was with the Plaintiff beyond all doubt," but it is contended, the sentence of condemnation precludes the plaintiff from asserting that fact. I yield to the cases cited, says he, " which shews that to a certain degree this court will support the proceedings in Foreign Courts, by presuming that their sentences are just; and will not make any exception at present of the proceedings of the French Courts of Admiralty. But when an attempt is made to pervert the justice of the case, it becomes necessary for us to see whether the decision of the Court at Guadaloupe, has so determined on the fact of neutrality that we cannot examine into it."

Geyer vs. Aquilar, 38 Geo. 3. The Chief Justice (Kenyon) " when this case was argued in the last term, the parties desired to have a second argument : to this the court readily acceded from

a vote, and in that case, we should have had no such principle to disgrace our code.

So far as respects our state, it was abolished by the legislature, by an act of 29th March, 1809. But it is to be regretted

an anxious wish that it might produce such arguments and reasons as would enable them to form a judicial opinion according to
their *individual feeling.* The situation of Judges is such that they
are some times obliged to decide against their own feelings as men.
We come to decide this case, says he, *bound and shackled* by certain rules from which we dare not depart. Civilized nations confess to be governed by certain rules, and the comity due from
courts in one country, to those in another, *induces them to give credit to one another's acts.* And so we must continue to act in this
country *until the legislature shall think fit to forbid it.* There is
the same comity between the different courts in this country.
Where there has been a proceeding in the exchequer, and a judgment *in rem*, as long as the judgment remains in force, it is obligatory on the parties who have civil rights depending on the same
question. Not long after Lord *Mansfield*, came into this court,
in an action brought against the officers of the customs or excise,
he was told by J. Denison that as the question had already been decided in the exchequer by a condemnation of the goods seized,
the judgment of that court was conclusive in favour of the defendant here ; at first Lord Mansfield doubted the propriety of that
opinion, but on enquiry finding that Mr. J. Denison was right, he
acquiesced, and always afterwards acted upon it. I admit the cases of
Mayne vs. Walter and Salucci vs. Johnston up to the full extent ; I
admit that if a foreign court of admiralty proceed on grounds contrary to the law of nations, their judgment ought not to have weight in
the courts of this country. But let us see what this case is : The
ground on which the courts in *France* proceeded was, that this
was a capture of enemies property ; and it certainly is not contrary to the law of nations to condemn a ship on that ground. Whether or not those courts arrived at that conclusion by proper means,
I am not at liberty to enquire ; here the question is whether they
have not stated as the ground of condemnation, a ground which
will bear them out, supposing it to be true ? And I am clearly satisfied that they have. They concluded from the evidence that
this was enemies property, not indeed in the formal language of
our courts of justice, but they say in substance " we think this
enemies property and therefore we condemn the ship and cargo."

that a *judiciary decision had not the credit of this reform in our jurisprudence.* I mean so far as respected the state courts, and what was within their jurisdiction.

Now that concludes this case; for as long as the foreign judgments are binding upon us, the conclusion we must draw from the judgment in this case in *France* is, that the property which was warranted to be *American* is found by that judgment not to be *American* property. I feel this however as the grossest injustice to *Americans.* The French courts seem to have proceeded in this instance on *Algerine* (nay on worse) principles; because they professed to proceed according to law, but in reality made the law a stalking horse for an act of piracy. But I cannot now question the legality of their decision; I am bound to decide according to the law; it is my duty *jus dicere et non jus dare."*

Ashurst, in this case : " Though most probably we should not have given the same judgment as the *French* courts gave, it is not open to us now to canvass that question.—As the French courts have already given a judicial opinion upon the question, it must govern us, whatever may be our opinions concerning the real merits of the case."

Groce, Justice ; " I feel myself bound to give judgment in favour of the defendant, and at the same time lament the necessity of so deciding."

Lawrence J. " If we could have examined the grounds on which the *French* courts determined this to be enemy's property, probably we should have formed a different conclusion : but we cannot review those judgments here. They have decided the question, though by no means according to my opinion : but having so decided, the rule undoubtedly is, that whenever a court of competent jurisdiction has decided any question, and the same question arises incidentally in another court, the latter is concluded by the former judgment. The case of Hughes v. Cornelius shews that this rule was not confined to judgments given in our courts; there, in an action of trover for a ship and goods, a special verdict was found setting forth a sentence in the court of admiralty in *France*, which was in favour of the defendant, and *per curiam*, agreed and adjudged that as we are to take notice of a sentence of a court of admiralty here, so ought we of those abroad by other nations, and we must not set them at large, again, for otherwise the merchants would be in a pleasant condition ; for suppose a decree here in the

exchequer, and the goods happened to be carried into another nation, should the courts abroad unravel this ? It is but agreeable
with the law of nations, that we should take notice and approve of
the laws of their countries in such particulars." " According to all
the authorities therefore I think we are concluded in this case by
the judgments given in France, however we may feel the impro-
priety of those decisions."

Here we have Hughes and Cornelius, and the reason given in
that case, 2 Show. 242 ; " suppose a decree in the exchequer, and
the goods happen to be carried into another nation, should the
courts abroad unravel this ?" The protecting the sales of property made under the order of their own courts, was the policy. But
could not that be done, without affecting the interests of persons
who did not claim under the sale ? There is no more reason in
this than to say the vendee shall not recover against the vendor on
eviction, or that a surety whose property has been sold under a
scire facias shall not recover against him, for whom he had been
surety, lest it should affect the sheriff's sale. We also again hear
of comity of nations, the reason given in the same case as reported
by Sir Thomas Raymond, that foreign courts will not regard our
sentences if we do not regard theirs. But do foreign courts exercise a reciprocal comity ? " The courts of France (says Martial
in his treatise on the law of insurance) do not carry their complai-
sance so far. The judgments of foreign tribunals have then, no
weight or authority whatever against Frenchmen ; and the case
must be again decided in the courts. And for this he gives the
authority of Emerigon, a French writer. These courts do not even
respect a sale made under the order of a foreign court ; or consider
it a change of property for aught that appears from this authority ;
nevertheless the British, for reasons of national policy, in their own
favour, which it is not necessary for us to examine, carry the comity on their part to the extent which has been decided, notwithstanding the embarrassments consequent upon the doctrines which
have laid them under the necessity of explaining and distinguishing in almost every case.

Christie vs. Secritan, 39 Geo. 3. The Chief Justice (Kenyon)
again says ; " in general there is no doubt but that the sentence of
a court of admiralty is conclusive as to the points which it professes to decide ; it was so ruled in the case of Hughes vs. Cornelius."
But he finds a variance between the warranty and the sentence,
and on that lets the plaintiff off from the principle.

Groce, J. " In considering that, we can only look at the ground of the sentence itself, and not at the previous reasons which are stated." The case of Bernardy and Matteaux, the Chief Justice (Mansfield) looked at the reasons in the process verbal, and laid the sentence aside, and got over the doctrine in that manner, hence the observation of Martial, 290 ; " In what cases such sentences shall be deemed conclusive evidence to falsify, or prove the forfeiture of the warranty, has been often found to be a very perplexing question, and has produced much litigation and many decisions, which are not easily reconciled, or reducible to any well defended principle."

43 Geo. 3. In the case of Lothian and others vs. Henderson and others, the question had arisen in the court of admiralty " in Scotland." The judge admiral decreed " in favour of the underwriters ;" which by implication involves the conclusion of holding the conclusiveness of the foreign sentence. The assured brought the merits of that decree before the court of session by an action of reduction where the Lord ordinary pronounced an interlocutor in favour of the insured, to which after a representation for the appellants he adhered. The appellants, the underwriters, having petitioned the whole court of session ; that court unanimously confirmed the interlocutor of the Lord ordinary ; whereupon the underwriters appealed to the house of lords.

We have now the sense of the judicial authority of Scotland against the conclusiveness of the foreign sentence ; and it comes to receive a consideration in the highest judicial authority of the Britis government. It was argued, May 1803, at the bar of the house of lords. On this argument the counsel on both sides not only spoke to the several questions ; but also argued at great length and with much learning, say the reporters, (3 Bosan. and Pul. 505) the admissibility in evidence of a sentence of a foreign court of admiralty in an action upon a policy of insurance, in order to falsify a warrant of neutrality.

After the argument, the lord chancellor, put the question to the judges involving this principle.

11th July, 1803, the opinions of the judges seriatim. I shall notice certain dicta in the opinions of some of them.

Baron Graham, speaking of the foreign sentence says, " I am relieved from the necessity of saying what I think of the disgraceful sentence ; and how far an English court of justice is bound to adopt their conclusions, when directly contrary to the premises from which they are drawn. To receive such sentences as conclusive, would be, in effect to say, that we give no credit to what they truly state, but absolute credit to what they falsely conclude."

Chambre, adverts to the embarrassing consequences of the doctrine; and which had been a question raised in that case, " whether on the event of condemnation, if the underwriters had given their bills, and before payment, the sentence of condemnation had arrived, they could legally have refused payment of these bills; or whether if the money had been actually paid, it could have been recovered back, which, taking the sentence to be conclusive, it must be conclusive to all purposes whatever, and so overturn every fact established by other evidence. If so, the bills would have been given under a mistake of what ultimately turned out to be really the fact, and then the consideration upon which they were given would have failed al initio." It is in this manner he would reconcile the doctrine with justice, and which difficulty the opinion drew along with it which he adopts. " I think," says he, " the sentence conclusive against the claims of the assured, agreeable to all the decisions on the subject, beginning with the case of Hughes vs. Cornelius, (confirmed as that was by the opinion of Lord Holt in two subsequent cases), and pursuing them down to the present period. It is true that in Hughes vs. Cornelius the question upon the foreign sentence arose in an action of trover, and not in an action on a policy of insurance where the non-compliance with a warranty of neutrality is in dispute. But from that period to the present, the doctrine there laid down respecting foreign sentences is considered equally applicable to questions of warranty in actions on policies, as to questions of property in actions of trover. It has been supposed indeed, that the cases warrant a distinction between those sentences which expressly take into consideration and ultimately decide the non-neutrality of the ship, and those in which the same point does not appear to have come so immediately under the consideration of the foreign courts. But I think wherever the courts in this country have been able to collect from the sentence that the point of neutrality has been decided, they have held themselves bound by that decision. Indeed the doctrine upon this subject is most ably summed up in the admirable judgment of the master of the rolls, in Kendersley vs. Chace. Had the *French* sentence in this case merely stated the *French* ordinance, without concluding as they have done, this case might have fallen within some of the late determinations of the Court of King's Bench. But the *French* court has gone further in their determination, and applying the facts and the ordinances, they have drawn a conclu-

sion which perhaps no court in this country would have done, but
by which they have decided that the ship *Catherine* being an *American*, had forfeited her neutrality. I am therefore of opinion
that the assured are bound by this decree of the *French* court.

The case of Hughes and Cornelius is still the leading case, in
which the decision was originally of proper extent, but like bad
report, the doctrine of this report has since grown to a monstrous
size.

Ingrediturque solo et caput inter nubila condit.

Le Blanc, J. in this case says, " that, these sentences are admissible and conclusive evidence of what they undertake to decide, *it seems not now safe to question.*"

The·doctrine is here put on the footing of precedent, and not
on the ground of legal reason or political relation.

Lawrence, J. discovers himself to be well aware of another
embarrassing consequence of this doctrine. It occurs to him as
it did to Chambre, that on the capture, the *right of abandonment
arises ;* the cause of action accrues ; but is liable to be defeated,
all effect of it divested by the subsequent sentence of condemnation. But a second difficulty occurs to find out, on this principle,
what it is *against which the insured insures,* if it be not the effect
of the capture, and what almost necessarily follows it, according
to the acknowledged practice of the French courts, we will add
British, a *condemnation.* He supposes it may be against the capture, wherever an acquittal follows ; because the voyage might be
defeated, and the assured be entitled to abandon, and call on the
underwriter as for a total loss.

I doubt whether it ever entered into the head of an insurer,
that it was only in the case of a capture, where an acquittal followed, that he could be entitled to recover.

Heath, J. says nothing of the conclusiveness of a foreign sentence, but puts the case before him, on the intention of the parties.
The object of the parties, says the Judge, " was to ascertain the
neutrality of the ship, in case of capture or seizure, by the medium
of such proof as would be sufficient in the case of a loss, by the pe-
rils of the seas. The manifest injustice practised by the *French*
courts of prize, at the date of this agreement was so public, and
notorious, and was the subject of so many suits in this country, that
I presume we may judicially take notice of it. If so, the meaning
of the agreement, as clearly and manifestly may be collected from
the terms of it, was to indemnify the insured against the iniquity
of these sentences, and for the underwriters, in consideration of

the high premium of ten guineas per cent. to take that risk on themselves; for this was a high war premium."

M Donald, Baron, places his decision on the special circumstances of the case; " but with respect," says he, "to the effect of those unjust sentences of the foreign tribunals, although I might have hesitated in concurring with some of the cases, it is now too late to encourage any doubts, as they have been acted upon to a very great amount."

Eldon, Chancellor, with the concurrence of Chief Justice Ellenborough, states, " it does not become me to impugn a practice acted upon for so long a series of years, and that by men in the judicial character, who must ever be looked up to with reverence in this country. I well know also how much property has been affected by this principle and how much more may now be afloat on the faith of that long train of decisions in Westminster hall, by which the principle in question has been sanctioned."

Chief justice of the common pleas, (Alvanly) " after the long series of cases in Westminster hall, in which foreign sentences have been received for the same purposes for which the French sentence in this, is now set up, and the long period of time during which those cases have been acted on by the commercial part of this country, and acquiesced in by the legal part of the community, I cannot admit that it is still open to this house to decide that foreign sentences are not admissible evidence in suits between the assured and the underwriters, in order to falsify the warranty of neutrality. Nor do I feel that opinion shaken by the consideration, that the point has never yet received the express decision of this house. At this late period, such a decision upon that point as the respondents now contend for, might almost induce the merchants of London to shut the door of Guildhall against the judges."

This is putting it, not on the ground of reason, but the fear of merchants, or a consideration of the effect of unhinging a principle. Prizes sold under the orders of the British Admiralty courts where the merchants were purchasers, could not be affected carrying the principle no farther than it originally stood in the case of Hughes and Cornelius, but this it is probable was in his mind; or if he looked only to the consequence of some adjudications being found to have gone upon a wrong principle, the merchants might complain. But by taking this distinction on the proceeding *in rem* and carrying it no further than to protect the sale, the jurisprudence of the country would have been less embarrassed than it now is in this particular; nevertheless common sense went down under an idea of the insuperable difficulty. An early oversight has become law in that country, and reason which had struggled long against it in the breasts of counsel and the heads of judges, has been over-reached by the imperceptible advances of original error: which has grown a monster in jurisprudence, and like usurpers of power in the governments of men, it maintains itself by the mischief it has done.

Let us see whether it has got such a footing in our jurisprudence here by the decisions of our courts.

Vasse vs. Ball, 2 Dallas, 270, at March term, 1797, in the supreme court, would seem to be the first case, where the point was made. The counsel for the plaintiff say, there is not in fact, any judicial determination of the English courts, antecedent to the American revolution, which declares that a sentence of a court of admiralty cannot be examined and controverted between persons who are not parties to it. It is not alleged on the part of the defendant, that there had been any other than English precedents to warrant the doctrine.

Shippen, J. expresses an inclination to think our courts bound by the foreign sentence, and where the decree proceeded expressly on the point.

M'Kean, chief justice, seems to have confined himself to the subject of the condemnation. "The idea," says he "that a sentence of a courts of admiralty is conclusive, arises from this consideration, that the court always proceed *in rem*. The decree naturally and necessarily binds the subject of the proceeding, a ship, or cargo; and any person purchasing under the decree will, of course, be secure. But this case was not determined on the general principle.—It is true, that the inclination expressed by chief justice Shippen, and the weight of that inclination would seem to have led to a general impression out of doors, that the doctrine of the English Courts would be adopted; for since that time, and before, owing to the English decisions, that had been done, which the Chief Justice of the Common Pleas, in Lothian and Henderson, suggests. "For," says he, "it being once known that such is the law respecting foreign sentences, those who do not choose to subject themselves to the caprice of a French Court, may stipulate in the policy that the evidence of a French Court shall not be aduced in evidence against their claim."

Our merchants have introduced these stipulations in their policies, that they might not subject themselves to the caprice of English Courts. But there need be no subjection to the caprice of either, if our Courts would not subject themselves to English decisions on a general principle, where error hath manifestly intervened, and which the very precautions of the stipulation prove to be contrary to common notions of convenience or justice.

Taking a decision to amount to more than mere evidence of what the law is, and of itself to be a ground of law, or to constitute the law, it has been shewn that at least it is not a clear case, that the decision in Hughes vs. Cornelius, went farther than has been stated; but even had it gone farther; and, that to the extent gone, it was to be considered in England as *a principle of the common law*, yet might it not be a question whether it was a principle of that nature which in our colonization we would carry with us. For though it hath been held, that if an uninhabited country be discovered and planted by English subjects, all the English laws then in being, which are the birth-right of every subject, are immediately there in force, " yet this must be understood" says Blackstone, " *with very many and very great restrictions :* and colonists carry with them only so much of the English law as is applicable to their own situation, and the condition of any infant colony; such for instance as the general rules of inheritance and of protection from personal injuries. *The artificial refinements and distinctions incident to the property of a great and commercial people,* are neither necessary nor convenient for them and therefore are not in force." But the obligation of the English laws over the colonists of Pennsylvania will depend upon the Charter to William Penn, which expressly provided as to this, Sec. 7. in these words " and our farther will and pleasure is that the laws for regulating and governing of property within the said province, as well for the descent and enjoyment of lands, as likewise for the enjoyment and succession of goods and chattles, and likewise as to all felonies, shall be and continue the same as they *shall be for the time being by the general course of the law in our kingdom of England,* until the said laws shall be altered by the said William Penn, his heirs and assigns, and by the freemen of the said province, their delegates or deputies or the greater part of them."

Considering that by this clause, authority is given to the decisions of English courts and that up to the revolution, they were as binding in this state as in England; yet this must be restricted to discussion upon such laws, as under the words of the Charter, became ours. Will it be contended that these laws include clearly and unequivocally such a principle as that in question; a principle of national policy; but is it a principle of the law of nations.

adopted by general usage or recognized by writers? But no de‑
cision even in the English courts; save that of Hughes and Cor‑
nelius, took place before the period of our revolution. That of
Mansfield in Bernardi vs. Matteaux as has been said, was after the
revolution. No decision has taken place in our own courts from
the period of our emigration, until the period of our revolution,
nor since, extending, or sanctioning this doctrine of the conclusive‑
ness of a sentence of admiralty in any case, much less to the extent
here contended. And if it did not make a part of the common law,
and is introduced *under that term* by the legislative act after the
adopting our first state constitution "that all laws in force at the
time of making, &c. *shall continue* ;" what foot-hold have we in ap‑
plying this late doctrine of the English courts? more especially
when from the decisions of foreign courts of admiralty in matters
of capture, all ideas of justice have been lost, and with regard to
French captures and condemnation even in the opinion of the Eng‑
lish courts themselves: in which we agree with them, that at
certain periods, libelling and condemnation were the same thing,
in the French courts. But we add, in the English courts of admi‑
ralty also. There were the forms of justice, but not the substance.
We had *monitions*, to save appearances, and even had appeals;
but it depended on the order and temper of the government from
time to time, what chance of liberation. These things being so,
and from the nature of things they will always be so, can it be a
matter of *sound discretion in our courts* to extend a dubious con‑
struction, or doubtful doctrine to our jurisprudence?

The United States v. Judge Peters.   5 Cranch, 115.

WOULD not this case seem to have presented an occa‑
sion, where it became necessary for the supreme court to
exercise an *original* jurisdiction in issuing a *mandamus*. It
may be said, that, in those cases "in which a state shall be a
party, *the supreme court shall have original jurisdiction.*" But
in this case there was no state nominally a party, nor could
the court know the state of Pennsylvania, the state suggest‑
ed to be a party, as being *in interest* before the court. An
amendment to the constitution had declared, " that the judi‑

cial power of the United States shall not be construed to
extend to any suit in law or equity, commenced or prosecuted against one of the United States by citizens of another
state, or by citizens or subjects of any foreign state." But
it was laid down by the court, chief justice Marshall's opinion, 141, " that the state of Pennsylvania had neither possession of, nor right to, the property on which the sentence of
the district court was pronounced ; and since the suit was
neither commenced nor prosecuted against that state, there
remains no pretext for the allegation that the case is within
that amendment of the constitution which has been cited ;
and consequently the state of Pennsylvania can possess no
constitutional right to resist the legal process which may be
directed in this case." The district court had not refused
a *mandamus to themselves;* for it would have been absurd
to have asked it. There could have been, therefore, no *appeal* from their judgment whether or not it ought to issue.
For it was this court that refused to do an act, *the issuing an
attachment.* It was *original* in the supreme court ; and in
the face of the case of Marbury v. Madison, the *mandamus*
was issued. I do not say the court erred in this case ; but
that in the case of Marbury v. Madison, they erred ; and
ought to have exercised an original jurisdiction in issuing
a mandamus.

The state of Pennsylvania was *incidentally* at least, and
in my opinion, *substantially concerned.* But I do not enter
into this question, having had it in view only to shew that
the court did in this case exercise an original jurisdiction in
issuing a *mandamus.*

The controversy was alarming at the time, and could not
but distress every good citizen. As to the state being the
real party interested, and substantially concerned, I subjoin
in a note, a publication on that side of the argument, and
which appeared *after the business was closed,* in the Democratic Press of the 15th March, 1810.

It is a point to which sooner or later we must come ; resistance to the jurisdiction of the federal courts, unless by an amendment to the constitution, the necessity of it is superceded. For

it is not to be supposed that these courts will not usurp; not that I attribute to the individuals who compose them, other dispositions than those common to the nature of man. But place any one in authority, and it will be natural for him to wish to extend his province. In the English courts, it is thought to be an excellence; and it is even laid down as a characteristic of a good judge, " to enlarge his jurisdiction." This is a maxim which has been attempted to be qualified, by a substitution of " to enlarge justice." But that this could not be the original maxim, is evident, from the absurdity of talking of *enlarging justice.* For in that case, it would become injustice. The meaning of the maxim is, that it is not the part of a good judge, to be squeamish in determining the extent of his cognizance.—And in fact, in the courts of England, they have not been squeamish. The court of *King's Bench*, is in strictness, a criminal court; yet by a fiction has drawn to itself the jurisdiction of matters of *meum and tuum,* which were originally the exclusive subject of the cognizance of the *common pleas.* We know the controversies that have existed on these heads, between those courts; as well as between the courts of common law in general, and the court of *Chancery,* in matter of jurisdiction. But this controversy can come to no dangerous result in that country; where they have an appeal; or a writ of error to the house of lords, where the question can receive an ultimate determination; this, not by the courts, claiming the jurisdiction; but by an independent tribunal; this tribunal, not perhaps, so well informed as either of the respective courts, claiming jurisdiction; but not having their opinions pre-engaged or their passions embarked in the controversy so that in the opinion of the people being more remote from bias, they are more likely to give satisfaction.

We have seen a late controversy in the state of New-York, between the supreme court and the jurisdiction of the chancellor in a matter of contempt.* The writ of error or appeal, I forget which it was, *lay* by the constitution of that commonwealth, to the Senate of the state. This tribunal not perhaps, correctly; but to the public satisfaction, because an independent tribunal, determined against the chancellor's authority; though it had been sanctioned by the opinion of the *majority of the supreme court.* Where a question of jurisdiction arises, there never will be satisfaction by a determination of the tribunal itself which claims the jurisdiction. And we know that the giving satisfaction, is a matter of

* *The Commonwealth* v. *Van Ness.*

much moment to the peace of the community, in the administration of justice. Hence it was, that in forming the federal constitution, there was no point upon which the ablest members of the convention, were more at a loss, than upon this, of the jurisdiction of the federal courts. After all, it was considered as a matter which must be left in a great measure, to future regulation; and was a principal ground of that clause of the constitution, which provides for an amendment.

It was impossible to foresee, perfectly, how this wheel would move; or what necessity there might be for the enlargement or the contraction of it. If the constitution had remained as it was, the judicial power of the union, extending to a case where a state was a party, there would have been less difficulty in ascertaining, the constitutionality or legal exercise of the power, there being no exclusion. But the amendment to the constitution of the United States necessarily introduced a difficulty, in all cases where a state might allege itself a party, the plea to the jurisdiction being made to the very power whose jurisdiction it was the object of the amendment to exclude. It is thus, that in the alteration of any structure or machine, an alteration of more is required than the particular part; and this, in order to adapt the proportions of the other parts to that which is altered. The amendment of the constitution in the particular in view, ought to have carried with it, *the establishment of some authority* to determine in what cases " the state was a party." This authority ought to be independent of that tribunal which was to take cognizance of the trial, supposing it to be a case where the state *was not a party*. This was a great omission. Of what use to exclude a jurisdiction, and at the same time to *leave it to itself to say whether it was excluded?* Admitting that it may be some check on the discretion of the power; yet it can constitute no certain bar. The state independency which was in the view of the amendment, is not secured in an effectual manner; but still subject to the federal judiciary.

It will be said what amendment could be thought of: what practicable. The most convenient that occurs to me to think of, and the most advisable to adopt, would be the *Senate of the Union*. These consisting of an equal representation of the states; interested equally in the conservation of their independence, would be the safest and most natural tribunal before whom a question of the state sovereignty could be brought. Without some such tribunal, what is a state to do in case of federal usurpation? If a municipal court usurps jurisdiction, it is justifiable to resist the process.

It is a principle of law, that the process of a court having no juris-diction of the case, is not merely voidable, but absolutely *void*. The officer with the process in his hand is a tresspasser; and may be resisted. Who is to judge whether the court has jurisdiction? The individual interested has a right to judge for himself. No man can question his right, but it must be at his peril. The state sovereignty, under this amendment, is placed as an *individual* in the union of the states. Has not the state a right to judge as an individual would have, of the jurisdiction of a court from which process issues? But it must be at its peril. I agree; and this proves that it must be the *state sovereignty itself*, that alone can take upon it to determine when and where its sovereignty has been in-vaded; and where it ought to resist. It must be a question of state decision, and no authority is competent to decide so as to act in consequence of a decision, but *the state itself*.

This proves that the judiciary of a state, being but a branch of the government, cannot be competent to decide on the jurisdic-tion of the United States courts; so as to liberate on a *habcas cor-pus*; for this would be drawing with it, an opposition to the laws of the United States by an act of the judiciary; and would be ad-mitting a power to involve the state in war, without the knowledge or consent of the sovereign power. Posse against posse, would be the same thing as a levied force, on the side of the executive of the state; and that of the union.

Had the State, in the case of Olmstead a right to decide for itself, on the jurisdiction of the United States? What doubt can there be of this? Has an individual a right to judge for himself, of the jurisdiction of a court to which he is called to answer? Doubtless. There is no lawyer, or law book, that will deny this. But it must be at his peril that he undertakes to decide. It will be the expediency that will be the only question. It will not be advisable perhaps where the court, whose process he undertakes to dispute will have a right to decide on his plea. He must look to the consequences, and count all the costs. In a community where his defence may come before a different tribunal, the prin-ciple not only holds of a *void* process; but it may be carried into practice, and acted upon by the people; it must be a clear case indeed, that will induce a man to resist where he means to insist upon the want of cognizance in the tribunal, from whence the precept may issue. He will suffer much, before he will ven-ture to kill or wound in opposition to the writ. The like prudence will be observed on the part of a sovereign state, who is as an individual in the community of states. Greater hesitation will be necessary where it can only be before the very court that issues the process, that the enquiry can be made of the want of jurisdiction. But if resistance is not made, it is waving a right on the ground of expediency; which may cease to have the appearance of a right, by the submission. It may grow into precedent, and be protected by the stare decisis of the law. For acquiescence is itself an evidence of right; and it is observable that in this very case of Olmstead, the decision of the court in the case of Doan *vs.* Penhallow; 3 Dall. 54, and the *acquiescence* of the state concerned, that of New Hampshire, is made a foundation whereon to rest, as to a particular of the decision then to be made. It is called *settling a matter where it has been once decided,* nor, with this principle of regarding precedent, do we find fault; but we shew the effect of a decision, and an acquiescence.

But what madness must it be in a state to resist where the presumption almost necessarily arises that the determination of the same court will be the same; it will be a bold daring, unquestionably, and must look like madness. In the case of an individual it may have the same appearance to resist the jurisdiction of a municipal court: especially where the government is known to make a point of having a law, or the construction of a law carried into effect. Yet John Hampden did resist the *levy of ship money;* and was indicted and convicted for that resistance; yet the resistance was not ultimately without a good effect; and though I say nothing as to the right; much less the expediency of resistance in Olmstead's case, yet I entertain the idea that it will be attended with the good consequence of leading the public mind to attend to the necessity of a provision for the removal of the grievance which gave rise to that expedient. I do not say our marshal did not do his duty in Olmstead's case; for there was but one other thing that he could have done (and this he was not bound to do) which was to return his writ with a *special indorsement of the opposition made to the execution of the process;* so that the court, on laying this before the executive of the union; and which by him, being laid before the representatives of the people, the grounds of the resistance of the state might be considered; and the expedience of an act of war on one of the state sovereignties might be the subject of deliberation. For it would behove the union to be as circumspect, and cautious in making war upon a state, as in a state to make opposition to the general government. It is true, a state is the weaker power; but the convulsion of a struggle would not be favourable to the permanence of the stronger. It is presumable that the Legislature of the state in enacting the law of 1803, acted under the idea that the matter might take such a turn as that which we have hinted; viz. a *special return of the marshal;* and which I humbly think might have been advisable, rather than a calling out the posse in the first instance. For I cannot think that the *ultima ratio,* directly looking at it, could be in view. It was too appaling to be contemplated, without more apprehension, than had generally pervaded the community. That the idea of resistance by means of the *civil authority,* could come into the mind of any one well informed, is impossible, because the absurdity of the consequence when drawn out, posse against posse; sheriff against marshal, shews the falsity of the proposition. But I take it, the mind of the Legislature was directed solely to the getting the matter brought before the Congress of the Union, in order to have it considered, whether it was a *casus belli,* or, just ground of the declaring war against a state; or in other words declaring that state in *rebellion;* and determining on a recourse to executive force to subdue it. For that the *posse* of the district, could have been competent if the opposition of the state had continued, is not to be supposed. The proportion of the force on one side, and on the other, rendered it morally, if not physically impossible. But the state thought it expedient to submit; and it did appear to me to be expedient. Enough had been done to attract attention; and this must have been the original object of the act of Assembly of 1803. But could not attention have been attracted by remonstrance on the floor of Congress, through the medium of our Representatives? that is one way doubtless; but it must have been in the shape of an *impeachment* against the Judges; and though I will not say that an assumption of jurisdiction, where it does not exist, is not impeachable; yet whoever could think of sustaining an impeachment where the error was merely that of the judgment, and no question of the purity of the intention? And I take it that in this case of Olmstead, no one has ever for a moment questioned the integrity of the United States courts; but the error of the judgment only. The human mind must incline so much in such a case to acquit, that the determination could not be as in a matter of meum and tuum of state right, and would be totally incompetent to ascertain with satisfaction to those concerned; or even to the public, the abstract justice of the case.

The legislature, I make no doubt, had all these considerations in their minds in the act of 1802, and their views were not directed ultimately to a conflict, but to a *negociation*. It was thought sufficient to break the case. The fact is, there are situations in the affairs of communities, where something palpable only can rouse. Lucretia's stabbing herself by her own hand, and Virginius stabbing his daughter, are instances of this in the Roman republic. What but the one could have roused attention to the tyranny of kings, and the other to that of the decemviri, so as to have produced a change, as no one has since doubted, *a happy amendment in the constitution of the government?* There is such a thing as a stage effect, in order to engage attention. The public attention must be excited a great deal by this transaction; and not the less perhaps, because it has not been carried farther; since it has been taken up in the legislature of the state, canvassing the authority of the power to call out the militia, and resist the process of the court. That the legislature must approve it, was unavoidable to be consistent with themselves; such of them as had been of the legislature and had actually voted for the law, for in that case, they had ordered it. They had not only enacted it in express terms, but it had continued a statute of several years standing. The legislature in session at the very crisis it began to be acted on, and no bill brought in, or motion made to modify or repeal it. As to the Governor having done what had been enjoined, there could be no question on a candid consideration of the words; nay, I am not able to put any face on a construction to the contrary, or to devise how it could have been avoided by him. It is a duty positively enjoined, and which admits of no evasion, from the express terms of the injunction. The Governor by the constitution of the state, or by law, has no command over the civil authority. He could not command a single justice to issue his warrant, to arrest the Marshal for a breach of the peace; if it could have been of any use to arrange the civil authority of the state against that of the union, under the idea of having a force competent to resist, or not involving the same consequence of a disruption of the *commune vinculum*, or cord which binds us together. The only means which the Governor had to *protect against the process of the federal court* was the *militia*. When the President of the United States tells the Governor, in his correspondence, that it was his (the president's) duty to execute the laws of the union, it was as much as to say, *just as it is yours to execute the laws of the state.*

If the question had been proposed in the state legislature, simply on the duty of the Governor, in executing the law, but at the same time involving by implication, no approbation, of the law itself, there would have been less difficulty, and of course less disagreement of opinion; for it cannot be contested with candor, but that *the duty of the Governor was imperative,* unless you allow him in his executive capacity a right *to judge of the obligatory force of a law;* and I could not infer from any thing I have heard, that any one would be willing to allow him that latitude.

Had I been a member of the legislature on the late occasion, I do not say that I would have been prepared to sanction by *implication,* the policy or expediency of the law; for that involves an extensive investigation. I lay out of the case what has been said of the matter ceasing to be a question of state concern by the *substitution of names,* or the *denomination of property.* For in this I think there is nothing solid. The subject of controversy was at first a vessel, the state on one side, and Olmstead on the other, claimants of the prize. This property was turned into money, that money deposited in the custody of the law, by bringing it into court. The state being a body politic could not take it out of court but by the agency of an officer. The treasurer of the state as her officer, did take it out, and the money was turned into *certificates.* Does this divest the state of its claim upon the property? Is it less a matter between the state and Olmstead than it was before? The treasurer indorsed on the paper that covered the certificates, "these will become the property of the state when" &c. What had Olmstead to do with the *certificates?* It was the money for which the vessel had been sold by order of the admiralty court, that was the subject of his claim. The passing this into certificates, was not his act. It was that of the state, of which act, he could not, in contemplation of law, be supposed to have any knowledge. It was the vessel, or the proceeds in money, that he could alone claim. If the money arising from the sale of the vessel had been converted into cattle, could he have claimed the cattle? Or if he did, could he have said, the money has now become cattle, and therefore the claim of the state is extinguished, and *she has ceased to be a party.* Yet this is the miserable quibble upon which the great legal characters that have canvassed this subject, on the part of Olmstead, have undertaken to put it. But it would seem to me that if nothing more solid can be advanced, the matter must be considered a state claim. The position is more tenable that the *amendment to the constitution does not extend to suits of admiralty, and maritime jurisdiction*. This position I will not undertake to canvass, because it is not necessary. For it seems to me that, since the adoption of the constitution, admitting that, *a parte post*, the United States courts draw the jurisdiction of all claims of right, or complaints of wrong *originating on the high seas*, let the parties be what they may, and this as a jurisdiction incident to the sovereign power ; yet this ground of claim was antecedent to the constitution, and not *surviving* to the new, because *not cognizable under the old*. Doubtless the jurisdiction had been assumed, or at least claimed under the old confederation ; but it was this very assumption or claim which the state at all times had protested against, and was unwilling to admit. It will not justify her to say that committees, or that congress under the confederation, had sustained the appeal ; but she called it a usurpation, and still calls it a usurpation, it being originally a mere matter of fact that was triable in the case of Ulmstead, and that having been found by a jury, and the state when she gave the appeal to congress in admiralty cases, expressly excepting *an appeal on a matter of fact ;* and the admiralty court of the *allied* states, before the ratification of the confederation having no jurisdiction, but by the express grant of each state, the confederation could not by relation, give such a power. To say the least of it, the jurisdiction assumed was extremely questionable, and it cannot be said by any candid man, but that there was strong ground whereon to rest an opposition. With respect to the *policy* of contesting or submitting, I say nothing ; and it is to be presumed the state might have acquiesced, but for the assumption of jurisdiction in other cases, which had excited considerable alarm, but of which I have no disposition to enter into an examination at present ; but at the same time, expressing my apprehension, that without some tribunal other than the courts of the United States themselves, it may be found difficult to go on without a schism. I propose the senate of the Union as this tribunal, and in order to secure all reasonable consideration in favor of the judiciary decisions, on questions of jurisdiction, let a majority of two-thirds be necessary to reverse a judgment of a court, *on a plea to the jurisdiction*, and this is the same majority which would be necessary to convict on an *impeachment*. Unless it is to be assumed as a principle that the United States courts " *can do no wrong*," their *jurisdiction* will be questioned, and when questioned, what can be done by an individual state but to resist? This may be done without looking forward to a disruption of the union as a *necessary* consequence.

On the resistance of the colonies to the mother country of Great Britain, at the commencement, and for a long period, there was no idea of a revolution, on the part of the colonies, but of bringing the matter to a negociation. This proves that resistance to an unconstitutional jurisdiction, does not necessarily involve an intention to dissolve the government. Remonstrance, and representation may be found ineffectual; and the only means left may be an opposition to the exercise of the assumed authority: and the only question will be, whether to wait until the invasions are so monstrous and palpable as to shock every mind; *or to resist the beginning* of usurpation.

This was done in the resistance by the colonies to the mother country of Great Britain. For it was not so much the weight of the oppression that was felt, but an *abstract principle* that was disputed, which gave rise to the revolution. The claim of binding the colonies by an act of parliament " *in all cases whatever.*"

The principal objection to the stopping short of resistance to an unconstitutional authority in the first aggression, is the danger of allowing precedents. It is now agreed in Olmstead's case, and made the foundation; and indeed the only ground that I see on the part of the United States courts, that the *recommendation of congress to institute Admiralty courts* by the individual states, and the individual states in that and other instances, submitting to these recommendations gave them the *force of law :* and the *qualifications* of adoption, are disregarded. The *exception* is thrown out of the case, and the whole power recommended, is assumed ; *and because it has been assumed, it has become legal.*

The states were united but sub-modo ; and they had no prize court. They actually had no power to establish a Judiciary tribunal in any state. Each state was a sovereign power itself, and but in the capacity of an *ally,* for the purposes of the confederacy. The prize court was that of the state, with a power of revision to the council of the confederacy, as far as the state had judged it necessary to concede it.

It was not necessary, save in the case of an *alien alleging the privilege of a neutral ;* and even in this case, not farther than the conclusion of law from *facts found.* But admitting it to be necessary, it was an argument why the revision, without *exception,* should have been given to the congress ; but it could go no length to prove, that it *had been given*. It has been said, that it was an incident to the *sovereignty ;* but this is begging the question, that there was a sovereignty to this extent. If it was an incident of sovereignty, why not establish admiralty courts by authority of the sovereignty? Why treat it as a matter of courtesy and recommend? It has been contended that to *recommend* was the same as to enact. Had the *recommendation* of congress, agreeably to the 5th article of the treaty with Great Britain the force of an act? There was not the least attention paid to it by any of the states, though this was after the ratification of the confederation in 1781; not until which had the congress any power whatever, but what they were *allowed* to *exercise*. The point is not tenable; and whatever may have been the *justice of the claim of Olmstead*, the committee of Congress formerly, or the courts under the present constitution, had no jurisdiction of the question.

I will admit, that where there is jurisdiction the courts will look at the justice of the case, on grounds of moral equity; and will be astute in saving it from the operation of a general rule. But on the contrary, in considering the question of jurisdiction, they will not be justifiable, in looking at the merits of the particular case; for they have no right judicially, to think upon the subject. Where the danger is of being trespassers to an awful extent, the endangering the peace of the union, it becomes them to stop short, rather than exceed. In applying their powers to a particular case, a strict construction is demandable. No wantonness of assumption in the face of a people, jealous of state rights. I will leave it to be considered by themselves for the present, whether there has been on all occasions, such delicacy in taking cognizance, as a mind perfectly awake to the importance of the consideration, would have thought it advisable to exercise.

The necessity of some tribunal to pass upon the question of jurisdiction of the United States courts, *where a state is concerned,* has been pressed upon the state of Pennsylvania, in the case of what is called *the actual settler under the act of Assembly* of the 3d April, 1792. The case of every actual settler under that act, is in fact a case where the state is concerned; and an ejectment, though nominally against the settler, is in fact against the state. Under the act of 3d April, 1792, a great tract of country was disposed of in consideration of money and settlement. The one half consideration, the *money part*, to be paid first, and the settlement to be made afterwards; or the settlement to be made first, and the one half consideration (money) to be paid with interest afterwards. In the case of him who has paid the one half consideration (money) and is to satisfy the remaining half by settlement, it is stipulated that it shall be in *a given time ;* as, otherwise he might never satisfy, at all, what remained due. This is stipulated to be *two years,* within which the satisfaction remaining due shall be begun to be made. And that, within that time, it shall be begun to be made, unless prevented by *the enemies of the state.* On the part of those who had paid the one half consideration (money) first, and were to satisfy the remaining one half of the consideration of the purchase, *the settlement,* within two years. It is said, they have been prevented by *the enemies of the state* from beginning *within two years* to make a settlement; and therefore are excused from satisfying the state as to the remainder of the consideration altogether. I say nothing of the absurdity of this construction of the *contract which the courts of the United States have sanctioned ;* because I deny, that, being a state claim, they had jurisdiction of the question.

For, in case of the remainder of the consideration, the *settlement,* not being satisfied, within the time, an entry is given to the state to have it made by such as shall make the settlement first, and pay money with interest afterwards. The state enters; which she cannot do, being an incorporeal body, but by *purchasers under her ;* or in other words, persons actually settling, and coming under the contract of satisfying as to the remainder of the consideration, (money) afterwards. The ejectment in that case is nominally against the actual settler, but in reality against the state. For if the actual settler is disturbed in his settlement, the state loses the half *original consideration of the sale.*

But how shall it appear to the United States courts, that the state is the party when she is not nominally on the record ? The answer is easy ; *by admitting evidence of the truth of the fact ;* and this to the courts themselves, who are to judge of the jurisdiction, on affidavit shewing the truth of the fact. The enquiring as to the real plaintiff or defendant in a case, is familiar in the courts, either with a view to the competency of testimony offered ; or as to the liability for costs ; and this is by facts disclosed to the court on affidavit, or otherwise. The operation also of a verdict, and judgment on the same point, and between the same parties really, though not nominally, can be reached only in the same way ; and it can be reached in this way, notwithstanding all shifts in the real party to put forward another name on the record by a collusive transference, or substitution, by any contrivance that the craft of the profession or the management of the suitors may devise. In such a case it is the duty of the court to endeavor to get at the fact; and to defeat the subtility of evasion.

In the amendment to the constitution, are the cases in view only those, where the state is *nominally* a party, and where the recovery must act directly upon it as a body politic? That is to say where money is recovered, the levy must be upon the money of the state, in the hand of the state treasurer: or upon public lands, and tenements such as a state house lot, or building. If that be so the amendment can in most cases be evaded. The suit for debt, if such be the nature of the demand, may be brought against the treasurer, as having that money in his hand to which the claimant has a right; or on an ejectment brought against a tenant of the public lot, a recovery may be had though it is the state that is actually put out of possession. If the courts cannot reach such a case; or if it cannot be pushed upon them so as to oust their jurisdiction under this amendment, my argument is gone, and the state prerogative thought to be saved, will be narrowed to a very small compass indeed. It can be applied only to cases, where the party cannot by any means give his claim such a shape, that he may pursue it *indirectly* without putting the state in his writ, or declaration.

The state of Pennsylvania never can be reconciled to what she conceives to be an unwarrantable assumption of jurisdiction of the United States court, under the act of 3d April, 1792, laying even aside the construction, monstrous and shocking, as it would seem to be, which they have put upon that act. She has been very near going as far in that case, as in the case of Olmstead, and by a legislative act providing against the effect of a judgment given in such a case, by directing the governor to *oppose force;* which if they were to do, I do not know how he could escape the duty but by resignation; and in that case he might be followed by an impeachment for a dereliction of his duty. It is under a sense of these difficulties, and appaling consequences, that I look forward to an amendment of the constitution, by providing a tribunal independent of the courts to decide in the case of a *contested jurisdiction.*

PENNSYLVANIENSIS.

Pierce v. Turner. 5 Cranch, 154.

ERROR to the Circuit Court of the District of Columbia, &c. case on a special verdict.

In this case Johnson, J. dissented from the opinion of the court; and on examination I am of opinion that he was right; and not only right in his judgment, but concise and correct in his reasons given. In page 170, he hits the point like a ball from a rifle, and knocks down the *fallacy* of the argument on the other side. Credit given on the *ostensible possession* of property; is the credit to be defeated by a deed that is concealed, and the person to be benefitted whose duty it was to have made it public. " The creditors, in order to maintain their action," (says the Judge) " prove first, the property in the wife before marriage; then her intermarriage with their debtor. These facts, in operation of law, upon her personal property, sustain their right of recovery. But, in opposition to their claim, the wife endeavours to avail herself of this deed; and the question is brought up on an exception taken by the creditors to its validity. The ground of their objection is, that it wants that evidence of authenticity which the law requires to make it, as to them, a valid instrument." I am decidedly of opinion with the dissentient member of the court; but I take the opportunity of saying that I do not like a dissenting judge saying, as in this case, I am *unfortunate enough to dissent*. For there can be no misfortune in the case. We know what is meant; it is as much as to say, I am sorry, that in this case, I have to run a little counter to the self-love of the court, and to wound their pride so far as my thinking them fallible, may affect. The sting is, that by this peace-offering to their *temper*, it should for a moment be thought possible, that it had been hurt, or pride wounded. It becomes a judge to have such self-denial, and to be of a mind so perfectly resigned to the love of truth and justice, as not to think of his situation, as to the cum quibus, he may be. This, may not be wholly in human nature; but I would have *appearances saved*, and those from whom one dissents, not supposed to have any feeling on account of it; nor one's own self to be in the least mortified, because he has not *the greater number on his side*. The maxim, cum Platone errare, quam cum aliis recte sentire, has been long exploded, as a self-degrading, and ignoble sentiment. To deliver the dissent, simply without apology, or compliment, is the best. Nothing need be said unless, that, in expressing the less, or more confidence with which the dissent is made, there may be the qualification of saying, *It would seem to me;* or, on the contrary, to say, *totis viribus contra.* " Go not with a multitude to do evil," is a maxim ; and it ought to be the same, go not with a multitude in thinking wrong.

These observations are not made for the sake of the judges of the supreme court ; for I have no idea that they will ever read them ; or perhaps come to hear of them ; but certainly will not be disposed to pay much regard to them. But it is for the sake of the *student* who may become a judge, that I give the hint. The fact is, I have been always dissatisfied with the apology, " it is my misfortune to dissent," &c. &c. &c. and, this, in so severe and stern a situation as the administration of justice. Will not the by-standing suitor feel a degree of indignation in hearing such declaration of " *misfortune to dissent ?*" For, it must be the language of his mind, " it is not your misfortune ; it is to your credit ; and it is your good fortune, to have the good sense to differ ; and so far from softening the matter out of deference to your brethren, you ought, or at least, it would have pleased me better, to have given your words the implication of some dissatisfaction at the error of the judgment of the majority. Not, as the expression would import, that you have had qualms in dissenting, which only arise from some apprehension, not so much of your own error, as of their displeasure. *The fear of man bringeth a snare.*"

Hepburn and Dundas v. Colin Auld. 5 Cranch, 262.

JUDGE Livingston, in page 273, expresses himself in a very manly manner. I concur with his observations.

LIVINGSTON, J. expressed his non-concurrence in the reasoning of the court, in the latter part of the opinion just delivered by the chief justice. He would dismiss the bill, even if a good title could now be given by the complainants. This court can no more dispense with punctuality *as to time* in any case, than with any other part of the agreement. But in this particular case, time was of the essence of the contract. The object was payment of a debt; and from the anxiety of the defendant to resist a decree for a conveyance, and the desire of the complainants to urge it upon him, it is to be presumed that the lands have fallen in value during this delay of the title. The remedy by a decree for a specific performance is a departure from common law, and ought to be granted only in cases where the party who seeks it has strictly entitled himself to it. It is said that by the English authorities, the lapse of time may be disregarded in equity, in decreeing a specific execution of a contract for land. But there is a vast difference between contracts for land in that country and in this. There the lands have a known, fixed, and stable value. Here the price is continually fluctuating and uncertain. A single day often makes a great difference ; and in almost every case time is a very material circumstance.

He dissented also from another part of the opinion, which intimates that if this were simply a deficiency of a few hundred acres, it would be considered as a case of *compensation*. This part of the opinion does not seem to be necessary, and does not affect the present case ; but this court can in no case compel a specific performance on terms and conditions. We cannot decree a special execution for part, and assess damages as to the residue.

This is like a contract for 5,000 bushels of wheat. A tender of 4,500 would not be good ; and we could not compel the purchaser to take a less quantity than he contracted for. So here the contract was for 6,000 acres. The complainants have a title to a part only ; we could not compel the defendant to take that part, and give him damages for the non-conveyance of the residue.

3 B

The United States v. Evans.   5 Cranch, 280.

IT will not be inferred that I approve of all the decisions of the supreme court, which I have not noticed.   Of some I do approve ; others I have not considered so fully as to have an opinion concerning them.   I have taken notice only of such as struck me, en passant, as exceptionable.   Amongst these I put down that of the *United States v. Evans.*   It was a writ of error to the district court for the Kentucky district.

In the court below, the judge at the trial rejected certain testimony which was offered by the attorney for the United States, who, thereupon took a bill of exceptions, and became *non suit ;* and, afterwards at the same term, moved the court to set aside the non suit, and grant a new trial, upon the ground that the judge had erred in rejecting the testimony ; but, the court overruled the motion, and refused a new trial ; whereupon the attorney for the United States sued out his writ of error.   By the court, " where there has been a *non suit,* and a motion to reinstate overruled, the court cannot interfere."

If the writ of error had been brought on the *motion* which had been overruled, I grant, the supreme court were right in not sustaining it.   But I should infer that the writ of error was brought on the *non suit,* and not upon the *motion* to set it aside.

But the *non suit* was *suffered ;* it was *voluntary.*   It was *voluntary* by *compulsion,* as the British make their fencibles. It was the rejection of the *testimony* by the court which occasioned it, and compelled, in its consequence, the suffering a *non suit.*   Non suit is a *judgment of the court,* where it is *ordered,* or directed ; and it amounts to the same thing where the suffering it, is a consequence of overruling testimony, without which the party cannot go on to the jury with a prospect of success in supporting his action.   That a court can direct a *non suit* where there is no *testimony,* volente, nolente, the party, is abundantly to be deduced from the English practice ; or if not from that practice, it is abundantly established from *principle* in cases in the " Constitutional court of errors and appeals, South Carolina, reported 2 Bay, 133, 187, 437, Edanus Burke, President; himself an host; *ipse agmen.* I cannot cite myself for an *authority,* but I can cite my *reasoning,* in a case, ut valeat quantum valere potest; and, on this head I refer to 5 Binney, 319.

Taking it that the party could refuse a *non suit,* that is to suffer it, when the court rejected testimony, what remained to be done, but to go through the form of taking a *verdict* which must, in that case, of necessity be against him, and then on a judgment for the defendant, to bring his writ of error, and assign the rejection of the *evidence* as the error which had been the cause of the finding by the jury? But, on principle, the non suit in consequence of a rejection of evidence, is the *court's act.* It is their *judgment,* and refusing to take off the non suit, leaves the matter just where it was; it can do no harm, if it has done no good, to have made the motion.

These matters are amongst the minutiæ of practice; and I do not at all wonder that the judges of the supreme court having their minds intent upon great objects, and principles of *general law,* a matter of *minute practice* should appear not to have been examined; but overlooked in a particular case; I should be surprized to find it otherwise. The proboscis of an elephant cannot take up a needle, though it can involve the trunk of a tree and bear it down. It is one of the most difficult things in the profession of the law, to acquire a knowledge of the *smaller rules,* and the reason of them—

Non equidem invideo, miror majus——

I am astonished that the judges of the superior court having so extensive a province of legal examination, can contract their minds at all to *a thing that lies in a nut-shell;* in other words, can make out so well as they do in subordinate questions. That they have erred in *local questions,* has been observed by professional men from other states, so far as I have had an opportunity of conversing with them. But nothing is inferred, detracting from the reputation of their *natural* powers, or acquired talents; but the impracticability of being competent to every thing that, under such extensive system, it becomes necessary for them to decide upon.

"Non omnia possumus, omnes."

Another consideration is, the judges of the supreme court have not time to read; commensurate with *the occasion for it.* They are half their time *carted* in stages, or running in *curricles,* from the one end of the continent to the other; and how can they have time to read?

It is the same thing with the judges of this state as to the riding, and the constant employment of their time; I mean as to the judges of the supreme court, and perhaps, in some degree, to all the others; to some of them I know it applies, *the judges of the mountainous districts;* and still I find I must explain myself, or strike out *stages* and *curricles,* so far as respects the judges of the *mountain districts.* For the roads are such that neither stages, nor curricles can run.

But as to judges of our supreme court, were it not that we are confined *to matters of a small compass,* our time being so much employed, we could not have leisure to read, what under other circumstances, might be necessary for our station. In all mouse-trap matters, as they may be called, we do pretty well, so far as I can infer from the not hearing much complaint from the profession, or the people.

O'Neal v. Thornton. 6 Cranch, 53.

THE judgment of the *circuit court* of the district of Columbia, was in this case *reversed* by the supreme court. In that case was introduced the construction of an act of Maryland, which authorized a *re-sale* of lots in the *city of Washington, as often as default should be made by any purchaser.* The court below had been of opinion, that the right to *re-sell* was co-extensive with the original power to *sell;* that every sale was a *new* sale, and within the statute; that the terms, " *new sale,*" " *first contract,*" " *original purchaser,*" " *second sale,*" and first purchaser, are all relative terms; that the expression in the second section of the act was extensive enough to comprehend all the *re-sales*. It was, "that on *sales of lots* in the said city by the said commissioners, under terms, or conditions of payment being made at a future day, &c. and, if the purchase money should not be paid, &c. the commissioners might sell the same lots at vendue," &c. That *sales of lots*, means on *any sales* of lots; that a *re-sale* was as much a sale as the *original* sales; that the act meant to give the commissioners the same right as to the sales of lots, which a vendor of personal property has in England; which is, that, "if the purchaser does not pay for the goods on the day stipulated, the vendor may sell them again at the risk of the first vendee."

The supreme court were of opinion "that a *single re-sale* only was contemplated by the legislature; and, that by such *re-sale*, the power given by that act is exercised." That is, that by a single execution of the power, the commissioners became functi officio; notwithstanding, a default of payment at the re-sale would produce the same necessity for a re-re-sale, that there had been for a re-sale.

A strict adherence to the *letter* of an *authority*, would, in human affairs, be vexatious, and would require such *specifications* and distinction in the mandate, as would embarrass all ordinary transactions; and, even in the highest, would lead to great inconvenience. To give an instance, in an ordinary transaction, I take one from the Jest book, Liber Facetiarum, where the master directed his servant to bring him a fish, which he did, but brought it as it was, without having undergone any process of cookery. Boil it, said the master, and bring it. This the servant did, but brought it in his hand. Whatever you bring me again, said the master to his new valet, who was a simple Scotchman, whatever you bring me again, said he, put a plate under it. In the evening calling for his slippers, the servant, sticking to the *strict letter* of what had been directed, brought them on a plate.

But, to give an illustration more directly applicable, the construction of the court, as to a single performance of an act, is, as if a master had ordered his servant to mount his horse, and ride him; and the servant had done so, but having been dismounted by some accident, he would not consider himself warranted in *re-mounting*, without a new instruction. The *toties quoties* he might say, was not within the letter of what he had been directed to do.

Blackstone in his commentaries, speaks of the *sullenness ;* or affected timidity of English judges, in the *narrowness* of their construction of powers given. I do not apply this to the honourable the supreme court; because I can easily see how they were misled in the construction put upon the act. It was by the equivoke of the word *purchaser*. He is a purchaser who *bids*, but he is *more* a purchaser who *pays*. All the *intermediate* biddings, between the "*first contract*," and the last, upon which the money is paid, pass for nothing, and ought to have been thrown out of view in the consideration of the case. All these biddings were a *fraud*, and the striking off ought not to have been spoken of as a sale at all; nor ought the *bidders* and note givers to have been called *purchasers*. They were speculators, swindlers, or what else name they might deserve; but they could not be called *purchasers*. What though a note was given? If forged, or the maker or person on whom drawn *insolvent ;* for it differs not as to the vendor; it amounted to no consideration paid; and if not a fraud in *fact*, was a fraud in *law*. In such a case, a *great national object*, the sale of lots with a view to raise funds for the public buildings of the city, in order to accommodate the national legislature, and the officers of government, a liberal construction of an act; an *amplitude* ought to have been given to it, as being an extraordinary case, and distinguishable from those to which general rules would apply. But even considering it a case, where only A and B were concerned on a private contract, I should think the construction and reasoning of the supreme court, as to this erroneous. But as to another point.

This was an action of assumpsit upon a promissory note, " given by O'Neale to Thornton, surviving commissioner of the city of Washington, for the money of lots No. 1 and

2. The defence was, that there was no consideration for the note, inasmuch as the superintendant for the city, &c. had abandoned, or rescinded the contract of sale, by having sold, and conveyed the same lots to *another person* in fee simple."

I will acknowledge that whether this sale to another person, was valid, or not valid, the surviving commissioner Thornton, to whom the *superintendant* had succeeded, was concluded from a recovery on the note, having parted with the *legal title* to another person, and it did not lie in his mouth to say that this re-sale was not valid. But the court unnecessarily introduce, in the opinion delivered, a principle of great importance, and, in which I conceive them to have *erred;* viz. that this sale to another person was not *valid*, because it was not a *re-sale*, but a *re-re-sale.* The *original*, and first sale had been to Morris and Greenleaf. It is admitted by the court that the re-sale was valid. Why not the re-re-sale? Because, say they, the *power* given under the act of Maryland was *functus officio*, upon the re-sale. This all turns upon the *equivoke* of the word *purchaser*, in the act. He cannot be considered as having purchased, or being really a purchaser within the meaning of the act, who does not comply with his undertaking, and pay the money. The term purchaser, may apply to the *original bidder*, because he paid some money, and, to a certain extent, complied with the contract. But the intermediate *bidders*, who had paid nothing, were not in the understanding of the act, or on any principle of law to be considered purchasers, but *baffiers;* or to use the Saxon term, *brockers*, at the sales. Had there been a thousand of these they would be laid out of the case; and even though they had given notes, and not paying at the day, the commissioners had a right to treat their pretence of purchasing as a *nullity*, and toties quoties, to set up again. What the commissioners, or the superintendant, in their places had a right to do, in *equity*, or what a *court of chancery*, would have decreed, they might do, the act of Maryland, exercising a chancery discretion, sanctioned, or prescribed the being done. It was a stepping out of the *ordinary course of legal remedy* by the legislature of Maryland; but it was doing no more than might be done by an ejectment at common law to compel payment, or what a court of chancery would do in order to reach the same object. The *exigency ; the great national object* justified the festinum remedium of an interposition. It would seem to me to be taking a narrow view of the *power* given by the act to confine it to any thing short of a sale that would raise the money. The mere *letter* of terms was not to be considered, but the substantial meaning and intendment of the act ; and I would not consider the power as functus officio, until a *real purchaser* was found, who would pay the money. I think it the more unfortunate that this construction did not take place, inasmuch as it was of great moment for the city of Washington, that the original object of the sales should be accomplished, the erecting public buildings, &c. and also for the purpose of settling *titles* for lots that these might be built upon, with safety by the real purchasers. The improvement of the city in all respects depended upon this.

I was led to consider this act the more, as a case was lately tried before me, at nisi prius, Philadelphia county, in which the case of a sale and re-sale, and re-re-sale of some of these lots came into view. It was an action on a bond given in consideration of a sale, or re-sale, or re-re-sale, for it made no difference with me, of some of these lots. The constitutional power of the state of Maryland to pass such an act was questioned, as being, in the first place, an act to *impair contracts*, and in the case before us, an ex post facto law. I was of opinion that an act to *hang* these speculators would have been in the nature of an ex post facto law ; for what they had done, was done before the act passed. But that as to impairing contracts, there was a wide difference between *annulling* a contract, and giving a remedy to enforce compliance with it. This a court of chancery will always do. There was nothing more, done in this case.

The Chesapeake Insurance Company v. Stark, 6 Cranch, 268.

THIS was error to the circuit court of the district of Maryland. The action was, covenant upon a policy of insurance of goods, &c. Defence, amongst other things, that *the abandonment was* not in due time.

Special verdict finding the facts. Marshall, chief justice, delivered the opinion of the court; and after observations on what did not so immediately, affect, goes on to say,

" The only point which presents any difficulty in the opinion of the court, is the objection founded on the omission, in the verdict, to find that the abandonment was made in reasonable time.

The law is settled that an abandonment, to be effectual, must be made in reasonable time; but what time is reasonable is a question compounded of fact and law, which has not yet been reduced to such certainty as to enable the court to pronounce upon it, without the aid of a jury. Certainly the delay may be so great as to enable every man to declare, without hesitation, that it is unreasonable, or the abandonment may be so immediate, that all will admit it to have been made in reasonable time : but there may be such a medium between these extremes, as to render it doubtful whether the delay has been reasonable or otherwise. If it was a mere question of law which the court might decide, then the law would determine, to a day or an hour, on the time left for deliberation, after receiving notice of the loss. But the law has not so determined, and it therefore remains a question compounded of fact and law, which must be found by a jury under the direction of the court.

In this case the jury have found an abandonment, but have not found whether it was made in due time or otherwise. The fact is, therefore, found *defectively ;* and for that reason a *venire facias de novo* must be awarded.

It may not be amiss to remark that the judicial opinions which we generally find in the books, on these subjects, are usually given by way of instruction to the jury, or, on a motion for a new trial, not on special verdicts. The distinction between the cases deserves consideration."

The facts being found by the *special verdict,* it *a question of law,* could not the court say what was the law arising from these facts? If a conclusion of reasonable time

from the facts must be drawn by the jury, in a special verdict, it is a conclusion of fact, and not of law. What
had the court to do with it, if a question of fact solely?
They have a right to assist the jury in weighing the evidence, and the power to set aside the verdict if against the
weight of it. But this does not make it a question compounded of law, and fact, if there could be such a *compound*.
Strictly speaking, we might as well talk of a compound of colour and sound; things judged of by different senses; and
which cannot be compounded.

But there is a conclusion of *fact* from *facts;* and a conclusion of *law* from that *fact*. As for instance, 1 and 1 make
2, which are two *facts*, making one. But 2 and 2 make 4,
which is a conclusion of *fact* from *facts*.

Again 1 and 1 make 2, which is a fact; but two are necessary to constitute a *conspiracy*, which is a conclusion of
law: three to make a *riot*, which is a conclusion of law also.
So, whether an entry with force and arms, is an indictable
offence, or a trespass merely, is a question of law. So that
strictly speaking it is not a compound question, but two questions of a different nature, and one of which must be resolved before the other. If the question is put to the jury,
they must resolve the question of fact first, in their own
minds, in the order of resolving, and then draw the conclusion of law, which, if they find a general verdict, they
must draw. If they give a special verdict, which in all cases
they may do, they draw the conclusion of fact only, and need
not go on to resolve the other question, viz. *what is the law
thence arising?* But it is but one question at a time, they
can resolve, and therefore the question is not *compound:*
save so far, as, that where the jury gives a general verdict,
they solve both questions at the same time and by one
answer. This has been the result of my investigation when
I have endeavoured to analize, and ascertain what could be
meant by a *compound question*.

But in the case before us, that *an abandonment must be
made*, to entitle to recover, is a question of law. That an
abandonment must be made in *reasonable time is a question of
law*. But the jury having found the *time*, is it a question of

law or fact, to draw the conclusion, and to say, whether or not that *time* was *reasonable ?* The court say it is a conclusion of law, why not then draw it? why reverse the judgment, and send it back to a jury, with costs, and the expence of a new trial? There appears to me *an inconsistency in the proceeding.*

If, as the chief justice lays it down in another case, 6 Cranch, 339, " that what is *reasonable time* for abandonment, is a question compounded of fact and law, *of which the jury must judge under the direction of a court,*" it is the only case that occurs to me where a reference to a distinct forum, cannot be had; the *jury finding the fact,* and *leaving the law to the court.*

Reasonable time, in the case of an abandonment, and in that of a *bill of exchange,* or in any other case, must be the same. In the case of a bill of exchange, the jury in a special verdict finding the *time,* will not the court in England, as a question of law, draw the conclusion? If the jury must do it as a conclusion of fact, what have the court to do? What direction could a judge on the trial give, but that if you find so, and so, then, in our opinion *reasonable time* had passed. When the jury have found so, and so, cannot the court say *reasonable time* had passed within which an abandonment ought to have been made. This, considering it a question of law, and not of fact, as the court have laid it down.

Notes relative to Judge Tucker's Commentary on the Constitution of the United States, &c.

I HAVE not entered into an examination how far the *constitution of the United States,* and the *acts of congress under it* have wrought a variation in the jurisprudence of the *state of Pennsylvania,* from the *law of England.* And this, not only because such operation has not an effect *peculiar to this state;* but also because *judge Tucker,* has noticed abundantly, what might be said on this head. The code of each state, so as it is affected by the constitution, or an act of congress, is lex

sub graviore lege, subject to a higher law; and must, so far
as it goes, be changed by it.   This observation is to be understood as going no farther than acts of congress within
the outward groove or orbit of the constitution.   I cannot
say that I have examined minutely the valuable commentaries of that civilian, so as to be able to point out mistakes,
if any had occurred to me; but a *learned jurist* has given
me a note of a few oversights, or miscontructions, as they appeared to him, which are to be met with in the comments of
judge Tucker, in his view of the constitution of the United
States.   If this publication, which is not very probable, should
at any time reach the notice of that judge, he will not be dis-
pleased with having it suggested to him, that he might reconsider. It is well known that judge Blackstone availed himself of
the observations of others, Junius, Priestly, Furneau, &c. to
change some things that had been given in the first edition of
his commentaries; and many alterations have been made
which would appear to have occurred to his own reflection. I
could point out one *particular of law*, which he had stated
so *equivocally* in the first edition, as to mislead; but which
in his later editions he has corrected.   It occurs 2 Com. 252.
Treating of the qualified property of the bailor and bailee,
" may all of them vindicate, says he, in their own right, this
their *possessory interest* against any stranger or third person, *according to their respective interests.*"   I have known
very learned counsel to contend from this authority, that
neither of them could recover otherwise than *according to
their respective interests.*   It would seem to have occurred
to the commentator that it was equivocal, and he has struck
out the expression, " *according to their respective interests.*"

Comparing small things with great, if it might be allowable to mention what I have written, there will be inaccu-
racies which may occur to myself, and much more to the
learned of the profession in the matters of this publication,
which I will have no pride to oppose, but the contrary, in
hearing of them being pointed out. The only consideration is, or rather *fear*, that not many learned in the law, and
capable, will do me the honour to examine and to note the

observations from reason, or from law, which may exist. With regard to the commentaries of judge Tucker, on the constitution of the United States, &c. the note of the learned jurist is as follows.

" The passages in Tucker's Blackstone which have struck me as inaccurate, are the following.

Tucker's Black. vol. 1. 181. The author states the cases in which he thinks that the judicial power of the United States is *exclusively* vested in the tribunals of the federal government, and enumerates them as follows :

1. All cases affecting ambassadors, other public ministers and consuls.

NOTE. This does not seem accurate, for an ambassador, &c. may sue in the state courts if he please, though he may not *be sued* there. Therefore the power is not entirely exclusive.

2. All cases of admiralty and maritime jurisdiction.

NOTE. If the author meant all cases which are *exclusively* of admiralty jurisdiction, such as prize and its incidents, he is right, but if he meant all cases of admiralty jurisdiction generally, including bottomry, mariner's wages, &c. he does not seem correct, for in all these cases there is a remedy at the common law, different in its form, indeed, and sometimes in its effects, from admiralty process, but still the common law takes cognizance of the subject matter, and the jurisdiction of the court of admiralty in such cases is even said to be only *permissive*, and ex rei necessitate et favore legis.

3. 4. 5. Seem correct.

6. Controversies to which the United States are a party.

NOTE. There appears nothing to prevent the United States from *suing*, though they may not be sued in a state court, nor indeed in any court, directly, and indirectly it is not clear that they may not be sued through their officers in a state court; I believe there have been instances (I think, in New-York) of a collector sued in a state court for torts committed under colour of his official duty. Of this, however, I am not sure, but upon the whole, Mr. Tucker's assertion seems too broad.

Again the decision of the chief justice on the habeas corpus in Blight's case, shews that state courts have taken cognizance of controversies to which the United States are real parties; for Blight's confinement was by the authority of a federal court, and the United States, or what is the same, the authority of its judiciary was clearly involved."

On the construction of Art. 4. Sec. 4. of the Constitution of the United States.

" The United States *shall* guarantee to every state in this union a republican form of government, and shall *protect each of them against invasion;* and, *on application of the legislature,* or, *of the executive,* (when the legislature cannot be convened) against domestic violence." This would seem to be an amplification of the power given to congress under head 15, of Sec. 8. Article 1. of the constitution, viz. " to provide for calling forth the militia to execute the laws of the union, suppress insurrections, and repel invasions." Under article 1. sec. 8. 15. The congress shall have *power to provide for calling forth,* &c. Under article 4. sec. 4. The United States *shall guarantee,* &c. The first gives the power to do; the last enjoins the doing in certain cases, which must, *in substance,* fall under the first head, at least so far as respects *the protecting against invasion;* and against domestic violence.

But, on a question put by governor Strong, of Massachusetts, to the justices of the supreme court of that state, these justices certified an opinion, inter alia, that, in calling forth the militia, " no power is given either to the president, or to the congress to determine that either of the said exigencies does in fact exist." Masachusetts Reports, 449. But it would seem to me unavoidably deducible, from sec. 4. article 4, that there is but *one case* where it is left to the legislature, or, to the executive, where it cannot be convened, to exercise the right of determining as to the exigency in which the militia may be called forth, and that is, " to protect against domestic violence." That is distinguishable clearly in section 4. article 4, from the *guarantee* of a republican form of government, and protecting against invasion. For, it is on application, &c. that *protection against domestic violence is to be given.* The other cases are left out of this clause, and precede it, and there is no application in such cases specified. The justices of Massachusetts would therefore appear to me to be erroneous in their opinion, that the president or congress have not the right to judge of the exigency of an *insurrection or invasion*.

Domestic violence is distinguishable from an *insurrection to resist a law of the United States*. It may be in opposition to a *law of the state;* or it may be a great riot without a specific object, but bidding fair to terminate in a dissolution of the government. With great propriety, it is left in this case to the legislature, or executive of the state in their absence, to say whether *such an exigence exists, as calls for the arm of the union*. But if the *violence* has for its object, a resistance to a law of the union, how shall the state officially know, that resistance is made. It must be communicated *through the medium of the general government*, to whose authority it is made; and does not this involve in it, *necessarily*, the judging of the exigency? can the state be supposed to have a negative upon this judging, and to say, *your law is not resisted;* you have raised a groundless clamour against these insurgents, and they *may go without day*. This is the law phraseology, when a complaint is dismissed; and the *defendants discharged from appearance.*

But who is to determine the exigency when a republican form of government is about to be put down in a particular state? It cannot be the legislature, or the executive, even if there had been the strongest *exclusion* as to this. For it must be a case where a republican legislature and executive had been overthrown, and the *one* or the *few* had usurped the government, that such an exigency could exist; and it would be an inconsistency to suppose that these would make an *application for the arm of the union to suppress themselves.*

It is in the case of *domestic violence* where the United States are not supposed to know of the outrage, or of the necessity of the interposition of the general government, that the application must be made, by the legislature, or the executive, of the particular state. The *necessity* of interposition must be judged of by the particular state; the

Dignus vindice nodus.

But in the case of "invasion;" who is invaded? Say state No. 1. who is to give notice of this to state No. 2?

Must it not come through the medium of the general government to No. 2 and to all the states? Does it not then follow that the general government, so far as respects No. 2. and all the rest, is to determine, whether or not, the exigency exists of *No.* 1 *being invaded?*

But admit the United States who are to *guarantee*, and *protect*, &c. have a right; and must of necessity, determine, in the first instance, whether an exigency exists; yet a particular state has a negative upon that determination, and may say, it does not exist. If so, *the outer wheel is then stopt by the cog-wheel, and the machine can no longer work.* It is assuming *false premises*, therefore, in the Massachusetts' justices to say, that the power is not delegated to congress, or to the president to determine when the laws of the union are resisted, insurrection on foot, or invasion made.

But who shall command the militia, in case of their being called forth? The president, or his lieutenant, doubtless. In this capacity Hamilton acted under Washington, in repressing the insurrection in the western parts of Pennsylvania, in the year 1794. I do not know that he acted under a commission eo nomine, but de facto, I saw him in the exercise of that command. General Lee was the ostensible lieutenant.

But may not the president appoint as his deputy; or, suffer to act, the officer who commands the *regular force on foot at the same time?* But can the officers of the regular force on foot, from him down, be substituted in the command of the militia for their officers? No: there is no necessity for it; nor, can it lawfully be done.

But who is to take the command when a regular force is on foot, and militia embodied at the same time; and the president is not present, nor has he any deputy, or lieutenant to command for him? I do not take that to be a case likely to happen, and I shall not enter into an examination of it. My mind has been chiefly intent upon the other questions.

But supposing the exigency of an invasion to exist, *according to the determination of the congress and president,* and the militia are *called forth to repel invasion;* or to *protect* against it; (for both these terms are used in the constitution, article 1, the term "*repelling invasion,*" is used. Article 4. "Protecting against invasion, is used.) *Can the militia be ordered beyond the boundary of the United States?* That will depend upon the question, if common sense and natural reason is to determine it, which of the two means will be the most effectual in repelling an invasion, or protecting against it; the stopping at the *limits, or carrying our arms into the country of the enemy.* Nations usually adopt this last mode, because it saves their own country from ravage, and it is more effectual to chace a fox or a wolf to his den, even though it is beyond a boundary, than to wait for a renewal of the depredations which they may have committed.

But————————————————

Here take notice, that I have heard it observed, upon close reasoning, that the word *but*, frequently occurs. I answer, that the course of reasoning, on any subject, is *syllogistic;* and, if it is worth any thing, cannot but in the nature of it, contain a syllogism; and though there is no major or minor formally stated, yet all course of reasoning on a *moral* subject, must partake of the nature of a demonstration in mathematics; and postulate, and axiom must be assumed; look at Euclid, and you will see a *but* at every new step that he takes in building up his structure. In Aristotle the same; first principles are assumed, and what is deduced from these, forces your acknowledgment, as you proceed, until the conclusion is wound up. I was proceeding then to say, *But,* ————Must not an enemy have invaded, before you can be justified in passing a boundary? To put the case in the strongest possible manner, let it be, that not *a single trespass has been yet committed* in any quarter of the *territory.* For if hostilities have been committed on any one quarter, it is a trespass upon the whole. I say, let it be, that, no act of hostility; no trespass, has been committed, by land, or by water; in that case, can it be allowable, under the constitution, to carry the militia beyond the boundary, even though it may appear, and actually be, the most effectual way to *protect* against invasion? In strictness of terms, it may, perhaps, be said not to come under the head of *repelling* an

3 D

invasion ; but, certainly it may come under the head of *pro-tecting* against it. The *practice*, which constitutes the *law* of nations will illustrate this. When an enemy is about to make war, or invade, when, or where is it hesitated, to anticipate hostilities, and to invade? Among pugilists, the *first blow is said to be half the battle*. It is by *boarding first, that we save ourselves from capture*, to use a nautical allusion, and *defend* the ship, when oftentimes by no other means could it be defended. The Romans passed over into Africa, to *defend* Italy, and to save Rome.

NOTES ON

BLACKSTONE'S COMMENTARIES, &c.

SECOND SERIES.

———

The customs of London are confirmed by an act of Parliament." I Bl. Com. 75.

THE *general law* of England, has nothing in it, of the nature of our attachment law, consisting of acts of assembly, and the adjudications of our courts. And in regard of *practice*, varies essentially from that under the custom of London. I refer the student to a treatise, by Thomas Seargeant, on the attachment law of our state, as an elementary tract, which would do credit to any lawyer, more especially to one so young in the profession, and in years. It is invaluable to the practising lawyer in our state; and, I should think, must be to those of other states who have attachment laws, as I presume all have. I will take the liberty of extracting from this publication, the preface to his work, as giving some view of the object of this very elegant and classical performance.

" The principles of the law relative to foreign attachment are important in Pennsylvania, not only from its frequent recurrence in practice, but from the circumstance of its being an *ex parte* proceeding, and therefore requiring to be conducted with regularity and precision. As it is also a proceeding against absent debtors, it is peculiarly interesting to the inhabitants of other states, who are frequently parties concerned. A means, therefore, of procuring information on this subject, although a branch of the local law of the state, seems calculated to be generally useful.

" Under these circumstances, a collection of the laws relative to foreign attachment appeared to be desirable. As our original acts of assembly, relative to attachment, were borrowed from the custom of London, and do not, in themselves, form an entire system, it has been usual to resort thither, to supply and illustrate them : and a system now exists in Pennsylvania formed partly from the custom of London, and yet differing from it in many important particulars. What was to be found in print lay dispersed ; and it was thought to be useful, if nothing more could be done, at least to bring together the different points decided, as a means of aiding a more entire view of the law upon this head, than can at present easily be obtained.

" This has been attempted in the present treatise. The writer has assiduously sought all the information on the subject that was to be found in print, and has obtained, through the kindness of his friends, some few, but important manuscript cases. In addition to these he has, for the reason before stated, introduced most of the law under the custom of London ; a considerable portion of which appeared to be applicable here ; and even that part which could not be so considered, tending to illustrate the grounds and reasons of the proceeding.

" He has felt the difficulty attending the formation of an elementary work, arising from the paucity of our own decisions on the subject : the only legitimate sources, from which the interpretation of the laws can be derived : particularly in what regards the practice, which varies essentially from that under the custom of London, and can be traced only in the decisions of our own courts."

" Penal statutes must be construed strictly." I Bl. Com. 87.

EXTRACT from Dodson's life of Sir Michael Foster, published, London, 1811.

" Sir John Eardly Wilmot, late lord chief justice of the court of common pleas, was the particular friend of Mr. Justice Foster : and Mr. Wilmot, in his memoirs of his very justly honoured father, has inserted some short correspondence on legal subjects between these friends, and spoken of Mr. Justice Foster in language significantly descriptive of his true character. Sir Michael Foster says he was conspicuous, not only for his knowledge of criminal law, but for every quality of an upright, enlightened, and sagacious magistrate.

" Although Sir Michael Foster generally concurred in opinion, with the other judges; yet, on several important questions, he differed from some, if not from all of the judges. A remarkable instance of this sort occurred in the case of John Midwinter and Richard Sims, who was tried before him at the lent assizes for the county of Gloucester, in 1749, for *unlawfully, maliciously, and feloniously killing a mare.* Midwinter was found guilty, and received sentence of death. But the judge having doubts as to the case of Sims, the jury, by his direction, found a special verdict with regard to him. The question in that case was, whether Sims, who was present, aiding and abetting Midwinter in killing a mare of the prosecutor, was ousted of the benefit of clergy by the statute 9 G. I. chap. 22, by which it is enacted, " that if any person, or persons, shall unlawfully and maliciously kill, maim, or wound *any cattle,* every person so offending, being thereof lawfully convicted, shall be adjudged guilty of felony, and shall suffer death, as in cases of felony, without benefit of clergy." Mr. Justice Foster thought that Sims was a felon, and a principal felon; but that, as aiders and abettors are not named, nor described in the statute; and the law requires statutes so penal to be construed *literally* and *strictly,* he was not excluded from the benefit of clergy. The other judges thought him to be *excluded;* and *some later judges* have agreed with them. But the argument of Mr. Justice Foster, whom Sir William Blackstone very justly styles a very great master of the crown law, and, who, as lord chief justice De Grey, upon an important occasion said, may be truly called the magna charta of liberty of persons as well as fortunes, amounts, in my opinion, to a demonstration, that all those learned judges have mistaken the law. Sims might deserve as severe a punishment as Midwinter, but no punishment which is not authorized by law, ought to be inflicted on any man; and the point is, whether the law in this case hath provided the same punishment for both. Mr. Justice Blackstone, it is material here to observe, adopts the distinctions which Mr. Justice Foster endeavours to establish, and he lays down these rules: That, " when the benefit of clergy is taken away from the offence (as in the case of murder, burglary, &c.) a principal in the second degree aiding and abetting the crime, is as well excluded from his clergy as he that is principal in the first degree. But that where it is only taken from the *person committing the offence,* as, in the case of stabbing, &c. his aiders or abettors are not excluded; *through the tenderness of the law,*

which hath determined that such statutes shall be taken literally.
1 Hale, P. C. 529. Foster, 356.

" In the appendix to the third edition of the crown law, I
inserted this case, which the author had most reluctantly omitted
in the first edition, at the pressing solicitation of lord Mansfield,
who, in February, 1772, wrote to him the following letter.

" I return your papers which I have read with great pleasure
and approbation ; but I very much wish *that you would not enter
your protest* with posterity against *the unanimous opinion of the
other judges* in the case of Sims. If the determination was contrary to *former authorities there is no harm in it.* Sims was, in
every view, equally guilty, and in the very same degree. In real
truth, and not by fiction of law, they both did the act. Midwinter
might not have been able to maim had not Sims holden, &c. The
authorities which you cite prove strongly to the contrary ; but
they seem to be founded in subtil nicety, and very learned interpretation ; and upon the large principles which you lay down, the
doing justice to the public, and adapting the punishment to the
degree of guilt, it is impossible to say that Sims was not equally
criminal ; and if his punishment was less, it could only arise from
a slip in penning the act. The construction is agreeable to justice ; and therefore suppose it wrong upon artificial reasonings of
law, I think it better to leave the matter where it is. It is not .

         " Dignus vindice nodus."

" If this case had been published agreeable to the author's determination, in 1762, it is probable that the lives of *three unfortunate*
men would have been spared. Seven men were indicted on the
statute of George 1. c. 22. being the same statute on which Midwinter and Sims, were indicted, for shooting at John Green, in
his dwelling-house ; and were tried at the Old Bailey, in 1768.
Three of them were proved to have been present when the
others fired, but they had not been seen to use any fire-arms themselves. The jury found them all guilty ; and the judges, on a reference to them, determined that the offence of all was capital, and
they were all executed. The words of the statute are, " if any
person, or persons shall wilfully and maliciously shoot at any
person in any dwelling-house, or other place, every person so offending, and being thereof lawfully convicted, shall be adjudged
guilty of felony, and shall suffer death as in cases of felony without benefit of clergy." This case is exactly similar to the case of
Midwinter and Sims, and if Mr. Justice Foster's opinion in that
case be well founded ; namely that the benefit of clergy is taken

away only from persons actually committing the offence, it follows necesarily that those men suffered a more severe punishment than the law authoriseth. Sims, as I have already said, might deserve as severe a punishment as Midwinter; but if by law the benefit of clergy be taken from the latter, and not from the former, the same punishment ought not to be inflicted on both. In such cases nothing ought to be left to the discretion of judges ; it is their province jus dicere, not jus dare. " The discretion of a judge is, as a great man hath said, *the law of tyrants*; it is always *unknown ; it is different in different men ; it is casual, and depends upon constitution, temper and passion*. In the best, it is *oftentimes caprice ; in the worst it is every vice, folly and passion to which human nature is liable*." See lord Camden's argument in the case of Doe v. Kersey. 5 Geo. III. 1765. in C. B.

" Bell's case was thus ; he was tried at the Old Baily, in 1753, on an indictment for high treason, grounded on the statute 8 and 9. William III. c. 26, for having in his custody a *press* for coinage without any lawful authority, or sufficient excuse, and was convicted. On a reference to the judges two questions were made.

" 1. Whether a press for coinage is one of the tools or instruments within that clause of the act on which this indictment is founded ?

" 2. Supposing it to be within the clause, whether the facts stated in the case amount to a sufficient excuse, so as to take the defendant out of the penalties of the act.

" Upon the first question, chief justice Ryder, was single, and thought that a press for coinage is not one of the tools or instruments within the clause of the act on which the indictment is founded. This opinion rests on a very slight foundation in point of law ; but it was probably occasioned by an excess of caution and tenderness, he having been attorney general at the time of the trial.

" Upon the second question, the majority of the judges thought that as the press was intended for coining Louis d'ors, and other foreign pieces not the current coin of this kingdom, his case was not within the act. But the other two judges were clearly of opinion, that as the press was intended to be used in coining, and was fitted as well for counterfeiting the coin of the kingdom, as any other coin, the prisoner's case was within the act. It would not be a defence, they thought, within the sense and meaning of the act, for him to say, I intended the press for a very wicked purpose, but not for the purpose it was adapted to ; I intended to commit a misprision of treason ; but not high treason ; the words *suffice* for an *excuse*, meaning in this act, as they do, in all language, an honest, a fair, a reasonable excuse, which an honest man may make without blushing.

" To a memorandum of this case, justice Foster has the following note.*

" This case was omitted by *the advice of Lord Hardwicke ;* I am satisfied that the chief justice, (Ryder,) upon the first question, and the other judges on the second, were totally mistaken. A great man, formerly of the profession, by whose advice it is omitted, told me that he hath no doubt upon either of the questions. I believe that his advice proceeded *from a regard to the judges ;* or from his fear of establishing a bad precedent by the authority of great names, though he did not explain himself fully upon that head.

" A sentence in a letter of lord Hardwicke, February 24, 1761, is the following, " Permit me to beg that you would reconsider whether it may be advisable to send into the world the case of John Bell. I forbear to express my reasons for calling your attention *once more* to this case."

" His lordship having conceived some doubts on the case of Earl Ferrers was very desirous to prevent the publication of it ; and with that view he endeavoured by a degree of *intimidation,* to prevail on the author to suppress that case ; and also the case of John Drummond, and captain John Gordon. But the author was so perfectly satisfied in the case of Earl Ferrers, that he could not comply with the importunate request of a man whom he loved and honoured. I am not, and I believe that Mr. Justice Foster was not apprized of lord Hardwicke's objections ; but I well remember to have been told by Mr. Justice Foster, that, in the opinion of his son, Mr. Solicitor General York, they were not well founded.

" From these instances of integrity and firmness, it may be seen that the compliment paid Mr. Justice Foster by the celebrated Churchhill, in his Rosciad, was not undeserved,

" Each judge was true and steady to his trust ;
As Mansfield *wise,* and as old Foster *just.*"

* *In his report of cases on the crown law.*

" The sheriff is an officer of very great antiquity in this kingdom.

————The deputy of the earl, or comes——

————The king by his letters patent committing custodium comitatus to the sheriff, and him alone.

————All the judges, together with the other great officers, and privy counsellors meet——

————The judges propose three persons to be reported (if approved of) to the king, who afterwards appoints one of them to be sheriff.

————Sheriffs were formerly chosen by the inhabitants of the several counties." I Bl. Com. 339, 340, 341.

THE sheriff in this state, from an early period, was elected by the people of the county, and commissioned by the governor; afterwards, to give the governor some selection, two persons were elected, and returned; one of whom was commissioned. Experience having shown abuses in the office, several successive acts of assembly passed regulating the election, and commissioning of sheriffs.

I have not the old acts of assembly by me to enable me to trace minutely these provisions; nor is it of moment to be particular on this head; as, whether the election, was at first annual, or triennial; or whether on the expiration of his term, the same person was re-eligible. This, however, I recollect from memory, that, at an early period, it was provided that two persons being elected, and returned to the governor, and one commissioned, the other should not act as *deputy* to him that was commissioned. This, doubtless, to prevent collusion, and, to use a mercantile phrase, joining stocks in the election.

It was afterwards provided, that no sheriff shall be re-eligible, but *at an interval of three years* from the time he had been sheriff; and farther, by an act before the revolution, that no one who had acted in the capacity of deputy to the sheriff *within one year* from the expiration of his office, should be eligible to the office of sheriff. This was a most salutary law, as precluding favour to a former sheriff to some extent; salutary————There are always rules to be taken upon sheriffs to return writs, pay money, &c. and attachments may be necessary to enforce these rules; and attachment to the person may be in the way of serving the attachments ordered by the court.

I do not find this act; I mean to say, that I cannot immediately turn to it, not having what are called the *province laws* in my office. It would not seem to have been brought forward in Dallas, Smith, or Purdon. Is it possible that it could have been repealed, or considered so? Governor M'Kean acted upon it in 1800, in the case of a *deputy* elected in Allegheny county. He rejected him who was *highest* upon the return precisely upon this ground.

An abuse of the office in another way, had taken place about this time; as will be seen by the following document taken from the docquet of the supreme court, and the papers filed in that office, or in the hands of the counsel; and my own note taken at the time.

Supreme Court, March Term, 1801.

Shoemaker v. Wilson——Judgment of March, 1797, *fi. fa.* to Septem. Testatum *fi. fa.* to Allegheny of Decemb. Levied on 280 tracts of land 400 acres each and 74 warrants 400 acres each. Sale of warrants as personal property for 720 dolls. On the 280 tracts inquisition held and land condemned. Venditioni exponas to March 1798. Land sold for the sum of 4000 dollars 81.200, less than 5 cents an acre,

3 March 1798, On motion of Joseph Thomas, and by consent of Thomas Collins, rule to shew cause why the sale of the 74 warrants under the *fi. fa.* and the sales under the venditioni exponas should not be set aside. 12 *May* 1798. *Deeds acknowledged in Allegheny and recorded the same day.*

Attorney Thomas absconding, nothing heard until March 1800. Duncan in support of the rule. Levy, inquisition, and the words James Sample, Sheriff, not in the hand writing of James Sample, but of Thomas Collins. *Warrants and Tracts put up and sold in bulk several at a time.*

No copy of the rule to set aside the sales, served upon the purchasers prior to making out the deeds. Proof that at the time of consenting to the rule, Thomas Collins expressly stipulated that a copy should be served upon the purchaser.

Alleged that *Thomas Collins was himself the purchaser*, and had notice of the rule. Postponed to give time to establish this.

March Term, 1801. J. Ingersol, Tilghman, Duncan in support of the rule. Dallas, and Reed in support of the sales.

Deposition of James Sample that his signature to the return of sales was in the hand writing of Thomas Collins, but that he supposed he had given him authority.

2. Deposition of J. Sample at a subsequent date and in the hand writing of Thomas Collins, that he (Sample) had given him authority to sign his name.

Allegation that Collins was the principal purchaser. And yet having notice of the rule had surreptitiously gone forward, and with a *haste which marks that knowledge*, procured the deeds to be acknowledged, and to be recorded the same day.

Dallas. It cannot be. That would be a ground not for setting aside the sales only, but the *Attorney himself*.

Depositions read establishing the fact that Collins was *interest- ed in the sales originally, and at the time of taking the rule. Sales set aside on the ground of irregularity, the setting up and selling more than one warrant and tract at a time.*

Here, it may be seen, was attorney at law, deputy she- riff, and purchaser in the same person. I believe I might say, that at the time of the transaction, 1797-8, there was *deputy prothonotary*, also.

Hence it will be seen, that if this act of Assembly, of which I speak, should, from some oversight, be found to be repealed, or considered so by some implication, it will be expedient to re-enact it, adding perhaps a section making it *penal* for an attorney at law to act as deputy sheriff, or deputy prothonotary, or be a *concealed* purchaser at a sheriff's sale.

It is true, it may be a long time, before such a combina- tion of characters, and combination of functions in one character, may again exist as did at this time in that western country.

—————

" For it is a principle of *universal law*, that the natural born subject to one prince, cannot, by any act of his own, no, not by swearing allegiance to another, put off or discharge his natural allegiance to the former: for this natural allegiance was intrinsic, and primitive, and antecedent to the other; and cannot be diveste ed without the concurrent act of that prince, to whom it was first due.   Indeed, the natural born subject to one prince to whom he owes allegiance, may be entangled by subjecting himself absolutely to another: but it is his own act that brings him into these straits and difficulties, of owing service to two masters; and it is unreasonable that, by such voluntary act of his own, he should be able at pleasure to unloose those bands, by which he is connected to his natural prince." 1 Bl. Com. 369.

I had passed over this dictum or position of Blackstone, seeing the very excellent note of judge Tucker in loco. Nor does it occur to me to add any thing, now, more than the sanction of my opinion, if that should carry with it any weight. I must therefore say that I concur in totis with what this American jurist has said upon the subject.   I did not wonder at that great man, the British commentator, laying it down to be the law of England, that the *natural born subject*, cannot put off his allegiance; but that he should lay it down to be a principle of *universal law*, is the ground of my astonishment.   But more astonishing still, is it, that, even some in this country, the United States, seem to have been led away with something like the same sentiment.   I can account for it only, in the case of intelligent men, on the ground of *political bias;* and this from not having a hand in the administration, or that party in the republic to whom they are attached, not having a hand in it.   For I admit that when Jefferson in his inaugural address, said " we are all federalists, all republicans," he spoke the truth, with the exception of *a few attached to foreign governments*.   But had he said, we are all *out;* all *in;* would this have been correct? I excuse the minority, on the ground of human passions.   But the time, in the nature of our government, cannot be remote when those that are *out*, will be *in;* and why suffer for a moment, the messuage to be dilapidated, and a single stone of the building lost.   I consider it, the losing a corner stone; the surrendering an essential right, if we admit for a moment the *degradation of our honour*, the lessening our privilege as an independent people, that we cannot *receive all that come to us without questions asked, save*

\so *far as we chuse to put them.* The law of that island (Britain) is " lex sub graviore lege,"

——Divisos orbe Brittannos ;

It is subject to the *divine* law, the law of *nature*, and the *law of nations. Universal* law, is directly the contrary of this lex loci, or feudal law of Britain. For what is that lex loci but an institution of barbarism, introduced by the Norman conquest? to whom is this allegiance due, of which they speak, but, to the *person of the sovereign ?* See *Calvin's Case.* How is it that the *exuere patriam,* has got into the place of the *exuere ligeantiam ?* William III. did not dare to confound them; and when he took the duke of Berwick* prisoner in the Low countries, did not venture to

---

* In the sketch of an historical panegyric of the marshal of Berwick, by president Montesquieu, prefixed to the memoirs of the marshal, the question is noticed, whether he had a right to become a Frenchman. This question says the president, Grotius, Puffendorf and all those writers who have influenced the opinions of Europe, have decided; and declared to him, that he was a Frenchman, and subject to the laws of France. In these Memoirs, the marshal mentions the case of a *general officer,* a Portuguese, while the war was carried on by him (the marshal) at the head of Spanish forces, on the frontier of Portugal, who wrote a note *by a countryman,* " to acquaint me, that although he was not known to me, yet he had so much respect for his catholic majesty, that he would give *me the intelligence of all that passed ;* and indeed he was very exact *in apprising me before hand of all the different movements,* the enemy intended to make, which was of great service to me. He sent word that he was very desirous of seeing me; *that* he could easily contrive it, when it was *his turn of duty,* under pretence of visiting the out posts ; and if I would send an officer to him at a certain spot, he would come there by night and visit me in my own quarters. Accordingly every thing was executed as he had proposed, and I held a conference of two hours with him, with which I was very well satisfied, from the accurate and particular account he gave me of the state of the enemy and their designs. This visionary man had taken it into his head, that he was serving the king his master by this *fine contrivance ;* for, said he, it is *against his interest to be at war with Spain ;* so that it is necessary that his eyes should be opened by

proceed against him on the footing of a traitor. The duke
of Berwick was England born, and a natural son of James
II. "The prince of Orange," says he, memoirs vol. 1. 117,
" certainly had a design of sending me prisoner to England,
where I should have been closely confined in the tower of
London, though that would have been contrary to all the
rules of war, *though he pretended that I was his subject, and
consequently a rebel.*"

But the lex loci of Britain considers a subject as the
king's or the *nation's* property ; and shall we be justifiable
in harbouring a slave ? I quote a case ad hominem ; that of
Somerset v. Stuart ; Loft's reports, 1. Somerset, a native
of Virginia, and a salve by the lex loci, but having been
brought upon English ground, a habeas corpus from lord
Mansfield issues, and he is pronounced *free.* Could he have
been retaken by the owner, out of a British vessel on the
high seas ? The floating domicile would have protected
him, as much as the clausum, or close on land. The *power*
of the government would protect him where the *municipal
law* could not reach.

Azuni has been quoted, as sanctioning the right of
search ; and that *the right of search, implies a right to take
the body of a man,* when found upon the high seas. But this
he does not say ; nor can it be inferred from the role d' e-
quipage, or *muster roll of the crew* being called for ; for
which he cites Hubner ; for this is only for the purpose of
ascertaining the character of the vessel, whether *neutral,* or
belligerent. The ship, or cargo may be made prize of war ;
but, are the *crew* ever taken to be the subjects of an admiralty condemnation, or of sale ? 2 Azuni, 213. N. York
edition, 1806, translated from the French. There is no carrying in, for adjudication ; or admiralty process to try, whe-

---

misfortunes." It may be on the same principle that citizens not
thinking the present war *just,* or expedient, may be more pleased
with our disasters than our *victories.* It is of moment therefore,
that the right of expatriation, which is at the bottom of our controversy, so far at least as respects the justice of the war, be explained ;
and it is with this view, that I have said any thing on the subject.

ther a person alleged to be a British subject, may not have been an American born.

It can be accounted for, only on the ground of prejudice, that such a violation of a right which Britain herself asserts against the world, the protecting her domicil, whether upon the water, or on terra firma, should not be considered a *just cause of war.* I say nothing of the *expediency* of putting ourselves in a situation, by our naturalization laws, to be under the necessity of suffering *national dishonour,* or protecting all whom we have naturalized. On this head I have already thrown out some ideas. For the *right* of an individual to expatriate, and any nation to naturalize, I may subjoin some authorities, and some reasonings in a proper place. I observe only here, that Britain would not surrender even a murderer from another power, that had taken refuge in her island. And can it be doubted, but that she would protect him on board a merchant ship, by her maritime law and power, as much as if at land by her municipal? In the one case a writ of habeas corpus would issue from the civil authority; and in the other, a demand would be made of the government trespassing; and the injury not being redressed, she would denounce war. She would consider the taking a single individual as a cause of war; not for the sake of the person, nor for the sake of the trespass, in the particular instance, but for the sake of the *principle which it involved,*

NOTE to me of a learned *jurist,* to whom I put the question as to his idea of the universality of the acknowledgment of *perpetual allegiance.*

It is said that this doctrine extends all over Europe, but nothing is less true. In the first place the word *allegiance,* though of French derivation, has obtained in England, and there alone, the sense in which we use it. In the French language the word itself is unknown, at least I never have read it in any book or found it in any dictionary. In its origin, it seems, it implied no more than the feudal relation between the lords and vassals of certain fiefs called *fiefs liges,* in which the vassal swore fealty to his lord, by putting his hands into his, in token of bodily subjection, and saying the words, *jeo deviens vostre home,* I am or become your *man,* alias your slave.—But all tenures were not of that description, and those who held no feudal lands, were not bound to swear hommage lige, were not liege men, and did not owe of course allegiance. In process of time flattery, in England, applied the word allegiance to the relation between king and subject.—It was at first a compliment, a word of course, but time-serving judges soon gave a legal sanction to its application, and the duty of allegiance as now understood in England became law. But the same was not done in any other country.

In France the legal effects of the relations between king and subject were left to the rules of the law of nations, and of the civil law, until the troublesome times of the revocation of the edict of Nantes, when the emigration of the protestants becoming considerable, tyrannical laws were made to check it. But those laws were always considered by the sensible men in France, as in England the treason laws of Henry 8.—And though a despotic government might sometimes use them as a rod, yet they were well understood to be the offspring of bad times.

Still those laws did not go so far as to establish the English doctrine of perpetual allegiance, they prohibited emigration without leave of the prince under certain penalties, one of which was that the emigrant should be considered as an *alien*, a proof that he was not thought to remain perpetually a subject. See Royal Edicts, August 1669, July 1682, August 1682, and July 1705, all made *flagrante prosecutione protestantium*.

Now see how these laws worked in practice. In the year 1747, Gen. Ligonier, born a French subject, but then in the British service, was taken prisoner at the battle of Lawfeldt, and brought to Lewis XV. The monarch invited him to dine at his table. Less than two years before, several Scotch and Irish officers in the French service, taken prisoners by the English, had been hanged, embowelled, quartered, and suffered the horrid punishment of traitors.

I copy the relation of Voltaire on this subject in his own words :

" Cet officier general des troupes angloises (Ligonier) etoit ne " son sujet ; il le fit manger a sa table ; et des Ecossois officiers " au service de France, avoient peri par le dernier supplice en " angleterre, dans l' infortune du prince Charles Edouard."

Volt. Siecle de Louis XV. p. 226. Edit. Kehl.

The late Edicts of Bonaparte, I take to be a violation of the fundamental laws of France, an act of wanton tyranny, that will expire with his power.

I know of no similar law in any other country in Europe.

The civilians are agreed that a subject may freely emigrate, except in certain cases, which are well understood.—See Heineccius, Grotius, Vattel, and all the host of publicists. Even Dr. Zouch, an Englishman, agrees with Grotius, that "extra hos ca- "sus (public danger and the like) credibile est ad liberam civium "discessionem populos consentire."—See Zouch, de jure inter gentes, part. 2 Chap. 12. See also SirLeoline Jenkins, who admits that natives of France, settled in a neutral country previous to a war, are to be considered by the British as neutrals. I copy his own words from his letter to the lords commissioners for prizes of the 17th Sept. 1666—in 1 Magens on Ins. 527.

"Among the Laders, my Lord, I found two names which I "guessed to be French, and the secretary who solicits this business "could not but acknowledge the persons (Du Prie and Heron) to "be Frenchmen born. But the salvo that he and the shipper gave "me upon oath, is that Du Prie had lived in Hamburg with his wife "and family for above these 20 years, and that the other had lived "there likewise these 8 years—*which, regularly, is sufficient in law* "*to excuse him, as I humbly conceive, from being subjected to the* "*same reprisals with the rest of his countrymen.*"

The case of Clark *sentenced* as a Spy, remarked upon.

Elijah Clark was convicted as a spy at a general court martial holden at the court-house in the village of Buffalo, on Wednesday 5th Aug. 1812, and continued by adjournment, from day to day, until Saturday 8th Aug. 1812.

The facts in evidence were, that he had, about 18 months before, removed with his wife to Canada; and that having crossed the lines " did linger about the encampments and army of the United States, for the purpose of spying out our state and condition; and of reporting the same to our enemies; and for these reasons the court are of opinion that the said Elijah Clark is guilty of the crime whereof he stands charged; and falls under the 101 article of the act entitled " an act for establishing rules and articles for the government of the armies of the United States," passed the 10th day of April, 1806.

And they do adjudge and sentence the said Elijah Clark, to be continued in the present place of his confinement until the 1st Friday of September next, and that he be at the hour of two o'clock in the afternoon of that day, taken from his said place of confinement, and hung by the neck until he be dead.

PHILETUS SWIFT, President.

GEO. HOSMER, Judge advocate.

Head-Quarters, Manchester, Niagara frontiers,
August 13, 1812.

GENERAL ORDERS.

Major general Hall, having doubt how far the prisoner (Elijah Clark) within named, comes within the description of a spy, by reason that he is within the *letter* of the second section of the 101 article of the act, entitled "an act for establishing rules and articles for the government of the armies of the United States," which excepts thereout, "all persons not citizens of, or owing allegiance to the United States of America," is pleased to order, and doth hereby order a suspension of the execution of the within sentence, until the pleasure of the president of the United States can be known thereon.

By order of the Major General,

GEO. HOSMER, A. D. C.

OPINION OF THE PRESIDENT.
War Department, Oct. 20, 1812.

SIR,

The proceedings and sentence of the general court martial, which was had in the case of Elijah Clark, conformable to your orders of the first of August last, and which were by you transmitted to this department, have been received and laid before the president. I have the honour to inform you that the said Clark being considered a citizen of the United States, and not liable to be tried by a court martial as a spy, the president is pleased to direct, that unless he should be arraigned by the civil court for treason, or a minor crime, under the laws of the state of New York, he must be discharged.

Very respectfully,
I have the honour to be,
Sir, your obedient servant.
W. EUSTIS.

Major General A. Hall, Niagara.

GENERAL ORDERS.

Consequent on the opinion of the president.

The pleasure of his excellency the president of the United States of America, in relation to the case of Elijah Clark, who was tried and convicted of being a spy, under and by virtue of general orders of August 1st ultimo, and whose execution was suspended by general orders of August 13th ultimo, having this day been made known to the major general through the honourable the secretary at war, therefore, in conformity to the directions of his excellency the president, it is hereby ordered " that the said Clark being considered " a citizen of the United States, and not liable to be tried by " a court martial as a spy, therefore, unless he should " be arraigned by the civil courts for *treason* or some *minor* " *crime* under the laws of the state of New York, he must " be discharged."

All officers and military authorities whatever, in whose custody the said Clark shall or may happen to be, for the cause aforesaid, are hereby directed to release him from his said arrest as a spy.

Lieutenant colonel Philetus Swift is particularly charged with the execution of the order.

By order of Major General Hall,
GEO. HOSMER, A. D. C.

Bloomfield, December 2d, 1812.

Once a citizen, and always a citizen, until the contrary be shewn; so that it did not follow that because Clark had removed to Canada, &c. he had expatriated, and considered himself a subject of the king of England. It was incon-

sistent with his safety to set up that plea; and therefore, it
may be presumed, that he did not set it up. By his temporary allegiance he could commit treason against the king of
England, even though he had not been naturalized, or had
put off the United States. But he could not be considered a
spy to the United States, in consequence of that temporary
allegiance; and, in this, the court had erred in taking cognizance of his acts in that point of view. If he had set up
the defence that he had become a subject of the British government in Canada, there would have been no difficulty :
he might have been hanged at once. It was not because he
could not have ceased to be a citizen; but, because he did
not allege that he had expatriated, that the civil authority
alone could interpose; and, to this, he was ordered to be
delivered.

I see no evidence in this, of President Madison giving
countenance to the idea of the *exuere patriam;* or of Clark
not having been able to put off his condition, or character
of a citizen of the United States. When he came before
the civil tribunal, he might plead his expatriation, and if
found for him, he could be remitted to the military jurisdiction to be hanged according to his *sentence*.

I can have no idea that president Madison would con-
trovert the doctrine of feudal allegiance according to the law
of England; but as to an American citizen not being able
to put off his allegiance to his government, it is quite another
matter. But even in England as to the extent of the claim
of perpetual allegiance to a subject who relinquishes his
feud, I presume he would question it.

The feudalist cannot put off his ligeance to his lord by a
law of the feudal system; but it is *ratione tenuræ*, that he cannot : the feud is the vinculum. But if he ceases to claim the
feud, what right has the lord to his homage? He owes services for the clod, while he claims the clod. But unless he
is adstrictus glebæ; or tied to the clod, like a serf, he can put
it off. Must a man who has no clod, or is willing to relinquish it, be tied to the *whole clod* of the dominium, so that
he cannot put it off?

That the feudalist cannot untie himself from his ligeance to the lord paramount the king, is a law of that system. But still, this is ratione tenuræ, and from his infeudation. That this principle should apply to such as have no feud, or are willing to shake off the *clod*, is contrary to the artificial reason of the system. Hence it is, that colonial emigration carries no such principle with it, that mere labourers, or persons merely merchants, or manufacturers, ought not to be considered as having any thing to do with it. Seamen, who plough the *wave*, what have they to do with a feud; or an adstriction to the *clod* of the kingdom? Their employment is not on terra firma; and it can only be by a *fiction* that they can be considered feudalists. Independent of an adstriction to the clod, the sovereign can claim them only so long as they are willing to stay on the land, or have contracted to stay. A contract cannot exist where their services have been impressed. The pride of an Englishman would be hurt, if he was told that he was a *serf* to his monarch; and what else can he be considered, if he cannot shake off his clog, but must be considered as tied to the island?

The *ultima ratio* must now determine the question as between the *United States*, and the *British empire*. It is brought to the test between the two governments, by *ordering to England for trial*, individuals taken in arms, and alleged to be the subjects of that power. The *retaliation* by a taking *in withernam*, as the common law terms it, individuals of that government, must bring it to the test; and I may therefore consider it, a little more fully. There can be no doubt, but that it has come to be considered their law, that a subject cannot put off his allegiance. In the charter of privileges, extorted from king John, liceat de cetero, unicuique de regno nostro exire, *salva fide nostra*, nisi tempore guerre, &c. *Fealty*, to the king, and the going *in time of war*, is the exception; the putting off the allegiance of the sovereign, makes no part of the privilege of going abroad, and this involves the not putting off subjection to the government. Being so, it is but the *cant* of poets, and orators, to say that an Englishman is *free-born*. Nevertheless, Daniel de Foe, in his poem, stiled, *the true Englishman*, though poetical licence might allow it, does not ven ture to say the *free Englishman.* The truth is, in strictness, the Englishman is not free-born. When we come to the *lawyers*, they will tell you, of a *general restraint*, under the charter; and a *particular restraint* by the writ *Ne exeat regno.* An English subject, is therefore confined to the *prison-bounds* of the island. I say island, because, that is the homestead of the government. A British subject is in legal strictness, as much confined to those limits of subjection, as the convicts at Castle William, on Governor's island, in Boston harbour. *Tufts and Burroughs* had the privilege of the island; but they were restrained from leaving it.

But do the British take subjects belonging to other countries? They are no slouches at this. But do they keep them too? Ay, defend them against all the world. They would think themselves degraded to give up even a *murderer*, a fugitive from justice from another country who had *taken sanctuary with them.* Does not this operate as an *estoppel*, which is a term of their own law, to say, that other people shall not have the same right? Will they admit that the United States have a right to reclaim a citizen expatriated, and take him out of a vessel at sea; or a port on land, and hang him? John Bull would roar like a mad bull, if this pretension was set up. I admit, that whether *derived* from the *German*, or, more immediately imposed by the Norman, the ne liceat exire, nisi *salva fide*, to the prince, is a law of their island. But when it comes to be a matter with *the right of another nation*, their own practice may be set up. But if it were not their own practice, there is another right to be consulted, that of another nation. This must be determined, by an appeal to the *law of nature*, and the *law of nations.*

The law of nature, does not acknowledge the *prohibition to expatriate.* The Roman law gave a right to the parent to put to death his offspring, either by exposing, or by capital punishment, when the child offended. Did this take away the right of a Sabine, a Volscian or a Samnite to protect the child, when he came amongst them? The Roman republic, even in the plenitude of her arrogance, when she came to her full majesty, did not affect this. We hear nothing of it, even in the times of the Cæsars, as a cause of war.

Extract of two notes of Mr. Duponceau, under the head of
allegiance, *from the American edition of the Edinburgh
Encyclopædia; 506 and 508.*

" The word allegiance is of modern date. In the ancient
books and statutes it is written legeance; and, from thence,
has been framed the barbarous latin word *ligeantia.* The
generally admitted derivation of these words, from the latin
ligare, or *alligare,* as expressive of the bond, or connection
subsisting between the lord and his vassal, has always appeared to us to be a forced etymology; because few of the
genuine terms of the feudal law have been borrowed from
the latin language; but their origin is rather to be sought
for in the idioms of the northern conquerors, who introduced that system into the provinces of the Roman empire.

Doctor Johnson very properly derives allegare from the
French word *lige,* which was itself the denomination of a
particular species of feud called *fief lige.*

The French and particularly the Angivins and Normans
said, *homme liege, vassal liege, hommage liege, fief liege;*
and out of the adjective, liege, formed the substantive *ligence;* from which the English made *ligeance,* and *ligeantia ,*
and afterwards *allegiance.*

The French as well as the English etymologists derive
the word *liege* from the latin *ligare;* but we cannot agree
with them in this opinion, and are inclined to trace that term
to another and more legitimate source.

The *fief liege* is defined by the French feudists to be a
species of *fief,* the tenure of which is called *ligence;* by
which the vassal is bound, not only to fealty, but to personal service, which distinguishes it from the *fief simple (fee
simple)* which binds the tenant to *fealty only.* Hence the
fief lige, is, by the French jurists, also denominated *fief de
corps,* in allusion to the *corporal service* which the vassal is
bound to perform; and the corporal oaths which he takes
on doing homage, by holding both his hands, between those
of his sovereign. Ferriere *Dict. de droit* verbo *fief lige.* Den-
nisart. Collect. de jurisprudens. eod. verbo. The difference

between *feudum ligeum,* and *feudum simplex,* is also well explained by Blackstone, 1 Com. 357.

We are for this reason strongly inclined to believe that the word lige takes its derivation from the Norman or Danish word *lig,* which signifies body, and thus, in the original language, as well as in the modern French, the true signification of *fief liege,* is a *corporal fief* or *fief de corps* as well on account of the *personal* services to be rendered, as of the *corporal oath* which the vassal was obliged to take."

" THE doctrine of perpetual allegiance is repugnant to the principle of republican governments. We are told by Plato that the Athenian citizens might freely expatriate themselves, whenever they became dissatisfied with their own country. Dialogue between Socrates and Crito. Sec. 8.

And Cicero considered the right of expatriation as the firmest foundation of Roman liberty. Every scholar has read and admired the beautiful apostrophe into which he breaks out upon this subject, in his oration for Balbus.

O, Jura præclara, atque divinitus a majoribus nostris comparata! ne quis invitus civitate mutetur, neve in civitate maneat invitus. Hæc sunt enim fundimenta firmissima nostra libertatis, sui quemque juris, et retinendi, et dimittendi esse dominum.

The same principle formerly obtained in the republics of modern Europe; and particularly in Holland and Switzerland. Indeed the publicists contended for the right of emigration, even under monarchical governments; and, the learned Binkershœck, has no hesitation in saying that it is lawful for the subject to emigrate *wherever the country is not a prison.* Quest. Jur. pub. lib. 1. c. 22.

In the United States the right of expatriation, has been solemnly recognized, by a decision of the supreme judicial authority; with these restrictions, however, that it must be exercised at such time, in such manner, and under such circumstances, as not to endanger the peace or safety of the

United States; and that the *bona fide* intention of the party to expatriate himself must be clearly proved, so that the act of emigrating be not made a mere cover to evade or violate the laws of our own country. Talbot v. Janson, 3 Dall. 133.

So far the general principle has become a part of our municipal law; but several important questions depending upon it, still remain to be determined. Among those the supreme court has reserved for future consideration, "whether a citizen of the United States can divest himself absolutely of that character, otherwise than in such manner as may be prescribed by *our own laws;* and whether his expatriation would be sufficient to rescue him from punishment for a crime committed against the United States." Murray v. the Charming Betsey, 2 Cranch, 64.

Such are the sentiments of Mr. Duponceau, whom all will admit, I take it, possesses the greatest knowledge of general law of any, in the U. States, and may be said to be the greatest universal jurist. From the preceding notes we have seen what his idea is as to the law of France, on the subject of the *ne exuere patriam*, which is a phrase unknown to all law heretofore, and has been foisted into language, as he observes, in the place of the *ne exuere ligeantiam*, and transferred by the British from the feudalist to every other subject. But it is not the law of France. That must appear from the Napolean code, art. 17th.

" The quality of a French subject shall be lost,

1. By naturalization acquired in a foreign country.

2. By the acceptance, not authorized by the emperor, of public functions conferred by a foreign government.

3. Finally, by every settlement made in a foreign country without the intention of returning."

This is the point upon which it ought to be put, the animus residendi. If Clark had alleged this, or if it could have been made out against him, he might have been hung as a spy. But it not appearing that he had gone to Canada with a view of not returning, he might be considered a citizen of the United States, and proceeded against by the civil authority as guilty of treason.

Upon the whole it is not consistent at the present day with the practice of nations, or with even that of Great Britain, to bring up this isolated, or, I might rather say, insulated doctrine of feudal origin, and force it upon the world. In the modern state of national society, it cannot be endured, or carried into effect; it is an outrage upon the law of nature itself, the improvement of the species, and the happiness of man. It is the offspring of a Barbaric code, which had its foundation in the military establishments of feudal invaders, and may be said to be functus officio, and to have gone to rest. We know that cannibals existed in Great Britain as well as in the islands of the South sea; and had it been the law still to cut breasts from women, and eat human flesh, would that bind us from protecting individuals from amongst that people, who had made their escape and taken refuge on our shores? In a case short of life, and liberty only, I refer once more to the case of Somerset v. Stuart; the negro slave rescued from the claim of his master, and set free. Because the law could know of no claim over a human being, but would *consider him as entitled to himself*, and upon that principle would defend him as sui juris, the moment he had set his foot upon the island.

———◦———

These are the principal distinctions between aliens, denizens, and natives: distinctions which it hath been frequently endeavoured, since the commencement of this century to lay almost totally aside, by one general *naturalization act,* for all foreign protestants. 1 Bl. Com. 374.

THE British government would seem to have no scruple about the right of *impatriation.* They take from whence they can get, without any restraint but considerations of policy, *so far as respects themselves.* And will they not protect by land, or *water, those whom they receive?*

I quote a sentence from a very able publication of that country, *Cobbett's* Weekly Register, Aug. 4, 1813. While in this country that editor of a paper here was no squeamish advocate of British claims; and no slight abuser of American character in general, and American characters. I had been sometimes disposed to apply to that writer, in my own mind, the language of king Henry V. in the case of Grey and Scroop.

" If that same demon that hath gulled thee thus,
Should, with his lion gait walk the whole world,
He might return to vasty Tartar back,
And tell the legions—I can never win
A soul so easy as that English man's."

But, as Don Quevedo, in his Vision of Hell, introduces the Devil preaching; (and it could not be denied, but that, though not a doctor of the Sorbonne, his doctrine, in that instance, was orthodox,) and was justifying himself against the charge of those that had come to that place, alleging that he had tempted them, whereas it was in a great degree their own evil passions that had impelled them; so I quote Cobbett, though not admitting him to be an authority in all cases; nor is what he says of much consequence, but as it is ad hominem, of the English *practice in impatriation.*

" It should be considered," says he, " that our own laws make exceptions as to *allegiance.* An American may become a British subject by marrying an *English woman.* From the time he marries, the law gives him the claim to all the rights enjoyed by Englishmen; and the same law imposes upon him all the duties of an *Englishman.* This law, of which no gentleman can be ignorant, has been, not long ago, acted upon by our government, as I understand, in this way. An American was *impressed* in our fleet.—He was claimed by the agent of the American government, as an American; and his discharge demanded accordingly. The *answer was,* that he was a British subject having married an English woman; and the demand of his discharge was refused accordingly."

This venerable body of men, being separate and set apart from the rest of the people, in order to attend more closely to the service of Almighty God, have thereupon large privileges allowed them by our municipal laws. 1 Bl. Com. 376.

MINISTERS of religion of every denomination, are exempted from militia duty by an act of assembly for the regulation of the militia, of the 9th April, 1807. And, by a decision of the supreme court of this state, July 12, 1813, nobis dissentientibus, "a clergyman who officiates as such is not bound to serve as a *guardian of the poor,* notwithstanding he so far attends to *secular business, as to keep a store for the sale of merchandize.*" The majority of the court thought themselves warranted in considering it a part of the common law introduced from England; or a usage here, amounting to common law by the tacit consent of the people, to *exempt the clergy from all secular duties.* The decision being so, I am content. But will it not be difficult to say who are *ministers,* so as to be exempted? Herman Husbands preached to his wife; and affected like saint Paul, at Rome, "in his own house, to receive all that came in unto him." Boden Teugh's Church consisted of four persons; himself and wife; and his son and wife. His grace was;

"God bless me and my wife;

My son John and his wife;

We four, and no more;

and let all the rest shift for themselves."

There wanted but a *denomination* to exempt these; and they might have taken that of Husbandists; or Teughites.

Now, that by this decision of the supreme court, it has come to be a rule of law, to exempt from all secular duties, having no church establishment in this state, some criterion must be fixed upon to distinguish. I should take it, that it might be *the living by the altar;* or making the ministering in holy ordinances, the *chief employment of their time.*

The court by this decision, would seem to have gone the whole length of the law of England. May it not then follow, that if the clergy are thus privileged, even from being a *guardian of the poor,* which is a duty connected with a charitable institution, the legislature may think it reasonable, that they be excluded from eligibility, or appointment to office of a profitable nature, which is the case in England. Perhaps the preachers of all denominations would rather say, in the language of the merchants to the king of France, Laissez nous faire; *let us alone;* the judges have not served us, by distinguishing farther than the act of assembly has done.

" There are two kinds of divorce, the one total, the other par-
" tial; the one *a vinculo matrimonii*, the other merely *a mensa et*
" *thoro.*" 1 Bl. Com. 440.

IN England, on a cause arising *ex post facto*, as intolerable cruelty, adultery, a perpetual disease, the ecclesiastical court administers the remedy of a divorce *a mensa et thoro;* but if the cause existed previous to the marriage, as consanguinity, corporeal imbecility, or the like, a separation *a vinculo matrimonii* may be decreed: 2 Bl. Com. 94.

In cases even of *adultery*, the party complaining is driven to parliament for redress. Coop. Just. 534.

In Pennsylvania, power was given to the governor, by an act of 1705, to grant divorce from bed and board, to the party complaining of adultery. But this power has been superseded by an act of the 19th Sept. 1785, which enables the supreme court to proceed, on complaint of a party, and grant a divorce not only from bed and board, but also from *the bonds of matrimony itself*, where " either party at the time of the contract was and still is naturally impotent or incapable of procreation, or that he or she hath, knowingly entered into a second marriage, in violation of the previous vow he or she made to the former wife or husband, whose marriage is still subsisting, or that either party hath committed adultery, or wilful and malicious desertion and absence, without a reasonable cause, for and during the space and term of four years."

By sec. 10, it is provided, that the supreme court may grant the wife a separation *from bed and board*, in case the husband shall maliciously either abandon, or turn his wife out of doors, or by cruel or barbarous treatment endanger her life, or offer such indignities to her person, as to render her condition intolerable, or life burthensome, and thereby force her to withdraw from his house and family.

By a supplement, passed, 2d Ap. 1804, the same powers are given also to the judges of the courts of common pleas.

In cases that are out of these provisions, application must be made to the legislature.

———•———

The constitution of feuds, had its original from the military policy of the northern, or Celtic nations——

It was brought by them from their own countries, and continued in their respective colonies, *as the most likely means to secure their new acquisitions.* 2 Bl. Com. 44.

THAT it was brought from their *own countries*, I incline to doubt. The contrary would seem to appear from Cæsar; Com. de bel. Gal. l. 6. c. 12. And this is the earliest historical document we have upon the subject. Plerique quum aut ære alieno, aut *magnitudine tributorum*, aut injuria potentiorum premuntur, sese in servitutem dicunt nobilibus.* From this we find that taxes were paid; and thence it may be inferred that *the tenure of lands was allodial, not military.*

Druides a bello abesse consueverunt, neque *tributa* una cum reliquis pendunt. *Militiæ* vacationem omniumque rerum habent immunitatem.† From hence it would seem that their establishment was the same with us in their republics; taxes, and militia duty.

Noticing the *customs* of the Germans, l. 6. c. 21. he says neque quisquam agri modum *certum*, aut fines proprios ha-

* The greater part when pressed with debt, or the weight of taxes put themselves in servitude to the nobles.

† It is customary for the Druids to be absent from war, nor do they pay taxes with the rest. They have an immunity from militia duty, and from all things.

bet. Sed *magistratus* ac principes, in annos singulos, gentibus cognationibusque hominum qui una coierunt, quantum eis, et quo loco visum est, attribuunt agri, atque anno post alio transire cogunt.* Thus we see not only that the assignment of grounds was of the civil authority, but that it was done by the magistrates, and principal men; the word *principes* not *duces*, is used. At the same time, there was no permanent *beneficium* or *military feud*.

But Tacitus, in that invalulable monument which he has left us on the manners of the Germans, gives us a much more minute account of the state of society, and customs amongst these people. Arva per annos mutant, says he.† Tacit. de mor. c. 26.

They could not therefore be considered as having each a particular portion of soil to which they were attached; and for which they owed service, homage, and *allegiance*. The distribution of soil, and establishment of military services was the result of the *new situation in which these* were placed. This new division of property, says Doctor Robertson, together with the maxims and manners to which it gave rise, gradually introduced a *species of government formerly unknown*. This singular institution is now distinguished by the name of the *feudal system :* 1 Rob. Cha. V. 10.

I yield therefore to the opinion of those who maintain that we have no trace of this system in the Saxon governments. It was introduced into England by the conquest of the Normans, and still remains, so far as it exists in England, a monument of that conquest.

"The last and most important alteration," says Blackstone, speaking of the effect of this conquest, "both in our civil and military polity, *was the engrafting on all landed estates*, a few only excepted, the fiction of *feudal tenure ;*

---

* Nor has any one a certain measure of land, or their own boundaries : but the *magistrates* and chiefs *every year* assign to the tribes, and kindred tribes that come together, as much as seems good to them, and in what place ; and year after year they oblige them to remove.

† They change grounds every year.

which drew after it a numerous and oppressive train of ser-
vile fruits, and appendages; the genuine consequences of
the maxim then adopted, that all the lands in England were
derived from, and holden mediately or immediately of the
crown," 4 Bl. Com. 418. and 438. He adds, " these slavish
tenures, the badge of foreign dominion." A legitimate principle of these tenures, was the doctrine of *unalienable and
perpetual allegiance.* It was not necessary that the emigrant to
these shores should carry *that principle* with them as applicable to their situation, having left, as will be admitted, this
badge of servitude, the feudal system behind them. Those
who give such a principle countenance, will deny that it is
peculiar to this law, and will endeavour to give it a foundation, as Blackstone would wish to do, on the general
grounds of *universal law.* But for this see the excellent note
of judge Tucker, in loco.

How far this system has been broken down in England,
and how far, what I consider to be a *root* of it, remains, this
doctrine of *inextricable allegiance,* the student will investigate. I may say something more of it in another place.
But God forbid that I should consider it as introduced here.
This vestige of the iron age, and vassalage of the *iron
crown,* our republican institutions have put, and will put
down.

———Si qua manent sceleris vestigia nostri
Irrita, perpetua solvent formidine terras.

———

" The last consequence of tenure in chivalry was *escheat;*
" which is the determination of the tenure, &c. by either natural
" or civil means." 2 Bl. Com. 72.

EXTINCTION of inheritable blood by civil means does
not take place in Pennsylvania. " No attainder shall work
corruption of blood, nor except during the life of the offender, forfeiture of estate to the commonwealth." State Const.
Art. 9, Sec. 19.

In default of heirs, land escheats to the commonwealth. In England the King, who is esteemed in the eye of the law, the original proprietor of all the lands in the kingdom, derives a part of his ordinary revenue from this source. 1 Bl. Com. 303. By our act of assembly of 29 Sept. 1787, entitled " An act to declare and regulate Escheat," it is provided, Sec. 1, that, " if any person who at the time of his or her death, was seized or possessed of any real or personal estate within this commonwealth, die intestate, without heirs or any known kindred, such estate shall escheat to the commonwealth *subject to all legal demands on the same.*"

The act goes on, and provides that " no escheat of real estate for want of heirs, shall be where brothers or sisters of the half blood, or father or mother, or grandfather or grandmother of the deceased, survive, to take the same."

The student will at once see that this provision of the act changes the law as it is in England, where land will rather escheat than ascend to parents, or go to the half blood, or to blood not of the first purchaser. The law of escheat is regulated by the law of distribution. Escheat, therefore, does not go to the commonwealth, in prejudice of aliens, who are enabled by act of assembly of 23 Feb. 1791, to acquire, to take, hold and dispose of real estates, by devise, or descent, and dispose of personal estates to which they may be entitled by testament, donation or otherwise. 2 Smith's laws, 425.

To complete the title by escheat, the English law requires the lord to *enter*, or sue out *a writ of escheat.*

By the act of Pennsylvania, 1791, 2d Smith, 421, provision is made to complete title by escheat to the commonwealth. Sec. 8. Escheator general to be appointed, with deputies. On information of any person dying without any known heirs, the escheator general, or deputy issues his precept to the sheriff or coroner, who issues his summons for an inquisition to be holden to ascertain the escheat, which inquisition shall be transmitted to the prothonotary of the supreme court, &c. &c. &c.

Hither might have been referred the advantages which used to arise to the king from the profits of his military tenures, to which most lands in the kingdom were subject, until the statute 12 Car. 2. c. 24, which, in a great measure *abolished them all.* 2 Bl. Com. 286.

BUT, a doctrine which I assert to be a *relict,* to pun upon a word, of this truly feudal system, and a principle of the military tenures, is, that a subject cannot throw off his allegiance when he quits the feud. This the government of England,* if not the jurists, assert not to be the offspring of that system, but to stand upon a broader base, that of the *common law,* antecedent to the introduction of feuds. They even attempt to prove it upon the basis of *universal law.* They are willing to admit, with all their eulogium on the rights of Englishmen, that an individual can no more escape from that kingdom, than a dog with a collar about his neck, but is liable to be restrained : or than if he were a slave that had escaped *ex ergastulo,* or work-house among the Romans. As between the government, and the individual, it is one thing; but when the protection of a foreign government attaches, it is another. As for the individual, it will be in vain for him to talk of the *natural right, and liberty of an Englishman,* when the crocodile has him in his jaws. But as to the foreign government which has received him, the only question will be the *right* to protect him, and the *power.* As to the *right* to protect him, I may consider it something farther, in the course of this publication. As to the *power,* I leave it to our administration; and can only say, that being myself persuaded of the *right,* I would give it up only with my last breath.

———Nisi cum vita simul amittet.

It is a principle, of the application of which the British are not aware, when they insist upon it.

Nescis quam legem in te sanciris iniquam.

* There would seem to be a chain still fastened to the foot of that people.

Does it not operate as in the nature of an *estoppel* to them, that they themselves *impatriate ?*

Will they venture in the face of this, or without having such a face, to carry that claim into effect, so far as respects *the protection of foreign nations.* They did not think it prudent in the revolutionary war, in the case of general Lee, nor in the case of Napper Tandy, nor will they think it prudent in any case in the present war. They have the example of Napoleon before them, as to this claim of perpetual subjection; but the example of the iron, or any other crown, will not paralize the American spirit, in contending for the freedom of mankind, in opposition to this *imprisonment of any one in an enchanted island.* *

"As to the power of charging lands with the debts of the owner." 2 Bl. Com. 289.

BLACKSTONE here speaks of the lien of a judgment as in the nature of a *pawn.* The judgment binds, and gives *a pledge, subject to discharge by the payment of the debt;* and such judgment binds *without limitation of time.* But by an act of assembly of 4th April, 1798, it is enacted, " that no judgment now on record in any court within this commonwealth, shall continue a lien on the real estate of the person, against whom the same has been entered, during a longer term than five years, from and after the passing of this act, unless the person who has obtained such judgment, or his legal representatives, or other persons interested, shall, within the said term of five years, sue out of the court, wherein the same has been entered, a writ of *scire facias,* to revive the same."

Sec. 2, provides " that no judgment hereafter entered

---

* See Mr. Duponceau's note, page 175, to his translation of Binkershoeck's Quest. jur. pub.

" It is lawful to emigrate from France, *and it is so wherever the country is not a prison.*"

&c. shall continue a lien, &c. during a longer term than five years, &c. unless the person, &c. shall, within the said term of five years, sue out a writ of scire facias, to revive the same."

Sec. 3. provides for the proceedings to revive a judgment, viz. " that all such writs shall be served on the terr-tenants, &c. and also on the defendant, &c. and where the land is not in the immediate occupation of any person, and defendant, &c. not to be found, proclamation shall be made in open court, at two succeeding terms, &c. and the court, unless sufficient cause to prevent the same is shewn at or before the second term subsequent to the issuing of such writ, shall direct and order the revival of any such judgment, during another period of five years, and so from period to period."

Sec. 4. disables from commencing or maintaining suit on bonds given as sureties for public officers, after the expiration of seven years from the time at which the cause of action shall have accrued.

The question has arisen under this act whether the purchaser of land which had been subject to the lien of a judgment and who had not *notice* of the judgment, was in any better situation than the plaintiff in the judgment. By the opinion of the supreme sourt of this state in the case of the bank of North America, v. Fitzimmons, it was decided, that notice or not notice had nothing to do with the act. 3 Bin. 343.

Mr. Smith in his note to this act, 3d. 332, takes no notice of this decision; whence, it is presumable that it was made *prior* to the decision in 3 Bin. He gives at full length the opinion of judge Washington of the circuit court of the United States, which was impliedly considered by the state judges (Tilghman and Brackenridge) to be erroneous, as having gone upon the mistake of an assimulation to the statute of enrolments, registry act, &c. in England. Judge Yeates being a stock-holder in the bank, did not give an opinion.

The next species of subordinate magistrates, whom I am to consider, are *Justices of the Peace.* 1 Bl. Com. 349.

THERE is no civil jurisdiction given to the *justice of the peace* by the law of England; but his authority is, as the title imports, merely *in matters of the peace.* But from an early period in Pennsylvania, jurisdiction of *civil controversies* had been given by successive acts of assembly; and from time to time, enlarging the sphere of jurisdiction, as to the nature of the complaint made; or, as to the sum demanded, whether on a contract, or in the case of trespass. The constitution of the state recognizes this, by Art. V. viz. the judicial power of this commonwealth shall be vested, &c. &c. &c. *in justices of peace.* This would seem to exclude, vi termini, the vesting *single justices* with any other jurisdiction *than that of the peace.* But the constitution must be supposed to use the term according to the well known, popular acceptation of it, as comprehending matters of a *civil* jurisdiction, as well as of *the peace.* The jurisdiction of the justices of the peace, therefore, extends beyond mere matters of the peace, and comprehends civil matters, in like manner with the county court, in England, "which is held every month, or oftener, by the sheriff, *intended to try little causes not exceeding the value of* 40 *shillings.*" So that the *civil jurisdiction of justices* is derived, entirely from positive law; and was originally confined, as the county court in England, to debts or *demands under* 40 *shillings.* Chief Justice Hale, in his considerations touching the amendment, or alterations of laws, Chap. 7, (Hargrave's Law Tracts, 249,) gives the reasons of such jurisdiction in small matters to the county court, and suggests an increase of jurisdiction. The heading of the *chapter* is, "The present inconveniences relating to courts of justice; and first touching the county court." He then proceeds;

"By the true and wise constitution of this kingdom, suites, where the debt or damage amount not to 40s. were not to be determined in the courts of Westminster, unless a title of land came in question; but they were to be determined in the county court hundred court, or court baron. And this was the ancient law. *Vid. stat. Glocest.* 6. *E.* 1. At that time 40s. was a considerable sum, 1. in respect of the intrinsecal value of the coin, for then 20d. made an ounce of silver, and at this day it is 5s. viz. sixty pence, and upon that single account forty shillings then, ariseth now to six pounds. But 2. that was not all; for, as I may say, money was at that time dearer than it is now, because there was not so much. And hence it is, that the prices of all things at this day, are much dearer now than they were then; because money is much more plenty now than it was then, as it will appear to any that looks into the proclamations of prices and commodities, both in the beginnings of iters and parliaments in the times of E. 1. and E. 2. *Vid. Rot. Parl.* 8. *E.* 2. *n.* 29. *in schedula*, a proclamation for the price of victuals, viz. a fat ox fatted with corn, 24s.—a fat cow, 12s.—a fat hog, 40d.—a fat mutton unshorn, 20d.—a fat mutton shorn, 14d.—a fat hen, 1d.—24 eggs, 1d. which evidences a great advance of the price of things at this day, besides the advance of the extrinsecal denomination of money.

"By this, that hath been said, it is apparent, 1. That it was the wise constitution of the common law, to keep small suites from the great courts at Westminster. 2. That if an equal proportion in the denomination of small suites were held, that if 40s. were the lowest measure of the suites to be commenced in these great courts, at least ten pounds would be the lowest measure at this day.

" And yet it is very apparent to any man that converseth with business, that, divide the suites that come down to the assizes to be tryed at the great courts, near one half thereof are under 40s. at least in some counties, besides those many, that are ended upon process serving and before they come to tryall.

" And yet there is not one of those suites brought to tryall, but at this day stands each of the parties in at least 10l. but if it pass for either, there is an allowance that recovers four times as much cost, as the principal amounts to, viz. at least eight pounds.

" And by this means, 1st. Suites are multiplied. 2. Expences and charges are multiplied. 3. Attornies and solicitors multiplied.

" There have been several attempts in parliament to remedy this, viz. the statute of 43. Eliz. cap. 6. 21. Jac. cap. 16. But they have proved ineffectual, partly by the mutual connivance of attorneys and practicers, to decline the benefit of these statutes, because it would abridge their employment and profit; partly by the influence of officers upon the practicers in the several courts, lest by that means their offices should decay; but principally, because, as the present constitution of the county courts and hundred courts stands, it were a kind of extremity to put these statutes fully into execution; for it were to drive men from the courts of Westminster, for small matters where they may have justice, unto inferior jurisdictions, where as they are at present constituted, they are like to have little or none.

" The first business, therefore, would be tò rectify inferior jurisdictions; and then we may with probable safety and advantage, abridge the courts of Westminster from these trivial and inconsiderable suites, where the ordinary costs, that are given to the party that recovers, exceed the value of what he recovers. Therefore I propound,

" (1.) That the county court may be established in this manner in all places. 1. That there be in every county court, a person learned in the laws, a barrister of at least seven years standing, that may be the steward of the county court, by grant from the king, *quamdiu se bene gesserit*, with a fee of   per ann. out of the perquisites of the county. 2. That the steward do try the causes at issue in the court by jury of twelve men, and be the judge to give judgment therein. 3. That the perquisites of the courts be answered to the king. 4. That there be also a sworn clerk to make and keep the records. 5. That there be a select number of attorneys, not exceeding the number of six in any one county, to be deputed, and upon cause to be removed, by the chief justice of the common bench for the time being; and none other to be the immediate attorneys to the court.

" (2.) That, although in a proportion as hath been observed, 10*l.* now is less than 40*s.* in the time of Ed. 1. yet I should not propound so high a measure for them, but they should hold plea of any debt, or debt, or damage, of the value of 5*l.* where the title of freehold, or lease for years, comes not in question.

" (3.) That where the sum in demand exceeds not that sum, the cause should not be removed from thence by any *recordari, certiorari, pone,* or *habeas corpus,* unless upon oath made, that the title of the land will come in question; and if upon that surmise and oath, a plaint or suit be removed by either party, and it appear to be untrue upon the pleading or triall, the party removing the suit to pay double costs.

" (4.) That the processes be only by summons, attachment,

and distress, and the execution by *fieri facias* or *levari facias*, and not otherwise.

" This being thus settled, I should propound, that the courts at Westminster should not hold plea of any suit for debt or damages under 5l. unless where the title of lands is concerned ; and that if upon the triall of any such cause, or otherwise it shall appear the debt or damages amount not to 5l. the plaintiff should recover no more costs than damages ; and if it be found for the defendant, that then he recover double costs.

" The greatest danger imaginable in this is, that it may give a handle to the erecting of country judicatures to the countermining of the kingdom. And I must confess, were this to be the effect of it, I think it were the most pernicious thing imaginable.

" But certainly this is but a vain fear, unless we were in such giddy times, that could not be contented with an ease and convenience to the people, without destroying the law and the government of the kingdom. For was not that law the same in the time of E. 1. and ever since, as to the point of the jurisdiction touching matters under 40s. and hath it any time introduced that inconvenience ? That which is propounded, is but to ease the county court of what makes it unuseful and burthensome to the people, and to render it serviceable and convenient, and to disburthen the courts of Westminster of these suits, wherein the costs to be recovered exceed the value of the thing in demand. Indeed there are some few alterations from the ancient constitution.

" 1. In the judge ; for the truth is, I think a person acquainted with the law, and sworn in the office, is fitter to be trusted, than a few ignorant, and it may be, concerned suitors.

" 2. In the triall, which I would have by the oath of twelve men ; and so in some counties it is used ; though in others, the triall of the fact is by witnesses, and the opinion of the major part of the suitors ; in others by wager of law. I hold the triall by jury returned, the best triall.

" 3. In the sum, which I have estimated to 5l. which is not so much even in intrinsecal value as 40s. in the time of E. 1. And upon the same account, the freehold of jurors hath been raised First in the time of E. 1. it was 20s. then by 2. H. 5. it was 40s. in some cases ; then by 27. Eliz. it was raised to 4l. and since to 20l.

" If men indeed will be giddy and unsteady, and if we should suppose parliaments not to be wisely sensible of their own, and the public concern, men may suppose that 5l. may in time arise to be

50*l.* and so the courts of Westminster be destroyed. He that sup-poseth this, may suppose things yet more dreadful. But, in my understanding, if things were reduced to this state with the county court, 1. It would be a great ease to the people. 2. It would disburthen Westminster-hall of many suites, which are indeed a reproach to the honour and dignity of it. 3. It would prevent multitudes of oppressive suites; many men suing for trifles, because, if they recover, the costs will crush and undo the defendant, being oftentimes forty times more than the principall. 4. It would accommodate the county court, to be admirably auxiliary and subservient to the great courts at Westminster. Writs of enquiry of damages, might be there executed by the sheriff, and in the presence, and with the assistance of the steward, and not by a jury packed by the under sheriff in a corner. Here outlawries might be proclaimed, tables of them set up, and tables of fine and infinite more accomodations; because it would be a place of note and resort, and things would be managed with order, and much more notoriety, than it is possible they can be now as the county court is constituted.

" That which seems to be the greatest objection against this is, that it will multiply suites, the jurisdiction being cheap and at hand.

" I answer, that it is regularly true, that this doth multiply suites, but yet these allayes with it.

" 1. If it were admitted, yet in respect of the sum propounded, it is apparently necessary, that some remedy should be provided for such sums: and it is apparently unreasonable, that they should be driven to sue at Westminster; for if the suit be necessary, he shall lose by his suite, though he recover, in respect of the expence he shall be put to.

" 2. Possibly at this day, many trifling and causeless suites are commenced at Westminster, to undo a defendant, with the costs in case of a recovery, or to put him to great expence; which would not be if the suits of this nature were in the county court thus qualified, where the defence would be as cheap for the defendant, as the suit is for the plaintiff; and the costs of recovery would not probably exceed the damage, but be probably less, which would be no great encouragement to vexation.

" 3. I suppose, that, in the progress of this discourse, something will be proposed evidently necessary to discourage vexatious suites, as well in this as in all other jurisdictions.

3 I

" 4. But if the judge of the court be such, as he ought to be for his learning and integrity, and the practicers sober and credible men, vexatious suites will not receive much countenance.

" I shall conclude this business with this farther observation, that by this means the students and professors of the law, which are now generally driven or drawn up to London, so that there are scarce any left in the country, will have some encouragement to reside in the country, and the country not left to the management of attornies and solicitors."

The above extract will give a view of the grounds upon which that great man, sir Mathew Hale, proposed extending the jurisdiction of the county courts, as to the sum in demand, except as to cases, *where the title to land came in question;* and this in consideration of the *depreciation of money.* There will be seen also, his unwillingness to take away the *trial by jury.* It is this very kind of *county court of common pleas,* that we had in Pennsylvania prior to the revolution, consisting of justices of peace, and since perfected under our present constitution by giving a person learned in the law as president. But Chief Justice Hale says nothing of annexing a civil jurisdiction to the office of justice of the peace, to act *without a jury.*

It was highly questioned by governor M'Kean, whether the increasing the jurisdiction of the justices did not affect the right of *the trial by jury as heretofore,* and which was secured by the constitution; and he even went so far as to put a negative upon a bill, which afterwards, passed into a law, by the constitutional two thirds of both houses of the legislature.

The question was afterwards brought before the supreme court, as to the constitutionality of the law, in the case of Emerick v. Harris, 1 Binney, 416, to the observations in which case I refer the student. I will acknowledge, that I have been at all times, more friendly to an increase of the jurisdiction of the justices, than to the system of unmanagable, and desultory arbitrations. I would check them by taking away *an appeal from him entering the rule of reference, and compelling the adversary to take that tribunal, unless in a case allowed by the court.*

I am friendly to a reasonable increase of the *civil jurisdiction* of the justices; and therefore I approve of the patronage of the general assembly to Mr. Bache, by authorizing the governor to subscribe for 1500 copies of his Manual. I think it money well laid out; *and would have no objection to them following up their blows in that way, and authorizing the governor, or the speaker of each house to take, for the use of the members, and the officers of government, a copy, each, of this publication,* which will about pay me for what I allow my amanuensis for transcribing; viz. 175 copies from the printer, *in boards,* and which *is all I get* for this edition of the work.

" An estate-tail may be *barred,* or destroyed by a fine, by a common recovery," &c. 2 Bl. Com. 116.

BY an act of 27 Jan. 1749-50, it was provided " that fines and common recoveries heretofore levied and suffered within the province of Pennsylvania, or which shall hereafter, &c. duly and according to the common and statute laws of England, &c. shall be of like force and effect," &c.

An act of 16th Jan. 1799, reciting that the mode of conveyance by common recoveries is attended *with a heavy expence,* provides in Sec. 1. " that any persons seized of any estate tail in possession, reversion or remainder, shall have full power to convey, &c. by such manner and form of conveyance or assurance, as any person seized of an estate in fee-simple may grant, bargain, sell, &c. and all such grants &c. shall be good and available against all persons whom the grantor, &c. could debar by any mode of common recovery, or by any means whatever."

Sec. 2. enables any person who has sold an estate-tail to a *bona fide* purchaser, for a valuable consideration, to confirm such sale by new deeds executed according to the act, provided that the intention to bar shall be stated in the deed.

I have already stated, ante, beginning page 143, reasons why I would think it not unadvisable to have the entailing of estates altogether taken away.

———

"By the statutes 31 Hen. 8, c. 1, and 32 Hen. 8, c. 32, joint tenants, either of inheritances, or other less estates, are compellable by writ of partition to divide their lands." 2 Bl. Com. 185.

THESE statutes are reported by the judges to be in force in Pennsylvania.

By an act " concerning writs of partition," passed 11th April, 1799; "the supreme court shall have original jurisdiction over the whole commonwealth, as to the granting and proceeding upon writs of partition, at the suit of any tenant in common, joint-tenant or co-partner."—And by an act passed 28th March, 1806, " the respective county courts of common pleas, shall have, and exercise all the powers which the supreme court *had* and *posessed* by the above act, as to the granting and proceeding upon writs of partition," &c. See 3d Smith's laws, 388.

By stat. 8 and 9 Will. 3, c. 31, no plea in abatement shall be admitted in any suit for partition of lands ; nor shall the same be abated by reason of the death of any tenant. 3 Bl. Com. 302.

This statute of William has not been reported by the judges to be in force ; but by an act passed 7th April, 1807, Sec. 4, " no plea in abatement shall be admitted or received in any suit for partition, nor shall the same be abated by reason of the death of any defendant."

Where there is any the least probable cause to found such prosecution upon. 3 Bl. Com. 126.

PROBABLE cause which shall *excuse* in an action for a malicious prosecution; or, in other words, shall constitute a *defence* in such an action, is sometimes said to be a *mixed question of fact and law.* I gave my sentiments on that head, on a *motion for a new trial* in a case of Lyon and Fox; and to which I will refer, having given it to Mr. Browne, amongst other papers, with a view to his reporting it. In that opinion I totally rejected the idea, or *expression* of calling it a *mixed question;* for it was calculated to mislead, and did mislead in the argument; and it became necessary to analyze and explain this principle. Lyon had been *committed*, in the first instance, and bail refused by the *magistrate committing;* and, in the second instance, on a habeas corpus by the chief justice, and other judges in term, *on a hearing*, bail was refused, and he was *remanded to custody.* If *probable cause* was a question of *law*, this must be considered as *concluding*, so far as to stand between the prosecutor Fox, and Lyon the accused. It was holden by me that it did not stand in the way of shewing *before a jury*, that notwithstanding all this, no *probable cause* existed; that the *weakness* or wickedness of a prosecutor; and what was more, the *error* of judges in thinking there was probable cause, did not affect the right of Lyon on a trial before a jury to shew there was no *probable cause.* And this doctrine I have understood to have been approved by the whole profession.

For my *reasoning and authorities* I refer to the report which Mr. Browne may publish. I add further, that even where a *grand jury* finds a *bill*, in addition to all that judges have done, in committing, it is still enquirable whether there was reasonable ground for the prosecution; and it can go only in mitigation of damages, even where nothing has been kept back by the prosecutor, in the investigation of the *probability* of a cause for commitment. I am not to be at the mercy of a judge, or a whole bench, who *at the instance of a prose-*

cutor, have thought there was *probable cause*. For I cannot sue them; or have redress, *otherwise than against him*. His misconception will not justify, by alleging the act of those who, pro hac vice only, and called upon by him, are to judge.

In the case of Lyon v. Fox, a new trial was granted; but on the ground only of *excessive* damages. We heard no more of it; I presume there was a compromise.

"An assize of nuisance."—3 Bl. Com. 220.

"A REMEDY which has been long antiquated in England, and which if ever pursued in this state, has certainly not been used more than once, or twice: indeed no precedent has been of its having ever been carried *completely through*." Chief Justice Tilghman, 2 Bin. 194.

The novelty of the case induces me to give a report of an *assize of nuisance*, which was carried completely through. It was that of Livezey and another, against Gorgas, and others. It had been removed by certiorari from the court of common pleas to the supreme court; and after a motion to quash the certiorari (see 2 Binney, 292) came before me at a court of nisi prius, holden for the eastern term, May 26th, 1811. Lewis for the plaintiffs. Rawle for the defendants.

December, 1807.—No. 33.

Philadelphia County, ss.

The commonwealth of Pennsylvania, to the sheriff of Philadelphia county.   GREETING.

WHEREAS, John Livezey, and Joseph Livezey, have complained to us that Benjamin Gorgas, Jacob Gorgas, John Weiss, George Horter, and Catherine his wife, Joseph Weiss, William Struper, and Jacob Weiss, unjustly and without judgment, have erected, levied and raised a certain wall and dam, thereby obstructing a certain mill race and water course, and have diverted a certain other mill race and water course in the township of Roxborough, in your county, to the nuisance of the freehold of them the said John Livezey and Joseph Livezey, situate in the same township and county, within 30 years last past; and therefore, We command you, that if the said John and Joseph shall make you secure of prosecuting their claim, then you shall cause 12 free and lawful men of the neighbourhood to view the said mill race, water course, and tenements, and the nuisance thereof done, and the names to be impannelled and summon them by good summoners that they be and appear before the judges of our court of common pleas, at Philadelphia, at our county court, there to be held, the 7th day of December next, together with the parties ready to recognize, &c. and put by sureties and safe pledges, the said Benjamin Gorgas, Jacob Gorgas, &c. if they be found in your bailiwick, so that they be and appear then and there before our judges aforesaid, ready to hear and recognize, &c. and have you then and there the names of those pledges and this writ.

Witness, Jacob Rush, Esq. President of the said court, at Philadelphia, the 26th day of September, 1807.

CHS. BIDDLE.

John Doe, } Pledges.
Richard Roe, }

John Denn, } Summoners.
Richard Fenn, }

SHERIFF'S RETURN,

Served the within writ upon the within named Benjamin Gorgas, Jacob Gorgas, and John Weiss—the within named George Horter and Catherine his wife, Joseph Weiss, William Struper, and Jacob Weiss, have nothing nor have any of them any thing in my bailiwick, by which they may be attached, nor are they or any of them found within—The residue of this writ to me directed, appears in a certain pannel hereto annexed. So answers

JOHN BARKER, *Sheriff*.

The names of the recognitors of an assize of nuisance between John Livezey and Joseph Livezey, plaintiffs, and Benjamin Gorgas, (ut supra)

1 Abraham Duffield,
2 Daniel Thomas, &c. in all 24,

(which number sheriff must summon in an assize. Co. Litt: 155, a " albeit the words of the writ be duodecim, yet by an ancient course the sheriff must return 24, and this for the expedition of justice.")

Sheriff's notice to John Weiss, who was the actual tenant to the precipe.

You are hereby informed that the recognitors of the within named assize will be and appear at the mill race, water course and tenements within mentioned, and the nuisance thereof, on the 19th day of the present month of October, at 10 o'clock, A. M. then and there to view the said mill race water course and the nuisance thereof done and you are summoned to be and appear before the judges within mentioned then and there ready to hear the recognition within mentioned.

JOHN BARKER, *Sheriff.*

———

Docket Entries in the Com. Pleas, of Dec. Term, 1807.—No. 33.

| John Livezey & Jos. Livezey,
vs.
Benjamin Gorgas, Jacob Gorgas, John Weiss, George Horter and Catherine his wife, Joseph Weiss, William Struper and Jacob Weiss.
Eject. Sept. 30, 1807. | Assize of Nuisance, Dec. 7. 1807 Proclamation made and recognitors of the assize called, 15 of whom appeared, the parties to the suit were then called—the plffs. appeared by Mr. Lewis their atty. and the said Benj. Gorgas, Jacob Gorgas, appeared by Mr. Rawle their atty. and protested |

against such their appearance being construed into an admission of the regularity of the plaintiff proceeding in any respect whatever, the said John Weiss saith he is seized of the premises in the count of the plaintiff mentioned, wherein the said dam, &c. are alleged to have been erected, and prays leave to present to the court an affidavit by him made, which is granted, and the said affidavit is read and filed. Whereupon the said John Weiss prays that the view in the said assize may be set aside, he the said John Weiss not having had a reasonable notice thereof, as he alleges. The court thereupon having heard the plaintiffs, by their counsel, and the said John Weiss, by his counsel, refuse the said prayer of the said John.

The action was then removed by certiorari to the supreme court.

Whereupon a summons to the recognitors issued from the said supreme court, as follows:

The Commonwealth of Pennsylvania, to the Sheriff of Phila-
  delphia County,   GREETING.

WE command you that you cause to come before our justices

of our supreme court, or one of them, at a court of nisi prius to be holden at Philadelphia, for the county of Philadelphia, on the 19th day of the present month of April, at 10 o'clock of the forenoon of the same day, the recognitors of assize, namely, Abraham Duffield, Daniel Thomas (inserting all their names) who were summoned and returned by the late sheriff of the same county as recognitors of assize in certain plaint of assize of nuisance prosecuted in our court of common pleas, for the same county by John Livezey and Jacob Livezey, against Benjamin Gorgas, (insert all the defendants) which said plaint of assize has been removed by our writ of certiorari from our said county court into our supreme court, when the same is still pending before our justices of the same court, so that the recognitors of assize may recognize, &c. and pass on the said plaint of assize between the parties aforesaid, and have you then and there this writ together with the names of the said recognitors as you shall answer.

Tested, &c. as usual in other cases.

RETURN.

April 2. 1811.

Summoned the within recognitors, viz. Abraham Duffield, Daniel Thomas, (ut supra) and nil habet as to Isaac Keen, and John Keen, who are dead.

So answers,

JOHN SNYDER.

Afterwards there issued a second summons to defaulting recognitors, (return ut supra.)

April 26, 1811, *Supreme court, nisi prius, coram* BRACKENRIDGE, *Justice.*

1. Recognitors being first called—writ of assize was read by Mr. Lewis.

2. Sheriffs' return then read—all of which papers were then filed.

3. Writ of certiorari read.

4. Return read.

5. Plaint read, as follows,

John Livezey and Joseph Livezey *v.* Benjamin Gorgas, and Jacob Gorgas, John Weiss, George Horter and Catherine his wife, Joseph Weiss, William Struper, and Jacob Weiss, *Defendants.* — In the supreme court of Pennsylvania, for Philadelphia county, of the term of March, A. D. 1808.

The assize cometh to recognize if Benjamin Gorgas, and

3 K

Jacob Gorgas, John Weiss, George Horter and Catherine his wife, Joseph Weiss, William Struper, and Jacob Weiss, unjustly and without judgment, have levied and raised a certain wall and dam, thereby obstructing a certain mill race and water course in the township of Roxborough, in the county of Philadelphia, to the nuisance of the freehold of John Livezey and Joseph Livezey, situated in the same township and county, within thirty years now last past; and therefore the said John Livezey and Joseph Livezey, by William Lewis, their attorney, complain that the said John Livezey and Joseph Livezey, on the first day of January, A. D. 1793, were and still are seized in their demesne, as of fee of and in one water mill, ten acres of meadow, ten acres of pasture, and ten acres of arable land, situated in the township and county aforesaid, together with a certain water course and stream of water, running along the said mill race and water course, and along the said ten acres of meadow, ten acres of pasture, and ten acres of arable land, to and from the water wheel of the same mill, which said water mill before the levying and raising of the said wall and dam, and the obstructing of the said mill race and water course, could by each day and night grind 200 bushels of bread corn; and the said John Livezey and Joseph Livezey, being so thereof seized, the said Benjamin Gorgas, and Jacob Gorgas, John Weiss, George Horter, and Catherine his wife, Joseph Weiss, William Struper, and Jacob Weiss, on the day and year aforesaid, at the county and township aforefaid, unjustly and without judgment, levied and raised a certain wall and dam, thereby obstructing the said mill race and water course, and the said stream of water running from said mill, by reason whereof the said mill cannot grind more than 20 bushels of bread corn by each day and night, to the nuisance of the freehold of the said John Livezey and Joseph Livezey, and so they, the said John Livezey and Joseph Livezey, say, they are injured and damage have sustained to the value of five thousand dollars, lawful money of the United States, and therefore they bring this assize.

Pledges to prosecute } JOHN DOE,
                      { RICHARD ROE.

6. Plaintiffs called, viz. John Livezey and Joseph Livezy, come forth and prosecute your writ of assize.

The plaintiffs appear by Mr. Lewis their attorney.

7. Defendants called, viz: Benjamin Gorgas, and Jacob Gorgas, John Weiss, George Horter, and Catherine his wife, Joseph

Weiss, William Struper, and Jacob Weiss, come into court or else this assize will be taken against you by default.

Benjamin Gorgas, Jacob Gorgas, and John Weiss appear by Mr. Rawle, their attorney.

8. The other defendants being called three times, and not appearing,. Mr. Lewis prays as follows.: Sir, I pray that the assize may be taken by default.

Per curiam. Let it be so.

9. Mr. Lewis then arraigns the assize by again reading the writ and the plaint, and then thus addresses the court:

" You well understand that John Livezey and Joseph Livezey have arraigned an assize of nuisance to their freehold in Roxborough, against Benjamin Gorgas, and Jacob Gorgas, John Weiss, George Horter, and Catherine his wife, Joseph Weiss, William Struper, and Jacob Weiss, and I pray, that, as to George Horter, and Catherine his wife, Joseph Weiss, William Struper, and Jacob Weiss, it may be taken by default."

10. Defaulters again called forth three times thus: Come forth or this assize will be taken by your default.

Mr. Lewis—Sir, I pray that this assize may be taken by default.

An agreement of the following kind was then filed.

" I agree not to object to the regularity of this case, proceeding in this court, in the record returned, by reason of the non-appearance of five of the defendants, who were returned nil habent, i. e. the record shall be considered in this court as fully as it was in the common pleas, but waving no other objection."

(Signed) WILLIAM RAWLE,
For B. and J. Gorgas, and John Weiss.

11. Mr. Lewis files the plaint and calls upon the defendants to plead; defendants, though entitled to an adjournment of some hours, agree to plead instanter saving their rights.

Plea,

Livezey,
v.
Gorgas.

And now, to wit, at this same term comes as well the said Benjamin Gorgas and the said Jacob Gorgas, by their attorney aforesaid, as the said John Weiss by his attorney aforesaid, and

defends the force and injury when, &c. and the said Benjamin and
Jacob, pray judgment of the writ aforesaid, because they say
that the said wall and dam, which they the said John and Joseph
Livezey above complain and unjustly allege, was erected, levied,
and raised by the said Benjamin and Jacob Gorgas, and the said
John Weiss, who is above impleaded jointly with the said Benjamin and Jacob, to the nuisance of the said John and Joseph, was
at the county aforesaid, erected, levied, and raised by a certain
John Gorgas, long since deceased, in and upon the freehold of
him the said John Gorgas, as well he might, and not by them the
said Benjamin and Jacob Gorgas, and John Weiss, or any of them,
which said John Gorgas afterwards, to wit, on the first day of
January, 1781, at the county aforesaid, died seized in his demesne,
as of fee of and in the said tenements whereof and wherein the
said wall and dam was erected, having first made his last will and
testament according to the form of the act of assembly in that
case made and provided, and thereby and therein devised the said
tenements, together with all his other lands, mills, tenements, and
hereditaments to his five sons and four daughters, to wit, John,
Benjamin, Jacob, &c. &c. &c. (reciting a chain of deeds and conveyances and the entry and seizin under each of them,) to a
certain John Weiss, and his heirs, who by virtue thereof entered
and was seized as the law requires; and so the said John Weiss
became in his lifetime seized of the whole of the said tenements whereon, &c. in his demesne as of fee and being so
thereof seized, the said John afterwards, to wit, on the ——— day
of July, A. D. 1803, at the county aforesaid, died so seized, after
whose death the said tenements descended to Catherine, the wife
of the said George, to the said John who is now impleaded, to
Joseph Weiss, to Ann who is married to a certain William
Struper, and to Jacob who is now an infant under the age of 21
years, the heirs of him the said John, by virtue whereof the said
Catherine and George, in right of the said Catherine, the said
John and Joseph, the said Ann and William, in the right of the
said Ann and the said Jacob, who is now an infant, then and there
before the   of the said writ into the tenements whereon, &c. entered, and whereof seized, as the law requires; and this
they are ready to verify. Wherefore they pray judgment of the
said writ, and of this they put themselves on the assize; and they
bring here into court the said several writs, deeds, and indentures
above mentioned, &c. and if not the said Benjamin and Jacob, by
their attorney aforesaid, defend the force and injury when, &c. and

say that the assize aforesaid between them and the said John and Joseph ought not to be taken, because they say that they did not erect, levy and raise the said wall and dam, thereby obstructing the said mill race and water course, and the stream of water running from the said mill, nor obstruct and direct the said mill race, water course, and stream of water, to the nuisance of the freehold of the said John and Joseph Livezey, in manner and form as the said John and Joseph have complained against them; and of this they put themselves on the assize.

And if not the said John by his attorney aforesaid, defends the force and injury when, &c. and says that the assize between him and the said John and Joseph ought not to be taken, because he says that he did not erect levy and raise the said wall and dam, thereby obstructing the said mill race and water course, and the stream of water running from the said mill, nor obstruct nor direct the said mill race and water course and stream of water to the nuisance of the freehold of the said John and Joseph Livezey, in manner and form as the said John and Joseph Livezey, have complained against him, and of this he *puts himself* on the assize.

Replication to be reduced to form hereafter.

13. The plaintiffs reply that the defendants, Benjamin Gorgas, Jacob Gorgas, John Weiss, and the other defendants, did levy and raise the said wall and dam, to the nuisance of the freehold of the said John Livezey and Joseph Livezey, in manner, &c. and of this in like manner put themselves on the assize.

And so issue was formed.

14. The assize was then called and each separately asked by the clerk if they had viewed the place—six or more having answered affirmatively, the clerk then administered to 12 of them the following oath or affirmation.

You shall well and truly try this matter of assize between the parties according to your evidence.

When the assize has sworn or affirmed.—They were thus charged by the clerk.

Gentlemen recognitors of assize,

You are to enquire whether the defendants, unjustly and without judgment, (as in the words of the plaintiff,) within 30 years last past, and if they did then you are to enquire what costs and damages the plaintiffs have sustained by reason of such levying, &c. (ut supra) and if they did not levy raise, &c. (ut supra) then you are to say so and no more and so stand together and hear your *evidence*.

The plaintiffs counsel then reads the plaint and opens the case going on first to prove the freehold to be in the plaintiffs, and 2ly, the nature of the nuisance done thereto—insisting that the defendants dam, &c. was not only an injury to the plaintiffs mill, but also injured his freehold and prevented him from building another mill.

Sheriffs' notice to the recognitors.

April 1. 1811.

Sꜰʀ,

You are hereby summoned to be and appear before the judges of the supreme court of Pennsylvania, or one of them at a court of nisi prius, to be held at Philadelphia, on the 19th day of the present month of April, at ten o'clock in the forenoon, as a recognitor of assize in an assize of nuisance wherein John Livezey and another are plaintiffs, and Benjamin Gorgas and others are defendants.

For Francis Johnston, Sheriff,

Thomas Elliot, deputy.

.Mr. Benjamin Cottman.

Lewis for plaintiff: contended that in cases of nuisance every man has 3 remedies: 1st, to prostrate it himself; 2d, to bring an action on the case and recover damages, and 3dly, to bring an assize of nuisance in order to remove the offending cause and to recover damages for the injury sustained in case of an obstinate person. The last was the only sure and adequate remedy. 3 Blac. Comment. 220. That the law was clear and undisputable that no man had a right to use his own property so as to injure his neighbours; that a man had no right to come to his neighbour's line and throw a cup of water or even spit upon his land; that if dedendant's dam, had raised the water an inch upon the plaintiff's freehold, it was a nuisance for which an assize will lie; it is comparatively festinum remedium, wherein the tenant must plead presently and no imparlance without good cause and if there be several defendants and any one of them do not appear upon the first day, the assize shall be taken by defendant against them. 1 Salk. 82-3. Enough in this action to declare for a nuisance to the plaintiffs' freehold generally, 9 Co. 53 b. 5 Co. 100 b. Consequential damage or preventing the plaintiff from exercising a right, was a nuisance as by overhanging his house, and preventing him from raising his higher, 9 Co. 54 b. Battons case and therefore preventing the plaintiff from buildng a new mill which he had a right to do was a nuisance to his freehold; plaintiff had a right to say defendant should not raise the water upon him one inch —although such raising produced no immediate and direct damage, and that when a plain right was clearly invaded, the actual amount of damage sustained was not the important point to be considered, 2. Ld. Rayd. 958, 6 Mod. An assize will well lie for the alienee against the alienee; for if a man by a wrongful act become liable to my action, he cannot by alienation of the premises whereon the cause of action still subsists, which alienation too is his own act, deprive me of my remedy; that the statute 13 Edw. I. c. 24. giving a writ in similar cases, expressly gives the action against the alienee; that the only difference was this, by virtue of that statute, the writ must be both against the wrong doer and the alienee. That every continuance was a fresh nuisance, and therefore the alienee who continues it, is equally liable with the alienee who first levied it; that a quod permittat must be against the alienee alone, because it must always be against the tenant of the freehold; but an assize must be brought against both. A quod permittat lies as well for the alienee as against the alienee, 5 Co. 100 b. That a descent is an alienation, and the nuisance may be laid to the damage of the freehold of the plaintiffs' ancestor, ibid. It follows then, that if the whole mischief had been done by the father of the Gorgas's, that the action will lie against them, together with the other defendant, John Weiss, the tenant of the freehold. Defendants say an assize lies only against tenant of the freehold, or his servant; it is admitted that the tenant of the freehold must be joined, which has been done; but if any thing be done on the soil of a tenant of the freehold by a stranger, it will well lie against the tenant and the stranger, F. N. B. 289, 290. 3 Vin. ab. 220. pl. 16. Lilly's Reports, 53. As to notice, an assize will lie without notice against him who did the wrong; but it is admitted that notice of some kind ought to be given to the alienee. The statute does not require notice; but the courts by an equitable construction upon it, to prevent a man from being sued without knowing of demand, or having been called upon to do what is right. But defendants have been called on; they have had notice and paid money on account of this very nuisance, brought to June, 1804; and this was superior to any notice that could have been given them. There are cases in which an action is the only proper demand, 1 Mod. 175. As to notice of bonds to executors, 2 Vern, 37. 88. 11 Viner, 350. pl. 13. 2 Bac. 434, old edition. But there is no case where action is not a proper notice and demand

If, upon this notice, defendants had removed the nuisance, it would have been a good plea to this assize. But John Weiss is himself guilty of levying and raising the nuisance; he increased the height of the dam, and repaired it, and this is levying, raising, and keeping up the nuisance ; for if it leaked, and the leak was stopt by him, he thus caused the water to raise upon the plaintiffs' freehold. If it be objected the word levying is not applicable to encreasing, it is answered by saying, that in an assize the plaintiff may abridge his demand. It is said the defendants' dam is no higher than is absolutely necessary for his own purposes ; but this is clearly no answer to our complaint. For if a man wishes to build a mill, and cannot do it without raising the water upon my freehold, he has no right to do it without my consent; and this privilege is as fair a subject of purchase, bargain, and sale as any other that can be imagined. The nuisance must be so abated as to completely redress the injury but must be done in a convenient manner, and the materials of which the thing abated is composed, belong to the defendant. Sir William Jones' Reports, 222-3.

Mr. Rawle for defendant, argued that Mr. Weiss was sole seized, and that the other defendants had no interest in the premises whereon, &c. since 1796. That the action was not maintainable by the alienee against the alienee, 2 Lutw. 1588, is so expressly, 2 Ins. 406. 404. 405. 12 Mod. 639, that a devise was an alienation, 2 Black. Com. 289, or transfer, 1 Dall. 170, that he who pursues a special remedy must pursue it strictly. If the father disseized, A. and died seized the disseizee is put to his writ of right, and cannot have an assize, 2 Roll. ab. 142. Assize lies against heir only, when he refuses to reform the nuisance, ibid—1 Vent. 48. 1 Mod. 27. 16 Vin. ab. 33. Jenk. Cent. 250—The plaintiff must precede his action by giving notice of what it is he requires to be done, and whereon the same previously requires a request, it must be proved, and no action lies till request. 1 Saund. 33. If he who originally erected the alleged nuisance had been living, he might have been joined with the alienee, but as he is dead, and his heirs or the alienee have done nothing to increase the nuisance, but used it as formerly, and as the alienee had notice to discontinue it. The assize as brought cannot be supported. That keeping a thing in repair, in the same state in which the tenant found it when he came into possession, can by no means be considered erecting it— No evidence to shew the plaintiff had suffered any damage. If there is water in the plaintiffs tail race, it is owing to a natural obstruction in the stream, which it is in the power of the plaintiff to recover.

That the assize would only enquire whether there was an actual damage at the time of bringing the assize, and that they had no right to take into consideration any pretended intention the plaintiffs might allege they had of erecting a new mill.

John and Joseph Livezey vs. Benjamin and Jacob Gorgas, John Weiss, and others.

Assize of nuisance; erecting a dam, obstructing a mill race and water course.

10th Oct. 1747, freehold in Thomas Livezey as to part. 9th Aug. 1760, freehold in Thomas Livezey as to the other part. This by title deduced from the proprietary.

15th June, 1790, devise of Thomas Livezey, Joseph and John Livezey.

30th Nov. 1807, notice to defendant to produce papers.

These produced, purporting to be receipts to defendant for money paid for the privelege of keeping up dam according to agreement.

The first, 19th April, 1775, Livezey to Gorgas, £15, privilege one year for swelling the water on a part of my land.

April 1776, receipt, £15 for like privilege.

31st March 1777, £15.

5th May 1781, £15.

29th May 1782, J. and B. Gorgas executors, £55 sum then due.

This just before repeal of tender laws (depreciation money.)

29th May 1791, £10.

June 1782, receipt.

April 1785, receipt for £10 in full for liberty of keeping up, &c.

Jan. 9th, 1793, record of action brought in common pleas for the nuisance.

8th March, 1802, 480 dollars damages.

17th March, 1802, 108 dollars remitted.

Before this there had been a reference.

John Huston (sworn.)

31st March, 1783, agreement shewn to the witness purporting to be between Thomas Livezey and J. and B. Gorgas.

The witness. (Benjamin Gorgas brought this draught
with him. I was desired to witness by B. Gorgas. Not
then executed, the deed not being according to the understanding of B. Gorgas. It was lowering their water more
than agreed upon.)

It is now offered to be read. It is a draught of a writing
to be executed with alterations in favour of Gorgas, in the
hand writing of J. Sergeant, who was of counsel for Gorgas.

It is admitted and read as *evidence of the sense* of the
parties at the time.

John Gorgas (sworn.)

As to Weiss repairing the dam, &c.

Earnest Felty (sworn) as to the nuisance.

Reading Howell (sworn) as to the nuisance.

Titus Yearkus (sworn) these as to the nuisance.

Suit of 1791, for this nuisance.

Nov. 1794, read suit vs. Gorgas.

Barker late Sheriff (sworn) as to holding the inquest under an order from the orphans' court for a valuation in partition of this mill and tract of land adjoining.

It is proposed to ask the sheriff whether an allowance
was not made in the partition in consequence of the reduced
value of the mill by this nuisance.

Question; whether he was not present with the jury in
fixing this value; and whether a reduction of some hundred
pounds was not made?

Exception to the question, as not the best evidence. P.
Curiam. If any note by the Jury appeared on the proceedings as the ground of valuation, this would be the best evidence. The next best evidence are the jury themselves; or
some of them. This is secondary and cannot be admitted.

Joseph Storm (sworn.)

Nothing taken into view as to this. I was one of the
jury.

Rawle pro def.

Gorgas (sworn) as to these being the only papers he has : article, &c.

George Ayres (sworn) was a referee in case of Gorgas and Livezey. Cannot say as to other papers laid before us.

Thomas Holmes (sworn) was one of the referees.; papers laid before us : both parties said these were all the papers.

Alexander Martin one of the referees. All papers laid before the referees. No complaint of any kept back.

10th Feb. 1782, deed ; Benjamin Gorgas to Jacob.

1st April, 1796, Jacob to Weiss and Thatcher, subject to all charges on the land.

6th October, 1800, Thatcher to Weiss, now seized of the whole.

July, 1803, Weiss (old) died leaving 5 children.

15th March, 1804, Petition to orphans' court, order and proceedings.

16th Aug. 1806, prior to proceedings on the assize, freehold in Weiss alone.

28th May, 1780, original will of J. Gorgas (read.)

Devise is an alienation. It will be contended no writ of assize in such case, there being here alienee of devisee ; that is alienee of alienee.

The statute which gave the writ casu consimili extends only to the alienee.

So a writ of assize does not lie versus alienee of alienee.

2d. Will insist that as against heir or alienee this writ will not lie, unless on request made to heir or alienee. Law respects descent cast.

It is not pretended that request has been made to J. Weiss, the son (present deft.)

3d. Defendant must be seized of the freehold, or be servants of those who are.

NOTE : This observed with regard to the others mentioned in the writ.

1774, J. Gorgas lived on the land ; Livezey, a representative in the legislature. Reference and the award. NOTE ; this to ground a presumption that Gorgas was overreached by Livezey in the arbitration ; article of agreement, &c. the one weak, the other wise.

Livezey v. Gorgas ; action brought.

Sept. 1794, Rule of reference ; report made ; exceptions for plaintiff overruled by court, and report confirmed. Writ of error

and appeal. Judgment reversed (supreme court.) Record remitted. Venire, issue, &c.

Declaration and plea in this suit, verdict of jury (read.)

Exception to the report being read, as it had been set aside.

The reading overruled. It is a nullity.

Andrew Hay, (sworn) to shew not a nuisance.

John Boyer, (sworn) to the same effect.

Richard Griffith, (sworn) to the same effect.

Samuel Gorgas, (sworn) to the same effect.

Benjamin Gorgas, (sworn) as to papers in his possession; has
no others to produce.

Authorities will be relied on.

Salk. 82, of the nature of assize.

3 Black. 220.

Take notice, &c.

10th October, 1797, Livezey purchased.

9th August, 1760, purchased other land. So, *proprietor of
land on both sides stream:* had in view to build another mill.
Barendollar, from whom he purchased on one side of the stream,
never disputed.

Andrew Heath, (sworn) must have been young, so might not
have heard of complaint.

Authorities continued.

2d Ray. 958, Right of vote in an elector.

6 Mod. The minimum of right in an election.

9 Coke, 54, b. An impediment to build is a nuisance; and remedied by him impeded, before he builds.

13th Ed. I. c. 24. As to remedy to be extended to alienee of
alienee.

Heir and devisee are alienees.

13th Mod. 639, assize must be versus alienee.

3 Wollaston, 189.

5 Coke, 100, b.

9 Coke, 53. Erected to the nuisance of the ancestor; descent
cast, &c.

Fitzherbet, Nat. brev. 289. Acts done by a stranger not tenant of the freehold. It lies against him who did the tort, and against
the terre-tenant.

3d Viner, 220, pl. 16.

Lilly's R. 53. Tenant of freehold must always be made defendant as well as those who did the wrong.

Per Curiam.

But in this case has not rent been paid by the son of Livezey to Gorgas; a draught of the article in their hand writing?

Rawle; I speak of request.

Lewis; I turn to the statute to show that it does not require it ; and it is only a conclusion by the court, as to what is reasonable. The bringing the action, a request. Action by plaintiff v. the two Gorgas's; reference, &c. June, 1804, an assize v. B. and J. Gorgas, and J. Weiss. Was not this notice? This three years before the present action.

1 Mod. 175. There are cases where as to notice it must be by action. But in all cases notice.

2 Viner, 27, 88, same. 2d Viner, 350, P. L. 13. Debt versus executors, &c. 2 Bac. 434.

This is notice to all three defendants. But Weiss has himself raised the dam and continued the nuisance.

Receipts by Gorgas shews, that while they continued to pay, it did not raise higher than height agreed upon. Maintaining and keeping up dam, is not that a trespass?

Rawle, in continuance.

Mill has not been impeded for an hour, or a minute.

But the present incumbrance is by an heir of the devisee; notice is necessary ; for

May 27th, 1780, devised by Gorgas to J. and B. Gorgas.

31st August, 1782, B. to J.

2d September, 1782. J. became seized of the whole.

1st April, 1796, deed to Weiss and Thatcher.

6th October, 1800, conveyance to Weiss, father of defendant, by Thatcher.

July, 1803, deed to G. Weiss.

Since April, 1796, J. and B. Gorgas had no concern. Weiss the now tenant of the freehold.

J. and B. Gorgas did not build a dam in the first instance, nor had any concern with a tenant.

Statute does not apply to alienee of alienee.

2 Lutwitch, 1588. Note, Stat. Will. 2. c. 24. which gives, does not extend to alienee.

2 Inst. 406, reading of Coke upon statute.

12 Mod. 639, if alienee dies, the party must have a writ of entry in the per, and not an assize.

2 Black. Com. 287.

1 Dall. 170. Transfer, a devise.

Now as to request.

2 Levintz, 153, case of notice which does not come up to request.

2 Rolle, 142, pl. 1. if a man erect, &c.

1 Vent. 48. 1 Mod. 27. 16 Vin. 33.

Jenkin's Centuries, 260.

P. C. This seems most to the point; but notice by action see.

1 Saunders, 33, demand necessary, if he originally erecting is still alive, he may be joined; but where dead, &c.

Dall. pro quer.

2 Questions.

1. What are the rights of the plaint?

2. What the remedy?

The bringing the action proves the law.

The elastic nature of the common law. ·

In an action on the case, can bring into view only damages before the suit brought.

Traces the chain of title; evidence of the nuisance. Compares the testimony, &c. &c.

Per Curiam, to the Jury.

The proprietor of the soil through which a stream runs, cannot divert it from its natural bed, save within his own bounds; and if even within his own bounds, he diverts it, he must be answerable that it is brought back to its bed before it passes the boundary below; nor could he divert it within his own bounds so as to waste it, and lessen the quantity that would have come to him below. He must use his stream so as not to diminish it to him to whom it is next to come. He cannot change its natural channel. The proprietor below has a right to the stream as it came to him by the usual supply of nature, so far as that no act of him above shall otherwise, than by a reasonable use, diminish it. The proprietor above cannot say, the stream is lessened, it is true, by the course I have given it, but it does you no damage; you have enough still. That answer will not suffice; it goes only to the *quantum of the injury, and the aggravation of it.* It is sufficient if the quantity of water is reduced unreasonably, that would otherwise have descended to him that is below. What is against his consent is a wrong.

He must be the judge of what he wants; and whether the lessening is a help or a hurt. This is not ideal. The owner of the soil above may have it in his power maliciously to waste the water, by turning it where it would sink in part and disappear; or he might, to serve another, turn the stream through his ground, and give it a new channel. I take it that an action on the case would lie for such a deprivation.

Be that as it may, the law is clear that the owner of the soil above has a right to the stream in its natural state; unincreased in depth by him below. That is, he has a right to the fall and current of the stream through his land, with the same descent at the boundary below that it had in its natural state. The proprietor below cannot increase the depth of the stream above by any impediment, so as to be justifiable.

But he cannot increase the depth above, otherwise than by flooding some of the soil, making that a part of the channel which was not before.

In the application of this principle it is true, as in the application of the principles of law in all cases, the maxim of, de minimis, occurs; the law will not regard small things. But what is the meaning of this maxim? It is that the law will not force us to put on glasses to see the minimum. But if seen it must be noticed. I will not say that the throwing back the water a single line would force itself upon you, and compel redress. For it must be an excess that is visible to the naked eye; that is discernable to every vision that will call for the interposition of the law. This reduces it to the practicable in the affairs of men.

But admitting that there is even a line of flooding on the land of another, or swell of the water, by reason of an impediment of the current, and that it is ascertained to be so, how can I say that it is not a trespass, and the subject of legal notice. Say an increase that but begins to be such, yet if it is such, how can I get over it? Give an inch, take an ell. Where shall we stop? Apply these principles to the case before us, and it will be seen whether a trespass exists. According to the testimony of some of the witnesses, it would seem to be a trespass not of lines; nor of inches; but of feet. The back water not only goes to the mill, the distance of many perches, but rises on the wheel three and one half inches; so that the wheel wades, as the phrase is, and is impeded in a revolution. If one inch at the mill, what must be the overflow at the division line? The how much goes to the quantum of damages, the overflowing at all goes to the trespass.

It has been alleged that the swell at the mill, is in part owing to rocks below within the plaintiff's own ground. That may be in part, but it is not wholly so.

As to the agreement that has been given in evidence, it goes to shew the understanding of the parties at the time, both as to what might be an overflowing, and a compensation for it. This will be considered. The question nevertheless is still open whether there actually was a raising of the dam in this case, to throw back the water and flood the soil of the plaintiff. Nothing that has happened by agreement, or otherwise, can bar the investigation.

I lay the legal questions out of the case. I reserve the points; though it would not seem to me at present that there is a great deal in them. A devisee may be considered as for some purposes, a transferee, or alienee; but is so identified in his interest with that of the testator, that his situation may seem to be different from that of a purchaser, so as to be considered such an alienee that the writ would not lie against him, or that notice should be necessary. But in this case there has been notice by action and otherwise; the lis pendens, the notoriety of the dispute; the defendant in doing acts himself, adding to the nuisance and continuing it. But these matters will be considered in bank. The jury need not charge their minds with a consideration of these at present. I will reserve them for the consideration of the judges in term; a mere matter of fact will at present be left to the jury; is there a trespass or nuisance, by the defendant, upon the land of the plaintiff, and how much the damages?

Livezey,
v.
Gorgas.
} May 3d, 1811.

Verdict.

And the recognitors of assize aforesaid, say, that the said John Livezey, and Joseph Livezey, were seized in their demesnes as of fee of and in the water mill, mill race, water course, stream of water, and lands and tenements with the appurtenances—in the said plaint mentioned, and as therein specified, and as the said John and Joseph Livezey, have above declared. And further the recognitors aforesaid, say that the above mentioned Benjamin Gorgas, Jacob Gorgas and John Weiss, unjustly and without judgment, the said certain wall and dam, in the view of the said recognitors placed, and in the said plaint specified, did levy and raise to the height of 2 inches and one half of one inch from a line 2 inches and a half below the lower edge of a certain hole of one inch diameter, bored in the rock at the eastermost end of the said dam thereby obstructing the said mill race and water course, and the said stream of water running from the said mill of the said John Livezey and Joseph Livezey, to the nuisance of the said freehold of the said John Livezey and Joseph Livezey, but not with force and arms, as the said John and Joseph Livezey, have above complained. And the recognitors aforesaid assess the damages of the said John Livezey and Joseph Livezey, occasioned by the obstruction and nuisance aforesaid, beyond their costs and charges, by them in their suit aforesaid expended at $ 533 and $\frac{33}{100}$ and for their costs and charges aforesaid, at 6 cents. And as to the other defendants, the recognitors aforesaid find in their favour.

" Whereby he is endamaged to such a value." 3 Bl. Com. 295.

ACCORDING to the old doctrine, *the sum must be certain, and declared upon as such.* Hence, it has been a question, whether, on a declaration on a bond, or covenant, a jury may not find damages, beyond the penalty. Whatever technical embarrassment there may have been, or may still be, in a court of law in England, as to this matter, there is none, and ought to be none, with us. But as to *the sum given by the verdict*, being *more* than the *sum* laid in the declaration, that is a technical objection which has received some countenance *by implication*, but on which I do not know of any decision. The *implication* I speak of, is, the *remititur* which, ex majore cautela, it has been usual to make. I have known counsel remit from an honest and fair demand, where, from some oversight, the sum laid, had happened to fall short; and it appeared to me to be one of those technical formalities, which are in the way of substantial justice, that was thought, to render this *remitting* necessary. The principles are correct, and further justice, that the writ shall agree with the precipe; the declaration with the writ; the evidence with the declaration; the verdict with the evidence; and that the judgment shall correspond with the verdict; and the execution pursue the judgment. But the less or more of the sum laid in the declaration ought not to affect. The more does not affect; and why should the less? It is as immaterial as the day laid, and ought to be so held. It is not what a plaintiff demands, but what he proves, that is, and ought to be the measure of his damages. In an action of slander, words spoken, since the action brought, that *are not of a nature to support a new action, and import a continuance of the same slander*, may be given in evidence, at least, according to some authorities, in aggravation of the damages, and these words may have been spoken, since the declaration filed. Be that as it may, I take it, that in an action for assault, battery, and wounding, evidence may be given of an injury consequent upon the battery, and the effect of it, even after the declaration filed; as the loss of an eye, or the use of a limb; and this may entitle to greater damages, than was in the contemplation of the party, at the time of the suit brought, or the filing of the declaration. But I do not see any principle of justice that could be in the way of a recovery, if it should have *so happened* that the suitor had omitted to make an application for leave to amend.

The idea of a plaintiff recovering no more damages than he counts for, held with great propriety and good reason, in

detinue and in debt; in *detinue*, because the judgment is to
have the thing detained; and damages, if the thing itself
cannot be had. The value which the plaintiff has, himself
set upon the article, must be taken to be the measure.
Jenk. 218, pl. 25. This principle has been transferred, without examination, into other actions, where the reason does
not apply. This, where the jury do not *first* look at the value of the thing in controversy, and then find damages as a
consequence; but, at the damages in the first instance, for
the wrong done.

" The whole of this process is denominated the pleading." 3
Bl. Com. 310.

THERE is a *variation* in the *practice* of the Pennsylvania
courts from that of England; not in principle, but in the lesser length of the *pleadings.* The *original process* is *shorter,*
because an *ac etiam;* or *quo minus;* or other *fiction,* is not
necessary to give a court jurisdiction; which is the case in
that of the king's bench, or exchequer, where jurisdiction is
taken of matters that properly belong to the court of *common
pleas.* But the process of summons, or capias, or other writ,
is the same, substituting the name of the *commonwealth* for
that of the *king.* The *declaration* also, which is the next
step in the cause, on the part of the plaintiff, is the same;
and therefore we take the English forms which are devised,
in the different kinds of action, to give a *statement* of the
demand in the fewest and clearest words possible; though
attornies will add count upon count, where a single one might
suffice. These will be sometimes necessary; because the
party, or the attorney for him, may not be able always to
know what he will be able to make out, or prove. As for
instance, in a count, or statement, he may allege that the defendant contracted to pay him *so much* for a certain article
which he sold, and delivered to him. He may not be certain that he will be able to make out that it was at such a

certain price; and, therefore, he will allege that having sold, and delivered such article, the defendant agreed to pay him *as much as it was worth.* The same in the case of labour, or service done and performed : the same in all cases, where if he should not be able to make out the demand in one way he might in another.

By our act of Assembly, 21 March, 1806, Sec. 5, it is provided, " That in all cases where a suit is or may be brought in any court of record within this commonwealth, for the recovery of any debt founded on a verbal promise, book account, note, bond, penal, or single bill, or all, or any of them, and which from the amount thereof may not be cognizable before a justice of the peace, it shall be the duty of the plaintiff, either by himself, his agent or attorney, to file in the office of the prothonotary, a statement of his, her or their demand on or before the third day of the term, to which the process issued is returnable ; particularly specifying the date of the promise, book account, note, bond, penal, or single bill, or all, or any of them, on which the demand is founded, and the whole amount what he, she or they believe is justly due to him, her or them from the defendant; and it shall be the duty of the defendant, at least twenty days before the next succeeding term to which the process issued is returnable, to file in the office aforesaid, either by himself, his agent or attorney, a statement of his, her or their account, if any he or she hath against the plaintiff's demand, and particularly specifying what he, she or they believe is justly due from him, her or them to the plaintiff; and it shall be the duty of the prothonotary to file, without the agency of an attorney, such statements; and it shall be the duty of the parties to appear in their proper persons, by their agents or attornies, on the third day of the next succeeding term, to which the process issued is returnable, when the term is for one week, and on the second Monday of the term when the same is to continue two weeks, before the court, which shall have issued the same ; but if the plaintiff or plaintiffs shall neglect to appear as aforesaid, the court shall order a non-suit to be entered; and if the plaintiff shall appear, but the defendant or defendants shall neglect to appear as aforesaid, and make defence against the demand of the plaintiff or plaintiffs, it shall be the duty of the court to give judgment by default against the defendant for the sum which shall appear to be due; but if the parties appear as aforesaid, and the defendant refuse to confess judgment, the cause shall be tried by a jury, or on the agreement of the parties, it may be referred agreeably to the provisions of this act; and the plaintiff's atttorney shall not be entitled to a judgment fee, in any action of debt, whether the judgment be confessed by the defendant or rendered on the report of referees, or on the verdict of a jury; and if the plaintiff on trial being had as aforesaid, does not recover more than the amount for which the defendant was willing to confess judgment, he shall not recover any costs that accrued on the cause subsequent to the offer of confessing judgment, excepting the costs of issuing and serving a writ of execution when the same may be necessary."

Our courts, in every case before this act, where the *declaration* was not sufficiently *explicit*, to enable a defendant to know what demand to meet, would direct a special *statement* of the items to be filed; and this in matters of account was always done, if the party demanded it. And, it was also a rule in most districts, that the declaration or statement should be filed at the *return of the process*, or during the term, if an appearance had been entered, or special bail to the action, if in a case that bail could be required.

I do not see any thing gained by this act; for surely the party might always have been his own attorney. It is provided by the constitution, that " he shall be heard by himself or his counsel."

The idea of the legislature was, to enable the better *every man to be his own lawyer.* But every man will not chuse to be his own lawyer, so far as respects *the conduct of a suit in court;* for he will not find his account in it; any more than in being his own *blacksmith* or *taylor.* For though there are no rules, merely *arbitrary* in *conducting,* or *defending* a suit in court, but all is founded in reason and good sense; yet, attention divided upon different objects, distracts; and the *habit* of doing a thing gives a *facility* in doing it. There is no magic in the thing, or mystery, but as the good man of *Auchtermuchty* found, according to the old tale, it was best to stick to his stots, (oxen) and let the housewife mind her kirn, (churn) and her children. But to go on with my observations to the student. Suppose yourself attorney or counsel for the defendant, what will you do on the return of process, say a summons; or rather, what can you do in any possible case?

Answer. I can object, on his behalf to the jurisdiction of the justice, or of the court, and allege that they have no cognizance of a matter in his case; he is not amenable to that tribunal. If that is overruled, I can say, he is entitled to *other process*, and move to quash the writ. If that is overruled, I can allege that the adversary has no right to sue, as being an alien enemy, or for other cause; or that the defendant ought to be sued at all, or alone, but with others, &c.

After the declaration filed, or statement made, in *abatement*, the preceding matter being overruled, I could demur to the declaration, or make a pause, and ask whether such a declaration or statement contained cause of action, &c.

This being overruled, I could plead, in bar, as we say, such as *a former recovery for the same cause of action.* All this course of proceeding, you will see in *Chitty on Pleading*, which I have just put into your hands.

Replication to your plea will be a step that may be taken on the part of the plaintiff. You demur, or make a pause and put it to the court to say, whether such a replication, is not a departure from the point, or can be made.

If this is overruled, you will rejoin, and make an answer to what he had replied to your plea. He may surrejoin until it comes to a point in issue between you. If you join issue, it closes the pleadings.

I state these things just to give an outline, and to shew that it is nothing more than bringing the parties to a point, that it may be seen what is the controversy between them.

At an early period, in England, all those matters took place at the trial when the parties came into court; and the altercation; saying that the party could not sue in that court; or sue at all from some disability; or that he could not sue alone; or that he the defendant ought not to be sued alone, but with another in the bond for instance; or that his action was frivolous, such as for grinning at him, &c. &c. But an improvement was made upon all this in due time, for the dispatch of business, and all these allegings and denials, and fending, and proving, as the phrase is, came to be put into writing. These might be in short minutes at first; but in due time, for the greater certainty, the statements came to be made, on both sides, at greater length.

All the difference then is with us that we take the midway, as it was in the second stage of the English custom, and are *entered in brief with us in Pennsylvania.*

——————

" A common jury is one returned by the sheriff according to the directions of the statute, 3 Geo. 2, c. 25, which appoints, &c.

As the jurors appear when called, they shall be sworn unless challenged by either party." 3 Bl. Com. 358.

BEFORE this statute, the sheriff summoned, *at his own discretion, unless in special cases,* inhabitants of the county. The law was the same with us in this state before the revolution and afterwards, but by acts of assembly on this head, provisions are made even in the return of a common jury, for the purpose of giving a fairer chance of an impartial selection and return.

By an act of 29th March, 1805, the sheriff and commissioners, or any two of them with the sheriff, shall meet in each county, at the seat of justice, at least thirty days previous to the first court of common pleas in each year, and select from the list of taxables, the names of a suitable number of sober and judicious persons to serve as jurors for that year, and write the name of each person so selected on a small piece of paper, each paper as nearly alike in size and shape as may be, so that the name does not appear; two wheels shall be provided, No. 1, and No. 2; the names for grand jurors shall be put in No. 1; those for petit jurors in No. 2. The wheels shall then be turned sufficiently to intermix the papers, and having first drawn from the proper wheels a number of names sufficient for the then next court, the wheels shall be locked up and sealed, &c. and so

in the same manner, thirty days previously to each succeed
ing court.

The name of each person summoned and impannelled
according to the provisions of the act, shall be written on a
distinct piece of paper, of an equal size and similar shape, as
nearly as may be, and rolled up and put into a box, and
when any cause shall be ready for trial, some disinterested
person, by direction of the court, shall in open court, after
having well mixed the papers, draw out one after another,
until a sufficient number shall appear and be approved.

A supplement to this act, passed 4th Ap. 1807, provides,
that whenever process shall be issued for summoning a jury,
the sheriff shall immediately give notice to the commissioners, who shall proceed to draw a sufficient number of jurors
for the next court.

By an act passed 4th April, 1809, it is provided, that, " in
all civil suits, each party shall be allowed to challenge two
jurors peremptorily; and in all criminal prosecutions wherein peremptory challenges have not heretofore been permitted
by law, the defendant or defendants shall be allowed to challenge four jurors peremptorily."*

By sec. 12, of the act of 21 March, 1772, which provides
the manner of giving possession to the landlord, where
tenant holds over, a jury of *substantial freeholders* is directed to be summoned.

In the case of special juries, our law is similar to that under the statute 3 Geo. 2, c. 35.

---

* This improvement in a trial by jury, and it is a great improvement, was on the suggestion, and at the instance of the lately
deceased Mr. Mountain, of Pittsburgh, of whom, *did the nature of
this publication* permit an eulogium on his personal *integrity* and
professional *talents*, I should have much to say, but the
              Sed nunc non erat his, locus———
will apply.

" Thus much for costs to which judgments are a necessary appendage." 3 Bl. Com. 399.

THE minute variations in the law of Pennsylvania from that of England, with regard to costs, are considerable. They must be collected from the acts of assembly, and the adjudications of the courts. In case of granting new trials, the act of 21 March, 1806, sec. 3, has made some variation from what the law was in this state before.

It is provided " that in all cases where a verdict of a jury shall be set aside, a new trial shall be had on the same conditions as to costs, and daily pay as are above prescribed, in cases of a new trial on the report of referees being set aside. If he shall prosecute his action, and not recover a sum equal or greater than was at first *awarded,* he shall not have judgment for costs, and shall pay the defendant seventy-five cents per day while attending on the same, and if the defendant file such exceptions, and the award be set aside by the court, and the plaintiff, by a new action, shall recover a sum equal, or greater than the original award, then and in that case, the plaintiff shall have judgment for all the costs accrued on that suit, together with seventy-five cents per day, whilst attending the same."

A new trial is granted by the English judges; and was with us before this act, on condition of paying the costs of the *former trial;* or costs to abide the event. That is, the costs of *the trial* to go into the bill; and whoever fails, pays *the whole costs in the cause.* It is to be remarked that the word *suit* is used in the act; and therefore it is the costs of the *whole proceeding* that are in question; not a particular part or portion, such as the costs which have accrued, from that *stage* to which the person applying for a new trial, wishes to be put back, which costs might be ordered to be paid down; or to abide the event.

But this section would not seem to have a reference to actions where *land* is to be recovered; for the words are, " not recover a *sum* equal or greater," which can only be in case where a *sum* is to be recovered. It would seem to be an omitted case, where land is *demanded;* and therefore the law must remain the same as it was before, *as to costs of suit,* on setting aside award, or a verdict in ejectment.

But, by the act of 20 March, 1810, considerable alterations from this act have been made, and in regard of costs. By sec. 9, " no appeal shall be allowed to either party, until the appellant pay *all the costs* that may have accrued on such *suit* or action." Quere, will not this amount nearly to *a denial of an appeal, to the poor man altogether ?* In a case lately brought from Luzerne county, by writ of error to the term at Sunbury, the costs of the different arbitrations, amounted, if I recollect right, to the sum of $ 276.

For the further amendments by this act, and the adjudications of the court upon it, I refer to 5 Smith's laws, 139.

" The king (and any person suing to his use) shall neither pay nor receive costs." 3 Bl. Com. 400.

THE acts of assembly have made a considerable alteration from the law as it is in England, with respect to costs.

By an act entitled " A supplement to the penal laws of this state," passed 23d Sept. 1791, it is provided, (sec. 11,) that costs accruing on bills returned ignoramus shall be paid by the county.

By sec. 13, of the act of 1791, the county shall pay the costs of unfounded charges, preferred before a justice of the peace or other magistrate having jurisdiction in the case.

By sec. 15, where a defendant shall be convicted of a crime punishable capitally or by imprisonment at hard labour, the county in which the crime hath been or shall be committed shall pay the costs, if defendant hath not property sufficient to discharge the same ; but where the same person hath been or shall be convicted of divers offences at the same term or sessions, the county shall pay the costs of one indictment only.

By a supplement to the penal laws of this state, March 20, 1797, " all costs accruing on all bills of indictment found by the grand jury of the city or any county in this common-wealth, charging a party with any felony, breach of the peace, or other indictable offence, shall, if such party be acquitted by a petit jury, on the traverse of the same, be paid out of the county stock, by the city or county in which the prose-cution commenced."

But it being found that these laws obliging the counties to pay the costs of prosecution where the party indicted was acquitted, tended to promote litigation, " an act to regu-late the payment of costs on indictments" was passed, 8th De-cember, 1804, which provides that " in all prosecutions, cases of felony only excepted, if the bill or bills shall be re-turned " ignoramus," the grand jury who returns the same shall decide and certify on such bill, whether the county or the prosecutor shall pay the costs of prosecution; and in all cases of acquittals, by the petit jury, on indictments for the offences aforesaid, the jury trying the same shall deter-mine, by their verdict, whether the county or the prosecutor or the defendant or defendants, shall pay the costs of prose-cution," &c.

There is an act, passed in 1805, explanatory of the act of 1804, which, as well as the *second section* of this " act ex-planatory" &c. is made perpetual by that of 29th March, 1809. See Smith's laws, in note, vol. 2, 548.

" To this real *sullenness*, but *affected timidity* of the judges, such a *narrowness* of thinking was added, that every slip (even of a syllable or a letter) was now held to be fatal to the pleader, and overturned his client's cause." 3 Bl. Com. 410.

BY the statutes of Jeofails in England, which had been adopted here, great relief had been given in case of slips of the pen or mispellings, &c. defects in process or declaration, pleading, &c. But by the 6th sec. of the act to regulate ar-

bitrations and proceedings in courts of justice, passed 21st
March, 1806, " suits brought in any court of record in this
commonwealth shall not be set aside for informality, if it
appear that process has issued in the name of the commonwealth, against the defendant for monies due, or for damages
ges by trespass, or otherwise, as the case may be, that said
process was served by the proper officer, and in due time, nor
any plaintiff non-suited for informality in any statement or declaration filed, or by reason of any informality in entering
a plea; but when in the opinion of the court, such informality will affect the merits of the cause in controversy, the plaintiff shall be permitted to amend his declaration or statement,
and the defendant may alter his plea or defence on or before the trial or cause, and if by such alteration or amendment the adverse party shall be taken by surprise, the trial
shall be postponed until the next court."

Obstinacy is the characteristic of an Englishman; irras-
cibility that of the Scot. Ea est pervicacia, says Tacitus of
the Germans. One would think, says Blackstone, that Tacitus was describing a modern Englishman, 4 Bl. Com. 171.
Per fervidum Scotorum ingenium, says Buchanan, in his
History of Scotland.

The truth is, *obstinacy* and *firmness*, spring from the same
root, virtue. It is *obstinacy* where the cause is bad; it is
firmness where the cause is good. What could make the
judges *sullen*, in regard of amendments which they had the
power to make, being within the province of the practice of
the law? I can conceive no cause, but *narrowness* of thinking, which Blackstone hints at; and, *the habit of travelling*
long in the same track. The ass is the most obstinate of all
animals; this from its nature; and, the habit of going in
the same path, produces with men a dread of innovation.
Hence the timidity of which Blackstone speaks. It is from
these reasons, that little improvement is to be expected from
the old in any theory of science. There is an attachment
to prescription in physicians, to *precedent* in lawyers, and
they are afraid to depart from rule. Old generals are afraid
of *accidents*, says Marshal Berwick in his Memoirs. They

have character to lose; and by according to what has been done before, they *risk less* than in departing from it; for they have precedent to justify. And it is in the application of the rule to the case, that the judgment errs. *Departure* from rule can be justified only by *success*.

Judges would not undertake to amend pleadings, because they had no precedent of this, or that, being amended; and hence at an early period the first statute of Jeofails, 14 Ed. 3. c. 6. viz. "That by the misprision, wheresoever it be, no process shall be annulled, or discontinued by mistaking in writing, *one syllable*, or *one letter*, too much or too little; but as soon as the thing is perceived by challenge of the party, or in other manner, it shall be hastily amended, in due form, without giving advantage to the party that challengeth the same, because of such misprision."

The timidity of judges arises a good deal from a respect for the profession; and strict practitioners, who are not always the most enlightened upon general principles, consider it as affecting the craft to lessen *mystery*, or to detract from *precedent*. With regard to these, it is to be observed, that, in some measure, small lawyers at least, find their account in it; and it may be said of them, hac arte vivitur; by this craft do they live. We see therefore the expediency of the provisions of this act of the legislature, which is more than has been provided by any of the English statutes; and is an improvement of the practice as it was before, in this state.

———————

"If the plaintiff recovers in an action real or mixed, whereby the seisin or possession of land is awarded to him, the writ of execution shall be an *habere facias seisinam*, or writ of seisin of a freehold——" 3 Bl. Com. 412.

BY the law of England, unless in the case of a chattel interest, which, upon a fieri facias, is taken possession of by the sheriff, he cannot make delivery to the purchaser; so that, in case of the sale of a *freehold* interest, the purchaser must recur to his ejectment; and, after recovery, must have an habere facias possessionem to enable the officer to give possession. In the case of the sale of a *lease-hold* interest, which is a chattel real, possession may be immediately given. The case in 2 *Shower*, 85, which lays it down, that, " on the sale of a *term*, the sheriff cannot turn out the tenant but the vendee must bring an ejectment, was cited in the case of Taylor v. Cole, 8 T. R. 298, and yet there, justice Buller gives it as his opinion, that the sheriff might turn out the tenant." Addison's Rep. 204, Pennsylvania v. Kirpatrick and Menaugh.

In this case possession had been taken by the purchaser under a sale by the sheriff without bringing an ejectment, and recovery, and writ of habere facias. But an indictment of forcible entry and detainer was the consequence; and there was *judgment for the commowealth*, and restitution awarded. The observations of judge Addison in that case led to an act passed 6 Ap. 1802, " To enable purchasers at sheriff's or coroner's sales to obtain possession," which provides, that where lands shall be sold by the sheriff, by virtue of an execution, the purchaser may give notice to the defendant, or person, in possession, and require him to surrender the possession within three months : on refusal to surrender, the purchaser may complain to any two justices of the county, who on due proof, &c. shall issue their summons to the sheriff, commanding him to summon before the justices, twelve freeholders, and also the defendant to shew cause why delivery of possession should not be forthwith made, and if on hearing the parties, or non-appearance of the defendant, the jury find against the defendant, the justices may make a record of the same, assess damages, and direct the sheriff to deliver full possession ; and no certiorari which may be issued to remove such proceedings, shall be a supersedeas, or have any effect to prevent, or delay the execution aforesaid, or the delivery of the possession agreeably thereto.

By an act of 21 March, 1772, the same proceedings are

provided for the landlord, where the tenant for *term of years*, *or at will*, unjustly holds over.

There are two British statutes, that of 4th Geo. 2, c. 28; and 11 Geo. 2, c. 19, by which the lessor or reversioner may recover by action of debt double the yearly value of the premises; and a proceeding by ejectment, but not our *summary proceeding* by ejectment, as under our act of assembly of 1772.

" And thus lastly, for the sake of a more beneficial and complete relief by decreeing a sale of lands." 3 Bl. Com. 439.

THE power of a court of chancery reaches all cases where a sale ought to be made for the purpose of fulfilling marriage settlements, and raising portions, or paying legacies or debts charged on the estate; and also reaches the case of *executing agreements* to convey. The heir or the *executor with a power to sell*, or whoever it is that can make the title, will be compelled to do it. With us, having no court of chancery to decree a conveyance on an *agreement* to convey; or in the case of the death of a vendor, to compel his representative to make a deed, an act of assembly was passed 31 March, 1792, " to enable executors and administrators, by leave of court, to convey lands and tenements contracted for with their decedents, and for other purposes therein mentioned."

There is no provision in the act to *compel* executors or administrators to a specific performance of the contract of the decedent; but the court is empowered to give leave on application by petition in a certain case, viz. where the heir is under age and the executors have no authority by the will.

The same power is given by this act to administrators.

By another act, 2 Ap. 1802, an executor or administrator *de bonis non* is enabled to execute a deed or deeds, &c. according to the contract of a *decedent* administrator.

By sec. 3, of the same act, where the administrator has

sold lands by order of the orphans court, and died intestate without executing a conveyance, and no person within three months shall be appointed administrator *de bonis non,* the orphans court, on petition of the purchaser, shall direct the sheriff to execute the necessary conveyance.

In England, administrators have nothing to do with the real estate. For the purpose of an *original* sale of lands, here, application must be made to the orphans court; and this by act of assembly with a view to the support of minors; and by the usage of the country, and the *construction* of the courts founded upon this usage, sale may be made for the purpose of defraying debts.

By the constitution, art. 5, sec. 6, the legislature are empowered to vest in the courts, such powers " *to grant relief in equity,* as shall be found necessary." This might seem to comprehend the power of decreeing a specific conveyance; but the power of the courts has not been yet enlarged to such extent; and therefore in all cases it must be by *action on the contract* where the party or his representative may refuse to comply; or by action of ejectment where the land will be recovered under the agreement to convey.

In England the king is the general guardian of the lunatic or non compos mentis. By our act of assembly of the 14th April, 1794, the contract of any person for the sale of lands, who after making the same, shall become lunatic or non compos mentis, it shall be lawful for the purchaser under such contract, to proceed to enforce the same against the person to whom the custody of the estate of such lunatic has been or shall be committed, in like form and with like effect, and the person having such custody shall have like remedy to recover the purchase money under such contract, as in case of contracts for the sale of lands.

By an act of the 12th March, 1800, it is declared, that the authority given by any last will and testament to executors to sell and convey real estates, shall be and remain in the survivors or survivor of them, unless otherwise expressed in the will.

By sec. 3d, administrators with the will annexed, have the same authority.

By sec. 4, administrators *de bonis non* may execute the power and authorities contained in any last will as fully as if all the executors had joined therein.

A supplement to the act of 1792, passed 12th March, 1804, provides that in all cases the executor of an executor, the admininistrator *de bonis non*, and so on *in succession*, shall have equal powers with executors and administrators in the first instance, by leave of court, to convey lands contracted for with their first decedents, agreeable to the act of 1792.

It is within the power of the court of chancery in England that the execution of no trust shall fail from the want of a trustee to execute the trust ; and therefore the court will appoint a trustee wherever any thing is to be carried into effect which equity requires should be done. These powers of a court of chancery therefore could only be given by act of assembly, and accordingly from time to time has been given in the case of representatives, such as executors, administrators, &c.

As supplying what a court of chancery in England might have reached, it is provided by an act of 28th March, 1786, that deeds, conveyances or writings, concerning lands and tenements when lost or defaced, may, on bill or petition, be supplied by the supreme courts, or any two of the justices thereof.

By an act passed 19th Jan. 1793, the same power is vested in the respective courts of common pleas of the proper counties.

----•◦•----

" An answer is the most usual defence that is made to a plaintiff's bill. It is given upon oath."——

" In almost every case, the plaintiff may demand the oath of his adversary." 3 Bl. Com. 446.

UNDER the chancery power, all papers, books and accounts to which the oath refers, may be called for, and must be produced.   Under our constitution, article 5, sect. 6, the legislature have power to vest in the courts, chancery powers to all extent, to compel a party to answer upon oath, as well as to produce books and papers, whether plaintiff or defendant.   They have not yet gone so far as to give the courts the power to reach the conscience, by compelling an answer upon oath; but by an act of the 27th Feb. 1798, it is provided, "That the supreme court, and several courts of common pleas in this state, shall have power, in any one action depending before them, on motion, and upon good and sufficient cause shewn, by affidavit or affirmation, and due notice thereof being given, to require the parties or either of them, to produce books or writings in their possession or power, which contain evidence pertinent to the issue; and if either party shall fail to comply with such order, and to produce such books or writings, or to satisfy said courts why the same is not in the party's power so to do, it shall be lawful for the said courts, if the party so refusing shall be a plaintiff, to give judgment for the defendant as in cases of non-suit, and if a defendant, to give judgment against him or her by default, as far as relates to such parts of the plaintiff or plaintiff's demand, or the defendant or defendant's defence, to which the books or papers of the parties are alleged to apply."

———

"By the ancient common law, there was a great latitude left in the breast of the judges to determine what was treason, or not so: whereby the creatures of tyrannical princes had opportunity to create abundance of constructive *treason*; that is, to raise, by forced and arbitrary constructions, offences into the crime and punishment of treason, which never were suspected to be such." 4 Bl. Com. 75.

IN the summer of the year 1794, an insurrection in the western counties of Pennsylvania, took place, in opposition to an excise law of the United States; and a number of those implicated; or, charged with being implicated, were arrested, and brought before the federal court for trial of the alleged offence. Being then a practising lawyer in the western country, I had an application from some of these persons to defend them; in consequence of which I had applied my mind to consider, a little, the *Treason law* of the United States; and the following is a note of the argument I had intended to have made on the law points which might arise in their case. But finding that my name was attached to the bills sent up against them, I declined the being of counsel, as there would arise the necessity of the counsel for the United States, *animadverting upon the testimony given.* To be called as a witness for the prosecution, and at the same time to manage the defence of the accused, would seem to involve some inconsistency; or, at least, it was a situation not pleasant, but to be avoided. The note of this argument which I had prepared, has appeared in print before, but I believe it has been little read. But at any rate I have thought proper to give it this chance for preservation, by subjoining it in a note at this place.*

* ON THE TREASON LAWS OF THE UNITED STATES.

TREASON by the common law is indefinite*: Restrained by 25 Edward III†: enlarged by 21 Richard II: restrained again by 1 Henry IV. chapter 10th, and brought back to that of 25 Edward III ‡: enlarged again by sundry statutes: it was brought back to that of 25 Edward III, by 1 Edward VI. chapter 12th; enlarged again by sundry statutes §: it was brought back by 1 Mary, chapter 1st ¶. I have noted the above to shew the rigour of the common law, and the fluctuation of the statute law of England, in regard of the extent of treason.

* *There was a great latitude left in the breast of the judges to determine what was treason or not.* 4 *Blackstone,* 75.

† *Whereas divers opinions have been entertained before this time, in what case treason shall be said, and what not, the king, at the request, &c.* Statutes at large, *p.* 117.

‡ *The preamble of the statute is, that,* " *Whereas in the said parliament, the said one and twentieth year of the late king Richard, divers pains of treason were ordained by statutes, in as much that there was no man which did know how he ought to behave himself, to do, speak, or say, for doubt of such pains, it is approved and assented to by the king, &c.* Statutes at large, 118.

§ *Statutes,* 632.

¶ *Statutes at large,* 709.

The fact is, the treason law of England, was, by the common law, to the last degree sanguinary ; and even as it has been softened by statute, it still remains bloody. Nothing could be more shocking than the condition of the subject du-

The table of treason in England at this present day, is that of 25th Edward III. By the treason law of the United States, this table is reduced to a single item ; viz. " that of levying war against the king in his realm, or being adherent to the king's enemies in his realm, giving to them aid or comfort in the realm or elsewhere."

The words of our act are, " if any person or persons, owing allegiance to the United States of America, shall levy war against them, or shall adhere to their enemies, giving them aid and comfort within the United States, or elsewhere."

My deduction now is, 1. That an immense softening has taken place in the law of England, from what it was by the common law, in regard of the extent of treason. 2. That by the treason law of the United States, it is softened still more as to the extent.

It will be seen, in the second place, what improvement there has been of the common law, in regard of trial. By the common law, no oyer of indictment was allowed before arraignment ; no copy before trial ; no counsel, except on point of law ; no process, to compel witnesses for the defendant to appear ; not upon oath, when they gave their testimony ; no limitation of the prosecution.

By 7th William III, it is provided that a copy of the pannel be given two days before trial.

Compulsory process for witnesses.

Limitation of prosecution to three years, contrary to the maxim of the common law, *Nullum tempus occurit Regi.*

By the common law of the United States the prosecution is limited to three years. " A copy of the indictment, and a list of the jury, and witnesses to be produced on the trial for proving the said indictment, mentioning the names and places of abode of such witnesses and jurors, is to be delivered to the accused at least three entire days before he shall be tried for the same." He is allowed counsel to be employed by himself, or if not able himself to employ, counsel to be assigned by the court ; he is entitled to compulsory process to procure the attendance of witnesses on his behalf ; and those witnesses are heard upon oath.

Thus the treason law of the United States, improves in some particulars, even the amelioration statute of William III.

ring the civil wars, in the contest for the crown, by the houses of Lancaster and York. The king de jure, and the king de facto provision softened it a little; but nevertheless the kingdom, for several ages, was but a Golgotha, or place

Let us see, in the third place, what has been the change in the nature of the proof necessary to fix the crime of treason.

By the common law one witness was sufficient. By 1 Edward VI. chapter 12, two witnesses are made necessary.* 1 and 6th Edward VI. chapter 3d: it is made necessary that the witnesses be brought face to face with the accused.†

By 13 Charles II, "Two lawful and credible witnesses, upon oath, upon trial," are made requisite.

While such was the process of legislative improvement in regard of proof in case of treason, did the judges keep an equal pace in favour of humanity in the construction of those statutes? No; their leaning constantly was against the accused; for near a century,‡ the statute of 1 Edward VI. was little regarded, or it was rendered nugatory, by the extraordinary resolution, "that one witness of his own knowledge, and another by hear-say, *from him*, though at third or fourth hand, made two witnesses or accusers within the act." Even in cases where the accused insisted strongly on the benefit of this act, the counsel for the crown has gone on in the method formerly practised, reading examinations and confessions of persons supposed to be accomplices; some living and amenable, others lately hanged for the same treason.

In succeeding trials, the prisoners have been told that the statutes of Edward VI, were repealed, particularly that which regards two witnesses face to face; "that this law had been found dangerous to the crown."

When the people of all ranks and parties in England had been learning moderation in the school of adversity, light began to dawn upon them. The judges were at length brought to attend to the statute of Edward VI; but gave it a construction unfavourable

---

* " Be accused by two sufficient and lawful witnesses, or shall willingly and without violence confess the same." Stat. 686.

† " Be accused by two lawful accusers ; which said accusers, at the time of that arraignment of the party accused, if they be then living, shall be brought in person before the party accused, and avow and maintain that they have to say against the said party, to prove him guilty of the treason or offences contained in the bill of indictment," Stat. 686.

‡ 17 Foster, 392.

of sculls, from the executions that took place. The accursed principle of the *ne exuere patriam*, followed even those that attempted an escape from the kingdom: a principle against which never enough can be said; but which, it is to be hoped,

to the accused: viz. " that admitting two witnesses to be necessary, yet one witness to one overt act, and another to another overt act, of the same species of treason, are two sufficient witnesses within the act." The judges drew the legislature after them in this illiberal construction of the statute, and by 7 William II, it is sanctioned by the clause, " on the oath or testimony of two lawful witnesses, either both of them to the same overt act, or one of them to one, and the other of them to another overt act of the same treason." But at the same time, the illiberal constructions of the judges are rectified and restrained in another very material particular; it is provided by section 4th, that where " two or more distinct treasons of divers heads, or kinds, be alleged in one bill of indictment, one witness produced to prove one of the said treasons, and another witness produced to prove another of the said treasons, shall not be deemed or taken to be two witnesses to the same treason.

Another error in the decision of the judges is corrected, or at least the construction given by them, is ameliorated by 7 William, chapter 3d, section 8th, by which it is provided, " that no evidence shall be admitted or given of any overt act, not expressly laid in the indictment."

By the treason law of the United States, a great improvement has been gained on the statute of 7 William. The proof demanded by our law is, " the testimony of two witnesses to the same overt act of treason, whereof indicted." And by our act, the construction given by the judges, at some period in England, to the clause of the statute of 1st Edward VI, is rectified. The " willingly and without violence confessing the same," had been construed to be a confession out of court, made however casually; this is fixed to a confession " in an open court."

It will be seen that the decision of the English judges have opposed the improving mind of the legislature; they have reduced it from time to time, contrary to the natural and humane meaning, by subtile and unreasonable construction. But in ascertaining the necessary proof of treason, the law of Congress has corrected all this, and fixed it on the basis of reason and humanity.

The only question now to be considered, or at least the only

will receive a death-blow, by the resistance made to it at the present time. It is astonishing how it came into the mind of an enlightened Englishman, such as Blackstone, to justify it, and to call it a principle of *universal law*, as he would

question which I shall consider, is, What shall be said to be a "levying war?" I shall state first what by the decision of the judges of England, has been construed to be a levying war.

It would strike the common mind, that the taking arms to dethrone the king, or to change the government, could alone amount to a levying war: that there must be not only an assembling in arms, but an *animus subvertendi*, or intention of overthrowing in the case. But it has been carried much further by the judges. To explain this, I cannot serve the public better, than by transcribing a chapter from the most sensible writer on this subject; that is judge Foster. It is chapter 2d, of discourse 1st, of high treason, on the clause *of levying war, and adhering to the king's enemies.*

"Lord chief justice Hale speaking of such unlawful assemblies as may amount to a levying of war within the 25 E. 3, taketh a difference between those insurrections which have carried the appearance of an army formed under leaders, and provided with military weapons, and with drums, colours, &c. and those other disorderly, tumultuous assemblies, which have been drawn together and conducted to purposes manifestly unlawful, but without any of the shew and apparatus of war before mentioned.

"I do not think any great stress can be laid on that distinction It is true, that in case of levying war, the indictments generally charge that the defendants were armed and arrayed in a warlike manner; and where the case would admit of it, the other circumstances of swords, guns, drums, colours, &c. have been added. But I think the merits of the case have never turned singly on any of those circumstances.

"In the cases of Damaree v. Purchase, which are the last *printed* cases that have come in judgment on the point of constructive levying war, there was nothing *given in evidence* of the usual pageantry of war, no military weapons, no banners or drums, nor any regular consultation previous to the rising. And yet the want of these circumstances weighed nothing with the court, though the prisoner's counsel insisted much on that matter. The number of the insurgents supplied the want of military weapons; and they were provided with axes, crows, and other tools of the like nature, proper for the mischief they intended to effect.

seem to have done in these Commentaries; though at the same time under the head of *parental subjection*, he admits that it has its limits. " To those," says he, " who gave us existence, we *naturally* owe subjection and obedience *during*

———*Furor arma ministrat.*

" Sect. 1. The true criterion therefore in all these cases is *Quo animo* did the parties assemble. For if the assembly be upon account of some *private* quarrel, or to take revenge on *particular* persons, the statute of treasons hath already determined that point in favour of the subject. " If, saith the statute, any man ride *open-* " *ly* [so the word *descouvert* ought to have been rendered] or se- " cretly with men of arms against any other to slay or rob him, or " to take and keep him 'till he make fine for his deliverance, it is " not the mind of the king nor his council that in such case it shall " be adjudged treason; but it shall be adjudged felony or trespass " according to the laws of the land of *old times used*, and accord- " ing as the case requireth." Then immediately followeth ano- ther clause which reacheth to the end of the statute; and provid- eth that, if in such case or *other like* the offence had theretofore been adjudged treason, whereby the lands of the offenders had come to the crown as forfeit; the lords of the fee should notwith- standing have the escheat of such lands, saving to the crown the year, and waste.

" I will make a short observation or two on those clauses.

" 1st, The first clause is evidently declaratory of the common law, it shall be adjudged felony or trespass *according to the law of the land of old time used*. The second hath a retrospect to some late judgments, in which the common law had not taken place; and giveth a speedy and effectual remedy to lords of the fee who had suffered by those judgments.

" 2dly, The words of the first clause descriptive of the offence, " if any man ride armed openly or secretly with men of arms," did in the language of these times, mean nothing less than the assembling bodies of men, friends, tenants, or dependents, armed and arrayed in a warlike manner, in order to effect some purpose or other by dint of numbers and superior strength. And yet those assemblies so formed and arrayed, if drawn together for purposes of a private nature, were not deemed treasonable.

" 3dly, Though the statute mentioneth only the cases of assem- bling to kill, rob, or imprison, yet these, put as they are by way

dur minority." 1 Bl. Com. 453. Rutherforth, and every other English writer, to *parental subjection* assigns the same limit. On principle of natural reason, the contrary supposition, would enslave descendants ad infinitum.

Adam came from his Creator, a *perfect man.* To the Al-

of example only, will not exclude others which may be brought within the same rule. For the retrospective clause provideth, that " if in such case *or other like* it hath been adjudged"—what are the other like cases ? all cases of the like private nature are, I apprehend, within the reason and equity of the act. The cases cited by Hale, some before the statute of treasons, and others after it, those assemblies though attended many of them with bloodshed and with the ordinary apparatus of war, were not held, to be treasonable assemblies. For they were not in construction of law, raised against the king or his royal majesty, but for purposes of a private personal nature.

" Sec. 2. Upon the same principle and within the reason and equity of the statute, risings to maintain a *private* claim of right, or to destroy *particular* inclosures, or to remove nuisances which affected or were thought to affect in point *of interest the parties assembled for these purposes,* or to break prisons in order to release *particular* persons without any other circumstance of aggravation, have not been held to amount to levying war within the statute.

" And upon the same principle and within the same equity of the statute, I think it was very rightly held by five of the judges, that a rising of the weavers in and about London to destroy all engine looms, a machine which enabled those of the trade who made use of it to undersell those who had it not, did not amount to levying war within the statute ; though great outrages were committed on that occasion not only in London but in the adjacent counties, and the magistrates and peace officers were resisted and affronted.

" For those judges considered the whole affair merely as a *private quarrel between men of the same trade about the use of a particular engine, which those concerned in the rising, thought detrimental to them.* Five of the judges indeed were of a different opinion. But the attorney general thought proper to proceed against the defendants as for a riot only.

" Sec. 3. But every insurrection which in judgment of law is intended against the person of the king, be it to dethrone or im-

3 P

mighty he owed his bringing up to manhood, and placing him where he was. We may suppose the first man bound, in like manner, to take care of his offspring, until brought to the same period; and in so doing, it was but the discharge of an

prison him, or to oblige him to alter his measures of government, or to remove evil counsellors from about him, these risings all amount to levying war within the statute; whether attended with the pomp and circumstances of open war or not. And every conspiracy to levy war for these purposes, though not treason within the clause of levying war, is yet an overt act within the other clause of compassing the king's death. For these purposes cannot be effected by numbers and open force, without manifest danger to his person.

" Sec. 4. Insurrections in order to throw down *all* inclosures, to alter the established law or change religion, to enhance the price of *all* labour, or to open *all* prisons, all risings in order to effect these innovations of a *public and general concern by an armed force*, are in construction of law high treason, within the clause of levying war. For though they are not levelled at the person of the king, they are against *his royal majesty*. And besides, they have a direct tendency to dissolve all the bonds of society, and to destroy all property and all government too, by numbers and an armed force. Insurrections likewise for redressing *national* grievances, or for the expulsion of foreigners in general, or indeed of any single nation living here under the protection of the king, or for the reformation of real or imaginary evils *of a public nature, and in which the insurgents have no special interest*, risings to effect these ends by force and numbers, are by construction of law within the clause of levying war. For they are levelled at the king's crown and royal dignity.

" Sec. 5. It was adjudged in the 16th Car. 1. a season of great agitation, that going to Lambeth house in a warlike manner to surprise the archbishop, who was a privy counsellor, it being with *drums* and a multitude to the number of 300, was treason.

" This is a very imperfect account of an insurrection, which hath found a place in the best histories of that time. The tumult happened on Monday the 11th of May, 1640, about midnight. On Thursday following the special commission under which the judges sat was opened and proceeded upon; and Benstead a ringleader in the tumult was convicted, and within a very few days afterwards executed.

obligation. It did not entitle him to the *perpetual service* of the descendant; or to authority and command over him. If the jus parentis, or patria potestas, must then have a limit, how can the right of a society attach, on his coming to be of

" It is not very easy from the short note of the case given by the reporters, to collect the true grounds of this resolution. But the history of the times will enable us to form a probable conjecture concerning them.

" On the 5th of May the parliament was dissolved to the general dissatisfaction of the nation. And, which greatly increased the ill humour of the people, the convocation was by a new commission impowered to continue sitting, notwithstanding the dissolution of the parliament. *And the blame and odium of both these unpopular measures were laid upon the archbishop.*

" On Saturday the 9th of that month, a paper was posted up at the Exchange, exhorting the apprentices to rise and sack the archbishop's house on the Monday *following.* And accordingly on that very day an attempt was made upon Lambeth house by a rabble of some thousands; with open profession and protestation, *that they would tear the archbishop in pieces.*

" It were to be wished that the full import of the libel posted at the Exchange, in consequence of which the attempt was made, had been set out: and also that we were informed what was the cry among the rabble at the time of the attempt, more than that they would tear the archbishop in pieces. These circumstances, could we come at them, would probably let us into the true reason and motives for the rising, and consequently into the reason and grounds of the opinion of the judges. For if it did appear by the libel, or by the cry of the rabble at Lambeth house, that the attempt was made on account of measures *the king had taken, or was then taking at the instigation as they imagined of the archbishop;* that the rabble had deliberately and upon a public invitation attempted *by numbers and open force, to take a severe revenge upon the privy-counsellor, for the measures the sovereign had taken or was pursuing;* if this may be supposed to be the case, I think the supposition is not very foreign, the grounds and reasons of the resolution would in my opinion be sufficiently explained, without taking that little trifling circumstance of the drum into the case. Upon such a supposition, the case came within the treason of Talbot's case, 17 R. 2, cited by Hale. And I think too within the rules laid down in the two preceding sections. But without an age to provide for himself, so as to preclude him from chusing another soil, or electing a different society with whom to find his happiness?

I have been led to these reflections when I have thought

the help of some such supposition, I see nothing in the case as stated by the report, which can amount to high treason.

" Sec. 6. But a bare conspiracy for effecting a rising, for the purpose mentioned in the two preceding sections and in the next, is not an overt act of compassing the king's death. Nor will it come under any species of treason within the 25 Edward 3. *unless the rising be effected.* And in this case the conspirators as well as the actors will be all equally guilty. For in high treason of all kinds, all the *participes criminis* are principals.

" It must be admitted, that conspiracies for these purposes have been adjudged treason. But those judgments were founded on the temporary act of 13 Eliz. which made compassing to levy war, declared by printing, writing, or advised speaking, high treason *during the life of the queen.*

" There was an act in the 13 Car. 2. to the same purpose on which some prosecutions were founded; but that act expired with the death of the king.

" Sec. 7. The cases of Damaree and Purchase for destroying the meeting houses of Protestant dissenters, being the last in *print* that have come in judgment upon the doctrine of constructive levying war; and having been ruled upon consideration of former precedent, I will state them somewhat largely from the printed trials.

" The indictments charged that the prisoners withdrawing their allegiance, &c. and conspiring and intending to disturb the peace and public tranquillity of the kingdom, did traitorously compass, imagine, and intend to levy and raise war, rebellion, and insurrection against the queen within the kingdom; and that in order to complete and effect those their traiterous intentions and imaginations, they on the   day of   at   with a multitude of people to the number of 500 armed and arrayed in a warlike manner, &c. then and there traitorously assembled, did traitorously ordain, prepare, and levy war against the queen, against the duty of their allegiance, &c.

" It appeared upon the trial of these men, which I attended in the students gallery at the Old Bailey, that upon the 1st March 1709, during Dr. Sacheverell's trial. the rabble who had attended

of the application of the law of treason, to those who in civil dissensions have endeavoured to withdraw themselves from the scene of tumult and of jeopardy.

But it will be said, let people expatriate, provided it is

the doctor from Westminster to his lodgings in the temple, continued together a short space in the King's Bench walks, crying among other cries of the day, *down with the Presbyterians.*

" At length it was proposed, by whom it was not known, to pull down the meeting houses, and thereupon the cry became general, *down with the meeting houses :* and some thousands immediately moved toward a meeting house of Mr. Burges, a protestant dissenting minister; the defendant Damaree, a waterman in the queen's service, and in her livery and badge, putting himself at the head of them, and crying, *come on boys, I'll lead you, down with the meeting houses.* They soon demolished Mr. Burges's, and burnt the pews, pulpit, and other materials in Lincoln's Inn Fields. After they had finished at that place, they agreed to proceed to the *rest of the meeting houses.* And hearing that the guards were coming to disperse them, they agreed for *the greater dispatch to divide into several bodies, and to attack different houses at the same time.* And many were that night in part demolished, and the materials burnt in the street.

" The prisoner Damaree put himself at the head of a party which drew off from Lincoln's Inn Fields and demolished a meeting house in Drury-Lane, and burnt the materials in the street; still crying they would pull them *all down that night.*

" While the materials of this house were burning, the prisoner Purchase who had not, for aught appeared, been before concerned in the outrages of that night, came up to the fire very drunk ; and with his drawn sword in his hand, encouraged the rabble in what they were doing. And incited them to resist the guards who were just then come to the fire in order to disperse the multitude. He likewise assaulted the commanding officer with his drawn sword, and struck several of their horses with the same weapon. And then advancing towards the guards, cried out to the rabble behind him, *come on boys, I'll lose my life in the cause, I will fight the best of them.*

" Upon the trial of Damaree, the cases referred to before in sect. 4. and 5. were cited at the bar, and all the judges present were of opinion that the prisoner was guilty of the high treason charged upon him in the indictment. For here was a rising with

not during war, for I admit this restriction, but let them not take arms against the parent country.   But, if the right to join another society, and become a member, is allowable, the duties to that society instantly arise, and it will have a right,

an avowed intention to demolish *all meeting houses in general;* and this intent they carried into execution as far as they were able. If the meeting houses of protestant dissenters had been erected and supported in defiance of all law, a rising in order to destroy such houses *in general*, would have fallen under the rule laid down in Keling, with regard to demolishing *all* bawdy houses. But since the meeting houses of protestant dissenters are by the toleration act taken under the protection of the law, the insurrection in the present case was to be considered as a public declaration by the rabble against that act, and an attempt to render it ineffectual by *numbers and open force.*

" Accordingly Damaree was found guilty, and had judgment of death as in cases of high treason.

" But he was pardoned and soon after restored to his badge and livery, which he wore to the death of the queen.   Her majesty's new advisers did not choose to have the dawn of their administration stained with the blood of one of Dr. Sacheverell's *ablest* advocates.

" With regard to the case of Purchase, there was some diversity of opinion among the judges present at his trial : because it did not appear upon the evidence, that he had any concern in the original rising, or was present at the pulling down any of the houses, or any ways active in the outrages of that night ; except his behaviour at the bonfire in Drury Lane, whither he came by mere accident, for aught appeared to the contrary.

" The jury therefore, by the direction of the court, found a special verdict to the effect already mentioned.

" Upon this special verdict, which in substance took in the whole transaction on the first of March, the judges unanimously resolved, that for the reasons mentioned at Damaree's trial, he and the others concerned with him in the demolishing and rifling the meeting houses, were guilty of high treason in levying war against the queen.

" As to the case of Purchase, chief J. Trevor, justice Powel, and baron Price were of opinion, that upon the facts found, he was not guilty of the charge in the indictment.   But all the rest of the judges differed from them.   Because the rabble was traitorously

to call upon, and compel the individual emigrant, to take
arms, if the sovereign authority of that society should command it. Here then will be a dilemma; and the right of
changing country, must fall; or the right of taking defence

assembled, and in the very act of levying war when Purchase joined them, and encouraged them to proceed, and assaulted the
guards, who were sent to suppress them. All this being done in
defence and support of persons engaged *in the very act of rebellion*,
involved him in the guilt of that treason in which the others were
engaged.

"This man likewise was pardoned. His case in point of law
and of real guilt too, came far short of Damaree's.

"Sec. 8. The joining with rebels in an act of rebellion, or with
enemies in acts of hostility, will make a man a traitor: in the one
case within the clause of levying war, in the other within that of adhering to the king's enemies. But if this be done for fear of death,
and while the party is under actual force, and he take the first opportunity that offereth to make his escape, this fear and compulsion will excuse him. It is however incumbent on the party who
maketh fear and compulsion his defence, to shew to the satisfaction of court and jury that the compulsion continued during all the
time he staid with the rebels or enemies.

"I will not say that he is obliged to account for every day, week,
or month. That perhaps would be impossssible. And therefore if
an original force be proved, and the prisoner can shew, that he in
earnest attempted to escape and was prevented; or that he did get
off and was forced back, or that he was narrowly watched, and all
passes guarded; or from other circumstances, which it is impossible to state with precision, but when proved ought to weigh with a
jury, that an attempt to escape would have been attended with great
difficulty and danger; *so that upon the whole he may be presumed
to have continued amongst them against his will, though not constantly under an actual force or fear of immediate death*, these
circumstances and others of the like tendency proved to the satisfaction of the court and jury, will be sufficient to excuse him.

"But an apprehension though ever so well grounded, of having
houses burnt or estates wasted or cattle destroyed, or of any other
mischief of the like kind, will not excuse in the case of joining and
marching with rebels or enemies.

"Furnishing rebels or enemies with money, arms, ammunition,
or other necessaries will *prima facie*, make a man a traitor. But

with a new society must exist.   Both cannot stand together.
It would be abominable, therefore, under our notions of the
rights of men, to consider him as *guilty of treason* who had
manifested his intention of changing one country for another,
and who had carried that into effect.

if enemies or rebels come with a superior force and exact contributions, or live upon the country at free quarter, submission in these
cases is not criminal.   For *flagrante bello* the *jus belli* taketh place,
'tis the only law then subsisting.   And submission is a point of the
highest prudence to prevent a greater public evil.

" And the bare sending money or provisions (except in the case
just excepted) or sending intelligence to rebels or enemies, which
in most cases is the most effectual aid that can be given them, will
make a man a traitor, though the money or intelligence should happen to be intercepted. For the party in sending did all he could :
the treason was complete *on his part, though it had not the effect
he intended**.

" The cases cited in the margin did not in truth turn singly upon
the rule here laid down, though I think the rule may be very well
supported. For Greg was indicted for *compassing the death* of
the queen, and also *for adhering to her enemies ;* and Hensey's
indictment was in the same form, and so was lord Preston's cited
in the last chapter. And the writing and sending the letters of intelligence, which in the cases of Greg and Hensey *were stopped
at the post office,* was laid as an overt act of both the species of
treason. So that admitting for argument's sake, which is by no
means admitted, that it was not an overt act of *adhering,* since
the letters never came to the enemy's hands, and consequently no
aid or comfort was actually given, yet the bare writing and sending them to the post office in order to be delivered to the enemy,
was undoubtedly an overt act of the other species of treason. In
Greg's case the judges did resolve that it was an overt act of both
the species of treason charged on him. And in Hensey's the court
adopted that opinion, and cited it with approbation.

" Though the cases of these men were in substance the same,
the charge against them varied in one particular. Greg's indictment chargeth that the letters were sent from the place where the
venue is laid *into* parts beyond the seas (IN *partes transmarinas)*

---

* *So ruled in the case of William Greg, and in the case of D*
Hensey.

To raise a *parricidal hand*, is the cry, against *the country which gave you birth.* Ubi libertas, ibi patria, where liberty is, there is my country. Must this maxim go for nothing? Is it an idle aphorism, and of no meaning in the mouth of

to be delivered to the enemy. Hensey's, with much greater propriety, and agreeable to the truth of the case, chargeth that the letters were sent from the place where the *venue* is laid, *to be delivered in* parts beyond the seas to the enemy. As the letters never went abroad, this was undoubtedly the safer way of laying the charge.

" Sec. 9. An assembly armed and arrayed in a warlike manner for any treasonable purpose, is *bellum levatum*, though not *bellum percussum*. Listing and marching are sufficient overt acts without coming to a battle or action. So cruising on the king's subjects under a French commission, France being then at war with us, was held to be adhering to the king's enemies, though no other act of hostility was laid or proved.

" Sec. 10. Attacking the king's forces *in opposition to his authority* upon a march or in quarters, is levying war against the king. But if upon a sudden quarrel, from some affront given or taken, the neighbourhood should rise and drive the forces out of their quarters, that would be a great misdemeanor, and if death should ensue, it may be felony in the assailants : But it will not be treason, because there was no intention against the king's person or government.

" Sec. 11. Holding a castle or fort against the king or his forces, if *actual force be used in order to keep possession*, is levying war. But a bare detainer, as suppose by shutting the gates against the king or his forces, without any other force from within, Lord Hale conceiveth will not amount to treason. But if this be done in *confederacy with enemies* or rebels, that circumstance will make it treason ; in the one case under the clause of adhering to the king's enemies, in the other under that of levying war. So if a person having the custody of a castle or fort deliver it up to the rebels or enemies, *by treachery and in combination with them*, this is high treason within the act : in the former case 'tis levying war, in the latter it is adhering to the king's enemies. But mere cowardice or imprudence, though it might subject a commander in such case to death by the martial law, will not amount to treason.

" Sec. 12. States in actual hostility with us, though no war be

3 Q

the great Franklin, whose motto it was said to be ?   Is man
like a vegetable, a fossil, that he must belong to a bed of
loam, or marl, just as he happens to originate ?   No; but it
is the society, it will be said, that attaches him by root, so

solemnly declared, are enemies within the meaning of the act.
And therefore in an indictment on the clause of adhering to the
king's enemies, it is sufficient to aver that the prince or state adhered to *is an enemy*, without showing any war proclaimed.   And
the fact, whether war or no, is triable by the jury; and public notoriety, is sufficient evidence of the fact.   And if the subject of
a foreign prince in amity with us, invadeth the kingdom without
commission from his sovereign, he is an enemy.   And a subject
of England adhering to him is a traitor, within this clause of the
act.   Or if an alien *amy* acteth in a hostile manner against us under a commission from a prince or state at enmity with us, he is an
enemy within the act.   And adhering to him is treason within this
clause.

   " So if a subject of England maketh actual war on the king's allies engaged with him against the common enemy, as was the case
of the States General in our wars against France in the time of
king William and the late queen, this is adhering to the king's enemies, though no act of hostility is committed against the king or
his forces.   For by this the common enemy is strengthened, and
the king's hands are weakened.

   " Sect. 13. In prosecution for these treasons, as well as for
that of compassing the death of the king, an overt act of the treason must, as I have already observed, be charged in the indictment
and proved.   This rule is grounded on the words of the statute,
which being a declaratory act must strictly be pursued.   The
words to this purpose are, " Where a man doth compass, &c.——
" or if a man doth levy war against our lord the king in his realm,
" or be adherent to the king's enemies in his realm, giving them
" aid or comfort in his realm or elsewhere, and thereof be [*pro-
" valblement*, i. e. upon full proof] attainted of *open* deed."   And
therefore it will not be sufficient to allege generally that the defendants did levy war or adhere.   But in the former case it must
be alleged that they did assemble with a multitude armed and arrayed in a warlike manner, and levied war.   And in the latter, acts
of adherence must be set forth.

   " But the particular facts done by the defendants, or a detail of
the evidence intended to be given, need not be set forth in either

that he cannot remove. It is his compact. How *compact?* Before he was born? No; but as soon as he was born. That cannot be, for he was incapable of contracting. But his parents contracted for him; and he is bound by their

case. The common law, as I have already said upon a like occasion, never required this exactness: and the statute of king William doth not make it necessary to charge particular facts, where it was not necessary before.''

The question will now occur; Are we bound by these decisions, founded in constructions given to the clause of "levying war?" The decisions of the judges are only evidence of law, not the law itself. Where the decision is unreasonable, it cannot be the law. There is a higher evidence against it, than the opinion in its favour; viz. the general reason of the human mind. Yet decisions ought to be regarded, as the judgments of wise men, *responsa prudentum,* and in some cases, to be followed as undeviatingly as the law itself. For instance, where under a decision, that has taken place, a principle has been settled in the tenure of estates, by grant, devise, or in personal contracts, which must be supposed in view, at the time of the grant, devise, or contract. It would operate with an effect, *ex post facto,* to depart from the decision. Nothing of this can exist in the case of a decision on the criminal code, where it is in favour of the accused. The court is, *quoad hoc* the government, and a rigorous construction does not bind. It may relax. But a liberal construction given, concludes against a more rigorous one in future cases. Because every person is supposed to know the decision, and to be told that in the cognizance of offences, hitherto the law will go, and no further.

Are we then at liberty to depart from the constructions given by the English judges to the clause of "levying war?" I have no doubt of it, nay think that pursuing the meliorating spirit of the constitution, and of our legislature, we are bound to depart from them in all cases, warranted by reason.

Are there any cases where the decisions appear unreasonable? There are.

In order to illustrate this, I first observe that a "war levied" is of two sorts, 1st. Expressly and directly, as raising war against the king, or his general and forces; or to surprize and injure the king's person, or to imprison him, or to go to his presence to enforce him to remove any of his ministers or counsellors, and the like. 2d. Interpretatively and constructively, as when a war is le-

contract. This brings it back to the jus parentale, or jus in liberos; and, unless it can be made out, that the parent has a right to perpetual service and subjection, the society cannot have it. For it is only from a carrying out the right of

vied to throw down enclosures generally, or to enhance servants wages, or to alter religion established by law, and many instances of like nature might be given. This has been resolved to be a war against the king, and treason within this clause.* The first resolution, says Sir Mathew Hale, that I find of this interpretative levying war, is a resolution cited by my lord Coke, in the time of Henry VIII. for enhancing servants wages; and the next in time was that of Burton, 39 Elizabeth, for raising an armed force to pull down enclosures generally. This is now settled by these instances, and some of the like kind hereafter mentioned. The proceeding against Burton and his companions, was not upon the statute of 25 Edward III, which required that in new cases, the Parliament should be first consulted; but upon the statute of 13 Elizabeth: for conspiring to levy war, which has not that clause of consulting the parliament in new cases, and therefore seems to leave a latitude to the judges, to make constructions greater than was left by the statute of 25 Edward III.

These resolutions being made and settled, we must acquiesce in them, *but in my opinion, if new cases happen for the future*, that have not an express resolution in point, nor are expressly within the words of 25 Edward III. though they may seem to have a parity of reason, it is the safest way, and most agreeable to the wisdom of the great act of 25 Edward III. first to consult the Parliament, and have their declaration, and to be very wary in multiplying constructive and interpretative treasons; for we know not where we will end.†

Will it not sound harshly in a common ear, to hear it said that in a wrong construction of the law, where even life is in question, we must acquiesce? yet this is the language of the humane sir Mathew Hale.

There was a special verdict found at the Old Bailey, 20 Car. II. That A, B, and C, with divers persons to the number of one hundred, assembled themselves, *modo guerino*, to pull down bawdy houses; and they marched with a flag upon a staff, and weapons, and pulled down certain houses in prosecution of their con-

* 1 Hale, 132.   † Hale. 132.

parents, into its deductions, that the society can have a right.
Rutherford, as I have said, and I cite an Englishman, because it is ad hominem, lays it down, 1 Inst. Nat. law, 170,
that " the law of nature cannot be supposed to fix any pre-

spiracy. This by all the judges assembled, but one,* was ruled
to be levying war, and so treason within this statute; and accordingly they were executed. But the reason that made the doubt
to him that doubted it, was 1st, Because it seemed but an unruly
company of apprentices, among whom that custom of pulling bawdy houses had long obtained, and therefore was usually repressed
by officers, and not punished as traitors.. 2d, Because the finding
to pull down bawdy houses, might reasonably be intended here or
there particular bawdy houses, and the indefinite expression in
materia odiosa, be construed either universally, or generally. And
3d, Because the statute of 1 Mary, chapter 12, though now discontinued, makes assemblies of above 12 persons, and of as high a
nature, only felony, and that not without a continuance together an
hour after proclamation made; as namely, an assembly to pull
down bawdy houses, burn mills, or to abate the rent of any manors,
lands, or tenements, or the price of victuals, or grain, &c.

Yet the greater opinion obtained as was fit, says the author,
and these apprentices had judgment, and some of them were executed as for high treason.

The decision in the case of pulling down the meeting-houses
of dissenters, by which decision it was construed treason, followed
the case of the bawdy houses. The distinction would have been
invidious, to have made it treason to invade brothels, and to make
it less, to demolish churches.

The construction was not equally rigid in the case of the insurrection of the weavers, in 1675, on which occasion the judges were
assembled to consider. Five of them thought this treason; five
dissented.† They thought it not like the design of altering religion, laws, pulling down enclosures generally, nor to destroy any
trade; but only a particular quarrel and grievance between men of
the same trade, against a particular engine that they thought a
grievance to them; which though it was an enormous riot, yet it
would be difficult to make it treason.‡ The five judges who were
for making it treason had relied on Burton's case. The decision

---

* *Sir Mathew Hale.*   † *Hale.* 133.

‡ 1 *Hale.* 146.

cise age, at which the absolute authority of parents shall, in all cases, cease, and all persons shall be looked upon to be capable of acting for themselves. Persons are then arrived at maturity, when they come to the use of their reason. But

in that of the bawdy houses, did not then exist; it was five years after.

I conceive the question fairly open for discussion; what ought to be the construction of the clause of " levying war." I mean taking up the subject, as certainly we have a right to do, unshackled by the decisions of the English Judges.

Taking up the subject on first principles, it might be said, that even a simple trespass tends to the subversion of the government; and every breach of the peace is said to be against the peace and dignity of the commonwealth. But where the trespass is with numbers, and with arms, it is arrayed more formally against the order of society, and might be construed treason. It was with a view to such construction that the statute of 25 Edward III. provides " if any man ride armed openly, or secretly with men of arms, against any other, to slay or to rob him, till he made fine for his deliverance, it is not the mind of the king, nor his council, that in such a case it shall be judged treason; but it shall be judged felony or trespass according to the law of the land, of old time used, and according as the case requireth."

It was on this principle the boundary of construction was settled by the judges generally; that, " risings to maintain a private claim of right, or to destroy particular inclosures; or to remove nuisances, which affect, or were thought to affect *in point of interest the parties assembled* for those purposes, or to break prisons in order to release *particular* persons, without any other circumstance of aggravation, have not been holden to amount to levying war, within the statute."

It must be therefore an insurrection which in judgment of law is intended against the government, to overthrow it; as you would break a machine to pieces, or to stop the motion of it, by breaking or obstructing some wheel or spring that is necessary for its operation. Yet resistance to an officer in the execution of his process, by the law of the land, is but an aggravated trespass. With a view to such construction, our statute has provided, " that if any person shall knowingly and wilfully obstruct, resist, or oppose any officer of the United States, in serving or attempting to serve, or execute any mesne process, or warrant, or order of

this happens at different times of life, in different countries : in some climates, *the mind* ripens faster, and attains to the use of reason sooner, than it does in others. In the same country too, it happens at different times of life to different

any of the courts of the United States, or any other legal or judicial writ, or process whatsoever, or shall assault, beat, or wound any officer, or other person duly authorised, in serving or executing any writ, rule, order, process, or warrant aforesaid, every person so knowingly and wilfully offending in the premises, shall, on conviction thereof, be imprisoned not exceeding twelve months, and fined not exceeding three hundred dollars."*

I would in the first place lay aside constructive treasons altogether, and confine the law to a direct attack upon the government, and in the second place I would confine it to an attack, *animo subvertendi*. Will it not be easy then to meditate the overthrowing the government, and go on to execute it by a resistance to a law, and by risings for indirect purposes, without a possibility of making proof of an *animus subvertendi*, or conspiracy to overthrow ? Let it be left to the jury to presume, or infer from the acts themselves, what the intention was ; but let it always be in view as the essence of the act, that there was a directly looking forward in the mind of the person, to a subversion of the government, before it be construed treason. Every outrage, without this essential expedient may be repressed, and punished under the idea of a riot, subjecting to fine, pillory, imprisonment, and hard labour. This will be more agreeable to the common sense and feelings of mankind, who must be struck with a sense that the outrage is a riot, but to whom it cannot be obvious, that it was meditated as an attempt upon the government itself, amounting to high treason. It is only by deduction and inference, that it becomes so.

There will be no evidence, that any of those concerned in the attack of the house of the inspector of the revenue, general Neville, ever thought of subverting the government, or had an idea that the act would be construed treason. Whatever the ultimate views of these may have been, who projected the taking the magazine at Pittsburgh, certain it is, that the bulk had no looking forward of mind to more than a redress of what they called grievances, under the government. If the construction therefore for

* *Laws of the United States.*

persons : all who live in the same climate, do not come to maturity of judgment, at the same age. No particular person, therefore, can be said *naturally* to have arrived *at years of discretion, or be capable of acting for himself ;* till we have

which I have contended, is supportable, either of these acts will amount to a riot only.

It will be said that our legislature, in excerpting the very words of the clause from the statute 25 Edward III. must be supposed at the time to have had an eye to the construction given to this clause by the decisions of the English courts ; and by adopting the terms, has sanctioned the interpretation. The presumption doubt‑less exists. But it does not necessarily follow ; and in favour of life, unless it necessarily follows, let not the construction govern. The legislature may have attended to the constructions, or they may not ; the question admits a doubt. This being the case, it is contrary to the law maxims of humanity, to establish the presumption. The legislature intent upon restraining the treason law to a single clause, may not at the same time, have pursued the constructions of that clause in their minds. It is not probable they did. It was not necessary. The judges had the power to construe these words, on principle of reason, with the same licence as if they never had been in a treason table of England. The ultimate question then will be, whether it be necessary for the preservation of the government, that the treason law be carried so far as to make the circumstances in the case of Neville's house, or the march to Braddock's fields, amount to that offence.

I admit that by the decision of the English judges, the attack upon the house of the inspector, is clearly treason. For though it was not destroying *all* inspection offices, yet it was for *a purpose of a public nature, and in which the insurgents had no special or individual interest,** exclusively of the community.

I also must admit that the march to Braddock's field, by the same construction, must be treason ; for though the expelling individuals would be but a violent trespass in itself : yet connected, as it was, with a view to the operation of a law which these men were supposed to countenance and support, it will be brought to the same thing. But the question may be made, whether it be necessary for the preservation of the government. that these or

* *Foster*, 211.

observed how that particular person behaves in common life. When he shews by his behaviour, that he has the use of his reason, then, and not till then, he is past his *natural minority.*

like cases be adjudged treason, where no evidence is alleged of an avowed intention to bring about a revolution.

Elementary writers, at the head of whom is the marquis de Beccaria, have with great plausibility, questioned the right of society to punish, by taking life at all. They stand on surer ground, who question only the necessity. By the Russian code, and that of Tuscany, it has been reduced to an experiment; and capital punishment is found not necessary. The only use of this at present, is to enforce a leaning of the mind towards a construction of the law, that will restrain it to the highest species of treason, and what alone ought to bear the name; a conspiracy to overthrow the government.

As our treason law stands, it is more the interest of the government in point of reparation from the offender, to have the act considered in the light of an aggravated riot only, than to have it made treason; in which case there is no forfeiture of property.* Reasons of policy would therefore lead to that construction of the clause, for which I have contended.

Nothing can be right that is contrary to the feelings of the human heart, and at which the reason of the common mind revolts. Let it be told one of these accused, that the essence of the charge against him is an attempt to shake the foundations of the government to which he had sworn allegiance, and to overturn as far as in him lay, the existing order of society, with all the advantages of security to person, property, and fame; and to bring about anarchy at first, and tyranny of one or a few in the end. He would say, I never had such a thought. Others will believe him; and they cannot feel an acquiescence with the law that would by construction fix this design upon him.

In every other crime, it is known and contemplated to the extent, what the individual is about to perpetrate. In homicide, he knows he is about to kill a man; in burglary, to break a house; in larceny, to steal an article. The fact in its nature and conse-

* " *No condition or judgment, for any of the offences aforesaid, shall work corruption of blood, or any forfeiture of estate.*"
Laws *of United States,* 151.

3 R

" Civil laws do, indeed, usually fix some certain age, as *the limit of minority* for all the subjects." The law of England has fixed this at the age of 21. Until this period, the parental authority exists, which is founded in the duty to

quences exist clearly to his mind. He is under no necessity of construing and inferring, in order to know what he is about. It is the *quo animo*, the mind with which a thing is done, that is at all times to be considered. And if it cannot be found that the mind meant the act, it cannot be considered as the act of the mind, which is the man.

I would therefore understand our law, as having in view only a fixed, formed, deliberate intention of subverting the government, as that offence which it will construe high treason, and punish with the loss of life itself. The accused had meditated death to the government, and the law in this case, and this case only, will meditate death to him.

The legislature of the United States contemplating precisely such a case as that of the insurrection of the western country, has provided for the suppressing it by an act of May 2d, 1790. " Whenever the laws of the United States shall be opposed, or the execution thereof obstructed in any state, by combinations too powerful to be suppressed, by the ordinary course of judiciary proceedings, or by the power vested in the marshal, by this act ; the same being notified to the president of the United States by an associate justice, or the district judge, it shall be lawful for the president of the United States to call forth the militia of such state, to suppress combinations, and shall cause the laws to be duly executed. And if the militia where such combinations may happen, shall refuse, or be insufficient to suppress the same, it shall be lawful for the president, if the legislature of the United States be not in session, to call forth and employ such numbers of the militia of any other state or states most convenient thereto, as may be necessary, until the expiration of thirty days, after the commencement of the ensuing session." The " opposing the laws, or obstructing the execution," are the phrases ; not that of traitorously conspiring to subvert the government. So that it would seem to have had in view, an insurrection for a purpose of an inferior nature, and calls it, " an unlawful combination," which though tending in its consequence to overthrow the government, yet had not that for its object in the contemplation of the actors. We are relieved, therefore, by this act, from an objection which

provide for the child. " This authority," says the same author, p. 168, " must necessarily cease, when the duty ceases upon which it is founded: after the child is able to think and to-judge for itself, it is no longer the duty of the parent to think and to judge for it; and consequently the will of the child is no longer under the absolute control of their will. However, they have still a demand upon it of gratitude, esteem, and reverence: it is still bound to honour them, by shewing all marks of respect, and more particularly by paying a deference to their advice and direction. For as they, from their longer experience, are more likely to judge rightly than the child is; so their former care of it, may convince it, that they are disposed to contrive for its welfare. But, notwithstanding the child owes them this duty of honour, they have not, as its parents, such authority over it, as to restrain its acts, because the obligations to these duties, are of the imperfect sort."

If the child, after coming to the years of maturity, and being at its own hand, if I may so express it, acquires property independent of the parent, has it not a right *to protect that property against the trespass of the parent, and go to law for that purpose ?* This proves, that by the law of nature, or society, it is not unlawful to resist the wrong of a parent, as injury to property, or person. Can it be unlawful then to resist the wrong of the society under which one was born, merely because it must be considered in the light of a *parent society ?* If it is lawful to emigrate at all, and become the member of a new community, it must be lawful to join in resistance to the parent society if it does wrong to

might exist, that unless such outrages as these were construed treason, the power of the federal government could not move to suppress them. On the ground, therefore, of the preservation of the union, I see no necessity to carry our construction of the clause of " levying war," so far as to embrace the late acts in the western country within the crime of treason.

If, in any case, proof can be directly made, or if the jury, from the facts themselves, cannot but presume that a subversion was intended, it may be so construed, but not otherwise.

the new community, and to *fulfil the obligations to that new society of which it has become a member.* If this reasoning is conclusive, it must be lawful to carry arms, defensive, or offensive, as the nature of the case may be, against the parent state. For this is necessary to the existing as a member of the new. To make it *treasonable,* therefore, after having become a member of a new, to bear arms, and being taken in arms to be punished capitally, *is contrary to the laws of nature;* as the being *taken prisoner, and put to death, is contrary to the laws of arms.* This is an extent, therefore, of the law of treason in England, beyond the law of Pennsylvania, as it was before the Union, or under the Union, exists here. Unless indeed chief justice Ellsworth's doctrine, in the case of Williams, should be considered the law, that in these states *no one can put off his allegiance to the government.* Chief justice Ellsworth, a great and upright man, I acknowledge, and for whose memory I have a high respect; did he never suffer the subject of a foreign government to be naturalized in his courts, and hear the oath of abjuration taken *renouncing all subjection, and allegiance, more especially to that sovereign, or state, of which the naturalized had been a member?* Did it ever come into his mind that one so naturalized, could owe but a *qualified allegiance* to these states, of whose supreme court, he was a judge?

Did it enter into the mind of the judge, that the *new citizen* was not equally bound, with all others, to do militia duty; and, if for the sake of offence, or defence, the sovereign authority, should order, he was not bound to obey? If so, could he say that the new citizen was not equally bound to be *protected, whether upon the sea, or upon the dry land?* Could a distinction be drawn between his rights and his duties, from that of any other member of the community? The truth is, it was an over-sight in the chief justice, and looking to what had been considered the law of England, he did not distinguish in the case. I excuse the judge, as being, I am confident, an inadvertency; but I lay it down as a *nefarious principle,* and outraging human reason to give it the least countenance. We have the right of every other independent country, to consider every one coming to our shores, and manifesting an ,intention of joining our society, as entitled to be received, and protected, by land, or water, within our *municipal jurisdiction, and beyond it*, by the arm of the nation. As to the *expediency*, I say nothing; I leave that to the politicians. I lay it down only, that *naturalization involves the duty, and the pledge of protection; and a citizen of the United States, chusing to expatriate, in time of peace, is not liable to our treason law, even though found in arms with a foreign force invading us.*

As to the *expediency*, I mean the policy, of naturalizing at all; and not repealing the whole body of the naturalization acts of congress; I do not mean to connect this, because I know it would be denying a *natural right* to those of a more populous country, emigrating to a country less populous in proportion to the soil, and it would be denying ourselves a right to take them; and it could be on the principle of *self-preservation* that we could dispense with the taking them. But as to the letting all go that chuse to go, I consider it not only their right, but our interest. We have no such *Merino-breed* of men, that there can be any thing in the way to hinder it. Those that emigrate from us, consult what they think their own interest, and we may be well rid of them. Whether Britain, were there not a matter of pride in the way, might not say the same thing, I leave it to her to determine.

But to return from my digression. The treason law of England has been rendered sanguinary by the construction of the judges. " One witness to one overt act, and a second witness to another overt act of the same species of treason," is an instance of this. But still more *the leaning of the judges to convict on a charge of treason.* I do not believe that in the whole state trials in England, there will be found a case, where there was not that leaning visible, where it was evident the crown wished a conviction, whether in a case of misdemeanor, or of felony of treason. In the case of Aaron Burr, with us, the leaning, if any, was the other way, and therefore I consider the principles laid down in that trial, as gaining much to the citizen of the United States, as a barrier against the application of British rules in the construction of treason. It contains some excellent land-marks, that may serve to guide in after times, when parties may prevail, and *judges may have the same leaning with the prosecutor for the state.* Not that I mean to insinuate any thing the least disrespectful, to the executive, or to the court, in this instance, but the contrary, and as a trial, in opposition, to all that we have seen in England, where the accused, for high treason, could scarcely ever be said, to have had a fair chance for his life.

" In civil cases, we have seen that every defendant is bailable ; but in *criminal matters it is otherwise.*"   4 Bl. Com. 296.

WITH submission to Dr. Blackstone, says Junius, " I think he has fallen into a contradiction, which, in terms at least, appears irreconcileable. After enumerating several offences not bailable, he asserts, without any condition, or limitation whatsoever, " all these are clearly not admissible to bail." Yet in a few lines after, he says, " It is agreed that the court of king's bench make bail for any crime whatsoever, according to the circumstances of the case." To his first proposition he should have added, *by sheriffs or justices ;* otherwise the two propositions contradict each other : with this difference, however, that the first is absolute, the second limited by a *consideration* of *circumstances.*" These were the words of the first edition of the commentaries upon which Junius animadverts ; a *contradiction ;* which I will acknowledge perplexed me not a little at an early period. But in a subsequent edition, the words, " *all these are clearly not admissible to bail,*" have been omitted. Nevertheless in another part, the words at the head of this note preserve the contradiction in some degree taken by themselves as they stand in the sentence. For if in all cases a defendant is bailable; but in criminal matters it is *otherwise*, it must follow that in *criminal matters*, *every* defendant is *not bailable*. He still should have added, that it is otherwise in criminal matters, *unless by a judge of the king's bench, or by that court.*

In his letters to lord Mansfield, Junius undertakes to prove that unless in a case *short* of being taken in the *mainor*, the Lord chief justice of England, has no more right to bail than a justice of the peace; that a person positively charged with felonies, stealing, and taken in *flagrante delicto*, with the stolen goods upon him is not bailable. I agree with Junius that if the lord chief justice did bail, it was an abuse of his discretion. And upon this principle our constitution has settled it: by Art. 9. Sec. 14. " All prisoners shall be bailable, *unless for capital offences*, when the *proof is evident or presumption great.*"

This I take it to have been precisely what the *common law* was before the provision of statute in England, or constitution here. But the constitution here specifies what the discretion of the judge at *common law* would have dictated to be his duty.

———

" All presumptive evidence of felony should be admitted cautiously." 4 Bl. Com. 358.

THERE is what is called *violent* presumption; that is where such circumstances exist as usually attend the fact. *Presumptive proof of this nature is held sufficient to convict.*

In a playful work published some years ago; and where I thought myself at liberty to support even a paradox, it being evident that I did not mean to be serious in *every thing*, I advanced some sentiments on this head, which, as not being continued in the second edition, I may here extract. It is from what I had entitled *Modern Chivalry*, Vol. I. p. 99; and is as follows.

" I doubt much whether *reason* or *experience*, (that is of conviction or presumptive evidence) approve the doctrine.

Reason tells us that there may be all the circumstances that usually attend the fact; and yet, *without the fact itself*. *Experience* evinces that it has been the case; for we have heard of persons convicted of a *capital offence;* and yet with their last breath, asserting innocence. Nay, in the very case of some who have been supposed to have been murdered; they have afterwards been found to be alive. But, on abstract principle, *a conclusion of certainty cannot be drawn from presumptive proof.* Because, in a case of the *most violent* presumption, there is still a *possibility* of innocence; and where there is a *possibility*, there must *be a doubt;* and will *you hang man, woman, or child, where there is a doubt ?*

"In all cases, there ought to be *complete proof*, because the convicted person is to be *completely hanged;* and the jury previous to this, must find a verdict upon oath; that is, must make *complete oath of the guilt.*

"It is the ground of the doctrine of presumptive proof, that where you cannot help suspecting, you ought to be positive; whereas the just conclusion would be, that where you cannot help suspecting, there you ought *to suspect still; but no more.*

"In algebra minus multiplied by minus, makes plus; but not so in arithmetic. In mathematics, the three angles of a triangle, are equal to two right angles: but these are all angles that are put together; they are things of the same kind; but the greatest angle, and the longest side, will never make a triangle, because there is no inclusion of space. There must be a number of things of the same kind, to make an aggregate whole; so that ten thousand possibilities, probabilities, and violent presumptions, can never constitute a certainty. It can never be made a question, how many uncertainties, will make a certainty.

"Semi plena probatio; or the going but half way towards proof, cannot amount to proof sufficient to convict. For a miss is as good as a mile. If the evidence is not positive to the fact, how can the jury find the fact; because *as the current cannot rise higher than the source,* so the verdict of the juror ought not to be more absolute than the oath of the witness. In all cases, therefore, short of positive testimony, what can be done but to acquit?

"These hints may be of service to weak judges; so, that honest people may not lose their lives, or be rendered infamous, without full proof of the offence. It is hard enough to suffer, where there is *full proof;* but to be in the power of a juror, or a judge's imagination, comparing, and construing circumstances, and weighing probabilities, contingencies, and what might have been; or what might not have been, as the humour, wheel or whim of the brain may suggest, is inconsistent with that fair trial, which in a free government ought to be allowed. Were I a juror, it would seem to me I should not find a verdict without *positive evidence* of the fact. For it would not be in my power to restore that fame or life which I had taken away; and if a guilty person should escape, it was none of my look out; but the business of providence to furnish proof; and if proof was not furnished, let providence take the matter on himself; and punish the culprit either in *this life*, *or in a future state*. Invisible things belong to the Omniscient; and it would seem great arrogance in man to take upon him to decide *in cases of uncertainty*. I can declare, that, in the course of my experience at the bar, I have known one hung, and two others within an ace of it, who were innocent. The one that was hung was a tory case, where the popular clamour was against the man, and *light* presumption became *violent* under such a charge, from the temper of the times, and that part of the country where the conviction took place."

So far the extract from this publication, and though I might not be disposed to lay it down at this time, to such extent; viz. that I would not *convict at all upon circumstantial proof in criminal cases*, yet *a great distinction ought to be taken in the consequence*. For though the life of man might not be safe, were it understood that nothing short of positive testimony should convict of murder; and circumstances are said to speak as strong as words or stronger even; yet, I should think that *death* in case of conviction short of po-

sitive evidence ought not to be the consequence; but imprisonment only. It might be left to providence to discover,
and bring to light a fact which might shew innocence; but,
after life shall be taken away, there is not this room left.
And we do know, from history, and trials in criminal
cases, many instances, where *providence* after the legally condemned, but innocent person executed, has brought to light
facts which have established the innocence; and in one case
at least, known in our reports, that no murder had been at
all committed. I refer to the case of the uncle and his niece.
She was heard to say, O! uncle do not kill me, after which
she was missing, because she had absconded with a relation
in a distant part of the kingdom. He was condemned upon
the presumption of circumstance, and was executed. She afterwards appeared to claim his estate.

I have not the book by me; nor do I know of more than
one copy in this country, " A report of criminal cases in the
high court of sessions, Scotland," by an advocate of that
court, a Mr. Arndt; but I will cite the outlines of one case
from memory.

A person convicted of murder upon *evidence from circumstance*, and the day of his execution fixed, solicited earnestly
a reprieve for three months; and that, if *providence* did not
in that time interpose for him by *bringing the truth to light*,
he would be resigned to the dispensation; but, that he had
a strong impression, *providence* would not resist his prayers,
which for the sake of his family, he had so earnestly put up.
A reprieve was obtained for this space of time; and the
lord president of the sessions going in the mean time, to a
summer residence in the north, overheard some men that
were at work in a stone quarry, under the hill by the road
side, say to one, why so down cast this day? What is the
matter? Matter enough said he. *There is a man to be hung
this day at Edinburgh, for a murder which I committed.* He
was apprehended, and confessed the whole, viz. *That had
been the day appointed for the execution of him who had been
reprieved.* The result was, if I recollect right, they were
both pardoned. The first because it had appeared that he

never ought to have been convicted; and the last because it would be an inconsistency in legal proceedings, to *hang one for a murder, which the law had said, had been committed by another.*

----*-----

Extract from Malcome's Miscellaneous Anecdotes; published, 1811.

THE following shocking article appeared in most of the newspapers of 1681.

" From Dublin we have an account, that at the last sessions there, an innkeeper being condemned for robbing on the highway, when he was at the gallows, confessed an horrid murder, complicated with most strange circumstances, which he had committed. The story, take as followeth. Last christmas, two persons, strangers to one another, came into his inn, the one of them having a considerable charge of money. After they were in bed and asleep, he took the sword of the person who had the least money, and killed the other, and put the sword into his scabbard again, all bloody. The person whose sword was made use of, arose in the morning early; called for his horse, and prosecuted his journey, so soon as he was gone, the innkeeper goeth into the room where the murdered person lay, and with a seeming amazement, cried out that one of his guests was murdered, and, upon search, found that his money was lost. Every one suspected the person who so lately rode forth; upon which he was pursued, overtaken, and, the innkeeper drawing his sword, it was bloody, which was so strong *a presumption* of guilt, that, being tried for his life, he was found guilty. But, on the other side, the innocence of his countenance, and behaviour when he was apprehended, and the extreme surprize he seemed to be possessed with at the sight of his bloody sword, and his not deviating from the right road to the place he overnight discoursed to be travelling unto, and the money lost not being found about him, the judge had some scruple upon his mind, and obtained a reprieve for him; and upon this confession of the innkeeper, a full pardon."

I add the following case in which I was of counsel, and the only counsel, for the defendants.

In Westmoreland county, Pennsylvania, in the year 1782, two persons by the name of Miller, and Cunningham, were indicted on a charge of murder before judges Pentecost, Cook and Hays, commissioned to hold a court of oyer and terminer, for that and other counties west of the mountains. Two hunters, the deceased one, coming early to the cabin of Cunningham (the son) were entertained by him, and his bottle of whiskey produced. After having drank what was in it, they wanted more; and, offered to buy a quart, that they might shoot at a mark, the loser to pay for it. He said that he had but a small quantity in a keg which he shewed, and had it for the use of people that were to come that day to put up a cabin for his brother-in-law, Miller, pointing to Miller who was there in the house with him, Miller's wife, the sister of Cunningham; and Cunningham the father, were the only persons then in the house. This the surviving of the hunters, and Cunningham the father testified on their examination, on the trial, as also what follows; viz. that the deceased of the Hunters, insisted on having a quart to shoot for with his companion, and they would pay for it. Cunningham persisted in refusing, and for the same reasons. Upon which the deceased drew his tomahack from his belt, and swore he would split the keg, unless he got the whiskey, and advanced seemingly in order to do it. Upon this Cunningham (the son) laid hold of him to prevent him, and a scuffle ensued. The deceased threw Cunningham across the fire; from which, by an exertion, he recovered, and got the deceased down. The surviving hunter, had in the mean time been interposing as he said to part the combatants; but as Cunningham, (the father) said, it was to *assist his companion;* under which impression the father laid hold of the surviving hunter, and endeavoured to put him out of the house; and did put him out, and the scuffle continuing some small distance out of the house, the surviving hunter, whose face was towards the house, saw his companion, the deceased, as he testified at the door; and just in the inside, as he had his hand upon the cheek door, he was knocked down with the but-end of his own rifle, as it afterwards appeared to be, and with which stroke the barrel was broke from the stock. In this case the blow could not have been given but by one of the three; the sister of Cunningham, the younger; Miller's wife; or by Miller himself; or by *Cunningham*, the younger. No one would think of the sister a very young woman, of apparent timidity, and delicate appearance; and the surviving hunter testified that she appeared much frightened on the occasion. Miller was put in the bill of indictment; but the suspicion did not attach so much to him, as to Cunningham, the younger, who had been in grips with the deceased, and had appeared to have the advantage in the struggle. Miller could not be called upon to *accuse* himself; nor to *accuse* Cunningham; for that would be the same thing as to *excuse* himself; or in other words, give testimony for himself; since one or the other of the two must have committed the homicide. The *sister*, the wife of Miller, could not be called upon to give testimony against her husband; nor against Cunningham, for that would be the same thing as testifying for her husband, since if *Cunningham* was the slayer, *Miller*, could not be.

I had asked Cunningham (the son) in whose favour would the sister lean in case she was called upon to give evidence. His answer was in favour of her husband. But if his father had a leaning, in whose favour would it be. His answer was it would be in favour of him the son.

From the narrative of Cunningham, the son to me, he stated that having got the deceased down, he desisted, and let him up, and that he the deceased had turned to go out, probably to join his companion out of doors, who was engaged with *old* Cunningham, who appeared by far the stoutest man of the whole. That Miller, in the mean time, had seized a rifle of the hunter, and turning the but-end, struck at the deceased; and with so powerful a blow, that it broke off the stock at the lock, *and killed him.*

In the communication of Miller and his wife to me, and of Cunningham, whom I heard separately, it was understood, that being counsel, I could not give testimony of it, or was not bound to do it; so that no danger could follow from a confession of the real truth of the case. Miller, or his wife, were silent, as to the manner in which the matter happened, but Cunningham gave a relation with simplicity, and perfect consistency with all the circumstances testified by his father, and by the surviving hunter. I had no doubt of his innocence. Nevertheless, *the opinion of the public was against him;* and the same jury passing upon Miller, found no difficulty in acquitting, but hung 18 hours upon Cunningham; but finally acquitted; not upon *any doubt* they had of Cunningham's guilt; but on my argument contending that so *outrageous a trespass,* and the necessity of self-preservation, made it justifiable.

In examining old Cunningham, I had asked him, whether, when the one with whom he was engaged out of doors, and who had disengaged himself, and was making to re-enter, in *appearance, to assist* his companion, had drawn his tomahack from his belt, and was advancing with it. He said no. But when he came to be sworn, he took care to add this circumstance, and to say that he had his tomahack drawn. The surviving hunter, said he had not; but the question was, which of these should be believed. In convicting both Cunningham and Miller, one innocent person must have suffered, and if one had been convicted, it would have been the innocent; and this from the presumption of circumstances.

This, I take it, was the only special commission of Oyer and Terminer, issued since the formation of the constitution, in 1776; and one person who was convicted of a capital offence, at this court, was afterwards pardoned; John Dickinson, who succeeded to the *presidency of the council,* having doubts as to the legality of such a commission issuing.

OBSERVATIONS

ON

ACTS OF ASSEMBLY THAT MAY BE REPEALED OR MODIFIED.

Act of 3d December, 1782.

THE act entitled an act to prevent the erecting any new and independent state within the limits of this commonwealth, 3d December, 1782, might be repealed; the occasion that gave rise to it having ceased to exist. It was a consequence of the cession made by Virginia to Pennsylvania of some part of the territory claimed, with a view to a compromise. The inhabitants of the territory ceded did not see the reason of such cession; nor were they willing to acknowledge the justice of it. The truth is, it involved a great question; viz. how far a state could cede territory, and another state acquire jurisdiction, with a view to a settlement of boundary. Nothing but what comes under the head of the *transcendental* right, as Burlamaqui stiles it, could excuse it, or justify; the salus populi suprema lex. I have no doubt now but that the people in that part of the state, at that time, had the right to have objected; and refuse submission to the Pennsylvania government. But I thought otherwise at the time, and took a decided part in support of the Pennsylvania jurisdiction. It was shortly after the cession in the spring of 1781, that I went to that country, entering on the practice of the law, having been before admitted in the court of common pleas of Philadelphia. The Pennsylvania courts were shortly afterwards established in that part of the country, the county of Washington, which comprehended the principal part of it, having been before

laid out. Conventions in the mean time were holden, and
the sense of the people taken as to submission or resistance.
The idea was to declare themselves independent of Virginia
or Pennsylvania, in the same manner as Vermont had done
of the states of Massachusetts and New York. It was suggested that a new state might be formed with a seat of government at Pittsburgh, having the Kanhaway on the one
side for a boundary, with Muskingum and Lake Erie on the
other, and to the eastward the Allegheny mountain. I will
not say that but for me this would have taken place; but I
certainly contributed very much to obstruct the proposition.
Could I have foreseen the want of support in the Indian war
from the state of Pennsylvania, or Virginia, or from the United
States, the people being left to defend themselves in a great
measure, I might have been disposed to think that an independent government would have been most advisable for their
support and preservation. But be that as it may, so it is that
a contrary policy was advocated and prevailed. It was at my
instance, and on my representation through the Pennsylvania representatives to the legislature, that the act in question
passed; and I believe it is the only act in the code which
contains a clause of *changing the venue.**

This act may be repealed, as now unnecessary under the
general government. See the constitution of the United
States, art. 4. sec. 3.

I have said, that I did not think but that it might have
been justifiable in the people of the territory ceded, to have
considered themselves as thrown into a *state of nature,* and
to have formed *a new and independent government;* because
what authority had states to cede, when in pursuance of the
9th article of the confederation then existing, a judicial tribunal was established, by which the controversy might have
been determined, the principle settled, and the actual boun-

---

* By a subsequent act, 31st August, 1785, the clause changing
the venue is repealed as contrary to the constitution, that trials
shall be by a jury of the vicinage. This would seem affirmatory
of the principle that the venue cannot be changed in a criminal
case.

dary ascertained ? The principle which governed me chiefly was the consideration suggested in the act ; viz. that the commonwealth of Pennsylvania had succeeded to the proprietary ownership of soil, and was pledged to pay a considerable sum in compensation to the charter proprietaries ; and the ungranted lands in that quarter was a fund for raising the compensation to be made ; and of which I thought it would be unjust to deprive the rest of the community. But if I had known the little account to which this turned afterwards by the mismanagement of the legislature, and the land office, and speculators intending a great deal, but making little for themselves ; and all these things obstructing the improvement and population of the country, I might have thought less of the value of my efforts on this occasion. Whatever they were, certain it is, that I encountered some danger in opposition to the popular current, on the Virginia side of the state. But it is not consistent with my object in the present book to go farther into what might be called a *matter of history rather than of jurisprudence.*

An act to regulate arbitrations, and proceedings in courts of justice. 21 March, 1806.

THE system of *arbitration* under this act, I have always considered as a matter of experiment ; and was well satisfied that the experiment was made, and a fair trial given it. For it appeared to me, that though it might not answer the expectations of the most sanguine, yet *some improvement might grow out of it.* I have considered the appeal as objectionable, so far as respects the party *who calls for the rule of reference being entitled to it.* And this, I take it, has been found, upon experiment, to be a grievance.

In the year 1807, on the circuit towards Lake Erie, I fell in with an inhabitant unknown to me, and, to whom I was unknown ; and entering into conversation with him, on the affairs of the country, I found him dissatisfied with it.

3 T

and disposed to leave it. His grounds of dissatisfaction, were a great variety of matters; but, amongst these, he spoke of the hills, the roads, the mountains as unpleasant; and the winds, the weather, and the seasons, as unfavourable : but most of all, the laws, the lawyers the justices, the judges, the courts and arbitrations. What of the *justices*, said I, you have an appeal in some cases, and where they do *wilful wrong*, there is a law enabling you to take depositions, and bring them to account. Ay, said he, but if we do get a hitch upon them, and bring them to the trig, *they plead ignorance, and who can dispute that ?*

But as to judges, said I, you have the presidents of districts; do not they do pretty well? Why, said he, they might be of *some use*, if they would let the jury take their own way, but this they will not do. They swear them; but dont swear themselves, and so are at liberty to say just what they please.

But said I, you have *circuit judges* that come trotting up here ; (circuit courts had not been then abolished ;) judges of the supreme court, they call them, what fault do you find with these? Why, said he, I have been at some of their courts; and have heard their charges; and they seem to steer pretty clear a while, in the trial of a cause; but towards the *winding up*, I have observed, that they *always lean a little more to one side than the other*.

As to the judges not being sworn, said I, presidents or circuit court judges, they are sworn *at first*, when they take the *oath of office*. That is, said he, like the man saying grace over a tub of beef which he salted up ; but none when he sat down to dinner.

But, said I, in the administration of justice, there is a way provided of *getting clear of judges ;* you have your *arbitrations ;* justice brought home to your own doors. If a cause is brought into court, you can take it out, and leave the judges sitting on their stools with nothing to do. Ay, said he, but they have *a trick of taking the cause back again ; so that we are just where we were at first, with more costs to pay.*

Though this illustration of the way of thinking of the people is introduced with a view of pleasantry not always suitable for a serious work, yet it did appear to me, and does now, that *appeals ought to be restrained, to the party called upon to refer.* Why shall he who calls for a reference, appeal from a *tribunal of his own chusing*, unless in the case of misbehaviour of parties, or of referees? This is *the common law ground of setting aside an award.*

Act of Assembly, 21 March, 1806. Sec. 13.

" That in all cases where a remedy is provided, or duty enjoined, or any thing directed to be done by any act, or acts of assembly of this commonwealth, the directions of the said acts, shall be *strictly* pursued, &c."

This is a section of an act entitled, " an act to regulate arbitrations and proceedings, in courts of justice." It is not improbable that the arbitration acts will receive a revision by the legislature at no distant day; and if so, I would recommend the striking out the word *strictly* in this section. It is not only a maxim of the common law, but is a *dictate of humanity*, and a maxim of reason, that penal laws be construed *strictly*, but remedial laws *liberally*. The courts have been much embarrassed with this word, and at a loss to know what to make of it. It certainly could not be the intention of the legislature to change the rule of construction in this particular; and yet it has the appearance of doing it. While therefore, we are endeavouring to reach the sense of the act in this particular, we are transgressing the *letter* of the provision. That I may explain what I mean, I will cite the language of Blackstone, on the liberal construction of terms. 3 Bl. Com. 430.

" A court of equity determines according to the *spirit* of the rule, and not according to the *strictness* of the *letter*. In general laws all cases cannot be foreseen; or if foreseen cannot be expressed; some will arise that will fall within the *meaning*, though not within the words of the legislature, and others, which may fall within the *letter*, may be contrary to his *meaning*, though not expressly excepted. These cases thus out of the *letter*, are often said to be within the *equity*, of an act of parliament; and so cases within the *letter*, are frequently out of the *equity*. Here, by *equity*, we mean nothing but the sound interpretation of the law; though the words of the law itself may be too *general*, too *special*; or *otherwise inaccurate* or defective. These then are the cases which, as Grotius says, "lex non exacte definit sed arbitrio boni viri permittit," in order to find out the true meaning of the law given, from every other topic of construction." 3 Bl. Com. 430.

We have an English statute, 28 Hen. 8. c. 7. Sec. 28, which provides "that the present act *shall be taken and accepted according to the plain words and sentences therein contained.*" It might as well have enacted that the words should be *plain*, and have no *ambiguity*; and the arrangement of a sentence or sentences, be so intelligible that no misunderstanding in the case, should take place; or have enacted that all *judges* whose province it was, to construe them, should have no *difference of opinion*; or, that all judges should have *legal knowledge, and good sense.* Notwithstanding such a statute, it might puzzle a king in that country, to find judges who would all agree, if they exercised their *individual* judgments; or, that would understand a statute *precisely*, as each one of the legislature might say, they had intended; for, perhaps even the members of parliament among themselves, might not agree, as to what, in their opinions, the meaning of the statute was.

The truth is, it is one of the most difficult things to express an idea in such manner that there can be no mistaking. Let any one think of giving an order, or *direction* to an agent; or, of having given instructions to an intelligent person relative to the most common business; and, how often will he find that he has not been sufficiently comprehended. Or, in the case of receiving instructions from an intelligent person, how often will he find that the meaning is somewhat to be guessed at. But how much will the chances of an uncertain meaning occur when the subject of the *direction* is on a matter not familiar to the *common mind*, and involves a great scope of action that is to be embraced by the rule. Cases that occur, will often prove that the highest powers of the human mind are not adequate to the anticipating of them. It is not in human nature to foresee every thing. It is under a sense of the difficulty, I have heard it said, that the wisest head could not frame a law, but a *cart and horses might be driven through it.* If it can be at all done, it must certainly be by one who understands *the use of terms ;* the *arrangement* of words; the remedy to be provided, or the *duty* enjoined; and *can foresee,* like a skilful general, when he lays the plan of a campaign, or disposes his troops for an engagement, where it is that the adversary may find a *weak part,* or make an *impression.*

But from the number of minds that are to be consulted before a bill can pass the chambers of the legislature, were it even drawn in the *most skilful manner,* it will be *disturbed by amendments.* According to the proverb, *many cooks spoil the soup.* In the nature of the case, it is impossible, always, to avoid *ambiguity* where *alterations,* by additions or by striking out, are made. There will be as many different meanings to be extracted, as there are spellings of the word *Sunbury* on the hand-boards, on the road from the town of Reading to that place. Of this we have a remarkable instance in the construction put upon the 9th section of the act of 3d April, 1792. The judges of the supreme court adhered to the letter; and even these differed among themselves. The judges of the state (supreme court) endeavoured to reach what they considered the *intention,* and even these as to the intention, differed ; some adhering less or more to the *letter,* others rejecting the *letter,* and following what they took to be the *meaning* altogether. The *ambiguity* of what is expressed, has led to much difference of opinion on the bench, and has been the source of litigation to the people. Where

"More is meant than meets the ear,"

will be the case, in all diction. But if the *letter* is to go-

vern; and if what is said must be taken *strictly*, the substantial *meaning* and *intention* will oftentimes be lost.

A difference of inclination to construe according to the *letter* or *intention*, divided the Roman lawyers. There were those " who contended for a strict adherence to the *letter* and *forms* of the law; others for a *benign interpretation of it*, and for allowing *great latitude* in the observance of its *forms.*" Butler's Horæ Juridicæ, 49.

I always thought, says lord Mansfield, in a report of the case of Perrin v. Blake, which has come into my hands, " that the *strict* adherence of courts of justice to the *letter* of the law, is productive of the worst consequences. In *all ages there will be strict lawyers.* But it is to be hoped that, in all ages, there will be lawyers of a different bent of genius, and a different course of education."

It cannot but be supposed, that there will be a wide difference between the penning of an act of the legislature, and that of a last will and testament. In the one case, great deliberation, and by men selected for their understandings; in the other, by the *individual* presumed to be inops consilii, or unassisted; and in many cases, in a great degree unlettered; and, it may be, in his last *sickness.* Yet the same principle will apply in one case, as well as the other, viz. that the *intention* is to govern. That it is oftentimes difficult to get at this *intention*, is certain. For where an unlettered individual himself draws or dictates his will, or rather dictates the heads of it; or where an *ordinary scrivener*, such as may occur, puts it into language, it must, in most cases, defeat his intention to be collected from the whole will, if the *letter* is to govern. I introduce the case of wills only to illustrate what I mean by construction according to *intention*, not that I would put an act of assembly to the same extent, on a footing with the construction of wills, for the reasons already given. For in wills there is oftentimes *great difficulty.* When Satan went on his voyage to the new world, our earth, Milton occupies the fallen angels in his absence, with discussing metaphyscis.

" Others apart sat on a hill retired,
In thoughts more elevate, and reasoned high
Of providence, fore-knowledge, will, and fate,
Fixed fate, free-will, fore-knowledge absolute,
And found no end in wandering mazes lost."

Had last wills and testaments been then, he might have given these to *construe*. Not that they might not be able to find out the meaning by the mumping, if the *intention was to govern*, but if adhering to the *letter*, they would find such contradictions, and inconsistencies, that it would be difficult to know what to make of it.

The English are divided on the subject of construing wills. All agree that the intention is to govern, save where a *technical* term occurs; and in this case some are governed by the *term;* or, in other words, by the *letter*. So that it is not what a man meant, but what he ought to mean by *the rules of art*, that is to guide. Nor is it even what *technical rules* will permit him to mean; but it is a compound of the two, what he meant, and what he ought to mean, that constitutes the enigma and comes to be unriddled. This will sometimes be a question worthy of Œdipus to the Sphynx. For in one case, it will be said, the intent controuls the *technical term ;* and, in another, the *technical term*, controuls the *intent*.

" I am sensible," says sir Joseph Jekyll, (master of the rolls,) 2 Peere Williams, 741, " there is a diversity of opinion among the learned judges of the present time, whether the legal operation of words, in a will; or the *intent* of a testator shall govern. For my part I shall always contend for the *intention;* and I think the strongest authorities are on that side. For if the *intention* is sometimes to govern, as it is admitted, it must, and not always give way to the legal construction; and, yet at other times, shall not govern, there will then be no rule to judge by; nor, will any lawyer know how to advise his client; a mischief which judges ought to prevent." And, by lord Mansfield, 2 Burr. 770. " No *technical* words are necessary to convey a testator's meaning; and, whenever that is doubtful, it must be collected from the *whole scope* of the *whole* will compared with the several

parts." And in Perrin and Blake's case, he says, " That
he always thought, that, as the law had allowed a free
communication of *intention* to a testator, it would be a
strange law to say, now that you have communicated that
intention so that every one understands what you mean, yet
because you have used a *certain* expression of art, we will
cross your *intention*, and give your will a different construction ; though what you meant to have *done* is perfectly legal ; and, the only reason for contravening your *intention*, is
because you have not expressed yourself like a lawyer."
Such was the judgment of a *majority* of the king's bench.
But, in the exchequer chamber, on a hearing, it was reversed. The majority of the judges stuck to the *strict letter*,
and the technical terms of the will.

In this country the bulk of judges have followed this decision of the exchequer, because it was that of the majority.
Judge Pendleton, in Virginia, did not follow it, as has been
already noted.

" Victrix causa diis placuit, sed victa Catoni."

Judge Tucker, in his notes on Blackstone, recognizes
this way of thinking of Pendleton. And in his judicial capacity, April, 1810, " that there are no precise words, no
precise arrangement of them, nor any thing, in any degree
technical, necessary to the discovery of the testator's real
and legal intention. Whenever, from the whole face, and
context of the will, we can collect the testator's *intention*,
we are bound to give it effect." 1 Munford, 541.

So far with respect to the construing last wills and testaments, with a view of explaining the difficulty of reconciling in all cases, *the pursuing the strict letter* of an act of assembly, with what they must obviously have *intended*. For
such is the imperfection of language, that *terms* are equivocal :
or vary in their meaning, according to their situation in a
sentence. There is also what the grammarians call an *ellipsis*,
in language ; words used in a preceding clause, which are
omitted in a second, and to be understood, or brought forward, and supplied. We have instances of this in last wills
and testaments, where the judges in early times, not the best

grammarians ; and seeing that the meaning required it, and not knowing how *otherwise* to reach it, have changed not a *letter* only, but a *word*, and substituted one *directly contrary;* as, or, for and ; and vice versa; and, for or. That is read the will so. I have no objection to this, but as it savours of what is *arbitrary*, and has the appearance of doing violence to language. It is something like the house-wife challenging her bag at the mill, P for John, and R for Patterson.

Were judges to pursue the *strict letter* of a statute, they would have less trouble. For it does not require much understanding to distinguish A from B. And this is according to the *letter*.

I have no idea that *tautology*, and *multiplying terms* contributes to perspicuity, and there is danger when it is undertaken to enumerate, that something may not be embraced as in the British parliament, where the word *person* was used in the bill, and a member moved an amendment, person, or persons; and another thinking to carry the matter still farther, and make sure, doubly sure, made a farther motion to add person, or persons, he, she, or they. Another in order to shew the danger of undertaking to specify particulars, concluded with moving that it be he, she, they, or it ; for there might be an *hermaphrodite*, in the case.

The truth is, that hæret in cortice, qui hæret in literæ; he sticks to the *bark* who *sticks* to the *letter* ; and it is only by penetrating through the rind, to the substantial wood, *that the meaning of an act can be ascertained.*

3 U

Act of Assembly, March 19th, 1810, prohibiting in courts of justice, the reading, or quoting British precedents subsequent to 4th July, 1776.

THERE is a British statute of an old date, I cannot immediately turn to it; and I cite from memory, prohibiting the judges from suffering themselves to be *feasted* when they go the circuit. The words are, "shall take no gift of any one, with the exception of food, or drink, *and of this very little.*" Under this minimum, or *very little*, I presume may be comprehended what was merely complimentary, on the score of respect, or friendship; as, in our times the libation of a glass of wine, or a dish of tea with the female part of the household; but no formal invitation to sup, or dine, or any thing like what might be called an *entertainment.* This statute must have been founded on some *experience* that such hospitalities operated as a species of bribery; for it is classed with the *accepting gifts;* and, doubtless, it is but a delicate mode of conciliating a pre-judgment. And hence it is that compliments to sup, or dine, are usually given to those whom we mean to conciliate, or pre-dispose. It was a paradoxical apothegm of the great Franklin, that the best way to gain a man, was *to take him by the throat.* And, when Aristippus was reproached by his brother philosophers, because he bent his knee when he presented a petition to Dionysius, " what can I help it," said he, " if that man *has his ears in his feet ?*" In the same manner it may be said by one who has a matter pending in court, and entertains, " how can I help it, if I know that judge, to have some part of *his hearing in his throat.*"

But would it not have been sufficient for this British statute to have prohibited only the accepting cards to sup, or dine, from a *suitor* in court? How could a judge ascertain whether the person giving the invitation was a *suitor,* not having at hand the court docket to evolve, or inspect; and it would be indelicate to ask the person, offering himself as a *host,* " pray sir, have you *a cause in court ?*" Besides, it might be rather *with a view to a cause* that he intended to bring, or expected to have brought against him, than to one *pending*, that the invitation was given. He might think of the rule of prudence, " Cast thy bread upon the waters, and thou shalt find it after many days." A cunning stager conscious to himself of a misdemeanor, or a felony committed, might apprehend an indictment, and be willing to save his *bacon* in one sense, at the expence of it, in another. Or to make an offering, not " of a turtle dove, and two young pigeons" to the *priest;* but of a duck, or a goose to the *judge.*

But, to say nothing of a *suitor*, might not something be done in that country of roast beef, through the medium of a barrister, or counsel in the cause, who might find out the weak side of a judge; whether he was to be gained by flattery to his understanding; or, deditus ventri, by food to his corporal taste. The exordium of an orator, according to Cicero, ought to be, " reddere auditorem docilem, attentum, benevolum." And were counsel to blame when they had discovered, that at least the *temper* of a judge might be soothed by using the means put in practice by the hero of the Æneid in his descent to Elysium, to soothe the centinel at the out-post?——

> Melle soporatam, et medicatis frugibus offam
> Objicit————

Oiling the springs of a machine makes it run smooth; and wine will put a judge in good humor; though the danger may, be that he will be put into too good a humor with one counsel *at the expence of another;* or at least *of the cause* which he supports.

It is not in the natural order of things, for men in authority who have *discipline* to support, to become *guests;* much less who have controversies to determine between man and man. There is a repugnance in a mind of *sensibility* in deciding against your *host*, if you can help it; and you will at least have a wish when his cause comes to trial, *that it may turn out good.*

But the principal obligation is the enabling the *unworthy to derive character from the station.* For though the judge himself may be neither pleasant in his manners, nor respectable for his understanding, yet, in contemplation of law, he is supposed to have at least *legal knowledge;* and his station carries with it *the majesty of the people;* and it is not proper that a knave should have it in his power to say, I had a judge, or the judges to dine with me.　And how can judges on the circuit know, in every case, what there may be against the man that appears to entertain them.

But, for their own sakes, on *account of regimen and command of time,* if for no other consideration, the judges will find it most advisable to decline invitations.　I do not think, therefore, it will be necessary to *provide by law,* as in England, at an early period they would seem to have done.

But of this enough; I go on to speak of that which was my main object, the *muzzling,* not the *mouth,* but the *mind* of a judge, in prescribing to him that he shall not take a nip of information come from whence it may.　What would we think of a British statute prohibiting the quoting precedents of our courts? It may be said, such an act of parliament would be unnecessary; for, my lords the judges of the English courts, are too self-sufficient to admit to be read our decisions.　There may be something in that; but, they would be startled at an act of the legislature prohibiting the reading these.　A liberal and enlightened chief justice of one of their benches would say, do we not hear occasionally read to us, the laws of other countries, or the decisions of their courts so far as they can throw light upon a matter before us; and why exclude the reasonings of a people, or the decisions on a law that is *common* to us both; nay even, why exclude reasonings on their acts of Assembly enacted *since our separation,* which have an analogy to our statutes made *since* or *before?*

I do not know whether the judges would permit a learned serjeant to quote a decision made in Pennsylvania, if it had a bearing on the point, as shewing what our *reason* was; yet, I should think it strange if they did not permit it, when it is pretty evident that they read these themselves; and what is more, profit by them.　That they read, at least, the New York reports would seem to appear from their

backing out, to use an American phrase, on the doctrine of
the *conclusiveness of a sentence* of a foreign court of admiralty. This doctrine was first shaken in the New York
state, by a decision of the high court of errors and appeals;
and followed up in Pennsylvania, on my part, in *the supreme
court ;** and afterwards in another case, by judge Cooper in
the high court of errors and appeals. If lord Ellenborough
had not read the reasoning in these cases, or heard them
read, he appears at least to have adopted a greater liberality
in his way of thinking on the subject than other judges, who
had sat on the same or other benches before him. See 1
Camp. 418. Park. 495. 6th edition. And 1 Camp. 429.
Park. 619.

On these and the like grounds, I incline to be of opinion
that the act in question, 19th March, 1810, ought to be repealed.

Were it not that my sentiments are known as having no
overweening attachment to British precedents, save so far as
they carry with them *natural*, or legal reason, I should be more
embarrassed in objecting to this act. But, were it not that I
should be unwilling to enter into a contest with the legislature, where public opinion, or prejudice is on their side, I
might be disposed to question *the constitutionality* of this act.
It would seem to be abridging the right of the judiciary, to
hear all reason on a question before them.

———————What is't to us
Though it were said byTrismegistus?

But if we are to hear the saying of a lord, years, or centuries ago; and before the 4th July, 1776, why not what
*another lord has said since, to explain or contradict the adju-
dication ?* The fact is, early decisions were, many of them

---

* I claim nothing but having been the precursor of judge
Cooper on the same side of the question; and this I have a
right to claim. But his *opinion*, published in a small octavo, I
would recommend to every American student, not so much for
the reasoning and ideas, as for the *analysis*, and *systematic comprehension of the subject.* It is a model that will deserve to be
admired.

narrow; and why drink out of the neck of a gourd, rather than out of an open goblet; more especially if the fountain was muddy, out of which the gourd was filled; the stream of law in that country, now runs more clear in particular cases than centuries ago; and it will always remain so, the law being an improvable science. I like exceedingly when a dictum of a judge, or an adjudication of a court, or tract writer of a semi-barbarous period, is cited, to have it shewn that a more enlightened, and liberal Mansfield; or Kenyon, or Ellenborough, has overruled, or scouted that doctrine. It is shewing from themselves, that they have been wrong; and why should not counsel have this privilege, when old decisions are cited on a point of common, or statute law?

To use a phrase, not meaning disrespect to the learned lords of England, when an old case is cited, contrary to all reason, or good sense, and a new one can be shewn contrary, in the modern decision of another judge, it is like curing according to the vulgar phrase, and vulgar notion, a bite in the case of madness, *with a hair of the same dog*.

ON THE JUDICIARY SYSTEM OF THE STATE.

I have said that I consider this system the first in the Union. I speak as to the *foundation* that has been laid; and improvements that have so far taken place. But some filling up is required to do it justice. What is that filling up? I shall not undertake to say what would in all things complete the building. I shall only go so far as to point out what I would conceive to be more *immediately necessary* to be done. This I do, not confident that it will be well taken, though confident that it is well intended; and meant for the best. And why should I undertake to point out what might be done, who am not of the legislative body; nor of the mass of the people, from amongst whom the representatives are eligible? But has not the legislature a right to the information, and suggestion of the different *functionaries* in their respective stations? For every individual must be supposed, to understand something of that department in which he is more particularly engaged. I shall venture to suggest, therefore, the expediency of what might be done, in the first instance, and at the present time, in carrying on the improvement of the system; though not without fear that coming from a judge, it may defeat the object: for it may be supposed that those immediately concerned in the discharge of duties, will be projecting something that will suit their own convenience. But as I take it, this will not appear to be the case in all the improvement that I shall suggest at present; I will venture it; and, it may go, for as much as it is worth. It will require a president or two more of the common pleas to be added, and that is all the *additional expence* that my propositions would involve.

The first is, a *second* president of the *district* court of common pleas of the city of Philadelphia, to sit *alternately* with the first. Nine months in the year is a length of sitting greater than any one president can long sustain; and it would require a constant sitting of that court to transact the business which comes before it. *It is a court which gives great satisfaction, and ought to be made perpetual.*

In the second place, I would propose another district of the common pleas to be added, in that part of the *mountainous* country, where the districts consist of *more than three counties*, while those of the less western, and in the level country do not consist of more than three. *It is monstrous that the duty should be so unequal;* both as to riding, and the weight of business, *while the salaries are the same. Advance of salary, or diminution of duty,* can alone, bring to an equality, or something like it, in this instance.

In the third place, I would propose the consolidating the two middle districts of the supreme court, into one at the seat of government; and the judges to hold two terms for this district, at an interval of six months; and on the first days of each sitting to deliver opinions on cases which had been argued at the other districts west of that, and which cases had been holden over *under advisement.* Cases of difficulty will be argued, upon which it will be impossible for the judges to make up their minds without time to examine, and reflect ; and a postponement of delivering their opinions on the case for a *whole year*, gives *great delay, and is a grievance.* If a judgment is to be *reversed*, the sooner the better ; that the party, if a plaintiff, may begin again, if the error appears to have been in the proceedings, or the trial ; and if the judgment is *affirmed*, the sooner known, the plaintiff can the sooner go on to *recover his right.*

I say nothing of taking away the *original jurisdiction* of the supreme court, in the county of Philadelphia, as it has been done, in the other counties ; nor of what has been sometimes suggested, an addition to the number of the judges of the supreme court, because that might look like over-stepping the limits proposed by myself, in saying nothing that might have the appearance of consulting my own convenience. The taking away the *original* jurisdiction of the supreme court in the county of Philadelphia, might lessen my riding, or sitting somewhat ; or the appointment of an additional number, the *original jurisdiction* remaining, might contribute to lessen, as the thirty-three weeks sitting alternately, would, in that case, be divided amongst more ; but as to the *Terms*, the sitting there would be the same.

Individuals, and even *professional* men, from our sister states are at a loss to conceive how we can go on without a court of chancery. I have referred them to the history of that court in England, that a necessity for it never could have existed, as a court distinct from common law jurisdiction, but for the narrowness of the common law judges. "Extending rather than narrowing the remedial effects of the writ (case) ; they might have effectually answered all the purposes of a court of equity ; except that of obtaining discovery by the oath of the defendant." They could have done that as we do here, by *damages* in actions on agreements for the sale of lands, compel, in most cases, a *specific execution.*

It was this *contractedness* of the minds of common law judges, that explains the maxim, boni judicis est, ampliare *jurisdictionem*, which some would amend by saying, *ampliare justitiam*. But this would be an inconsistency; because *justice* cannot be enlarged or diminished, without *ceasing to be justice*.

A court of *chancery* must sit at *some one place in a state*, and this is irreconcilable with the principle adopted, [in Pennsylvania; and which *ought to be adopted*, of *bringing home justice*, as much as it is possible, *to every man's door.*

HINTS TOWARDS A GENERAL LAW ON THE SUBJECT OF
WRITS OF ERROR.

IN England a writ of error is not grantable ex débito justitiæ, or of right, in *treason and felony*. Application must be made to a judge of the superior court, or to the superior court itself, to allow it; which may, or may not be done, according to the idea of the judge, or court, as to the probability of there being error. With us, by act of assembly, 13 April, 1791, no writ or certiorari, or writ of error, shall be available to remove an *indictment, or stay execution of the judgment*, in any *criminal case;* unless the same shall he *specially* allowed by the supreme court, or one of the justices thereof, upon sufficient cause to him shewn; or shall have been sued out with *the consent of the attorney general.* Some time must intervene before application can be made to a justice of the supreme court; or, to that court; and before the writ of error can be heard; and in the mean time the sentence must go into *part execution*, which is a little like a person, so far as this goes, being hanged, or whipped first, as the phrase is, and *tried afterwards*. For where there was *error*, there can not be said in strictness, to have been a *trial*. The expence to the county in keeping in confinement, until the application can be made to a judge, or to the court, and the writ of error, if allowed, heard, is in the way. But might not bail be taken in the mean time, with condition to surren-

der after hearing; this at least, in *case of misdemeanors,
and offences short of felony?*

A writ of error lies where a party is aggrieved by any error in the *foundation, proceeding, judgment, or execution* of
a suit. But might it not be provided that no error shall
be assigned in the *foundation,* as for instance, want of *jurisdiction before a justice;* or of a court, unless exception taken,
or pleaded to the *jurisdiction,* at the *proper stage* for taking
the exception, or entering the *plea;* and the judgment of
the justice, or court given expressly upon the point. The
same in the case of exception to proceeding, judgment, or
execution? This is an amendment which would seem to be
absolutely necessary, both for the sake of the justice, the
court, and the party. It is not uncommon to have a judgment reversed from error upon the *face of the proceedings,*
though the court below could, but *constructively,* be said to
have passed upon that, in which error is assigned. This is
a matter of which *the judges of the court below* complain, and
have great reason to complain. But, the court above have
thought, that, it is competent only for the legislature to make
an alteration of what the judges of the supreme court have
conceived to be the law, as to this particular. It is a matter
of surprise to me, that for the sake of their own reputations,
the presidents of the district courts, have not before this,
suggested an alteration of the law on this head. It is unfair that they should be supposed *to have decided a point that
was never made to them.* And yet, *constructively,* they are
in contemplation of law, supposed to have sanctioned errors,
which were never noticed by the party, or the counsel. For
it is the law, that, for errors of form, or substance, appearing
on the *face of the proceedings,* error may be *assigned* after
the record comes up; notwithstanding, they had not been
objected to, or noticed before.

In civil cases, writs of error are of course, subject only to
the party " making *oath or affirmation,* that the same is not
intended *for delay.*" This is a temptation to perjury, and
ought to be abolished. The oath, or affirmation, is, almost
of course, made. For, a very slight matter, will satisfy the

conscience, such is human frailty, or perverseness, where, in a case of money to be paid, it is not convenient to pay. The *bringing the money into court*, with the costs of suit, would be the true *test* of the writ of error being brought for the purpose of delay; or, with a solid expectation of being able to reverse the judgment. But in the case of money brought into court, it lies unproductive to both parties; and it might be provided that the plaintiff should take it out on entering into a recognizance, with security to refund, in case of a reversal of the judgment, under which it was paid into court.

In assigning errors in the charge of the court brought up by a bill of exceptions, to the charge; (for in no other way can it answer any end to bring it up; because otherwise it would come unaccompanied with the facts of the case, on which the law laid down in it was predicated,) error is alleged in *the reasons of the law laid down*, though the result of the charge as to the law itself be correct. On a writ of error, therefore, let it be provided, that where the jury are directed correctly on the point of law, on which the case turns, the judgment shall not be reversed, on account of *reasons given in the charge;* unless the law laid down, bearing on the issue, was erroneous. I entertain the expectation that this act calling upon judges to file opinions, will be repealed. The profession themselves, at whose instance it was brought forward, will see the inutility of it. With a view to a bill of exceptions, *questions*, as formerly can be put to the court, and answers to these can be given, and incorporated by the counsel themselves, when they draw up the bill. That there may be no dispute, when they come to draw up the bill, let the judge at the instant put his answers in writing, or express them with such deliberation, that the counsel may have the opportunity of taking them down. But to render it *absolutely necessary*, for a judge to write any thing, is absurd. It was no part of the *common law;* for even *signing his name*, was not necessary to a bill of exceptions. His seal was sufficient. His report of a case tried before a judge of the supreme court at *nisi prius*, might have been memoriter; and his notes now, are not for the counsel or the party, but for his brother judges who sit at the term; and nisi prius, and

circuit courts being taken away, except in the city of Philadelphia, notes are not necessary for any purpose, but as the
judge chuses to take them. As to presidents of districts, but
for this act it would not be necessary that they should write
any thing, unless their names, in taking the acknowledgment
of deeds. No man can take a note with more *fidelity*, or
quickness, than I can; but I despise the mechanical drudgery; and as it detracts from the strength of thinking, I would
wish none of it in a judge before whom I was to plead. Let
him give me his *eye*, and his *intellect;* not with his head
down, and his hand busy; because I could not drive my
words through his scalp; and it always discouraged me to
see a bare, or a covered poll, presented like a battering-ram,
while I was endeavouring to reach his mind with my observations. I despise drudgery; not that I undervalue mechanics, or mechanism; but, because handicraft labour, is
out of place here; and a Jack of all trades is proverbially
a bungler. Though I state this playfully, yet there is truth
in it; I wish a judge to be *obliged* to write as little as possible. For the fact is, that it rarely happens that one can
combine *clerkship*, and the application of the *mental* faculties
with the utmost force at the same time. Persons that have
written much, *pursuing the rapidity of their thoughts*, contract what the common people call a cramped hand; and
studious men, from their sedentary lives are *nervous;* and
the nerves are affected by the contraction of the fingers in
writing; this adds also to the contractedness of the chirography. To oblige the judge to write out the reasons of
his judgment, whenever any one may chuse to call upon him,
is a novelty in the history of juridical duties. This much
may suffice as to this act which ought to be repealed, more
especially as it falls heaviest, in the accumulation of their
labours, upon *the judges of the inferior courts, and increases
the fund on which a writ of error may be brought.*

There is a defect in the law of England; 2 Tidd, 1155,
and I take it, unless I have overlooked the provision, the
same defect exists with us, " That on a writ of error by the
defendant, and a reversal of the judgment against him, he

is not entitled to costs;" which is unreasonable, while the plaintiff in the like situation, could claim costs.

It will not be understood that I have applied my mind to consider all provisions that might be in the case of writs of error; but give such hints as at present occur to me.

———◆———

Opinion on a curious question of practice, made at the term of the western circuit, September, 1803.

Robert Galbraith and others } In case.
   vs.
  Judah Colt, }

   In the circuit court of September, 1803.

THE following state of this case is agreed upon by both parties, and the judgment of the court prayed thereon.

At the Allegheny court of quarter sessions, of September, 1797, several bills of indictment for riots were found against James Lowry and others. Three of these indictments are No. 2, 4, and 5, of that term. Judah Colt, as agent for the Pennsylvania Population Company, was the private prosecutor of these indictments, and at the said sessions, by the advice and direction of the court, he entered into a stipulation to pay costs, in case of a verdict for the defendants.

These indictments were continued from term to term until September term, 1798, when the defendants pleaded not guilty to all the indictments, and were tried and convicted upon indictment No. 2.

After this conviction it was agreed between the defendants and the attorney for the commonwealth, with the consent of Judah Colt, the private prosecutor, that a nolle prosequi should be entered against defendants in the indictments, Nos. 4 and 5, upon the payment of costs by the defendants. This entry was accordingly made upon the docket, and endorsed upon the indictments, together with an agreement by the attorney for the commonwealth, with the consent of Judah Colt, that the recognizance of defendants in the indictment should not be sued until after the next ensuing term.

The bill of costs when taxed by the clerk of the sessions, was disputed by the Lowreys as being too high, ard was thereupon referred, by their consent and request, to the president of the court of quarter sessions.

Before the president delivered his opinion the Lowreys refused to pay any costs, and no recognizance of theirs could be found upon which they could be sued.

Process was issued by the attorney for the state, to bring in the defendants, upon indictments, Nos, 3, 4, and 5, of September 1797, and they were accordingly brought in to answer at September, 1799. This process was issued by the direction of the attorney for the state, without the knowledge or consent of Judah Colt, other than his having requested that the bills for attendance of witnesses on part of prosecutor might be collected, and process was issued to compel Judah Colt to appear and give testimony on these indictments against defendants. And the prosecution was revised as the most efficacious mode of recovering the fees and prosecutors bills due on the judgments.

On the trial of the indictments No. 4, and No. 5, at September term 1800, the defendants were acquitted and the costs taxed (prout bills of costs.)

These costs are now demanded of Judah Colt upon his stipulation of September term, 1797, and he refuses to pay, conceiving himself discharged from his stipulation. The court of quarter sessions have given no opinion on this question, and the plaintiffs have brought this suit to try whether Colt is liable to pay the bills as taxed, or any part of them.

HENRY BALDWIN, *Attorney for Plaintiffs.*
THOMAS COLLINS, *Attorney for Defendant.*

I understand the first question in this case to be, whether an appeal is sustainable by this court from the opinion of the circuit court, which was given on a case stated under an agreement of which I have not been furnished with a copy along with that of the statement of the case; but which I understand to have been, to submit to the opinion of the two judges then holding the circuit court, and that opinion to be conclusive; provided that the argument could be heard by those two judges from the interference of other business at the time. In strictness then, I would take it, there not having been time for hearing by those two judges, from the interference of other business at the time, there was an end to the agreement; and without an accommodation of the agreement to a hearing in another manner, it was coram non judice and the hearing void. Much more so when a change in the constitution of the court gave the advantage of but one judge at a circuit court instead of two; and more especially when a reason which might have weighed, and it is presumable did weigh, in the agreement on the part of either of the parties, was, that the court being constituted of but four judges, in the case of a reference to two, there could not be a majority out of four to reverse the opinion of two; a reason which it is well known did operate much at the nisi prius courts to prevent appeals or motions in bank from that which we had discovered to be the sense of the one half of the court who had already heard the matter, considering such a motion or appeal to be unavailing; so that an agreement to acquiesce in the opinion of two as conclusive, even under the constitution of the circuit court, was not giving up much. For though the other two judges in bank might reverse the opinion of the two circuit judges, yet the presumption was strong against it, the number being equal in both cases, and the presumption of understanding the same. There is therefore a great difference in the agreement to submit to two under the former constitution of the circuit court, and a submission to one under the change which has taken place.

But it may be said the arguing the case stated before the single judge, by implication, carries with it the agreement that the opinion of the single judge, shall have the effect which the agreement contemplated, which was that of a decision by two; and if such was not the understanding of the party defendant, it behooved him to have had the agreement accommodated to his ideas, by an alteration as to that part of it which respects the conclusiveness of the effect. On the contrary, I would take it, that it behooved the party plaintiff to have had an alteration made as to the submission to one judge, if he meant to avail himself of the conclusiveness of the opinion of one.

It may be said, there is an astutia here to defeat the plaintiff in the advantage he has gained by the opinion of the

single judge, and to relieve the defendant from the decision
of which he complains. It may be so; but may it not be
justifiable? It would seem to me; as I must acknowledge it
does; that the single judge has erred in his judgment in
this case; and, even on this preliminary question, it seems
to me, that it is proper to overreach it in the contemplation
of the mind, and to enquire what has been the decision of
that judge. It is allowable then, at least I have done it, to
look at the case stated, even in determining the first point.
For astutia, in an endeavour to get at justice, is allowable;
and to admit a rigorous or liberal construction of an agreement, with a view to that object I have been disposed to do
so in favour of the defendant. For it would seem to me that
the defendant ought to be considered as relieved from the
stipulation as to the costs of the prosecution in question.
My memory does not serve me with a positive recollection;
but it seems to me, that in the course of my reading I have
seen something which has led me to doubt the power of the
court to impose the stipulation; and on principle there
would seem reason to doubt it. For though in fact, in a
forcible entry, there is a private, as well as a public wrong;
and oftentimes the injured party resorts to the indictment
merely with a view to his private wrong, yet I should be at
a loss to conceive, that the power of the court could oblige
him to stipulate for costs in this more than in any other criminal case when the statutes have not done it. If so the
stipulation would be void, and on that ground the defendant
would be relieved. But supposing the stipulation legal and
binding, it respected *an acquittal on trial.* But here by the
agreement on the part of the commonwealth with the defendant, the prosecution is arrested short of a trial; a nolle
prosequi is entered *on payment of costs.* It is true the prosecutor assents to it. But nevertheless it is the agreement
of the attorney for the state with the defendant; and I would
take it, that the agreement takes the case as to costs out of
the stipulation, and puts it wholly on the *recognizance.* The
prosecutor, the stipulant, directed the proceeding for costs;
but what could he be supposed to mean, but that the proceed-

ing should be on the recognizance of the defendant; and
for the purpose of costs only, and not for the purpose of
trial. But no recognizance had been taken, as stated in the
case. This was the oversight of the officer of the commonwealth, and for which the prosecutor the stipulant is not
answerable. If the officer is reduced to the necessity of recurring to a process to bring in the body of the defendant,
and going on to trial, from the default of a recognizance, it
would not seem to me reasonable that he should hold the
prosecutor to his stipulation, who, in consequence of the
agreement of the attorney of the state with the defendant,
had given up the prosecution.

It is under these impressions that I may be disposed to
give the stipulant the advantage of any want of conformity to
the agreement on the strictest construction of it, in order to let
in a consideration of this point. Justice is the great object of
us all, and when that does not certainly appear to have been
attained, the mind is not satisfied, more especially if all advantage has not been had in the hearing by such tribunal, in
the first or last resort, as it may have been in the contemplation of the party to have had, who thinks himself agreed by
the determination.

It is possible that on hearing the matter argued, I might
think with the judge who has given an opinion; and in order to get at this, if the party to the agreement on the one
side, will hold the other to the conclusiveness of the effect
of the opinion, I would hold him to the strictness of the
agreement as to the tribunal before whom it was agreed to be
heard, and unless he would consent to waive the conclusiveness, and give the advantage of a hearing on appeal, I would
turn round to begin again, on the case stated, or leave him
to his action as it was commenced, and the ordinary progress
of the suit.

3 Y

THE following was delivered in the case reported, 3
Bin. 69. It was a case which had been holden over for advisement, and I had made out my opinion, but from oversight,
I had omitted to deliver it to the reporter; not that it was
of much moment to insert here, more than to shew that I
had considered the case; and did not merely *concur*, as it
stands in the report, but delivered reasons. There are a
number of other cases, some of them reported, and some not,
where I made out opinions; though at an early period, I
was more in the habit of delivering them, not from written
notes : some of them which had been written out, I did not
deliver, because, finding that we concurred, it was left to the
chief justice; to deliver the opinion of the court.

Some of these which I had drawn up, I threw into the
fire, as having been always averse to the trouble of keeping
papers, where *it was not absolutely necessary. My notes in
other cases*, I have given to some of the bar, or have lost.
To Mr. Mountain, of Pittsburgh, I gave a number; and
when on that circuit last fall, I thought of enquiring for them
with a view to this publication, thinking to insert some. But
I was unwilling to give him the trouble of looking them up,
if he had preserved any of them. Seeing his bodily weakness, and knowing that the business of the term must at that
time press upon him; and for which all the strength that he
had, was necessary. In a number of cases, I had given the
opinions I had drawn up, to some one or other of the judges; to chief justice Tilghman, one in a case of the *first impression*, Dessebats v. Berquier, which I had drawn up with
some pains; but it was mislaid, or handed over by him to
some other of the judges; or it is possible to myself; but
which I could not find at the time the court delivered their
opinions, or since; and therefore I could only express my
concurrence with the sentiments they had delivered, at least
it was not necessary to take up time in doing more. For
they were to the same effect with reasons that had occurred
to me.

There is one note upon an important question, the case of Starrer v. Shetz, which I could wish to have had, in order to insert it here. It was argued in the high court of errors and appeals, in which court I had taken a seat, to hear the argument. But some idea being expressed, that I had given an opinion in the court below; (the supreme court) I withdrew, though I had not so understood it myself. The fact is, it had been argued before I came upon the bench of my supreme court; but at the delivering of an opinion on the case by that court, I was on the bench, and may have said something as approving of their way of thinking, but did not consider myself as sitting in the case, but only observing upon the reasons which they had given. There was a misunderstanding in the case some way, either on my part, or on that of the counsel concerned, and I gave up my own recollection of the fact, and yielded to them. All I know, is that I had not considered myself as having given an opinion, &c. But having withdrawn from the hearing of the cause in the court of errors and appeals, I made a note afterwards, of what, as at that time advised, I should have been disposed to have thought of the case. I gave to judge Smith, that note together with his own notes to me, of the argument of counsel on the former opinion, when heard in the supreme court. His notes containing what I probably had written, are not now to be found amongst his papers; and probably must be in the hands of some gentlemen of the bar. I have not had an opportunity of enquiring.

What is the use of all this; it may be said, the profession can go on, and justice be administered, and the law understood without a report of your opinions; but it concerns myself to increase the evidence of my industry, and attention to the duties of my *trust and station*.

It may be said that there is an inconsistency with this, in my *throwing into the fire many things*, which, I acknowledge I had drawn up with some care. The truth is, had I expected that I should have had any opportunity of giving them to the public, I might have preserved some of these; but Mr. Dallas, had, in a great degree, withdrawn himself from reporting cases, his professional business occupying his time; and, this accumulating fast upon him, in the courts of the United States, from his office as district attorney; and, from his great, and still opening talents. Mr. Binney had not yet offered himself as a reporter, and therefore not seeing a prospect of publicity to my labours, I consigned them, I was going to say, to the tomb of the Capulets; but, that figure not agreeing, I will say, to the funeral pile of the Cæsars.

Mr. James Mountain, of whom I have spoken in this note, is, I understand, much regretted, even, by those of the profession not friendly to his way of thinking on political questions. He argued two cases during the term, which unquestionably accelerated his dissolution; the exertion being more than he could bear; we may be said, on that occasion, to have heard the words of the *dying swan :* he died in three days after the Term.

The following are the words of the will on which the law point made in this case arises: " My wife, &c. shall continue to live in the house with her children until the term of the lease is expired, and she must observe the agreement which was made, &c. The executors namely W: L: M: and R. shall be empowered to sell my land in, &c. *When my debts are paid,* if any thing *should remain,* my wife shall keep, &c. and my oldest son shall have £5 per advance; and then each child shall have an equal share, and my wife shall have the third part, and if my wife cannot bring up and maintain the children properly, then the executors shall take the children away and put them out to good people, that they may be brought up. And *in order that my last will and testament may be executed I constitute as executors W. L. M. and R.*"

The sale in the case before us has not been by W. L. &c. but by some of them; others having refused to act. The question then will be, can the sale be made by fewer than the whole. Looking into the books I have extracted some authorities which I will note before making any observations of my own.

" It can scarcely be imagined that a testator when he intrusts his executors with a power of selling land, should mean to have those for whose benefit he directs the sale, disappointed by the death of one of the persons invested with an authority, which the survivor is equally capable of executing." Coke Lytt. 113. Hargrave's note.

" Where a naked power is vested in two or more nominatim without any reference to an office in its nature liable to a survivorship, as an executorship is, it would be a contradiction to the general rule, to allow the power to survive : but where a power of selling is given to executors, or to persons *nominatim* in that character, it is not wholly irreconcilable with the rule, to deem a surviving executor a person within the description. For by the death of one executor the whole character of executors became vested in the survivor, and the power being annexed to the executors, ratione officii, and the office itself surviving, why should not the power annexed to it also itself survive, as well as where it survives by reason of being coupled with an interest ? But whether lord Coke's notion of the power not surviving, or the opposite one most conformed to strictness of law, is not now of any great importance, as such a power though extinct at law, *would certainly be enforced in equity.* His distinction is taken in case of a devise that passes no interest, or estate to the executors ; but merely a power or authority : but, though admitted in point of law, it would not avail in a court of equity, as this jurisdiction, notwithstanding the extinction of the power at law, would compel the execution of it, for the sake of those for whose benefit the power was given." Idem..

Powel on devises controverts the correctness of taking no distinction between a devise that executors shall *sell land,* and devise of land to executors *to be sold,* which had been doubted by Hargrave. This on ground of naked authority and of an authority coupled with an interest. And he points out a case of a bona fide purchase from the heir, where a court of equity would not compel a surviving executor to execute a sale, who had had but a naked authority,

whereas they would compel where it had been coupled with
an interest which others had in the execution of it.   But he
admits that, " take the law to be that all persons endowed
with a naked authority must unite in the execution of it, it
is with an *unless where the* evident intent of the testator renders a contrary construction absolutely necessary."   Powel,
310.

" If one make three executors and devises lands to be
sold by his executors, and one of them die before the time
of the sale, the other two may sell ; because in that case
the intent of the testator is taken to be that such executor
who shall be alive at the time when the land is to be sold,
shall sell ; and where this construction seems to accord
with the words of the will and *the intent of the testator."*
Idem.

" Where the devise is to bring up and educate children,
this is an authority coupled with an interest.

To pay debts, to perform legacies, is an authority coupled with an interest : an interest in the executor by devise,
and not an authority or confidence only." Idem.

Having made the above citations, I assume it, that a refusing or renouncing executor, is the same as a defunct executor. For he is defunct quoad hoc. I mean as to acts
in which he refuses to join, because he has refused to take
the administration of the will.

But it is evident to me on a view of this will, that the
power to sell is not merely nominatim to W. L. &c, as trustees
for the mere purpose *of sale ;* but in the capacity of executors, ratione officii, *to sell.*   There were other purposes for
which they were constituted than the mere sale of the land.
And what is more, the authority in this case, is not naked,
but coupled with an interest ; debts are to be paid ; remainder after sale, if any thing, to be distributed to wife, a third
part ; to each child, an equal share ; if wife cannot bring up
and maintain children properly, the executors to take them
away, &c.   In order that my will may be executed, I constitute as executors, &c. So that upon all grounds I can
have no doubt of the power to sell in this case.

I add only that I sanction so far as the *weight* of my opinion may go, the doctrine, that, on an ejectment, we will consider that done which would have been ordered to be done by a court of chancery; and where an executor has sold who could have been compelled by a court of chancery to sell for the purposes of a trust, the sale will be supported. It is to be presumed in this case that the trusts could not have been executed without a sale; for the testator contemplated the necessity of it in directing a sale.

One observation more, and I have done. I take it that where any thing directed by the testator to be done, cannot be done, but by a sale, it is strong evidence of his intent, that such of his executors shall sell, as remain, or who do not refuse the administration. I know no distinction between *a refusing or renouncing, and a defunct executor;* but this, that an executor may refuse as to the real estate, but may act as to the personal; or after renouncing the living executor, may be allowed to announce his willingness to act, and come in to an agency in the execution of the will, whereas the defunct, cannot.

RESPUB. vs. M'LEAN.

THIS case had come before the court at an early period; 1801 or 1802. Chief justice Shippen, Yeates, Smith, and Brackenridge, on the bench. The court were divided on the question, which had been argued at great length and with great ability. C. J. Shippen, and Brackenridge, of opinion that the justice falling into a new county could not act by virtue of his old commission; Yeates, and Smith contra; so that no decision could take place. Chief justice Shippen, and justice Smith, having deceased, left the bench still equal, and opposed in their sentiments. But on the appointment of chief justice Tilghman, the matter was re-argued, and the court's opinion delivered. It was by the casting voice of chief justice Tilghman, decided that *he could not act.*

I have not the opinions of chief justice Shippen, Yeates or Smith, nor that of chief justice Tilghman, but I give my own, which may serve to give some idea of the reasoning on at least one side of the argument.

OPINION.

M'Lean the defendant was acting as a justice of the peace in Adams county. Rule to shew cause why an information in the nature of a writ de quo warranto shall not issue against him.

Brackenridge J. A county is a *corporation*, with commissioners, treasurer, coroner, sheriff, constables, justices of the peace, judges of the courts, &c. It is struck off, from the state at large, and may be, as in this case, within the bounds of an old county; but it becomes a distinct and independent body.

Can the commissioners, treasurer, coroner, sheriff, &c. of the old county, continue to act within the new? Not unless the authority is specially saved, in the act of incorporation of the new. This has been done in the erecting many counties. It has been done as to certain officers in erecting this county: " The sheriff, coroner and public officers of the county of York shall continue to exercise the duties of their respective offices, within the county of Adams, until similar officers shall be appointed agreeably to law within the said county of Adams." 4 State laws, 533. Is a justice of the peace, such an officer, as is within the meaning of this act? If so; he is, at least, supersedable, and superseded at all times, by the elections, or appointments of others of the same description and authority, in the ordinary way, provided by the constitution, and the laws of the commonwealth.

But can an officer of the old county, the justice of the peace in question, falling as to residence within the new, act within the new, independent of any legislative act? How can he become known to the new? There seems some *copula* wanting to connect him with it.

It may be matter of authority, to consider what has been the legislative construction in the case; by implication we have abundant evidence.

Our first legislative act is that of erecting Lancaster county. By this act it is provided, "that the county of Lancaster shall enjoy all and singular the jurisdictions, powers, rights, &c. which any other county doth, or may or ought to enjoy." But nothing is said, specially, of the appointment of the justices. 1 State laws, 242.

The act erecting York county, specially provides even for the jurisdiction of the supreme court, and justices (meaning county justices) shall be commissioned by the governor. 1 State laws, 326.

In erecting the counties of Cumberland, Berks, Northampton, Bedford, Northumberland and Westmoreland, it is provided, in the same words as to the Supreme court and as to the justices. 1 State laws, 328, 352, 562, 607, and 663.

These acts were under the proprietary government.

In erecting the county of Washington, under the constitution of September 28th, 1776, the jurisdiction of the supreme court is preserved, and it is directed that justices shall be elected in the townships and commissioned by the president and council. 1 State laws, 874.

In erecting the county of Fayette, provision is made, in like manner, and also for the first time, it is provided in the act of incorporation, " that the justices of the peace commissioned at the time of passing this act and residing within the county of Fayette, or any three of them, shall and may hold courts of general quarter sessions of the peace and general jail delivery, and county courts for the holding of pleas, and shall have all and singular the powers, rights, jurisdictions, and authorities, to all intents and purposes, as other the justices of courts of general quarter sessions and justices of the county courts for holding of pleas, in the other counties may, can or ought to have in their respective counties." 2 State laws, 155. It is observable, that it is as judges of courts, authority is given them, not as justices of the peace, generally, for the keeping of the peace and the recovery of *debts*. By the constitution of 1776, chap. 11, sect. 26, the legisla-

3 Z.

ture may establish courts, and under this power it may have
been, that they undertook to establish judges.

In erecting the county of Franklin, it is provided, "that
the justices of the then present county of Cumberland, which
will *hereafter be within the said county of Franklin*, shall be
justices of the peace for the said county until the expiration
of their several terms for which they were respectively appointed." This goes the whole length of the power of a
justice of the peace. 2 State laws, 216.

In erecting the county of Montgomery, power given to
justices commissioned in the old to act as judges in the new.
2 State laws, 221.

In erecting the county of Dauphin, justices already commissioned, are authorized to act as judges. Power is not
given to act as justices of the peace generally. 2 State laws,
254.

In erecting the county of Luzerne, provision made for
the electing and commissioning justices. Nothing said relative to justices already commissioned. 2 State laws, 466.

In erecting the county of Huntingdon, the justices of the
peace commissioned at the time of this act and residing within the bounds and limits of the said county, shall be justices
of the peace for the said county during the time for which
they were so commissioned. 2 State laws, 527.

By the act erecting Allegheny county, provision is made
"that justices now commissioned and within the limits of the
new county may hold courts." 2 State laws, 595.

By an act erecting Mifflin county, "justices commissioned at the time and residing, &c. shall be justices of the peace
for the said (new) county." 2 State laws, 718.

By the act erecting the county of Delaware, "the justices
then in commission are authorized to hold courts; and *that
all* public officers, *other than justices of the peace*, shall continue to exercise the duties of their respective offices, until
similar officers shall be appointed. 2 State laws, 732. This
clause implies several things. 1st, That a justice of the peace
might be comprehended under the term "public officers."
2dly, That he could not act without the aid of the legislature.

It had been doubted and might well be doubted, whether as a justice of the peace deriving his *constitutional* existence from the commission of the president and council, he could derive any extension of authority, from an act of the legislature. So far as respected their authority as justices of the peace, generally, this legislature excepted it.

The act of assembly enacting the county of Lycoming, is the first act, erecting a county, after the constitution of 2d Sept. 1790. It is provided that the president of the third district, of which district the said county of Lycoming is hereby declared to be a part, shall have like power, &c.; but no notice taken of associate judges that might fall within it, nor justices of the peace. 3 State laws, 716.

In erecting the county of Wayne, it is provided "that, the sheriff, coroner, and other officers of the county of Northampton, *other than the justices of the peace*, shall continue to exercise the duties of their respective offices, within the county of Wayne, until similar officers shall be appointed agreeably to law within the said county." 4th State laws, 242. This act is under the constitution of 2d Sept. 1790.

In the act erecting Centre county, the jurisdiction of the supreme court, as in all the other acts is extended, and that of the district president; but no notice taken of justices of the peace. 4 State laws, 542.

In erecting the last counties in the state, those of Beaver, Butler, Mercer, Crawford, Erie, Warren, Venango, Armstrong, the authority of the judges of the supreme court, and district president, is extended, but no reservation of the power or authority of *associate judge, or a justice of the peace.*

Expressio unius exclusio est alterius. The question will then come to this, can the justice of an old county act in the new, without the *reservation* of their authority, by the legislature, in the *incorporating act?* How can he be known to the new county? Can the justice of York county, in his commission, begin his precept "Adams county, scilicet?" In this case he might act in both counties. In the old county by the authority of his commission and in the new by virtue of his residence.

But is not his commission during good behaviour; and can the legislature, by erecting a new county, in fact, abolish it? It does not affect his commission. It abridges or takes away the sphere of action only. His commission was taken, subject to the eventual sub-division of the county: a power, which the legislature has and must exercise. And, I take it, there is no privation of right in the case. And, that independent of the aid of the legislature, to say the least of it, a justice acting in one county under colour of a commission in another, is a trespassor.

The strongest thing that occurs to me to be said to the contrary, is the term "public officers," in the act for erecting the county of Adams. "The sheriff, coroner, and public officers of the county of York, shall continue to exercise the duties of their respective offices within the county of Adams, until similar officers shall be appointed agreeably to law, within the said county of Adams."

In the acts for erecting the counties of Delaware and Wayne, there is the like provision with an exception "as to justices of the peace," which exception, I take to be explanatory and not implicatory, that under the term, "public officers," justices of the peace could be comprehended. It is as much as to say, by public officers we do not mean justices of the peace. Independent of the explanation, it must have been evident, as in the case before us, that the legislature could not mean these. The reservation of authority is in favour of "public officers," until similar, shall be appointed. The provision, therefore, must respect officers, supersedable by the appointment of similar. But justices of the peace, hold their commissions, during good behaviour, and are not supersedable by the appointment of similar. Under the term, "public officers," therefore, I take it, justices of the peace are not comprehended. There being no legislative act in conservation of their authority and extension of it to the new county, it can be known only to the old.

The argument comes to this, that the commission of the justice for the old county does not enure for the use of the new, unless there is a saving of his jurisdiction in the erection of the new, that is, the new county erected subject to the jurisdiction, if this could be done. It does not lie upon me to say that it could. But, a fortiori, it cannot be without. And in this case there is no saving, but the new county laid out without respect to the jurisdiction of the justice. He may remain a justice of the old county, therefore, and may withdraw within it, and act, but has no connection with the new. He is not known to it *de facto ;* nor by operation of law, nor by legislative exception or recognition, or new commission from the governor by virtue of his signature to a law, directly, or by implication, authorizing them to act, if the signature could be supposed to have that effect, which it is not necessary for me to say that it has, but certainly without it there cannot be authority for an officer dismembered from an old county to act in a new.

On the granting new trials.

MY mind had got a set against granting new trials, and this on two grounds.

1. *Appeals* from the circuit courts on motions for a new trial which had become pretty nearly *a matter of course ,* and trials in the first instance, passed for nothing; at least for very little. I saw that in the nature of things we could not go on, so as to give satisfaction to the country. In the 2d place also I was impressed with what I thought a too great facility with the court, in sustaining of this kind and granting new trials contrary to the sense of juries on *matters of fact,* on the ground of the verdicts being against evidence. This more particularly in some cases which had occured in the western district on the subject of what are called *improvement rights.* It was under this impression that I delivered the following in the case of Laughlin v. Maybury, at

the sittings in term, for the western district, Sept. 1807. I will not say that these sentiments delivered here, or expressed to the same effect elsewhere, contributed to have *the circuit courts abolished;* but this soon afterwards took place.

I have been led to consider a little the *origin* and *nature* of granting *new trials*. It succeeded *the writ of attaint:* This writ was founded on an allegation of *perjury; (a)*

(a) St. Westm. 1. 3. Ed. I. c. 38. An attaint shall be granted in a fee of land.

For as much as certain people of this realm, doubt very little to make a false oath, which they ought not to do, whereby much people are disinherited, and lose their right; it is provided, that the king of his office, shall from henceforth grant attaints, upon inquests in plea of land, or of freehold, or of any thing touching freehold, when it shall seem to him necessary.

This statute is in affirmance of the common law. 2d, Inst. 236. But though an attaint, did lie upon a false verdict before this, yet because in plea real, remedy of a higher nature, the king sometimes refused to grant it.

Brief of conviction, old name for writ of attaint. Stat. of Marl. c. 14.

The witnesses named in the deed, should be joined with the inquest.

But if they, of their own head will say, that it is disseizin, their verdict shall be admitted at their own peril.

13. Ed. I. c. 30. That the justices assigned to take assizes, shall not compel jurors to say precisely, whether it be disseizin or not, so that they do show the truth of the deed, and require aid of the justices.

By Statute, 14 of Ed. II. distress is given in case of default of jury of attaint to bring them.

1. Ed. III. c. 6. It is provided that for the great mischiefs, damage and destruction that hath happened to divers persons, by the false oaths of jurors, in writ of trespass, from henceforth writ of attaint shall be granted, as well upon the principal as upon the damages, and the chancellor shall grant without speaking to the king.

34 Ed. III. c. 7. Here it is awarded against the falsehood of jurors, to the poor without fine,

and this allegation was founded on *express* proof, or on a *presumption* of corruption in the jury, *by the party*. Hence at common law where the writ must be against the whole jury, the defendants could not have been fewer than thirteen. This appears from the recital in the statute of 15 Hen. VI.

The presumption of corruption in the jury by the party, where it was matter of presumption, and not of express proof, must have *been drawn from the glaring injustice of the verdict*. That it *must have been a case of manifest wrong*, will appear, from the greatness of the punishment on conviction. This wrong could more easily appear, when the matter in issue to the jury was simple, as at an early period it was in all cases. As questions became more complicated, the wrong could not always so manifestly appear ; and hence the *presumption of corruption*, did not so necessarily arise. The punishment of course, became disproportioned to the evidence ; conviction did not follow, and the attaint ceased to be a remedy. It was attempted to be helped out by statute, reducing the punishment : yet reciting in all cases, the reason and ground of the writ, to be that of *corruption by the party, and perjury* in the jurors. But the questions submitted to a jury becoming every day still more complicated in evidence, and intricate in law, from the removal of restraints in the alienation, of real estate ; or from the relations and transactions of a more improved state of society, the unreasonableness continued more and more to be felt, of

9 Rich. II. c. 3. Attaint given upon a false oath, and also writ of error on the judgment.

11 Hen. VI. Complaint of the great damage and disherison that cometh by the usual perjuries of jurors, the which perjury doth abound and increase more than it was wont, for the great gifts that such jurors take of the parties, &c. costs and damages given on conviction.

15 Hen. VI. Great perjury which horribly continueth, &c.

11 Hen. VII. c. 21. Whereas perjury is much and customary used among such persons as pass upon issues, &c.

23 Hen. VIII. c. 3. Att. v. persons giving, &c. and v. party, &c. 20*l.* 5*s.* ½ to king ½ to party, &c. fine and ransom by the discretion of the justices, before the false sacrament shall be found.

considering that as *a crime* which might be no more than a *mistake:* the writ of attaint with all the softening of statutes in the penal consequences of conviction, ceased to be a reme‑ dy; for no conviction would follow; *the feelings of the heart and the reason of mankind revolted against it.* It is now a *mere name;* and the inference of *perjury* has ceased to be drawn, even in a case *of glaring injustice;* because *defect of intellect,* or *of attention,* in the course of a long examination, or pre-conceived, and imperceptible bias, may be sufficient to account for it; and I take notice of this early mode of ques‑ tioning the verdict of the jury, only with a view to show that originally it could not be questioned upon *slight* grounds.

In place of the writ of attaint which was now disused, recourse would seem to have been had in *extreme cases* to the court of chancery, where, under a consideration of the circumstances of the case, *new trials* were directed: this led to the *courts of law* themselves entertaining motions for new trials. Motions of this nature, had been always enter‑ tained on the ground of *misbehaviour* of the jurors or par‑ ties; or *irregularity* in the finding, or delivery of the ver‑ dict; and the reason why we do not hear more of these mo‑ tions at an early period, is because " the old report books do not give any accounts of the determinations made by the court upon motions." 1 Bur. 394. In Stade's case, Style, 138. which is our first on the subject of *granting new tri‑ als,* it was moved that judgment be stayed upon a certificate of the judge, that the *verdict had passed against his opinion;* and that there might be a new trial; for that it had been done theretofore in like cases. But Rolle, (chief justice of the king's bench) said " that it ought not to be stayed, though it have been done in the common pleas; for *that it was too arbitrary for them to do it.*"

Nevertheless, (though, at first, with great strictness) the practice of the common pleas would seem to have prevailed; " and of late years," says lord Mansfield, 1 Bur. 395, " the courts of law have gone more liberally into the granting new trials; and not only after trials at *nisi prius,* but also after trials *at bar,* as readily as after trials at nisi prius; or indeed rather more so, as the latter must be done upon what could have actually and personally appeared to a single judge only, whereas the former is grounded upon what must have manifestly and fully appeared to the whole court." As a reason for granting new trials he further observes, " that as most general *verdicts include legal consequences, as well as propositions of fact ;* in drawing these consequences, the jury may mistake, and infer directly contrary to law." This was the beginning of his doctrine, which led to the making *propositions of fact,* in some cases, *legal consequences;* and finally to the exclusion of the jury in some instances, from the province of drawing *legal consequences* at all. I impute it to his introduction, that in subsequent practice, more liberty hath been taken with the verdicts of juries, than, it would seem to me, principle would warrant. It became fashionable to allege, and indeed tracts (Eunomus, &c.) have been written to prove, that the juries were, in no case, *judges of the law;* that if they did not determine the law, it was because, on a general issue it was *incidental* to the finding the fact, and involved with it; that the courts had not only discretionary power, but were bound to control the juries in their verdicts; that if juries were to give *an hundred verdicts* against what the judges took to be law, new trials should be granted; for juries ought not to be considered as having even a concurrent right to judge of law, but, *as directed by the court:* that the direction of the court was the only evidence they could have of law; the only *speculum* through which they could look at it.

On this I observe, that, in every general verdict, two things must be involved, the *fact,* and *the conclusion from the fact.* Hence it cannot be that the jury are judges of law. Whence then the maxim, *ad questionem juris,* &c. *?(b)* The

(*b*) That decantatum in our books (as my lord Vaughan calls it) Ad questionem facti, &c. is true; for if it be demanded, what is the fact? The judge cannot enter it. If it be asked, what the law is in that case? The jury cannot answer it. But upon the general issue, if the jury be asked the question, guilty or not? Which includes the law, they resolve both law and fact in answering guilty

maxim means, that where the *legal conclusion can be separated from the fact, it shall be drawn by the court.* This can be done only by the pleadings, in the course of which, the facts are admitted, and the conclusion alone remains to be drawn.

In drawing the conclusion, the mind thinks of some general principle under which the fact may come; and in this operation of the mind, the court must necessarily travel into

or not guilty. So as though they answer not singly to the question, what is the law? Yet they determine the law in all matters where issue is joined and tried, but where the verdict is special But in such cases the judge of himself cannot answer or determine on the particular of the fact, but must leave it to the jury, with whom let it rest and continue forever, as the best kind of trial in the world for finding out the truth; and the greatest safety of the just prerogatives of the crown, and the just liberties of the subject; and he which desires more for either of them is an enemy to both. If the court might charge the jury *to find* for the defendant; because, though the jury will generally respect the sentiments of the court on points of law, they are not bound to return a verdict conformably to theirs. Per. judge Iredell. 3 Dal. 33.

It is the peculiar province of the jury *to infer facts from the evidence.* Cushing justice, 3 Dal. 33.

On questions of fact, it is the province of the jury; on questions of law, it is the province of the court to decide. But, it must be observed, that by the same law which recognizes this reasonable distribution of jurisdiction, the jury have nevertheless a right to take upon themselves to judge of both, and to determine the law as well as the fact in controversy. On this and on every other occasion, however, we have no doubt you will pay that respect which is due to the opinion of the court; for as on the one hand it is presumed, that juries are the best judges of fact, it is on the other hand presumable that the court are the best judges of law. But still *both objects are lawfully within your power of decision.* Sup. C. United States, Jay, Chief justice; 3 Dal. 4.

Can it then be the right of the court to set aside a verdict *indefinitely?* It will be to say, you may determine the law; but your determining is nothing. Yet this must be the result of the doctrine of an *arbitrary power in the* court to set aside a verdict on the ground of being against law.

the *fact* from which the *conclusion* is drawn. They cannot but, in the first instance, make an inference from the evidence of what the fact in the case is. It does not follow, therefore, that it is only matter of law of which the courts judge in granting a new trial. In every case, on a general verdict, they must judge of the fact first. *(c)* Hence the imperfection of their judgment, in judging of the justice of the verdict. And it follows, that they are not bound, and cannot be justified in granting new trials *against the sense of successive verdicts.*

Where a mind has the faculty of reasoning, and that faculty is strengthened by the exercise of reasoning, as is presumed to be the case with a judge, great power is acquired in separating, and comparing ideas; and where a knowledge of general rules enables to determine under what rule the facts of a case come, we approach the nearer to something like certainty : yet such is the diversity of transactions, that the application of a general rule in all cases, would work injustice. *(d)* How then can a judge know, or undertake to say with certainty that, where a jury departs from what he would call a general rule ; there is not something in the nature of an exception in the case, which attaches the feelings of the heart, and forces a verdict contrary to the direction of the court who apply the general rule. For this reason *a verdict of a jury ought not lightly to be questioned, even though it has gone against the opinion of a judge.*

(c) Co. Lit. sec. 368. Also in such case where the inquest may give their verdict at large, if they will take upon them the knowledge of the law upon the matter, they may give their verdict generally, as is put in their charge ; as in the case aforesaid they may well say that the lessor did not seize the lessee if they will, &c.

(d) There is an excess of discrimination in investigating the qualities of things, which in legal as well as other objects of critical disquisition, tends only to draw out a question to infinity. That the foundation of every rule must of necessity be imperfect, and that it is impossible to bound the scope of its application to a mathematical point. Rob. on Frauds, cites 2 Atk. 41, 42.

It is with less confidence that a court ought to advance in granting a new trial on the ground of being *against evidence.* " And one reason for this (which can never be answered) is, that the judge cannot fully know upon what evidence the jury gave their verdict, for they may have other evidence than what is shewed in court ;" Tri. Per pais, 274. That is to say, the impressions of a jury of what they themselves know of the parties, or witnesses ; or *what is collected from the manner in which the testimony is given*, cannot be communicated, and makes no part of the evidence before the judge. To say that the evidence therefore, in the language of judge Foster, 1 Bur. 397, greatly preponderates against the verdict, is a matter which in no common *case can be done.* I am therefore not disposed to think that in every case, " Where there is a reasonable doubt," (which is the expression of Lord Mansfield,) we are justifiable in setting aside a verdict.

The granting a new trial must involve the idea, that the court so exercising the power *have the evidence all before them, from which the fact was inferred by the jury.* Unless therefore in the case of a judge *before whom the evidence was given*, there cannot be the same evidence that was given to the jury. For though the whole be taken down by the notes of the judge, literatim as to written evidence, and verbatim as to the oral testimony, yet the impression cannot be communicated. For " as much may be frequently collected from the manner in which the evidence is delivered as from the matter of it." 3 Black. 373.

" The law's delay" is proverbial; it is enumerated by the poet amongst the evils of life. It furnishes an argument against the turning the successful party round to another trial. Nor is it him that it delays only, but other suitors. There is greater delay in this state, from the granting new trials, than under the judiciary system of that country from whence we derive the practice. There, the four terms occur every year, to which the motion for a new trial can be made, and the cause may go to trial at the sittings after term ; or at a nisi prius court, allowing only reasonable time for the commission to issue, and the jury to be summoned; and the new verdict may be had in three months. Here, so far as respects the nisi prius, the delay of a new trial, ordered at March term, must be until December, and in all the circuit courts, it cannot be less than a year. So that the delay of judgment and execution, independent of the merits, is of itself an object for a motion for a new trial. Hence it is that in the circuit courts the motion for a new trial, where the verdict is for the plaintiff, is *a thing of course*, an appeal being given from the judge refusing a new trial, and the delay of course obtained. It being thus a thing contemplated by the judge before whom the cause comes to be tried, that a motion for a new trial will be made, he is led to delay the trial by taking down the written evidence at great length, and to ' chronicle the small beer' of the testimony ;* endeavouring to reach the whole body of the evidence ; so that the time allotted for the circuit is taken up with sometimes little more than a single cause ; and when a new trial is granted, the judge who comes the next year, has the same cause to occupy his chirography, and prepare for the motion that is to be made again. This may be said to be in some degree the fault of the system; but the court must take the system as it is, and in matters of practice must look to it ; and the reason ab inconveniente must weigh with them in all that is within the province of *discretion*.

Our legal discretion must have respect to the rights of other parties who are waiting in the country for a hearing of their claims. And at a time when the cry of delay is loud against the administration of justice ; it would seem to me that it is our duty to consult despatch in the trials ; and to refuse, unless in *extreme cases*, the throwing the matter back upon another jury. The public sentiment as far as I can collect it, is with the juries, and we hear less of the *injustice of verdicts*, than of the *delay* of trials. If a more sparing interference of the courts should be exercsied ; it may come to be felt by the people, and lead to a reform in a system, which does not give time for those revisions of verdicts

---

* To suckle fools, and chronicle small beer.　　　　　*Pope.*

which the constitution and holding of the English courts
admits. Is it a time for the courts of this country to be
stretching to the utmost extent the control of verdicts, when
the *struggle is, whether there shall be law judges at all?* Rules
of law are to be regarded, as much as the principles of any
other science; but a great part of these rules which we call
law, are but the dictates of natural feeling, or moral reason applied to the case before us; principles of equity and justice
resulting from the relations or contracts of men. The judge
in the plenitude of his pride, is apt to arrogate to himself,
as having alone the capacity to judge of these, or to *apply
them, which is but the exercise of reason.* A consideration of
these particulars ought to give respect for the deductions of
even uneducated men, so as not lightly to set aside what
they have thought the justice of the case.

A knowledge of rules is the result of reading, or of hearing: but the application of them requires a different faculty, and which we denominate *common sense;* now it is allowed on all hands, that a man may have at least the reputation
of a great judge, and yet be deficient in the knowledge of
human nature, and in *natural understanding.* It is the province of a court to assist with the knowledge of rules; and
of a jury to assist in the application of them. This gives a
jury a wider field than the mere finding of a fact, even supposing them excluded from determining what the law is.
The sense of a jury in the application of law to the fact, is a
great help to the court, and a great support. *Consilium simul,
atque auctoritas adsunt. (e)* [*Tacit de Mor. Germ.*] A pas-
sage which expresses the case, and perhaps shews the origin of juries. I never therefore find the verdict in agreement with my way of thinking, as to the justice of the case
before me, but I draw from it strong confirmation of my
opinion; nor, ever find it against it, but I go a great way
in taking it for granted that I was wrong. And with good
reason; for it has been rare, that I have not observed in the

---

*(e) Liguntur in iisdem consiliis et principes qui jura per
pagos vicosque reddunt, concilium simul atque auctoritas adsunt.*

jury all due deference to the judgment of the court, and it must be a strong sense of right or wrong, that will lead them to dissent. It is this experience, and this course of thought that has given me some renitency to applications for new trials. It has been perhaps increased by the time taken up in arguing them, and the making them in the circuit courts, mere matter of course; so that every cause must be tried, *with a view to a new trial,* and the judge is more concerned to get the evidence forward to the hearing in term, than to infer from it in the first instance.

So much with respect to the province of the jury in drawing a conclusion of law, and the province of the court, in controling this conclusion in setting aside a verdict. But in matter of fact the conclusion of a jury is still more to be respected. I will not say that it is exclusively their province; but it is peculiarly their province and likely to be invaded. It must be a strong case that would make me easy in throwing the parties upon the country for a new trial, where there has been no surprise; where there has been a full hearing, and with the advantage of learned counsel. But when the motion is made merely on the ground that the verdict is against evidence; and where the judge who has tried the cause, and before whom the verdict was taken, and sanctioned it with his judgment, and now declares himself satisfied with it, I am nearly prepared to say, that to interfere, is a power which I will not undertake to exercise, at least I am prepared to express a wish, that the legislature may interfere and take away the appeal in such cases from the circuit court altogether. In order to prevent delay this must be done, or the system must be changed.

But under the head of granting new trials on the ground of being against evidence, I do not comprehend cases, where looking through the evidence, it may be seen that in the nature of the case there is evidence behind, which had not been before the jury, or in the words of the chief justice of the common pleas, 3 Bos. and Pul. 495, " some facts might be established which are left equivocal;" or where an evident oversight of some facts appears, a party may be allowed, in the language of Chambre, 3 Bos. and Pul. 372, "the opportunity of taking the opinion of another jury."

Having made these preliminary observations, I shall now consider in a few words the case before the court. It may be said to involve a question of law; for that an actual settlement is necessary, to support the claim of the plaintiff, or to protect the defendant, is matter of law; and it may be that what shall be construed an actual settlement may be considered as matter of law; but this consideration in the nature of the thing, is so involved with the conclusion to be drawn from the facts, that it amounts to the same thing; for the question will be, whether the facts of the case constitute an act of settlement. The legal conclusion, and the conclusion from the evidence cannot be separated. The verdict can therefore be considered only on the ground of being against evidence. Here then we have the conclusion of a jury, and the sanction of the judge before whom the cause was tried; and what weighs still more with me, that judge, after reflection and a lapse of time, declaring himself satisfied with the verdict. I shall therefore not be disposed to disturb it; but to concur in refusing a new trial.

OBSERVATIONS TO THE STUDENT ON THE PRACTICE OF THE LAW.

SINCE I wrote what I had said, "might be called an introduction," &c. I have seen the preface to the *American edition* of lord Erskine's speeches, New-York, 1813. The editor is of opinion, "that it can be demonstrated, that there is actually a greater aggregate amount of talent exhibited at the American, than at the English bar." He founds this upon reasons *a priore*, that there ought to be. "For, in this country," says he, "there is no other outlet for the first rate talent of her children, than that of *the profession of the law*. That, the nature of our political institutions forbids any hope of our statesmen acquiring any permanent power or extensive wealth and influence in the community; and consequently, offers no adequate inducement for the primary talents of the country to devote themselves, exclusively, to a life of politics; whence the government, whether national, or of each single state, seldom, or never commands for its permanent service, the first rate abilities of America; that the pulpits of America are not sufficiently favoured by public opinion to offer an adequate bounty of stipend, reputation, and influence to conciliate to their service the life-efforts of paramount, comprehensive talents; that the navy and army of the country have not yet grown up to a sufficient size and extent of magnificence, to vindicate to themselves the highest order of American genius; and, that in no country of the globe have trade and mechanics, or the plough taken to themselves permanently, very commanding abilities."

I am not able to say what may be the relative merit of English, and American lawyers; but this I have uniformly found, that the inhabitants of all states, and even districts of a state, are in the habit of conceiving that the lawyers of their states, or districts are the first, in legal knowledge and in eloquence. Said an individual of New-York to me some years ago, with whom I happened to lodge in an hotel, " We have lawyers in our state that will go you back *an* hundred years;" he meant, in citing cases. But we have, said I, some with us in Pennsylvania, that will *go you back two.*

Even professional men will naturally be disposed to overrate the talents of each other, where they have only themselves to compare with. But, in proportion to the opportunity they have of seeing, and hearing advocates elsewhere, their respect, or admiration must be reduced, in some degree, for those they have at home. The publication of our American reports, of sundry of these states, must tend to enlarge the minds of professional men, as well as of others, with regard to the relative legal knowledge, or talents of advocates.

I should be very happy to believe, that, from whatever cause it may be, our lawyers are not behind those of England, if not before them, in professional ability; and I should have no objection to believe it to be the case, that our judges are not behind those of England. For, having the honour to be a judge, I should, in that case, be included. Nor can I see any reason why we should be behind them, unless we suffer our minds to be subdued by an opinion of their superiority, and the precedent of their opinions; and, if we are inferior, I could assign no stronger cause, than such subjection. And it has been no small cause of my object in this publication, to give a spring to the mental faculties of the student, and teach him to free himself from the shackles of great names; and, *my lords upon a king's bench.* A student that is taught to think for himself, not slighting, or undervaluing the wisdom of those before him, bids fair to rise to eminence, his mind being strengthened by reflection. But there is a medium in all *admiration, or undervaluation.* I have thought the judges with us have been too much fettered with English decisions; not distinguishing what was decided, from the reason of it. As, for instance, in the case of Perrin and Blake, where, merely because the *technical construction in* a devise prevailed, we neglect the reasoning, and good sense of those who support the contrary, that *intention* shall *alone govern.* Hargrave, in his dissertation on the rule in Shelly's case, has abundantly shewn the fallacy of the application of it to the case of technical expression in a devise. And yet there are courts and judges that still stick to it, not considering the greater latitude that we have here in shaking a decision, or retaining it. The case also, of distinguishing between what shall give *real* property, and personal, in *full interest, such as the testator had,* is an instance of this narrowness which is still retained. I see that it has been put down in Virginia by Tucker and Fleming, in the high court of errors and appeals, Roan sticking like a barnacle to the bottom of the old doctrine. At the same time I do not mean to undervalue judge Roan. His argument in the case of Reed v. Reed, 1 Munford, Appendix, shews him to possess supereminent abilities. But as to this point, the construing a devise, I am with the majority. Judge Tucker, in the case of Wyatt v. Sadler's heirs, 1 Munford, 537, observes, " that there is one reason which does not exist in England, why the *intention* of the testator in the distribution of his lands among his children ought to be referred to an estate of inheritance, unless the contrary intention manifestly appear." It is, that lands were the property most easily *acquired in this country*, as well as most necessary to the support of a family. A father often had *nothing* else to *give.* In distributing it, he must be presumed to do a father's part among his children by *giving an estate of inheritance.* The contrary construction has still some foothold in this state, but it must soon go. It will certainly go by a legislative provision, unless the decisions of the courts render it unnecessary for the legislature to interpose. But, to return from whence I have digressed.

I have no idea that either judges or lawyers here, are inferior, *in natural powers*, to the lawyers or judges of England. For I take *the man of America*, I do not mean the aborigines, to be at least equal to *the man of the European countries*, whence we have emigrated. But I am not sure that we have equal advantages of acquiring legal information, and becoming eminent. Their *law lectures by professors in the universities*, is an advantage in the course of academial studies. But still more, the opportunity they have of studying at what are called the Inns of court, I should conceive to be a pre-eminent advantage, having the opportunities of familiarly conversing with learned serjeants ; and more especially with each other; and whetting the appetite for study, and exercising the faculties of the mind in legal research, and investigation. Besides all this, the opportunity of attending the courts, and seeing and hearing trials, and the manner in which they are conducted, is an advantage. We have not the same advantage here, in all places.

But a great drawback with us in the profession of the law, is that here, every man *must be his own attorney*, and sometimes *his own conveyancer* in the course of his practice. He must attend with unceasing vigilance to watch

the court docket, and take notice of the entry of rules, &c.
Settling dockets, and putting down causes, and all matters
preparatory to the trial takes up a great deal of time. The
examination of witnesses, beforehand, where the witnesses
for his client are willing to attend him, and the making out
his own brief from these, with his cases, must also be at the
expence of time. For, all these matters preparatory to the
trial are indispensibly necessary to the knowing what can be
proved, and what demand to urge, or defence to make.

The first thing that a practising lawyer ought to do,
when a client applies to him, is to take a note of what he
will undertake to prove; or will probably be able to prove,
and to read it to him, lest he should afterwards say, or at
least, think, you have deceived me; you thought I had a
good cause and would succeed. The answer is, take notice
my friend, we are both deceived; your witnesses have not
proved up to *the statement you made to me.*

The examination of your client's witnesses immediately
before the trial, is of moment that they may understand
to what point it is that you call them; that they may not
take up the time of the court, by a cock and a bull story, as
the phrase is, but come to the point at once. A man of conscience or of honour would not wish to drill them farther
than this, even were they disposed to go farther. But his object would be to get the truth from them, and let them understand what circumstances are irrelevant, and to be thrown
out of the case, and which a court itself would exclude if the
testimony of a witness could be got at without such unnecessary appendages. As to an adversary's witnesses a man of
delicacy would scorn to interfere with them lest he should be
supposed to have tampered with them, or to have misled.

Of the moyens de parvenir, or means of getting forward
in the practice, I have already said something; viz. the qualifying for a discharge of the trust of an advocate by previous
legal studies, and still more by diligence, and attention in
business. It is impossible but the capable counsel will always have the ear of the court, unless something offensive in
his manners, should occasion him to be frowned upon, and

prejudice even against his reasons; for it is not in human nature, but that a judge will be repelled even though in a degree imperceptible to himself, from a patient hearing to an ill-behaved person of the bar. And there will be *petulant* advocates at all times, as well as impatient, or perhaps arrogant judges. But it is impossible for a judge however well disposed personally to the counsel, to bear with him, in the unskilful management of a cause, or a desultory, and still more, a tedious harangue. The decies repetita, is not a motto for a serjeant's ring. Knock down your argument on that point of law, or fact, I have thought sometimes, while an advocate has had it a long time under the hammer, like an auctioneer; *it will fetch no more.* Tediousness, is generally the effect, not so much of a want of talents to be brief, as of a want of previous study of his case, and due preparation. The firstlings of all men's thoughts ought to be *double distilled* in the alembic of the brain, to make full proof.

I come now to give a hint, that is worth a Jew's eye, as the phrase is, to the young practitioner of law : this is to endeavour to recommend himself to the older, and abler of the profession, by shewing that he can be serviceable in a cause into which he may have had the good fortune to be introduced. It cannot be expected of him to do much in the higher department of conducting a suit, or arguing the cause, upon a point of law. And perhaps not much in convincing a jury as to the conclusion of fact which his client's interest requires to be drawn. For it requires an intimate knowledge of the human heart, from reflecting upon the operations of our own passions, or from our experience, and observation of those of others, to enable to persuade the mind ; and to this, in the nature of the case, the young cur of the profession cannot but be greatly incompetent. But, it may be expected, and ought to be expected of him, that he will do. what he can do, and to which, until he acquires experience, he may be competent. And this is the taking care of the docket ; watching the entries of rules ; searching the docket ; copying a declaration, or statement ; or a notice ; or a paper book for a court of error, &c. Giving audience to a

client, and keeping him off from the leading counsel who is
otherwise engaged in his behalf, and to better purpose than
listening to him, though the client may not be able to comprehend this. Nevertheless, it is what the younger practitioner can do. For as to the client, he measures your attention
to his cause, and the interest you take in it, by the hearing
you give him. The younger in the practice, may take all,
or some of these matters on himself. For, it is the maxim,
and ought to be, " Juniores ad labores." Matters of mere
labour let the junior take.

In the course of all this business, the younger counsel
will find himself well rewarded by the information he will
acquire of the practice, from the corrections, and directions,
of the older in the profession. But it is oftentimes the case,
that the younger will be for doing what they are not capable
of doing; and, from a false sense of honour, and obstinacy
of silly pride, they will not do what it may be in their power to do. The consequence is, the elder counsel will not
find his account in being coupled with them, and therefore
will neither take the pains to instruct, nor exert himself to
get them employed, and brought forward in a cause.

The false pride of the younger counsel may take the
alarm at being thought to act a subordinate part in all these
inferior matters ; and especially the being thrown as a tub
to the whale, to keep the client off; but he will find his
account in it; for, by his hearing patiently, and seeming to
understand, he will gain the good will, and confidence of
the client, who will very probably attribute to him his success in the cause, if he should happen to succeed. In the
petit guerre of the trial, there will be occasions when a judicious leading counsel may safely suffer him to speak. For
the discharge of artillery even where there is but flash and
smoke, may do something by the sound ; it may check the progress of an enemy, until the column is formed in another
quarter. At the same time, by managing the piece, the
young artillerist will acquire a facility, though he has but
powder ; and may be the better able to direct it, when he
comes to have ball.

It is the county and circuit courts chiefly, that I have in my eye in giving these prescriptions, where, in the country a great deal of business presses all at once upon the counsel, and it is of moment to have some person in the cause, that will do the hearing business, without which a client will not be satisfied. He will sit by you even in court, and injure himself by disturbing you. I once was out of humour by one who interupted me in this manner at an important point, an exception to evidence. He jogged me, and I gave him a pretty smart jog in return. He was what is called a back-woods man, and a hunter; I had him, the opponent, in my eye, said I, his defeat in my eye; my rifle raised; and now by that jog on the elbow I have lost my shot.

But I have another hint to give which will avail the young practitioner when he has got into business; and that is *to try to keep it.* For be assured it is much more easy to get into business, than to keep it. Assiduity, is the se-cret of this, in illustrating which, the bargeman rowing up the stream presents himself to me as a similitude. For, if he loses a single stroke, the boat is carried back by the cur-rent proportionably to the loss of that stroke; for, says the the poet,

" Non aliter quam qui adverso vix flumine lembum
Remigiis subigit: si brachia forte remittit,
Atque illum in præceps prono rapit alveus amni."

Nor is it so difficult to keep, as to recover professional practice when *once lost.* The idea of a new lawyer has some charm with it; but having lost business by neglect, the charm is worn off, and the presumption arises, that he will neglect it again.

The going into the legislature may perhaps not injure before a young lawyer gets much into practice. It may be a means of increasing it after a short absence and return to the bar. But it is dangerous unless managed solely with this intent, and with a view to this.

As to the moyens de parvenir, or coming forward at the bar when you have got practice, so far as respects public speaking in a cause, you must speak when there is an occa-

sion, or necessity for it, and perhaps sometimes when there
is not; and this with a view to *improve the faculty*. It is
only by frequent speaking that a habit is acquired; and
without some habit, it is impossible to have *a facility*. It
need be no discouragement that you make out badly the first
time. I would consider hesitation as a presage of future
eminence; at least I would consider it as no evidence
to the contrary. I would not object to the writing, and reducing thoughts on the case to notes; but no procemium, or
common place introduction to declaim from; for you will
soon come to the edge of the bank from which you must
step down, and every one will discover the tumble you must
make. The tones of a declaimer are usually unnatural; nor can the diction be sustained, when you come to the
expression of your sentiments as they occur, extempore. It
is better to begin without any set speech, even though your
confusion should be as great as that of the mayor delivering
the address of his corporation to Charles II. who made his
apology, and had occasion for it, that he had begun at the
wrong end.

As shewing the natural progress of the eloquence of
him who thinks, I give the model of Ulysses, according to
Homer:

> When Atreus' son harangued the listening train,
> Just was his sense, and his expression plain,
> His words succinct, yet full, without a fault;
> He spoke no more than just the thing he ought.
> But when Ulysses rose in thought profound,
> His modest eyes he fix'd upon the ground,
> As one unskill'd or dumb he seem'd to stand,
> Nor rais'd his head, nor stretch'd his scepter'd hand
> But when he speaks, what elocution flows!
> Soft as the fleeces of descending snows
> The copious accents fall, with easy art;
> Melting they fall, and sink into the heart!
> Wondering we hear, and fix'd in deep surprize;
> Our ears refute the censure of our eyes.

I would rather hear a young lawyer faulter and stammer

(and without habit, it will be the case with every mind of
sensibility) than to hear him run on with a flippancy in the
first instance, that argues the having committed a speech to
memory, or the having little depth of thought to embarrass
the current of his diction. The exercise of extempore speaking is every thing; but no committing to memory, or declaiming is of any use at the bar, but the contrary. Deba-
ting societies of students of the law, with a view to this, is
of great use, when the point proposed, is studied with attention, and a just eloquence cultivated, grounded on a knowledge of the subject.

It may be seen that Ulysses did not come forward with
a set speech, but had the images in his mind, and a perfect
understanding of his subject. It was not until his mind
heated by the essaying to utter, *that feeling gave him action,
and a flow of elocution.* Coming warm from the heart; it
is this kind of eloquence that reaches the heart. All else is
but the recitation of an unimpressed person. I set no store
therefore by the gestures taught in the schools, or declaiming
with attitudes of raising hand and lifting foot; I would rather
have a dancing master, that would confine himself alone to
teaching the postures of the limbs, and the bearing of the body.
A drill seargeant would not be amiss as to all this. Extempore
speaking with the gestures that the feelings excite, is alone the
language, and the eloquence of nature. Coming from a breast
full of the subject it is irresistible. A speech condensed and
written, and committed wholly to memory, is another matter;
but this can have no place in the eloquence of the bar. Because, except as to a common place introduction, it cannot
be known what to say, but as the occasion of the evidence,
or argument calls for the oratory.

On being applied to, for the purpose of advice as to the
bringing a suit for a client, you will doubtless advise according to the best of your judgment. But take it to be the
case that you have been consulted, and the evidence fairly
disclosed to you, and you have approved the bringing suit,
the plaintiff in your opinion, having the law clearly in his favour. But, upon trial, though he proves all that he had un-

dertaken to prove, and the defendant nothing to overthrow
it, so as to change the law, which you had pronounced to be
in his favour, yet the decision of the court has been against
you, what are you then to do. I will not say what you are
to do, but I will state to you the address of a young practitioner whom I once knew, not overburthened with legal
knowledge, at least not the greatest lawyer in Christendom,
who happened to be in the predicament of which I speak,
and being upbraided by his client with the usual language,
" did you not tell me, I had the law on my side ?" And did
I not tell the court so too, says the advocate ; did you says
the client. Ay, did I ; to their faces ; I told them you
had the law on your side. The governor can give commissions, but nature only can give sense. What could a client
have more to say ?

In such a case the instinctive impulse of self-preservation will lead the advocate to lay the blame upon the judge,
or upon the whole court if the decision should have been
unanimous. Where a single judge decides for him, he is
safe enough, but where the whole court is against him, what
can he do, but insist upon them being wrong; and it is not
impossible but that they may have erred. When at the bar,
I have been as much shocked at the decision of a court, on
a point of law, as I have ever been at the verdict of a jury
on a matter of fact. In contemplation of law, the court are
always right, but in contemplation of reason and common
sense, they may have erred. But though a counsel has a right
in self-defence with his client, or to others, to assert his
own judgment against a judicial opinion, it is a matter of
extreme delicacy as to the mode and manner of arraigning
the decisions, and as to the language used. Insinuations
against the integrity of a judge, or court, may lead to the
penal consequence of being struck off the roll ; and at all
events is a great imprudence ; for, coming to the ear of a
court or judge, it is not in human nature, that he can be so
well disposed to listen to you and take an interest in your
success at the bar. It is always of great moment to a practising attorney to be thought to stand well with a judge or

court. For in general it is an evidence that he deserves to stand well; and this *from his legal knowledge and attention to business.*

But I come now to say a little, on perhaps, a more important point; that of self-preservation from bad habits. These are frequently acquired from mere imitation, or the idea of being a fashionable fellow; such as smoking segars, which is detestable in a young person, and never fails to exhibit to me the evidence of a bad family education, or indulgence. Or, if not proceeding from that source, the effect of puppyism, which bespeaks a mind naturally little, and of the petit maitre kind. Imitators are contemptible every where; such as at London, or Paris, your opera-glass coxcombs. The wearing spectacles, some years ago, was common in Philadelphia, among the young men, because there happened to be a few great men there, in the profession of the law, that wore spectacles; Wilson, Lewis, Coxe, and Wilcox. They wore them because they needed them; on account of the convexity of the visual orb. But the use of glasses by their imitators, when they walked the streets, was from an affectation of being thought learned men, because they resembled such in a nearness of vision, and the necessity of using lenses on the nose. It was more pardonable in a blind man whom I once knew, who wore spectacles to make people believe that he could see.

But the segar excites thirst and leads to intemperance. When the mouth is parched, you must wet the whistle; recourse must be had to something to moisten it. That which was at first unnecessary, and mere wantonness of indulgence, becomes a habit, and cannot be got rid of, but increases until the individual becomes the slave of tobacco, and of spirituous liquor. I never see a young person with a segar in his teeth, but I give him up, as one that will never come to much. In early life there can be no necessity for narcotics, or use in them, as a sedative; nor is there any necessity for the use of stimulants, when the animal spirits are of themselves, gay, and sufficiently volatile. These things ought all to be reserved for a more advanced age, if used at all, and the beginning too soon with the use of them is unnatural, and destructive.

The situation of the greatest danger to a young practitioner of law is a remote county town, where amusements are few, and a literary society is wanting. The attending the courts is to all, a scene of inducement to intemperance, it being the lawyer's harvest, and as on that occasion, as with agricultural men, so on this with the lawyer, there is a latitude of mirth, and convivial indulgence, to which those are the most exposed, whose society, from wit or song, or other talent is the most courted. There can be no profession where it behooves to be so much upon guard, in these respects, as the practitioner of the law. Intemperance of living at the county courts, and sitting up, perhaps at cards, " *hath cast down many wounded; many strong men have been slain by it.*" It is owing to these causes, and circumstances, in a great degree, that so few succeed in the profession of the law, which, I will admit, will, in a republic, where the law governs, always have the first place as *an order or rank of men.* Political science constitutes no order or rank, for the standing, to an individual is but occasional, not permanent.

Nor do I speak of agriculture, for that does not come under the denomination of a profession. That of arms does; and, inter arma silent leges; in time of war the soldier occupies the whole attention of the public; but a standing army, on a great scale, has never been favoured in a republic. It is contrary to the genius of it, and will be certainly depressed, and frowned upon, perhaps more than it ought to be. For though a militia is a proper organization for a time of peace, and the preservation of civil liberty; yet, for the purposes of actual service in a war with a foreign enemy, whether of offence, or defence, an army enlisted for, and during such war, is the only efficient force. It must be made a man's business, to be in camp, to make it his home; and it must be made his home, to keep him contented in it. That *subordination* is necessary in a stated body of troops, which cannot be found in a militia.

The *navy* unquestionably, in a republic, will always occupy the next grade in rank to the civil authority, and those connected with it; the one supporting the laws, and the administration of justice in the interior; the other protecting from without. For, commerce, to a people that live upon the water, will be sought; and to protect commerce a navy, a permanent navy, is essentially necessary. I do not know to whom to attribute the depression of ours, at an early period after it had begun to be cultivated; but to that source I attribute all our national humiliation for a length of time, and, all the calamities of the present war. If we had gone on as we had begun, to build seventy-fours, and frigates, we should have had no tribute to pay to Barbary powers; no *constructive* blockades from the English government, which was the earliest aggression; no Berlin decree, or orders of council; or Milan decree following these; no *British* captures, nor *French* spoliations; no necessity for embargo, a measure which it was expected to relieve us from the necessity of war. But what is more, we should have had no impressment of American seamen, under a pretence of being British seamen; nor would Britain, with all her wave-ruling boasts, have dared to question our right of *impatriation*, which she herself exercises, in its fullest latitude, and protects in *her employment, naturalized or not, as she would her own subjects, without asking questions as to the service in which they had before been; or the country to whom they might have before belonged.* The means of defence, and the spirit to defend, is the only preservative of peace to a nation, as it is of safety to an individual.

With such a force upon the ocean, as we might have had before the present war, to protect our own trade, and *annoy that of Britain,* she would have been cautious with regard to the Indian in our neighbourhood, or the suffering trading companies, for the sake of gain, and a monopoly of fur, and peltry, to excite men to hostilities with our frontier settlements. For I will not charge her with more, *in the first instance,* than suffering these traders to excite an Indian war against us; however she may have come, in *the next instance,* to acknowledge them as allies; and to close the cli-

max by the *ne plus ultra of degradation, and national barba-
rity, to place the scalp with the speaker's mace, in the capital
of Upper Canada.*

But now to conclude what I have to say to the student.
You will not understand me as at all conceiving that what
I have suggested in the preceding notes, and observations,
is, in all respects correct. For even the great Lyttleton,
concludes his treatise upon tenures with a caution which
must much more become such a jurist as I can pretend to
be, even though writing upon matters less profound than
those upon which he wrote, viz. to use his own language,
" Know my son, that I would not have thee believe that all
which I have said in these books is law ; for I will not presume to take this upon me. But, of those things that are
not law, enquire, and learn of my wise masters learned in
the law. Notwithstanding, albeit that certain things which
are moved and specified in the said books, are not altogether
law, yet such things shall make thee more apt, and able to
understand, and apprehend the arguments and the reasons of
the law, &c. For by the arguments, and reasons in the law,
a man more sooner, shall come to the certainty, and knowledge of the law." The first thing I would recommend you
to do, when this book shall have been published, and you
obtain a copy, is to have it bound up with blank leaves, and
in them enter your remarks, as to the errors, that may seem
to exist after due examination, and your practice which may
suggest them ; but much more the remarks which the learned in the law may make upon them, whether coming from
a judge upon the bench, or a counsellor at the bar, whose
opinions are as much to be regarded, so far as respects what
is extra-judicial, and out of court. The profession form a
a body like a general council of the church, but, with this
difference, that what the council determine is, eo instante,
to be accounted orthodox ; but, in the opinions of the profession, make their way, progressively ; nevertheless, never
fail to control all judges, just as the vox populi in a commonwealth must ultimately prevail. It is immaterial, whether what is contrary, is put down by general sentiment, and
public opinion in one case, or the other.

THE CONCLUSION.

THIS book has been written raptim, et carptim; at snatches of time in the intervals of business; and these intervals have been short, never exceeding ten days at a time. For, though I have been two or three times in a year, near three weeks at home, yet the greater part of that interval has been taken up in making out statements of causes tried at nisi prius, for the sake of the court in Term, where there were motions for a new trial, on ground of misdirection; or on reserved points; or, on the ground of the verdict being against evidence. But, still more, my time has been occupied, when at home, in considering cases *holden over under advisement* from the Term, and examining the authorities cited by the counsel in the argument. For it is only at the intervals of which I speak, from these occupations, that there can be leisure to make notes or observations upon collateral subjects, and abstract matters of law. Nor would there be leisure for this, at these intervals, were it not that I abstract myself wholly from company, and neither visit, nor receive visits of ceremony, and, see no one, but upon business; except a literary character, or professional man, to whom I am always at home, and perpetually disengaged. Because from them I may derive something; information, or instruction. Drawing near the end of my pilgrimage, I consider all time lost that is not employed in leaving some memorandum of my existence, and that may be useful to men, either by contributing to *mental enjoyment*, or to instruct. I state this with a view to *exclude the conclusion* that this publication can be evidence of my having little to do, in my immediate official occupations. For, it is rather an argument to the contrary; and that I must have been industrious and attentive to the discharge of my trust, since the whole subject of the book, has a relation to the study and the practice of the law.

I will acknowledge, as I have already hinted, that I have intended it, a good deal, for the legislature, with a view to assist them in the amendment of the Pennsylvania code; and, this, by giving, as far as my understanding would lead me; a broad view of the state of their law as improved, from that of England, or variant from it; or, how far still defective in our provisions by acts of assembly, or in the filling up, and completing our excellent judiciary establishment. It will be seen also, that I have given a glance at the encroachments of the national government, whether by acts of congress, or judicial *construction*, upon state rights. Not that I mean, in the most distant degree, to shake the confidence of the state in the national government; on the contrary, my object is to preserve it by confining legislative acts, and construction, to the constitutional orbit. " Esto perpetua," may it last forever, would be my wish. But this, in the nature of things, cannot be expected. I look for its dissolution, I am afraid at *no distant day.* The late symptoms of schism in the northern states, seem to bespeak an approaching catastrophe. I consider the opinion of the Massachusetts judges, in answer to the questions of governor Strong; together with the order from Martin Chittenden, governor of Vermont, to withdraw *the militia from under the command of the United States, as fraught with the seeds of death, and destruction.* It behooves every good man to endeavour upon great and enlarged principles, to conciliate and reconcile rather than to oppose, and enter into a contest. If the northern states will have the administration of the general government, in God's name let them *take a turn at the helm;* for my own part I have approved of all the measures of the present administration of the general government, so far *as respects foreign powers,* but I do not chuse to go farther, because, if I did, I would have *to make exceptions.* But I have approved of the war with Britain; I say nothing as *to the time, or the preparation for it.* For I am not about to write a chapter upon politics. But I had no idea of a war with any power but that of Britain, at the present time. Because France had either been drowned in the ocean like a rat, or had been driven from it; and it would be unworthy of our spirit to be pursuing a dead animal; and dead she is as to the sea, and external commerce. Unless we go upon the land, (the continent of Europe) what spoliation can she make? Britain is our rival on the seas; and, for that reason, our natural enemy. Take John Bull by the horns, however much we may be injured in the first instance, is our *policy,* as well as an adversary worthy of our prowess, and our arms. I would fight her for a thousand years, rather than surrender to her injustice, and abominable claims of the dominion of the sea. It is upon the sea, only, that we come in contact with any nation worth regarding. It is there, the wheel of our government rubs with that of any other; and France has no wheel there for hubs to touch; she is worthy making war with until we can find time to attend to the depredation of Barbary powers, or French depredations. But if it would reconcile us amongst ourselves, *to make war with France, make it and put an end of the difference.* For the dispute actually has been, so far as I have been able to discover, which adversary we should take; or, whether or not we should not take both. For all seemed to agree prior to the declaration of war, that we were a humiliated and degraded race, devoted to the love of gain, and having no spirit to resent our injuries. And certain it is, as I have been as-

4 D

sured frequently, that Americans abroad were ashamed
to acknowledge that they belonged to the United States.
I believe it will not be the case now, and that even in
Britain, some respect has began to be entertained for us.
There is no animal in the system of nature, but can make
itself respectable, provided it has the spirit to resent injuries.

What injuries have we sustained from Britain ? The
very insults of her negociations in our endeavours to conciliate peace, is a cause of war. For a nation that will
treat with *contempt* our allegation of wrongs, is come to
that height that it behooves to resent. I say this because
I do not enter into the question of her injuries ; these,
a fortiore, will justify our declaring war ; and unless she
is brought to terms—interminable war.

But the cry is with those who think otherwise, where
shall we be, if Britain should go down ? Where *are we
now*, if she stands up ? And where will we be, if her *dominion of the sea* is not reduced ? That is our present
concern ; and when it comes to be reduced below an
equality upon the ocean, what hinders us to throw ourselves into the scale in her favour. If Bonaparte takes
her island, which God avert, and of which I have not the
least apprehension, he cannot, at the same time take
her fleet ; and without a fleet he cannot come to us.
The truth is, all apprehension of France, is absurd, except, as to the spoliations of our trade that comes into her
ports ; and having combatted the Leviathan, we can notice France as a Shark, that will be scarcely worthy of
our harpoon.   As to all external commerce, or power upon the sea, she is a dead fish already.   She has not a boat
to swim upon the ocean, that can be worth mentioning.
But I arrest myself.   There are those who think differently, both upon the policy, and the justice of the war
with England ; and *respect is due to the opinions of men.*
But while

The good, the brave,
The brave, the good,

are *acting* in the cause, may not I be allowed to use words? This I will only say to *the student*, that I have examined the causes of the present war, and I think it *justifiable*, and, on ground of policy *absolutely necessary*, as much so as was the war of the revolution, which gave us independence; and I can have no doubt, but that the heroes of this war will add their names to those of seventy-six; and, in future time be equally regarded;

The ever green shall flourish where they ly,
And everlasting be their memory.

As to the merits of this publication itself, in a literary point of view, or as a didactic work, so far as respects legal investigation, and comment, it is submitted, to the legitimate judges, the constituted authorities, the people, and particularly the profession, who may be led more immediately to examine, and to form an opinion.

"Discite justitiam moniti, et temnere Divos."

The people are the gods in a republic. All are amenable to this tribunal; and, as the gallery is the Olympus of the Theatre, so it belongs to the high and low to approve, or disapprove, in this greater Theatre, and it is not always the best judges that make the most noise in the first instance. But, ultimately, it must be the opinion of men of sense that will fix a decision, and determine whether what has been executed, is a thing of utility or of small amount towards the attainment of legal science, or the improvement of any part of the legal code of this state, or that of the United States, or any hint thrown out which may contribute to the administration of justice in the decisions of courts, who are constituted, and intrusted for that purpose.

FINIS.

Memorandum as to the *errata* of this publication.

IT has been in my power to revise very little of it after being printed off, and, doubtless, errors from the copy of my notes, not the most legible hand-writing ; or from my dictation, which was a considerable part, must have occurred. These, in addition to errors of the press, might require a table. But this I cannot attend to, and must leave it to the reader to supply and correct. I notice two, which struck me in a part which I had an opportunity of casting my eye upon. The one occurs in page 167, Cottom Mathew, *for* Cotton Mather ; *the other in page* 216, per capita, *which should be* per stirpes ; *which, currente calamo, was a lapsus in my language, a great blunder, and more especially requires to be noted.*

In page 402, *I have spoken of an act prohibiting the eligibility of a* deputy sheriff *to the office of sheriff, &c. The act of* 14th Feb. 1729-30, sec. 20, *is not what I mean. By this it is provided,* " *that no sheriff within this province shall continue in his office of sheriff, or occupy the said office above three years ; and that no man who hath been sheriff or* under-sheriff *of any county by the space of three years, shall be chosen sheriff of that county again within three years next ensuing.*" *I mean an act, and such I think did exist, which provides, and goes more to the root of the evil, that no one who has acted as* deputy within the space of one year, *shall be eligible.*

In page 389, *for* observations, *read* aberrations. *In page* 413, *for* true Englishman *read* true-born Englishman. *In page* 414, *for* free Englishman *read* free-born Englishman. *In page* 448, *for* recover *read* remove.

INDEX.

A.

ERRATA CONTINUED.

Page.	Line.			
58	23	*for*	juste	*read* justi.
115	8	—	the only remedy,	—— a remedy.
146	19	—	would	—— could.
155	2	—	and	—— et.
181	2	—	receives	—— receive.
198	25	—	errors	—— error.
200	7	—	degree	—— stage.
219	11	—	mulctatur	—— mulctetur.
Ibid.	9	—	dic	—— die.
224	3	—	Deuris	—— Dennis.
223	15	*from the bottom*,	illicito	—— illicitè.
230	11	—	would	—— could.
225	20	—	ever	—— even.
230	8	*from bottom*,	authorities	—— author.
232	3	*from bottom*,	would	—— could.
234	20	—	in	—— if.
232	4	—	and	—— or.
357	20	—	have	—— not have.
438	1	—	have	—— having.
469	1	*supply the word*	acting.	
515	2	—	view	—— vein.
526	19	— *supply the word*	canine.	
539	2	—	Starrer	—— Hauer.
558	2	*from bottom*,	Liguntur	—— Leguntur.
552	24	—	Stade's	—— Slade's.
574	6	*from bottom, strike out the word*	In.	
565	8	— *from bottom,*	young cur	—— younger.
569	19	— (in some copies)	declaring	—— declaiming.
578	4	—	began	—— begun.
579	19	—	temnere	—— non temnere.
Ibid.	30	—	or any hint	—— or whether any hint.

457 Assize of Nusance. Livesey, *v.* Gorgas & Others. *Omitted* entry of judgment, which was of December term, 1810; and execution thereupon of the same date, reciting the proceedings to the judgment, and returnable the third Monday of March then next. Sheriff's return; PROS-TRATED, AND REMOVED THE WALL AND DAM AS WITHIN COMMANDED; costs received—so answers Francis Johnston.

I.

R.

S.

T.

FINIS.